INTERNET, MAIL, and MIXED-MODE
SURVEYS

THIRD EDITION

INTERNET, MAIL, and MIXED-MODE SURVEYS

The Tailored Design Method

DON A. DILLMAN

JOLENE D. SMYTH and

LEAH MELANI CHRISTIAN

WILEY

John Wiley & Sons, Inc.

Library of Congress Cataloging-in-Publication Data:

Dillman, Don A., 1941–
    Internet, mail, and mixed-mode surveys : the tailored design method. – 3rd ed. / by Don A. Dillman, Jolene D. Smyth, Leah Melani Christian.
        p. cm.
    Rev. ed. of: Mail and internet surveys / Don A. Dillman. 2nd ed. c2007.
    Includes bibliographical references and index.
    ISBN 978-0-471-69868-5 (cloth)
    1. Social surveys. 2. Questionnaires. I. Smyth, Jolene D. II. Christian, Leah Melani. III. Dillman, Don A., 1941– Mail and internet surveys. IV. Title.
    HM538.D55 2009
    300.72'3–dc22

                                                                        2008033213

Printed in the United States of America.

10 9 8 7 6

To

James F. Short Jr.

Who continues to honor us
with his presence and perspective

Contents

Preface

IT HAS been 30 years since the first edition of this book appeared in print. That book, *Mail and Telephone Surveys: The Total Design Method* (Dillman, 1978), introduced and helped to legitimize both mail surveys, which were considered inferior to face-to-face interviews, and telephone surveys, only rarely used for surveying before that time. This first edition provided step-by-step instructions for obtaining high-quality responses for both of these modes.

The second edition, *Mail and Internet Surveys: The Tailored Design Method* (Dillman, 2000a), introduced new electronic modes of surveying: the Internet, e-mail, and interactive voice response. It also discussed the need to move beyond using the same procedures for all surveys and articulated the importance of tailoring survey designs to the topic, population, and survey situation. An update of this edition (Dillman, 2007) recognized the rapid changes in survey practices with respect to web and mixed-mode surveys and presented new evidence about how visual layout and design affects people's answers to survey questions.

This third edition is a nearly complete rewrite of the second edition. We begin by discussing how surveying has developed and changed in the past 75 years and explore the trajectory of each major survey mode. We consider how telephone interviewing has come to face major challenges; how Internet surveying has expanded enormously within the past decade; and why, despite its expanded use, the Web is not yet a satisfactory replacement for telephone or mail in many survey situations. These developments now have the survey world in a state of considerable turbulence that motivates the perspective and practices for survey research discussed in this book.

In contrast to the second edition, which gave only limited attention to the Internet, the use of this mode of surveying is emphasized in each of the chapters, and specific guidelines are presented for the design and conduct of web surveys. This edition also places front and center the design and implementation of mixed-mode surveys that combine Internet, mail, and sometimes telephone, interactive voice response, and face-to-face methods. Moreover, this edition thoroughly integrates into this discussion the substantial knowledge gained in recent years about applying visual design principles to communicate more effectively with survey respondents both within and across modes.

Two coauthors, Jolene Smyth and Leah Christian, are also introduced in this edition of the book. The writing of this book has followed 7 years of intensive collaboration on multiple research projects, the results of which have been published in a series of journal articles and book chapters. This collaboration began while both Jolene and Leah were graduate students at Washington State University (WSU) and has continued following the completion of their doctoral degrees and their moves to their present positions.

This book has benefited from the efforts of many individuals and organizations. We wish to thank the National Science Foundation Division of Science Resources Statistics and the U.S. Department of Agriculture National Agricultural Statistics Service. Since 2002, cooperative agreements with these agencies and WSU have encouraged and made possible extensive survey experimentation on mode effects and how the visual layout and design of survey questionnaires and individual questions influences respondents' answers. These experiments have been linked to specific challenges facing these agencies and others as some of their surveys have transitioned from paper to Web or been developed for mixed-mode designs. All three of us and this book have benefited greatly from the willingness of these agencies to link these activities in a productive way. In particular, we wish to thank Lynda Carlson, Ron Fecso, Dale Atkinson, Mary Frase, Nancy Leach, and other professionals in these agencies who provide leadership for a number of important national surveys. The questions they have asked us to pursue in our research have guided the rewriting of this book in an incredible number of ways, for which we thank them. We also thank the Gallup Organization for their support of some of the research reported here.

We also express appreciation to Stan Freedman of the Energy Information Administration; James Fields, formerly of the Government Accountability Office; Rick Clayton and Clyde Tucker of the Bureau of Labor Statistics; Rick Rosen, formerly of the Bureau of Labor Statistics; James Marsden and Phyllis Simard of the U.S. Census Bureau; and Betsy Martin, formerly of the U.S. Census Bureau. Each of these professionals provided assistance at various times to help us better comprehend the dynamics associated with specific government surveys.

We cannot thank enough the staff of the Social and Economic Sciences Research Center (SESRC) at WSU who served as a continuous source of innovative ideas through all three editions of this book and who made it possible to develop many of the ideas reported here. We wish to thank in particular Thom Allen, Nik Ponomarev, Vincent Kok, Kent Miller, Bruce Austin, Marion Schultz, and Leona Ding. Their amazing skills and patience guided us through many challenging experiments and analyses and helped to advance the ideas discussed here. We also thank John Tarnai, Danna Moore, Rita Koontz, and Sandy Johnson for many years of administrative support and for making the SESRC a wonderful place to work. The SESRC is a unique center of innovation and collaboration without which the scientific work that undergirds this book could not have been done. In addition, faculty and students in the Department of Sociology and elsewhere at WSU engaged us in collegial fashion in the series of experimental tests that are part of this book. They include Tom Rotolo, Michael Stern, Taj Mahon-Haft, Arina Gertseva, Nicholas Parsons, Bryan Rookey, Mallory McBride, and Allison O'Neill. For this we thank them.

We would also like to thank Thom Allen at WSU and Kristen Olson at the University of Nebraska–Lincoln, both of whom provided helpful reviews and comments on selected chapters in this book. In addition, Allison O'Neill and Rayna Sage were there when push came to shove to help transform draft chapters into finished drafts, and all the while with great humor. We appreciate enormously their help and support under difficult time constraints.

Appreciation is expressed by Don Dillman to the Department of Community and Rural Sociology at WSU for its financial support of the research reported in all three editions of this book and for providing an appreciative context, consistent with WSU's land grant mission, for linking research with practice in serving the people and organizations of Washington State. Thanks also goes to the members of western region projects (W-183 and WERA 1001) on rural and agricultural surveys who for 2 decades have encouraged and critically reviewed many of the research efforts mentioned in this book. He would also like to thank more than 150 graduate students who have taken "Soc 525," the survey research practicum, and who have been sounding boards for many of his most preliminary ideas.

Jolene Smyth would like to thank the faculty of the Survey Research and Methodology Program and the Department of Sociology at the University of Nebraska–Lincoln for their patience and support in the later stages of the writing of this book and for engaging in helpful and informative methodological discussions, many of which are reflected in these pages. She would also like to thank the graduate students in her Spring 2008 Questionnaire Design course who attentively listened to many of the ideas contained herein, read and provided feedback on selected chapters, and asked thought-provoking questions that helped us think through many of the subjects discussed in these pages.

Leah Christian would like to thank the Pew Research Center for its support and for the unique experiences she has gained with political polling and landline and cell phone surveys since starting there. Specifically, she would like to thank Scott Keeter for his engaging conversations on methodological issues during the final stages of completing this book. Lastly, she would also like to thank the Carl Vinson Institute of Government at the University of Georgia for the practical experience she gained in managing a variety of survey projects while working in the Survey Research Unit there.

We also wish to thank one another. The intense collegial interaction that has characterized nearly 7 intensive years of work together and led to the creation of ideas and approaches that none of us were likely to have generated alone has been a unique and wonderful developmental experience. We are thankful for the opportunity to work together, and our collaboration underscores to us the importance of a continuing process of listening, learning, and critiquing (as well as rewriting the umpteenth draft of) papers and chapters. We hope it benefits this book and your use of it.

This book is dedicated to James F. Short Jr., Professor Emeritus at WSU and founding director (1970–1985) of the Social Research Center (renamed the Social and Economic Sciences Research Center in 1986) that for nearly 40 years has contributed to the survey research education, accomplishments, and success of university faculty, staff, and graduate students. His inspiration and support for researching and writing the first edition of this book is remembered, and his continuing presence and perspectives on our work are warmly felt and deeply appreciated.

DON A. DILLMAN
Washington State University
Pullman, Washington

JOLENE D. SMYTH
University of Nebraska–Lincoln
Lincoln, Nebraska

LEAH MELANI CHRISTIAN
The Pew Research Center
Washington, DC

CHAPTER 1

Turbulent Times for Survey Methodology

FOR MORE than 75 years, sample surveys have remained a remarkably useful and efficient tool for learning about people's opinions and behaviors. The characteristics of millions of people can be estimated with confidence, then as well as now, by collecting information from only a few hundred or thousand respondents selected randomly from carefully defined populations. To estimate within 5 percentage points the preferences of 100 million U.S. voters, one needs only to survey 400 randomly selected voters. Or, if one wants greater precision, for example 3 percentage points, about 1,150 voters need to be surveyed, as is commonly done for predicting the outcomes of national elections.

But beneath this commonality in sampling a small proportion of the population to estimate the views of many, huge changes have occurred in the past 8 years in how surveys are conducted and in the modes available to survey researchers. These transformations, which have occurred incrementally over time, have changed substantially the levels of human interaction and trust between surveyors and respondents, the time and attention individual respondents are given, the level of control respondents have, and the likelihood of response. The sample survey has been transformed from being a comfortable face-to-face conversation to a highly impersonal experience that with increasing frequency is mediated by an electronic device. The nature of this new experience, and its consequences, are intricately linked with cultural transformations and technological innovations occurring in industrialized societies throughout the world.

To understand surveying in the early twenty-first century requires comprehending the nature of this great transition, which is the focus of this chapter. These turbulent times that now exist dramatically influence the practice of survey research, and the impact of these changes is likely to continue to affect how surveys are conducted in the coming years. We describe these changes here in order to provide needed context for discussing the procedures for conducting high-quality Internet, mail, and mixed-mode surveys in today's rapidly changing survey environment.

Figure 1.1 provides a way of looking at some of the changes in surveying and the ways that human interaction, trust, time involvement with each respondent, and the locus of control has changed over time. We discuss these aspects of change in more detail throughout this chapter.

Figure 1.1   Seventy-five years of change in respondent involvement and control over the survey process.

Characteristic	Through the 1960s	1970s through 1980s	1990s to the Present
Human interaction	High: Face-to-face through in-person visits to respondent homes	Medium: Remote through a telephone connection	Low: Encounter is more likely to be with a machine or its products
Trust that the survey is legitimate	High: Encouraged by interviewer presence, appearance, and sincerity	Medium: Encouraged through voice inflection and ability to listen and request additional information	Low: Because of possibility that survey is fake and potentially harmful to respondent
Time involvement with each respondent	High: Interviewer goes to respondent and obtains information one-on-one	Medium: One-on-one, but contact effort is minimal	Low: Minimal to no time with individual respondents
Attention given to each respondent	High: Because of time to find and interview each respondent	Medium: Because of placing calls one after another	Low: Mass e-mails
Respondent control over access	Low: Households generally accessible	Medium: Unlisted numbers, voice mail, and call monitoring	High: Caller ID, call blocking, e-mail filters
Respondent control over whether to respond	Low: Required breaking off human interaction	Medium: Ease of hanging up telephone	High: Increased disclosures required to be communicated and social support for refusing

SURVEYING THROUGH THE 1960S

During the first two thirds of the twentieth century, there existed only one generally accepted mode for conducting surveys: the in-person interview. When the science of drawing random samples to represent entire populations was developed and applied in the 1940s and 1950s, it was carried out by sending interviewers to people's homes or places of work. To do this efficiently often required quite complex sampling methods such as drawing samples of households in stages, and clustering locations for interviews in order to reduce costs. Planning and conducting such studies was laborious. Months and sometimes years were needed to justify the importance of a particular survey and obtain the resources to carry it out. Data collection itself took additional weeks or months, as every aspect of the survey had to be physically transported from place to place. Under these conditions the sample survey was reserved for only the most important of survey needs.

Prior to the 1960s, a respondent guided by prevailing norms of politeness would be approached by an interviewer, usually a woman who was dressed appropriately to sit as a guest in one's home and engage in a fairly comfortable conversation. A survey methodologist at the U.S. Census Bureau summed up the situation by describing efforts to train interviewers in the 1930s and 1940s on putting respondents at ease by asking ice-breaker questions such as "How is your family?" (D. Rothwell, personal communication, 1975). The respondent would often be persuaded by the interviewer to answer the questions at length, giving substantial detail and explanation. Getting people to answer thoroughly was the hallmark of a good interviewer. Responses would be recorded by paper and pencil, and the respondent would be made to feel at ease and good about the experience, as if the interviewer were genuinely interested in the respondent as a person (and she often was). Response rates of 70%, 80%, and even 90% were common.

During this time period, telephone and mail modes were only occasionally used to conduct surveys. Both were considered inferior methods, in large part because of the botched *Literary Digest* prediction that Alf Landon would emerge victorious over Franklin Roosevelt (55% to 41%) in the 1936 presidential election. This prediction was based on a mailing of straw vote ballots to more than 10 million people sampled from telephone directory listings (36% of U.S. households had telephones at the time) and auto registrations, for which only a 20% response rate was achieved. More than 2.3 million ballots were returned and, when tallied, predicted that Landon would win the election. When the election was over, however, Roosevelt had won by a margin of 61% to 37%, an outcome that was in the opposite direction and much larger in magnitude than *Literary Digest* had predicted. This botched prediction cast a shadow over the use of both mail and telephone surveys for many decades.

The *Literary Digest* blunder provided a tangible example of some of the shortcomings of telephone surveying, but problems during this time period went much deeper than just limited telephone coverage and low response. There were also large technological and cultural problems that had to be overcome before the telephone could become a survey mode to be taken seriously. One problem was that area codes did not exist, making it necessary to place calls through operators, with multiple operators sometimes being needed to complete a single call. Long-distance calls were also enormously costly and the voice quality of conversations poor, with people often having to shout to be heard over poor connections. In addition, many portions of the U.S. population were on party lines, so their neighbors could, and often did, listen in on calls, making confidentiality difficult. Culturally, people viewed the telephone as a short-conversation device, and long distance, in particular, tended to be reserved for sending or receiving critical information. Until the 1960s picking up a telephone and hearing the operator say "I have a long-distance call for you" was tantamount to being warned that something bad had happened to a friend or relative. Moreover, the idea that one would reveal personal information, from health problems to income, over the telephone to a person they had never met was close to unthinkable.

The situation for mail surveys was a little different in that they began being used extensively in the 1940s, but generally only for specialized populations. Adequate household lists did not exist for conducting general public surveys, and selecting people within households seemed impossible to accomplish. In addition, response rates tended to be quite low. As a result, methods texts consistently rejected the mail mode for important surveys (e.g., Kerlinger, 1965; Parten, 1950). However, as with the telephone, the problems with conducting mail surveys extended well beyond these methodological concerns. For one, manual typewriters were the only means of preparing questionnaires, and they significantly limited the composition possibilities. In addition, duplicating copies of questionnaires was a cumbersome task that could only be done by ditto or mimeo machines, which produced poor-quality copies. These challenges meant that the normal procedures for conducting mail surveys were incredibly time consuming, required extraordinary effort (especially for more than one mailing), and were often ineffective.

As a result of these technological and cultural difficulties as well as their diminished reputation attributable to the *Literary Digest* poll, neither the telephone nor mail enjoyed the status of a respected survey mode in these early days of conducting surveys.

SURVEYING IN THE 1970s THROUGH THE 1980s

By the mid to late 1960s, however, a number of cultural and technological changes were on the horizon that would foreshadow great opportunities for telephone and mail surveys. As these changes began taking place in the early 1970s, the development of modern telephone and mail survey methods began in earnest (Dillman, 2005a; 2005b). In the late 1960s, area codes made direct dial calls possible, and long-distance charges decreased significantly in part because of the development of Wide Area Telecommunication/Telephone Service (WATTS). Telephone line quality was also greatly improved so that it was possible to have a conversation in a normal tone of voice. Moreover, by 1970 about 87% of U.S. households had telephone service. Also at about this time random-digit-dialing (RDD) procedures were being developed that made it possible to randomly select households, and once someone answered the phone, an interviewer could ensure that the proper person in the house-hold was interviewed.

Yet for some time the perception persisted among surveyors that people would not allow themselves to be interviewed over the telephone, and for this reason the telephone was still viewed as leaving much to be desired as a way of collecting survey information from the general public. This perception turned out to be more myth than reality, though, as it was soon discovered that norms of conversational politeness carried over to telephone interviews (Dillman, 1978). It soon became evident that responses quite similar to those obtained through in-person interviews could be obtained via the telephone and that competitively high response rates could be achieved as well (Groves & Kahn, 1979).

However, telephone interviewing changed the respondent experience dra-matically. Telephone calls now came without warning, usually in the early evening hours, as fewer and fewer households had anyone home during normal working hours. Upon picking up the phone, the respondent often heard a script read by a stranger in an emotionally uncharged, rather than conversational, way. The respondent was also oftentimes unfamiliar with the organization from which the call originated and had to decide in only a few short seconds whether or not to proceed with the interview based upon only the sound of the interviewer's voice. If he decided to participate, he was read scripted questions and had to provide answers in predesigned ways. Open-ended questions were often eliminated because of the high time and coding costs. Elaborations or extra explanations were often discouraged, as the re-spondent became someone to be managed for the sake of calling efficiency.

During this same time period, key breakthroughs were also made in the technologies needed to make mail surveys more efficient. One such devel-opment was the invention and widespread availability in the 1970s of copy machines that could quickly produce quality copies on normal white paper. Electronic typewriters and better printing methods also became available. The impact of these technologies is that they allowed surveyors to efficiently com-bine multiple survey elements such as personalization and multiple mailings that could produce far higher response rates than those previously obtained (Dillman, 1978).

Both the telephone and mail methods that were developed during this time allowed surveys to overcome distance, thus reducing the need to develop the complex multistage sampling schemes required for in-person interviews and greatly reducing survey costs. As a consequence, it became possible, from a cost perspective, for more surveys to be conducted and for smaller organizations from nearly any location to conduct them. Given these changes, it was not surprising that in the early 1980s the dominant mode of surveying for government surveys approved by the Office of Management and Budget was mail. A total of 69% of all approved surveys in 1981 relied exclusively on mail, and another 11% used mail in conjunction with other methods (U.S. Office of Management and Budget, 1984). Nor was it surprising that in the early 1980s the telephone, with its advantage of speed, almost completely replaced in-person interviews for surveys of the general public, such as election surveys.

For a time in the late 1980s it appeared that three modes of surveying were destined to share responsibilities for the conduct of sample surveys—telephone, when national household samples were needed; mail, when postal address lists were adequate and costs a concern; and in-person, when even small coverage omissions could not be tolerated (e.g., the Current Population Survey, which makes monthly employment estimates for the United States). The survey environment at this time might, however, be compared to the quiet surface of the sea in which everything seems orderly, but underneath currents of change are beginning to shift and overhead a storm is beginning to form.

TURBULENT TIMES: THE 1990s TO THE PRESENT

The time from 1990 to the present has been marked by a number of fast-paced cultural and technological changes that have demanded equally fast-paced innovation on the part of surveyors to keep data quality high. One aspect of the changing currents was the trend toward gated communities and locked apartment buildings that made it more difficult for interviewers to gain access to people's homes. Another aspect was the move toward unlisted telephone numbers, and the removal of postal addresses from telephone books, making these listings less representative of populations that had been traditionally accessed through them.

Many of the currents of change in this time period had dramatic effects on telephone surveying. For one, sellers of products quickly found telephone calls to be an effective way of marketing their products and services, and they found that many of the methods used to improve response rates in surveys (e.g., time of day to call) worked for them as well. Receiving calls during the "dinner hour" became a distasteful phenomenon, regardless of whether for marketing or surveying purposes. The increased use of telemarketing had the consequence of increasing greatly the number of unsolicited calls people were receiving and making it more difficult for respondents to determine when a call was for legitimate research purposes and when it was a marketing effort. Indeed, in some instances marketing calls were made under the guise of survey research.

As the number of unsolicited calls increased, so too did mistrust of callers, and people began looking for ways to avoid unwanted calls. This tendency was likely magnified by the surveyor tactics of using repeated call backs at different times of the day to contact hard-to-reach respondents and implementing refusal conversion call backs for respondents whose initial refusal was delivered in a friendly rather than angry or terse tone of voice. People soon found relief from unwanted calls through a number of new technologies including unlisted telephone numbers, answering machines, caller identification, and call blocking. These technologies let respondents take charge of whether any interaction at all occurred. The culture of response was changing significantly, with people learning to say "no" to almost all telephone requests. Additionally, people's tolerance of long interviews was on the decline, a factor that spurred many firms to limit the length of the surveys they conducted by telephone.

At the same time that people became less willing to accept unsolicited calls, the addition of extra telephone lines to many homes for fax machines and computer dial-up modem connections made it increasingly difficult to sample households adequately by telephone. However, the sampling challenges raised by these trends were minor compared to the challenge that would soon arise with the development of cellular telephones. As cellular telephones became more popular and accessible, the telephone came to be viewed less as a household device and more as an individual device. This cultural and technological change made it more difficult to call a household and select a respondent, as calls now went to individuals. As a result, one of the tenets of scientific surveying that allowed generalizing from hundreds of sampled households to millions of other households—giving all members of a population an equal (or known, nonzero) chance of being selected—became increasingly difficult to achieve. In addition, per-minute charges to the respondent and the disconcerting possibility of trying to interview someone while that person was driving a car added to the concern that the telephone was not working well as a survey method. Taken together, these cultural and technological shifts have resulted in significant reductions in both the proportion of the population that can be reached by telephone and the proportion that is willing to comply with a survey request over the telephone (Lepkowski et al., 2008).

During this same time period, significant advances in computer technology also had substantial impacts on survey methodology, from making mail survey production more efficient to combining with other modes to improve data collection. One of the earliest applications of computer technology to another survey mode was *computer-assisted telephone interviewing* (CATI), in which a telephone interviewer follows a script on the computer to administer a questionnaire and then enters the respondents' answers directly into the computer. Other ways that computers have been combined with telephones for interview purposes are through *touchtone data entry* (TDE), whereby respondents can provide responses to a computer by pressing keys on their telephone keypad; and *interactive voice response* (IVR), in which a computer administers an interview and can register vocal as well as keyed respondent answers.

As computers went mobile (e.g., laptops and handhelds) *computer assisted personal interviewing* (CAPI) became possible. With CAPI, an interviewer enters responses directly into a computer program on a laptop computer or other small computing device. *Computer-assisted self-interviewing* (CASI) occurs in much the same way, except that the respondent runs the computer. The advantages of using computers in these ways are that they help standardize the interview, eliminate the need for interviewers to administer skip patterns, and efficiently combine interviewing and data entry into one step.

Although each of these applications of computer technology has had significant effects on survey methodology, perhaps the biggest storm of change has been caused by the development of the Internet survey. To place Internet surveying in perspective, it is important to recall that before 1980, the personal computer was not readily available for purchase by individuals and was also quite costly. Even by 1990, e-mail communication was mostly a novelty. The idea of going to a computer in one's home to access a distant computer in order to complete a questionnaire was impossible for most people to fathom. Yet by the mid-1990s, surveyors were beginning to post web surveys for people to complete, though mostly for those who were associated in some way with online communications.

From very early on it was apparent that the potential for web surveys was enormous. The cost savings were particularly appealing, as interviewer wages, long-distance charges, postage, printing, and keypunching costs associated with telephone and mail surveys are essentially eliminated. Thus, it should not be surprising that surveyors have rushed to embrace the Web as a data collection methodology just as consumers have rushed to accept computers and other uses of web technology. As a result, the use of the Internet for surveying people has increased dramatically during the past decade.

However, since the beginning, web surveying has faced a number of challenges, not the least of which have been major gaps in computer and Internet access rates and lack of computer skills among some segments of the population. Although both access and computer operation skills have improved substantially in recent years, significant proportions of the U.S. population remain without the technology or ability to go to a web page and complete an Internet survey. The lack of standards for creating e-mail addresses that would make it possible to develop sampling algorithms is also a problem. Likewise, there is no systematic list of Internet users from which to draw a sample (these issues are dealt with in more depth in Chapter 3).

Because of these challenges, use of the Internet as a survey mode has been largely limited to surveying specific populations of interest with high Internet access rates and skill levels, such as members of professional associations, students in universities, employees of certain organizations, purchasers of certain products and services, and similar targeted groups. For these populations, Internet surveys can be designed and implemented and results reported faster than with any of the traditional survey modes and often at lower costs. However, even these surveys are subject to the inability to ensure that each respondent receives the same visual stimulus from the questionnaire because of the myriad combinations of hardware and software configurations currently in use.

As with the previous technological innovations, the rise of the Internet has also been accompanied by cultural shifts that have real consequences for survey methodology. One such shift has been in the way people have viewed the Internet itself. Over time there has been an increasingly widespread distrust of Internet communications and interactions resulting from the increased occurrence of cyber crimes including phishing scams, identity theft, and the danger of receiving a computer virus. Because of this distrust, as well as unwanted and oftentimes offensive e-mail appeals, many people now avoid responding to unsolicited e-mails or to invitations from unrecognized sources to go to web sites, especially when they involve clicking on links in e-mails.

Another cultural change that has accompanied the growth of the Internet has been a shift in preferred ways of communicating with others. E-mail has become the standard method for communicating in most work organizations and for many individuals. The growing preference for e-mail means that telephones are even less likely to be answered by individuals, and when messages are left, people often respond by e-mail. E-mail has also replaced postal mail for many letters and memos. The shift toward e-mail as the communication mode of choice for significant sectors of the population is somewhat ironic as it is one of the very factors that make Internet surveys possible, but it is also making surveys by traditional modes more difficult to complete.

The development and widespread implementation of these communication technologies in recent years has meant that surveyors have to take extra steps to distinguish their surveys from the countless other contacts (mail, phone calls, e-mails, text messages, etc.) one receives on a daily basis. Additionally, the wedding of surveys to high-technology devices requires surveyors to give additional consideration to how different populations interact with new technologies. For example, although younger people may be more familiar with new technology, they may also be more inundated with contacts and appeals for their time and attention. In fact, the 18- to 30-year-old demographic segment is probably the most difficult group to get to respond to surveys by any mode.

In summary, the past 2 decades have seen in-person interviewers lose access to secured apartment buildings and neighborhoods, and telephone surveying become less representative of the general population because of the disconnection of home landlines in favor of cellular phones and the increased likelihood of refusal. In addition, emergent web surveying suffers from a whole new set of technology-related problems (e.g., access, skills, etc.) as well as low response rates. Although there is some evidence that mail surveys have also undergone modest decline (Connelly, Brown, & Decker, 2003), there is also evidence that response rates can be maintained (Dillman & Carley-Baxter, 2001; Dillman & Parsons, 2006). As a result, in a situation opposite of what was seen 30 years ago, mail surveys can now achieve higher response rates than the typical telephone survey.

The respondent experience has also been significantly transformed. Now when the respondent answers the telephone she might be met by a voice recording or electronically contrived voice rather than a real person. Rather than speak her answers, she may punch keys on her phone or other mobile device to register them. Instead of receiving a paper questionnaire in the mail to fill out with pen or pencil, she may now be asked by e-mail to fill out an electronic questionnaire using a mouse and keyboard. In deciding whether to respond she now also has to consider the risk involved in responding to an unsolicited e-mail. And if she chooses not to respond by one mode, she is likely to receive a request to respond by another mode altogether. Or she might be given the option to choose from among several response modes from the very beginning. The respondent experience is now highly impersonal and is increasingly controlled by respondents who feel less obligated to provide requested information and for whom refusing is now more socially acceptable.

GETTING BEYOND THE TURBULENCE

Decisions are being made every day that reflect what is wrong with some survey modes as well as what is right with others. The days are far behind us when surveyors would simply declare that the in-person mode is the best mode or when the telephone was viewed as the heir apparent to such interviews. The reality of today is that certain survey modes are better for some populations, survey topics, and survey sponsors than are others, and even choosing the "best" mode may leave one far short of being able to collect quality data. Consequently, one of the most significant changes within survey methodology in the past 15 years has been the shift from using predominantly single-mode surveys to using multiple modes in the same data collection effort to compensate for the inadequacies of each. This ability is largely facilitated by the computerization of society, which has made it possible to transform questionnaires easily from one survey mode to another.

In the preceding century many survey methodologists were able to specialize in a single survey mode, leaving it to others to grapple with the intricacies of other modes. In this new mixed-mode era, such specialization is no longer possible. When surveyors decide from the beginning that achieving good results requires using multiple modes, questions must be written that achieve the same measurement across modes, and modes must be implemented in ways that support one another and maximize response rates. These requirements mean that survey methodologists must be competent in multiple survey modes.

Despite all of the change and turbulence, in this new survey environment the goal remains the same as in the past: to design scientifically sound data collection systems that allow us to obtain precise estimates of the behaviors and attitudes of all people in a population by sampling and obtaining results from only a fraction of them. However, the means for doing so have changed in a number of ways.

In preparation for writing the third edition of this book, interviews were undertaken with professionals in a number of survey organizations. When asked at the beginning of these interviews how surveying had changed since the publication of the second edition in 2000, the first three people who were interviewed stated at the outset that surveys are now respondent driven, rather than driven primarily by the needs of the survey organization. For example, the administrator of one large government survey stated, "We are trying to give respondents what they want, but still do valid surveys. That means giving people a choice." As this administrator's comments reflect, the survey world today is different than it was even 10 years ago in ways that make it critical not only to understand the elements of doing valid sample surveys, but to better understand the role of respondents in producing such responses.

FROM TOTAL DESIGN TO TAILORED DESIGN

The first edition of this book (Dillman, 1978) introduced mail and telephone survey methods as cost-effective alternatives to in-person interviews and provided step-by-step procedures for conducting such surveys. The subtitle of the book, "The Total Design Method," was chosen to describe the need to give attention to designing every aspect of a survey that in some way touched respondents. However, the total design method had a one-size-fits-all orientation, advocating the use of the same procedures for all populations and survey situations (Dillman, in press). That orientation was in part a reflection of the mass society orientation of the time, which emphasized standard procedures and production methods. It was also a reflection of the rapid developments in mail and telephone methodologies that had not yet allowed for research and development of different procedures for different populations and situations.

In the 1990s it became apparent that massive changes in the design and implementation of sample surveys were occurring. Surveyors began to carefully match their selection of survey mode to characteristics of the population, the survey topic and length, and the sponsor's situation as well as to take advantage of the new availability of electronic modes of data collection (Internet, interactive voice response, portable computers, etc.). These changes were introduced in the second edition of this book as the beginning of the wide-scale use of tailored design strategies for designing surveys (Dillman, 2000a). The tailored design strategy involved a significant methodological shift from a one-size-fits-all approach to one in which solutions were tailored to most effectively and efficiently deal with the contingencies of different populations and survey situations. In the second edition, discussion of the telephone was removed because of space constraints in favor of discussion of the Internet and other electronic modes that share many similarities with mail methods (e.g., visual communication and self-administration).

In addition to these changes, the criteria for successful surveying were expanded from the focus on response rate concerns in the first edition to simultaneously reducing four sources of error—coverage, sampling, measurement, and nonresponse. The second edition also introduced, somewhat tentatively, the importance of mixing survey modes and consideration of how visual layout concepts might influence people's answers to survey questions, both of which are dealt with in somewhat more detail in an updated version of the second edition (Dillman, 2007).

In the 9 years that have now elapsed since the publication of the second edition of this book, more change has occurred in how sample surveys are designed and implemented than had occurred in the 22 years between the first two editions. These 9 years can be described as a period of intense confrontation between technology and culture. On the one hand, the Internet has reached nearly all businesses, but it is still unavailable in many homes. In the meantime the telephone, although reaching its maximum penetration of more than 97%, has changed from being a household device to belonging only to an individual within the household. On the other hand, human culture in the United States and a large number of other countries has changed, so responding to surveys has become much more a matter of respondent choice, both with respect to allowing oneself to be contacted in the first place and with respect to the ability and willingness to say "no" to survey requests. Thus, one of the ironies of modern surveying is that there now exists more means of reaching people and doing so more quickly than ever before, but there is a greater likelihood of people not allowing certain means of access, whether through mail, Internet, or telephone. We have entered an era of choice not just for surveyors, but also for respondents.

In response to these changes, this third edition of this book retains the tailored design focus introduced in the 2000 edition but takes this concept considerably further in order to address some of the difficulties that arise out of increased respondent choice as well as the availability of more survey modes, greater differences in the resources available to survey sponsors, changes in the contact possibilities for potential respondents, and differential respondent access to resources. More so than either of the previous editions, this edition sees surveyors confronted with an era of enormous variation in how surveys are designed. As a result, this edition expands on the previous editions in three important ways.

First, since the second edition of this book was written, enormous resources have been devoted to developing and testing ways of designing web surveys and to simplifying the tasks of accessing and completing them. At the same time, the power of computers and Internet connections and cultural understanding of computers have increased dramatically. Therefore, whereas in the previous edition only one chapter was devoted to the Internet, in this new edition the Internet has been integrated throughout—from coverage and sampling to writing questions and obtaining high response rates.

Second, the recognition that all survey modes face challenges and that none alone may be sufficient for getting adequate responses has led to many surveys being conducted using multiple modes. In the first edition of this book, virtually no mention was made of mixed-mode surveys. In the second edition, a chapter was devoted to the mixing of survey modes, and *unimode design* (i.e., unifying the way in which questions are asked across survey modes) was advocated. In this edition, mixing modes becomes a central issue throughout the book. Even when a surveyor limits the design to a single mode, as remains warranted in many instances, we believe it is prudent to keep mode comparisons in mind because researchers often wish to compare data collected by different survey modes from different populations. In addition to unimode or unified design, we also build the case for mode-specific design that takes into account the occasional need to construct questions differently in order to obtain comparable results across survey modes.

The third change of major significance in this book is the discussion of visual design concepts and their importance for designing surveys. Whereas telephone interviews must rely entirely on aural communication and paralanguage, web and mail surveys must rely on visual communication made up of words, numbers, symbols, graphics, and their properties (color, contrast, location, etc.). The consequences of these differences, though recognized for many years, were not systematically researched until the late 1990s and were only preliminarily dealt with as controllers of navigation in the previous edition of this book. Since the publication of that edition, however, research has shown that visual layout affects respondents in many different ways. These effects were the main focus of the 2007 update (Dillman, 2007) and are developed further throughout this third edition of the book.

In addition, we also devote a chapter to longitudinal surveys and a new kind of tailored design, the Internet panel survey. In that chapter we discuss the unique challenges faced by each of these types of surveys as well as some challenges that are common to both. Another new chapter discusses how sponsorship affects survey design, with an emphasis on the regulatory impacts of institutional review boards and the Office of Management and Budget.

CONCLUSION

When interviewers walked city streets or traversed the countryside by car in the 1940s to sample households and interview the people who lived in them, they were pursuing the same objective that would later be pursued by surveyors in the 1970s who sent written questionnaires to postal addresses or who called telephone numbers randomly to contact people, and by surveyors in the 2000s who sent e-mail requests asking people to complete a survey on the Internet. The scientific tenets of surveying—that is, getting a sample of a few hundred or thousand respondents to allow estimates with known precision to be made for the population from which they are selected—have remained the same. However, the methods used for asking questions and obtaining answers and knowledge of the factors that influence the accuracy of those answers and the proportion of people who will provide them have changed dramatically.

This book is about obtaining high-quality responses in the early twenty-first century using the technology available and results of decades of research on factors that influence people to answer survey questions and to respond accurately. Each of the remaining 12 chapters covers some aspect of data collection and how to tailor to different survey populations and situations. We begin in Chapter 2 with the tenets of tailored design, focusing on scientific and theoretical knowledge about what makes people likely to respond to surveys and how to create effective interaction with respondents to encourage cooperation and valid answers to survey questions.

CHAPTER 2

The Tailored Design Method

CONSIDER FOR a moment the following examples of the enormous variety of circumstances surveyors now face, each of which captures a situation we have encountered recently:

- Each month a federal agency conducts a survey of thousands of businesses about their number of employees. The survey is very short, only six questions, but the agency has to collect the data and report it in less than 2 weeks.
- A television rating organization collects people's viewing habits from each of the nation's several hundred television markets to describe those habits accurately for each market for a specific week of the year.
- The elected leaders of a U.S.-based professional organization changed the program for its annual meeting and now wants to know whether attendees liked or did not like the change. One challenge was that the number of attendees from other countries had increased significantly, and the leaders wanted to survey enough of them to know whether their satisfaction level was different from that of U.S. participants.
- A federal agency that is surveying universities faces the challenge of collecting information that is known in individual academic departments but is not generally available from a centralized office.

It should be apparent, even from this small list, that the same procedures will not work for all surveys. But how does one go about deciding which procedures to use and not use, and by what criterion does one choose certain methods for collecting data over others? Also, under what conditions should one choose a single survey mode, and under what conditions is it better to use multiple modes?

At first glance, this situation may hardly seem different from that faced for decades by survey researchers. However, the dizzying array of mode possibilities now available, individually and in combination with one another and each with quite different cost implications, adds to the complexity of the situation. In addition, the dramatic changes described in Chapter 1 with regard to the presence or absence of human interaction, trust in the legitimacy of the survey, and changes in respondent control over whether and how they can be contacted, make what once may have been a simple survey design situation much more difficult. In this chapter we introduce tailored design as a means of helping sort out survey procedures that are effective from those that are ineffective given specific survey contexts.

Tailored design involves using multiple motivational features in compatible and mutually supportive ways to encourage high quantity and quality of response to the surveyor's request. It is developed from a social exchange perspective on human behavior, which suggests that respondent behavior is motivated by the return that behavior is expected to bring, and in fact, usually does bring, from others. It assumes that the likelihood of responding to a self-administered questionnaire, and doing so accurately, is greater when the respondent trusts that the expected rewards will outweigh the anticipated costs of responding.

Underlying this general approach are three fundamental considerations. First, tailored design is a scientific approach to conducting sample surveys with a focus on reducing the four sources of survey error—coverage, sampling, nonresponse, and measurement (Groves, 1989)—that may undermine the quality of the information collected. Second, the tailored design method involves developing a set of survey procedures (including the contact letters or e-mails to respondents and the questionnaire) that interact and work together to encourage all people in the sample to respond to the survey. Thus, it entails giving attention to all aspects of contacting and communicating with respondents—few, if any, aspects of this process can be ignored when using a tailored design strategy. Finally, tailoring is about developing survey procedures that build positive social exchange and encourage response by taking into consideration elements such as survey sponsorship, the nature of the survey population and variations within it, and the content of the survey questions, among other things.

REDUCING TOTAL SURVEY ERROR

Conducting surveys that produce accurate information that reflects the views and experiences of a given population requires developing procedures that minimize all four types of survey error—coverage, sampling, nonresponse, and measurement (Groves, 1989). Reducing survey error means selecting the survey mode or combination of modes that provides adequate coverage of the entire population (low coverage error) and from which a large enough random sample of the desired population can be drawn (minimizes sampling error), designing an implementation system that encourages most people in the sample to respond (reduces nonresponse error), and approaching respondents in the contacts and the questionnaire itself in a way that encourages and enables them to provide thoughtful and honest answers (decreases measurement error).

Coverage error occurs when not all members of the population have a known, nonzero chance of being included in the sample for the survey and when those who are excluded are different from those who are included on measures of interest. Coverage error can occur because the choice of survey mode may not provide adequate coverage of the population, as is the case with Internet surveys where a significant number of people in many populations do not have access to the Internet. It can also occur when the list from which the sample is drawn does not include everyone in the population, such as when a sample frame based only on households with listed telephone numbers is used or when a list is not current and excludes people who moved or joined in the last year (for a more in-depth discussion of coverage error, see Chapter 3).

The extent to which the precision of the survey estimates is limited because not every person in the population is sampled is described as the *sampling error*. The power of random sampling, which is discussed in detail in Chapter 3, is that estimates with acceptable levels of precision can usually be made for the population by randomly surveying only a small portion of people in the population. For example, a researcher can survey about 100 members of the U.S. general public and achieve estimates with a margin of error of ±10%, with a 95% confidence level (i.e., 95 out of 100 times the estimate will be within ±10%). Surveying 2,000 people reduces the margin of error to about ±2%. Surveying 100, or even 2,000, people rather than the approximately 303 million who live in the United States represents an enormous and desirable cost savings, but doing so means that one has to be willing to live with some error in the estimates. In other words, sampling error results from surveying only some rather than all members of the population and exists as a part of all sample surveys.

Another source of error, nonresponse error, stems from not getting everyone who was sampled to respond to the survey request. *Nonresponse error* occurs when the people selected for the survey who do not respond are different from those who do respond in a way that is important to the study. For example, a survey of voting intentions for a presidential election would be rife with nonresponse error if Democrats were significantly less likely to respond than Republicans. Minimizing nonresponse error (a topic covered in considerably more depth in Chapter 7) involves motivating most of the people sampled to respond so that one receives completed questionnaires from people of different sociodemographic groups or with other characteristics that may be important to the study (i.e., from different types of people).

Lastly, *measurement error* occurs when a respondent's answer is inaccurate or imprecise. Measurement error is often the result of poor question wording or design and other aspects of questionnaire construction (see Chapters 4–6). Because interviewers are not present to help respondents navigate the survey and understand the meaning of the questions in self-administered surveys, questionnaire layout and the design and wording of individual questions are extremely important in ensuring that respondents give accurate and precise answers.

Figure 2.1 presents four surveys, each of which failed to achieve its objectives as originally designed but for very different reasons. These surveys illustrate how each of the four sources of error can undermine survey projects and how designing effective surveys involves paying attention to reducing total survey error.

PERSPECTIVES ON WHY PEOPLE RESPOND TO SURVEYS

THE ECONOMIC EXCHANGE VIEW OF SURVEY RESPONSE

Several years ago an investigator for a very large and well-financed national mail survey about the retirement resources and plans of the survey population called to ask a single question: "I am doing a mail survey that will ask about people's retirement resources and will be about 16 pages long. How much do I have to pay them in order to get them to respond?" His question was framed from the perspective of economic exchange, much like one might ask what price needs to be set in order to get everyone to buy a book, a piece of software, or even a meal in a particular restaurant.

There are several problems with attempting to set a price for what responding to a survey is worth to a respondent and with using money as the primary motivation for seeking a response. People's price points, if they have one, are likely to vary widely, so that the responses of those who judge a given payment as adequate may differ significantly from the responses of those who do not. In addition, very few surveyors have the resources to pay an amount that would guarantee a response from most or all respondents, so in general economic exchange is not a usable model for surveyors. Furthermore, considerable research (discussed in detail in Chapter 7) suggests fairly substantial payments to respondents are not as effective in raising response rates as small token cash incentives given in advance. Also, many survey sponsors in widely different settings—government, universities, and the private sector—have adopted deliberate policies not to use such payments for

Figure 2.1   Why surveys fail.

A designer of health rehabilitation devices wanted to understand potential demand for its products among the U.S. general public and how having health insurance might affect the ability to purchase those devices. They commissioned a survey of more than 10,000 people who were members of a volunteer Internet panel.

Why did this survey fail? About 30% of Americans do not have access to the Internet, and the Internet panel mostly included very young and highly educated people. This was of particular concern for this study because health needs and insurance coverage have been shown to differ by age and education. Therefore, the sponsor could not accurately assess the demand for the products or the influence of having health insurance on purchasing them.

    Coverage error results from all members of the population not having a known, nonzero chance of being included in the sample and from those excluded differing from those included.

A PhD student working on her self-financed dissertation spent many months designing a survey of high school students to compare differences across schools. However, the student could only afford to mail out 100 surveys, with no reminders, for each randomly selected school in her sample. Because of these limitations, it was likely that only 25 to 30 students from each school would respond.

Why did this survey fail? The largest difference the student expected to find among the surveyed groups was 10 percentage points, and most differences were likely to be even smaller. The small completed sample from each school meant that the margin of error for her estimates ($\pm15\%$) was larger than the differences she expected between schools, meaning that significant differences could not be detected.

    Sampling error results from surveying only some, rather than all, members of the survey population.

A vice president at a major university administered a 40-minute web survey to all faculty, staff, and students at the university. The survey used a standard questionnaire that was used at other universities and that contained a long series of questions about bias and harassment repeated for many different minority groups found throughout the country. In addition the survey required an answer for each question.

Why did this survey fail? Early survey takers became upset at the length of the survey and at being forced to answer questions about minority groups that were not present, or that they did not know about, at their university. This dissatisfaction became a topic of conversation in offices and classes, with the result that others were discouraged from completing the survey. In the end, only people who were very interested in the topic completed the survey, so only their experiences were represented in the final data.

    Nonresponse error results when people selected for a survey who do not respond are different in a way that is important to the study from those who do respond.

To encourage careful thinking about each question in a customer satisfaction survey conducted by a public agency, response scales were varied across questions. On one page, a scale began with very satisfied and ended with very dissatisfied, but a later scale on the same page began with not at all satisfied and ended with completely satisfied (i.e., different labels and ordering of categories). Later, respondents were asked to enter a numeric response into a box with 5 meaning very dissatisfied and 1 meaning very satisfied.

Why did this survey fail? People made mistakes when responding to the questionnaire, sometimes marking a satisfied response while intending to register dissatisfaction because the scales were not listed in the same direction across questions and because their expectation that larger numbers are associated with the higher end of the scale was not met. Additionally, the use of different category labels for different services undermined the ability of the sponsor to compare satisfaction across the services.

    Measurement error results from inaccurate answers to questions and stems from poor question wording, survey mode effects, or aspects of the respondents' behavior.

their surveys. Finally, there are many other influences on whether people will respond to a survey, and focusing on only one while ignoring others would seem to unnecessarily limit one's ability to obtain responses.

Nonetheless, as Internet surveying has grown and surveyors increasingly find themselves with e-mail but not postal addresses of respondents, the practice of offering cash payments contingent on receiving a completed questionnaire and a postal address has increased substantially. In addition, panel surveys (discussed in Chapter 9) often recruit people based on promises of such postsurvey payment for each survey. When a European conductor of one such panel was asked in late 2006 about the normal payment, he responded without hesitation, "1 Euro for 10 minutes is the norm." An economic exchange with a singular focus on cash payment contingent upon response is not the model we follow in our social exchange framework.

GENERAL PSYCHOLOGICAL MODELS OF SURVEY RESPONSE

Others have attempted to apply general psychological models to understanding survey response. The foundations of these models come from a variety of sources, many of which (e.g., behavior reinforcement, Maslow's hierarchy of human needs, and cognitive dissonance) were described by Cape (2006) with respect to their potential application to survey methodology. The general premise here is that people are motivated by many different considerations, both extrinsic and well as intrinsic, in developing their responses to different situations.

In an early application of a psychological model to survey response, Groves, Cialdini, and Couper (1992) applied Cialdini's (1984) influence theories to the conduct of interview surveys. Cialdini argued that concepts such as scarcity of opportunity, consistency with previous behavior, desire to reciprocate, enjoyment of task, and social proof (i.e., what other people have done or are perceived as doing in the face of similar opportunities) are all social psychological elements upon which one draws in deciding whether to comply with a request to do an activity. Groves et al. argued that these elements influence decisions about survey requests in particular and, based on this, made the case that they should be built into the survey process whenever possible to encourage higher response.

In another approach, Comley (2006) used transactional analysis, a psychoanalytic theory developed by Eric Berne, to develop specific recommendations for how one should and should not interact with respondents throughout the survey process. In particular, Comley pointed out that to maintain their sense of well-being people need units of positive recognition but that surveyors often use an adult-to-child interactional style that turns respondents off rather than an adult-to-adult style that would give them the positive recognition they need. For example, telling respondents "Some of your answers are invalid. Please review all the questions on this page" is an adult-to-child-style message that will likely leave some respondents cold and increase nonresponse.

THE LEVERAGE-SALIENCY THEORY OF SURVEY RESPONSE

Building upon the ideas developed through the application of Cialdini's work to the survey setting, Groves, Singer, and Corning (2000) developed the leverage-salience theory, in which they proposed that respondents in interview surveys are differentially motivated to respond by different aspects of the survey (i.e., leverage) and by how much emphasis is put on each aspect by the surveyor (i.e., salience). For some, cash incentives may be important, but for others, topic and sponsorship or personal community involvement may be important. Each design feature will have varying amounts of leverage on the decision to cooperate for different people. In addition, the amount of emphasis that the survey sponsor puts on a design feature (i.e., how salient the sponsor makes it) will interact with the importance the respondent places on it in affecting the final decision to respond or not. If the respondent is strongly influenced to participate by the topic of the survey and the surveyor makes the topic very salient throughout the implementation process, the respondent will be highly likely to respond. If, however, the topic of the survey is a turn-off for the respondent and the surveyor makes the topic very salient, the respondent will be highly unlikely to respond unless some other aspect of the survey or the request to complete it exerts enough positive leverage on the respondent and is made salient enough to overcome this negative effect. Using this approach, Groves et al. (2000) argued that advance letters from the sponsoring organization may have more effect on some than others based on the legitimacy of the sponsoring organization. They also proposed that young people may respond differently than older people to various incentives, and some may be more greatly affected by whether the interview is by telephone or whether they are given the possibility of a data collection mode that offers more privacy.

The leverage-saliency approach suggests that an overemphasis on a single appeal that is attractive to some potential respondents but not others may produce serious nonresponse error if it is related to an important variable of the study. Additional research on the leverage-saliency theory was conducted to determine whether an appeal based upon topic would produce nonresponse bias (Groves, Presser, & Dipko, 2004). Although people interested in the topic were much more likely to respond, the impact on survey estimates was mixed. The main implication we draw from this very productive line of research is that it is important for appeals to respondents to be broadly based in an attempt to encourage all types of survey recipients to respond.

SURVEY RESPONSE AS A SOCIAL EXCHANGE

Social exchange theory underlies the tailored design method and provides the overarching framework within which we attempt to identify and implement ways of increasing the likelihood of response. As it was first applied to survey methodology in the 1970s (Dillman, 1978), social exchange, like leverage-saliency, focused on appealing to potential respondents in multiple ways. However, in this revision we have sought to update the social exchange perspective on survey nonresponse with knowledge gained from the various frameworks mentioned previously and, in particular, to place an emphasis on utilizing more mutually supportive response-inducing factors in an attempt to appeal to the many different types of respondents that can exist within any survey population.

At the most basic level, social exchange posits that people's voluntary actions are motivated by the return these actions are expected to, and often do, bring from others (Blau, 1964). People engage in a social exchange with others when the perceived rewards outweigh the expected costs. *Rewards* are what one expects to gain from a particular action, and *costs* are what one will have to give up, or spend, to receive the rewards. Entering into social exchanges requires *trust* that the other party will provide a valued reward in the future, although not necessarily to the respondent. In other words, trust is the expectation that the sponsor will carry through on the promises made.

As discussed previously, social exchange should not be equated with economic exchange. Social exchanges are different from economic ones both because there is only a general expectation of a return and because they involve various types of rewards and costs. In contrast, economic transactions rely exclusively on the exchange of money, where exact monetary values are used to measure worth and explicit time periods are often specified for when the rewards should be provided. In social exchanges, the exact nature of the benefits and when they will be provided are often not specified in advance; instead, they are left open to the discretion of the person providing the reward. For example, after hosting a dinner party for a group of friends, one may expect others to reciprocate but cannot specify when or what type of party they should have or even guarantee that others will have a party at all.

An example of how social exchange differs from economic exchange can be illustrated by the research on providing survey incentives. Small token incentives provided with the request to complete the survey significantly improve response rates, whereas a promise to pay people after completing the survey has minimal or no effects on whether people respond (Church, 1993; James & Bolstein, 1990, 1992; Johnson & McLaughlin, 1990). Providing people an incentive in advance encourages participation because people feel they should reciprocate for the reward they receive by completing the survey. This research is discussed in more depth in Chapter 3.

APPLYING SOCIAL EXCHANGE TO SURVEY DESIGN

Social exchange is a subtle but powerful method for motivating people to respond to surveys and is particularly useful for surveyors because the rewards that they can typically offer are relatively small. The theory of social exchange suggests three key questions about how the design of the questionnaire and the implementation process can motivate people to respond to the survey:

1. How can the perceived rewards for responding be increased?
2. How can the perceived costs of responding be reduced?
3. How can trust be established so that people believe the rewards will outweigh the costs of responding?

There are many different ways to establish trust and increase benefits while decreasing costs; our suggestions were developed based on traditional elements of social exchange as developed originally by Blau (1964), Homans (1961), and Thibaut and Kelley (1959) and on more recent ideas about influence in a social context from others whose works were reviewed previously.

Ways of Increasing the Benefits of Participation

According to social exchange, people are motivated to act by the benefits they expect to receive. As people receive more and more requests to complete surveys, the rewards of participation in any one survey may decrease. People who have already participated in one or two surveys may feel they have done their part as survey participants (Groves & Magilavy, 1981). Thus, surveyors must work hard to distinguish their survey request from other requests and emphasize the benefits of responding to the survey.

Provide Information about the Survey

Sending information to potential respondents about the survey and how the results of the survey will be used to benefit them and others can encourage survey participation (Groves et al., 1992). In particular, sending items such as prenotice letters and informative brochures that explain why the survey is being conducted and that highlight the importance of participation can influence people's decision to participate.

Ask for Help or Advice

Many people feel a sense of reward from knowing they have helped others (Blau, 1964; Homans, 1961). Appealing to people's helping tendencies or norms of social responsibility can encourage them to respond to the survey (Groves et al., 1992). Survey requests that ask people for their help and advice demonstrate how respondents' assistance is needed and subordinate the survey sponsor to potential respondents. For example, Mowen and Cialdini (1980) found that including the phrase "it would really help us out" at the end of their survey request increased survey participation by 19 percentage points.

Show Positive Regard

Similar to asking for people's help, showing positive regard can also encourage people to participate in the survey. Thibaut and Kelley (1959) noted that many people feel rewarded from being regarded positively by another person. Personally addressing contacts, providing a toll-free number to call with questions, and providing various ways for people to respond can show positive regard and respect for potential respondents, which may help motivate them to participate in the survey.

Say Thank You

Verbal appreciation can be an important reward in social exchanges (Blau, 1964). Phrases such as "We appreciate your help" or "Many thanks in advance" can be added in contact e-mails or letters to increase the likelihood of people responding. In addition, a postcard follow-up designed as a thank you for the prompt return of "the important questionnaire we sent to you recently" has been found in some surveys to increase survey participation almost equal to the initial mailing with the questionnaire (Dillman, Christenson, Carpenter, & Brooks, 1974).

Support Group Values

Most people identify with certain groups, such as being an American citizen or a dues-paying member of the Nature Conservancy. By tailoring communications to the survey population, sponsorship, and topic, one can appeal to values shared widely by those in the group. Supporting people's values can convey a sense of reward in them (Blau, 1964). Showing support for shared values also underlies efforts to appeal to potential respondents on the basis of a study's social usefulness (Dillman, 1978; Slocum, Empey, & Swanson, 1956).

Give Tangible Rewards

As discussed earlier, providing potential respondents with token financial incentives (ranging from $1 to $10) with the survey request has been shown to significantly increase the number of people who respond. Other types of incentives, such as charity donations and ballpoint pens, have also been shown to have modest effects on response when provided with the request to complete the survey. Providing token incentives in advance evokes a sense of reciprocal obligation such that people feel the need to respond to the reward they received by completing the survey.

Make the Questionnaire Interesting

Designing questionnaires with questions that a wide variety of people find interesting will encourage higher response rates. Liking to do something can be a powerful determinant of human behavior (Cialdini, 1984). When the topic of the survey is highly salient to potential respondents, they are more likely to complete the questions than when the topic is of low salience (Heberlein & Baumgartner, 1978). Even when not all potential respondents may be interested in the topic, questionnaires can be made more interesting by improving their visual layout and design, ordering questions so that more engaging ones are placed early in the questionnaire, and crafting questions that are easy to understand and answer.

Provide Social Validation

Knowing that other people similar to themselves have completed the survey can strongly influence people to participate in a survey (Groves et al., 1992). Because people frequently use the actions of others as standards of comparison for their own actions and feel rewarded when they see themselves as similar to most others in a group, they are more likely to comply with requests when they believe others like them would as well. For example, in follow-up contacts, telling people that many others have already responded encourages them to act in a similar way and respond to the survey.

Inform People that Opportunities to Respond Are Limited

People perceive rewards as more valuable when opportunities become scarce (Groves et al., 1992). Telling people, in a friendly and nonpatronizing way, that there are relatively few opportunities to respond and that they may not have an opportunity to respond unless they do so quickly can encourage them to participate (Petrie, Moore, & Dillman, 1998). Likewise, explaining to potential respondents how only a small number of people are selected for the survey can have a similar motivating effect.

WAYS OF DECREASING THE COSTS OF PARTICIPATION

Oftentimes reducing the costs of participating in a survey is closely related to increasing the rewards. However, there are also particular strategies that surveyors can use to decrease the perceived costs of responding to a survey independent of rewards.

Make It Convenient to Respond

Perhaps one of the most effective ways of decreasing costs is making it as easy as possible for people to respond. This may involve offering a desired mode of responding that fits the population or, for web surveys, e-mailing people and including a link that, when clicked, will open their browser and take them directly to the survey to make it more convenient for them. Likewise, including a prepaid return envelope with postal questionnaires has been shown to increase response rates because it is easier for respondents to return the completed questionnaire when they do not have to find, address, and stamp an envelope (Armstrong & Luske, 1987).

Avoid Subordinating Language

People prefer not to feel that they are dependent upon others, and Blau (1964) argued they will expend great effort to avoid feeling subordinated. Consider these contrasting statements that might be included in a letter or e-mail to potential respondents:

- "For us to help solve the school problems in your community, it is necessary for you to complete this questionnaire."
- "Will you please be a part of helping to solve the school problems in your community? Your responses can assist this community in fully understanding the issues facing schools here."

The first statement subordinates the respondent to the surveyor using what Comely (2006) might consider an adult-to-child style, whereas the second statement makes the respondent feel that the surveyor is dependent on him or her. Asking a person for help or assistance subordinates the sponsor to the potential respondent rather than vice versa and is one way to decrease the costs and increase the rewards of participation.

Make the Questionnaire Short and Easy to Complete

Questionnaires that appear short and easy to fill out reduce the perceived costs of responding. For most people, one of the biggest costs of responding to survey requests is the time it takes to complete the survey. Research has shown that longer questionnaires achieve slightly lower response rates (Heberlein & Baumgartner, 1978) but does not confirm that using more pages for the same number of questions decreases response rates (Leslie, 1997). Other research has shown that respondent-friendly questionnaires, with carefully organized questions in easy-to-answer formats, can improve response rates (Dillman, Sinclair, & Clark, 1993). Thus, designing questionnaires to enhance usability and minimize respondent burden, as well as keeping questionnaires short, can decrease the costs of responding to the survey.

Minimize Requests to Obtain Personal or Sensitive Information

Many survey questions ask for information that some people do not want to reveal to others. For example, surveyors often ask people about their income and other financial information, their health and medical history, and their past sexual behavior or drug use. Surveyors should only include requests for sensitive information when the responses are essential to the survey's objectives. When these types of information are an important part of the survey, efforts can be made to provide explanations for why responses to these questions are important and how the information will be kept confidential or even anonymous. In addition, the choice of question wording can help "soften" the requests for personal information.

Emphasize Similarity to Other Requests or Tasks to Which a Person Has Already Responded

People have a strong desire to appear consistent in their attitudes, beliefs, and actions. Therefore, people who have committed themselves to a position are more likely to comply with requests to do something consistent with that position (Groves et al., 1992). This inclination to behave consistently means that arguments can sometimes be offered that point out how responding to a particular survey is consistent with something one has already done. For example, a survey of members of a particular organization may include the following statement: "We really appreciate your support through the recent payment of dues, and we want to be responsive to your expectations. Completing this web survey will give us guidance on how best to serve you and your fellow members."

The need to be consistent may also explain why, in panel surveys, once people respond to the initial request, it is much easier to get them to respond to subsequent requests (Otto, Call, & Spenner, 1976). Consistency may also explain why the "foot-in-the-door" technique, where people are more likely to perform a large task if they are first asked to perform a smaller task, is effective (Mowen & Cialdini, 1980). A survey of national park visitors successfully used this technique by first asking people to respond to three short questions upon entering the park and then asking them to complete a questionnaire at the end of their visit (Dillman, Dolsen, & Machlis, 1995).

WAYS OF ESTABLISHING TRUST

Because social exchange involves future obligations, one must trust that the other party will follow through and provide the return or reward as expected. Under conditions of social exchange, there is no way to ensure that what the survey sponsor has promised as a benefit of the study will actually occur. For example, if a surveyor says "This survey will help our company do a better job of providing service to its customers," or "This survey will help state legislatures make decisions about how to allocate funding for higher education," there is no way to guarantee that the results of the survey will actually deliver the return as expected. Thus, potential respondents are more likely to complete the survey when they trust that the sponsor will provide the rewards as promised. Trust is critical to believing that in the long run the benefits of completing the survey will outweigh the costs of doing so.

Obtain Sponsorship by Legitimate Authority

People are more likely to comply with a request if it comes from an authoritative source that has been legitimized by larger society to make such requests and expect compliance (Cialdini, 1984; Groves et al., 1992). Therefore, it is not surprising that government-sponsored surveys achieve higher response rates than those sponsored by marketing research firms (Heberlein & Baumgartner, 1978). In addition, the unique authority that some government agencies have to inform people that their response to a survey is mandatory helps improve response for government surveys of both businesses (Tulp, How, Kusch, & Cole, 1991) and individuals (Dillman, Singer, Clark, & Treat, 1996). A more complete discussion of sponsorship can be found in Chapter 11.

Provide a Token of Appreciation in Advance

A few dollars included with a survey request increases rewards, but it also creates value in the social exchange process by establishing trust. By providing the incentive with the request, before the survey is completed, the researcher demonstrates trust in potential respondents—who can pocket the money without completing the survey—and encourages their trust by demonstrating that the surveyor will provide the promised rewards. In addition, emphasizing that the incentive is a "small token of appreciation" is consistent with conveying trust and respect for the respondent.

Make the Task Appear Important

Many surveys try to appeal to people on the basis that something important will ultimately happen as a result of the survey. Making each contact appear important can help establish trust in the survey sponsor and that the results will have the impact the surveyor says they will. Printing personalized cover letters on letterhead stationery, including a carefully chosen color picture on the front of the questionnaires, and providing brochures or other materials about the survey project can make the survey appear credible and help establish trust in the survey sponsor. In contrast, form letters produced on copy machines and questionnaires that are poorly designed or contain questions that are difficult to understand suggest that a survey, and the sponsor, is relatively unimportant.

Ensure Confidentiality and Security of Information

Of considerable concern for some survey respondents is how the information they provide will be used and who will have access to it, particularly if they are disclosing information that is personal or sensitive. The rise of the Internet has also brought increased attention to the security of information transmitted via the Web, especially with respect to whether surveyors can guarantee that people's responses will remain confidential and secure. One way of establishing trust is by explaining the efforts that will be taken to ensure the confidentiality and security of people's survey responses.

Box 2.1: Trust at the Industry Level

The issue of trust is one that extends far beyond any one survey sponsor, respondent, group of respondents, or even survey project. Establishing and maintaining trust is a fundamental concern for the survey industry as a whole, and it is an area in which the industry is constantly being challenged, as the following example demonstrates.

The year 2004 saw one of the closest state gubernatorial elections in U.S. history, with the disputed winner edging out her opponent by a mere 129 out of about 2.9 million votes cast. The final result was a contentious one, reached only after three ballot recounts and a state supreme court ruling. During the political wrangling over the election, some absentee voter ballots were questioned, resulting in these voters signing affidavits to ensure their ballots were counted. The election outcome was still in contention in January and February 2005 when backers of the losing candidate sent a "Home Ownership Survey" to more than 400 residents who had signed the affidavits in one particularly debated county in the state. Along with the three-question survey, the sponsors sent a $10 incentive check. The survey, it turned out, was a ploy. When respondents returned their signed surveys or endorsed and cashed their incentive check, these signatures were compared to the signatures on their ballot affidavits. If they did not match, the sponsors alleged that the respondent's vote was fraudulent (Postman, 2005). When the story of this survey ploy was run in the largest newspaper in the state, several respondents explained that they use different signatures for different purposes. Others explained that their spouse signed and cashed the check for them. Nearly all were upset at the dubious nature of the survey, as undoubtedly were many un-surveyed residents of the state who learned of the ploy.

This example, although somewhat sensational, is only one of many. In fact, some scams utilizing surveys are so common that they have their own names within the industry.

- *Frugging: Fundraising under the guise of survey research.* In 2003, both the Republican and Democratic parties sent voters "surveys" asking for their views on central party issues. Embedded within the surveys, however, were appeals for sizable financial contributions to the parties. Similar

(continued)

tactics have been used by a whole slew of groups ranging from local media outlets to wildlife and parks organizations.

- *Sugging: Selling under the guise of survey research.* A prominent DVD marketing company sent out a survey and as thanks for filling out the survey told respondents they could pick 5 DVDs of their choice for just $0.49 each. The fine print, however, revealed that those who returned the survey would be automatically entered into a club and obligated to buy more DVDs.
- *Phishing: Tricking people into providing personal information, usually over the telephone or Internet.* In 2007, unsuspecting taxpayers were sent e-mails that appeared to come from the Internal Revenue Service. The e-mail explained that they had been randomly selected to participate in a customer satisfaction survey and promised to pay $80 for their participation. Embedded in the survey were requests for personal information that would presumably be used to contact respondents and transfer the $80 to them. Instead, the information was to be used to access the respondents' bank accounts, run up their credit card bills, and take out loans in their names. The respondents were to become victims of identity theft.
- *Push polling: "A form of negative campaigning disguised as a political poll"* (AAPOR, 2007). A recent one-question poll of 9,000 people within a school district asked whether respondents supported a construction project "that will result in higher taxes, while not improving education." The goal of the poll, admittedly, was not to collect public opinion. Rather, it was to back certain candidates in a local school board election by influencing public opinion about the construction project.

Each of these self-serving scams abuses the public's trust and undermines the credibility of legitimate survey research. As such, each impacts the ability of all survey sponsors, from the U.S. Census Bureau to the unfunded graduate student, to conduct good survey research. Therefore, as individuals, we all have a vested interest in working to eliminate these scams. Such scams are addressed by the following organizations: the American Association for Public Opinion Research (AAPOR), the Council for Marketing and Opinion Research (CMOR), and the Council of American Survey Research Organizations (CASRO).

THE IMPORTANCE OF USING A VARIETY OF APPEALING SURVEY FEATURES

One of the features of a social exchange that is sometimes overlooked is how communication between people should change over time as one person tries to encourage the other person to comply with a request. Repeating the same request over and over in everyday conversations is unconventional, can be quite irritating, and is unlikely to be effective. The following set of requests can be illustrative here:

Week 1: Ted, I need the book that I loaned to you.
Week 2: Ted, I need the book that I loaned to you.
Week 3: Ted, I need the book that I loaned to you.
Week 4: Ted, I need the book that I loaned to you.

In this case, the request for Ted to return the book is being made in the same way over and over. However, if Ted does not comply with the request the first time, the stimulus in this type of request is used up and, therefore, is unlikely to be effective the second and third times it is used. Another way that requests are often made is illustrated in the following set of appeals to Ted:

Week 1: Ted, this is to let you know that I will require that new Harry Potter book that I loaned to you back by Friday.
Week 2: Ted, I just wanted to remind you that you have not brought back the Harry Potter book that I informed you needed to be returned last Friday.
Week 3: Ted, did you forget to return the Harry Potter book that is overdue? It was not that I really needed it then, but some people do not respond as quickly as they should.
Week 4: I suppose you still have not remembered the Harry Potter book.

Here the request is varied throughout the contacts, but each includes negative, demanding, and somewhat patronizing wording that is reminiscent of the adult-to-child conversational model described by Comley (2006). Perhaps most insulting is the final communication, which says in a defensive way that it is okay not to respond. In contrast, the following set of requests shows a more conventional, positive way of encouraging Ted to return the book:

Week 1: Hi Ted, have you had a chance to read that book? I hope you are enjoying it.
Week 2: How are you doing with the new Harry Potter book? Carolyn was asking me if I had a copy, and I said I would check and see if you were finished.
Week 3: Hey Ted, did you watch the playoff game last weekend? By the way, when you are finished with the Harry Potter book, I have another one that I think you would like.
Week 4: I need your advice on a project report. Carolyn thought you could be helpful on it. Oh, she also asked me about the Potter book. I know she is eager to read it.

Here the stimulus is varied over time, and Ted is respected in each contact. This final strategy is consistent with both the leverage-salience approach to making requests and the tailored design approach.

Although survey requests do not lend themselves to the informal conversation and introduction of side topics to the extent shown in this final set of examples, it is equally important to vary the stimulus in order to appeal to different types of respondents and to write requests in an adult-to-adult conversational style. Comments from respondents to a recent mail survey illustrate well the importance of attending to multiple design and implementation features in order to attract different types of respondents. In the fall of 2006, the survey "Family Farming and Ranching in Washington: A Woman's Perspective" was sent to a random sample of cattle and wheat operations across Washington State. Several measures were taken in the implementation of this survey to make its appeal as broad as possible. First, both the survey title, which was displayed prominently on the cover page of the 12-page booklet-style questionnaire, and the message in the accompanying cover letter stressed the importance of hearing the opinions of farm and ranch women. A shortened description of the survey ("Women's views on farming and ranching survey") included in the return address carried this same message over to the envelope the survey was sent in. Second, an appealing picture of a mailbox mounted decoratively on a very old piece of farm equipment and set next to a green wheat field was displayed on the front cover. Third, a $2 token incentive was included with the initial questionnaire mailing. Fourth, because Washington State University (WSU) is the well-respected land grant university in the state and offers many services to the state's agricultural sector, and because the survey was being conducted from there, the WSU logo was included on the outgoing envelopes and the letters were printed on university letterhead. Finally, the back cover of the 12-page booklet-style questionnaire was devoted almost entirely to space for respondents to write any additional comments or opinions they may have had that could not be expressed in the more structured survey questions (Smyth, 2007; for more information, see "Family Farming and Ranching in Washington Research Results" at www.crs.wsu.edu/1-07-farmranchwa.pdf).

Several respondents took advantage of this final feature to make comments that can shed light on what features of the survey and implementation materials convinced them to respond. Some comments included "Go cougs!" (a phrase commonly used by supporters of WSU and its Cougar athletic teams, which was left by several respondents), "Thank you for giving me the opportunity to vent!" "Thank you, thank you for asking farm women for their opinions on their farm lives," "Thank you for the $2 bill. Here I can only afford my 2¢," and "Your $2.00 could have been sent in pennies. It would have taken me less time to count the @%#& pennies than to fill out your study. Your $2.00 was an insult for as much time as it took, but I did want a woman's voice heard." These comments suggest that for some of the women it was the connection to WSU that influenced their decision to respond. For others the focus on women's opinions—communicated in the survey title, in the cover letter, and on the outgoing envelope—was important. For others, the $2 bill caught their attention and made a positive impression. Still others were offended by the $2 bill but felt the topic of the survey was important enough that they should respond.

This last case, in particular, demonstrates very strongly the importance of drawing on multiple features of questionnaire design and implementation to persuade as many sampled respondents as possible to complete and return the survey. Yet when looking at letters used to encourage people to respond to surveys, one often sees virtually, if not completely, identical letters used for multiple follow-ups, and in many instances the letters are so formal and distant that all aspects of humanness on the surveyors' end of a survey get omitted. Another common tendency is for surveyors to use incentives in both the initial contact and the follow-up contacts. However, consistent with the argument we are making here, research has shown that in most survey situations the repetition of an incentive in a questionnaire replacement mailing does not increase response over what can be obtained with a reminder alone (Tortora, Dillman, & Bolstein, 1992). Thus, as both the leverage-saliency approach and the tailored design perspective would suggest, it is important to change the look, feel, and content of later contacts rather than repeat the same requests over and over.

DEVELOPING A TAILORED SURVEY DESIGN FOR THE SITUATION

In considering how to apply social exchange ideas for tailored design, it is important to realize the breadth of the opportunities for changing a survey to increase rewards and trust and minimize costs. Tailored design and social exchange are not limited simply to the cover letters that one addresses to the recipient. In fact, beautifully composed and executed cover letters may be nullified by poorly designed questionnaires, poor timing, and a host of other poorly designed survey features. Here are some examples of inquiries we have received that illustrate a singular focus:

- I need responses to a web survey within 24 hours. Is it okay to send two reminders the same day we send the first e-mail?
- I am only going to send one mailing. I need to know how much my response rate will improve if I use a colorful commemorative stamp.
- We have a lot of nice pictures. Will using them improve our response rate?
- What color paper or background colors should I use to get the best response?
- How many questions can I include and still get good response?

These requests and dozens more like them have included only a few details (and sometimes none at all) about other aspects of the survey plan, but the answers we might provide will often differ depending on other aspects of the survey design. Generally, we would like to know who is being surveyed and by what mode or modes, how respondents will be contacted, how many contacts are planned, the anticipated timing of contacts, what (if any) incentive will be sent, what the topic of the survey is, and how many questions will be asked. For the specific inquiries above, we might also ask why the survey has to be done in one day, why only one mailing is being used, what else besides nice pictures will be used, and so on.

Once we understand more about the overall survey design, we can better answer people's questions about particular aspects of their survey and make practical suggestions to fit their situation. When asked about whether they should contact nonrespondents by telephone, we might suggest instead including a token incentive with the first contact. Or after hearing about their overall design, we might conclude that a telephone follow-up would work or that they should also offer a web option to encourage people to respond who may not otherwise. Similarly, we might recommend varying the background color in a web survey because the cost is minimal, but designing a mail survey with the questionnaires printed on white instead of colored paper to save money and so that the front page can include a color picture that resonates with members of the population.

When developing a tailored survey design for self-administered questionnaires, surveyors need to consider a number of survey features and their effects on potential respondents and to keep in mind that when one specific social exchange feature cannot be used in a particular survey situation, many others can likely be used instead. In Figure 2.2 we present some examples of essential features that should be considered when devising a survey plan and different ways each feature can be tailored to the particular survey situation. As the figure suggests, an effective survey design is the result of many decisions that need to fit together and support one another in a way that encourages most people to respond. As a result, although the merits of each individual survey feature should be considered carefully given one's particular survey situation, it is also important to consider how each feature fits into the larger survey system. After all, whether an action evokes a sense of cost, reward, or trust is related to how it interacts with other features of the system, not just how it appears in isolation (e.g., a well-designed questionnaire may never be viewed if it is mailed in a poorly designed envelope that makes it look like junk mail).

Applying the tailored design approach to each feature in Figure 2.2 requires consideration of rewards, costs, and trust as well as recognition that some survey features may invoke multiple social exchange elements within one's specific survey situation (e.g., an advance incentive is a reward, but because it

Figure 2.2 Features of the survey design that can be tailored to the situation.

Survey mode	• Choice of mode or any combination of modes
Sample	• Type of sample (random, stratified, etc.) • Number of units sampled
Contacts	• Number of contacts • Timing of initial contact and between contacts • Mode of each contact • Whether each contact will be personalized • Sponsorship information • Visual design of each contact • Text or words in each contact
Incentives	• Type of incentive • Amount or cost of incentive • Whether to provide before or after the survey is completed (pre or post)
Additional materials	• Whether to provide them at all • Type of materials (brochures, pamphlets, research reports, etc.) • Visual design of the materials • Text of the materials
Questionnaire	• Topics included • Length (duration, number of pages/screens, number of questions) • First page or screen • Visual design and layout of pages/screens • Organization and order of questions • Navigation through the questionnaire
Individual questions	• Topic (sensitive, of interest to the respondent, etc.) • Type (open vs. closed) • Organization of information • Text or wording • Visual design

is sent in advance it also promotes trust). Because what constitutes a reward or cost often depends on the survey context, it is important to take into account and plan around differences in survey content, sponsorship, and populations through the use of different social-exchange-inducing features.

For most surveys, for example, it is typical to receive only one or maybe two contacts in a 10-day period; any more begin to become irritating. However, people who have been asked to keep a diary of the specific television programs they watch in a given week might not find it unusual or too burdensome to be contacted five times in a 10-day period. First they would be mailed an introductory letter, followed quickly by a questionnaire, and then a postcard to tell them their "diary week is about to begin." Then midweek they might get a call to see if they are having any difficulties, and finally another postcard would be sent indicating that their diary week is over and thanking them. This sequence, which is similar to the one used for many national television viewing and other diary surveys, makes perfect sense in this context in which respondents are being asked to record their behavior each day for a specific week. In other survey situations, this same contact strategy may have the opposite effect and turn people off because it is so intense.

Another example is that sending a token financial incentive to individuals can greatly improve response; however, sending incentives to business respondents may not have the same effect because they may think that there is an ethical problem or that they may have to complete extensive paperwork to accept the money. In this case, what seems like a reward from the sponsor's perspective may actually produce a cost for some recipients.

How a survey is designed and administered should also depend on the length and topic of the questionnaire, as both influence respondents' perceptions of rewards and costs. Longer questionnaires or those about particularly dry or sensitive topics increase costs to the respondents. Getting people to respond to these types of surveys often requires extra effort, perhaps an added incentive, extra explanation as to why their participation is important, additional follow-up contacts, or administration through a survey mode that provides more anonymity (i.e., self-administered instead of interviewer administered). Adding more interesting questions, changing the order and format of questions to make them more interesting, or easing into sensitive topics are other tactics that might be used with these types of questionnaires. As a slightly different example, a topic requiring a respondent to read a detailed statement before answering or to evaluate a lengthy list of response options may be better suited for self-administered surveys where the respondent can review the information several times, if needed, before responding.

Sponsorship can also influence people's motivations to respond. Government sponsorship of surveys is likely to improve response, whereas market research sponsorship is correlated with lower response. Government surveys can appeal to legitimate authority, avoid the use of financial incentives, and often require that people respond. In contrast, market research organizations generally have little "legitimized" authority, so they may need to send incentives for people to respond. Sponsorship can also interact with question topic to influence participation decisions. For example, it is understandable that market researchers might ask about one's affinity for different brands and where one likes to shop, but it might seem more of an intrusion if they ask for detailed financial information. However, people might be willing to provide detailed financial information to the U.S. Census Bureau.

Tailored design also involves tailoring procedures to the particular population being surveyed. Knowledge about the target population or other similar populations can help surveyors develop effective design strategies that motivate response. For example, some populations can only be given questionnaires if they are handed to them in person: visitors to museums or national parks, or voters exiting the polls. In some situations, members of the population may only have access to one mode of communication, which greatly limits how they can be contacted. In other situations, it may not be possible to survey all of those sampled from the population using a single mode, so multiple modes may need to be used. Compared to surveys of the general public, surveys of more specialized populations, such as students, employees, or military personnel, usually achieve higher response rates.

In addition to these larger population considerations, it is important to consider differences among potential respondents within the population and how different aspects of the survey design may have different amounts of leverage on respondents' decisions to participate (Groves et al., 2000). When deciding whether to respond to a survey, each person evaluates the survey request based on his or her own values and beliefs, positions in society, current emotional state, and other psychological dispositions. Because of these differences, each feature of the survey design may be more important to some people than to others and can have positive or negative influences on people's decisions to respond. A summary of the tailored design method can be found in Figure 2.3.

The examples that follow show how some surveyors have successfully tailored their surveys to address the various types of issues that have been introduced throughout this chapter and how multiple concerns have been brought together to achieve desired results.

- An organization was interested in using the Internet to the extent possible (i.e., to reduce costs) to survey a large number of respondents from the general public on a variety of topics. To get a probability sample, they used a random-digit-dial telephone contact followed by a mail questionnaire to create a panel of many thousands who were willing to complete surveys every 2 to 3 weeks either by mail or Web depending

Figure 2.3   Overview of the tailored design method.

A. Tailored design is the development of survey procedures that work together to form the survey request and motivate various types of people to respond to the survey by establishing trust and increasing the perceived benefits of completing the survey while decreasing the expected costs of participation.

B. Successful tailored design attends to the multiple sources of survey error—coverage, sampling, measurement, and nonresponse—with a focus on minimizing overall survey error.

C. Tailored design involves customizing survey procedures for each particular survey situation based on knowledge about the topic and sponsor of the survey, the types of respondents who will be asked to complete the survey, and the proposed budget and time frame for reporting the results.

D. Multiple aspects of the implementation process and the questionnaire can be combined in different ways to encourage respondents to participate by creating trust in the sponsor and influencing the perceived expectations of the benefits and costs of responding to the survey.

To establish trust	To increase benefits of participation	To decrease costs of participation
■ Obtain sponsorship by legitimate authority	■ Provide information about the survey	■ Make it convenient to respond
■ Provide a token of appreciation in advance	■ Ask for help or advice	■ Avoid subordinating language
■ Make the task appear important	■ Show positive regard	■ Make the questionnaire short and easy to complete
■ Ensure confidentiality and security of information	■ Say thank you	■ Minimize requests to obtain personal or sensitive information
	■ Support group values	■ Emphasize similarity to other requests or tasks to which a person has responded
	■ Give tangible rewards	
	■ Make the questionnaire interesting	
	■ Provide social validation	
	■ Inform people that opportunities to respond are limited	

on their Internet access, frequency of computer and Internet use, and stated preferences (i.e., they reduced coverage error by including both people with and without Internet access). The surveys by mail and Web (two visual modes) contained identically worded questions and were constructed similarly to minimize potential measurement differences. To maintain interest in the panel and to encourage respondents to complete surveys (i.e., to minimize nonresponse and panel attrition), they routinely thanked panel members for their responses, occasionally sent token gifts, and sometimes gave summaries of results from earlier surveys in which the respondents had participated. For more information on such panels, see Chapter 9.

- A graduate student wanted to survey community leaders throughout two states for her dissertation, but like many other PhD students, she faced budget constraints because her project was self-financed. She first sampled communities across the two states and then used the Internet to identify key community officials who she would then ask to complete the 12-page mail questionnaire containing 50 questions (some with subparts). To distribute her labor and financial costs over several months, she divided the sample into three subsamples, which made it possible for her to do all of the mailing preparations herself, including multiple follow-ups (i.e., reducing nonresponse). Follow-ups were sent by mail in most cases; however, to get several sample members to respond she had to send the questionnaire as an e-mail attachment. Sending the same questionnaire, but with a different mode of delivery, helped reduce nonresponse while minimizing measurement error. She completed the survey with a 72% response rate (360 of 500; Crowe, 2008).

- A 25- to 30-question annual Internet survey about the undergraduate student experience at WSU was conducted six times from 2002 to 2007 with response rates consistently reaching the 50% to 60% level despite a number of shortcomings in the sample frame from which students were randomly selected. In particular, many students did not update their contact information after being admitted to the university. Moreover, a number of students did not use their university-provided e-mail address, and only 60% to 70% provided the university with a different e-mail address through which to contact them. As a result of both of these problems, implementation procedures were developed whereby a small $2 token of appreciation was sent (i.e., reducing nonresponse) via postal mail (i.e., reducing coverage error that would have resulted from using e-mail contacts) along with letters requesting that students go to the Web and complete the survey (i.e., using only one data collection mode eliminated the possibility of mode effects in the data). For students with known e-mail addresses, an e-mail was also sent after the letter to provide a more convenient hyperlink for accessing the survey (i.e., reducing nonresponse). Finally, up to two follow-ups by postal and/or e-mail were sent at 2- to 3-week intervals to encourage students to respond (see Smyth, Dillman, Christian, & Stern, 2005, for a more complete description of the methods used).

None of these surveys were perfect; however, each represents a deliberate effort to contemplate and minimize errors due to coverage, sampling, nonresponse, and measurement. Each of them involved multiple contacts that were carefully constructed to encourage the sampled individuals to respond. Some involved the Web only, some mail only, and some used both modes, but in every case the design was tailored to the situation, including the goals of the particular study, respondent preferences, what contact information was available, and the resources budgeted for the project.

CONCLUSION

Tailoring to the population, survey sponsorship, mode considerations, and other features of one's survey situation is not something one does just in the cover letter or e-mail. Nor is it something one does in just the questionnaire or in the decision to use or not use an incentive. It starts when one is making a decision to do a survey and should occur throughout the entire process of designing and implementing the survey. It is not something one does by attending to only a few parts of the survey process; it is something one thinks about when designing each and every part.

Recently we described the use of the social exchange framework and tailored design to a class of students. After summarizing the major trends of the past decade toward greater impersonalization in the survey process, less time spent focusing on each respondent as an individual, greater automation of the survey process, and the use of mass appeals that now characterize many web surveys, one student seemed perplexed. She then asked if applying social exchange was consistent with the times or if attending to so many details was akin to getting water to run uphill. Her question was reminiscent of the time when the original total design method book was written, and when the mass society technologies of the time made focusing on individual respondents difficult. Our response: Now that we have improved technological ability, perhaps part of the solution to the growing problem of decreasing response rates and their effect on nonresponse error is to change the trajectory of how we as survey researchers attempt to relate to respondents and their needs.

CHAPTER 3

Coverage and Sampling

A GRADUATE student came into the office one day and announced with enthusiasm, "I now know how to do the perfect survey on discrimination and harassment against minorities at this university." This particular student was very comfortable with large data sets, had recently learned to program web surveys effectively, and understood that access could be obtained to university e-mail address files. The rest of the conversation unfolded in the following way:

QUESTION: How will you make it perfect?

ANSWER: It's simple. Instead of surveying a sample of some kind we can just get all of the faculty, staff, and student e-mail addresses and ask them all to fill out a web survey. It's only 25,000 people, and surveys that big and even bigger are now done all the time because it's so easy to send mass e-mail and collect data on the Web.

QUESTION: Can you get everyone's e-mail address, and will all of them use their e-mail?

ANSWER: Well, the university gives everyone an e-mail address, so they must be able to use them.

QUESTION: What about some of the staff who work at the physical plant and others who choose not to use their university e-mail address? And also, what about people who have kept their e-mail address after leaving the university?

ANSWER: I don't think that would be a big enough problem to worry about, and a good survey can't do everything.

QUESTION: Do you think you would get a good response rate?

ANSWER: That's the beauty of it: Even if only 2,000 (8%) or so respond, that's enough to be accurate within 2.5%. So response rate isn't really a problem.

QUESTION: Do you think there is any danger that the 92% who don't respond will be different from the 8% who do respond?

ANSWER: Well, even if they are different, surely we would have responses from those who are most concerned about discrimination.

QUESTION: How likely is it that their answers may differ from those of nonrespondents?

ANSWER: I don't know, but we would still have responses from a lot of people, and surely that information will be useful because of there being so many respondents.

During the past few years, most survey methodologists have probably experienced a conversation with some of these features. The excitement of being able to contact enormous numbers of people for little or no cost has led many organizations to design and implement mass web surveys. Often these are sent to everyone associated with an organization or firm and use the same long questionnaires and questions as those being used in organizations elsewhere, regardless of their applicability to the specific group being surveyed.

A well-done sample survey provides the ability to estimate with known statistical precision (based on probability theory) characteristics of all members in a carefully defined population. But many mass surveys compromise the ability to estimate characteristics of a population because, in their eagerness to take advantage of new technologies, they ignore the fundamental premises of sample surveys. This was the case with the enthusiastic graduate student in the above conversation. This conversation illustrates some of the common flaws in thinking about what types of people to survey, how many people to survey, how to sample them, and how to survey them (e.g., assuming that e-mail lists are exact representations of a population, surveying the entire population, focusing on the number of completes, ignoring nonresponse, etc.). In essence, these elements of the survey process boil down to minimizing coverage and sampling error, which are the focuses of this chapter. We return to the student's mistakes in the conclusion to this chapter.

ESSENTIAL DEFINITIONS AND THEIR USE

Discussing coverage and sampling, even in a cursory way, requires a common understanding of certain terms.

- The *survey population* consists of all of the units (individuals, households, organizations) to which one desires to generalize survey results.
- The *sample frame* is the list from which a sample is to be drawn in order to represent the survey population.

- The *sample* consists of all units of the population that are drawn for inclusion in the survey.
- The *completed sample* consists of all of the units that complete the questionnaire.
- *Coverage error* results from every unit in the survey population not having a known, nonzero chance of being included in the sample.
- *Sampling error* is the result of collecting data from only a subset, rather than all, of the members of the sampling frame.

A community survey conducted in 2007 illustrates the use of these concepts. The goal was to estimate characteristics for residents in the adjacent communities of Lewiston, Idaho, and Clarkston, Washington (Dillman, Smyth, Christian, & O'Neill, 2008). This group of approximately 40,000 people constituted the *survey population*. The *sample frame* consisted of mailing addresses from the U.S. Postal Service Delivery Sequence File (DSF). From this list a random *sample* of 1,800 households was selected to represent the survey population. Letters to 109 of these households were returned undeliverable from the post office, leaving 1,691. To get from the household level of the DSF to the individual level of the target population, the survey contacts asked that the adult (at least 18 years old) in the household with the most recent birthday complete the questionnaire. Questionnaires were returned by respondents from 1,041 households, or about 62% of the contactable sample (i.e., AAPOR COOP2) (American Association for Public Opinion Research, 2008).

The completed sample size of 1,041 individuals composed the data set for statistical analysis. Because the sample was randomly selected, this completed sample size can be used to determine the amount of *sampling error*, and therefore the likely precision of the estimates for the entire survey population (i.e., residents of the Lewiston/Clarkston communities) can be made. For a completed sample of this size, one could have statistical confidence that the estimates based on sample results were within about ±3 points of the "true value" of the population, assuming there is no additional error from other sources.

COVERAGE CONSIDERATIONS

THE CURRENT STATE OF COVERAGE AND SAMPLING

Telephone Coverage

From the 1980s through the 1990s, the telephone was widely regarded as the best survey mode for general population surveys because nearly everyone in the United States (more than 90%) had telephone service (i.e., high coverage), random-digit-dialing (RDD) procedures allowed these persons to be randomly sampled, and people were generally amenable to answering survey questions over the telephone. However, the development and increasingly widespread adoption of the cellular telephone has begun to significantly reduce telephone coverage rates. In 2003, nearly half of all people in the United States used wireless telephones (Blumberg, Luke, & Cynamon, 2006), and 2.8% entirely substituted wireless service for their residential landline phones (Blumberg & Luke, 2006). By late 2007, however, nearly 16% of U.S. adults had fully replaced their landline phones with wireless service, and growing evidence shows that these people lead substantially different lifestyles than their landline counterparts (e.g., they are more likely to be young adults, living with unrelated roommates, renting their homes, living in poverty, and living in the South; Blumberg & Luke, 2008). When one combines these wireless-only individuals with those who do not have any telephone service, the estimate is that about 18% of the U.S. adult population is missed by traditional RDD sampling. Some surveyors have sought ways to incorporate cellular telephone numbers into their samples, but the complexity of this practice is beyond the scope of this book. So that we can focus here on self-administered surveys, we refer readers to a 2007 special edition of *Public Opinion Quarterly* devoted to this topic (Lavrakas, 2007) and a recent volume titled *Advances in Telephone Survey Methodology* (Lepkowski et al., 2008). The main point here is that telephone coverage rates, long considered the primary strength of this mode, have become questionable, thus eroding the power of RDD sampling, which has long been considered the gold standard of cost-effective survey sampling. As a result, many are now turning to self-administered survey modes in search of alternatives to RDD sampling.

Internet Coverage

One way that surveyors have tried to circumvent the problems of telephone coverage and nonresponse (as discussed in Chapter 1) is through the use of web surveys. However, although the Internet is a useful mode for conducting surveys targeted at very specific populations such as college students and certain professionals, it too has significant coverage gaps in the general population. According to the Pew Internet & American Life Project, in September 2007, only about 71% of the U.S. population used the Internet at least occasionally, and only 67% had Internet service in their homes. Moreover, only 47% of the U.S. population had a high-speed connection at home; 23% used dial-up, and the remaining 29% did not have Internet access (Horrigan & Smith, 2007). That means 29% are left out of Internet surveys altogether, and more than half of the population does not have Internet service that is sufficient to operate many web surveys. Moreover, 2% of those who use the Internet use it only at work (Horrigan & Smith, 2007), where there are oftentimes restrictions on the way it can be used that might inhibit users' ability to participate in web surveys.

The lack of Internet service for 29% of the population and high-speed service for 53% of the population is complicated by differences between those who have and do not have these services. Non-Whites, people 65+ years old, people with lower incomes, and those with less education have lower Internet access rates than their counterparts, and, therefore, are more likely to be left out of Internet surveys (Pew Internet & American Life Project, 2007). These same groups, as well as those living in rural areas, are also underrepresented among those with high-speed Internet service (Horrigan & Smith, 2007).

Internet access rates have grown steadily since the 1990s and continue to grow; however, as is the case with many new technologies, it appears that the growth may be slowing. Nevertheless, even if every household in the United States were to have high-speed Internet service, the Internet may still be inadequate for general population surveys for several reasons. First, there is no list of all (or even most) known members of the population (i.e., a sampling frame). Second, there is no simple procedure available for drawing samples in which individuals or households have a known, nonzero chance of being included. This inability is partly the result of widely different e-mail address structures. Examples of the many ways one person's address might vary range from complete full name or nickname to a descriptor that has nothing to do with one's name. For example: Elizabeth.Fern.Thompson@domain.com, EFT@domain.com, thompsonef@domain.com, ethompson@domain.com, thompson005@domain.com, liz@domain.com, FloppyEars@domain.com, and busymom@domain.com. In addition, some people share e-mail addresses with a partner or spouse (e.g., lizandhank@domain.com); and many individuals have multiple addresses, sometimes from different providers (e.g., xxxxx@yahoo.com, xxxxx@university.edu, xxxxx@msn.com). Currently there is no equivalent to the RDD algorithm of randomly selecting numbers (e.g., 509-555-xxxx) from local telephone exchanges. Third, whereas most people have the ability to use a telephone, people's ability to use the Internet varies significantly, even within households that have good Internet access, making any within-household selection processes quite difficult to implement effectively.

Moreover, even if such addresses could be sampled, there are legal and cultural barriers to contacting randomly generated e-mail addresses. Because Internet service providers are private rather than public providers, surveyors do not have the assumed right to contact people as was the case with telephone, nor do professional associations of surveyors support sending e-mails to populations with which the surveyor has no preexisting relationship. The Council of American Survey Research Organizations (CASRO), for example, states in its code of standards that "Research Organizations are required to verify that individuals contacted for research by e-mail have a reasonable expectation that they will receive e-mail contact for research" (2007, p. 8). A preexisting relationship is necessary for respondents to have such a "reasonable expectation."

In response to these challenges, web surveyors have increasingly come to rely on self-selected panels of respondents. People willing to join panels and fill out surveys provide their contact information voluntarily and are thereafter asked to respond periodically to surveys on a variety of topics until they leave the panel. Some web panels contain tens and even hundreds of thousands of active panel members at a time, which has helped many surveyors circumscribe the challenges discussed above of finding and contacting web survey respondents. However, many web panels are not representative of the general population. Moreover, the easy access that web panels provide to large numbers of willing potential respondents and the very low marginal costs for collecting data from each additional panel member have led to a "bigger is better" mentality, such that enormous numbers of panel members are sampled for each survey. In these instances, even if only a small proportion of the sampled panel members complete the survey, the completed sample size is still quite large. This all too often leads to the unfortunate situation where reporting that surveys have been completed by tens of thousands of people gives the impression that estimates are quite precise. However, what gets overlooked in many of these cases is that it is not possible to calculate sampling error because of the nonprobability nature of the sample to begin with, and in almost all cases there is a substantial risk of high nonresponse error. Web panels are a topic to which we return in more detail in Chapter 9.

Mail Coverage

Telephone directories, which included complete mailing addresses, once provided a reasonable sampling list for households in many regions of the United States, but by the early 1990s the proportion of households with unlisted telephone numbers had increased dramatically to about 25% nationwide (Survey Sampling, personal communication, August 19, 1999). In addition, cell-phone-only households are not listed in such directories, and many of the households for which landline telephone numbers are now provided are listed without a mailing address. Furthermore, the trend toward spouses not changing last names when they marry has meant that wives and husbands with different last names are both likely to be listed in directories, giving these households a higher probability of being selected in a random sample. As a result of these changes, telephone directories are inadequate for general population surveys, which for a number of years made the mail mode an unlikely candidate for large-scale national surveys. However, mail surveying has recently reemerged as a possible mode for conducting random-sample, general population surveys because recent advances in computer technologies have enabled the creation and maintenance of large-scale address lists.

One particularly promising *address-based sampling* list that has been made available in recent years is the U.S. Postal Service DSF. The DSF is an electronic file containing all delivery point addresses serviced by the U.S. Postal

Service. In other words, it contains the address of every delivery stop on every postal carrier's route, with the exception of general delivery (i.e., having mail held for pickup at the post office); however, it does not contain any names associated with the addresses. Some advantages of the DSF are that it contains a variable to differentiate between business and residential addresses (a task that is problematic in RDD surveys), and it can be geo-coded for stratified sampling or targeting specific populations.

The DSF also has some weaknesses as a sampling frame. For one, it is available only through private list vendors, each of whom has different protocols for managing and updating the lists, resulting in some list differences across vendors (Link et al., 2005). Missing addresses for multiperson dwellings such as apartment complexes can also be problematic because they can result in large groups of people being left off the list.

Only a small handful of studies have examined the quality of the DSF as a sampling frame, but initial evaluations have shown that it provides up to 95% coverage rates (Iannacchione, Staab, & Redden, 2003). However, coverage rates tend to be lower in rural areas, in areas in transition, and on Native American reservations and military bases than in more densely populated areas (Link et al., 2005; O'Muircheartaigh, English, & Eckman, 2007; Steve, Dally, Lavrakas, Yancey, & Kulp, 2007). Whereas households in these areas are underrepresented, households that have multiple mailing addresses, such as both a post office box and a street address, are overrepresented because both addresses are contained on the list, thereby giving these households a higher probability of being selected.

One study compared results to the Behavioral Risk Factor Surveillance System survey across parallel RDD landline telephone surveys and DSF mail surveys conducted in six states (California, Illinois, New Jersey, North Carolina, Texas, and Washington; Link, Battaglia, Frankel, Osborn, & Mokdad, 2008). In this study, the DSF mail survey (with a reminder mailing), resulted in response rates that were 4 to 7 percentage points higher than those achieved in the RDD survey. A comparison of characteristics of both the DSF and RDD respondents to the 2003 Current Population Survey, which is considered by many to be the most accurate benchmark for comparison of demographic characteristics in the United States, revealed that both the RDD and DSF surveys overrepresented White, non-Hispanic individuals; individuals with high education levels; and married persons. In addition, the RDD survey overrepresented people with children, and the DSF survey overrepresented those with incomes of $50,000 or more. Both surveys underrepresented those living with three adults in their household, and the DSF also underrepresented those living outside of metropolitan statistical areas (Link et al., 2008).

Another important difference was that whereas the RDD landline survey did not include cell-phone-only respondents and those with no telephone service, 6.5% of the DSF mail survey respondents reported cell-only status and an additional 1% reported having no telephone. Thus, the DSF mail survey was able to collect data from those who cannot be contacted via RDD landline surveys. Finally, cost estimates revealed that the DSF mail data collection effort saved more than $8,500 per 1,000 respondents compared to the RDD data collection (Link et al., 2008). The savings would have been even larger if the surveyors had attempted to include cellular telephone numbers in the RDD versions.

Thus, based on the limited research that has been conducted thus far, the DSF appears to have a number of appealing aspects, but also a number of important shortcomings that must be kept in mind. Overall, the DSF and address-based sampling lists provide promising opportunities for conducting random-sample surveys of the general public, but more research is needed on just how promising these lists are.

Other alternatives to telephone directories and the DSF also may exist for more local general population surveys (i.e., at the regional, state, or county level). In some states, sampling for general public surveys can be accomplished by obtaining driver's license lists. Although these lists do not include individuals without licenses, thus biasing results against those segments of the population who do not obtain driver's licenses, they provide a reasonable approximation of the general public and make respondent selection within households unnecessary. However, increasingly states do not require that driver's licenses be renewed each year and these lists have a tendency to age, with mailing addresses becoming less reliable as the required time between renewals increases. Another possibility is to consider the use of registered voter lists. For community issue surveys aimed at predicting election results, such lists may be quite adequate. Yet the high proportion of those who do not register to vote may make them unacceptable for most other purposes. Utility lists have also been used, but they often include the owners or management companies that pay the bills rather than the people who occupy rented units, thus exhibiting the potential for coverage error.

Krysan, Schuman, Scott, and Beatty (1994) evaluated a means of sampling general public households without using lists. Previous in-person probability surveys of the same geographic area were used to create a sample frame by having interviewers record residential addresses adjacent to where any interview had taken place. Mail surveys were later sent to these newly sampled addresses. Using a five-contact strategy that included a prepaid $1 bill and final contact by 2-day priority mail, quite similar to the basic model described here in Chapter 7, they achieved a 74% response rate in predominantly White Detroit suburbs compared to 75% by face-to-face interview. This method did not work as well in predominantly Black areas of Detroit, where only 46% response was achieved compared with 83% by face-to-face interview. In both strata the mail survey was 5 to 10 minutes long compared with about an hour for the face-to-face interview, which included many additional questions. Nevertheless, this method of sampling offers promise for overcoming the major coverage challenge for general public mail surveys.

Increasingly, general public lists are being compiled by combining information from a large variety of sources: credit card holders, telephone directories, city directories, magazine subscribers, bank depositors, organization membership lists, catalog and Internet customers, and so on. Although these lists are not representative of the population and, therefore, should not be used as sampling frames, the information they contain can sometimes be linked with samples drawn from more representative lists such as the DSF. For example, by matching addresses from a DSF-based sample with addresses on these lists, it may be possible to learn names of respondents who live at the address or to obtain a phone number or e-mail address associated with the address that can be used for follow-up contacts with nonrespondents.

REDUCING COVERAGE ERROR

Although the issue of finding a good general population sampling frame is of concern to the larger field of survey methodology and to those who field large-scale national surveys, by far the largest portion of people administering self-administered surveys are interested in specialized groups such as store customers, employees of organizations, members of special interest organizations, and service subscribers. Computer technologies have made it possible to compile and maintain enormous up-to-date lists for these types of populations.

Developing and maintaining lists has become a specialized activity that is typically done in response to the diverse needs of organizations, particularly their mail-out needs. Sometimes legal and ethical concerns cause certain information to be added or subtracted from a list. Some people have telephone numbers and e-mail addresses, whereas others do not. Sometimes the list is divided into sublists for typical mailing needs, with the result that individual names may appear on several of the sublists. Lists are often formatted for particular mailing equipment in a way that makes their use for other purposes difficult. Some lists are formatted entirely in capital letters, which need to be changed for writing cover letters. Knowing the ins and outs of how a specific list is compiled, maintained, and managed is essential for understanding what type of list exists and how it can be used. Becoming this familiar with a list oftentimes requires one to seek out the office or person who keeps the list. Following are five questions that should be asked about any potential sampling list.

Does the List Contain Everyone in the Survey Population?

One of us was once given a list that was described as including all members of a health maintenance organization. When he asked how the list was compiled, the list keeper reached for an enrollment form on his desk that included a box that allowed members to check if they wished not to have their home address revealed to any outside organization. The list he was being given was one sometimes provided to outside organizations, and the sponsors of the proposed survey had simply forgotten that not all members were on the list. Had he used the list, he would have had an obvious coverage problem, and the sponsor would not have been able to claim that the sample survey results represented all members of the organization.

An essential first step in evaluating the list is to determine whether all members of the survey population are on it. If they are not, then one should determine whether getting the remainder of the people on the list is possible or evaluate the likely coverage consequences of not obtaining the excluded names.

Does the List Include Names of People Who Are Not in the Study Population?

Many years ago, when asked to survey graduates of a university, one of us was given the alumni mailing list from which to sample. Only when returns started coming back did he learn from some questionnaires that the respondents had not attended that university. Further inquiry with the sample provider revealed that for convenience in mailing university publications, the list had been expanded to include contributors to the university. He also learned that spouses were left on the list after alumni died. In addition, this survey included many questions about what each alumnus had done after graduation. It was only after surveys were returned that the surveyor learned that the definition of alumnus included anyone who had attended the university for at least one semester, regardless of whether he or she had graduated.

This experience points to the critical need to know exactly whom a list does or does not include and to develop different ways of dealing with any deficiencies. When the surveyor learned that the list included people who were not in the intended population, he also learned that the names of donors, spouses, and nongraduates could be deleted from the data file. However, had it not been possible to delete them, prior knowledge of the list's complete structure would have allowed many of the questions to be structured so that ineligible individuals would have been screened from inappropriate questions. For example, nongraduates would have been directed to skip the question on what year they had graduated from the university.

Sometimes it is possible to partly recover from undetected problems of this nature. For example, responses from nongraduates might have been discarded. However, learning ahead of time exactly who is on the list and why would have caused less embarrassment for both the survey sponsors and the recipients of the questionnaire, and it would have saved valuable resources.

How Is the List Maintained and Updated?

Lists are maintained in many different ways. Sometimes address lists are actively updated by regularly resending undeliverable correspondence with address correction requests. Likewise, updates may occur once a year when memberships are renewed. In other instances, a list sits unused for years, with only new names and addresses being added, so that names added in earlier years are less likely to have current addresses. Finally, in many cases updating contact information is left up to individual list members, thus eliminating the costs to the organization of having to employ people to update the list. As just one example, university students are often responsible for reporting any address and phone number changes to the university. Unfortunately, many never do, resulting in poor-quality lists. Knowing these characteristics of a list allows one to evaluate the likelihood of unintended coverage biases (e.g., fewer good addresses for older members on a survey about retirement saving) creeping into one's survey results. In difficult cases of this nature, we have sometimes sent letters to a sample of list members, or even the whole list, with "Address Correction Requested" on the envelope in order to learn from the U.S. Postal Service how many addresses were invalid.

Are the Same Sample Units Included on the List More than Once?

When doing customer surveys, we have sometimes been given lists that have the same address, or nearly the same address, for several names. Investigation of this phenomenon for one such list revealed that the list was compiled from customer orders made over the course of several years. Each time an order was taken, the purchaser was asked to give an address, and sometimes different household members purchased goods from the same source. The variations in addresses and names also stemmed from people giving their name or address in a slightly different way on different orders, and the process of eliminating only exact duplicates allowed those variations to remain on the list. This problem appears to be decreasing as companies increasingly check for previous orders for an address and make corrections when accepting orders.

A district-wide survey of the parents of school children presented the problem of duplication in a different way. The keeper of the list created a separate listing for each parent. If a child had two parents living in separate residences, usually as a result of separation or divorce, each parent had a separate entry on the address list. However, if the parents lived together, they were listed as one entry. The sample was designed on the basis of individual children being the sample unit, so that all children were to have an equal chance of their parent (or parents) being drawn in the sample. The result of the sampling from this address list would have given each child with separated or divorced parents twice the likelihood of being included in the sample as children with parents living together. The solution required matching parent names to each child and then deciding randomly which parent should be asked to respond to the survey.

Does the List Contain Other Information that Can Be Used to Improve the Survey?

Increasingly, mixed-mode surveys are being used to improve response rates for studies. In addition, a follow-up contact by a different mode, such as telephone, is particularly effective in identifying ineligible units in the population. Such individuals are probably less likely than others to respond to repeated contacts by mail. For this reason, it is useful to determine whether telephone numbers (daytime or evening), e-mail addresses, fax numbers, or other information that might facilitate contact by another mode is available.

In addition, some lists contain information such as age or gender that might be used in a postsurvey analysis to evaluate nonresponse error. Other information, such as number of orders submitted during the past year, year of initial organization membership, or perhaps level of membership may be available for analyzing nonresponse errors in ways more pertinent to specific survey objectives or sponsors.

What to Do When No List Is Available

Visitors to national parks and museums, users of airports, and attendees at open houses are examples of groups for which no list may exist. For such populations, coverage is not a problem if people can be sampled as they experience the place or activity of interest. Procedures for sampling, delivering, and retrieving self-administered questionnaires from unlisted populations are one of the tailored applications discussed in Chapter 10.

RESPONDENT SELECTION

Sometimes letters are addressed to an individual within the household or organization who is not necessarily the person who should complete the questionnaire. For household surveys, just as the goal is to give each household a known chance of selection, it is often desirable to give each adult in the household a known probability of selection. Letters intended for households that are addressed to an individual provide a special problem in this regard because that person may immediately "take ownership" of the questionnaire. When the first edition of this book was published, general public samples drawn from telephone directories typically produced a higher proportion of male respondents than female respondents even though letters requested that an adult female complete the questionnaire in half the households. The overrepresentation of male respondents stemmed from the fact that men's names were more likely to be listed than their spouses' names, so the envelopes were often addressed to them (Dillman et al., 1974). In contrast, women were somewhat more likely to participate in telephone surveys because they were more likely to answer the telephone, and it was sometimes difficult to get access to another household adult.

Commonly used respondent selection methods such as the Kish (1949) method, which requires listing members of a household by age and gender, do not work well in household mail and Internet surveys because of the complexity of the request and the need to collect information that may be considered sensitive before allowing respondents to become engaged in the questionnaire. An alternative method that is sometimes used is the most recent birthday method. A sentence is inserted in the cover letter and sometimes on the questionnaire that makes a request of this nature: "In order for the results of this survey to accurately represent all adults in the state, it is important that the questionnaire sent to your household be completed by the adult (18 years or older) who currently lives there and who has had the most recent birthday."

This technique, when used over the telephone, has produced an over-representation of women (Groves & Lyberg, 1988), which may occur because women are somewhat more likely than men to answer home telephones. Similar findings have been reported for mail surveys (Battaglia, Link, Frankel, Osborn, & Mokdad, 2005). Moreover, in both telephone and self-administered modes, there is some risk that the request for the person with the most recent birthday will be ignored or misunderstood, resulting in the wrong person being selected (Battaglia et al., 2005; Gaziano, 2005; Lavrakas, Stasny, & Harpuder, 2000). Nevertheless, in the absence of better alternatives that can be easily understood and executed by respondents, the most recent birthday method seems to be among the best within-household selection methods for self-administered surveys.

Some household surveys are not aimed at obtaining a representative sample of the adult population. Instead, the topic of interest may be a household behavior, in which case the person with the greatest responsibility for that area of activity should complete the questionnaire. For example, a survey on telephone service appropriately requested the following: "The adult most responsible for making decisions about the telephone services provided to your household should complete the enclosed questionnaire." This line of reasoning can be extended to many areas of activity, from shopping for groceries to purchasing automobiles to making investment decisions. It also applies to businesses where the desired respondent may be the one most responsible for recommending or making decisions about, for example, the purchase of computers. In these types of surveys, the coverage issue is thereby limited to the household or business level.

COVERAGE OUTCOMES

The hoped-for outcome of the coverage considerations we have discussed here is that every unit in the survey population appears on the sample frame list once (or can otherwise be available by its appearance at a sampling location). As a result, each unit will have a known chance, and in most cases the same chance as any other member of the population, of being selected into the survey sample to receive a questionnaire. The survey population is thus prepared for actual sampling.

Frequently, a coverage analysis of potential sample frames produces a conclusion that no list is completely adequate for one's purpose. The surveyor is then faced with a decision about whether plans for the survey should be abandoned or whether a certain amount of coverage error is acceptable. Such decisions usually involve a consideration of whether any alternatives exist (frequently they do not), the cost of those alternatives, and whether any methods exist for evaluating the extent of any resultant error.

One alternative that many surveyors have turned to in recent years is the use of mixed-mode surveys, which is discussed at length in Chapter 8. The goal of this strategy is to compensate for the coverage weaknesses of one mode with another and vice versa. For example, one might conduct a survey primarily via the Internet but send a paper questionnaire through the mail to those in the sample who do not have Internet access, thus minimizing the possibility of coverage error attributable to lack of Internet access. Additionally, mixed-mode surveying provides one solution to the challenge of respondents exercising more and more choice about what contact information they make available and of different people providing different types of information.

PROBABILITY SAMPLING

The remarkable power of the sample survey is its ability to estimate closely the distribution of a characteristic in a population by obtaining information from relatively few elements of that population. Sampling error is the type of error that occurs because information is requested from only a sample of the members of the population rather than from everyone in the population. It is highly dependent on sample size and, in contrast to the other three types of survey error, can usually be estimated with considerable precision.

Drawing a sample can be remarkably complex or fairly simple. When the dominant mode of collecting survey data was face-to-face interviews, samples were typically drawn in several stages: first selecting geographic areas, then choosing subareas (e.g., census tracts) within those areas, segments within subareas, residences within segments, and finally individuals within residences. The benefit of drawing a sample in this way was that the costs of interviewing could be reduced enormously by reducing the distance for interviewers to travel between sampled households. For mail and web surveys, the geographical distance between respondents usually has no effect on costs. This fact alone makes it possible to avoid some of the potential complexities of this type of sampling for self-administered surveys.

Because the concern in this book is to be able to generalize results of a survey from the sample that completed the questionnaire to the survey population, we are necessarily talking about probability as opposed to nonprobability methods of sampling. We also exclude explanation of the complexities of how to develop alternative sampling designs or the statistical theory and proofs that underlie the development of such designs from our sampling discussion. Many excellent texts describe these aspects of conducting a quality survey (Lohr, 1999; Maxim, 1999). In addition, one may also consult the classic sampling texts by Kish (1965) and Cochran (1977). Our focus here is on the general relationship between sample size and the reduction of sampling error in the context of simple random sampling.

Sampling error is defined as error stemming from the fact that only a subset of the entire population is surveyed. It is possible to survey a targeted subset of the general population that is large enough theoretically to make fairly precise estimates for the population as a whole, but that would be unacceptable for making inferences about the general population for other reasons. An example is surveying 1,200 residents from only one community and claiming the completed sample is large enough to estimate within about 3 percentage points the opinions of the nation as a whole. A well-trained surveyor would never attempt to make such a claim. Yet we frequently hear of survey sponsors or media outlets attempting to generalize results to the entire population from web surveys of whoever happened to find the site and volunteered to fill it out, questionnaires distributed in magazines and returned by the tiny percentage who were interested, or questionnaires given to whomever was willing to complete them. Still, understanding the number of properly selected respondents necessary for generalizing results to the population is the first essential step in drawing a survey sample.

How Large Should a Sample Be?

When one is first confronted with the question of how many respondents is enough, the answer may seem quite nonintuitive. If, for example, one wishes to estimate the percentage of people who have a college education in a small county of 25,000 adults within 3 percentage points of the actual percentage, a completed sample of about 1,024 respondents is needed. If one wants to estimate this characteristic for a small state of 2 million adults with the same confidence, then about 1,067 respondents are needed. If, however, this information is sought for the entire United States, then the same number—1,067—is needed. These examples demonstrate one of the primary characteristics of probability sampling: It is the size of the sample, not the proportion of the population sampled, that affects precision. The formula below can be used to determine what size of a completed sample is needed, taking into account (a) how much sampling error can be tolerated within a given confidence level (i.e., desired confidence interval width or margin of error), (b) the amount of confidence one wishes to have in the estimates, (c) how varied the population is with respect to the characteristic of interest, and (d) the size of the population from which the sample is to be drawn:

$$N_s = \frac{(N_p)(p)(1-p)}{(N_p - 1)(B/C)^2 + (p)(1-p)}$$

Where: N_s = the *completed* sample size needed for the desired level of precision.

N_p = the size of the population.

p = the proportion of the population expected to choose one of the two response categories.

B = margin of error (i.e., half of the desired confidence interval width): .03 = ±3%.

C = Z score associated with the confidence level (1.96 corresponds to the 95% level).

To explain further, N_s is the sample size needed for the size of the survey population and N_p is the number of units (people, households, etc.) in the survey population from which the sample is to be drawn (i.e., the city, county, state, nation, etc.). The term $(p)(1-p)$ is a measure of the expected variation in answers to the question of interest. This term is set at the most conservative value possible (i.e., the expectation that 50% of the people in the population answer "yes" to a question and 50% answer "no"). B represents one half of the width of the confidence interval one desires the estimate to fall within—for example, being able to estimate the value of a characteristic of the population within a range of ±3 percentage points. Finally, C is the corresponding Z score associated with the amount of statistical confidence one desires to have in the estimates, a level that is commonly set at 95%. Using the 95% confidence level ($C = 1.96$) means that one can be statistically confident that 95 out of 100 times that a random sample is drawn from the population, the estimate obtained from the completed sample will be within the stated confidence interval ($B = .03$; ±3 percentage points in this example).

Thus, for a question with a 50/50 split in a population of 800 people, a completed sample size of 458 cases is needed to be sure that the estimate of interest will be within ±3 percentage points 95% of the time:

$$N_s = \frac{(800)(.5)(.5)}{(800-1)(.03/1.96)^2 + (.5)(.5)}$$

$$N_s = 458$$

To put it another way, one can conclude for a yes/no question in which one expects respondents to be split 50/50 (the most conservative assumption that can be made about variance) that 19 out of 20 times that a random sample of 458 people is selected from the total population of 800, the true population value for the question will be within 3 percentage points of the sample estimate.

But not all questions are yes/no items. Moreover, the amount of variation that exists in a population characteristic differs from one population to another. For example, the variation in age of first-year students at a major university may be quite small, mostly 17- to 19-year-olds, whereas in the general public age variation is quite broad. The greater the variation, the larger the sample size needed for making population estimates. For this reason, the examples presented here assume maximum heterogeneity (a 50/50 split) on a proportion in the population from which the sample is to be drawn.

If we experiment with different parameters in the equation above, we discover several somewhat nonintuitive premises about sample size that need to be understood in order to make wise sampling decisions. These premises are reflected in Figure 3.1, which was derived from the sample size

Figure 3.1 Completed sample sizes needed for various population sizes and characteristics at three confidence interval widths (i.e., margins of error).

	Sample Size for the 95% Confidence Level					
	± 10%		± 5%		± 3%	
Population Size	50/50 Split	80/20 Split	50/50 Split	80/20 Split	50/50 Split	80/20 Split
100	49	38	80	71	92	87
200	65	47	132	111	169	155
400	78	53	196	153	291	253
600	83	56	234	175	384	320
800	86	57	260	188	458	369
1,000	88	58	278	198	517	406
2,000	92	60	322	219	696	509
4,000	94	61	351	232	843	584
6,000	95	61	361	236	906	613
8,000	95	61	367	239	942	629
10,000	95	61	370	240	965	640
20,000	96	61	377	243	1,013	661
40,000	96	61	381	244	1,040	672
100,000	96	61	383	245	1,056	679
1,000,000	96	61	384	246	1,066	683
1,000,000,000	96	61	384	246	1,067	683

equation above. The figure is presented here less because of its practical use for surveyors than for the general perspective it provides about sample sizes needed for doing self-administered surveys.

Premise 1: Relatively Few Completed Questionnaires Can Provide Surprising Precision at a High Level of Confidence

This is the reason that survey sampling is such a powerful tool. Figure 3.1 shows that if one could be satisfied with knowing whether an estimate from a sample survey is within ±10 percentage points of the true population value, that estimate could be calculated by obtaining completed questionnaires from a random sample of only about 100 individuals. What this means is that in a properly conducted national survey with a completed simple random sample of 100 households, in which 60% of the respondents say they own the home in which they are living, one could state with 95% confidence that between 50% and 70% of the entire population owns the home in which they live, assuming there is no error from nonresponse, measurement, or coverage.

Premise 2: Among Large Populations There Is Virtually No Difference in the Completed Sample Size Needed for a Given Level of Precision

This premise is also reflected in the sample size numbers presented in Figure 3.1 and is shown visually in Figure 3.2, which graphs the completed sample sizes that are needed to make estimates within ±3, ±5, and ±10 percentage points by population size. For each of these lines, when the population size gets large (i.e., 6,000+), the lines level off considerably, meaning that the differences in the needed completed sample size are quite small

Figure 3.2   Completed sample size needed by population size and desired margin of error (95% confidence level with 50/50 split).

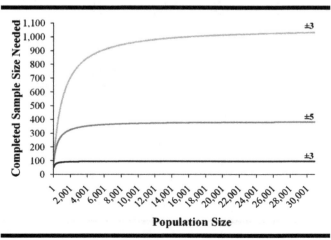

among large populations. It is only when the population size decreases to a few thousand or less that the number of completed questionnaires needed for a given confidence interval width begins to change significantly. It is for this reason that one can estimate within ±3 percentage points the percentage of people who have a high school education in a small county of 25,000 adults with 1,024 completes and can measure the same thing among the entire U.S. population of more than 300 million by obtaining only 43 more completes.

Premise 3: Within Small Populations, Greater Proportions of the Population Need to Be Surveyed (i.e., Completed) to Achieve Estimates within a Given Margin of Error

Frequently survey sponsors ask why, if about 1,200 people will provide an estimate within 3 percentage points in a national poll, they cannot get by with only a small fraction of that number when their entire survey population is only one county or small city. This question returns us to our original claim that it is not the proportion of the population that is sampled, but the size of the sample, that matters. The proportion that must be sampled changes across population sizes and is much higher among small populations.

This raises the question of whether one should sample at all, or instead attempt to survey everyone in smaller populations. This question is especially critical for self-administered surveys, in which the marginal costs of contacting additional people are usually less than for interview surveys. In these cases, survey sponsors frequently make quick decisions to survey everyone in their small populations, but as a consequence they usually have to spread their resources thinner, so that other sources of error do not get minimized to the extent possible. However, there is nothing to be gained by surveying all 1,000 members of a population in a way that produces only 350 responses (a 35% response rate) versus surveying a random sample of only 500 in a way that produces the same number of responses (a 70% response rate), because the potential of nonrespondents being different from respondents on important survey items (i.e., nonresponse error) may be greater when the response rate is lower. In cases like this, considering only the relationship between *completed sample size* and statistical precision, and overlooking the potential for nonresponse error, leads to unwise decisions in which survey sponsors simply trade small amounts of sampling error for potentially large amounts of nonresponse error. This brings us to our next premise.

Premise 4: At Higher Levels of Sample Size, Increases in Sample Size Yield Smaller and Smaller Reductions in the Margin of Error

This premise is demonstrated in Figure 3.3, which shows the margin of error that can be expected as the completed sample size increases from 1 to 1,000 in a population of 1,000 (50/50 split, 95% confidence level). This graph shows

Figure 3.3   Rate of decrease in margin of error resulting from increases in completed sample size in a population of 1,000 (95% confidence level with 50/50 split).

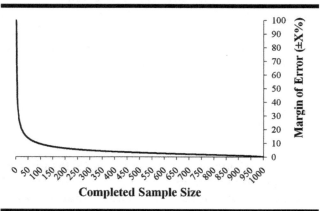

that the margin of error is drastically reduced from ±98 points to ±13.5 points as the completed sample size increases from 1 to 50. As the completed sample size is increased from 50 to 100, the margin of error continues to decrease, but much less drastically, to ±9.3 points. In this example, the sampling error drops below 5 percentage points at a completed sample size of 278. Surveying the entire population would require one to survey hundreds more, thus substantially increasing costs, but could only reduce the margin of error 5 percentage points under the best conditions. As pointed out above, the additional resources might better be allocated to improving response rates among a smaller sample.

Premise 5: Completed Sample Sizes Must Be Much Larger if One Wants to Make Precise Estimates for Subgroups of Populations

The discussion up to this point has assumed that the surveyor is interested in making estimates only for the survey population as a whole. If, in a statewide survey of adults, one desires to make estimates for women only with a precision of ±3 percentage points using the 95% level of confidence, then one needs slightly more than 1,000 women respondents in the survey. If one wants this much precision at the same level of confidence for women who are between 18 and 35 years old, the same reasoning applies (i.e., one needs more than 1,000 women who are within that specific age group). The desire for substantial precision in making estimates for subgroups of populations is typically a powerful factor in pushing samples as high as the sponsor can afford. Indeed, in most cases, determining sample sizes is far more likely to be based on the amount of funds available than on a strict calculation of the limits of sample sizes.

How to Draw a Simple Random Sample

Face-to-face interview surveys often require using multiple-stage sampling to minimize costs. Telephone surveys require generating random lists of numbers. In contrast, self-administered surveys are most likely to begin with lists of names, postal addresses, or e-mail addresses and, because of the insensitivity of such surveys to distance costs, allow the use of very simple sampling methods.

The most common type of sampling used for self-administered surveys is simple random sampling, in which every member of the sample frame (or list) has an equal chance of being selected. This can be accomplished in several different ways. One way is to assign a different number to every respondent, write each of those numbers on a slip of paper, put them into a hat, and draw a sample of the size one wants. However, doing so is fairly laborious, especially if the population is larger than a few hundred units. The much simpler and now most common way is to use a computer program that numbers and randomly selects respondents.

In the past, systematic samples were often drawn for self-administered surveys. That is, members of the population were numbered consecutively from 1 to the highest number (say 10,000). Then an interval was determined based on the desired size of sample (say the desired sample size is 1,000). A sample of this size from this sample frame meant that every tenth name needed to be selected, so the sampling interval became 10. The researcher then randomly drew a number within the interval of 1 to 10 to determine the starting point. The hat method would work fine for determining the starting point. If the selected starting point was seven, then every tenth number from that point forward (i.e., 17, 27, 37, to 9,997) would be selected for inclusion in the sample. Systematic samples are adequate if there is no periodicity (i.e., a characteristic that appears with the same frequency as the selected interval) in the list. A traditional example of this problem was selecting every tenth person in the U.S. Army with squads of 10 soldiers in which the first listed person in each squad, and the one drawn, was the squad leader. Alphabetized lists normally do not exhibit a problem of this nature. Systematic sampling methods are far less likely to be used today than in the past. The likelihood of having sampling lists in electronic files means that random selection methods can usually be used in which the computer generates random numbers.

Mailing costs for questionnaires sent within the United States are about the same regardless of distance. Consequently, there is often no advantage in general public surveys to using more complicated sample designs that cluster households together geographically and draw samples in stages (e.g., area of country followed by geographic chunks within areas, and segments within chunks). However, when faced with designing such surveys for groups that cannot be listed, more complex designs may save money and perhaps be the only way that such surveys can be undertaken (Lohr, 1999). An example is a national survey of school teachers, for which there is no list. Rather than compile a list for a study, one might sample states, geographic areas within states, and schools within geographic areas. Then teachers within selected schools could be listed and sampled. In addition, survey objectives for making estimates for subgroups in a population are often best achieved by oversampling some groups and undersampling others, thus using disproportionate sampling and weighting. Such designs are beyond the scope of this book, and we recommend the use of the sources mentioned at the beginning of this section as well as assistance from a sampling statistician.

The definition of *coverage* includes the expression "known, nonzero chance of being selected" rather than "equal chance" because sometimes a surveyor wishes to give some elements of the population a greater chance to be included in the survey. For example, a survey of employees in a very large organization may have as an objective to estimate differences between the opinions of employees who have worked for a firm for less than 6 months (say, 5% of all employees) and the opinions of longer time employees (95% of staff). In this case, longer time employees have 20 times the chance that new employees have of being selected for inclusion in the survey sample. In order to have enough people in each group to make acceptable estimates, the surveyor can simply separate the groups, a process known as *stratification*, and draw separate (and disproportionate) samples so that a large enough number of new employees is drawn to allow acceptably precise estimates to be made. The texts listed at the beginning of this section describe stratification methods (of which there are many) for surveys, and the reader is referred to them for discussions of when, why, and how to implement stratified sample designs.

WHEN ARE SURVEY RESULTS "GOOD"?

Because sampling error can be calculated by applying mathematical formulas, some people tend to use it as the primary standard for drawing conclusions about survey quality. Others tend to focus solely on survey response rates (i.e., the ratio of completed sample to total sample) as the quality indicator, reasoning that low response rates equate to high nonresponse error and therefore poor survey quality. Both of these practices are problematic. Relying on sampling error alone ignores the fact that precision may also be affected by the presence of *coverage error, nonresponse error,* and *measurement error.*

Similarly, focusing solely on response rates as measures of survey quality ignores potential error attributable to sampling, measurement, and coverage. In addition, nonresponse error is not a direct function of low response rates (Groves, 2006). Rather, nonresponse error results from those who do not return the survey *differing in attitudes, beliefs, behaviors, and characteristics* from those who do return the survey *on the item or items of interest.* It is possible, therefore, for a survey with a very low response rate to adequately represent the survey population or for a survey with very high response rates to fail to represent the intended population. Likewise, it is possible, and quite likely, that the amount of nonresponse error within a single survey will differ across questions and question topics (Groves, 2006).

Although technically larger is always better from the standpoint of sampling error, it is important to balance the expenditure of resources for minimizing sampling error against potential expenditures for reducing the other three sources of error. It makes little sense to push sampling error to an extremely low level if it comes at the cost of not trying to lower levels of other types of error. Conducting quality self-administered surveys means simultaneously attempting to hold error levels of all four types low, an endeavor that requires an optimal allocation of resources as discussed in detail by Groves (1989). Minimizing all four types of survey error is perhaps the most difficult challenge of surveying, and as of yet there is no accepted way of providing a meaningful combined measure of the effect of the four sources of error on overall accuracy.

CONCLUSION

The example that opened this chapter illustrates well the common confusion that exists with respect to sources of survey error and, in particular, coverage and sampling error. The eager graduate student, in his haste to take advantage of new technologies, was planning not to sample at all, yet wanted to be able to treat the results as if they were a representative sample of all faculty, staff, and students at the university by making statistical statements of confidence about the results. Yet no statistical basis for making such statements existed. Coverage concerns were also being ignored. Many affiliated with the university do not use their university-provided e-mail accounts, and others choose to continue using them even after their formal affiliation has ended, meaning that some eligible people would not have been contacted and some ineligible people would have been. Moreover, this student's singular focus on completed sample size (although there really was not going to be a sample) and sampling error (even if misunderstood) resulted in his ignoring the enormous potential for nonresponse bias. Had this study been carried out as the student envisioned, the results would most likely have been significantly biased and potentially misleading in important ways.

Understanding coverage and sampling error is central to one's ability to conduct a quality survey. Coverage error tends to be idiosyncratic to particular populations and sample frames, and there are no standard formulas for success. We have summarized the current states of coverage among the major self-administered modes, but these will very likely change considerably, even in the short term. In contrast, probability sampling is theoretically well developed, with formulas for measuring sampling error and determining needed sample sizes that are applicable to most types of surveys and survey populations. In addition to providing an introductory discussion of sampling theory, we have attempted to offer some strategies for putting it into practice. Yet for a survey to truly be successful, one has to give attention to other sources of error as well: All four sources of survey error have to be reduced to acceptable levels. In the next four chapters we turn our attention away from coverage and sampling error and focus instead on strategies for minimizing measurement error through effective survey design and nonresponse error, first through survey design and then through implementation procedures.

CHAPTER 4

The Basics of Crafting Good Questions

ON THE surface, writing a question may seem simple. For example: "How many hours per day do you typically study?" Yet the decision to ask such a question immediately raises a whole host of issues. Will the question produce different answers in different modes? Should one provide answer categories or an open space where respondents can write their answer however they desire? If one chooses to provide answer categories, what should they be, how should they be ordered, and how should they be arranged on the page?

Underneath these questions are more fundamental methodological questions. From what does a respondent draw meaning when reading and interpreting a question? How can all parts of the question work together? How do the words and the visual layout influence how respondents comprehend and ultimately respond to the question? Does it make a difference what the specific categories are? Are answers influenced by providing other categories? Do some question structures produce higher nonresponse than others? These challenges are illustrated by a recent experiment we conducted (Smyth, Dillman, & Christian, 2007a).

We asked three randomly selected subsets of a sample of students the number of hours per day they studied in three different ways:

1. A low range consisting of five categories from 0.5 hours or less to 2 to 2.5 hours plus a sixth category for those who studied more than 2.5 hours.
2. A high range consisting of an option for those who studied 2.5 hours or less plus five categories for those studying from 2.5 to more than 4.5 hours.

3. An open-ended answer box with no categories at all so that the respondent could choose what to report.

Technically, all three ways of asking the question could accommodate students studying anywhere from 0 to 24 hours, but as Figure 4.1 demonstrates, the scales emphasized different, slightly overlapping portions within that range whereas the answer box did not emphasize any of the range.

As a result of these differences in construction, the percentage of students reporting in a web survey that they study more than 2.5 hours per day ranged from 30% when the low scale was used to 71% when the high scale was used. This is a difference of 41 percentage points! The answer box version produced a more moderate estimate: 58% of students reported studying more than 2.5 hours. When the same experiment was conducted over the telephone, the results were very similar in that students who received the high scale were much more likely to report studying more than 2.5 hours per day than were those who received the low scale.

A previous mail experiment reported in the second edition of this book found a similar result, with 23% of respondents to the low-scale version reporting that they study 2.5 hours or more per day and 69% of respondents to the high-scale version reporting studying this much (Dillman, 2000a,

Figure 4.1 Percentage of students reporting studying $2^1/_2$ hours or less and more than $2^1/_2$ hours for three different question formats.

	Low Scale	High Scale	Answer Box
Up to 2½ hours	½ hour or less From ½ to 1 hour From 1 to 1½ hours From 1½ to 2 hours From 2 to 2½ hours	2½ hours or less	☐
More than 2½ hours	More than 2½ hours	From 2½ to 3 hours From 3 to 3½ hours From 3½ to 4 hours From 4 to 4½ hours More than 4½ hours	

Percentage Reporting Studying Up to and More than 2½ Hours by Format			
Up to 2½ hours	70%	29%	42%
More than 2½ hours	30%	71%	58%

Source: "Context Effects in Web Surveys: New Issues and Evidence" (pp. 427–443), by J. D. Smyth, D. A. Dillman, and L. M. Christian, in *The Oxford Handbook of Internet Psychology*, A. Joinson, K. McKenna, T. Postmes, and U. Reips (Eds.), 2007a, New York: Oxford University Press.

pp. 32–34). Clearly, the way these questions are constructed influences the ability to accurately measure the number of hours students study. But why? What is producing such differences?

If respondents use only the words in the question stem and the category numbers to interpret the meaning of the question, the answers across these three versions of the question should be the same. Because the answers vary widely, it is apparent that respondents are drawing extra information from the response categories and using that information to help formulate their answers. In other words, respondents are using information well beyond the numbers that are provided to define the parameters of each response option.

For many students, knowing exactly how many hours per day they study is not something they can recall in the same way that they can recall whether they live in a student dormitory or own a car. As a result, they probably have to estimate how many hours per day they study, and doing so probably requires them to average across days during the week and on weekends and probably even across times of year (i.e., a normal day vs. a day during the week of final exams). When respondents have to do this type of mental work to formulate their answers, they often look to the question and its accompanying response options for clues.

When asked how many hours per day they study, respondents might assume that the range emphasized by the scale represents how many hours most students study. As a result, someone who gets the low scale might conclude that *most* students study between 0.5 and 2.5 hours, whereas someone who gets the high scale might conclude that most students study between 2.5 and 4.5 hours. Another assumption that respondents may make is that the middle option(s) represents the amount that the *average* student studies; thus, those who receive the low scale might assume that the average student studies between 1 and 2 hours, but those who receive the high scale would assume that the average student studies from 3 to 4 hours. Rather than actually counting the hours they study, respondents can instead decide whether they study more, the same, or less than most typical students. In this type of estimating, different assumptions made based on the scale range and midpoint are bound to influence answers.

This example illustrates the challenge of crafting good survey questions that every potential respondent will be willing to answer, will be able to respond to accurately, and will interpret in the way the surveyor intends. Stated quite simply, one must think about many things at once to write a good question, and failure to do so can have significant effects on how the question performs. Factors to consider include what type of question to write (e.g., open- vs. closed-ended, single vs. multiple answer, etc.), how to word the question stem, what response options to offer and how to word them, how to visually present the questions, what type of answer spaces to provide, and whether and where to provide additional sources of information (i.e., instructions).

In this chapter, we address how to answer these questions and others that may arise when developing survey questions. First we describe a holistic approach to crafting survey questions that considers what question format is best and how multiple aspects of the question wording and layout need to work together to reliably provide accurate data about the concept of interest. Then we discuss general guidelines for question wording and visual presentation that apply to nearly all survey questions. In the chapter that follows, we turn to more specific guidelines for particular types of questions. However, before we start with guidelines, we discuss four issues that need to be considered for each question.

ISSUES TO CONSIDER WHEN CRAFTING SURVEY QUESTIONS

1. WHAT SURVEY MODE(S) WILL BE USED TO ASK THE QUESTIONS?

How one writes a survey question should depend strongly on how that question is going to be delivered to respondents. The key point to keep in mind here is that different survey modes rely on different communication channels. In telephone interviews, respondents give and receive information through spoken words and the hearing system, whereas on the Web and in mail questionnaires, information is transmitted through the visual system. As a result, words take on extra importance in telephone surveys, and memory becomes a significant factor to be considered. In mail and Internet surveys, visual design elements become important. In this chapter we focus mostly on writing questions for mail and Internet surveys, with only brief comments on telephone surveys. We discuss writing questions for mixed-mode surveys in Chapter 8.

2. IS THIS QUESTION BEING REPEATED FROM ANOTHER SURVEY, AND/OR WILL ANSWERS BE COMPARED TO PREVIOUSLY COLLECTED DATA?

The answer to this question will influence how much, if any, the question can be changed. If a particular question has been used in another survey and the main objective is to replicate the previous survey or make the new results comparable in some other way, usually no changes or only minimal changes can be made. Examples are government surveys that have asked the same question repeatedly, sometimes for decades, to produce time-series data. For self-administered surveys, this means trying to replicate not only the question wording but also the other aspects of the visual design and layout of the questions. Thus, it is important to ask whether questions will be repeated from other surveys or previous waves of data collection and, if so, whether they can be changed.

3. WILL RESPONDENTS BE WILLING AND MOTIVATED TO ANSWER ACCURATELY?

Ensuring that respondents are motivated to respond to each question is a major concern in self-administered surveys because there is no interviewer present to encourage respondents to carefully select and report complete answers. Without proper motivation, respondents may ignore instructions, read questions carelessly, or provide incomplete answers. Worse yet, they may skip questions altogether or fail to complete and return the questionnaire.

In some instances motivational problems stem from poor question design, such as when questions are difficult to read and understand, instructions are hard to find, or the response task is too vague. In other instances, the question topic itself may be the source of motivational problems. This is often the case with questions pertaining to personal financial information. For example, people are more likely to report their income when provided with broad categories from which to choose rather than asked to provide an exact value; however, sometimes a survey, such as the U.S. Decennial Census, requires an exact number, and anything else is unacceptable.

Respondents are also often reluctant to answer questions about certain behaviors that they may find embarrassing or threatening, such as sexual or criminal activity. When asking for sensitive information about people's past or current behavior, changing the wording of the question can encourage reluctant respondents to answer. For example, instead of asking "Have you ever shoplifted anything from a store?" one might ask "Have you ever taken anything from a store without paying for it?" Another strategy is to include the question with others, such as "How often do you go shopping?" and "What types of stores do you shop at?" so that it may appear in context and seem less objectionable. Although steps can be taken to improve the design of sensitive questions, it may still be difficult to collect accurate information from all respondents.

4. WHAT TYPE OF INFORMATION IS THE QUESTION ASKING FOR?

It is easier to get accurate answers for some types of survey questions than others. For example, almost everyone knows how old they are, as people are frequently asked to give that information to others. Because people already have an answer in their head when asked about their age, assuming they are willing they can easily provide it and can do so in a number of different ways, as shown in Figure 4.2. Because the information is readily

Figure 4.2   What type of information is the question asking for?

A question that people can easily answer regardless of how it is asked

What year were you born?

[   ] Year born

How old are you?

[   ] Age

What is your date of birth?

[ ] [ ] [   ]
Month   Day   Year

A question for which people are often more likely to be influenced by context

In your opinion, how effective do you think citizens groups are in helping to solve environmental problems?

☐ Very effective
☐ Somewhat effective
☐ A little effective
☐ Not at all effective

In your opinion, how effective or ineffective do you think citizens groups are in helping to solve environmental problems? (Please mark an "X" on the line.)

◄──────────────────────────►
Very effective   Very ineffective

In your opinion, how effective are citizens groups in helping to solve environmental problems?

☐ A great deal
☐ A fair amount
☐ Not very much
☐ Almost none at all

---

available to the respondent, most surveyors can accurately collect such data as age and other *factual or demographic information* regardless of how they ask for it; however, as we discuss later in this chapter, people can still be encouraged, through question design, to report the answer in a particular format.

Surveys also frequently ask for information that people may have thought little about and will need more time to answer, such as questions about *attitudes and opinions*. The second example in Figure 4.2 provides an example in which respondents are asked how effective they think citizens groups are in helping to solve environmental problems. Most respondents will not have a ready answer available for this type of question and may have to do considerable work to formulate one. Some may consider generally whether they think people can effect change, whereas others will think about examples of environmental citizens groups or various types of environmental problems that people have tried to help solve. For these types of questions, more so than for factual or demographic questions, respondents can be substantially influenced by the context of the question as they work their way through the question–answer process of comprehending the question, recalling relevant information, forming a judgment, and reporting their answer (Tourangeau, 1992). Different elements of the question that can influence the answering process include what type of response is being asked for (e.g., choose one category, mark an X on the scale), the wording of the question and response options (e.g., "a great deal" or "somewhat effective"), and visual layout.

Other questions that are prone to such context effects are those asking about *behaviors and events*. Surveyors often ask about many aspects of people's behavior, such as what they have done, how often (number of times or relative frequency), and when. Frequently survey designers want respondents to provide far more detail about past behaviors than can be recalled and, as a result, they write questions respondents find difficult, if not impossible, to answer. Doing this causes respondents to draw even more on features of the questions' context rather than their real experiences in formulating their answers, as is the case in Figure 4.1. To avoid this tendency, surveyors should consider three recall problems. First, memory tends to fade over time. Second, individual episodes or occurrences of regular and mundane events are generally not precisely remembered (Rockwood, Sangster, & Dillman, 1997). And third, people usually do not categorize information by precise month or year. Given these limitations, respondents are unlikely to be able to accurately report how many days they drove more than 5 miles during the past 6 months. But they can probably very accurately report how many days they drove their car during the past week or drove more than 200 miles at a time in the past 3 months. Asking questions about behaviors that people can easily recall because they are recent or more memorable can help improve the accuracy of the information people report. In addition to choosing an appropriate reference period for the type of behavior, using definitions and examples can also help improve recall (Schaeffer & Presser, 2003). However, definitions must be easy for respondents to understand, and examples should be selected carefully so as not to influence respondents' answers in unintended ways.

A HOLISTIC APPROACH

Throughout this and the next chapter, we discuss a holistic approach to crafting effective survey questions for mail and Internet surveys. By holistic we mean that multiple aspects of the wording and design of the question need to work together to convey meaning. This approach considers what type of question structure best measures the concept of interest, how questions are composed of multiple parts that work together, and how both the words and the visual presentation of questions are important.

CHOOSE THE APPROPRIATE QUESTION FORMAT

There are two broad types of question formats: open-ended and closed-ended questions. *Open-ended* question formats provide a blank space or box where respondents type or write in their response using their own words (or numbers), whereas *closed-ended* question formats or *scalar* questions provide respondents with a list of answer choices from which they must choose to answer the question.

The strength of the open-ended question format is that it allows respondents to freely answer the question as they want without limiting their response. Thus, this format is preferable when the surveyor does not want to influence respondent answers by providing a set of answer choices; when the goal is to collect rich, detailed information from respondents; and when the surveyor is questioning about topics for which little information is known ahead of time. Additionally, an open-ended format in which respondents provide a numerical response can sometimes be easier for respondents and yield more precise information because respondents report an exact number rather than choose from categories with vague labels or ranges of values.

However, there are also several limitations to open-ended question formats. In self-administered surveys, more respondents skip open-ended question formats than closed-ended formats because the former require more work to answer. Issues of item nonresponse bias arise because some types of respondents may be more likely to skip these questions than other types. If respondents do answer the question, they may provide only a short response. In addition, responses to open-ended questions must be entered and coded before they can be analyzed; however, web surveys make this less time consuming because the responses are already in electronic form. In addition to the time to code responses to open-ended questions, there is often a lot more variation in respondents' answers, so it may be more difficult to analyze and interpret the data, and a variable may not be able to be created based on the responses. In contrast, responses to closed-ended questions can be analyzed immediately (or with minor transformations to the data), and data results can be produced quickly.

Closed-ended question formats should be used when surveyors want respondents to provide an answer after considering or evaluating a set of answer choices. Because researchers provide answer categories in closed-ended questions, the response options they choose have significant impact on how respondents interpret the questions. Closed-ended question formats can utilize nominal or ordinal scales. In *nominal* scalar questions, respondents are asked to compare a set of categories with no natural order underlying the categories. Because the categories lack an inherent ordered relationship, the difficulty of processing nominal scales increases as the number of categories that need to be compared at one time increases. An adaptation of the nominal closed-ended format allows respondents to select multiple answers (e.g., check-all-that-apply and ranking questions). Examples of nominal variables include grocery stores one has visited, web sites one frequently visits, and brands of personal care products purchased. Surveyors may order these variables alphabetically or group them by type, but any such ordering or grouping is subjective and is usually to help make answering the question easier for respondents. One difficulty discussed below is that such ordering and grouping can sometimes have unintentional effects on answers and actually make responding more difficult.

In contrast, *ordinal* scale questions provide an ordered set of answer categories (but the intervals between categories is unknown), and respondents must decide where they fit along the continuum. Because there is an inherent order to the categories, respondents are particularly influenced by how the categories are distributed and by the overall layout of the response scale. A common ordinal scale asks about levels of satisfaction (e.g., completely satisfied, very satisfied, somewhat satisfied, not at all satisfied), where each category represents a higher degree or level of satisfaction. Someone who is "completely satisfied" is more satisfied than someone who is "very satisfied," but it is not necessarily known how much more satisfied. Another common type of ordered scale asks about frequency of behaviors or events (e.g., all of the time, most of the time, some of the time, none of the time), where each category represents a greater or lesser frequency. One concern with ordered closed-ended questions is that researchers often use vague quantifiers to describe the answer categories. For example, some people may consider walking every day to be "all of the time," whereas other people may consider walking three times a week to be "all of the time."

One of the fundamental writing tools that exists for creating survey questions is to shift questions from one format to another. Having a working knowledge of different question formats can help surveyors craft effective survey questions because often questions that do not work in one question format can be converted to another format to more effectively measure the concept. For example, one of us was once asked to help a university committee that was preparing a questionnaire to evaluate a dean's performance. All of the questions proposed by the committee were nominal closed-ended questions with unordered response categories, similar to the question structure commonly used in student examinations. The first question, shown in Figure 4.3, asked about both leadership and innovation in a way that

Figure 4.3   Choosing the appropriate question format.

Nominal closed-ended

Which of these five statements best describes the dean?
- ☐ Innovative but lacking leadership qualities
- ☐ About the same on innovation and leadership qualities
- ☐ Stronger on leadership than innovation
- ☐ A born leader
- ☐ A real innovator

Ordinal closed-ended for each concept

To what extent has the dean demonstrated strong leadership qualities?
- ☐ All of the time
- ☐ Most of the time
- ☐ Some of the time
- ☐ None of the time

To what extent has the dean demonstrated an ability to innovate?
- ☐ All of the time
- ☐ Most of the time
- ☐ Some of the time
- ☐ None of the time

Nominal closed-ended—revised to achieve direct comparison of concepts

Which one of the following do you feel best describes the dean?
- ☐ A strong leader
- ☐ A strong innovator
- ☐ Both a strong leader and innovator
- ☐ Neither a strong leader nor innovator

Open-ended for each concept

How would you describe the dean's leadership abilities?

How would you describe the dean's ability to innovate?

would have made it difficult to interpret the results. The proposed solution to the university committee was to break the question apart and to ask two ordered closed-ended questions that focused on how often or to what extent the dean had demonstrated leadership and innovation. Then ask people a nominal closed-ended question where the dean's abilities to lead and innovate are directly compared. Separating leadership and innovation into separate questions and asking the direct comparison question allowed the committee to test its stated objectives of finding out how the faculty evaluated the dean separately on leadership and innovation and on which attribute she performed better.

Another option for revising the question would have been to replace it with two open-ended questions that asked separately about the dean's ability to lead and innovate and perhaps still follow up with the direct comparison of leadership and innovation in the nominal closed-ended question. Which strategy should be used depends on the ultimate purpose for asking the question. The open-ended questions would have produced more descriptive data on how faculty evaluated the dean's abilities independently; however, the ordered closed-ended questions would have allowed the committee to measure the dean's abilities using a common scale so that results could be easily summarized and compared.

A partially closed question format is a hybrid of the open- and closed-ended formats that includes a set of response categories and an "other" response, thus allowing respondents who do not fit into the provided response categories to specify a different category that they do fit. This format is often used when it would be too burdensome to ask respondents about the entire set of items. For example, in the question in Figure 4.4, if a respondent's favorite sport were basketball, she would select that sport and move to the next question; however, if her favorite sport were rowing, which is not one of the options provided, she would select "other" and write or type "rowing" in the adjacent answer space. The value of this question format is that it reduces the number of items respondents have to consider at once and still collects data for the key items of interest. However, respondents are more likely to select the options provided than to write or type their own other responses. Hence, categories should be included for all of the key items of interest, and care should be used in drawing conclusions about volunteered categories versus those that are explicitly provided (i.e., it is not accurate to

Figure 4.4 Example of a partially closed question format.

Which of the following is your favorite college women's sport?

☐ Basketball
☐ Gymnastics
☐ Soccer
☐ Softball
☐ Swimming
☐ Tennis
☐ Volleyball
☐ Other: Please specify [   ]

Figure 4.5   Example of new web response mechanisms.

Automatic calculation tools

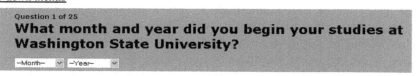

License type: **Physician**

Question 4 of 19
During a _typical_ week, _approximately_ how many hours do you spend in the following professional Physician activities? *(Do not include on-call time)*

8	Direct patient care (including patient education)
4	Administration of clinical practice
	Teaching (Physician education)
	Research
	Other professional Physician activities
12	TOTAL (add above items - this should represent your typical weekly hours of work)

[Next >>]   [<< Back]

Drop-down menus

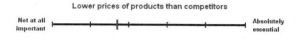

Question 1 of 25
What month and year did you begin your studies at Washington State University?

—Month— ▾   —Year— ▾

Visual analog scales

Next, we'd like to change topics and ask you a few questions about grocery stores.

For the aspects of a grocery store listed below, how important would each be in determining at which grocery store you would shop?

On the lines below, click on the position that best reflects how important you consider each to be.

Lower prices of products than competitors

Not at all |————+————|—+————+————| Absolutely
important   essential

Source: Visual analog scale image courtesy of "A Comparison of Visual Analog and Graphic Ratings Scales," by R. K. Thomas and M. P. Couper, March 2007, paper presented at the General Online Research Conference, Leipzig, Germany.

draw conclusions that compare listed to unlisted options, such as "respondents were 10 times as likely to say basketball is their favorite sport than rowing").

In web surveying, new response mechanisms such as automatic calculation tools, drop-down menus, and visual analog scales have been developed (see Figure 4.5). Each of these formats uses one of the question formats we discussed above, but the way that respondents report their answers differs in each case. *Automatic calculation tools* are usually composed of a series of numerical response open-ended questions for which the computer helps calculate a running total to make responding easier and reduce the number of errors made by respondents.

A *drop-down menu* provides respondents with a list of options where they select one or sometimes multiple responses, similar to a nominal closed-ended question or a multiple-answer question. The main difference is that respondents cannot view the options until they click on the menu, and then they often have to scroll to find the answer they want to select. Heerwegh and Loosveldt (2002a) and Couper, Tourangeau, Conrad, and Crawford (2004) found that response times were not significantly different between a radio button format and drop-down box. However, Couper et al. (2004) also found that respondents were more likely to select the visible response options when provided with a drop-down box with half of the response options showing than when presented with a drop-down box where they had to scroll to see the response options. Thus, it is important to not preset drop-down menus with only some response options visible. Instead, one should label the boxes with what type of information is being requested and only make specific items visible once the box is clicked, such as in the example in Figure 4.5.

Visual analog scales usually use an ordinal closed-ended question format in which the respondent can interactively slide a marker to the position on the scale that best describes his or her answer. The parallel in a paper survey would be placing a mark such as an X on a continuum. In two recent studies of visual analog scales on the Web, Couper, Tourangeau, Conrad, and Singer (2006) found no differences in the response distributions for visual analog scales than for scales presented horizontally with radio buttons, and Thomas and Couper (2007) found similar validity and self-reported accuracy ratings between visual analog scales and scales presented as a list of options vertically with radio buttons. Both studies found that the visual analog scales took longer to complete than the scales with radio buttons.

Although these new response mechanisms provide alternative ways for respondents to report their answer or help them provide an answer, many of them are not new question formats, so we discuss them with the specific question structure to which they apply.

THE ANATOMY OF A SURVEY QUESTION

Survey questions are made up of multiple parts that must work together in concert to produce high-quality data about the topic of interest. If one part of the question fails or provides a conflicting message with another part, it can undermine the accuracy of responses. Crafting good survey questions requires understanding how each component of the question conveys meaning independently to respondents as well as how all of the parts work together to convey meaning.

The most important part of any survey question is the *question stem*, or the words that form the actual query itself. In Figure 4.6, the question stem is "How many years have you lived in Washington?" The question

Figure 4.6   Examples of the components of open- and closed-ended question formats.

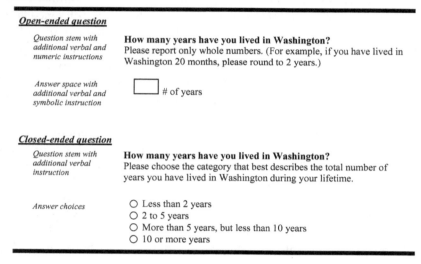

<u>*Open-ended question*</u>

Question stem with additional verbal and numeric instructions

How many years have you lived in Washington?
Please report only whole numbers. (For example, if you have lived in Washington 20 months, please round to 2 years.)

Answer space with additional verbal and symbolic instruction

[ ] # of years

<u>*Closed-ended question*</u>

Question stem with additional verbal instruction

How many years have you lived in Washington?
Please choose the category that best describes the total number of years you have lived in Washington during your lifetime.

Answer choices

  O Less than 2 years
  O 2 to 5 years
  O More than 5 years, but less than 10 years
  O 10 or more years

stem provides the most explicit and direct information about what the question is asking (e.g., how long have you lived in Washington) and how respondents should provide their answer (e.g., in years). It may also include *additional instructions,* definitions, or examples that will help respondents comprehend the meaning of the question or of key concepts. Additional instructions might include verbal instructions (e.g., "select only one" or "please round to the nearest whole year"), or they may consist of numbers, graphics, or symbols that further inform respondents how to answer (e.g., $, #, YYYY). Each question has *answer spaces or choices* that provide additional information to respondents about what responses are possible and how to record their answer. Answer choices limit the available possibilities from which respondents can choose (e.g., less than 2 years, 2–5 years, etc.) and often provide cues about the type and number of answers to provide (e.g., size of answer space, reminder of units requested). Throughout this chapter and the next, we use the specific terms italicized above for each of the particular parts, and we use the term *question* to mean the entire anatomy of the survey question, including all of the parts.

Words used in the question stem, additional instructions, and response options are the primary sources of meaning that respondents draw upon when comprehending the meaning of survey questions. In addition, numbers, symbols, and graphics can also influence how respondents answer questions. Finally, the visual layout and presentation of questions can also have significant effects on how respondents interpret and answer questions in mail and web surveys. Thus, in open-ended questions, respondents draw meaning from the question stem, any instructions that accompany the stem or answer spaces, and the visual display of the answer spaces (e.g., size, location, etc.). In closed-ended questions, both the wording and the visual display of the answer choices, in addition to the question stem and any instructions provided, can influence how people respond. Therefore, crafting survey questions involves both choosing words to form the questions and deciding how to visually present the questions, including each of the component parts, to respondents.

In the remainder of this chapter, we present guidelines for crafting survey questions that apply to nearly all types of survey questions. First we discuss guidelines for choosing words and writing good survey questions. Then we discuss further how the visual layout of survey questions can influence responses to questions in mail and web surveys. Lastly, we present general guidelines for the visual presentation of survey questions that apply to nearly all types of survey questions.

GUIDELINES FOR CHOOSING WORDS AND FORMING QUESTIONS

Guideline 4.1: Make sure the question applies to the respondent

Imagine you are responding to a survey that asks "What type of Internet connection do you have in your home?" but you do not have an Internet connection. How do you respond? What if you ate dinner at a restaurant last night but are asked "If you made dinner at home last night, about how many minutes did it take to prepare the meal?" (see Figure 4.7). Sometimes people who write questions for mail surveys try to reduce the number of

Figure 4.7   Make every question require an answer.

A question that does not require an answer from every respondent

If you made dinner at home last night, about how many minutes did it take to prepare the meal?

☐ minutes

A revision that uses a filter question

Did you make dinner at home last night?

☐ Yes
☐ No

If yes, how many minutes did it take to prepare the meal?

☐ minutes

questions (i.e., save space) and avoid skip instructions by asking questions such as these.

These two questions have a common problem (i.e., they do not require answers of every respondent), but the source of the problem is slightly different for each. The first question contains an embedded assumption of having an Internet connection that may not be true for all respondents. The second avoids making assumptions by including an "if" statement but does not apply to those who do not fit the "if" criteria. Even if a "does not apply" box were provided, the use of the word *if* implies that no response is needed from those who ate out the previous night.

This type of question can be particularly damaging in web surveys when respondents are required to enter an answer for every question before they are allowed to advance to the next question. In this situation, the respondent has to choose between two bad options: knowingly entering false information or quitting the survey altogether. However, questions that do not apply to every respondent are still problematic in questionnaires that do not require answers. Aside from potentially confusing respondents, the methodological problem with these questions is that it is impossible to distinguish between those who did not respond because they were unmotivated (i.e., nonrespondents) and more motivated people who, nonetheless, did not respond because the question did not apply to them. Moreover, in order to be able to estimate the distribution of a characteristic in the sample population, the surveyor must give respondents the opportunity to answer every question they are asked. Therefore, a good rule to apply is that in order for an inquiry to constitute a survey question, it must require an answer from each person of whom it is asked. The two questions above should only be asked of respondents who answer "yes" to filter questions such as "Do you have an Internet connection in your home?" or "Did you make dinner at home last night?" (see Figure 4.7). Techniques to ensure that respondents follow the required skip instructions properly are discussed in Chapter 6.

Guideline 4.2: Make sure the question is technically accurate

Asking a question that is not technically accurate can confuse respondents and make answering difficult. For example, many avid horse people might be confused by this seemingly simple question: "How many feet tall is your horse?" This is because horses are often measured in a different unit—hands (one hand equals 4 inches). A more appropriate way to ask this question would be "How many hands tall is your horse?" Ensuring that questions are technically accurate becomes more challenging when one is asking questions about topics that apply to very specialized populations such as equestrians or business executives. Failing to do so, however, can compromise the quality of responses as well as diminish the perceived credibility and authenticity of the surveyor, possibly resulting in reduced motivation or even break-offs on the part of respondents.

Guideline 4.3: Ask one question at a time

On first take, the advice to ask one question at a time seems like a no-brainer, yet it is striking how often what appears to be one question actually contains two components about which respondents may feel differently. Consider, for example, the question in Figure 4.8. This question actually contains two questions: "Do you subscribe to any periodicals, magazines, newsletters, etc. . . . ?" and "Do you regularly read any periodicals, magazines, newsletters, etc. . . . ?" As this question is written, it poses problems for respondents who subscribe to but do not regularly read these items, or for those who regularly read them but do not subscribe. Such respondents will not know for which component to provide their response. The question also poses a problem for the survey or anyone using the resulting data, as they will not know which component the respondents were referring to when they marked "yes" or "no."

One possible solution to this problem, as demonstrated in the first revision, is to untangle the original question by asking the two questions separately. If even more precision is desired, each of the two questions can be written in a forced-choice style so that respondents are asked to indicate whether they subscribe to and whether they read each type of literature, as shown in the second revision in Figure 4.8.

Guideline 4.4: Use simple and familiar words

One way to establish legitimacy and credibility with respondents is to present them with a formalized and professional questionnaire. Generally this is good practice. One way it can backfire, however, is if efforts to formalize the questionnaire lead to the use of complex words or phrases and technical terminology that not all respondents will understand. Many complex words and phrases can be easily replaced by more generally understood terms, as seen in Figure 4.9. When drafting questions it may be advisable to consult a grammar book or writing manual, as they commonly provide more extensive lists of replacement terms for complex words and wordy phrases. A good rule of thumb is that when a word exceeds six or seven letters, a shorter and more easily understood word can probably be substituted. However, it should not automatically be assumed that all shorter words are acceptable. For example, it would not be advisable to substitute "deter" for "discourage."

Another common tendency, especially in government surveys, is to inadvertently use abbreviations or specialized phrases that are commonplace for the survey sponsor but require some translation for respondents. An example is shown in Figure 4.10. Although the survey sponsors may know what Form SS-4 is, many respondents may not. Others may not immediately know

Figure 4.8   Ask one question at a time.

A double-barreled question

Do you personally subscribe to, or regularly read, any periodicals, magazines, newsletters, etc. that are specifically related to your occupation?

☐ Yes
☐ No

A revision to ask each question separately

Do you personally subscribe to any periodicals, magazines, newsletters, etc. that are specifically related to your occupation?

☐ Yes
☐ No

Do you regularly read any periodicals, magazines, newsletters, etc. that are specifically related to your occupation?

☐ Yes
☐ No

Another possible revision to collect more specific information

Please indicate whether or not you personally subscribe to each of the following sources of information specifically related to your occupation.

	I do subscribe	I do not subscribe
Periodicals	☐	☐
Magazines	☐	☐
Newsletters	☐	☐

Please indicate whether or not you regularly read each of the following sources of information specifically related to your occupation.

	I regularly read	I do not regularly read
Periodicals	☐	☐
Magazines	☐	☐
Newsletters	☐	☐

what IRS stands for, further confusing them and making it even harder to figure out what form SS-4 is. A clearer statement of the question is provided in the revision, in which the form is referred to by its full name and "IRS" is replaced with "Internal Revenue Service."

In most instances it is desirable to replace complex and specialized words, but there are instances when this is not necessary. Virtually all occupational groups share a particular vocabulary that is not understood by outsiders but that facilitates efficient communication within the group. Replacing this specialized vocabulary with simpler words would only confuse matters for these groups. In a survey of city planners, for example, it seems quite reasonable

Figure 4.9 Words and phrases that can be simplified.

Replacing complex with simple words

Exhausted.....................Tired

Candid..........................Honest

Top priority.................Most important

Leisure.........................Free time

Employment.................Work

Courageous ....Brave

Rectify.........................Correct

Replacing complex with simple phrases

Occupants of this household.....................People who live here

Your responses..Your answers

Post-school extracurricular activities.........What you do after school

Subnational region ....Area of the country

to talk about "annexation" instead of "an addition." Similarly, in a survey of physicians it seems reasonable to talk about "pharmaceutical companies" instead of "companies that sell medicines." To do otherwise may even suggest a lack of knowledge and understanding of the topic of the survey.

However, the fact remains that people who write questionnaires are far more likely to overestimate than underestimate the knowledge and vocabulary of respondents. Thus, when in doubt, it is prudent to use the simpler of the available alternatives. Ultimately, though, the best way to determine if the vocabulary is appropriate is to pretest questions with members of the population of interest to identify potential difficulties, a topic we return to in Chapter 6.

Figure 4.10 Use of simple and familiar versus complex or specialized words.

Unnecessary use of specialized words and abbreviations

Have you filed Form SS-4 with the IRS?

☐ Yes
☐ No

A simplified revision

Have you filed an application for an employer identification number (Form SS-4) with the Internal Revenue Service?

☐ Yes
☐ No

Guideline 4.5: Use specific and concrete words to specify the concepts clearly

Suppose you are interested in different elements of family cohesiveness and you pose the question in Figure 4.11 to a sample of mothers with school-age children. One strength of this question is that it clearly specifies a reasonable time referent and the units in which one should report an answer. The problem, however, is that it contains several vague concepts. What does "eat" mean? Should we count snacks? What if we all gathered for a smoothie a couple hours before dinner; does that count, even though it is a thick drink? And what does "together as a family" mean? Does the lunch we got from the drive-thru and ate in the car on the way to grandma's house count? What about the pizza we ate in the living room while watching a movie on Saturday night? Do we count the end-of-season potluck for the baseball team at which we were all present but interspersed with other families?

One respondent might take a very liberal interpretation of this question and include all gatherings where her whole family was present and food or drinks were consumed, whereas another may take a very conservative view and count only full meals for which the family was gathered at home around the kitchen table. The problem is that the two interpretations would most likely result in quite divergent answers that are due to different interpretations of the question, not differences in family cohesiveness. This question could be improved by specifying that you are interested in meals consumed at home, as in the first revision. It could be made even more specific by specifying that you are interested in sit-down meals shared as a family, as in the second revision.

Figure 4.11   Use specific and concrete words to specify the concepts clearly.

Question with vague concepts

How many times did you eat together as a family last week?

[   ] # of times

A revised question with more specific and concrete concepts

How many meals did you eat together as a family at home last week?

[   ] # of meals

A more specific revision

How many meals did you sit down to eat at home as a family last week?

[   ] # of meals

This example illustrates a common problem for many writers of survey questions. Once the units are specified, many concepts such as age, height, and weight are very straightforward. Others, however, are not as straightforward as they seem. It seems like everyone would know what it means to eat together as a family, but as the example shows, once one begins to factor in the complexity of family life in this day and age, the concept of eating together as a family is opened up to much interpretation. Thus, it is important to make sure the concepts in survey questions are clearly defined and communicated in order to minimize the amount of interpreting and defining that respondents need to do.

Guideline 4.6: Use as few words as possible to pose the question

Part of keeping questions simple is keeping them short and to the point. The longer the question, the more information the respondent has to take in and process, and the higher the likelihood for misunderstanding or misreading. When presented with the question in Figure 4.12, for example, one respondent in a cognitive interview answered, "I don't have any idea how many people live in the United States." As a result of this and other interviews, the well-intentioned second sentence that explained the reason for the directions about who to include and who to exclude was removed (Dillman & Allen, 1995).

The goal of keeping questions short sometimes contradicts the previously stated goals of using familiar and simple words and using specific and concrete words to specify concepts clearly. Substituting several simpler words for a more complex word or carefully specifying concepts can lengthen questions. In these instances, we recommend subordinating the

Figure 4.12 Use as few words as possible to pose the question.

Long question with potentially confusing information

How many people were living or staying at this residence on Saturday, March 3rd, 2000? To make sure each person in the United States is counted only once, it is very important to:

> **Include** everyone who lives here whether related to you or not, and anyone staying temporarily who has no permanent place to live;
> **But not include** anyone away at college, away in the Armed Forces, in a nursing home, hospice, mental hospital, correctional facility, or other institution.

A shorter revision with potentially confusing information removed

How many people were livingor staying at this residence on Saturday, March 3rd, 2000? Please:

> **Include** everyone who lives here whether related to you or not, and anyone staying temporarily who has no permanent place to live;
> **But not include** anyone away at college, away in the Armed Forces, in a nursing home, hospice, mental hospital, correctional facility, or other institution.

Figure 4.13   Eliminating wordy and redundant expressions.

Due to the fact that............................	Because
At this point in time...........................	Now
A small number of..............................	A few
A considerable number of.................	Many
Small in size......................................	Small
Has the ability...................................	Can
Ascertain the location of..................	Locate
Concerning the matter of..................	About
If conditions are such that................	If
In the majority of instances..............	Usually
Make a decision................................	Decide
Take into consideration....................	Consider

goal of keeping the question short to the goals of using simple and familiar words and using specific and concrete words. Once one is sure that any words chosen are understood by virtually all respondents and the concepts are clearly specified, one can attempt to keep the question short.

There are several ways to do this. One way is to replace wordy and redundant expressions such as those shown in Figure 4.13 with simpler wording. More comprehensive lists of commonly used wordy expressions and their replacements can be found in most grammar and writing manuals.

Another technique is to avoid including answer categories in the question stem, as in the following example: "Are you very likely, somewhat likely, somewhat unlikely, or very unlikely to visit Glacier National Park again?" If the respondent will be able to see the response options after reading the question stem, it is unnecessarily redundant to include these options in the stem as well. Such redundancy across many questions is a particularly strong indicator to respondents that it is okay to skip words, and it may result in the rest of the sentence also being unevenly read. Therefore, this question should be shortened to "How likely or unlikely are you to visit Glacier National Park again?" However, it is important that this technique only be used in single-mode self-administered survey designs in which respondents will be reading the question for themselves. In surveys where an interviewer administers the survey or when self-administered surveys are combined with interviews in mixed-mode studies, the answer categories may need to be included with the question stem for better respondent comprehension and consistency across modes (see also Chapter 8).

Guideline 4.7: Use complete sentences with simple sentence structures

It is tempting to save space by using incomplete sentences for paper surveys. It is true that few people will misunderstand "Your name" or even "Age."

Figure 4.14 Use complete sentences.

Common use of incomplete sentences

Number of years lived in Idaho

[ ] Years

Your city or town

[ ] City or Town

Your County

[ ] County

A revision using complete sentences

How many years have you lived in Idaho?

[ ] Years

In what city or town do you live?

[ ] Name of City or Town

In what Idaho county do you live?

[ ] Name of Idaho County

However, the series of questions in Figure 4.14 once caused many respondents to provide erroneous answers to the second and third questions. Nearly 20% of the respondents listed the number of years they had lived in the city or town and the county. In addition, several other respondents listed "United States" for *county,* a word that is only one letter different from *country.* Writing each question as a complete sentence would have helped solve both problems. In addition, in the revision "county" is changed to "Idaho county" in order to minimize the possibility of listing the United States as the respondent's county of residence.

Using complete sentences is even more important in web surveys with page-by-page construction. When there is only one question per screen, respondents can easily lose track of the context in which an inquiry is made. Here, incomplete sentences become isolated in ways that can make their meaning even less clear.

When asking for very specific information it is tempting to add extra clauses onto the sentence to help specify the focus of the question; however, these may confuse respondents or result in their misunderstanding the question. The problem with doing this is that reading sentences with multiple clauses or a complex sentence structure requires more skill than reading sentences with simple structures. Just as with wording, it is advisable to avoid complex sentence structures and replace them instead with simple structures.

Guideline 4.8: Make sure "yes" means yes and "no" means no

It seems obvious that questions should not include double negatives, or, in other words, require a respondent to say "yes" to mean "no" as in the following question: "Should the city manager not be directly responsible to the mayor?" Yet such questions are commonly asked in surveys. One of the reasons they are so prevalent is because voters are often asked in elections to vote for measures where a yes vote would result in something not being done, as illustrated by the tax approval question in Figure 4.15. Surveyors are often reluctant to pose the question differently than it will be expressed on the ballot. However, because people tend to read questions quickly, it is likely that some people will miss the word "not." In addition, the mental connection of favoring a "not" is difficult for most people.

Two different solutions for this problem might be considered. The first revision simply asks whether people favor or oppose requiring 60% approval by voters in order to raise state taxes. To help clarify, the answer categories specify what favor and oppose mean for the purposes of this question. This

Figure 4.15   Make sure "yes" means yes and "no" means no.

A question containing a double negative

> Do you favor or oppose not allowing the state to raise taxes without approval of 60% of the voters?
> ☐ Favor
> ☐ Oppose

A revision with no double negative

> Do you favor or oppose requiring 60% approval by voters in order to raise state taxes?
> ☐ Favor
> ☐ Oppose

A revision that preserves important wording

> In the September election, you will be asked to vote on this referendum: "No state tax can be raised without approval by 60% of those voting in a statewide election." If the election were held today, would you vote for or against approval?
> ☐ For
> ☐ Against

wording would seem appropriate during discussion of an issue before it has reached the ballot measure stage. A second revision, indicating that a vote will be taken, specifies the measure exactly as it will appear on the ballot and asks whether respondents are for or against approval of the measure. The switch of categories from favor/oppose to for/against is also an attempt to bring the language of the question more in line with that of the voting situation.

Guideline 4.9: Be sure the question specifies the response task

Another way of stating this guideline is that the response task should be clear to the respondent after having only read the question stem. There are two pieces to this guideline. First, *the question stem has to clearly state the response task.* This means that the question stem needs to ask for exactly the kind of information and level of detail (e.g., units) the surveyor wishes to collect. Second, *the response format and/or options provided must match the task as it is stated in the question stem.* In other words, do not change the rules in the middle of the game. A yes/no question should only have "yes" and "no" as substantive response options (nonsubstantive options such as "don't know" or "not applicable" are still appropriate). Similarly, if the question asks how many days something occurred, the response options should be numbers appropriate to the time referent (e.g., 0–7 if the referent is a week) or a number box labeled "number of days." Asking for the number of days in the question stem and then providing options such as "Always," "Most of the time," "Sometimes," "Rarely," and "Never" represents a mismatch between the question stem and the response options that forces the respondent to undertake the extra, and sometimes difficult, step of determining which category fits best (i.e., is 5 days "most of the time" or "sometimes"?).

HOW DOES THE VISUAL PRESENTATION OF SURVEY QUESTIONS MAKE A DIFFERENCE?

Prior to the 1990s, most of the survey methodology research focused on how the wording of questions influences how respondents answer them; the visual design and layout of questions was mostly viewed as an art form. Since then, researchers have drawn on research from the science of visual perception (Hoffman, 2004; Palmer, 1999; Ware, 2004) to formulate theoretically based rationales for how the design of questions and questionnaires can be improved to help respondents process survey questions and navigate through self-administered questionnaires (Christian, Dillman, & Smyth, 2007a; Jenkins & Dillman, 1997; Redline & Dillman, 2002; Redline, Dillman, Dajani, & Scaggs, 2003). In addition, a growing body of experimental research has demonstrated how the independent and combined effects of manipulating

various aspects of the visual design and layout of survey questions influence how people respond to paper and web surveys (Christian & Dillman,
2004; Dillman & Christian, 2005; Smyth, Dillman, & Christian, 2007b; Smyth,
Dillman, Christian, & McBride, in press; Smyth, Dillman, Christian, & Stern,
2006b; Tourangeau, Couper, & Conrad, 2004, 2007).

Visual design and layout influences respondents as they organize information presented in the survey questionnaire and as they focus their attention
on responding to individual survey questions. Visual design features can
help guide respondents to self-administered surveys, much like an interviewer would do in a face-to-face or telephone survey, to ensure that each
respondent receives the same question stimulus delivered in the same way.
Thus, this research is requiring survey methodologists to apply new visual
design concepts to the practice of crafting survey questions and constructing
questionnaires.

In this chapter, we briefly introduce the visual design concepts, summarized in Figure 4.16, necessary for understanding how survey respondents
process and respond to survey questions. We follow this discussion with
guidelines that can be applied to the visual presentation of all types of survey questions to help ensure that respondents attend to each component and
process the parts of the question in the intended order. In Chapter 5, we
present guidelines for the wording and visual presentation of specific types
of open- and closed-ended questions. We continue our focus on visual design
in Chapter 6, where we describe how respondents visually process and navigate entire questionnaire pages. There we present guidelines for questionnaire construction to help respondents organize the information presented
on each questionnaire page and to encourage them to process questions in
the intended order.

Survey questionnaires include four types of visual design *elements* that
communicate meaning to respondents: words, numbers, symbols, and
graphics. *Words* are the most powerful source of meaning that respondents
draw upon when answering survey questions; however, *numbers* used in the
question stem, in instructions, and in or as labels for answer choices also
communicate additional meaning to respondents. *Symbols* can also be used
to add special meaning, often without occupying very much physical space.
For example, an arrow may communicate to respondents where to focus their
attention next. Finally, *graphics* (e.g., text boxes, squares, html boxes, circles,
and radio buttons) are another type of visual design element that can be used
in designing survey questions. In addition, graphics can include more complex images and logos that layer various elements. The use of these types of
graphics has increased, particularly in web surveys, because of the ease and
affordability of including them, but also in mail surveys because the cost of
printing them has decreased.

Figure 4.16 Visual design concepts that guide question design.

Visual design elements that communicate information to respondents

Words are the fundamental source of meaning that help respondents understand what is being asked of them.

Numbers are used to convey meaning and sequence or order to respondents.

Symbols are figures that add special meaning based on what they represent to respondents.

Graphics are shapes and visual images that can be simple or complex and convey meaning to respondents.

Visual design properties that modify how elements are presented visually and the meaning respondents assign to them

Size: Changes in the size of elements influence how elements are perceived and whether they stand out visually.

Font: Changes in the shape and form of elements influence the legibility of words and how elements are perceived.

Brightness/Contrast/Color: Changes in shading and color influence how elements are perceived and whether they stand out visually from the background.

Location: How near or far elements are from one another (the spacing and alignment) influences whether they are perceived as related or unrelated.

Gestalt grouping principles that guide how respondents perceive relationships among information

Pragnanz: Elements that are organized into the simplest, most regular, symmetrical objects will be easier to perceive and remember.

Proximity: Placing visual elements closely together will cause them to be perceived as a group.

Similarity: Elements sharing the same visual properties (color, shape, size, orientation, etc.) will be grouped together.

Elemental connectedness: Elements connected by other elements will be grouped together.

Common region: Elements within a single closed region will be grouped together.

Continuity: Visual elements that can be seen as continuing smoothly will be perceived that way.

Closure: Elements that together create a "closed" figure will be perceived that way.

Common fate: Elements that move or imply movement in the same direction will be grouped together.

Each of the four visual design elements (words, numbers, symbols, and graphics) can be presented in different ways: They can be large or small, light or **dark**, close to one another or far apart, static or in motion, grayscale or in color. Thus, in addition to using the four types of visual design elements, surveyors can also manipulate the *properties* of each of these types of elements to increase or decrease the attention and change the meaning respondents assign to them. Visual design properties include size, font, brightness or contrast, color, location or proximity, shape, orientation, and motion. For example, attention can be drawn to particular words, numbers, or symbols by changing their size, contrast, or color in relation to the surrounding text (e.g.,

bolding or *italicizing* an important word or phrase in the question stem). A dollar symbol ($) could flicker (motion) to remind respondents to report their income in dollars. Symbols can also be located in proximity to the answer spaces where respondents will need to use them at the time of response. In addition, differently shaped graphics for response scales, for example a ladder versus a pyramid shape, can influence how respondents interpret and respond to the scales (Schwarz, Grayson, & Knäuper, 1998).

When respondents are presented with a questionnaire, they first take in the entire scene and organize the information presented to them. During this process, respondents begin to distinguish the various visual elements on the page, and the properties of these elements influence whether they are noticed (Ware, 2004). After respondents organize the information on the page, they focus on answering the questions. Here, the visual processing is attentive and conscious, the visual field narrows to about 2 degrees or 8 to 10 characters in width (the *foveal* view), and attention is focused on only a few elements (for definitions of *attentive processing* and the *foveal view*, see Figure 6.4 in Chapter 6). During focused attention, the properties of the visual design elements or how they are displayed can strongly influence the meaning respondents assign to them.

The Gestalt psychology principles of pattern perception can help survey-ors understand how respondents perceive groups among visual elements with shared properties and then assign meaning by viewing the grouped elements as conceptually related (see Figure 4.17). According to the principle of *proximity,* locating elements that should be grouped closer to each other

Figure 4.17   Examples of Gestalt grouping principles.

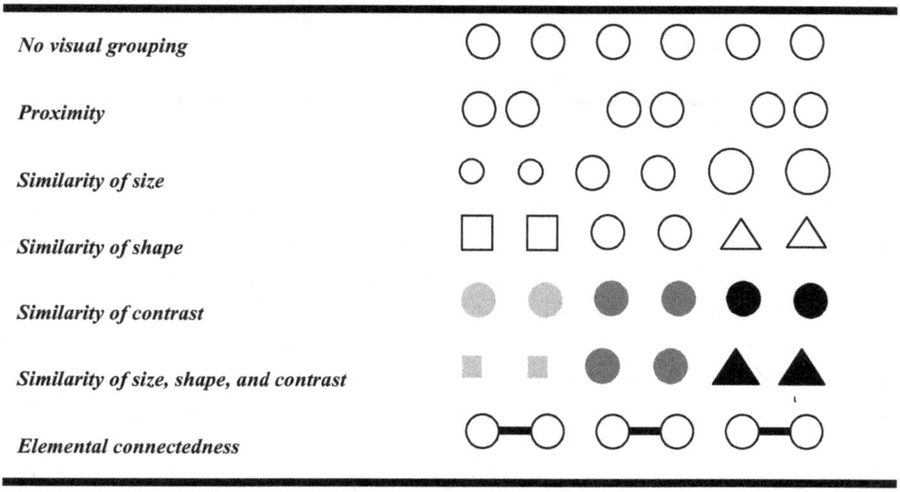

than to other elements encourages respondents to perceive them as related. Surveyors can also use *similarity* of contrast, color, size, or shape to encourage respondents to perceive elements as a group. Respondents also perceive elements that are enclosed in a *common region*, such as a box or an area with a common background color, as a group. Likewise, connecting visual elements by using another element, such as a line, encourages respondents to perceive the *connected* elements as a group. Finally, elements that continue smoothly will be perceived as a group; *continuity* is probably used in surveys mostly in presenting complex graphics where multiple elements are layered in a continuous manner so that they are perceived as a group. These Gestalt principles can help surveyors in deciding how to present visual design elements and which properties to apply to them. In addition, using two or more of these principles to layer properties on the same element(s) can send a stronger stimulus to make them appear as a group than varying only one property of the elements.

The following example illustrates how visual design elements and properties used in accordance with the Gestalt grouping principles can improve responses to a simple survey question. In a recently published article based on a series of experiments, we found that visual design changes to the question "What month and year did you begin your studies at WSU?" increased the percentage of respondents reporting their answer in the desired format (i.e., two digits for the month and four digits for the year) from 55% to 96%, an increase of 41 percentage points (Christian et al., 2007b). In a follow-up study, Christian (2007) reported the sequential impact of a series of visual and verbal manipulations to the same question. The results of her study can be seen in Figure 4.18. In the initial version at the top of Figure 4.18, respondents were provided with two equal size boxes for the month and year, and only 44% provided their answer using the desired format. However, when the size of the month box was reduced by half (consistent with the expectation that the month be reported in half the number of digits as the year), more respondents reported the year using four digits, raising the percentage using the desired format to 57%. Thus, the size of the answer boxes communicated additional meaning to respondents, beyond the graphics alone, about how many digits they should use in providing their answer.

In the next manipulation, adding the verbal instruction to "Please provide your answer using two digits for the month and four digits for the year," resulted in a 21 percentage point increase, bringing the percentage using the desired format to 78% and demonstrating that respondents were processing the words in the instruction and applying them when providing their response. Providing the verbal instruction directly after the question stem helped to ensure that respondents would see and process it just prior to providing their answer. Finally, replacing the word labels "Month"

Figure 4.18 Example of the influence of visual design on how respondents report date information.

Experimental Treatment	Used desired format (2-digit month, 4-digit year)
Question 1 of 30 **What month and year did you begin your studies at WSU?** ■■ ■■ Month Year	44%
Question 1 of 30 **What month and year did you begin your studies at WSU?** ■ ■■ Month Year	57%
Question 1 of 30 **What month and year did you begin your studies at WSU? Please provide your answer using two digits for the month and four digits for the year.** ■ ■■ Month Year	78%
Question 1 of 30 **What month and year did you begin your studies at WSU? Please provide your answer using two digits for the month and four digits for the year.** ■ ■■ MM YYYY	94%

Source: How Mixed-Mode Surveys Are Transforming Social Research: The Influence of Survey Mode on Measurement in Web and Telephone Surveys, by L. M. Christian, 2007, Pullman, WA: Washington State University. Unpublished doctoral dissertation.

and "Year" with a symbolic instruction MM YYYY beneath their respective boxes increased the percentage using the desired format to 94%. The symbolic instruction was designed so that the letter M was used to represent month and Y to represent year, with the number of letters indicating the number of digits to use when reporting the month and year. In this version, respondents gained additional meaning from the symbolic instruction about the number of digits to use in their response. Locating the instruction near the answer spaces and within their foveal view also helped to ensure that respondents would notice and apply the instruction when reporting a response.

In the previous experiment reported by Christian et al. (2007b), providing the symbolic instruction with the answer spaces had the highest impact on use of the desired format (increased use by 35 to 42 percentage points in the two experiments), but there was no additional instruction presented with the question stem. That the instruction was so important in Christian's (2007) experiment (see Figure 4.18) without the MM YYYY symbol to indicate the desired number of digits suggests that verbal instructions are particularly effective in the absence of adequate visual information. Results of telephone experiments confirm this conclusion: The instruction to use the desired format on the telephone, where there is no visual information available, raised the percentage reporting in the desired format from less than 1% to 59% (Christian, 2007). Nevertheless, in self-administered surveys, it is now clear that the use of visual information is key to obtaining desired responses and can contribute to this effort above and beyond question and instruction wording.

GUIDELINES FOR THE VISUAL PRESENTATION OF SURVEY QUESTIONS

Because the visual presentation of survey questions influences how people answer them, choosing words and forming clear questions is not enough; surveyors also need to think about how to put all of the components of the question together. We now turn to describing general guidelines for the visual presentation of survey questions that apply to designing nearly all types of questions. We continue to use the visual design concepts we just discussed in presenting these guidelines.

The poorly designed question in the top panel of Figure 4.19 would undoubtedly turn many respondents off. Some might not even be able to understand that this is a survey question or what it is asking, making it difficult for most respondents to provide an answer. For the next five guidelines, we use this question as an example. The overall problem with this question is that it is unorganized and cluttered, so there is no clear message sent by the visual design. But such a broad observation does not necessarily give us enough information to start revising the question. When we look closer, however, we can identify a number of more specific problems that we can begin to address:

- It is difficult to tell where the question stem ends and the response options begin.
- The response options run together.
- It is not immediately clear how one should mark an answer.
- Certain options stand out more than others, making them more likely to be selected.

Figure 4.19   Implementing general visual design principles to construct individual questions.

Poor design

Which one of the following best **describes** the reason for your most *recent visit* to the Southgate Mall? ♡ **Shopping** for fun/entertainment ▷ Shopping for a needed item [ ]MALL WALKING/Exercise ☐ Other _____ ◯Dining at the mall ☆Hanging out with friends Meeting new people ⚭   CONDUCTING BUSINESS

Revision with improved design

Which one of the following best describes the reason for your most recent visit to the Southgate Mall?
☐ Shopping for fun/entertainment
☐ Shopping for a needed item
☐ Mall walking/exercise
☐ Dining at the mall
☐ Hanging out with friends
☐ Meeting new people
☐ Conducting business
☐ Other _____

Poor design

How much do you favor or oppose implementing a merit-based pay system for elementary school teachers? ☐1 Very much in favor ☐2 Somewhat in favor ☐3 Neutral ☐4 Somewhat oppose ☐5 Very much oppose

Revision with improved design

How much do you favor or oppose implementing a merit-based pay system for elementary school teachers?
☐1 Very much in favor
☐2 Somewhat in favor
☐3 Neutral
☐4 Somewhat oppose
☐5 Very much oppose

- The purpose of the bolding, underlining, and reverse print are unclear.
- One would have to process the "other" option before processing all of the options provided by the surveyor.

The revision is clearly an improvement on the original design. To construct it we used the following five guidelines.

Guideline 4.10: Use Darker and/or Larger Print for the Question and Lighter and/or Smaller Print for Answer Choices and Answer Spaces

The first thing we needed to do was create subgrouping within the question. Good subgrouping helps the respondent quickly recognize and process the parts of the question. We used the design property of *contrast* to create separation between the question stem and the response options. To create differences in contrast, we bolded the question stem but not the response options. This is the standard use of bolding that we have adopted for most of the examples throughout this book. If we wanted to reserve bolding for another purpose in our questionnaire, however, another property we could manipulate is text size (see the bottom example of Figure 4.19). Increasing the size of the text in the question stem but not the response options helps differentiate these two parts of the question.

Guideline 4.11: Use Spacing to Help Create Subgrouping within a Question

The Gestalt psychology principle of *proximity* states that items located close to one another will be perceived as belonging to a group, and items located farther apart will be perceived as not belonging together. We applied this principle to help reinforce the subgrouping within the question. We started by moving the first response option onto its own line of text and adding some extra space between it and the question stem. We then moved each response option onto its own line and arranged them vertically underneath the question stem so that they would no longer blend together. To help create the impression that the response options were all part of one group, we placed them in close vertical proximity to one another and spaced them equally. We also indented them a few spaces to the right underneath the question stem to reinforce the subgrouping we were creating. Grouping and subgrouping of multiple questions is discussed in more depth in Chapter 6.

Guideline 4.12: Visually Standardize All Answer Spaces or Response Options

Another problem with the poor design that we needed to address was that some response options stood out visually more than others, making them more likely to be seen and selected. "Shopping" stood out because it was bolded, "dining" because it was in reverse print, and "hanging out with friends" because it was underlined. Our solution to this problem was to standardize the design properties of all of the response options. The first thing we did was make sure they were all the same readable size with the same character spacing. We then changed them all to the same font.

We chose Times New Roman because of its readability and professionalism (i.e., compared to the 𝒟𝒾𝓈𝓃ℯ𝓅 𝒮𝒸𝓇𝒾𝓅𝓉 used for "conducting business"). Finally, we removed variations due to color, contrast (bolding), underlining, and reverse print. The resulting uniformity makes the response options easier to process and helps ensure that they will be processed equally. Incidentally, the similarity across response options also helps them appear as a subgroup within the larger question group (i.e., the Gestalt psychology principle of *similarity* says that items that appear regular and similar will be perceived as belonging together). In addition to making these changes, we reordered the response options so the "other" option was located at the end of the list so that respondents would process all of the response options before getting to it.

Guideline 4.13: Use Visual Design Properties to Emphasize Elements that Are Important to the Respondent and to De-Emphasize Those that Are Not

In the poor design, the words "describes" and "recent visit" in the question stem are emphasized with bolding and italics, respectively. However, these words seem no more important to the respondents' understanding of the response task or the question than any others in the stem. As a result, the bolding and italics were removed in the revised design. Instead of emphasizing these words, we opted to use underlining to emphasize the word "one" in order to draw the respondents' attention to the fact that they should select only one of the response options. The choice of underlining for this purpose works quite well for paper surveys but should be carefully considered for web surveys because underlining already has a predefined meaning on the Internet, especially when combined with the color blue. Underlining on the Web often denotes a clickable link, although many web designers use underlining inconsistently, and sometimes links are not underlined.

Nevertheless, we use underlining in the same way in the merit-based pay example in the bottom of the figure to draw respondents' attention to the fact that this question is about elementary school teachers only. In this example we also face another common problem: the need to include extra information for survey processing reasons. In this case, the extra information is numbers located inside the check boxes to assist with data entry. Because they are unimportant to the respondent, these numbers should be deemphasized if they cannot be eliminated altogether. We do this by manipulating the properties of size, contrast, and location. The numbers are made smaller and lighter to make them less obvious but still visible to the astute data enterer. They are then relocated from the center to outside the check box, where they are less likely to be noticed by respondents but can still easily be used for data entry.

Guideline 4.14: Use Design Properties with Consistency and Regularity

This general guideline may be the most important. Even if the meaning of a design element or property is not immediately intuitive, the respondent has a better chance of learning its meaning and applying it throughout the questionnaire if it is used consistently, both within and across questions. However, if design elements and properties are used inconsistently, like the use of the bolding in the shopping mall example, the respondent has to relearn their meaning at each use. Doing so may require more patience and mental energy than some respondents are willing to expend.

A good rule of thumb is to use each design element or property for only one purpose. For example, no matter what question or what part of the question it is used in, underlining is only used to draw attention to important words, white square boxes are only used as answer spaces, bolding is only used to distinguish between the question stem and the answer options depending on the particular needs of one's survey. One can choose to use these design properties to convey different meanings than in this example, but the important thing is that they be used with consistency and regularity.

Taken together, these visual design guidelines (4.10–4.14) helped us organize all of the information in the questions in Figure 4.19 to make these questions more easily perceived and processed and, most important, to make it easier for respondents to provide a response. In addition to easing the response task, these changes also added an air of professionalism to the questions, thereby increasing the likelihood that they would be taken seriously by potential respondents (i.e., perhaps increasing rewards and trust). In the remainder of this section we present several more general guidelines dealing with instructions, the response task, and organization.

Guideline 4.15: Make Sure the Words and Visual Elements that Make Up the Question Send Consistent Messages

One of the biggest lessons we have learned since the last edition of this book was published is just how influential visual design elements can be. We know of multiple cases where surveyors made design decisions with the intention of easing the response task but with the result that the design features they introduced biased the results. In one national survey, for example, the designers sorted related response options into two groups based on their content. Pretesting revealed that the subgrouping caused respondents to make mistakes in answering the question. Many respondents attempted to mark multiple answers, but because the survey was only designed to accept one answer, they inadvertently erased their first response when they entered their second.

Figure 4.20 shows examples of this type of design from a set of web survey experiments we undertook to examine the effects of subgrouping response options in this way (Smyth, Dillman, Christian, & Stern, 2006b). When the response options were subgrouped with no instruction to select the best answer (not shown in figure), 70% of respondents marked answers within both groups compared to 41% when the response options were not subgrouped. Adding the instruction "Please select the best answer" to the subgrouped version reduced the number of respondents marking answers within both groups to 66%. The instruction also reduced the mean number of options respondents selected, as more respondents limited themselves to selecting

Figure 4.20 Make sure verbal and visual design elements send a consistent message.

Instruction and visual arrangement of response options contradict one another

Q18. What best describes the benefit of the Student Recreation Center? Please select the best answer.

Health Benefits
- ☐ The variety of physical fitness offerings
- ☐ The health and wellness offerings
- ☐ Helps reduce stress

Academic Benefits
- ☐ Improves academic productivity
- ☐ Enhances learning experience
- ☐ Provides information for students to learn about their health

- ☐ Don't Know

66% of respondents marked an answer in both the top and the bottom half of the response options

A revision with instruction and unnecessary subgrouping of response options removed

Q18. What best describes the benefit of the Student Recreation Center?

- ☐ The variety of physical fitness offerings
- ☐ The health and wellness offerings
- ☐ Helps reduce stress
- ☐ Improves academic productivity
- ☐ Enhances learning experience
- ☐ Provides information for students to learn about their health
- ☐ Don't Know

41% of respondents marked an answer in both the top and the bottom half of the response options

Another possible revision reincorporating instruction

Q18. What best describes the benefit of the Student Recreation Center? Please select the best answer.

- ☐ The variety of physical fitness offerings
- ☐ The health and wellness offerings
- ☐ Helps reduce stress
- ☐ Improves academic productivity
- ☐ Enhances learning experience
- ☐ Provides information for students to learn about their health
- ☐ Don't Know

Source: "Effects of Using Visual Design Principles to Group Response Options in Web Surveys," by J. D. Smyth, D. A. Dillman, L. M. Christian, and M. J. Stern, 2006b, *International Journal of Internet Science, 1*(1), pp. 6–16.

one option from each subgroup instead of multiple options from each subgroup. Overall, these findings suggest that the subgrouping communicated to respondents that they should select answers from both subgroups. Within this context the instruction to select the best answer appears to have been interpreted as "select the best answer *from each subgroup.*" In other words, the visual information provided by the subgrouping influenced how the instruction was interpreted.

This experiment provides an excellent example of how verbal and visual elements can contradict one another, leading to errors in responses. Perhaps more important, though, it demonstrates the importance of stepping back and looking at question construction holistically to ensure that both the words and the visual design of the question are sending a consistent message about the meaning of the question and the response task. In many ways the guidelines we present in this chapter and the next provide the tools for doing just that.

Guideline 4.16: Integrate Special Instructions into the Question Where They Will Be Used Rather than Including Them as Free-Standing Entities

Frequently it is necessary to provide a special instruction to clarify a question. This leads to the undesirable practice of placing instructions outside of the question and emphasizing them with boxes or perhaps a different color. The problem with this practice is that once people have gotten into the routine of completing a questionnaire, the marking of an answer leads to the immediate search for the next question. As a result, free-standing instructions tend to be skipped entirely. The example in Figure 4.21 shows that such instructions are most likely to be properly applied if they are expressed as part of the query itself rather than placed as a separate entity (Christian & Dillman, 2004).

In the first layout, an instruction to skip this question and move on to the next if it does not apply is located below both the question stem and the response options. In this design, 40% of respondents marked "no" and only 5% left the question blank and moved on. In the second layout, the instruction is moved up to a more integrated location between the question stem and the response options. Placing the instruction here resulted in 19% of respondents marking "no" and a full 26% leaving the question blank and moving on. When the instruction was located where it was needed to help respondents decide whether and how they should answer the question, more people were able to successfully apply it. In contrast, when the instruction was located as a free-standing entity outside the question stem and answer categories, many respondents had probably already marked an answer before they even noticed it. The fact that 11% of respondents to this version (compared to 3% when the instruction was integrated) left the next question (Question 9) blank suggests that when some respondents got to the instruction located below the response options, they applied it to the wrong question altogether. The third layout, which has shown some promise in cognitive interviews, is another possible way the instruction could be integrated with the question stem.

As this example demonstrates, it is not enough to simply move instructions from the front of the questionnaire or from a separate booklet into the

Figure 4.21   Integrate special instructions into the question stem.

Instruction placed outside of the navigational path

8. Have one-on-one meetings with professors contributed significantly to your WSU education?

☐ Yes
☐ No

40% marked No
5% left Question 8 blank
11% left Question 9 blank

If you haven't had many one-on-one meetings, just skip to Question 9.

A revision with the instruction placed within the navigational path

8. Have one-on-one meetings with professors contributed significantly to your WSU education?

If you haven't had many one-on-one meetings, just skip to Question 9.

19% marked No
26% left Question 8 blank
3% left Question 9 blank

☐ Yes
☐ No

Another possible revision with the instruction integrated with the question stem and visually distinguished using italics

8. Have one-on-one meetings with professors contributed significantly to your WSU education?
If you haven't had many one-on-one meetings, just skip to Question 9.

☐ Yes
☐ No

Source: "The Influence of Graphical and Symbolic Language Manipulations on Responses to Self-Administered Questions," by L. M. Christian and D. A. Dillman, 2004, _Public Opinion Quarterly, 68_(1), pp. 58–81.

appropriate question subgrouping. Rather, even within a single question, in order to be effective, instructions need to be strategically located where they will be used (the location of instructions is discussed in more depth with respect to establishment surveys in Chapter 12).

Guideline 4.17: Separate Optional or Occasionally Needed Instructions from the Question Stem by Font or Symbol Variation

When respondents begin to fill out a questionnaire, they are learning how the questionnaire works, including what must be read and what can be skipped. Requiring them to read through a great deal of material that does not apply or that can be skipped without negative consequences encourages the habit of skipping words and phrases. For these reasons a distinction should be made between words that are essential for every person to read and those that may be needed by only some respondents. There are many different reasons that reading a particular instruction may be optional. Perhaps it is because the instruction "put an X in the appropriate box" is the same instruction used for a previous question, and many respondents will remember that. It may also be that only a few respondents need the information, such as in the case of the instruction used in Figure 4.21 ("If you haven't had many one-on-one meetings, just skip to Question 9"). To avoid presenting information that respondents already know, or that applies to relatively few of them, distinguish this information from the query by the use of either italics (as shown for the second revision in Figure 4.21) or a symbol variation (e.g., putting it in parentheses).

Guideline 4.18: Organize Each Question in a Way that Minimizes the Need to Reread Portions in Order to Comprehend the Response Task

The goal underlying this guideline is efficiency for the respondent. In Figure 4.22, a recreated excerpt from the 1993 U.S. Census of Agriculture, it is inefficient for respondents to read in great depth about what land to consider in their answer before even knowing what the question is asking. The inevitable result is that it will be necessary to reread the information after discovering what the question is asking. The drawback to such inefficiency is that respondents may become frustrated and unwilling to retrace those steps and therefore may give a wrong answer or no answer at all. In this case, the problem is confounded by a visual layout that makes it somewhat unclear what navigational path is to be followed (i.e., what information is to be read in what order).

A more effective organization of the information is shown in the revision in the bottom panel of Figure 4.22. The revision allows respondents

Figure 4.22   Poor information organization with unclear navigational path.

Poor information organization and lack of navigational path

CENSUS USE ONLY	035	036	037	038	039	040	041	042

SECTION 1   **ACREAGE IN 1992** – Report land owned, rented, or used by you, your spouse, or by the partnership, corporation, or
organization for which you are reporting. Include ALL LAND, REGARDLESS OF LOCATION OR USE – cropland, pastureland,
S1   *rangeland, woodland, idle land, house lots, etc.*

If the acres you operated in 1992 changed during the year, refer to the INFORMATION SHEET, section 1.
1.   All land owned ....   None   Number of acres 043 ☐

Better information organization and creation of clear navigational path

1. **How many acres of land did you own in 1990? You should report all land (crop land, pasture land, rangeland, woodland, idle land, house lots, etc.) regardless of location, owned by you, your spouse, or by the partnership, corporation, or organization for which you are reporting.** *(If the acres you operated in 1990 changed during the year, refer to the information sheet, Section I.)*

_____Number of acres owned

to know at the beginning that they are being asked to report the number of acres they own; they are then given instructions on what to include and exclude. The important implication of this principle is that no amount of visual redesign can compensate for poorly worded questions or unorganized information, which, once read, leave the respondent unclear about precisely what to do.

Guideline 4.19: Choose Line Spacing, Font, and Text Size to Ensure the Legibility of the Text

Even a very well-worded question can be difficult for respondents to process if it is not designed in a legible way. Enhancing legibility means choosing an appropriate font, font size, and line length. With respect to fonts, one should avoid script fonts because they can be very difficult to read (e.g., *Brush Script MT*, *Walt Disney Script*, *Edwardian Script ITC*, *Freestyle Script*). Instead, serif or sans serif fonts should be used. Examples of serif fonts are Times New Roman, Garamond, Century, and Georgia. Each of these fonts has added detail, or *serifs*, at the end of the strokes that make up the structure of the letters. In contrast, sans serif fonts do not have the added details (e.g., Arial, Verdana, Tahoma, and Latha). Although both serif and sans serif fonts work well on paper, sans serif fonts are commonly preferred for web readability. Generally, one should also choose proportionally spaced fonts (e.g., Arial or Times New Roman) rather than monospace fonts (e.g., Courier New).

To some degree, the font size one chooses will depend on the survey population. A good rule of thumb is to use 10- to 12-point fonts for most populations but larger fonts for older populations. An additional consideration for web surveyors is that font preferences are often set on the user's computer, giving the designer little control. Additionally, font sizes appear different on screen than on paper, and the same font size may appear larger or smaller depending on factors such as the user's screen resolution. Thus, web designers are advised to seek additional resources on how to ensure legibility of text (more on this in Chapter 6).

With respect to line length, readers may have difficulty tracking along the lines, reading evenly, and finding their place at the beginning of the next line on the return sweep when text lines are too long. In comparison,
excessively short
lines of text require
almost constant eye
motion and frequent
return sweeps that
can become overly
burdensome.
Thus, a more moderate line length of 3 to 5 inches is recommended.

CONCLUSION

Although crafting survey questions may seem simple, we have demonstrated in this chapter how it requires attending to many details at once to help ensure that respondents process all of the component parts and comprehend the question as intended so that they can report an accurate answer. We have also discussed a holistic approach that highlights the many aspects surveyors need to think about when crafting survey questions. This approach considers whether an open- or closed-ended question is best for each concept of interest in the survey and requires thinking about how all of the components of a question (the question stem, any additional instructions, and answer spaces or response options) work together to form the entire question stimulus.

Drawing on the considerable amount of research on the importance of the visual design and presentation of survey questions, we have demonstrated how crafting effective survey questions for mail and web surveys involves not only choosing words to form clear questions but also deciding how the components of the question are presented visually to respondents. Within this holistic framework, we have offered general guidelines to help surveyors as they choose the words to form questions and visually design and present the components of the question. This second step is an important one that is often neglected in other guides for crafting questions.

The guidelines we have presented in this chapter apply to nearly all survey questions. However, this is only the first of two chapters devoted to crafting survey questions. In the next chapter we shift our focus to crafting specific types of open-ended and closed-ended questions. Because each of these different question types has a different goal and a slightly different configuration of question components, each is subject to its own strengths and challenges. Although the general guidelines presented in the current chapter still apply to these question types, we take them a step further to focus on both the wording and visual presentation of the question stem, any additional instructions, the answer spaces, and response options that are unique to these question types.

LIST OF GUIDELINES

Guidelines for Choosing Words and Forming Questions

Guideline 4.1: Make sure the question applies to the respondent
Guideline 4.2: Make sure the question is technically accurate

(continued)

Guideline 4.3:   *Ask one question at a time*
Guideline 4.4:   *Use simple and familiar words*
Guideline 4.5:   *Use specific and concrete words to specify the concepts clearly*
Guideline 4.6:   *Use as few words as possible to pose the question*
Guideline 4.7:   *Use complete sentences with simple sentence structures*
Guideline 4.8:   *Make sure "yes" means yes and "no" means no*
Guideline 4.9:   *Be sure the question specifies the response task*

Guidelines for the Visual Presentation of Survey Questions

Guideline 4.10:   *Use darker and/or larger print for the question and lighter and/or smaller print for answer choices and answer spaces*
Guideline 4.11:   *Use spacing to help create subgrouping within a question*
Guideline 4.12:   *Visually standardize all answer spaces or response options*
Guideline 4.13:   *Use visual design properties to emphasize elements that are important to the respondent and to deemphasize those that are not*
Guideline 4.14:   *Use design properties with consistency and regularity*
Guideline 4.15:   *Make sure the words and visual elements that make up the question send consistent messages*
Guideline 4.16:   *Integrate special instructions into the question where they will be used rather than including them as free-standing entities*
Guideline 4.17:   *Separate optional or occasionally needed instructions from the question stem by font or symbol variation*
Guideline 4.18:   *Organize each question in a way that minimizes the need to reread portions in order to comprehend the response task*
Guideline 4.19:   *Choose line spacing, font, and text size to ensure the legibility of the text*

CHAPTER 5

Constructing Open- and Closed-Ended Questions

TO SUCCESSFULLY undertake almost any task, one has to attend to many details at once. For example, going for any type of bicycle ride requires attention to balance, pedaling, and steering. Failure to properly attend to any one detail (especially balancing!) can have significant and far-reaching consequences. However, to have a *great* bicycle ride, one has to look far beyond these common details and focus on how the mechanics of the specific bicycle work with the type of ride desired. If the bicyclist wants to ride on flat paved roads, she would need smooth thin tires, a light frame, and high gears to have the best ride. The same bike, however, would not hold up to mountainous terrain. For this type of riding, she would need wide and knobby tires, a sturdier frame, and lower gears to get the best ride.

There are many parallels between planning for a great bicycle ride and constructing survey questions. A set of common guidelines, such as those discussed in Chapter 4, is useful in that it provides a general framework within which to craft all types of survey questions, but, as with the bicycle example, constructing a set of great survey questions also requires carefully designing each component of every question in light of its unique measurement goals. Just as a bicycle rider needs to put the right components together in the form of different types of bikes for different types of rides, a survey designer needs to know how to put together the components of different types of survey questions to effectively measure different types of constructs. In this chapter, we pay detailed attention to how different types of questions—open-ended, closed-ended nominal, and closed-ended ordinal—need to be constructed to perform optimally. We continue to apply the techniques discussed in Chapter 4 to make sure the questions are easy to read and comprehend and are well designed visually; however, we shift our main focus in this chapter to the unique design considerations that arise due to the specific characteristics and measurement goals of each of these question types.

OPEN-ENDED QUESTIONS

When many people think of open-ended questions, only one type comes to mind: the *descriptive question*, in which respondents are asked to provide in-depth information on the topic of the question. An example might be a question asking how a local restaurant can improve the dining experience it provides. However, in addition to this type of open-ended question there are two other circumstances in which surveyors ask respondents a question and provide them with an open-ended box in which to answer. Perhaps the most common of these circumstances, and one that many overlook when they think about open-ended questions, is when the surveyor asks respondents to report a *numerical response* such as a date, frequency, monetary value, count, amount, or scalar value in an answer box. Another circumstance in which open-ended answer boxes are provided is when surveyors ask respondents to provide a *list of items* such as grocery stores they frequent, favorite brands of clothing, or businesses they would like to see move into their town.

Each of these types of open-ended questions provides the respondent with an immense amount of flexibility in the answer that can be provided. As a result, they also have in common the fact that the answers provided are strongly influenced by the visual design of the answer boxes that accompany the questions. However, the measurement goal of each question is very different: In one only a number is desired, in another only a list of items is desired and any extra elaboration or description is unnecessary, and in the third the surveyor wants as much elaboration and description as possible. As such, the design strategy that must be employed for each type, including both question wording and visual design, differs substantially.

Open-Ended Requests for Numerical Responses

The usual goal of a numerical response open-ended question is to get the respondent to enter a single number or amount into the answer box. A parallel goal is to discourage the respondent from entering invalid responses, including numbers outside of any prespecified range, the wrong units, or additional interpretive information that may cause confusion during data entry and data cleaning. Several strategic design practices can be undertaken to discourage invalid responses and to help ensure that the respondent clearly understands how to answer such questions.

Guideline 5.1: Ask for the Specific Unit Desired in the Question Stem

In an open-ended question, making sure that the question communicates the type of answer desired takes on extra importance because of the ability respondents have to enter whatever comes to mind into the answer box. Take, for example, the question posed in Figure 5.1: "In an average week, how often do you cook dinner at home?" Some respondents to this question might answer using a number, as was intended by the researcher (e.g., "5"). Others may provide more vague responses, such as "most of the time" or "rarely." Still others may get very specific: "I cook dinner at home on Monday, Tuesday, and Thursday. My partner cooks dinner on Wednesday, Friday, and Sunday. We eat out every Saturday night." The first revision for this question should encourage respondents to report their answer in number of days per week, because this expectation is established in the question stem.

Figure 5.1 Open-ended number box questions.

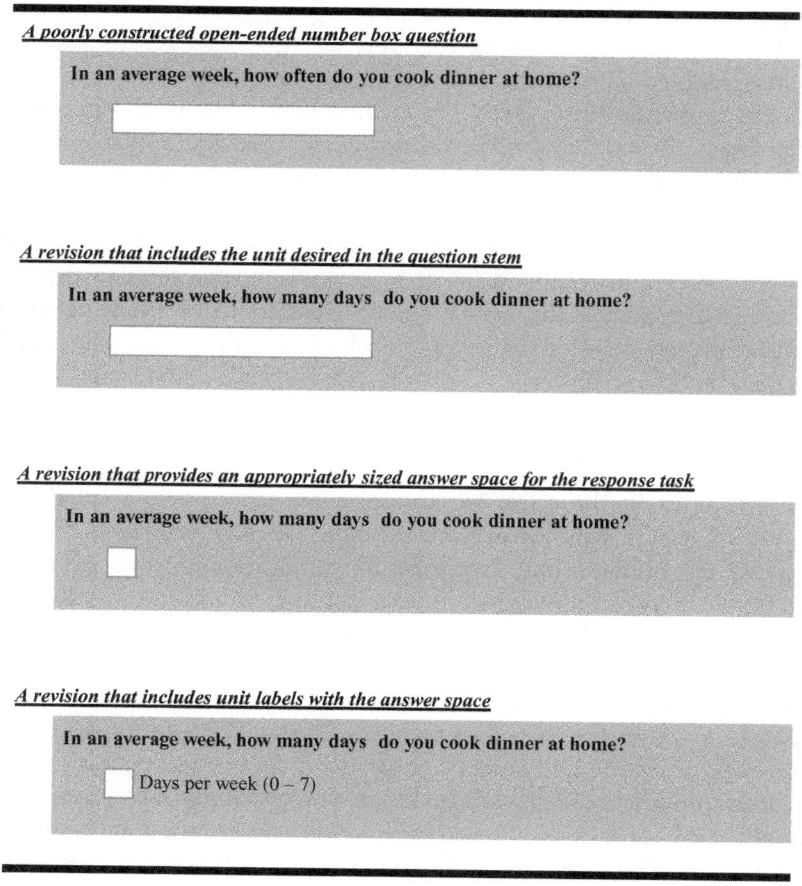

A poorly constructed open-ended number box question

In an average week, how often do you cook dinner at home?

A revision that includes the unit desired in the question stem

In an average week, how many days do you cook dinner at home?

A revision that provides an appropriately sized answer space for the response task

In an average week, how many days do you cook dinner at home?

A revision that includes unit labels with the answer space

In an average week, how many days do you cook dinner at home?

Days per week (0 – 7)

Guideline 5.2: Provide Answer Spaces that Are Sized Appropriately for the Response Task

Another way to encourage respondents to answer in the way desired and to discourage them from providing invalid answers is to appropriately size the answer space for the type of information desired. Research has shown that when answer boxes are too large for the information that is supposed to be entered into them, respondents are more likely to enter extra information. In one study discussed in Chapter 4 (Christian, 2007; Christian, Dillman, & Smyth, 2007b), people were more likely to enter the requested number of digits for a date question (two digits for the month and four digits for the year) when the month box was half the size of the year box. In another study, respondents were asked how many of the 10 people they socialize with most are of each of the following races or ethnicities: White/Caucasian, African American, Asian, Hispanic, and Other races or ethnicities (Couper, Traugott, & Lamias, 2001). A programming error resulted in some respondents getting answer boxes that were appropriately sized for the response task (two digits wide) and others getting boxes that were significantly larger than needed. About 11% of respondents who received the small box entered an invalid response, such as "about three" or "between four and five" in one or more of the boxes. In comparison, nearly 21% of those who received the large box did so. The likely reason that the size of the answer box can influence responses so strongly is that respondents look to it as a clue for how much information they are expected to provide. A small answer box tells respondents that very little information is needed, whereas a large answer box implies that the surveyor expects to receive a lot of information. Therefore, in the second revision in Figure 5.1, the answer box is resized to be more appropriate for the expected one-digit responses and to discourage respondents from entering invalid responses.

Guideline 5.3: Provide Unit Labels with the Answer Spaces

Providing units in the question stem and an appropriately sized answer box will go a long way toward encouraging the proper type of responses, but some respondents may overlook the units requested in the question stem. Others may initially register the units but get distracted thinking about the topic of the question and forget them. It is for these reasons that we also provide the unit labels with the answer spaces in the final revision in Figure 5.1. To help ensure that the respondent sees the unit label, we locate it very close to the end of the answer space so that as the respondent processes the answer space, the unit label is within the foveal view. Locating the labels this close to the answer space also creates the perception of grouping (i.e., the Gestalt principle of proximity), or that the labels belong with the answer space, thus helping to ensure that respondents perceive them as important to the response task. In addition to the unit labels, we also provide the range of values one is expected to enter to help clarify the intent of the question.

OPEN-ENDED REQUESTS FOR A LIST OF ITEMS

The question in the top panel of Figure 5.2 is a typical list-style open-ended question. The implicit expectation here is that respondents will provide a list of businesses they would like to see in the area without providing a lot of extra information or description. This response task, however, can be made more explicit in a number of ways.

Figure 5.2 The effect of answer spaces on responses to list-style open-ended questions.

	Number of Items Listed	
A list-style question as commonly designed	**3+**	**5+**
Question 22 of 27 — What businesses would you most like to see in the Pullman and Moscow area that are currently not available?	32%	12%
List-style questions with multiple answer boxes		
Question 22 of 27 — What businesses would you most like to see in the Pullman and Moscow area that are currently not available?	47%	5%
Question 22 of 27 — What businesses would you most like to see in the Pullman and Moscow area that are currently not available?	44%	18%
A list-style question with labeled answer boxes		
Question 22 of 27 — What businesses would you most like to see in the Pullman and Moscow area that are currently not available? (Business #1, Business #2, Business #3)	51%	2%

Source: Improving Response Quality in List-Style Open-Ended Questions in Web and Telephone Surveys, by J. D. Smyth, D. A. Dillman, and L. M. Christian, May 2007b. Paper presented at the annual conference of American Association for Public Opinion Research, Anaheim, CA.

*Guideline 5.4: Specify the Number and Type of Responses Desired
in the Question Stem*

As with numerical open-ended questions, the first step to sending a clear and explicit message to respondents about the question's response task is to specify in the question stem the number and type of answers desired. So, for example, we might reword the question stem from Figure 5.2 as follows: "Please name three businesses that you would most like to see in the Pullman and Moscow area that are currently not available." Reaching this level of specificity in the question stem is particularly important for those conducting telephone surveys or mixed-mode surveys with a telephone component. In fact, in one experiment we did, the percentage of respondents reporting three or more businesses over the telephone increased by 32 percentage points when they were asked "What three businesses would you most like to see" rather than "What businesses would you most like to see" (Smyth et al., 2007b).

*Guideline 5.5: Design the Answer Spaces to Support the Type and Number
of Responses Desired*

Another similarity with numerical open-ended questions is the importance of providing appropriately designed answer boxes. However, the different goal of the question means different aspects of the answer box are important. In particular, as the second panel in Figure 5.2 shows, the expectation of multiple answers can be effectively communicated by providing multiple answer boxes arranged as one might arrange a to-do or grocery list. In an experimental comparison, the number of students listing three or more businesses in response to the question in Figure 5.2 increased by 15 percentage points when they were provided with three individual boxes rather than one large box (Smyth et al., 2007b). Likewise, among respondents who were given three individual boxes, only 5% listed five or more businesses, but among those provided with five individual boxes, 18% listed five or more businesses. Moreover, responses contained less unnecessary extra detail and elaboration in the multiple-box treatments than in the single-box treatment. These findings were confirmed in two additional experimental comparisons. One caveat, however, is that providing too many boxes may make the response task appear too burdensome. Indeed, increasing from three to five boxes in the aforementioned experiment resulted in a nearly 5 percentage point increase in item nonresponse for this question.

*Guideline 5.6: Provide Labels with Answer Spaces to Reinforce the Type
of Response Requested*

Finally, it is also advisable in list-style questions to communicate response expectations by verbally labeling answer spaces as is done in the bottom panel of Figure 5.2. The verbal labels increase the percentage of respondents providing three or more items, but, perhaps more important, they also help respondents focus their answers substantively. In three experiments comparing unlabeled to labeled boxes, students reported significantly fewer general business types and, in two of the three experiments, significantly more specific business names when the boxes were labeled (Smyth et al., 2007b). In hindsight, the students could probably have been helped even more by more specific labels such as "Business Name #1" or "Business Type #1."

OPEN-ENDED REQUESTS FOR DESCRIPTION AND ELABORATION

When many surveyors think about descriptive open-ended survey questions, they think high costs. Some of their high cost stems from the physical space such questions require on the questionnaire, but even more costly is the additional time and labor that has to be invested in processing and coding the responses so that they can be analyzed in a meaningful way. As a result of these costs to the surveyor, many mail survey designers have opted to save space and money by cutting these questions or by providing only small boxes for respondents to provide their answer. Similarly, if web surveyors include them, they also often provide only small answer spaces under the assumption that web respondents know they can write beyond the boundaries of the box (i.e., scroll).

Descriptive open-ended questions are also "expensive" for respondents in the sense that answering them requires a significant investment of time and effort on their part. Many respondents are simply not willing to make that large of an investment, especially in self-administered surveys where there is no interviewer to encourage them or to whom they feel accountable. As a result, response quality for these questions is typically quite poor.

However, evidence now shows that people provide better open-ended responses containing more information in web-based surveys than in traditional pen-and-paper surveys. In a nonexperimental comparison of responses to a question that was administered first in a paper survey and then several years later in a web survey (two different samples, but from the same population), we found that the web respondents provided substantially longer answers (by 10–15 words) that contained both more themes and more elaboration or detail than did the paper respondents (Smyth, Dillman, Christian, & McBride, in press, 2006). This finding paralleled an experimental comparison reported by Schaefer and Dillman (1997), in which they found that e-mail respondents used an average of 30 more words to answer open-ended questions than did paper survey respondents. In addition, as the following guidelines demonstrate, a number of methods have been developed to motivate respondents to give higher quality responses to these questions. Together, these developments provide great hope for the reemergence of this question type and consequently improved possibilities for combining qualitative and quantitative data collection and analyses.

Guideline 5.7: Provide Extra Motivation to Respond

One of the fundamental problems with descriptive open-ended questions is that they take a lot of work on the respondents' part (i.e., increase costs). Where this is most obvious is in the reporting stage of the answering process. Whereas closed-ended questions require respondents to tick off an answer space, descriptive open-ended questions require them to write or type their ideas, preferably at length and with lots of descriptive and explanatory information. Providing good answers to these questions takes lots of time as well as both mental and physical energy. Providing a short and very basic answer is much easier. As a result, respondents may need extra motivation to answer descriptive open-ended questions well.

One way to keep motivation for these questions high is to use them sparingly and only for important topics about which descriptive information is necessary. Another way is to provide clarifying and motivating material with the question, as we have done in the revision in Figure 5.3. In one research example we asked university students the following: "In your own words, how would you describe your advisor(s)?" A randomly selected subset of the students received the following introduction prior to the question: "This question is very important to understanding the [Washington State University] student experience. Please take your time answering it." In two different comparisons we found that including the additional explanation increased response length between 5 and 15 words and the percentage of respondents who elaborated in their response between 12 and 20 percentage points. Respondents who received the motivational explanation also took more time

Figure 5.3   Open-ended questions asking for description and elaboration.

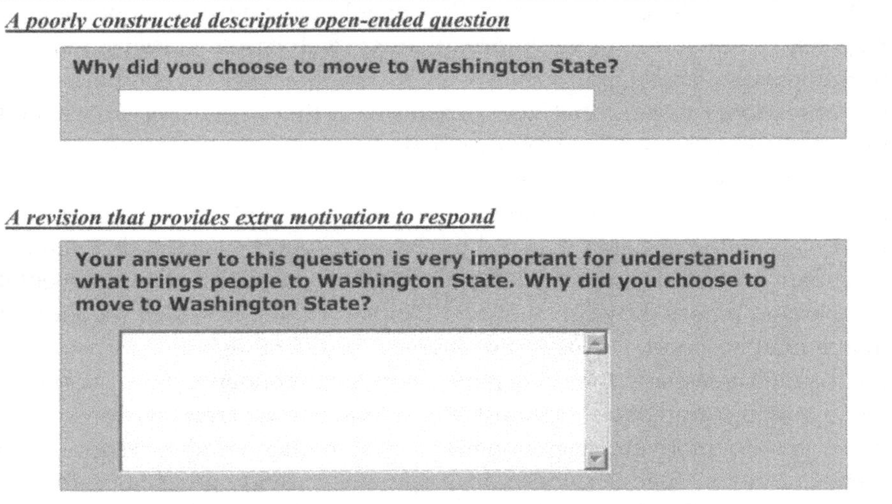

A poorly constructed descriptive open-ended question

Why did you choose to move to Washington State?

A revision that provides extra motivation to respond

Your answer to this question is very important for understanding what brings people to Washington State. Why did you choose to move to Washington State?

to provide their answers (between 20 and 34 seconds; Smyth et al., in press, 2006). If space is an issue, further research into the use of introductions has shown that using a shorter introduction (e.g., "This question is very important to understanding the [Washington State University] student experience") has nearly the same benefits as using the longer version (i.e., the introduction above with "Please take your time answering it"). Informing respondents that their answers are important and clarifying why they are important gives respondents a reason to expend the time and energy needed to produce good open-ended responses.

Guideline 5.8: Provide Adequate Space for Respondents to Completely Answer the Question

The goal of this type of question is to collect thick, rich, descriptive information. This means respondents are going to need space to write. Answer boxes, therefore, should be sized appropriately for the amount of information desired. A small box such as the one shown in the top example in Figure 5.3 communicates to respondents that the surveyor is looking for a short answer. In comparison, the larger box shown in the revision suggests that a longer answer is desired.

One of the earliest studies of the effects of answer box size of which we are aware was somewhat of an accident. In 1954, Gallup and the National Opinion Research Center (NORC) jointly fielded the same survey. Although they used a common questionnaire, in the printing process NORC provided 5 times more space for recording open-ended answers than did Gallup. When the data came back, the answers recorded by interviewers on the NORC questionnaires were 4 to 10 words longer than those recorded on the Gallup questionnaires (Smith, 1993).

In more recent experimentation, Christian and Dillman (2004) compared answers in a mail survey from three questions for which respondents were randomly assigned to receive either a small box or a large box. They found that responses in the large box, which was twice the size of the small box, were two to six words longer and contained more themes than responses in the small box. Another study using a mail survey compared responses to open-ended questions with seven different box heights ranging from 0.28 to 1.68 inches. This study also found that as box size increased, so too did response length (Israel, 2005).

In additional research, we found that increasing answer box size on the Web can encourage better answers from late responders (i.e., those who put off responding until late in the fielding period and therefore probably already lack motivation to respond; Smyth et al., in press, 2006). In comparisons of responses to small- and large-box versions of four questions there was no difference in the words, themes, or elaboration (i.e., extra explanation about a topic) entered by early responders. Among late responders, those who received the large box gave answers similar to those of early responders. However, those who received the small box gave responses that were three to seven words shorter and contained fewer themes. The percentage of late responders who elaborated on their responses was also 5 to 17 percentage points lower when they received the small box. It appears, from these findings, that larger box sizes can encourage better answers from the least motivated respondents.

Guideline 5.9: Use Scrollable Boxes on Web Surveys

One of the great qualities of web surveys for open-ended questions is that answer box space is not as constrained as it is in paper surveys. In a paper survey, the boundaries of the answer box are real boundaries: Once printed, answer box space cannot be shrunk or stretched. In contrast, a text box on the computer is made up of virtual space, meaning that even though respondents can see boundaries in much the same way as on a piece of paper, they can oftentimes exceed them. If the text box is programmed to allow it, respondents can enter responses that well exceed its size and then scroll up and down in the box to see all that they have entered. Working with virtual space in this way means that even if visual space is scarce (i.e., there is only room for a small answer box), one can still provide plenty of "space" for respondents to record their answers. One simply provides them with scrollable boxes.

In this situation, however, there is the problem that the small visible space may suggest to respondents that only a short answer is desired. It is possible, although we have not tested it, that the scroll bar that appears on the side of the scrollable box (as in the revision in Figure 5.3) provides a visual cue to computer-savvy respondents, informing them that they can enter text beyond the boundaries of the box. However, the danger is that respondents who are not as familiar with computers may miss this cue. To overcome this problem, we have experimented with including the following explanation: "You are not limited in the length of your response by the size of the box." Two experimental tests of this explanation resulted in response length increases of 6 to 19 words, more themes, and increases in elaboration on the scale of 20 to 26 percentage points (Smyth et al., in press, 2006).

Guideline 5.10: Consider Programming Probes to Open-Ended Responses in Internet Surveys

A new body of research in the area of web surveys has begun to explore the effects of using interactive design features. Examples include progress indicators, automatic calculators that sum numerical responses, and error messages. Another interactive feature that can be programmed into a web survey is an open-ended question probe. In a survey about a new undergraduate major (Latin American and Caribbean Studies) being offered by the University of Georgia, undergraduate students were asked two open-ended questions to gauge their interest in topics related to the major. For each question, once they submitted their answer, a probe appeared asking

Figure 5.4 Example of probing on descriptive open-ended questions.

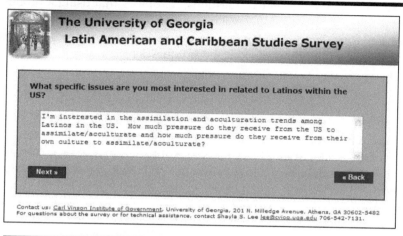

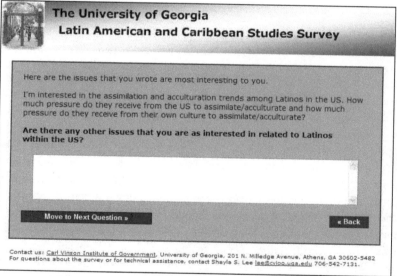

Source: "The Influence of Interactive Probing on Response to Open-Ended Questions in a Web Survey," by J. Holland and L. M. Christian, October 2007, Raleigh, NC. Paper presented at the Southern Association for Public Opinion Research Annual Conference.

for more information. An example of one of the questions can be seen in Figure 5.4. Results of the study indicated that compared to a version without the probe, the version with the probe produced significantly longer answers with significantly more themes, but no increases in elaboration (Holland & Christian, 2007). That the percentage of respondents elaborating was not increased significantly is probably due to the fact that the probe was worded in a way that elicited more themes but not necessarily more elaboration. Thus, for very important open-ended questions, it appears that using a probe can improve response quality. However, inasmuch as such probes may increase the burden of an already burdensome question type, it is advisable to reserve this technique for only the most important questions.

CLOSED-ENDED QUESTIONS

We now turn our attention to closed-ended questions. As discussed in Chapter 4, closed-ended questions can have unordered (nominal) or ordered (ordinal) response categories. They can require only one answer or, in the case of some nominal questions, multiple answers. As with open-ended questions, each of these different types of closed-ended question has its own specific design guidelines. Before we get to those, we present a few more general wording and design guidelines that apply to all closed-ended questions.

Box 5.1: Drop-Down Boxes

A new response format that is unique to web surveys is the drop-down box (see the example below). This format is frequently used on the Web for closed-ended questions with long lists of response options. Utilizing drop-down boxes for these types of questions reduces download times and is a more efficient use of screen space. However, using drop-down boxes requires respondents to perform multiple mouse clicks. They must first click on the menu to reveal the response options and then scroll down the list to the one they want to select (or use the keyboard to type in the first letter of the word they are looking for). Many people find this multiple-step response process considerably more difficult than the single-step process required for more standard web question formats (Heerwegh & Loosveldt, 2002a). Moreover, if the box is programmed to allow it, respondents can select multiple answers by holding the Ctrl or Command keys while clicking each response, but this added response step is often difficult for inexperienced computer users. Thus, drop-down boxes are typically recommended only for questions asking for one answer, unless it can be expected that respondents will be experienced computer and Internet users. Also, because they can be difficult for some respondents to maneuver, drop-down boxes are not recommended for questions for which people can easily type in a numeric response (e.g., year of birth) or for which they need to see the response options to help them understand what the question is asking.

Because respondents must select from the list of options and the lists are often quite lengthy, they tend to have difficulty finding the appropriate option when the options are illogically ordered (Altheimer & Dillman, 2002). As a result, the drop-down format is best used for lists that can be ordered in a way that respondents can easily comprehend after reading only a few options (e.g., an alphabetical list of states or countries).

Research has shown that respondents are more likely to select options that they do not have to scroll to see than those that they do have to scroll to see (Couper et al., 2004). As a result, drop-down boxes should be designed so that no response option is visible before the respondent initiates the process of selecting an answer. Placing a verbal instruction in the box, as in the example below, is one way to avoid privileging the first response option, and it also helps inexperienced respondents figure out how to answer. Additionally, it can serve as a reminder to respondents that they have not yet selected an answer, which can be particularly helpful if there are several drop-down boxes on one screen.

Q20. What is your major?

Click for area of study ▼   Click for major ▼

Next Question

Guideline 5.11: State Both Positive and Negative Sides in the Question Stem When Asking Either/Or Types of Questions

It is tempting to reduce the number of words in questions by mentioning only one side of an issue. For example, the question in the top panel of Figure 5.5 asks only if one favors congressional term limits without any mention that one might oppose them. Stated this way, the appropriate response to the question is actually "yes" or "no." In addition to creating a mismatch between the question and response options, a question written this way implicitly suggests that favoring term limits is the "right" answer. This implicit message, in combination with the cultural tendency in many societies to agree or acquiesce, may lead more people to report favoring congressional term limits than actually do. Stating both sides of the question, as is done in the improved design, rebalances the question so that neither favor nor oppose is given priority.

Similarly, the question in the bottom panel of Figure 5.5 asks the extent to which people agree with a statement but leaves out any mention of disagreement. Structured in this way, the question may encourage people to think of a scale ranging from *not at all* to *strongly agree*. Substituting "agree or disagree," as in the improved design, conveys to the respondent that the scale has a greater range. It also lets the respondent know that disagreement is an acceptable answer. Mentioning both sides of a scale is even more important when the terminology of a scale changes from one end to another, as it would for a scale that goes from *strongly favor* to *strongly oppose*.

Figure 5.5   State both positive and negative sides in the question stem.

Poor designs	*Improved designs*
Do you favor congressional term limits of four years?	Do you favor or oppose congressional term limits of four years?
☐ Favor ☐ Oppose	☐ Favor ☐ Oppose
To what extent do you agree with this statement: "It is easier for people to find work in this community than it was about one year ago."	To what extent do you agree or disagree with this statement: "It is easier for people to find work in this community than it was about one year ago."
☐ Strongly agree ☐ Somewhat agree ☐ Somewhat disagree ☐ Strongly disagree	☐ Strongly agree ☐ Somewhat agree ☐ Somewhat disagree ☐ Strongly disagree
	How do you think that the task of finding work in this community has changed since about one year ago?
	☐ It is easier ☐ It is about the same ☐ It is more difficult

However, in light of the fact that agree/disagree questions are particularly prone to acquiescence, the second revision would seem to be a better solution. This revision maintains the use of the closed-ended ordered categories but removes the categories from the agree/disagree framework and replaces them with categories that would seem to be less prone to acquiescence: easier, the same, or more difficult (as discussed further in Guideline 5.21).

Guideline 5.12: Develop Lists of Answer Categories that Include All Reasonable Possible Answers

The question in Figure 5.6, which asks respondents to choose one answer that describes how they heard about a tornado, suffers from several very common problems. One of the most notable is that it is missing some important news sources: the Internet and newspaper. Inasmuch as both the Internet and newspaper are common sources of news, they too need to be offered as options in this question, as is done in the revision. Otherwise, people who heard about the tornado from these sources would have great difficulty answering this question. To avoid encouraging respondents to skip questions at will, every question should include all reasonable possible answers so that every respondent can find an applicable answer.

Figure 5.6 Exhaustive and mutually exclusive questions.

A question that is not exhaustive or mutually exclusive

From which one of these sources did you first learn about the tornado in Derby?

☐ Radio
☐ Television
☐ Someone at work
☐ While at home
☐ While traveling to work

A revision that is exhaustive and mutually exclusive

From which one of these sources did you first hear about the tornado in Derby?

☐ Radio
☐ Television
☐ Internet
☐ Newspaper
☐ Another person

Where were you when you first heard about it?

☐ At work
☐ At home
☐ Traveling to work
☐ Somewhere else

Guideline 5.13: Develop Lists of Answer Categories that Are Mutually Exclusive

The image that often comes to mind when one discusses the lack of mutually exclusive categories is that a clerical error has been made, as in age categories such as the following: 35 or younger, 35 to 50, 50 to 65, and 65 and older. Although the overlap is minor, it can be very annoying to people who happen to fall on the line.

In some instances we have seen deliberate, though minor, overlap created when attempting to ease the task of the respondent. For example, income categories of *less than $15,000, $15,000 to $19,999, $20,000 to $29,999, $30,000 to $39,999,* and so on have sometimes been changed to read *$15,000 up to $20,000, $20,000 up to $30,000,* and so on. The latter categories are easier for interviewers and respondents to read than the former ones and make virtually no difference in the ability of respondents to choose an appropriate category. The sensitivity of reporting income is such that the gain from ease of reading (especially for interviews) probably outweighs the mutual exclusivity concern about the few people whose incomes happen to fall exactly on the dividing line.

Our main concern with mutual exclusivity is when it is used for response categories of survey questions where there is considerable likelihood that its presence will go unnoticed. To illustrate this point, we return to Figure 5.6. Another problem with the question in its original form is that the choices include both sources of the news and location. Therefore, in addition to adding missing response options, the revision breaks the one question into two: one about source and the other about location.

It may seem from this example that mutual exclusivity is only an issue in single-answer questions. But drawing the conclusion that mutual exclusivity does not matter in multiple-answer questions would be a mistake. On the contrary, lack of mutual exclusivity in multiple-answer questions can cause significant bias in responses. In the Spring of 2003 we administered a student experience survey that contained the following question: "Which of the following resources have you used at [Washington State University]? Please check all that apply." This was followed by 10 university resources, the group of which was taken from the university's web page (see Figure 5.7). When the response options were presented in their original order, the first option was "libraries" and the ninth option was "library instruction." In this order, 1 in 5 respondents checked that they had used library instruction. When we reversed the order of the options so that "library instruction" appeared in the 2nd position (and "libraries" in the 10th), substantially more respondents selected it—about 1 in every 2. A similar pattern of results was also found in a forced-choice version of this same question.

When "library instruction" appeared after the broader category of "libraries," many respondents interpreted it narrowly, as a part of the broader set of services offered in the library. Because they had already selected "libraries," they did not need to select "library instruction" unless they had, in fact, used this very specific service. When "library instruction" appeared first, however, respondents seemed to interpret it more broadly (i.e., as libraries) and therefore selected it, not realizing that the category "libraries" was going to be an option later in the list. Additional analyses suggested that some respondents caught their mistake. Respondents who initially checked the first library option they came to were 7 times more likely to go back and uncheck it when they got to the second library option when "library instruction" appeared first than when "libraries" appeared first (Stern, in press). In this case, having response options that lacked mutual exclusivity drastically altered the results so that they more strongly reflected the poor design of the response options than actual use of resources at the university.

A similar type of result was obtained from Florida beef producers in a question about what forages were fed to cattle in winter months (see the bottom panel of Figure 5.7; Israel & Taylor, 1990). Switching the "native range" option from first to fourth on the list decreased the percentage checking that answer from 70% to only 30%, a 40 percentage point drop. "Winter pasture"

Figure 5.7 Subtraction effects in multiple-answer questions.

Which of the following resources have you used at WSU? Please check all that apply.

Original Order	Percent Endorsing	Reverse Order	Percent Endorsing
Libraries	95	Counseling services	
Computer labs		Library instruction	52
Student health center		Campus-sponsored tutoring	
Academic advising		Career services	
Student recreation center		Internet/e-mail access	
Internet/e-mail access		Student recreation center	
Career services		Academic advising	
Campus-sponsored tutoring		Student health center	
Library instruction	20	Computer labs	
Counseling services		Libraries	93

Which of the following forages are used during the winter months to feed your cattle? (Check all that apply.)

Original Order	Percent Endorsing	Reorder	Percent Endorsing
Native range	70	Silage	2
Deferred grazing (save pasture for fall and winter)	37	Deferred grazing (save pasture for fall and winter)	48
Hay	84	Winter pasture	36
Silage	1	Native range	30
Winter pasture	29	Hay	79
Other	14	Other	15

Source: Top Panel from "The Use of Client Side Paradata in Analyzing the Effects of Visual Layout on Changing Responses in Web Surveys," by M. J. Stern, in press, *Field Methods.* Bottom Panel from "Can Response Order Bias Evaluations?" by G. D. Israel and C. L. Taylor, 1990, *Evaluation and Program Planning, 13,* pp. 1–7.

and "deferred grazing," which were moved to the third and second positions, respectively, were both subject to increased endorsement. The likely reason for this change is that "native range" is such a broad category that, when listed in the first position, respondents who would otherwise have selected "winter pasture" or "deferred grazing" picked it and then mentally subtracted that from the answers they would have otherwise given. By comparison, "silage," which is a distinctively different type of livestock feed from any of the other pasture choices, received the same proportion of endorsements regardless of whether it was in the fourth or first position.

Guideline 5.14: Maintain Spacing between Answer Categories that Is Consistent with Measurement Intent

Like category order and response labels, the spacing between answer categories conveys extra information about what a category means. This is especially true for scalar questions that use vague quantifiers for answers. Giving one category more space suggests that its portion of the scale is greater than that of the other categories and thereby encourages more people to use it.

Consider the example in the top panel of Figure 5.8, in which the response options are spaced closer together on the left than the right side of the scale. Experiments with spacing like this have resulted in more people choosing the options on the right side of the scale than occurs when options are evenly spaced, as in the revision (Tourangeau et al., 2004). In this case, the options on the right appear to account for a larger portion of the scale. In addition, the option to the immediate right of the midpoint appears closer to the spatial midpoint of the scale, thus making it seem less extreme and making it more likely to be endorsed. In fact, several studies have now shown that respondents draw heavily on the visual midpoint of scales in interpreting the meaning of scale points (Christian, Parsons, & Dillman, in press; Tourangeau et al., 2004).

Another example with nominal rather than ordinal response options is shown in the bottom portion of Figure 5.8 (Christian & Dillman, 2004). When the unevenly spaced version of this question was administered to university undergraduates, nearly 38% chose the option "To have a life partner with whom you have a satisfying relationship." In comparison, only 31% chose this option when the evenly spaced version was administered. Thus, it appears the extra space associated with this option drew more people to it. Findings such as these reinforce the importance of providing equal spacing between answer categories for both ordinal and nominal questions.

CLOSED-ENDED QUESTIONS—NOMINAL SCALES

A nominal scale might best be thought of as measuring a qualitative variable. In other words, the categories of a nominal scale contain no natural ordering. There is no difference in magnitude between them. One example of a nominal variable is the kind of car one drives: Chevrolet, Ford, Honda, Subaru, Toyota, Volkswagen, and so on. Another example is the restaurants one frequents: Red Robin, Olive Garden, Red Lobster, Pizza Hut, and so on. Other examples are sex (male, female) and race and ethnicity. One can order any of these variables by any number of criteria: alphabetical order, country of manufacture, type of food served, and so on. But any such ordering is completely subjective. In other words, it is based on sets of criteria that are external to the categories themselves; the categories have no natural ordering.

Figure 5.9 shows examples of four types of closed-ended questions with nominal response options, and it also illustrates the range of ease and difficulty that can accompany nominal questions. The first question, for example, is quite simple as it contains only two options from which to choose. The most common question of this type is the yes/no question (e.g., "Do you

Figure 5.8   Spacing response options evenly.

Uneven spacing of answer choices in an ordinal question

Compared to other veterinary services you have received, how would you rate the pricing at Pet Vet?

Very over- priced	Somewhat over- priced	Slightly overpriced	Average	Slightly underpriced	Somewhat underpriced	Very underpriced
○	○	○	○	○	○	○

Revised even spacing of answer choices

Compared to other veterinary services you have received, how would you rate the pricing at Pet Vet?

Very overpriced	Somewhat overpriced	Slightly overpriced	Average	Slightly underpriced	Somewhat underpriced	Very underpriced
○	○	○	○	○	○	○

Uneven spacing of answer choices in a nominal question

Thinking about your life after completing your education, which one of these do you consider most important

☐ To have a life partner
　with whom you have a
　satisfying relationship   38% selected the first option
☐ Enjoy your work
☐ Earn a high income
☐ Raise a family

Revised even spacing of answer choices in a nominal question

Thinking about your life after completing your education, which one of these do you consider most important

☐ To have a life partner with whom you
　have a satisfying relationship   31% selected the first option
☐ Enjoy your work
☐ Earn a high income
☐ Raise a family

Source: Bottom Panel from "The Influence of Graphical and Symbolic Language Manipulations on Responses to Self-Administered Questions," by L. M. Christian and D. A. Dillman, 2004, _Public Opinion Quarterly, 68_(1), pp. 58–81.

own a car?"). Choosing from among many categories, however, can be quite complex, as suggested by the second and third questions in Figure 5.9. Responding to either of these questions requires a lot of effort. Answering the question about the highway bypass requires absorbing considerable detail, identifying differences between the choices, and then selecting the most preferred route. The final question requires respondents to compare eight groups,

Figure 5.9   Examples of closed-ended questions with unordered response options.

Most simple form: Two categories

While growing up did you live mostly on a farm or mostly elsewhere?

☐ Farm
☐ Elsewhere

A more difficult form: Multiple complex categories

If the highway bypass is to be built on one of these routes, which would you most prefer?

☐ A north route that starts west of the city at Exit 21 (Johnson Road) off Highway 30, crosses Division at North 59th Street, and reconnects to Highway 30 three miles east of the city at River Road.

☐ A modified north route that starts further west of the city at Exit 19, crosses Division at 70th Street, and reconnects to Highway 30 three miles east of the city at River Road.

☐ A south route that begins west of the city at Exit 19, crosses Division at South 24th Street, and reconnects to Highway 30 east of the city at River Road.

*Another difficult form: The ranking question**

Which of these do you believe are the largest and smallest problems facing residents of the Lewiston & Clarkston area? Use "1" for the largest problem, "2" for second largest problem, and so forth until you have completed all eight.

☐ Lack of community involvement

☐ Taxes are too high

☐ Lack of affordable health care

☐ Lack of money for local schools

☐ Lack of affordable housing

☐ Lack of good jobs

☐ Too much crime overall

☐ Too much drug use

---

*Source: *How Use of the Internet Impacts Community Participation and the Maintenance of Core Social Ties: An Empirical Study,* by M. J. Stern, 2006, Pullman, WA: Washington State University. Unpublished doctoral dissertation.*

then seven, then six, and so forth to complete the ranking. In both cases, providing answers requires substantially more effort than is usually the case for closed-ended questions with ordered categories. Yet these are precisely the types of questions that can sometimes provide the most useful information to survey sponsors.

Guideline 5.15: Ask Respondents to Rank Only a Few Items at Once Rather than a Long List

In ranking questions, such as the community problems question in Figure 5.9, each answer choice adds another concept that must be compared with other choices. Ranking questions such as these can be incredibly difficult for respondents to understand and complete correctly. As an example, when the community problems question was administered to a random sample of community residents, nearly a quarter of them failed to complete it correctly (Stern, 2006).

On paper or on the screen, a question that lists 15 items to be ranked from top to bottom may not look much more difficult than one that has only 6 items to be ranked, but the respondent demand is obviously far greater. If all 15 options need to be presented, then the question might be simplified by asking for a ranking of only the top three. Another alternative is to present respondents with a paired comparison in which they are asked to compare only two options (and thus two concepts) at a time until they have compared each option against each other option. The surveyor can then use the results to form the ranking for the respondent.

As an abbreviated example, let us assume a respondent is given the following comparisons and asked to indicate which item in each pair is the more important problem facing residents of her community. The underlined options are the ones our hypothetical respondent feels are most important.

<u>Lack of community involvement</u>	<u>Taxes are too high</u>
Taxes are too high	<u>Lack of affordable health care</u>
<u>Lack of affordable health care</u>	Lack of community involvement

We can now use these results to form a list that ranks the importance of these items for this respondent from most to least important:

1. Lack of affordable health care.
2. Taxes are too high.
3. Lack of community involvement.

Sometimes it is also possible to make ranking questions less burdensome through creative use of technology. For example, the items to be ranked in a paper survey might be printed on peel-and-stick labels that the respondent can peel up and place into a ranked order, a method that has been used by Rokeach (1973) to assess 18 competing values. Such a method allows respondents to actually locate each item relative to the others and as such provides a clearer visual reminder of their ordering as they work through the items. Physically rearranging the items in the desired order makes it much less mentally burdensome for respondents to keep track of their ordering than trying to keep track of a numbering system applied to items that are physically out of order. A similar technique for ranking questions is now being used on the Web, including a study in which respondents are asked to rank the same 18 competing values as originally ranked in Rokeach's work. Using computer and Internet technology, respondents are asked to drag and drop items into the desired order (Neubarth, 2008). Considerations of whether to employ these technologies should carefully weigh the impact they will have on download times, the likelihood that respondents' computers will be enabled to operate them, and respondents' computer and Internet skill levels.

Guideline 5.16: Avoid Bias from Unequal Comparisons

Closed-ended questions with unordered categories can become unbalanced, thus biasing responses. Consider the wording of the question in Figure 5.10 designed to find out what respondents think is most responsible for outbreaks of violence in schools. The term *irresponsible* places a value connotation on the first category that is not present in the other choices. Although it is unclear whether unbalancing questions in this way leads to more or less frequent selection of such categories (Schuman & Presser, 1981), the credibility of responses to such questions is inevitably open to critique.

The difficulty of revising such questions is that true balance may be extremely difficult to achieve. The first revision uses less emotionally charged words (i.e., "the way children are raised by parents") but results in a category with many more words than the school and television choices. The last two categories could be made more specific by mentioning school discipline policies and violent television programs, but it is unclear without extensive pretesting whether that would improve or detract from the balance. The challenge of achieving balance on such closed-ended questions often leads to reducing choices to simple nouns (*parents, schools, television*), a solution that also increases the vagueness of the categories. One might, for example, wonder what aspect of television is being referenced: its use in schools, how much television children watch, or the content of the programming. Still another revision that might be considered is to completely restructure the question, converting to a closed-ended ordinal question structure with a detailed concept presented in the stem of the question, as shown in the final revision offered in Figure 5.10.

Guideline 5.17: Randomize Response Options if There Is Concern about Order Effects

Sometimes the order that response options are placed in can affect their likelihood of being selected. Two examples of order effects due to the content of the options are demonstrated in Figure 5.7. Another potential cause

Figure 5.10   Avoid bias from unequal comparisons.

Unequal comparison

Which of the following do you feel is most responsible for recent outbreaks of violence in America's schools?

☐ Irresponsible parents
☐ School policies
☐ Television programs

A revision with more neutral response options

Which of the following do you feel is most responsible for recent outbreaks of violence in America's schools?

☐ The way children are raised by parents
☐ School policies
☐ Television programs

A simplified revision

Which of the following do you feel is most responsible for recent outbreaks of violence in America's schools?

☐ Parents
☐ Schools
☐ Television

Still another revision retaining more complex descriptions

To what extent do you feel that the way children are raised by parents is responsible for recent outbreaks of violence in America's schools?

☐ Completely responsible
☐ Mostly responsible
☐ Somewhat responsible
☐ Not at all responsible

And so forth for the remaining concepts.

---

of response category order effects can be memory and cognitive limitations. In self-administered surveys, early response options may be processed more deeply, and thus may be more likely to be selected, because respondents' minds become more cluttered as they continue through a list and have more information to keep track of (Schuman & Presser, 1981). Another potential cause is lack of motivation. Respondents with low motivation levels or those who have to finish quickly because of some other obligation may choose the first defensible answer they come to rather than the best answer (i.e., they may satisfice) just to get the survey finished (Krosnick, 1991).

The dynamism of the Internet, and now of advanced database and printing technologies for paper surveys, provides surveyors with the ability to randomize response options to get around such order effects. Randomizing response option order does not eliminate order effects; rather, it averages them out. In other words, any effect due to being located early in the list for some respondents will presumably be cancelled out by the effects of the same option appearing late in the list for other respondents.

Guideline 5.18: Use Forced-Choice Questions instead of Check-All-That-Apply Questions

A multiple-answer question can generally be asked in one of two formats, and traditionally these two formats have been used interchangeably under the assumption that they elicit similar answers. In the check-all-that-apply format, respondents are provided with a list of items and asked to check each one that applies to them. An example is shown in the top panel of Figure 5.11. The check-all format has traditionally been used in paper and web surveys because it is space efficient and easily processed and completed. The forced-choice format, by comparison, has traditionally been used in interviewer-administered surveys. In this format the respondent is presented with one option and asked to make a judgment about it before moving to the next. An example is shown in the bottom panel of Figure 5.11. The advantage of the forced-choice format for telephone surveys is that it lets the respondent focus memory and cognitive processing efforts on one option at a time.

Although these two question formats have long been used interchangeably, a close look at them reveals that they require a fundamentally different response task. Whereas the check-all format provides respondents with a group of items and asks them to choose those that apply from the group, the forced-choice format requires respondents to make an explicit judgment about each item independently. To satisfy the requirements of a check-all question, a respondent simply has to mark a few of the options, but to satisfy the requirements of a forced-choice question, a respondent has to consider and come to a judgment about every item.

Recent comparisons of these two response formats have provided evidence that they are not as interchangeable as was once assumed and that their differences may trace directly back to the different response tasks that underlie them. In one study, we compared 16 questions in both web and paper surveys and found that the forced-choice format consistently resulted in more options being endorsed (Smyth et al., 2006a). The upper left pie chart in Figure 5.12 shows that 61% of the 198 individual items within these 16 questions were marked affirmatively significantly more often when they appeared in the forced-choice format than when they appeared in the check-all

Figure 5.11 Examples of closed-ended questions with unordered response options.

<u>*Check-all-that-apply formatted question*</u>

Which of the following varsity sports would you consider yourself to be a fan of? Please check all that apply.

☐ Men's baseball
☐ Women's basketball
☐ Men's basketball
☐ Women's cross-country
☐ Men's cross-country
☐ Men's football
☐ Women's golf
☐ Men's golf
☐ Women's rowing
☐ Women's soccer
☐ Women's swimming
☐ Women's tennis
☐ Women's track and field
☐ Men's track and field
☐ Women's volleyball

<u>*A revision converting to the forced-choice format*</u>

Do you consider yourself to be a fan of each of the following varsity sports?

Yes	No	
☐	☐	Men's baseball
☐	☐	Women's basketball
☐	☐	Men's basketball
☐	☐	Women's cross-country
☐	☐	Men's cross-country
☐	☐	Men's football
☐	☐	Women's golf
☐	☐	Men's golf
☐	☐	Women's rowing
☐	☐	Women's soccer
☐	☐	Women's swimming
☐	☐	Women's tennis
☐	☐	Women's track and field
☐	☐	Men's track and field
☐	☐	Women's volleyball

Source: "Comparing Check-All and Forced-Choice Question Formats in Web Surveys," by J. D. Smyth, D. A. Dillman, L. M. Christian, and M. J. Stern, 2006a, *Public Opinion Quarterly, 70,* pp. 66–77.

format. The pie chart in the upper right corner shows that 37% of the 46 items compared in an additional comparison of four multiple-answer questions were marked affirmatively significantly more often in the forced-choice format. In both of these sets of experiments, no items were marked affirmatively significantly more often in the check-all format. Additional analyses revealed that the difference in endorsement across these two formats came from about

Figure 5.12   Endorsement outcome for individual items within check-all and forced-choice experimental comparisons.

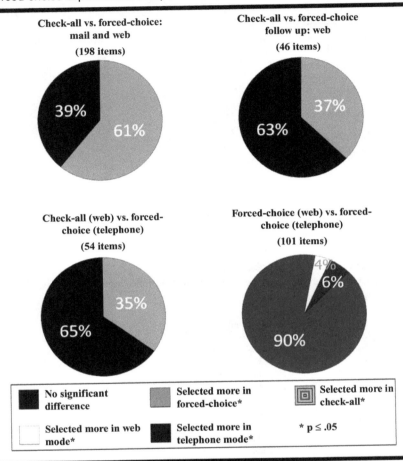

Source: "Comparing Check-All and Forced-Choice Question Formats in Web Surveys," by J. D. Smyth, D. A. Dillman, L. M. Christian, and M. J. Stern, 2006a, *Public Opinion Quarterly, 70,* pp. 66–77; and "Does 'Yes or No' on the Telephone Mean the Same as 'Check-All-That-Apply' on the Web?" by J. D. Smyth, L. M. Christian, and D. A. Dillman, 2008, *Public Opinion Quarterly, 72,* pp. 103–113.

66% of respondents to the check-all format. These respondents seemed to be using a satisficing response strategy. They answered relatively quickly and were more likely to select the items appearing in the top half of the list than the bottom, regardless of what those items were (i.e., primacy). In contrast, respondents to the forced-choice format, even those who responded quite quickly, appeared to have processed all of the response options.

The pie chart in the bottom left corner of Figure 5.12 shows similar results with respect to the use of the forced-choice and check-all formats across telephone and web surveys. In the forced-choice format in a telephone survey, 35% of 54 items were marked affirmatively significantly more often than in the check-all format in a web survey. Subsequent experimentation has also shown that the forced-choice question format transfers very well across web and telephone modes (Smyth, Christian, & Dillman, 2008). In nine comparisons of this format across web and telephone surveys, only 4% of the items were selected significantly more often in the web mode, and only 6% were selected significantly more often in the telephone mode (see the bottom right pie chart in Figure 5.12). These numbers are close to what one might expect by chance out of the total of 101 response items. These results indicate that the forced-choice question format works very well in both telephone and web surveys, and, combined with the evidence that the check-all format is prone to satisficing response strategies, they form the basis for our recommendation to substitute the forced-choice format for the check-all format in most instances. However, in the rare circumstances when the information being asked is very factual and respondents are likely to know their answers without having to read the list of items, it may be advisable to retain the check-all format because it is less burdensome.

Guideline 5.19: Consider Using Differently Shaped Answer Spaces (Circles and Squares) to Help Respondents Distinguish between Single- and Multiple-Answer Questions

Mail survey designers have traditionally used the same answer space throughout their entire questionnaire, most commonly a square check box. In contrast, early web survey designers tended to use round radio buttons or square check boxes depending on the function of the answer space. With radio buttons respondents can typically only select one response option. If they attempt to select another, their original answer is erased and replaced with the new one. Check boxes, in contrast, allow respondents to select multiple answers.

The distinction between radio buttons for single-answer questions and check boxes for multiple-answer questions was most likely originally the result of programming limitations. However, we believe it serves another unintended but important function. It provides a visual cue at the location of the response that the response task is changing, and it can work in combination with clear question wording to help clarify the response task.

Consider, for example, the two questions presented in the top panel of Figure 5.13. In these designs, there is very little indication that the two questions differ in the number of options one can select. Unless respondents read very carefully, they are unlikely to catch the fact that the one on the left is a single-answer question and the one on the right is a multiple-answer

Figure 5.13   Use answer spaces to help distinguish between single- and multiple-answer questions in Web surveys.

Little distinction between single- and multiple-answer questions

1 Of the following considerations, which is the most important to you when purchasing a new car?

☐ Price
☐ Color
☐ Exterior condition
☐ Interior condition
☐ Amenities

2 Of the following considerations, which three are most important to you when purchasing a new car?

☐ Price
☐ Color
☐ Exterior condition
☐ Interior condition
☐ Amenities

A revision with answer spaces designed to help differentiate between single- and multiple-answer questions

1 Of the following considerations, which is the most important to you when purchasing a new car?

○ Price
○ Color
○ Exterior condition
○ Interior condition
○ Amenities

2 Of the following considerations, which three are most important to you when purchasing a new car?

☐ Price
☐ Color
☐ Exterior condition
☐ Interior condition
☐ Amenities

Examples from a popular online survey host site

Of the following considerations, which is most important to you when purchasing a new car?

● Price
● Color
● Exterior condition
● Interior condition
● Amenities

Of the following considerations, which three are most important to you when purchasing a new car?

● Price
● Color
● Exterior condition
● Interior condition
● Amenities

Of the following considerations, which is most important to you when purchasing a new car?

▪ Price
▪ Color
▪ Exterior condition
▪ Interior condition
▪ Amenities

Of the following considerations, which three are most important to you when purchasing a new car?

▪ Price
▪ Color
▪ Exterior condition
▪ Interior condition
▪ Amenities

question. In comparison, the differently shaped answer spaces in the revised version of these questions provide a visual cue that the response task has changed. In addition to altering the answer spaces, these questions could be further improved by rewording the single-answer version as follows: "Of the following considerations, which *one* is the most important to you when purchasing a new car?"

If web survey programmers were still largely limited to radio buttons and check boxes, including this guideline in this edition of the book would be unnecessary. But web programming has become much more sophisticated in recent years, allowing designers more latitude to alter the properties of answer spaces. A somewhat alarming trend that has arisen out of this new programming ability is the standardization of design properties across single- and multiple-answer spaces. Examples from an online survey host service are provided in the bottom panel of Figure 5.13. Here, depending on the overall design theme surveyors choose for their survey, they get either round or square answer spaces regardless of whether the question allows only one or multiple answers. To be fair, there are slight differences in the properties of the answer spaces. Properties such as coloring and shadowing are applied to the single-answer spaces to make them appear as if they protrude off the screen, whereas those applied to the multiple-answer questions make them appear more flat. But compared to differences in shape, these are very subtle and could easily be overlooked, especially in page-by-page survey constructions where the two types of answer spaces cannot be immediately compared.

At this point in time we adhere strongly to the convention of providing radio buttons for single-answer questions and check boxes for multiple-answer questions in web surveys. Our stance on the shape of answer spaces for paper surveys is less absolute, however. Although we believe it is useful to provide a visual cue that the response task is changing here as well, no research of which we are aware has examined the effects of doing so in paper surveys.

CLOSED-ENDED QUESTIONS—ORDINAL SCALES

Closed-ended ordinal questions are one of the most commonly used types of survey questions because they can measure gradations of a variety of opinions, attitudes, behaviors, and attributes. These scales can be used to analyze levels of something (e.g., satisfaction, importance, success, frequency, etc.) where, for example, someone who is "very satisfied" is more satisfied than someone who is "satisfied," or "all of the time" is more than "some of the time." *Unipolar* ordinal scales measure gradation along one dimension where the zero point falls at one end of the scale (e.g., *very successful* to *not at all successful*—see Figure 5.14). By comparison, *bipolar* ordinal scales measure gradation along two opposite dimensions, with the zero point falling in the middle of the scale (e.g., *very satisfied* to *very dissatisfied* or *very likely* to *very unlikely*—see Figure 5.14). In other words, bipolar scales measure both level and direction. Ordinal scale questions are used in all survey modes, although they are often constructed differently for different modes. For example, all of the categories are usually verbally labeled in self-administered surveys and longer scales are often used, but oftentimes telephone surveyors prefer to label only the endpoints to ease administration or to shorten scales because there is no visual display to help respondents.

Figure 5.14   Types of scalar questions and scale length.

A 5-point bipolar scale

How likely or unlikely are you to make a monetary donation to the Red Cross this year?

☐ Very likely
☐ Somewhat likely
☐ Neither likely nor unlikely
☐ Somewhat unlikely
☐ Very unlikely

A 7-point bipolar scale

How likely or unlikely are you to become a Red Cross volunteer this year?

☐ Very likely
☐ Somewhat likely
☐ Slightly likely
☐ Neither likely nor unlikely
☐ Slightly unlikely
☐ Somewhat unlikely
☐ Very unlikely

A 4-point unipolar scale

How important do you feel it is to volunteer your time with organizations like the Red Cross?

☐ Very important
☐ Somewhat important
☐ Slightly important
☐ Not at all important

A 5-point unipolar scale

How successful do you feel the Red Cross has been at getting assistance to natural disaster victims?

☐ Completely successful
☐ Very successful
☐ Somewhat successful
☐ Slightly successful
☐ Not at all successful

Because scalar questions are used so frequently in all survey modes and for a variety of topics, there are many different viewpoints on how to construct them in ways that produce accurate responses. An enormous amount of research over the years has been devoted to this issue, including how to design ordinal scale questions for mixed-mode surveys. This research suggests that because respondents often assign meaning to each category in relation to the other categories offered, how the categories are presented in the response scale and the labels for the categories themselves contribute to how respondents interpret and respond to the scale. For example, responses can be expected to be different depending on the number of categories presented, the verbal and numeric labels assigned to the scales, the order in which the categories are presented, and the layout of the categories (Christian, 2007; Christian & Dillman, 2004; Christian, Dillman, & Smyth, 2008; Dillman & Christian, 2005; Krosnick & Fabrigar, 1997; Schwarz, Knauper, Hippler, Noelle-Neumann, & Clark, 1991; Tourangeau et al., 2004, 2007).

Thus, constructing ordinal scale questions involves making several decisions, such as how to structure the question stem, how many response categories to provide, whether to label all or only some of the categories, what types of labels to choose, and how to visually present the scale to respondents. As these questions illustrate, designing scalar questions involves thinking about how all of the components of the question are working together, and in mail and web surveys, particular attention must be paid to the visual presentation of the scale and how the verbal and visual design elements work together to impact people's responses. In developing the guidelines that follow for constructing ordinal scale questions in mail and web surveys, we continued to use a holistic approach (presented in Chapter 4) that integrates recent research on the impact of visual design. We also drew heavily on an extensive set of experiments in which we tested the effects of a number of different ways of constructing ordinal scale questions in mail, web, and mixed-mode surveys. In addition to the discussion here, we return to the topic of ordinal scale questions in Chapter 8, where we focus on ordinal scales in mixed-mode surveys, and in Chapter 10, where we discuss their use in various types of customer satisfaction surveys.

Guideline 5.20: Choose an Appropriate Scale Length—In General, Limit Scales to Four or Five Categories

Ordinal scales can measure as few as 2 points and as many as 10 or even 100 points. The challenge in choosing an appropriate scale length is to provide enough categories that respondents will be able to place themselves on the scale but not so many that the categories begin to lose their meaning or become ambiguous (which will result in clustering of responses around certain points). In addition, respondents can only hold a limited number of categories in their head at once, so offering fewer categories can help reduce the cognitive complexity involved in providing a response. In other words, one must provide a scale that is long enough to represent the entire continuum of possible answers but without so many categories that they begin to burden respondents or that the difference between any two categories becomes so small as to be practically meaningless (Krosnick & Fabrigar, 1997).

For bipolar scales, which measure both the direction (e.g., satisfied or dissatisfied) and the intensity (e.g., very, somewhat) of the construct, the optimal number of response categories seems to be either five or seven, which allows for two or three levels of differentiation on either side of the middle or neutral category. For unipolar scales, which measure different levels or gradations (e.g., very, somewhat, not too, not at all) but not direction, optimal scale length is four or sometimes five categories. Scales of these lengths have been shown to be more reliable and valid (more scale points yield only modest gains in reliability and validity) as well as to provide meaningful distinctions for analysis (i.e., differentiation of the construct; Krosnick & Fabrigar, 1997). Figure 5.14 shows examples of 5- and 7-point bipolar scales and 4- and 5-point unipolar scales.

Guideline 5.21: Choose Direct or Construct-Specific Labels to Improve Cognition

Oftentimes surveyors ask respondents a question that does not match the response scale or for which respondents have to convert their responses from how they were asked in the question stem to the categories offered in the scale. For example, the first example in Figure 5.15 shows two ways of attempting to measure the accessibility of students' instructors outside of class. Putting this question in the agree/disagree framework requires respondents to process an extra concept because they first have to decide how accessible their instructors are and then convert that judgment into a 'different concept (i.e., how much they agree or disagree that their instructors are accessible) to report their response. In the revised construct-specific measurement, the question stem and response options both focus directly on the construct of interest, thus directly measuring levels of accessibility/inaccessibility and easing the response task for respondents. Research has shown that construct-specific scales reduce acquiescence response bias and cognitive burden, making it easier for respondents to map their judgment to the response options, resulting in less measurement error (i.e., higher reliability and validity; Saris & Krosnick, 2000).

Writing a construct-specific question requires one to very clearly define the construct of interest and its dimensions. We offer two other examples in Figure 5.15 to help surveyors think about how they can ask about different concepts using construct-specific scales. In the second example, the first version focuses on satisfaction/dissatisfaction with the durability of a mountain bike, whereas the construct-specific version goes directly to the concept of interest—the durability of the bike—by asking respondents to rate the durability of their newly purchased bikes. Again, the difficulty with identifying construct-specific measurements is determining which construct one is actually trying to measure. In the mountain bike example, if one wants to know how durable a recently purchased bike is, the proper question to ask is the construct-specific one in Figure 5.15. Other research goals may dictate the use of other types of questions and response options. For example, one might elect to use the satisfied/dissatisfied question if the goal were to determine how much durability (as prerated at the bike shop) is required to satisfy customers.

The third example in Figure 5.15 provides a slightly different scenario in that the scale is unipolar and the construct of interest is the frequency of a behavior instead of an opinion. Here the problem is not multiple concepts (i.e., the question is easy to answer); rather, it is that the categories are so imprecise that they can be interpreted differently by respondents and may not provide meaningful results. For example, in some religions, "regularly" implies once a week, whereas in others it may imply several times daily. Thus, one respondent may think of regularly as implying at least once or twice a week, whereas another may think that annual attendance at holiday services is regular attendance. Changing the answer categories to actual frequencies as shown in the revision eliminates the possibility of widely varied interpretations of the scale labels because it focuses on the number of times in a specific period and thus can provide more precise measurement of the construct.

Figure 5.15   Use construct-specific scales whenever possible.

Questions with multiple constructs	*Construct-specific questions*

Construct of interest: Accessibility of instructors

To what extent do you agree or disagree that your instructors are accessible outside of class?

☐ Strongly agree
☐ Agree
☐ Neutral
☐ Disagree
☐ Strongly disagree

How accessible or inaccessible are your instructors outside of class?

☐ Very accessible
☐ Somewhat accessible
☐ Neutral
☐ Somewhat inaccessible
☐ Very inaccessible

Construct of interest: Perceived durability of mountain bike

Our records show that you recently purchased a Trek Mountain Bike at our Yakima, Washington store. How satisfied are you with the durability of the mountain bike you purchased?

☐ Very satisfied
☐ Somewhat satisfied
☐ Slightly satisfied
☐ Neither satisfied nor dissatisfied
☐ Slightly dissatisfied
☐ Somewhat dissatisfied
☐ Strongly dissatisfied

Our records show that you recently purchased a Trek Mountain Bike at our Yakima, Washington store. How would you rate the durability of the mountain bike you purchased?

☐ The best
☐ Very high
☐ Somewhat high
☐ Average
☐ Somewhat low
☐ Very low
☐ The worst

Construct of interest: Frequency of attending religious services

How often did you attend religious services during the past year?

☐ Never
☐ Rarely
☐ Occasionally
☐ Regularly

How often did you attend religious services during the past year?

☐ Not at all
☐ A few times during the year
☐ About once a month
☐ Two to three times a month
☐ About once a week
☐ More than once a week

Guideline 5.22: Provide Scales that Approximate the Actual Distribution of the Characteristic in the Population

Many respondents use the response scale as a guide to help them formulate their answer. One way they do this is by assuming the scale represents the full range of responses and that the middle category reflects the average position. Respondents then may formulate their answer based on how they think they compare to the value in the middle position. Such was the case in the example at the opening of Chapter 4 in which a scale that emphasized lower values in the range suggested a significantly different estimate of how much time the average student spends studying than did a scale that emphasized higher values in the range. Students' reports of how many hours they study were affected enormously by the difference in the range of categories offered. Likewise, when asking about household income using an ordinal scale, care should be taken when selecting the range of responses offered, and the middle category should reflect the mean or median income for the population under study. Thus, it is important to provide category ranges that will allow all respondents to find an acceptable answer but that also approximate the expected distribution of the characteristic of interest in the population.

In addition, it is important to remember that respondents may draw conclusions about the distribution of a characteristic in a population based on any visual representations of the scale that are provided. Researchers have found, for example, that people report lower ratings when they are provided with (a) a pyramid-shaped scale graphic in which 10 boxes are stacked vertically but the lower boxes are wider than those in the middle and on top rather than (b) a ladder-shaped graphic in which 10 equal-size boxes are stacked on top of one another (Schwarz et al., 1998; Smith, 1993). The pyramid-shaped graphic suggests that more of the population, and indeed the average, is in the lower categories on the scale, whereas the ladder graphic suggests equal distribution throughout the entire scale so that the average corresponds to the middle category. These findings suggest that graphical representations of scales should be used only when necessary, should also resemble the distribution of the characteristic in the population, and should be designed and pretested carefully to evaluate the effects of the visual representation on respondents' answers.

Guideline 5.23: Provide Balanced Scales Where Categories Are Relatively Equal Distances Apart Conceptually

Another important element in choosing category labels is ensuring that all of the verbal labels are relatively equal distances apart conceptually and that the scales are balanced, with an equal number of positive and negative categories (so that the positive half of the scale is labeled symmetrically to the negative half of the scale). Consider, for example, the question about the quality of service provided by the local water utility company on the upper left side in Figure 5.16. The scale provided with this question is unbalanced, such that three categories are positive ("excellent," "very good," and "good"), one is about average ("fair"), and only one is negative ("poor"). In addition, the conceptual distance between "excellent" and "very good" is much smaller than the distance between "fair" and "poor." To understand and answer this question, respondents would have to apply extra effort, and chances are it

Figure 5.16 Provide balanced scales with categories that are evenly spaced conceptually.

Unbalanced scales with uneven distance between categories	*Balanced scales with more even distance between categories*
How would you rate the quality of service provided by your water utility company?	How would you rate the quality of service provided by your water utility company?
☐ Excellent ☐ Very good ☐ Good ☐ Fair ☐ Poor	☐ Very good ☐ Good ☐ Fair ☐ Poor ☐ Very poor
To what extent do you favor or oppose the death penalty?	To what extent do you favor or oppose the death penalty?
☐ Strongly favor ☐ Slightly favor ☐ Neither favor nor oppose ☐ Slightly oppose ☐ Mostly oppose ☐ Entirely oppose	☐ Strongly favor ☐ Somewhat favor ☐ Neither favor nor oppose ☐ Somewhat oppose ☐ Strongly oppose

would produce artificially positive responses as a result of the extra positive category. The revision in the right side in Figure 5.16 provides two positive and two negative categories on each side of the average, or middle, category, making it a more balanced scale. It also has equal distances between all of the categories on the scale, both of which will help to ease the response task (Krosnick & Fabrigar, 1997) and can provide more accurate results.

In the second example in Figure 5.16, which asks about the death penalty, the scale on the left is unbalanced with two positive categories and three negative categories. In addition, respondents who are moderately in favor of the death penalty will likely have difficulty selecting a category that represents their view. Because the conceptual difference between "slightly" and "strongly" is so large, these respondents will either have to overstate (by selecting "strongly") or understate (by selecting "slightly") their opinion. The revision on the right is balanced with two positive and two negative categories, and moderate respondents will probably have an easier time placing themselves on this scale because "somewhat" favor/oppose is a much more moderate category than "slightly." Most likely, both those who just barely tip either way off the midpoint and those who are moderately in favor of or opposed to the death penalty will feel comfortable selecting "somewhat," as the conceptual distance between the categories is more equal in this revision.

Another option would be to provide an additional degree of differentiation to break up the large conceptual distance. Rather than replacing "slightly" with "somewhat," a "somewhat" category could be added between "slightly" and "strongly" on both sides of the scale. Providing this extra category equalizes the distances between the points and allows respondents to express their opinions more precisely. As an added consideration, providing relatively equally spaced categories is a prerequisite for treating scalar results as interval-level variables (i.e., assign a 1 to strongly oppose, 2 to somewhat oppose, a 3 to neither, etc.) in data analyses (Krosnick & Fabrigar, 1997).

Guideline 5.24: Consider How Verbally Labeling and Visually Displaying All Response Categories May Influence Answers

The ordinal scales we have discussed up to this point are all fully labeled and have verbal labels for each response category (see first question in Figure 5.17). However, telephone surveyors often shorten scales by having respondents report a number that corresponds to their answer and verbally labeling only

Figure 5.17   Fully labeled and polar-point-labeled scales.

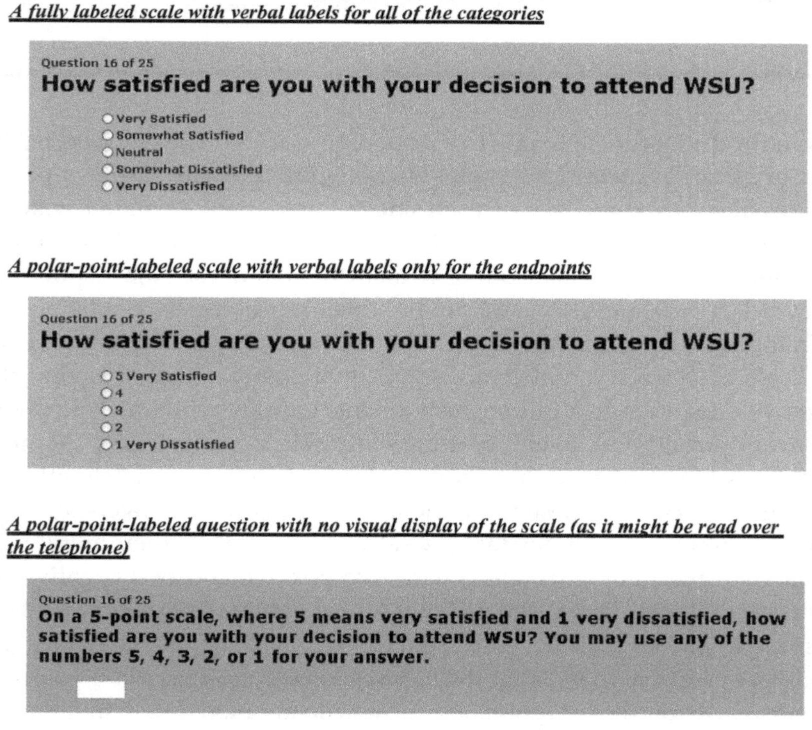

A fully labeled scale with verbal labels for all of the categories

Question 16 of 25
How satisfied are you with your decision to attend WSU?
○ Very Satisfied
○ Somewhat Satisfied
○ Neutral
○ Somewhat Dissatisfied
○ Very Dissatisfied

A polar-point-labeled scale with verbal labels only for the endpoints

Question 16 of 25
How satisfied are you with your decision to attend WSU?
○ 5 Very Satisfied
○ 4
○ 3
○ 2
○ 1 Very Dissatisfied

A polar-point-labeled question with no visual display of the scale (as it might be read over the telephone)

Question 16 of 25
On a 5-point scale, where 5 means very satisfied and 1 very dissatisfied, how satisfied are you with your decision to attend WSU? You may use any of the numbers 5, 4, 3, 2, or 1 for your answer.

Source: "The Influence of Visual Layout on Scalar Questions in Web Surveys," by L. M. Christian, 2003, Pullman, WA: Washington State University. Unpublished master's thesis. Retrieved April 1, 2006, from www.sesrc.wsu.edu/dillman/papers.htm.

the endpoints or positive and negative categories of the scale, particularly for longer scales (as shown in the third revision in Figure 5.17). Polar-point scales are easier for interviewers to administer over the telephone, and some surveyors argue that a numeric range is easier for respondents to hold in their memory than a full set of verbal category labels. We discuss polar-point and fully labeled scales here because both formats are used in mail and web self-administered modes as well as in mixed-mode surveys that include mail or web.

One difficulty with polar-point-labeled scales is that the meaning of the unlabeled categories is open to respondents' interpretation, and different respondents can interpret the middle categories differently, often increasing measurement error. In contrast, verbally labeling each category on the scale gives the surveyor more control over how the points are interpreted and helps ensure that respondents interpret them similarly. In addition, each category is given the same verbal and visual weight so no one category stands out more or less compared to the other categories. Lastly, because few people hold or express their opinions in numerical terms, numbers can be removed from fully labeled scales to eliminate the extra processing step of converting opinions to numeric terms. For these reasons, surveyors tend to prefer fully labeled scales, and these can be used effectively in all survey modes for most scales containing from 2 to 5 points. In addition, fully labeled scales rate higher on reliability, validity, and respondent preference, and they are less susceptible to context effects (Krosnick & Fabringer, 1997).

Previous research has shown that fully labeled scales elicit more positive ratings than polar-point scales in mail, web, and telephone surveys (Christian, 2003; Christian & Dillman, 2004; Christian et al., 2008; Dillman & Christian, 2005). Thus, we suggest using caution when switching between the fully labeled and polar-point-labeled scales, either within a questionnaire or between questionnaires where data will be compared. It is important for surveyors to be consistent in how scales are formatted, particularly when comparing their responses to those from other surveys.

In self-administered surveys, visually displaying the response categories can help respondents more easily understand the overall layout of the scale. Removing the visual display, as in the third question in Figure 5.17, can make the question more difficult for respondents as they first have to think whether they are satisfied or dissatisfied, and they then have to figure out what number best corresponds to how satisfied or dissatisfied they are. Moreover, research has shown that respondents to scales with no visual display have trouble determining which end of the scale is positive and which end is negative, may have difficulty matching a number to a category label, and take more time to respond (Christian & Dillman, 2004; Christian et al., in press; Dillman & Christian, 2005). However, for mixed-mode surveys involving telephone, this format may be used in mail or the Web because it most closely approximates the stimulus that telephone respondents receive (discussed in more detail in Chapter 8).

Guideline 5.25: Carefully Evaluate the Use of Numeric Labels and Their Impact on Measurement

Another tendency that some people have when creating scales is to provide numeric labels, either in addition to the verbal labels or instead of some of the verbal labels, as discussed in the previous guideline. Numbers are often used to reinforce to respondents that the categories are intended to be equal distances apart.

Unless there is a specific and intentional purpose behind including the numbers, we recommend against this practice as the numbers are simply one more piece of information respondents must attempt to make sense of, and doing so adds significantly to response time (Christian et al., in press). Respondents who are following the norms of conversation will expect each contribution made by the researcher to be unique and relevant (Schwarz, 1996). Thus, they will try to make sense of both the verbal and numeric labels provided with scales. If a survey designer is unaware of what the numbers mean, chances are respondents will also be confused by them or, worse yet, will attribute unintended meaning to them that will affect responses, thus negatively impacting how well the question performs.

If numeric labels are provided, the effects on respondents' answers need to be evaluated carefully, as numbers can be powerful sources of information respondents draw upon when responding to ordinal scale questions. One of the best examples of how including numbers can affect measurement comes from studies on the use of only positive versus positive and negative numbers. Of respondents who were presented with a scale ranging from 0 to 10 on a show card, 34% rated themselves between 0 and 5 (Schwarz et al., 1991). When presented with the scale ranging from −5 to 5, only 13% rated themselves in the comparable categories of −5 to 0. Further experimentation revealed that respondents interpreted the label "not successful at all" to mean the absence of success when it was accompanied by a 0 but to mean the presence of explicit failure when it was accompanied by −5. The decidedly negative connotation of "explicit failure" seemed to push people higher up the scale. Thus, the numbers selected to anchor this scale entirely changed the way the scale labels, and thereby the entire scale range, were interpreted. Tourangeau et al. (2007) confirmed this effect in web surveys but found that the effect of the numbers was reduced when all of the categories were verbally labeled.

In attitude scales, respondents also expect the highest numbers to be associated with the most positive ratings. Research has shown that contradicting this expectation by associating high numbers with negative ratings does not necessarily, in and of itself, have negative effects (Christian et al., in press). Respondents usually figure out what happened and their answers are not affected, unless they are being asked to enter a number into an open-ended space or number box (Christian & Dillman, 2004). However, any numbering needs to be done consistently across questions. Switching the way the numbers are assigned within a questionnaire will affect responses, as some respondents will miss the fact that a switch was made and will continue to answer as if the direction had not changed.

Guideline 5.26: Align Response Options Vertically in One Column or Horizontally in One Row and Strive for Equal Distance between Categories

Because the categories in ordinal closed-ended questions have an inherent order, they need to be presented in a way that supports that order. Presenting the response options vertically in one column (or horizontally in a row, particularly if multiple questions with the same scale are grouped into a grid) with equal distances between the categories reinforces the linearity of the scale and the evenly spaced category labels (see Guideline 5.23). In addition, respondents will be able to quickly perceive how the options are presented and will process them in the intended order.

In contrast, presenting response options in multiple-column, double- or triple-banked formats may result in respondents selecting different answers depending on whether they process the categories horizontally or vertically and depending on how the designer organizes the categories. For example, in the first example in Figure 5.18, respondents who are pretty satisfied with the education they are receiving and who process the options horizontally may choose "good" because it is the first option they come to that captures their view. Other respondents with the same view of the quality of their education who read vertically will probably mark "very good" for the same reason. Although their judgments are the same, the way they map them onto the response scale differs because they process the options in a different order.

Likewise, the way that the survey designer arranges the options in columns and rows may also affect what answers are selected. In the top panel of Figure 5.18, a respondent who reads horizontally may choose "good" as a reasonable answer. However, the same respondent, when presented with the options arranged as they are in the middle panel of Figure 5.18, may instead choose "very good." Results from both paper and web experiments indicate that respondents process the categories differently when they are presented in multiple columns and that people are more likely to select the second category on the first row, regardless of its label (Christian, 2003; Christian & Dillman, 2004; Toepoel, Das, & van Soest, 2006).

The simple solution to these problems is to retain the inherent order of the categories in the visual layout of the scale by presenting them equally spaced in one vertical column, as is done in the final example in Figure 5.18, or in one horizontal row. Doing so encourages respondents to process categories in a consistent manner from top to bottom (or left to right). Even if some

Figure 5.18   Align response options vertically in one column.

Triple-banked answer categories—Vertical

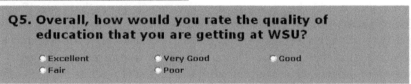

Triple-banked answer categories—Horizontal

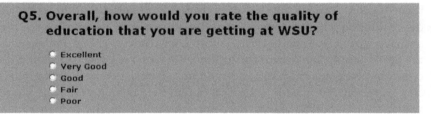

A revision with vertically aligned answer categories

Source: "The Influence of Graphical and Symbolic Language Manipulations on Responses to Self-Administered Questions," by L. M. Christian and D. A. Dillman, 2004, *Public Opinion Quarterly, 68*(1), pp. 58–81.

respondents choose to process the list from bottom to top, they will not be skipping categories, and they will be processing the list in a way that reflects their natural ordering from lowest to highest or highest to lowest.

We are often asked whether to present the positive or negative end of the scale first. Research on *primacy* (i.e., respondents being more likely to choose the first option when the scale is presented visually) and *recency* (i.e., respondents being more likely to choose the last option when read aurally) is quite mixed. Tourangeau et al. (2004) suggested that most respondents expect the most positive category to be presented first ("up means good" heuristic). However, recent research has shown that there were no differences in responses in a web survey when all of the scales were presented with the most positive category or the most negative category first (Christian et al., in press), but respondents answered the question more quickly when the positive category was presented first.

Guideline 5.27: Place Nonsubstantive Options at the End of the Scale and Separate Them from Substantive Options

Oftentimes, "not sure," "don't know," "no opinion," or other types of responses may need to be offered when some respondents will not be able to answer the question (or if an answer is required to move to the next web screen, although we usually do not recommend this practice—see Guideline 6.27 in Chapter 6). When offered, it makes a great deal of difference where the "not sure" or "don't know" category is placed. An experiment by Willits and Janota (1996) compared results from the placement of an "undecided" category in the middle and at the end of the following scale: strongly agree, somewhat agree, somewhat disagree, strongly disagree. When the "undecided" option was located in the middle of the scale, an average (across 13 questions) of 13% of respondents selected it compared to only 5% when it was located at the end of the scale. Locating the "undecided" option at the end of the scale encouraged neutral respondents to choose a substantive option because they had to read through these options first and presumably only those who were truly undecided selected that option.

Equally important as locating nonsubstantive options at the end of the scale is graphically separating them from substantive options. Experimental work by Tourangeau et al. (2004) has shown that respondents utilize a number of interpretive heuristics in processing survey questions. One of those heuristics ("middle means typical") reflects the assumption, discussed above, that the middle category reflects the average or typical. However, their experimentation has indicated that respondents are more heavily influenced by the *visual* midpoint of the scale than by the *conceptual* midpoint. In fact, respondents seem to assume that the visual and conceptual midpoints are aligned, as is the case in the first question in Figure 5.19. Thus, when a scale is changed visually but not conceptually, respondents continue to use the visual midpoint as their reference point, thus skewing results.

One way that the visual and conceptual midpoint of a scale can become unaligned is by adding response categories such as "don't know" and "no opinion" directly onto the end of the scale, as in the second example in Figure 5.19. In this example, the conceptual midpoint of the scale is still the "neither" option, but because the nonsubstantive options increase the visual length of the scale, the visual midpoint has shifted down to the "somewhat disapprove" option. Tourangeau et al. (2004) showed that when shifts like this occur, respondents are more likely to select the "somewhat disapprove" category (i.e., they are drawn to the visual rather than conceptual midpoint). In other words, shifting the visual midpoint down the scale causes respondents to give more negative responses.

The final question in Figure 5.19 shows how separation of nonsubstantive options from the substantive scale can shift the visual midpoint back up into alignment with the conceptual midpoint. In this case we used

Figure 5.19   Align the conceptual and visual midpoints of the scale.

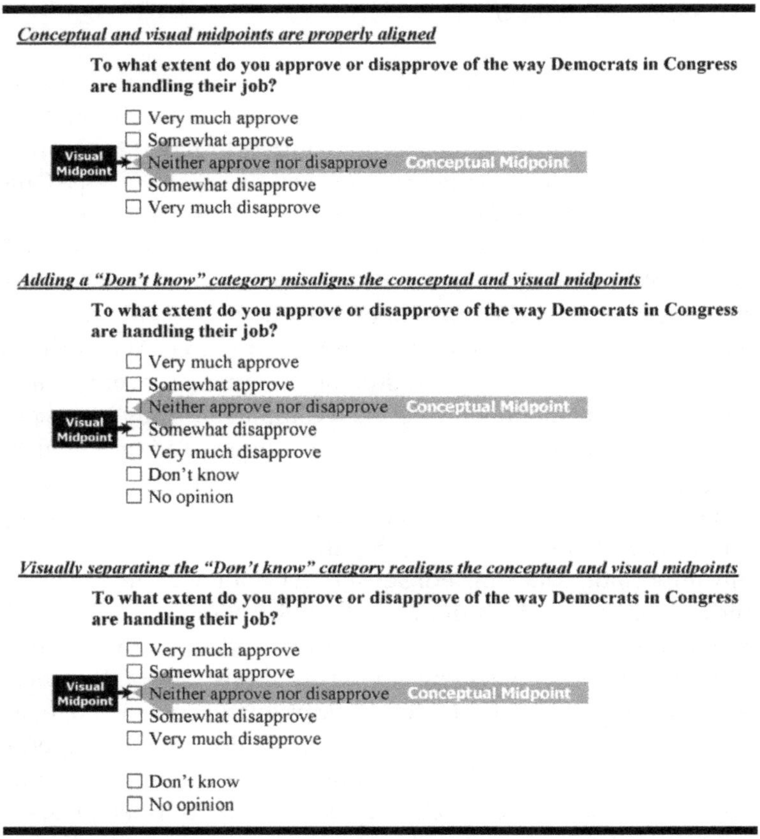

Conceptual and visual midpoints are properly aligned

To what extent do you approve or disapprove of the way Democrats in Congress are handling their job?

☐ Very much approve
☐ Somewhat approve
Visual Midpoint → ☐ Neither approve nor disapprove   Conceptual Midpoint
☐ Somewhat disapprove
☐ Very much disapprove

Adding a "Don't know" category misaligns the conceptual and visual midpoints

To what extent do you approve or disapprove of the way Democrats in Congress are handling their job?

☐ Very much approve
☐ Somewhat approve
☐ Neither approve nor disapprove   Conceptual Midpoint
Visual Midpoint → ☐ Somewhat disapprove
☐ Very much disapprove
☐ Don't know
☐ No opinion

Visually separating the "Don't know" category realigns the conceptual and visual midpoints

To what extent do you approve or disapprove of the way Democrats in Congress are handling their job?

☐ Very much approve
☐ Somewhat approve
Visual Midpoint → ☐ Neither approve nor disapprove   Conceptual Midpoint
☐ Somewhat disapprove
☐ Very much disapprove

☐ Don't know
☐ No opinion

additional space to create the separation. Another way to do this is to insert a horizontal separator line between the substantive and nonsubstantive options. Subsequent research has shown that varying the distance between the middle category and the other categories on each side of the midpoint does not impact responses as long as the visual and conceptual midpoint remain aligned (Christian et al., in press).

CONCLUSION

In Chapters 4 and 5, we discussed many factors that influence how respondents process questions and whether they can provide accurate answers to them. Our overarching theme has been that it is important to consider both the question wording and the visual design of every component of every question. In this chapter, we narrowed our focus and provided guidelines for the development of some of the most commonly used specific types of questions: open-ended, closed-ended nominal, and closed-ended ordinal questions. Together, these three question types provide an enormous capability for surveyors to accurately assess respondent opinions and behaviors, and, as such, they form the backbone of many surveys. Knowing the specifics of designing each of these types of questions is as important to survey success as having the right type of bicycle is for the success of a road ride. The details matter a great deal! We now turn to a third critical step, that of putting the questions together to build a questionnaire. This step requires surveyors to consider additional issues, such as how to order the questions, what technology to use, and how to help respondents make sense of the questionnaire at a more global level.

LIST OF GUIDELINES

Open-Ended Requests for Numerical Responses

Guideline 5.1: *Ask for the specific unit desired in the question stem*
Guideline 5.2: *Provide answer spaces that are sized appropriately for the response task*
Guideline 5.3: *Provide unit labels with the answer spaces*

Open-Ended Requests for a List of Items

Guideline 5.4: *Specify the number and type of responses desired in the question stem*
Guideline 5.5: *Design the answer spaces to support the type and number of responses desired*
Guideline 5.6: *Provide labels with answer spaces to reinforce the type of response requested*

Open-Ended Requests for Description and Elaboration

Guideline 5.7: *Provide extra motivation to respond*
Guideline 5.8: *Provide adequate space for respondents to completely answer the question*
Guideline 5.9: *Use scrollable boxes on web surveys*
Guideline 5.10: *Consider programming probes to open-ended responses in Internet surveys*

General Guidelines for Closed-Ended Questions

Guideline 5.11: *State both positive and negative sides in the question stem when asking either/or types of questions*
Guideline 5.12: *Develop lists of answer categories that include all reasonable possible answers*

(continued)

Guideline 5.13: *Develop lists of answer categories that are mutually exclusive*

Guideline 5.14: *Maintain spacing between answer categories that is consistent with measurement intent*

Closed-Ended Nominal

Guideline 5.15: *Ask respondents to rank only a few items at once rather than a long list*

Guideline 5.16: *Avoid bias from unequal comparisons*

Guideline 5.17: *Randomize response options if there is concern about order effects*

Guideline 5.18: *Use forced-choice questions instead of check-all-that-apply questions*

Guideline 5.19: *Consider using differently shaped answer spaces (circles and squares) to help respondents distinguish between single- and multiple-answer questions*

Closed-Ended Ordinal

Guideline 5.20: *Choose an appropriate scale length—in general, limit scales to four or five categories*

Guideline 5.21: *Choose direct or construct-specific labels to improve cognition*

Guideline 5.22: *Provide scales that approximate the actual distribution of the characteristic in the population*

Guideline 5.23: *Provide balanced scales where categories are relatively equal distances apart conceptually*

Guideline 5.24: *Consider how verbally labeling and visually displaying all response categories may influence answers*

Guideline 5.25: *Carefully evaluate the use of numeric labels and their impact on measurement*

Guideline 5.26: *Align response options vertically in one column or horizontally in one row and strive for equal distance between categories*

Guideline 5.27: *Place nonsubstantive options at the end of the scale and separate them from substantive options*

CHAPTER 6

From Questions to a Questionnaire

THERE IS a huge difference between a list of unordered survey questions and the questionnaire that delivers them to respondents effectively. The design of a questionnaire must consider how to motivate someone who receives it to become a respondent and complete the survey. It must also avoid many measurement problems, ranging from unintended order effects to unnecessarily high item nonresponse. This chapter describes how to transition from a list of questions to a respondent-friendly questionnaire that will maximize response and minimize measurement error.

Many of the challenges of transforming questions into a questionnaire are illustrated by the now infamous butterfly ballot experience from the 2000 presidential election. A dramatic controversy emerged over whether some voters in Palm Beach County, Florida, had mistakenly voted for Pat Buchanan for president while intending that their punch on the butterfly ballot be for the Democratic nominee, Al Gore (see Figure 6.1). C. R. Fox (2000) showed that about 2,800 unintentional votes were recorded for Buchanan, whereas 2,300 incomplete punches and 11,000 double punches were recorded that invalidated intended votes for Gore. These arguments are supported by data showing that the votes recorded in Palm Beach County for Pat Buchanan in that election were proportionally much greater than those recorded in other Florida counties based on the number of registered Reform Party voters, votes for Bush, total votes cast, and votes for Buchanan in the 1996 primary (see Figure 6.2). In addition, Wand et al. (2001) concluded from a detailed postelection analysis that these anomalies were not found among absentee voters in Palm Beach County who did not use the butterfly ballot and that Buchanan's support in Palm Beach County tended to come from more Democratic precincts.

Figure 6.1   Palm Beach County butterfly ballot.

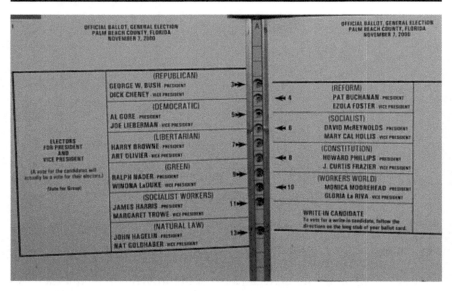

Based on these analyses, there can be little doubt that the design of the butterfly ballot produced (a) many votes for a candidate for which voters did not intend to vote and (b) many votes that could not be counted at all. The consequences of these errors for the outcome of the 2000 presidential election make this perhaps the most dramatic and consequential example ever of poor design of an election ballot, which is quite similar to a survey questionnaire. It is likely that a number of characteristics of the ballot caused the voting errors:

Figure 6.2   Votes for Buchanan in all Florida counties in 2000 presidential election, relative to the number of registered Reform Party voters.

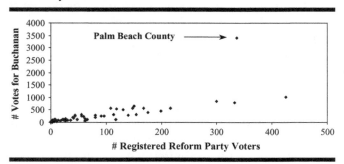

Source: Based on Data Reported by Sebago Associates, 2000.

- The use of punch pins for marking questionnaires is unusual. People do not typically encounter them, except when they vote, and for many voters the previous election was likely a distant memory. Thus, the attention of voters was likely divided between making sure they punched the ballot correctly and that they registered their choice correctly.
- Most voters knew which candidate they planned to vote for before they went into the voting booth, so they probably stopped reading choices once they found their preferred candidate.
- Research has shown that people typically start to read in the upper left-hand corner of the left-hand page and proceed down the page, much as they would read a book. Thus, George Bush's name was likely seen first, followed by that of the second listed candidate, Al Gore.
- It is unusual to list the candidates for one office (or answer categories in a survey) in two different groupings on two different pages. Voters as well as questionnaire respondents are used to having all answer choices in a single, defined group on the same page.
- The lines around candidates on each page visually suggest that the candidates on the first page should be considered as a separate grouping from candidates on page 2.
- It is even more unusual to have answer choices on two separate pages "share" a column of answer spaces in the middle between them, so that answers must be punched to the right of candidates listed on the left page and to the left of candidates listed on the right page.
- When some people who wanted to vote for Gore saw his name and tried to figure out how to vote, their eyes were likely drawn to the word "Democratic" and the line immediately above it, which led directly to the second box in the answer column. It was logical for a voter to mark that second box because the first box in the column was for Bush, the Republican candidate.
- Once the second hole was punched and voters pulled away their hand, it would not be surprising that some voters noticed the arrow in the Democratic space and considered the possibility that they may have punched the wrong hole. To remedy the problem, some probably marked the second hole beside the Gore "rectangle," thus producing a "double punch."
- It is unlikely that someone will raise his hand in a polling place and ask for the attention of poll workers to get a new ballot. Most voters would likely be embarrassed by having to announce to voting precinct workers that they may have made a mistake on the ballot. In addition, a few voters may have thought it was appropriate to mark two punches because both a presidential and vice-presidential candidate were listed in the Democratic space. For these reasons, it is not surprising that double punches far outnumbered the "extra" votes for Buchanan.

The experience of the butterfly ballot in Palm Beach illustrates many of the problems associated with developing a questionnaire from a list of questions. First, respondents must understand how to register their responses given the appropriate technology. For questionnaires the technology used may range from optically processed paper questionnaires that may require marks to be made in a particular way and in a particular location (e.g., fill in the bubble, or place an X in a box) to web surveys where some respondents may be unfamiliar with navigating between pages and registering their responses correctly. People often have to learn the technology of how to record their responses at the same time they are trying to understand the question and decide on a response.

Second, designing a questionnaire involves ordering the questions in a logical way so that the effects of earlier questions on later questions are diminished. The presidential preference question is particularly complex because both the presidential and vice-presidential candidates were displayed as one choice and also because there were 10 groups of candidates to choose from, even though people are used to thinking of only two major party candidates. Had this complex question appeared later in the ballot, it is likely that people would have already learned the ballot format and, therefore, would have been less likely to make such a significant error.

Finally, respondents answering questionnaires or ballots are responding to subtle visual clues as to what constitutes a question and how they should answer it based on how they typically process written information on a page. The butterfly ballot was particularly poor in this regard, making it difficult for voters to know where the presidential preference question ended and how the answer spaces were associated with the names of candidates. A detailed analysis of how visual design played a role in the butterfly ballot has been presented elsewhere (see Dillman, 2007, pp. 463–472).

In this chapter, we discuss three fundamental aspects of questionnaire design: the effects of technology, deciding question order, and using visual design principles to construct questionnaires. We present guidelines for ordering the questions and visually designing questionnaires that are common to both mail and the Web. Because of the different technologies used to construct mail and web questionnaires, we then introduce specific guidelines for developing each. Finally, we propose means of pretesting mail and web surveys, a process that we believe involves more similarities than differences for these two survey modes, and the aim of which is to provide a final check to prevent problems such as those that occurred with the butterfly ballot.

HOW TECHNOLOGY MAKES A DIFFERENCE

At first blush, web and mail questionnaires may appear to have monumental differences. On the Web, questions can be asked one page at a time, whereas in mail that is inefficient and seldom done. Instead, paper questionnaires are often printed in booklet format to help respondents navigate between the pages. Using color on the Web is as inexpensive as constructing in black and white, but not so for paper, where each questionnaire must be printed. Web surveys can use answers to early questions to ask follow-up questions and even customize the question wording (e.g., "When you began work at 'Safeco,' how long was your daily commute?"), whereas paper questionnaires cannot. In addition, branching constructions must be explicit and easy for respondents to follow in mail questionnaires, whereas for web surveys respondents need not, as a general rule, even know that branching has taken place.

Constructing web questionnaires involves learning how to program items so that they appear on the respondent's screen in the same way they appear on the designer's screen. Moreover, web programming will be transmitted to software and hardware that may be quite different and through electronic connections that can range from quite limited and slow to incredibly fast, and these differences can have substantial effects on the final appearance of the questionnaire. Developing paper surveys requires learning about printing capabilities, optical scanning and image requirements (which vary widely among survey organizations), postal regulations that constrain what respondents can receive and respond to, and processing of the questionnaires once they are returned.

Other seeming differences between mail and the Web no longer exist. For example, both technologies now allow variation to be built into questionnaires for specific recipients. Through intelligent printing, one mail respondent might be asked the following question referring to a 5% increase in local taxes, whereas another is asked the same question but with the 5% changed to 10%: "Would you be willing to pay '#%' more in local taxes if a new multipurpose basketball arena were to be built in Seattle?" Respondent identification numbers can then be used to identify which version of a question each respondent completed so one can evaluate the effects of the different question wording. In addition, the order in which questions are asked or in which response categories provided can also be varied and even randomized by both modern mail and web survey design technology. Now, even small survey organizations can obtain these capabilities.

It is also important to recognize the substantial differences that now exist in the electronic world of surveying. Handheld devices are proliferating with tremendous speed, raising the prospect that certain surveys will be answered, but not on a traditional desktop or laptop computer with a large screen. In addition, fillable PDF files are emerging as a substitute to interactive web surveys to facilitate printing, sharing, and responding, especially in the world of business surveys. Brief web surveys are also sometimes embedded within e-mail messages to facilitate not having to click on a link or go to the Web to provide a response. Thus, web and mail surveys are now, at best, general terms that describe tailoring questionnaire construction to people on the move who can answer in different places and situations using different technologies.

The differences that currently separate web from mail survey construction tend to mask equally large similarities in how people respond to visual stimuli. Both the Web and mail use visual channels to communicate with respondents. Nearly a decade of research has shown remarkable consistencies in how visual layouts of questionnaires produce similar answers on paper and on the Internet. For example, whether scalar questions are asked in linear or nonlinear formats, whether needed instructions about how to respond appear with response categories rather than only in the stem of questions, and whether questions are asked in a check-all format versus a forced choice format all affect answers similarly across web and mail surveys (Dillman, 2007).

Moreover, the objectives of good questionnaire design remain the same across these two modes. The first objective is to reduce nonresponse. Respondent-friendly questionnaires have been shown to improve overall response rates, but only to a moderate degree (Dillman et al., 1993). More important, some research has shown that making a questionnaire respondent friendly is most likely to improve response among people who are least likely to respond to surveys, thus helping to reduce nonresponse error. For example, in a 1992 test of respondent-friendly U.S. Decennial Census questionnaires, response was improved by only 2.9 percentage points in areas of the United States with high response to the previous Census compared to 7.5% in areas with low response (Dillman et al., 1993). Specific design choices, such as which question to ask first, can also contribute significantly to the reduction of nonresponse error by getting people to whom the survey questions do not apply to return their uncompleted questionnaires.

In addition to obtaining acceptable response rates, another objective of good questionnaire design is to reduce measurement error. Good questionnaire design helps encourage all respondents to read and process questions and their component parts completely and in the prescribed order, and it minimizes the influence of one question on the measurement of subsequent items. Poor design of individual questions and of the questionnaire can increase item nonresponse by causing questions to be overlooked because of where they are located or other design properties. Effective questionnaire design, in contrast, can help reduce item nonresponse. In addition, poor design can result in some questions or response options being interpreted differently than intended. Thus, respondent-friendly questionnaires should help guide respondents as they complete the questionnaire.

The design of the questionnaire, which is intended to encourage and motivate people to respond, invokes all three of the social exchange elements discussed in Chapter 2. Questionnaire design can improve rewards by making the questionnaire appear interesting and socially important. The costs associated with participating in the survey can be reduced by making the questionnaire easy to navigate and complete. Trust is encouraged through paying attention to detail and by making the questionnaire look and seem important and professional. All of the issues we address in this chapter, from the order of questions to the visual design of the questionnaire and pretesting, are important to designing a good questionnaire that encourages response and reduces measurement error.

ORDERING THE QUESTIONS

A questionnaire should be organized much like a conversation, which typically evolves in accordance with societal norms (Schwarz, 1996). Most conversations tend to follow a logical order in which people respond to what other people are saying and contributing to the conversation. If someone jumps to a new topic immediately after every response you give, it appears that they are not listening to or caring about what you said. Consider for a moment receiving the following questionnaire, which was proposed for a self-administered survey. We have presented it here in abbreviated form, but with the order of the questions unchanged:

- What was your total family income in 2007?
- Do you like to play golf?
- What is your opinion on global warming?
- Are you married?
- How many times have you gone bowling during the past year?
- What is your political party preference?
- Do you favor or oppose these measures to reduce environmental pollution?
- What is your occupation?
- Please describe your favorite recreational activity.
- How adequate is your present health care?
- Which political party does the best job of promoting economic growth?
- How old are you?
- Has your health gotten better or worse during the past year?

Imagine the difficulty of trying to respond to these questions in the current order where questions about personal characteristics, political issues, recreation, and health care are all intermingled and where the questions are not grouped in the way your knowledge of the topics is likely to be organized.

Guideline 6.1: Group Related Questions that Cover Similar Topics, and Begin with Questions Likely to Be Salient to Nearly All Respondents

Grouping related questions makes it easier for respondents to answer and more closely approximates an actual conversation. Switching between topics means that people's answers are less likely to be well thought out, as new topics are more likely to evoke top-of-the-head responses. In addition, constantly changing topics back and forth within a questionnaire, such as in the original question order listed previously, makes it appear that no effort was made to order the questions in a meaningful way (i.e., the questionnaire appears unprofessional and therefore unimportant). Once related questions are grouped, it is often best to begin with questions that are most salient and interesting to the potential respondents and then move to questions that are less salient (Groves et al., 2006; Heberlien & Baumgartner, 1978). Asking the more salient questions first will help get respondents to commit to the questionnaire.

The following example demonstrates the importance of ordering questions and beginning with salient questions that will be of interest to people who will be asked to respond. One of us was once asked to provide advice for a particularly difficult survey of licensed commercial salmon fishermen that focused mostly on the size of their boats and investment in their equipment. After much discussion with the survey sponsor, an introductory section was added to the survey that asked about the fishermen's views of the future of salmon fishing, whether they would advise young people to enter this occupation, and other issues that were described as the "gut" issues facing the business. The response rate for this study of individuals, many of whom had not completed high school, was well over 50%.

Guideline 6.2: Choose the First Question Carefully

No single question is more crucial, especially in web surveys, than the first one, as it is most likely to determine whether people will respond to the survey or choose not to participate. This is not the place for a question that is long, boring, difficult to understand, tedious to answer, or potentially embarrassing. Whereas a mail respondent may be able to page through the entire survey to get a sense of length and content, the first question in a web survey (especially one with a page-by-page design) must stand alone as an invitation to continue to respond.

The first question should apply to everyone and be easy to read, comprehend, and answer. In addition, it should be interesting and reflect the purpose of the questionnaire as it has been previously explained to the respondent. A first question that is applicable to respondents communicates to them that the entire questionnaire is relevant to them and encourages their participation. Likewise, a first question that is interesting will encourage response by increasing the perceived rewards of completing the survey and reducing the perceived costs. In addition to being applicable and interesting, a first question that is simple helps to set the framework that the rest of the questions will be relatively easy to answer and will not require a lot of effort from potential respondents, thus reducing perceived costs. And finally, a first question that is clearly connected to the purpose of the questionnaire as it was explained in contact letters gives the survey a feeling of consistency and can help promote trust.

In the salmon fisherman example discussed in the previous guideline, the first question asked whether the respondent felt that the benefits of being a salmon fisherman were getting better, getting worse, or staying about the same. This was a simple closed-ended question that all respondents could answer easily and that would be interesting to the salmon fishermen being surveyed, which would help encourage them to continue with the survey.

Although it is desirable to choose a first question that applies to everyone, is easy to answer, is interesting, and connects to the implementation materials, special situations may override the search for a first question that meets these criteria. The most common is when respondents must meet eligibility requirements up front in order to complete the survey. In these instances, we use the first question to determine eligibility and to inform both those eligible and those not eligible to return the questionnaire if they are completing it by mail (eligibility criteria are also sometimes communicated in the cover letter—see Chapter 7). Asking people to complete a question about eligibility and then return the questionnaire even if they do not complete the remainder of the questions is helpful for understanding coverage, sampling, and nonresponse issues. Otherwise, the ineligible person would be counted as a nonrespondent. If they are answering a web questionnaire, those who are determined to be ineligible are politely thanked for their willingness to participate and informed of their ineligibility.

Guideline 6.3: Place Sensitive or Potentially Objectionable Questions near the End of the Questionnaire

In addition to choosing the first question carefully, it is also important to place sensitive or potentially objectionable questions near the end of the questionnaire after respondents have had an opportunity to become engaged with the questionnaire, to establish rapport with the surveyor, and have answered the more salient and interesting questions. Respondents who have already responded to several questions and spent 5 to 10 minutes answering the questionnaire are less likely to quit if asked potentially objectionable questions. Moreover, some questions may seem less objectionable in light of questions already answered, and placing sensitive questions near the end avoids interrupting the flow of the questionnaire as would happen if they were asked abruptly at the beginning or in the middle. Pretesting can help identify questions that people might object to answering, such as those about income, sexual behavior, criminal activity, medical history, and so on.

Guideline 6.4: Ask Questions about Events in the Order the Events Occurred

An effort should also be made to order questions in a way that will be logical to the respondent. In particular, people find it easier to respond to questions about events in the order the events happened. For example, if asking a series of questions about previous and current employment positions, it can be helpful to walk through the different positions with respondents in chronological order (i.e., from the past to the present or from the present to the past). Asking about events in the order they occurred is helpful because autobiographical memories are often hierarchically linked in a network so that remembering one event can facilitate accurate recall of the next event in the sequence (Belli, 1998). In addition, more accurate and complete recall about each position can be facilitated by having respondents answer where they worked, in what position, the nature of the position, and how long they were in that position before responding to questions about what they liked most or why they left the position.

Guideline 6.5: Avoid Unintended Question Order Effects

Many surveyors think of each of their questions as standing alone; however, respondents often draw on surrounding questions as they attempt to interpret and answer a given question. The effects of earlier questions on answers to later questions are referred to as *question order effects*. Although the cause of a question order effect can vary, the outcome is usually one of two types: a *contrast effect*, whereby the responses to questions become more different; or an *assimilation effect*, whereby the responses become more similar. Both of these types of effects become increasingly likely to occur when the questions are closer to one another, both in terms of topic and in terms of physical proximity on the page or screen.

Figure 6.3 summarizes various causes of assimilation and contrast effects. As the figure illustrates, question order effects can occur when early questions influence the cognitive processing of later questions (i.e., a *cognitive-based order effect*) or when early questions invoke a social norm that affects the way later questions are answered (i.e., a *normative-based order effect*). The following examples illustrate how each of the effects in Figure 6.3 can occur in a survey.

Priming

Researchers randomly assigned respondents to the National Health Interview Survey on Disability to six condition checklists in an attempt to measure the prevalence of chronic conditions in the population. After the checklists were administered, all respondents were asked questions about disabilities, including whether they had a disability and, if so, what caused it. In response to the question about what caused their disability, nearly 49% of respondents who had previously been asked about sensory impairments reported such conditions as the cause of their disability compared to only 41% of those who had not been asked about sensory impairments. The same pattern held for a number of other types of chronic conditions. Overall, respondents who reported having disabilities were more likely to attribute their disability to conditions they had been asked about previously in the interview than to alternative conditions (Todorov, 2000). The early questions made certain

Figure 6.3 Common cognitive- and normative-based sources of question order effects.

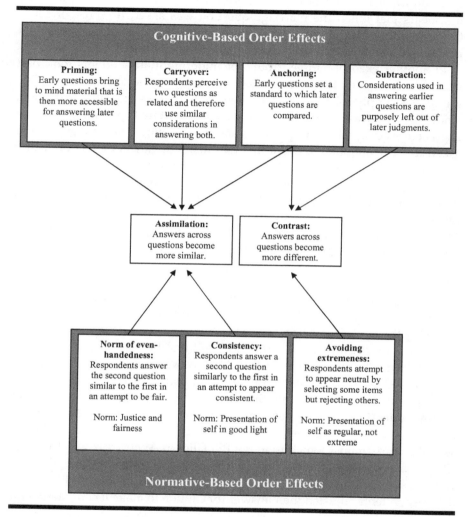

conditions more accessible for consideration in the later questions, a priming effect that resulted in assimilation.

Carryover

Respondents were presented with two questions: "How would you describe your marriage?" and "How would you say things are these days?" Answers to these two questions varied greatly depending on which was asked first. When the marriage question was asked first, 70% said their marriage was very happy (compared to pretty or not too happy), and 52% went on to say they were very happy in response to the general question. But when the general question was asked first, only 38% answered that they were very happy. Thus it appears that when the marriage question was asked first, respondents' thoughts about the happiness of their marriage were carried over into their general judgments about how things were going (Schuman & Presser, 1981).

In another example, three groups of undergraduate students took part in a study in which they were asked about their general well-being. One group was simply asked about their general happiness and life satisfaction. Another group was asked to write about a life event that had made them feel good before being asked the questions about well-being. The third group was asked to write about a life event that had made them feel bad before being asked about their well-being. Overall, participants who wrote about positive life events reported being more happy and satisfied with their lives, whereas those who wrote about negative life events reported less happiness and life satisfaction (Schwarz & Clore, 1983). In both of these examples, respondents carried over considerations from an early question or task into their answer formation for a later question, resulting in an assimilation effect.

Anchoring

A Gallup poll conducted in early September 1997 contained two questions: "Do you generally think Bill Clinton is honest and trustworthy?" and "Do you generally think Al Gore is honest and trustworthy?" When respondents were asked about Bill Clinton first, 50% indicated that he was honest and trustworthy, and 60% then answered that Al Gore was honest and trustworthy. When asked about Gore first, 68% indicated that he was honest and trustworthy, and 57% answered that Bill Clinton was honest and trustworthy. In the first order (Clinton first), respondents had to answer about Clinton based on their own frame of reference, but in the second they could use Al Gore as a standard against which to judge Bill Clinton. When this was the case, Clinton benefited (+7 percentage points) from the Gore standard. Because Clinton and Gore at that time were generally viewed as a team, it appears that respondents adjusted their answer for Clinton to make it consistent with their answer for Gore (Moore, 2002). The result was an assimilation effect.

Results from an earlier Gallup poll (March 27–29, 1995) show how anchoring can also lead to a contrast effect. In this poll respondents were asked to indicate whether a number of characteristics and qualities described Newt Gingrich (then Speaker of the House) and Bob Dole (then Senate Majority Leader). When Gingrich was mentioned first, 41% of respondents said that he was honest and trustworthy, but when he was mentioned after Bob Dole, only 33% indicated that he was honest and trustworthy. Having Bob Dole as a standard against which to compare led to fewer people thinking Gingrich was honest and trustworthy. The opposite happened for Dole. When he was listed first, 60% indicated that he was honest and trustworthy, but when Gingrich formed the standard against which he was compared, even more people (64%) found Dole honest and trustworthy (Moore, 2002). Whereas in the previous example people tended to focus on the similarities between Clinton and Gore, resulting in an assimilation effect, here they tended to focus on the differences between Gingrich and Dole, resulting in a contrast effect. In both of these examples, the standard formed by the subject in the first question was applied to the second question, resulting in an anchoring effect.

Subtraction

Mason, Carlson, and Tourangeau (1994) asked respondents how they would describe the economic situation in their communities over the next 5 years and how they felt about the economic situation in their state over the next 5 years. They found that more people (7%–10%) said the state economy would get better when the state economy was presented before the community economy question. The reason for this difference is that once people answer the first question, they tend to "subtract" out reasons used to justify their answer from their reasoning on the second question. In this particular case, when the question about the community economy came first, new industry was a factor that strongly influenced respondents to say that their community's economy would get better. New industry also strongly influenced responses about the state economy when that question came first, but when the state economy question came after the community question, new industry did not play as large of a role for the state question (i.e., it was subtracted out of the considerations). The result was a subtraction effect, whereby important considerations used to answer an earlier question are taken out of considerations for a later question.

Norm of Evenhandedness

Students at Washington State University were asked two questions about the consequences of plagiarism. One asked whether a student who had plagiarized should be expelled. The other asked whether a professor who had plagiarized should be fired. When the professor question was asked first, 34% indicated on the following question that a plagiarizing student should be expelled. However, when the professor question was asked second, only 21% indicated that the student should be expelled (Sangster, 1993). The likely cause of this difference is that once the students had judged someone from outside their group harshly for plagiarizing (i.e., by recommending firing), they then felt they must apply the same standard to someone within their group. This phenomenon of adjusting answers to be evenhanded or fair was first noticed in a classic study in 1948 (Hyman & Sheatsley, 1950) in which respondents were asked whether communist reporters should be allowed to report on visits to the United States and whether U.S. reporters should be allowed to report on visits to the Soviet Union. When the question about communist reporters reporting on visits to the United States was asked first, only 37%

of respondents said yes. However, when this question followed the question about U.S. reporters reporting on trips to the Soviet Union, 73% said yes.

Consistency

Dillehay and Jernigan (1970) administered three questionnaires pertaining to policies toward criminals to three sets of students. One was strongly biased toward leniency for criminals, another was strongly biased toward harshness for criminals, and the third was constructed to be neutral. All of the students were then asked to complete scales measuring their opinions about criminals. The results indicated that those who initially completed the questionnaire biased toward leniency later displayed more lenient opinions toward criminals than did those who initially received the harsh or neutral questionnaire. Thus, it appears that these students, after being swayed by a biased questionnaire into supporting a very lenient stance toward criminals, adjusted their answers to opinion questions about criminals to be more consistent with their original responses.

Avoiding Extremeness

As part of an experiment, a group of students were told the study they were taking part in was concerned with language and the structure of speech. The students were then introduced to the topics of euthanasia and reduced training for doctors through a questionnaire that asked them whether they stood for or against these controversial practices. Half of the students were then informed that they would be participating in a face-to-face interaction with another participant about either euthanasia or reduced training for doctors. They were told the topic they would be discussing as well as the position the other participant would take. The other half were informed that they would be listening to a recording of another participant's views on one of the two topics, and they were then informed of their particular topic and the other participant's views. All of the students were then told that more information was needed before beginning and were asked to complete a set of four questions on each topic. The results from these questions showed that students who expected to have to talk in person with another participant about their topic rated that topic more moderately than those who expected to only have to listen to a recording (Cialdini, Levy, Herman, & Evenbeck, 1973). When confronted with a more social situation, respondents avoided presenting themselves as extreme by moderating their answers.

In addition to these question order effects, a body of research has emerged that summarizes the effects of asking general or summary items, such as "How would you rate the overall quality of life in your community?", prior to and after asking about a number of specific domains such as streets and roads, education, and police protection. Studies have found that the summary question tends to be scored lower by respondents when asked before a list of specific domain questions and higher when asked after the specific domain questions (Willits & Saltiel, 1995).

Much of the research that has been conducted on question order effects predates the development of web surveys, but, for the most part, one can expect these effects to be very similar in web surveys as in mail surveys. However, the way that surveyors program their web surveys can magnify or minimize order effects. For example, presenting all of the questions on one screen allows the respondent to scroll back and forth throughout the survey, making it easier to identify relationships between questions (much as is the case with a mail survey). In contrast, using page-by-page construction separates the questions and makes moving back and forth through them more cumbersome, if it is allowed at all. In this case, one would expect fewer question order effects, as it is more difficult for the respondent to carry the context and memory of previous questions across screens. In fact, Tourangeau et al. (2004) showed that items are more highly correlated when they appear together on one screen as opposed to being spread across several screens.

Another programming capability of web surveys that is relevant to question order effects is the ability to control, and vary, the order in which questions are presented. One can present the same questions in the same order to all respondents or can vary the order for random subsamples of respondents. Varying the order can range from flipping the order of two questions that are expected to produce order effects to randomly ordering all of the questions (although we generally would not recommend the latter without good reason).

Schwarz (1996) detailed how, in the normal give-and-take of regular conversations, people tend to give answers that take into account things they have already said. Thus, answers to individual questions are less complete, or less able to stand alone, than the writers of those questions probably intended. Although order effects are probably larger with questions that immediately follow one another, there is limited evidence that effects also occur when questions are widely separated. Consequently, it is important to recognize early on that a questionnaire cannot be viewed as a compilation of completely independent questions that have no effects on one another. Each question must be evaluated not only on the basis of its individual content but also with regard to the larger context that often adds or subtracts meaning. When one anticipates including questions like those described previously, it may be judicious to consider constructing half the questionnaires with one order and half with another, or at a minimum recognize in reports of findings the possibility of question order influence on respondent answers.

CREATING A COMMON VISUAL STIMULUS

We discussed in Chapter 4 how visual design and layout influences people when they are responding to survey questions, and we provided guidelines for the visual presentation of individual questions. In this chapter, we continue that discussion but introduce additional visual design concepts to help surveyors understand how respondents perceive entire questionnaire pages, organize information on the page, and navigate the survey questionnaire.

Ensuring that every respondent perceives the survey questions in the same way is considered essential for obtaining quality survey data. However, creating a common stimulus for all respondents is far more difficult in self-administered surveys because the respondents, rather than interviewers, control the order in which they answer the questions and whether they process all of the questions and their component parts. Even though interviewers are not present to guide respondents through the questionnaire, effective visual design can help respondents gain entry into the page so they will want to respond to the questionnaire and will understand how the information is organized. In addition, visual design can be used to encourage respondents to process all of the questions in the desired order and to navigate between sections and individual questions.

HOW DO RESPONDENTS MAKE SENSE OF INFORMATION PRESENTED IN A SURVEY QUESTIONNAIRE?

When a person is presented with visual information, whether in a newspaper, web site, or survey questionnaire, many separate actions take place very quickly as the eye takes in the information and the brain processes it to make sense of the page or screen. The ways in which people perceive and attend to survey information are determined by innate tendencies of visual information processing as described in recent work by Palmer (1999), Hoffman (2004), and Ware (2004). People do not assign meaning to information all at once. Instead, they process and give meaning to visual elements and their properties in multiple steps, although often quite quickly. The way people process visual information can be divided into three stages: (1) understanding the basic layout of the page, (2) organizing the information on the page, and (3) focusing on completing the task. During the first two stages, the information on the page is processed on a global level, and in the third stage, the focus is narrowed to processing parts of the page in more detail. In Figure 6.4, we define the three stages and the types of processing that occur in these stages.

When respondents first view a paper or web questionnaire, they quickly scan the page and notice visual properties, such as color and size, to understand the *basic page layout*. This stage occurs mostly prior to conscious attention at the level of *preattentive processing*, where one gains a general understanding of the scene by noticing certain visual properties (e.g., number, size, shape, contrast, enclosure, color hue and intensity, etc.) that "stand out" from other information on the page. In addition, this stage is dominated by *bottom-up processing*, where only the visual scene itself influences how information is perceived.

Figure 6.4   Visual design concepts that guide questionnaire design.

Three stages of visual processing

Basic page layout: In the first step, respondents quickly scan the page and preattentively process basic visual properties, such as color and size, to gain a general understanding of the basic layout of the page. This stage is dominated by bottom-up processing.

Information organization: In the second step, respondents begin to organize the information by segmenting the page into basic regions, differentiating individual visual elements from the background, and perceiving groups or relationships among elements. The stage involves both preattentive and attentive processing, and respondents move from bottom-up to top-down processing.

Task completion: In the final step, attention is on the task of answering individual questions where survey respondents focus on a smaller area of the page and begin attentively processing the components of each individual question. Top-down processing occurs in this stage where the survey context and respondents' prior knowledge influence interpretation.

Attention and visual processing

Preattentive processing: Broad, rapid visual analysis of the entire field of available information that determines which visual elements are attended to in later stages according to certain properties that are noticed subconsciously and "stand out" because they deviate from other information on the page.

Attentive processing: Conscious visual processing where the visual field narrows and the focus is on a few elements that enter visual working memory and are more easily recalled.

Foveal view: When respondents are focused on individual survey questions during attentive processing, their field of view shrinks to about 2 degrees or 8 to 10 characters in width.

Bottom-up processing: Visual information is quickly processed by the visual system alone, and only the visual stimulus itself influences perception.

Top-down processing: Visual information is processed based on the context of the situation and the viewer's cultural knowledge, prior experiences, and expectations.

Figure/ground orientation: The organization of the visual scene into what is object and what is background, determined by the contours of the visual elements, and determining order of attention during processing, with figures attended to first.

In the *information organization* stage, respondents divide the page into basic regions according to their shared visual properties, a process called *segmentation*. Once the page is divided into regions, the contours and boundaries help the respondent distinguish figure from ground and differentiate individual visual elements that are used in further visual processing. Then, respondents begin to perceive groups among visual elements, using the Gestalt grouping principles, as discussed in Chapter 4. Grouping information helps speed up processing and improves comprehension. For example, respondents might begin to perceive elements of similar contrast that are located close in proximity, such as a set of response options, as a group. This is an in-between stage where the elements that are preattentively processed in Stage 1 and early in Stage 2 are now actively attended to and cognitively processed. Meaning is determined by the visual scene, but *top-down processing* also begins, so that the context of the situation and respondents' cultural knowledge, prior experiences, and expectations also influence the meaning assigned to visual information.

After respondents perceive and organize the basic visual elements of the questionnaire, they begin the third stage, *task completion.* It is during this stage that respondents shift their focus from the entire page to a much smaller area (the foveal view) for more focused processing and that they first begin to read the text on the page in any detail. During this *attentive processing,* respondents sequentially attend to the components of each individual question (the question stem, any additional instructions or definitions, the answer spaces and/or response options), and these components enter working memory and are more easily remembered.

How respondents perceive the information in the question influences the remaining four steps of the response process as described by Tourangeau (1992): comprehending the meaning of the question, recalling important information, forming a judgment, and reporting a response. The task completion stage is dominated by top-down processing, where the survey context and the respondents' prior cultural knowledge and experiences influence how they interpret the visual information. For example, symbols such as currency symbols can have different meanings based on cultural expectations, and symbols such as boxes and circles have different meanings in web than in mail surveys because on the Web, check boxes allow multiple responses and circular radio buttons only one.

In Figure 6.5, we demonstrate how respondents process a questionnaire by showing images of what respondents perceive in each of the three stages. During the first stage, respondents notice the basic horizontal and vertical layout of information on the page; distinguish changes in contrast and color; and notice the dark, medium, and light gray and white areas on the questionnaire page (the Stage 1 image in Figure 6.5). Respondents perceive multiple dark gray features of different shapes and sizes (a circle, rectangle, and five small squares), three medium gray rectangles of different sizes at the top of the page, and white spaces in the lower right and bottom areas of the page.

We show two images of Stage 2 in Figure 6.5 to differentiate early Stage 2, where preattentive and bottom-up processing still dominate, late Stage 2, where more active attention begins and respondents use top-down processing. In early Stage 2, respondents use the boundaries and contrast to segment the page into two regions. Once the page is segmented, respondents focus on the darker gray and white elements and let the light gray recede into the background (the Stage 2a image). In this early stage, respondents notice even more elements located in different areas of the page and their varying sizes, shapes, and contrast. In late Stage 2 (the Stage 2b image), respondents attend to these various elements, grouping them and using prior knowledge and experiences to assign meaning to them. Respondents distinguish the header region with the logos identifying the sponsor and the contact information, the title of the survey, and the instructions to respondents. In the question region, respondents perceive the section heading and instructions, five questions, one with four subcomponent parts, and the answer spaces (respondents may also briefly notice the "office use only" area in light gray at the bottom of the page).

In the final task completion stage, respondents focus their attention on perceiving and comprehending the words in the first question stem so they can then retrieve the relevant information, formulate a judgment, and report a response in the accompanying answer space (Stage 3 image in Figure 6.5). Then respondents move on to focus on processing and answering the next question.

Once respondents can easily get into the pages, they can then focus on answering the individual questions. The following guidelines help make sure that respondents to self-administered questionnaires can understand the basic layout of the questionnaire pages and the organization of information contained within them in order to process questions and navigate through them in the intended order.

Guideline 6.6: Establish Consistency in the Visual Presentation of Questions (across Pages and Screens), and Use Alignment and Vertical Spacing to Help Respondents Organize the Information on the Page

We have seen many questionnaires in which it is not clear to respondents where they should begin and how questions are organized. In these questionnaires, respondents have to search the page to figure out how to navigate between questions. In addition to presenting the components of the question consistently and creating clear grouping and subgrouping (discussed in Chapter 4, Guidelines 4.10–4.12), displaying questions consistently across questionnaire pages and screens can help respondents as they move from question to question and page to page.

The Gestalt principle of pragnanz, introduced in Chapter 4, posits that visual information that is regular is easier to process and remember. In addition, repeated observation in cognitive interviews of respondents to both web and paper questionnaires shows a rhythmic quality in people's response patterns. The respondent goes somewhat automatically from the answer space of one question to the beginning of the next appropriate question. Arranging questions similarly with the parts in the same order for each item helps respondents be more efficient in sequentially processing the information in the questionnaire. Once respondents are into the rhythm of responding, deviations from this format often lead to misunderstandings. Figure 6.5 (Stage 2b)

Figure 6.5 How respondents perceive a questionnaire page during each stage of visual processing.

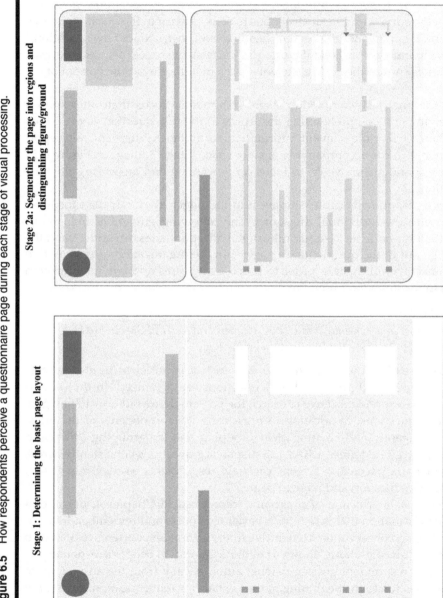

Stage 1: Determining the basic page layout

Stage 2a: Segmenting the page into regions and distinguishing figure/ground

Source: "'Achieving Usability in Establishment Surveys through the Application of Visual Design Principles," by D. A. Dillman, A. Gertseva, and T. Mahon-Haft, 2005, *Journal of Official Statistics*, 21, pp. 183–214.

Figure 6.5 (*Continued*)

Stage 2b: Grouping and organizing the information on the page

Stage 3: Perceiving and answering individual questions

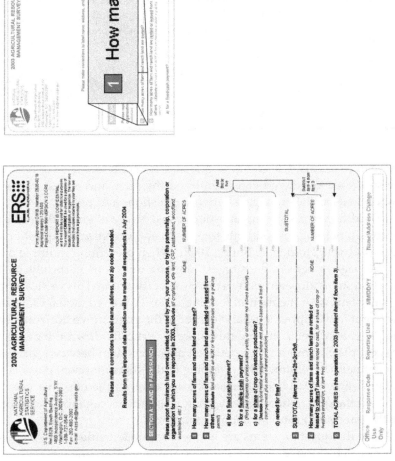

Figure 6.6   Example of consistent page layout for a web questionnaire.

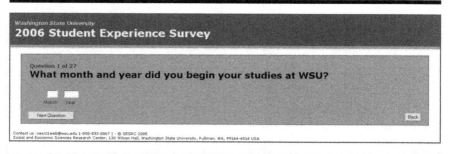

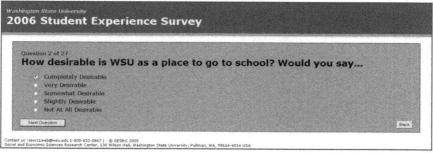

and Figure 6.6 display examples of a mail and of a web questionnaire where questions are displayed consistently on the page and across pages to help respondents as they navigate between questions and pages.

In addition to displaying questions consistently, aligning them is a powerful tool in helping respondents to process and organize the questions on the page (Lidwell, Holden, & Butler, 2003). When presenting multiple questions on the page or screen, we suggest aligning questions vertically, so that the question stems all begin along a common vertical line. This vertical alignment is consistent with the natural reading order in many languages, where people begin in the upper left-hand corner of the page, move horizontally across the page, and then continue this process vertically down the page. We also suggest placing more space between questions than between their subcomponent parts to reinforce the grouping of the subcomponent parts, discussed in Guideline 4.11. We cannot emphasize enough the effective use of blank space in the questionnaire for helping respondents organize the information on the page and group related information.

Once the question stems are aligned on the left side of the page, answer spaces can be located along another common vertical line further to the right on the page, as shown in Figure 6.5 (Stage 2b). Alternatively, we prefer indenting the answer spaces or response categories and locating them underneath the appropriate question stem (see example in Figure 6.6). This format helps respondents to easily establish a hierarchy (Lidwell et al., 2003), where they first process the query, then the categories or answer spaces, before moving to the next question.

If only one question is shown per page, as in many web surveys, it is helpful to begin each question in the same place on the screen so respondents know where to focus their attention on each page. Also, indenting the answer spaces or response categories underneath the question stem, as shown in Figure 6.6, is often helpful when there is only one question per page because respondents do not have to move their eyes all the way across the screen to perceive the answer spaces.

Overall, displaying questions consistently throughout the questionnaire and aligning questions and their corresponding answer spaces or categories vertically helps respondents organize the information on the page and maintain a sense of order as they move across questions. Perhaps even more important, a vertical alignment helps encourage respondents to process the questions in the intended order and decreases the likelihood that items will be inadvertently missed.

Guideline 6.7: Use Color and Contrast to Help Respondents Recognize the Components of the Questions and the Navigational Path through the Questionnaire

Color is a powerful tool for helping people organize information and understand the meaning of specific visual elements (Lidwell et al., 2003; Ware, 2004). Using color consistently throughout the questionnaire can help respondents clearly identify related information and can ease the task of answering the questions. Color can also contribute to respondent motivation and the overall visual appeal of the questionnaire. When color cannot be used, contrast can be varied in grayscale.

A lightly shaded background can help respondents in several ways. First, it creates a region in which the respondent can focus attention. The use of regions to assist processing is discussed in Guideline 6.8. Second, a shaded background allows for the use of white answer spaces, the benefit of which is discussed below. Finally, black font color for the text can easily be perceived on a variety of lightly shaded backgrounds so that respondents can easily see and read the text of the question and its component parts.

Lighter shades of blues and greens are often used as background colors in surveys because they are more pleasing and calming. Oftentimes darker shades of the background color (or a darker gray) can then be used for keypunch codes or other information used by the surveyors. For example, 20% of a certain shade of blue might be used for the background, and then 80% of that same shade can be used for agency information in order to make it visible to someone looking for it (e.g., a coder or data entry person) but to reduce the likelihood that it will be seen and used by the respondent.

When smaller white answer spaces are enclosed within a lightly colored or shaded area they tend to be perceived as a figure, or the elements that people focus their attention on, and the larger colored area recedes into the background (Dillman, Gertseva, & Mahon-Haft, 2005; Hoffman, 2004). Consistently displaying all answer spaces in white on a lightly colored background will, therefore, help respondents quickly and clearly identify where they should record their answers and can also help them identify the navigational path in the early stages of visual processing. Moreover, white answer spaces can help respondents more easily focus their mouse, pencil, or pen on the space, and in paper surveys they can encourage respondents to constrain their marks within the answer spaces, thereby enhancing legibility and facilitating optical processing. Lastly, having all answer spaces appear in white helps respondents quickly scan their responses to see if they have completed all of the question(s) on the page.

Figures 6.5 (Stage 2b) and 6.6 show a mail and web survey that both used a black font color with white answer spaces against lightly colored green backgrounds (although the images are shown here in grayscale).

Guideline 6.8: Visually Group Related Information in Regions through the Use of Contrast and Enclosure

Grouping information into larger "chunks" helps respondents to easily process and organize the information on the page (Lidwell et al., 2003). Dividing the page into visually separate regions through the use of contrast and enclosure helps respondents to perceive the elements within the region as more related to one another than to other elements outside the region. Regions can be used to group related information, such as the title and introduction to the survey, or to group related questions into sections. However, regions need to be chosen carefully so they aid in the completion process. It is important not to group questions or other information into arbitrary regions that have little or no meaning to respondents.

Many questionnaires contain sections of questions that are more related to one another than they are to items located elsewhere. For example, the 2010 Decennial Census will use questionnaires in both English and Spanish. By using one background color for Spanish and another for English, and by placing boundaries around the questions with the different languages, the regions become an effective guide as to who needs to fill out each part of the questionnaire.

Another effective use of regions is from the 20-page U.S. Department of Agriculture Agricultural Resource Management Survey, a 2.5-hour long paper survey that asks detailed questions about farm operations. Grouping related questions into regions and sections is especially important in this survey because some sections do not need to be filled out by specific types of farmers, and the sections are unlikely to be filled out in a specific order or at one time (e.g., some farmers may complete all of the sections they can without consulting records and then leave the remaining sections to be completed once they have compiled the relevant information). The first page of this questionnaire, shown in Figure 6.5 (Stage 2b), has three regions: the first region contains the title, sponsorship information, and general instructions; the second region groups several related questions (and labels that area "Section A"); and the third region groups several spaces for agency use only (see Guideline 6.10 for more information about visually deemphasizing this type of information). The regions are defined using enclosure, where a large rectangle with contoured edges groups the related information. Contoured edges help these regions lift off the page and become the objects of visual attention (Hoffman, 2004). In addition, lightly colored shading is used to demarcate the two regions on which respondents need to focus their attention, whereas no shading is used for the agency-only information to help this area recede from respondents' attention.

Regions can also play a powerful role in helping respondents organize information in web surveys, even when only one question is shown per page. Figure 6.6 shows two question screens where a consistent page layout is used across screens and related information is grouped into three main regions. The top region includes the title and sponsor of the survey, the middle region contains the question and component parts as well as the navigation buttons, and the bottom region includes information about how to contact the survey sponsor. These three regions are visually defined by enclosing the related items in a rectangle with different background shading and making changes in the fonts used for the text.

The top region is repeated from one web page to the next and is likely to be ignored by respondents after the first screen or two, similar to the "banners" included on many web pages. Enclosing the components of the question in a common region helps respondents easily process them as a group. In addition, a colored background is used to encourage respondents to focus their attention on this area and on the task of answering the question. Lastly, the bottom region uses a white rather than shaded background to help decrease its visual importance but still provides the contact information for respondents who need it. Cognitive interviews have shown that respondents who completed a 25-item questionnaire using this screen layout do not recall having seen any information in the survey about how to contact the sponsor.

Guideline 6.9: Consistently Identify the Beginning of Each Question and/or Section

Although paper designers almost always use numbers or letters to identify each new question, web designers have often been reluctant to do this for two reasons. One is that when page-by-page construction is used, numbers are not needed for knowing which question is next because each question appears on its own page and the next question appears after the previous one. The second concern is that respondents are often branched over questions that do not apply to them and may notice that some question numbers were skipped (and may even go back and modify their responses to see if they are then asked the questions they were previously branched past). Thus, many web designers avoid numbering questions, even if their questionnaires do not involve complex skips.

However, there is considerable value to numbering items in some web surveys. Not only does numbering help respondents easily identify the beginning of each question, it can also be useful when a respondent has a question about an item and wishes to easily identify the question when communicating with the survey sponsor. Numbering can also help respondents know where they previously left off when they return to a survey. Numbering questions in web surveys is also useful when a paper questionnaire is to be used by respondents to prepare answers ahead of time that will then be entered into a web survey. This is particularly common in establishment surveys where information may need to be compiled across multiple people or even divisions within an establishment (see Chapter 12). In addition, it is possible in many cases to use a combination of numbering or numbering and lettering (e.g., 2.1, 2.2; or 2a, 2b) to keep overall number sequences intact so that skip patterns are not so easily noticed by those being skipped past questions.

We have noted some surveys in which the value of a starting point is recognized, but the designers do not want to use numbers and so opt to place a large graphical question mark at the beginning of each question. However, this may confuse rather than help respondents as punctuation, such as question marks, is normally used at the end of a sentence rather than at the beginning. If a strategy such as this is to be used, it would be more desirable to mark the beginning of each question with a black square or circle. One can also signify the start of the new question with consistent placement of the question (horizontally and vertically) on each web page or the use of a larger, darker font for the question stem.

Thus, in both paper and web surveys, it is important to clearly identify the beginning of each question and the beginning of each section (if sections are used to group questions). In Figure 6.5 (Stage 2b), reverse print is used to display question numbers and section letters and titles. The consistent use of reverse print to identify the beginning of each section and each question helps respondents to easily navigate through the questionnaire. We often suggest numbering questions simply and consecutively from beginning to end and using letters for each section in order. Restarting numbering in each section should be avoided, especially when references need to be made to questions in other sections. For web surveys, we also recommend consecutive numbering for more simple surveys (e.g., Figure 6.6 shows a simple numbering of "Question __ of __" to tell respondents not only what question number they are currently completing but also how many total questions they will be expected to answer). However, one can clearly identify the beginning of each question by using location or a common shape when question numbers are omitted.

Guideline 6.10: Use Visual Elements and Properties Consistently across Questions and Pages/Screens to Visually Emphasize or Deemphasize Certain Types of Information

It is easier for respondents to navigate the questionnaire and complete the questions when similar types of information are presented consistently across pages. Elements that appear similar in color, size, and shape are perceived as related. When the same type of information is presented similarly across questions and pages, it helps respondents connect related information and enhances the usability of the questionnaire (Lidwell et al., 2003). This can ease the task of comprehension and speed up the answering process.

For example, it is distracting and frustrating to respondents when they are expected to provide their response to the same types of questions in different ways, such as checking answer boxes in one section, putting marks on answer lines in another section, and circling numbers in yet another section. Yet we have often seen such changes in formats on different pages of questionnaires for no apparent reason. Thus, one way to ease the task for respondents is to have them report responses to similar types of questions in the same way throughout the questionnaire.

It is even more common for questionnaire designers to use underlining or bolding to emphasize words or phrases in a question in one part of a questionnaire and then use capital letters or even italics for the same purpose later in the survey. Each time the property applied to the word or phrase changes, respondents have to take time to understand why the visual presentation is different and what the change in presentation means. When these visual properties are used inconsistently, it often undermines the purpose of using them in the first place (i.e., to help simplify the response task).

Questionnaires vary enormously in the challenges they present for providing information consistently. Some questionnaires focus mostly on the opinions of one person and tend to ask brief questions with few answer choices. In these cases, layouts are often simple to construct. Other questionnaires are more complex, and exceptional care needs to be taken when designing these pages.

Not only do visual properties need to be manipulated in a consistent manner, but properties should be varied strategically to visually emphasize information respondents need to complete the task and deemphasize information that is less important or that they will not need at all. In the examples shown in Figure 6.5 (Stage 2b) and Figure 6.6, information that respondents will not need or only a few respondents will need does not appear visually prominent to respondents. The keypunch codes in Figure 6.5 (Stage 2b) are in gray, rather than the black font used for the questions, and are located outside of the answer spaces. In addition, agency-only information in the questionnaire in Figure 6.5 (Stage 2b) and contact information in Figure 6.6 are presented in a gray font against a white background and are located at the bottom of the page to help this information recede from the respondents' attention. As these examples demonstrate, several properties can be manipulated at one time (e.g., contrast, location, and font style) to help deemphasize information that none or only a few of the respondents will need. In addition, layering manipulations by bolding and increasing the size of a word or phrase can make the word or phrase appear more visually prominent, emphasizing its importance.

For each survey, we recommend setting rules for when to use various visual properties (underlining, capital letters, italics, bolding, reverse print, size of text, color, etc.) so that information is presented similarly throughout the questionnaire. Often a construction "rule book" describing which properties will be manipulated to display certain types of information can help ensure consistency in how visual information is presented, particularly for longer or more complicated questionnaires. For example, when redesigning the Agricultural Resource Management Survey mentioned earlier, surveyors created a rule book to guide the consistent and regular use of visual information, which then could be applied by all those working on the questionnaire (Dillman et al., 2005). Many of the rules for visual presentation may be the same from one questionnaire to the next; however, some rules are created for specific issues in a survey and may not apply for other questionnaires, and thus construction or design rule books are likely to vary from questionnaire to questionnaire.

Guideline 6.11: Avoid Visual Clutter

It is important to view the questionnaire from the respondent's perspective and eliminate or reduce the prominence of any information that is not necessary for completing the survey. We often see questionnaire pages designed such that too much information is jammed onto the pages and different items on the page compete for the respondent's attention. Some designers may use only an 8-point font so they can fit more questions on the page. Others see questionnaires as an opportunity to promote branding and include logos and text that prominently identify the sponsor(s), the client, the type of software used, the security features, and other extraneous information on the web pages. Variously sized logos and images compete for respondents' attention and often distract them from completing the task at hand.

There are several ways to reduce clutter on the page. Reducing the number of items on the page and increasing the amount of blank space can help respondents gain entry into the page and organize the information presented to them. It is particularly important to remove any images, unnecessary lines, or other information that may draw attention away from the task of answering the questions and that may make it more difficult to respond. Complex groupings of questions, such as grids and matrixes (and particularly unnecessary lines within grids or matrixes), also interrupt the flow of the questionnaire and tend to introduce more complexity, as people have to connect information across columns and rows. Also, reducing the variety of different elements on the page helps to reduce complexity. For example, including five questions of the same type may be fine for one page, but including five questions that ask respondents to respond in five different ways and that include different types of elements (e.g., answer spaces, check boxes, drop-down menus, and a slider scale) makes it much more difficult for respondents to perceive where to begin and how to navigate between questions.

Another strategy for reducing clutter is to selectively emphasize only a limited amount of information. Because visual information is processed in relation to the other information on the page, it is recommended to highlight or visually emphasize less than 10% of the total visual scene (Lidwell et al., 2003), as emphasis is less effective as the percentage of highlighted information increases. As a greater number and variety of elements and their properties are manipulated, it becomes more difficult for the viewer to distinguish the ones that deviate from the other elements on the page (Ware, 2004). For example, if red is used to draw attention to a particular word or phrase, it will become more difficult for the respondent to easily process the change in color as the number of other colors on the page increases. Overall, reducing visual clutter improves the visual appeal of the questionnaire, increasing people's motivation to respond and helping them to focus on the task of answering the questions.

Guideline 6.12: Minimize the Use of Matrixes and Their Complexity

Matrixes represent one of the most difficult question formats to answer for three reasons. First, they require people to match information in rows with questions in columns (or vice versa), a task that is quite complex. Second, the request to fill out a matrix and the instructions for how to do so are often difficult to understand, in part because of the complexity of the task. Third, the structure of the matrix leaves it up to the respondent as to whether to navigate the matrix and fill in answers primarily in columns or rows or some combination of both. Moreover, because of all three of the previous difficulties, items are more likely to be missed when they are arranged in matrixes than when individual questions are posed sequentially in a vertical layout, resulting in higher item nonresponse.

Recent research on the American Community Survey has shown that a two-page matrix that asks for name, gender, age, relationship to one another, ethnicity, and race for all of the people living in the respondent's household produces a lower mail response rate and greater item nonresponse for some items than does asking for responses to be made to all questions for one person at a time, as is achieved by placing questions for each member of the household in their own vertical column (i.e., not a matrix; Chestnut, 2008). The latter method of asking for all information for one person at a time clarifies the navigational path for answering rather than leaving it up to the respondent as to whether to work vertically or horizontally to complete the matrix.

Even with these substantial difficulties in mind, we propose reducing rather than eliminating the use of matrixes because in some surveys the complexity of the information asked for can best be communicated in simple matrixes, and some survey populations are used to thinking about information presented in this format (e.g., accountants responding to establishment surveys). However, we have seen matrixes that required the respondent to remember as many as seven different specifications (through the use of subheadings in both columns and rows and additional definitions or instruction booklets) in order to fill in a single cell of the matrix (Dillman, 2000a, p. 344). Most people can only remember four to five pieces of information at once, and the likelihood of errors being made when so much information must be connected is enormous.

The Web has had conflicting impacts on the use of matrixes. On the one hand, the fact that many web pages are built using tables has encouraged the use of relatively simple matrix formats, although they are often exceedingly long. In addition, inappropriate shading and the failure to suppress gridlines may make matrixes difficult for respondents to process. For example, one survey we saw recently had 19 items on a single screen, and each item was to be rated on a scale of 1 (*poor*) to 10 (*excellent*). That's 190 radio buttons on one screen! Even though their overall structure is quite simple by comparison to some matrixes, the length of many such matrixes is highly burdensome and tedious for respondents, and connecting information from rows and columns is still quite difficult for some. On the other hand, the Web has decreased the use of very complex matrixes with multiple specifications for each column and row. The Web is simply not conducive to such matrixes because they would require both horizontal and vertical scrolling in order to fully comprehend the questions being asked. Such scrolling adds an additional layer of complexity that has negative effects on response. Paper surveys, especially those used for business surveys, have exhibited a tendency to use formidable matrixes in order to reduce the number of pages and costs of mailing. Inasmuch as many business surveys that use matrixes are now made available in a printable format or paper alternative, the reduced tendency for using exceedingly complex matrixes on the Web is reducing their use on paper as well.

When matrixes cannot be avoided, conscious efforts should be made to control the number of pieces of information that must be processed in order to provide a single answer. Moreover, the use of visual layouts that are constructed so as to encourage easy processing both horizontally and vertically is essential and can improve the quality of responses. An example of a matrix used in an individual-person, general public survey to encourage thoughtful consideration of only two items of information is provided in Figure 6.7. A more complete explanation of a similar matrix is provided elsewhere (Dillman, 2008). Examples of other effective matrix layouts are provided by Dillman et al. (2005) and Morrison, Dillman, and Christian (in press).

Figure 6.7 Example of a matrix format used effectively in a household survey on community issues.

30. Please think for a minute about three relatives who do not live with you but with whom you communicate most frequently, and answer these questions. It may help to list their first name or initials in the line provided.

	Relative 1 ▼	Relative 2 ▼	Relative 3 ▼
First name/Initials (optional)	_____ (name)	_____ (name)	_____ (name)
Does this relative live in Lewiston/ Clarkston?.....................	☐ Yes ☐ No	☐ Yes ☐ No	☐ Yes ☐ No
If no: about how far away from Lewiston/Clarkston do they live?	_____ Miles	_____ Miles	_____ Miles
About how old is this relative?.....................	_____ Years	_____ Years	_____ Years
Approximately, how often do you communicate with this relative?.....................	☐ Every day ☐ Every week ☐ Once a month ☐ Less than once a month	☐ Every day ☐ Every week ☐ Once a month ☐ Less than once a month	☐ Every day ☐ Every week ☐ Once a month ☐ Less than once a month
When you want to communicate with this relative, which of the following do you use most often?.....................	☐ Personal visit ☐ Postal mail ☐ E-mail ☐ Cell phone ☐ Other telephone	☐ Personal visit ☐ Postal mail ☐ E-mail ☐ Cell phone ☐ Other telephone	☐ Personal visit ☐ Postal mail ☐ E-mail ☐ Cell phone ☐ Other telephone
Is this relative in any of the same organizations, clubs or groups as you?	☐ Yes ☐ No ☐ Don't know	☐ Yes ☐ No ☐ Don't know	☐ Yes ☐ No ☐ Don't know

Source: "The Logic and Psychology of Constructing Questionnaires" (pp. 161–175), by D. A. Dillman, in *International Handbook of Survey Methodology,* E. D. de Leeuw, J. J. Hox, and D. A. Dillman (Eds.), 2008, New York: Psychology Press.

GUIDELINES FOR DESIGNING MAIL AND WEB QUESTIONNAIRES

The guidelines we have presented up to this point on ordering the questions and creating a common visual stimulus apply to both mail and web questionnaires. We have highlighted how some of these guidelines may be implemented differently in paper and web surveys; however, the common principles underlying these guidelines are the same for both modes. Because of the underlying technological differences in mail and web surveys and how people relate to these different technologies, we now turn to discussing guidelines for questionnaire construction that are specific to either mail or web surveys.

THE MAIL QUESTIONNAIRE

When the first edition of this book was published in 1978, the possibility of using graphical design features effectively for guiding respondents through questionnaires was quite limited. Paper questionnaires were typically produced by typewriters, which did not allow for bold versus light type and on which shapes (e.g., check boxes) were difficult to create. Vertical spacing, dotted lines to connect text (e.g., opinion items on the left side of page with answer choices on the right), and hand-drawn lines were among the few features that could be easily used in most questionnaires. Black-on-white printing was often the only practical choice.

When the second edition was published in 2000, computers had made possible the use of varied shapes, fonts, and graphical displays. However, printing remained predominantly black on white partly because of the higher costs associated with color printing. We are now in an era when full-color printing has become widely available and less expensive, so even smaller organizations can use color in their questionnaires. Moreover, the linking of computers with printers now offers the possibility of intelligent printing, whereby variable information can be inserted into questionnaires while they are being printed so that each paper questionnaire can, in essence, be a unique document identified by an assigned identification number. The availability of so many different possibilities for printing and improvements in the technologies for achieving the possibilities now give surveyors choices that were considered impossible less than a decade ago and have increased the use of mail surveys in combination with other modes. Color can be used effectively in both web and mail surveys, and rotating and completely randomizing questions or response options are also possible in both modes.

However, mail surveys also have certain limitations that distinguish this mode from others. If people are to be directed to different follow-up items depending upon their answer to a particular question, they must be provided with very specific directions to guide them. In addition, it is not possible to incorporate answers to earlier questions into later questions in order to make later questions clearer and easier to answer as is the case with web surveys and computer-assisted telephone interviews. Neither is it possible to provide automatic totals or feedback when answers to questions are inconsistent with answers to previous items (e.g., when current age is inconsistent with year born). Also, later questions cannot be completely hidden until earlier questions are answered. In addition, it is easy for paper respondents to peruse the entire questionnaire to get a sense of topics covered and length, which may be more difficult to do on the Web.

Guideline 6.13: Determine whether Keypunching or Optical Imaging and Scanning Will Be Used, and Assess the Limitations That May Impose on Designing and Processing Questionnaires

Keypunching (i.e., entering the data from a questionnaire into an electronic spreadsheet) has become an increasingly significant cost for those using paper questionnaires. It is now possible to avoid much of that cost by using software to design, scan, and process questionnaires optically; however, the use of optical scanning places certain limitations on the design of questionnaires. In the past, optical questionnaires were not respondent friendly as they were not visually pleasing, nor were they easy to complete because of the limitations imposed by the technology. For example, the answer spaces needed to be printed in red or other bright inks that contrasted with the black ink used for the answer options with which they were grouped, and there were limitations on which parts of each page could be used for answer categories as well as what kind of mark needed to be made by the respondent. Significant improvements have occurred in optical scanning design software and in the capabilities of scanners during the past decade. In addition, there is no evidence that well-designed questionnaires that can be optically scanned will obtain lower response rates compared to other questionnaires. Several options are available now so that responses can be accepted on any part of the page (except for the extreme margins), and respondents are not as constrained in how they can respond.

Efficiency in processing has advanced significantly as software has made it possible to image the entire questionnaire into a computer. The imaged information can then be processed efficiently by software that is set to make probability decisions on the quality of marks, accepting the likely ones and flagging the questionable ones for a computer operator to examine and make judgments about the respondent's intentions. Scanning entire questionnaires improves the speed of processing because many of the responses can be processed by the software program, and the images are easily viewable for verification when responses cannot be recognized.

Figure 6.8   Graphical designs of answer spaces that affect respondent writing and make optical scanning more effective.

• ●	Small circles or ovals encourage respondents to completely fill the space with a pen or pencil.
☑	Small boxes encourage the making of check marks that are less constrained and may cause difficulties for optical scanning.
☒	An optimally sized box (3/16″ square) encourages respondents to write X's within the box instead of check marks.
☑	A rectangle encourages people to make checks instead of the desired X's.
✓	A large oval encourages the use of a constrained check (or tick). Moreover, it is more acceptable than a box in certain cultures because an X is associated with receiving a bad mark in school.
apple	Undivided blank spaces encourage respondents to write in cursive, the result of which is to make it harder for optical image systems to read the response correctly.
A P P L E	Partially or completely segmented spaces encourage the use of printing (instead of cursive), which can be read more easily by optical image systems.
A P P L E	Segmented spaces printed against a colored background encourage respondents to restrict marks to within the answer spaces.
A P P L E	Segmented square spaces make it more difficult to write characters and numbers because of the unnatural height-to-width ratio.
A P P L E	Too much spacing between spaces requires unnatural hand shifts, thus making it more difficult to provide an answer.

Although different software packages require different kinds of marks, it is important to recognize that the shape and size of spaces one provides send a message about what kind of mark is desired. For example, as shown in Figure 6.8, a small circle (or oval) answer space tends to encourage respondents to fill in the space entirely with a pencil or pen, whereas large ovals tend to encourage tick or check marks. Check marks are a preferred mark in some cultures because of X's being associated with receiving a bad mark in school. When one wants respondents to use an X as is desired in other cultures, a $\frac{3}{16}$″ square box encourages the use of such marks. However, a smaller box encourages the use of check marks as respondents attempt to "hit" the small box with the bottom of the check mark. Such marks are often problematic for processing because of their less controlled nature, which results in the long line after the point reversal producing large marks that interfere with the reading of nearby answer spaces. In addition, it has been found through intensive observation of completed questionnaires that rectangles encourage the use of check marks that produce similar interference with nearby response areas.

A significant barrier to the development of effective optical questionnaires was the entrenched belief that respondent handwriting would be too divergent to ever allow the reading of most people's handwriting. In retrospect this turned out to be a case of defining a problem incorrectly. Instead, people needed to be encouraged to write more clearly, for example by printing instead of using cursive. The use of narrow lines or tick marks to segment answer boxes into a series of connected one-character spaces encourages people to print letters rather than use cursive (Dillman, 1995). It has also been observed that the use of colored backgrounds to surround white answer spaces encourages further improvements in writing by helping people stay inside the desired answer spaces. However, it is important that spaces for printed characters and numbers have greater height than width to accommodate people's natural way of writing. Thus, good questionnaire design has become a way to facilitate intelligent reading of characters, words, and numbers. The recording and processing of longer responses to open-ended questions is facilitated by providing larger blank spaces in which people can write their responses in cursive, which for many people is faster than printing. Once the entire field is imaged into a computer, a trained data entry person can simply process all of the answers to a particular question as a group, typing or coding one answer after another (Dillman, 2000a).

Guideline 6.14: Construct Paper Questionnaires in Booklet Formats, and Choose Physical Dimensions Based upon Printing and Mailing Considerations

To put it simply, questionnaires should be presented in conventional formats that people are used to handling when reading several pages of information. In U.S. culture, the most common format is a book or booklet with pages that are taller than they are wide and that people are used to opening and reading from left to right, top to bottom (and turning pages from right to left). Formats that deviate from this, such as questionnaires with pages that are printed on both sides and stapled in the upper left corner or pages with multiple folds and unusual shapes, should be avoided.

When working on the U.S. Decennial Census in the 1990s, one of us was asked to design alternative one-page forms that could be unfolded so that answers to all of the questions could be scanned in a single operation. Although many formats were extensively tested (including accordion folds, soft-folds [first in half and then in quarters], and a booklet with a single fold-out page), none worked as well as a simple booklet (Dillman, Jackson,

Pavlov, & Schaefer, 1998). A somewhat frustrated participant in these projects, after observing pages left blank and refolded questionnaires that would not fit into envelopes, noticed that when questionnaires look like maps, people treat them like maps and are unable to refold them in their original form. It is also important to print questions in a portrait rather than landscape format. When the paper is longer than it is wide, it helps to reinforce the vertical format and conventional reading patterns.

When using booklets, it is important to factor in several issues related to designing, printing, and mailing differently sized booklets. It is important to realize that when one uses booklet construction, pages have to be added or deleted in units of four. The decision to add or delete a sheet of paper (i.e., 4 pages) often has consequences for the costs of mailing and printing the questionnaires. Many office printers can now print and staple booklets, although paper size requirements may need to be met. For example, some common printers will print questionnaires on legal-size paper (8.5″ × 14″) with two pages on each side, fold, and then staple the resulting booklet so that individual questionnaire pages are 8.5″ × 7″ (see Figure 6.9). These questionnaires can then be folded lengthwise to fit into regular #10 business mail envelopes (4.125″ × 9.5″), which is an envelope size commonly used for correspondence.

A more common format prints the questionnaire pages using 11″ × 17″ paper, which can then be folded into a conventional 8.5″ × 11″ booklet and fit

Figure 6.9 Example of booklet questionnaire made from legal-size paper (8.5″ × 14″).

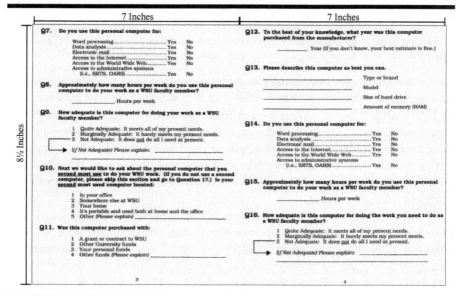

into 9″ × 12″ clasp envelopes for mailing. This size booklet is more commonly encountered by respondents, and its larger size often makes it easier for respondents to use. If one chooses to go to a professional printer, one's options are expanded, and even more paper and color options may be available. However, it is important to assess the effect of the size of the questionnaire on printing and mailing costs, as discussed in more detail in Chapter 7, Guideline 7.8.

Guideline 6.15: Decide Question Layout and How Questions Will Be Arranged on Each Page

Once the size of the booklet has been decided, the next step is determining the graphical layout of individual pages. In the legal-size folded format shown in Figure 6.9, the questions are aligned in a single column on each page. If the larger size booklet is used with questionnaire pages that are 8.5″ × 11″, the page can be divided into two columns so that the span of type being read does not extend entirely across the page. The example in Figure 6.10 shows relatively short questions for which the two-column format works well because it allows more questions per page and contributes to more accurate reading and comprehension of each question (see Guideline 4.19 in Chapter 4).

A one-column format can also be used with the larger size booklet, particularly when longer or more complex questions are included; however, this format can be difficult for some respondents as lines of text extend all the way across the page and a larger eye motion is needed to move from the end of one line to the beginning of the next. One benefit of this format is that it can more closely emulate web survey screens, which are usually constructed with questions that read all the way across the width of the screen. In addition to using a one-column format, the example shown in Figure 6.11 encloses each question in a separate region, more similar to how questions would appear in a page-by-page web survey. This format was developed for a mixed-mode survey that is discussed in considerably more depth in Chapter 7.

All three of these different formats can be developed using common word processing programs that are available to most surveyors. The examples shown in Figures 6.9 through 6.11 incorporate the guidelines for visually designing questionnaire pages discussed earlier, although in somewhat different ways. Overall, the most important decisions to make when constructing paper questionnaires are how the questionnaire will be presented to respondents (in a booklet format or not), what size the questionnaire will be, and how the questions will be arranged on the page.

Grouping questions on one page in paper questionnaires presents both problems and opportunities. One problem is that there is a considerable risk that when people turn pages, they do not carry over information well from the previous page. A second problem is that sometimes related questions, such as a series of queries about one's job experiences after college graduation, need to

Figure 6.10 Example of a double-column page from an 8.5″ × 11″ booklet questionnaire.

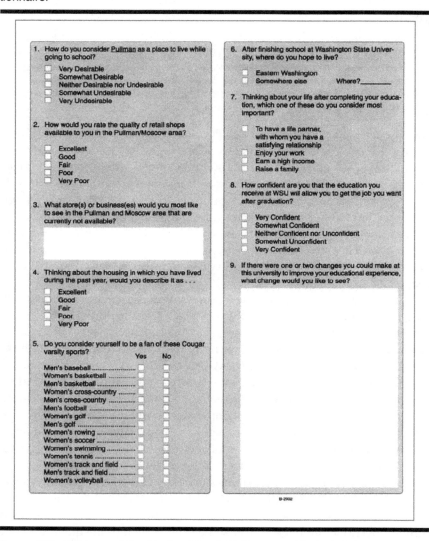

Source: "The Influence of Graphical and Symbolic Language Manipulations on Responses to Self-Administered Questions," by L. M. Christian and D. A. Dillman, 2004, *Public Opinion Quarterly, 68*(1), pp. 58–81.

be grouped on one page or in one section. In these situations, it is important to design questionnaires so that the entire sequence can be viewed on one page or on two facing pages. Requiring respondents to turn pages within these sequences or sections can interrupt them and impact their responses. When several related questions need to be viewed on one page in web surveys, they

Figure 6.11 Example of a paper questionnaire designed to emulate a page-by-page web questionnaire for a mixed-mode study (8.5″ × 11″ booklet).

Q1. Approximately how many years have you lived in the Lewiston-Clarkston area?

☐ Years

Q2. Overall, how satisfied are you with living in this area?

O₁ Very satisfied
O₂ Somewhat satisfied
O₃ Neutral
O₄ Somewhat dissatisfied
O₅ Very dissatisfied

O₆ Not sure

Q3. How attached do you feel to the Lewiston-Clarkston area?

O₁ Very attached
O₂ Somewhat attached
O₃ Slightly attached
O₄ Not at all attached

O₅ Not sure

Q4. During the past five years, how much better or worse do you think Lewiston-Clarkston has become as a place to live?

O₁ A lot better
O₂ Somewhat better
O₃ No change
O₄ Somewhat worse
O₅ A lot worse

O₆ Not sure

Q5. How much better or worse do you think the local economy has become in the past five years?

O₁ A lot better
O₂ Somewhat better
O₃ No change
O₄ Somewhat worse
O₅ A lot worse

O₆ Not sure

Q6. How much better or worse do you think the area's natural environment has become in the past five years?

O₁ A lot better
O₂ Somewhat better
O₃ No change
O₄ Somewhat worse
O₅ A lot worse

O₆ Not sure

1

Source: "Will a Mixed-Mode (Mail/Internet) Procedure Work for Random Household Surveys of the General Public?" by D. A. Dillman, J. D. Smyth, L. M. Christian, and A. O'Neill, 2008, May, New Orleans, LA. Paper presented at the annual conference of the American Association for Public Opinion Research.

are often grouped together on one screen so that respondents need to scroll down to view the later questions (see Guideline 6.23 for a discussion of the paging of web surveys).

In contrast, placing information on different pages allows items to be separated when there is concern about respondents referring back to earlier questions when answering later ones or when surveyors prefer that one question does not immediately impact the context for another related question. In sum, it is important to contemplate individual page content as both a problem and an opportunity for which a balanced solution needs to be found. Unfortunately, responding to this challenge is sometimes made more difficult when using booklet designs where two pages are often viewable at a time; however, these facing pages are more conducive for complex series of questions where multiple pages are needed to present all of the questions in the sequence.

Guideline 6.16: Use Symbols, Contrast, Size, Proximity, and Pagination Effectively When Designing Branching Instructions to Help Respondents Correctly Execute Them

One of the most significant differences between web and paper questionnaires is that branching instructions for paper surveys must be executed by the respondent so they need to be made explicit. Getting some people to skip questions they should not answer while convincing other respondents not to skip ahead remains one of the most perplexing problems facing mail survey designers. Two experiments—the first, a classroom experiment with 1,267 respondents; and the second, a field test of about 12,500 households in the 2000 U.S. Decennial Census—have now been conducted on how to achieve this goal (Redline et al., 2003). The first experiment involved a specially constructed questionnaire that was four pages long and included 52 questions, 24 of which contained branching instructions asking respondents to answer different follow-up questions depending on which answer category was initially selected. The second experiment was built based on the lessons learned in the first and was embedded in the Census Long Form, which contained 53 questions, 19 of which included branching instructions (Redline, Dillman, Carley-Baxter, & Creecy, 2005).

In both studies, a combination of factors designed to get people to follow branching instructions correctly were tested. One procedure, the *detection method*, involved using an arrow symbol in a large, dark font to direct people from their answer either to the next question or to an appropriate instruction that was written in a larger, darker font than the questions. Words were used at the beginning of the next question to remind respondents who should and who should not answer it (e.g., "If Yes"). A second procedure, the *prevention method*, moved the answer boxes from the left of the answer categories to the right so that skip instructions could be located within the respondent's

Figure 6.12 Examples of different branching instruction designs used in class-room experiment and national census test in the 2000 Decennial Census.

Treatments:		Classroom Error Rate (%)	Census Error Rate (%)
Control form: Standard format used in Decennial Census with written instructions	30 a. LAST YEAR, 1999, did this person work at a job or business at any time? ☐ Yes ☐ No → *Go to 31* **b. How many weeks did this person work in 1999?**	22.3	25.8
Prevention method: Advanced verbal warning; shift answer box to right; and larger, bolder font	30 Attention: Remember to check for a "Go to" instruction after you answer the question below. a. LAST YEAR, 1999, did this person work at a job or business at any time? Yes ☐ No ☐ → *Go to 31* b. How many weeks did this person work in 1999?	11.3	17.5
Detection method: Arrows, larger and bolder fonts plus verbal feedback	30 a. LAST YEAR, 1999, did this person work at a job or business at any time? ☐ Yes ☐ No → *Go to 31* b. (If Yes) How many weeks did this person work in 1999? *Count paid vacation, paid sick leave, and military*	12.3	21.7

Note: Error rates shown here include commission errors (not skipping ahead when directed) and omission errors (skipping ahead when not directed). Advanced verbal warning used only in the Classroom Experiment. Statistically significant difference in total error rates between the control form and each of the two methods with p<.01 for both experiments.

Source: "The Influence of Alternative Visual Design on Respondents' Performance with Branching Instructions in Self-Administered Questionnaires" (pp. 179–196), by C. D. Redline and D. A. Dillman, in *Survey Nonresponse,* R. Groves, D. Dillman, J. Eltinge, and R. Little (Eds.), 2002, Hoboken, NJ: Wiley.

foveal view when focusing on the answer box. These instructions were written in larger, darker print and were placed against a darker background. The control instructions were written in the same font as the questions, as shown in Figure 6.12.

In the Decennial Census experiment, the detection method reduced the proportion of branching errors significantly, lowering *commission errors* (i.e., not skipping ahead when directed to do so) from 21% to 13% and *omission errors* (i.e., skipping ahead when not directed to do so) from 5% to 4%. The total error rates (commission and omission error rates combined) were lower for both the detection and prevention groups compared to the control group, where errors were made nearly 26% of the time (see Figure 6.12). The conclusions drawn from these experiments were that both of these methods were effective in helping respondents follow the desired navigational path. They also provide evidence of the substantial effects that the combined use of symbols, wording, size, contrast, and proximity can have on task-oriented processing. This research also revealed that branching instructions would most likely be ignored when they extended from one page to the next (Redline et al., 2005). These findings have led to the practice of making strong design efforts to avoid having the last question on a page branch any respondent somewhere other than to the first question on the next page, even if a slight reordering of questions is needed in order to avoid that situation.

Guideline 6.17: Create Interesting and Informative Front and Back Cover Pages that Will Have Wide Appeal to Respondents

In the 1990s a national survey being designed at the U.S. Census Bureau was being proposed as a replacement for the Decennial Census Long Form, which every 10 years had collected detailed demographic information for 1 in 6 households. The long form made it possible for virtually all jurisdictions in the United States, even quite small ones, to obtain information about the education, occupations, commuting behavior, and income of the people who lived there. The new survey that was proposed to replace it was to be mailed by the Census Bureau to several hundred thousand households each year. The large title placed on the cover was "The Continuous Measurement Survey." When it was pointed out to the director of the Census Bureau that the title, while technically correct, was unappealing to most people, a decision was quickly made to change it to "The American Community Survey," which it remains today.

Often, when surveys are designed, they are assigned functional names that may describe the purpose from the perspective of the surveyors but that have no meaning whatsoever to respondents. Titles need to describe what a survey is about but also have broad appeal to the respondents who receive it. At the same time, care must be taken not to use a title that makes the questionnaire appeal to some types of respondents while being a turn-off to others. Thus, one would not title a survey on political views "The Problems with the Current Presidential Administration." That would seem likely to attract people who do not like the president and turn off those who do.

This challenge of choosing a title and cover page that appeals to sample respondents was faced in a recent survey of a small metropolitan area, the focus of which was to understand key issues affecting the quality of life in the area and use of communication technologies, particularly Internet and cell phones (Dillman et al., 2008). The title of this survey became "Lewiston and Clarkston Quality of Life Survey," as shown in Figure 6.13. A brief statement describing the study in general terms as well as contact information for the sponsor were also included on the front cover, as was a color picture of the region depicting where the two communities meet, an image that is immediately identifiable to anyone living there.

The back cover of the questionnaire thanked respondents for completing the questionnaire and asked for any additional comments about the study. The address to which respondents should mail the questionnaire was also repeated on the back page. Additional color photos of other key aspects of both communities were selected for the back cover to continue the appeal to survey respondents.

It is important to design questionnaire covers that look interesting and appeal to as wide a spectrum of the survey population as possible. The cover pages should (a) have a clear title respondents can understand, (b) identify the sponsor, and (c) encourage respondents to want to open the questionnaire and complete the survey. It is also important for the questionnaire covers to connect to the other implementation materials, as is discussed for web opening screens in Chapter 7 (Guideline 7.25).

Guideline 6.18: Avoid Placing Questions Side by Side on a Page so that Respondents Are Asked to Answer Two Questions at Once

In Chapter 4 we discussed the importance of not asking respondents to answer more than one question posed as a single question. Here we are concerned with the related, yet distinctly different, issue of arranging two or more questions on a page (i.e., page layout). Questionnaire designers are often tempted to ask respondents to simultaneously answer two or more different questions that are arranged side by side on a page. To some extent this practice is a holdover from the days when paper questionnaire designers did everything possible to reduce questionnaire page length by simultaneously introducing two questions that used some of the same information and then displaying them so that respondents were encouraged to process both at the same time. For example, Figure 6.14 shows a multiple-part question in which women in farm and ranch families were first asked how often they do each job and then were asked if they would prefer to do each job less, the same, or more.

Such questions exhibit two problems. One is that they require a respondent to make a choice between toggling back and forth between items or answering one question and then reprocessing each item over again to answer the other. Some respondents choose one path, whereas others go a different route, in essence exposing themselves to a different sequence. In addition, frequent testing of such questions has led us to the conclusion that they are difficult and more likely to produce item nonresponse. In this particular example, 11% of respondents left at least one item in Question 11 (frequency of doing the job) unanswered, and fewer than 1% skipped the question entirely. However, 35% of respondents left at least one item in Question 12 (preferred frequency) unanswered, and, even with the additional reminder to go back and answer this question, 5% skipped it altogether.

Although number of pages is less of a concern with web surveys, the horizontal orientation of computer screens sometimes tempts designers to place questions side by side in this manner. The larger design issue that discourages this practice is the desire to design a single vertical navigational path through the questionnaire that all respondents are encouraged to follow so that they process questions in the intended order.

Figure 6.13 Examples of interesting and appealing front and back cover pages designed to appeal to sample members.

Source: "Will a Mixed-Mode (Mail/Internet) Procedure work for Random Household Surveys of the General Public?" by D. A. Dillman, J. D. Smyth, L. M. Christian, and A. O'Neill, 2008, May, New Orleans, LA. Paper presented at the annual conference of the American Association for Public Opinion Research.

Figure 6.13   (*Continued*)

Thanks again for completing this survey!

If you have any additional thoughts about any of the above topics or the survey itself, please share them here.

Social and Economic Sciences Research Center
Washington State University
PO Box 641801
Pullman, WA 99164-1801

THE WEB QUESTIONNAIRE

In less than a decade, the survey world has been turned upside down by the introduction of web surveys. Now more surveys than ever are being conducted because of the low cost of many web surveys. The beauty of a web survey is that once it is launched it can, in principle, be completed very

Figure 6.14   Example of double question grid format.

11. Please indicate whether you regularly, occasionally, or never do each type of work listed below. If a type of work is not done on your farm/ranch, please mark Does Not Apply and continue to the next type.

Type of Work	Does Not Apply	How often do you do each job? Reg.	Occ.	Never	Would you prefer doing each job... Less	Same	More
Plowing, disking, planting or harvesting	☐	☐	☐	☐	☐	☐	☐
Applying fertilizers, herbicides, or insecticides	☐	☐	☐	☐	☐	☐	☐
Driving large trucks	☐	☐	☐	☐	☐	☐	☐
Doing fieldwork without machinery	☐	☐	☐	☐	☐	☐	☐
Caring for horses	☐	☐	☐	☐	☐	☐	☐
Doing farm/ranch work with horses	☐	☐	☐	☐	☐	☐	☐
Checking cattle	☐	☐	☐	☐	☐	☐	☐
Calving/pulling calves	☐	☐	☐	☐	☐	☐	☐
Feeding cattle	☐	☐	☐	☐	☐	☐	☐
Vaccinating cattle	☐	☐	☐	☐	☐	☐	☐
Branding, dehorning, or castrating cattle	☐	☐	☐	☐	☐	☐	☐
Running farm/ranch errands	☐	☐	☐	☐	☐	☐	☐
Fixing or maintaining equipment	☐	☐	☐	☐	☐	☐	☐
Making major equipment purchases	☐	☐	☐	☐	☐	☐	☐
Marketing products	☐	☐	☐	☐	☐	☐	☐
Bookkeeping, records, finances, or taxes	☐	☐	☐	☐	☐	☐	☐
Supervising the farm/ranch work of others	☐	☐	☐	☐	☐	☐	☐
Caring for garden or animals for family use	☐	☐	☐	☐	☐	☐	☐
Caring for children or elderly family members	☐	☐	☐	☐	☐	☐	☐
Working on another family/in-home business	☐	☐	☐	☐	☐	☐	☐

12. Now, if you haven't already done so, please return to the list of jobs above and indicate in the right hand columns whether you prefer to do each job less, the same amount, or more than you currently do.

Source: Doing Gender When Home and Work Are Blurred: Women and Sex-Atypical Tasks in Family Farming, by J. D. Smyth, 2007, Pullman, WA: Washington State University. Unpublished doctoral dissertation.

quickly by large numbers of people and at low cost. Thousands or even tens of thousands of questionnaires can be completed in a single day and the results released. As a result, as discussed in Chapter 1, many surveys have shifted from being an interviewer–respondent conversation over the telephone or in person to being a visually delivered request over the Internet. However, in practice, there are many barriers to web survey success.

Although web surveys were conducted a decade ago when the second edition of this book was written, there were many significant technical and social barriers to their widespread use, and response rates were often low. Only a third of households in the United States had Internet connections, connections were very slow (it sometimes took many minutes for questions and answers to be sent back and forth) or would break off entirely, and there was huge variation in the technology used by both respondents and surveyors.

Much has changed since 1998, and the majority of U.S. households now have access to the Internet, many of them through high-speed connections, as discussed in Chapter 3. In some populations, nearly all members have high-speed connections. Although some problems remain (e.g., some surveys are too sophisticated for the hardware and software available to many respondents, and many users do not update their browsers), a tipping point has been reached for many populations. As the examples throughout this book have shown, some surveys can now be done entirely on the Web without concern about people being unable to respond.

Along with these new capabilities, there are also challenges that are yet to be solved. The Web remains an unsafe environment and one that many respondents fear. The anonymity of the Internet allows people to pretend to represent other legitimate organizations, such as banking and credit card companies or government entities, to try to gain access to financial or other sensitive information, to send bogus offers of rewards for going to certain web sites, and to encourage people to purchase products that are never sent and sometimes do not even exist. Thus, surveyors have to be careful to ensure that their survey requests are not viewed suspiciously or thought to be an effort to trick the respondent into taking a computer action that will deliver a computer virus or worm. Techniques for doing this are discussed in more detail in Chapter 7.

To provide context for understanding the guidelines that follow, it is useful to start with a brief introduction to the Internet and how web surveys are conducted. The Internet consists of many independent networks around the world that use a standard protocol (TCP/IP) to exchange information electronically. The World Wide Web (www) uses a standard hypertext transport protocol (http) to exchange information over the Internet, and web pages are formatted using hypertext markup language (HTML) and other programming technologies and stored on web servers. Users, or potential respondents, connect their computers to this network through a telephone cord, cable wire, or satellite and through software on their computers called a *browser* (e.g., Internet Explorer, Firefox, or Safari). Once respondents open their browsers, they can connect to a specific server and web page by entering a web address or uniform resource locator (URL). That server then sends the web page associated with that URL to the user's computer in the form of code, which the browser translates into a viewable web page.

A web survey is made up of a web page or series of web pages containing survey questions formatted most commonly in HTML that are stored on a server so that respondents with the proper URL can access them through their computers and the Internet. Survey sponsors send requests, often by e-mail but also by mail or telephone, to the person (or unit) from whom a response is desired and provide the URL for the web survey (and often an individual identification code). After respondents enter the URL into the browser's address bar, they are usually first routed to a welcome or introductory screen that briefly describes the survey and asks them to proceed with the questionnaire. Once respondents begin the survey and answer the questions, their answers are sent back to the web server after they press the "submit" or "next" button. Their responses may be reviewed by the survey software and are stored in a database on the server. What this means, in essence, is that surveyors have to translate their questionnaire designs into computer code to be stored on a server. They also have to design databases that will store survey responses in an accurate, organized, meaningful, and accessible way on the server.

Another factor that has contributed to the growth in web surveying is the wide variety of ways that technical aspects of building and hosting a web survey can be managed. Perhaps the simplest and least expensive is by using one of several free or inexpensive software applications provided on the Web. In this case, the surveyor designs the survey and contacts using point-and-click software available via the Web through a specific company. The surveyor makes a series of very simple and limited design decisions, which the software then translates into the proper computer code that will be needed to form the web pages and the database. The survey is then hosted on the company's servers and, when complete, the surveyor can access the data or data reports, depending on the level of service initially selected. Although easy and inexpensive, many such services have a number of limitations that should be considered very carefully, such as limited design options, implementation procedures and control over the actual data.

Another option is to use off-the-shelf software that allows people to design, host, and implement web surveys without needing to have high-level programming skills. In recent years there has been rapid improvement in this type of software, including more options of software to use and more design options within many of the programs themselves. In addition, numerous organizations have emerged that will serve as a host for one's survey, allowing one to build the questionnaire following the rules of the host organization, which will collect the data. Both of these options often limit the control that surveyors can have over the design and hosting of the survey as well as the contacting of potential respondents.

A final option is to program and host the survey from scratch. Many people have the programming skills needed for designing and implementing surveys as well as an understanding of the methodological issues involved (or they work with people who have the methodological understanding), so many organizations are now able to program and host their own surveys. Some organizations have even developed their own software and systems for collecting and analyzing data. Some of these systems are quite sophisticated, allowing one to innovate new ways of collecting and processing data, whereas others are more rudimentary. Conducting surveys from the ground up in this way provides the most design flexibility and ability to innovate, but it is also often the most expensive option.

The guidelines presented here are aimed at helping surveyors work their way through the development and design of a web survey in ways that will encourage responses from many types of respondents. These guidelines address many of the technological issues of constructing web surveys as well as decisions about formatting and displaying the questionnaire to respondents. Although the design and implementation of web survey questionnaires are related, we discuss specifics about implementing web surveys in the next chapter.

Guideline 6.19: Decide whether an Electronic Alternative to a Web Survey Is More Appropriate (e.g., Fillable PDF or Embedded E-Mail Survey)

The advancement of computer and web technologies has resulted in various electronic alternatives to the traditional web survey. For example, fillable PDF forms are often used to survey establishments where respondents may print off a paper copy of the questionnaire that they can pass or carry around to all of the appropriate people to answer the questions or where they may need to keep a paper copy for their records. Software is also now available to allow respondents to enter answers electronically into a PDF file that can then be e-mailed back to the surveyor for data entry. Moreover, some software that is available for designing such fillable PDFs also has the capability to read responses into a data set, thus eliminating manual data entry. One advantage of fillable forms is that respondents can download the entire document and complete it on their computer; however, they do need to install Adobe Acrobat Reader on their computer to be able to complete the survey in this format (this program is free, and many people already have it on their computers). Although PDF forms can be quite handy in some situations, one drawback is that responses are submitted to the server all at one time, so respondents must complete the entire form and submit it for responses to be registered.

Another alternative to the traditional web survey is to embed questions directly into an e-mail that is then sent to the survey population. This methodology was discussed in the previous edition of this book as a possibility, but it was argued that e-mailed surveys are mostly impractical because as answers are entered, text in the questions moves, making the final document difficult to process. In addition, the visual appearance of the e-mail survey may differ for respondents depending on how they read their e-mail—online through one of many Web-based e-mail providers, or through a software program on their own computer. On the flip side, it is now possible to send HTML (rather than plain-text) e-mails that include more advanced formatting so that the questionnaire appears more like a traditional web format and images can be included in the e-mail. However, some e-mail providers will accept only plain-text e-mails or may caution respondents before images or other advanced formatting are displayed (for more on this, see Guideline 7.22 in Chapter 7). Overall, it is important to evaluate whether one of these formats may be more appropriate for one's survey needs, as they are often less costly than fully interactive web surveys.

Guideline 6.20: Choose How the Survey Will Be Programmed and Hosted Commensurate with the Needs, Skills, and Sponsorship of Each Survey

It is important to assess whether an organization has the capability of conducting and implementing a web survey that meets the desired goals. Some people have the training that allows them to design and program all aspects of their own web surveys and are located in an organization that provides the needed server capabilities and protection (including backups) to host the survey, receive the data, and send e-mail contacts to potential respondents. In addition, they or others in the organization can troubleshoot and manage survey and technical issues that may arise in the process. If one's organization does not have the capabilities to design, host, and implement a wide range of web surveys, there are several other alternatives, as we discussed earlier, for programming and hosting a web survey. Designing and hosting surveys has also become an activity in which some people and organizations have become specialists. It may be necessary to contract out the programming and hosting of the survey to these people or organizations. Others may instead decide to purchase a software package that can help with designing and managing the implementation of the survey, particularly if they plan to conduct a large number of web surveys. Thus, it is important for surveyors to think about the expectations they have for collecting data and choose from these alternatives for designing and hosting web surveys commensurate with those needs.

Guideline 6.21: Evaluate the Technological Capabilities of the Survey Population

It is important to design the web survey with the survey population in mind. Survey populations vary in their access to the necessary technology to complete a web survey and their understanding of how the technology and the process works (see elaboration in Chapter 3). Some people may not be familiar with completing surveys on the Web and will need more instruction about how to access and complete the survey (see Guideline 7.24). In addition, as computer technology expands, there is a wide variation in the types of devices available to people for accessing the Internet, including desktop computers, laptops, and handheld or other types of devices (all with varying screen sizes and with a range of processors, memory, and hard drive sizes). Although more people are getting high-speed Internet connections (T1, DSL, and cable) as discussed in Chapter 3, a large number of respondents are still using dial-up connections (56k and even 14.4k modems), which are much slower. Moreover, high-speed connections often vary in how fast respondents can download and upload information. In addition, the availability of new browsers has expanded as more people are online, and most browsers are constantly providing updates and new plug-ins that are required to view specific web pages. However, some people may not have the most updated version of their browser or may not have installed these additional plug-ins. Lastly, there is also wide variation in user settings, and as people become more computer savvy, they are more likely to customize their settings, which expands the variation. Thus, it is important to assess the technological capabilities of the population for each survey that is conducted, recognizing the speed at which technological changes are being adopted across many populations.

Guideline 6.22: Take Steps to Ensure that Questions Display Similarly across Different Platforms, Browsers, and User Settings

Because of differences in hardware and software configurations and in individual user settings, the way that web surveys are displayed can vary widely across respondents. As a result, it is necessary to take additional steps to try to control the effects of configurations and settings on the visual display of questions in an effort to try to ensure that every respondent receives the same stimulus. One step that can be taken in the web survey programming is to separate the content of the survey from the stylistic elements (e.g., fonts, font sizes, color, widths, alignment, and other aspects of visual presentation) by using cascading style sheets (CSS). Cascading style sheets allow the programmer to specify the order and precedence in which various styles should be applied depending on user configurations and settings such as screen resolution. In other words, they allow the programmer to tailor how information is presented to different types of browsers, handheld devices, and other equipment used to display web surveys in an effort to minimize variations in how web pages appear visually. As a simple example, if one respondent has a high screen resolution, which makes items on the screen appear small, the CSS programming will make the survey pages display with a larger font (e.g., 20 point). If another respondent has a very low screen resolution, which tends to make items on the screen look big, the CSS programming will make the survey pages display with a smaller font (e.g., 12 point). Despite the respondents' different screen resolutions, the size of the text will appear very similarly for both of these respondents because the CSS programming adjusts the display to make up for differences due to resolution. Thus, it is important for web surveyors to use CSS and other newer advancements in web programming to have greater control over how web questionnaires appear to survey respondents.

Another programming tool that can be used to help standardize the appearance of web survey screens across various user configurations is the HTML table. In essence, the survey content is programmed into tables where the column widths are set as proportions of the screen so that they adjust appropriately if the browser window size is changed. What this does is help minimize the effects of changes in browser window size on the visual appearance of the web page.

Guideline 6.23: Decide How Many Questions Will Be Presented on Each Web Page and How Questions Will Be Arranged

One of the most important decisions in designing a web questionnaire is how many questions will be presented on each screen or page. Web surveys can present one question per page, multiple questions per page, or all of the survey questions on one page. However, several important implications need to be considered when deciding how many questions will be presented on each page.

When all of the questions are presented on one page, the web questionnaire more closely approximates a paper survey because the respondent can preview the entire questionnaire before answering questions and then scroll forward and backward within it while answering (Dillman, 2000a). It has been argued that respondents can make a more informed decision about whether to complete the survey when they can see the entire questionnaire (Crawford, Couper, & Lamias, 2001). However, this format also has several limitations. Depending on the length of the survey, respondents may have to scroll through lots of questions in the questionnaire, thus increasing the chances that they will miss questions or even entire sets of questions. Branching formats or skip patterns may also be difficult for respondents to execute, similar to paper surveys. In addition, responses are usually not submitted to the server and stored in the database until the respondent completes all of the questions and clicks a button to submit the responses; no data are captured for respondents who break off after completing only a portion of the survey. JavaScript or other programming technologies can be used to capture responses more often in scroll designs, but some people disable scripting on their computers. Their data will be lost if they break off without submitting at the end of the survey. Lastly, this format limits the ability to use many of the interactive features of web surveys (e.g., asking follow-up questions based on previous answers, performing automatic calculations, etc.) for the same reason. That is, many interactive features rely on JavaScript or related programming that can be disabled by respondents, so no-script backup options must be provided for these people.

Some web surveyors are using a hybrid of this scrollable web survey format in which more interactive features can be programmed into the survey and responses can sometimes be saved before the entire questionnaire is completed. In this hybrid version, respondents start with several questions on the page, but after they enter a response or sometimes press a "submit" button, subsequent questions will appear (on the same page) or questions already on the page may be modified based on their responses. An example of a fairly long questionnaire that used this hybrid scrollable format was developed for potential use in the 2006 New Zealand Census. In this questionnaire, if a respondent answered a question in a way that made later questions inapplicable, the inapplicable questions were "grayed out," in effect deemphasizing them and signaling the respondent to skip them (Potaka, 2008; Statistics New Zealand, 2006). But once again, such interactive features depend on JavaScript or related programming that can be disabled by respondents.

In contrast to presenting all of the questions on one page, web surveys can present each question on its own page and require respondents to click a button to move from page to page. In this format responses can be saved to the server database each time the "submit" button is pressed. One of the main strengths of this construction is that surveyors receive responses to each question even if respondents choose not to complete the entire survey (which can be helpful in understanding where, and sometimes why, people are terminating the survey). Because of this continuous interaction with the server, more interactive capabilities can be utilized, such as automatically branching respondents to subsequent follow-up questions, modifying questions based on responses to previous questions, or collecting certain paradata for each question (see later discussion under Guideline 6.32). The page-by-page design format may be best for questionnaires with complex skip patterns because it gives the surveyor control over which questions come next rather than having to rely on the respondent to correctly interpret instructions. An additional benefit is that with page-by-page construction it is often easier for respondents to know where to focus their attention because every question can appear in the same location (horizontal and vertical alignment) on the pages, an element of consistency that can reduce item nonresponse.

On the negative side, questionnaires that are constructed with each question on its own page often take longer to complete (Couper et al., 2001; Manfreda, Batagelj, & Vehovar, 2002). In addition, because the questions are viewed in isolation, respondents may have difficulty remembering the context established by previous questions and may need to review their previous responses to remind themselves of that context. Likewise, respondents who need to remember their answers to a previous question in order to answer a subsequent question or ensure they are not being redundant will face extra difficulty because reviewing previous questions in the page-by-page format is much more difficult than in a scrolling design. Moreover, respondents who temporarily quit the survey and then come back later to complete it may have difficulty remembering where they left off or the context of the questions. Thus, it is important for respondents to be able to move both forward and backward in the survey and to be able to see their previous answers when questions are presented on their own pages. However, even when respondents can move backward in the survey, effort needs to be made to make sure each question can stand alone (i.e., can be understood without needing to refer to previous questions).

A final format for constructing web questionnaires, and one of the most commonly used, is that in which multiple questions are presented on one page and respondents navigate between multiple web pages. This format is often used when surveyors want to group related questions (e.g., several questions about a current job position) or questions that use a common scale format. Grouping questions can help respondents as they answer the questions and can reduce the number of pages that respondents need to navigate (particularly with longer questionnaires). However, similar to findings on paper surveys (Schwarz, 1996), research on web surveys has shown that when questions appear on the same page, there is a higher correlation among answers across the items (Couper et al., 2001; Tourangeau et al., 2004). Thus, when choosing to group multiple questions on the page, it is important to select questions that are related, otherwise respondents may try to make connections across questions that the researcher does not intend.

In today's world of web surveying, which of these formats is used depends on the particular needs of each survey. Presenting all of the questions on one page is usually used for shorter questionnaires for which only a limited number of questions need to be answered. Presenting each question on its own page is also typically used for somewhat shorter surveys (where navigation between screens does not get too cumbersome) or when complex skip patterns or other interactive features need to be included. Constructing web surveys with multiple questions per page is often used for longer surveys and for surveys in which grouping questions on a page can help respondents process them.

Guideline 6.24: Create Interesting and Informative Welcome and Closing Screens that Will Have Wide Appeal to Respondents

When web survey respondents enter the survey URL into their Internet browser or click on the link provided in the e-mail, they first see the opening screen. This page helps orient respondents by providing a description of the survey and instructions for how to proceed. It also serves much the same function as the cover page of a mail questionnaire in that it is the first experience the respondent gets with the actual questionnaire, and for many ambivalent respondents it is where they either make a commitment to start the survey or decide against doing so. As a result, the opening screen must provide immediate and clear confirmation that the respondent has accessed the correct page and be welcoming and encouraging in ways that have wide appeal to potential survey respondents.

One of us recently received a survey in which the first text on the opening screen stated the following: "No parts of this survey may be copied or used without written permission of [company name]. Requests should be mailed to [company name and address]. Use of this survey without written permission is punishable by law." Starting off with this somewhat cold tone is not what one wants to do if trying to convince undecided respondents who have reached the opening screen to go ahead and launch into the questionnaire. It immediately subordinates the respondent to the interests of the surveyor in a quite threatening way and implies that the respondent and the surveyor have conflicting interests. If this type of information must be included to protect proprietary survey measures (as was probably the case in this instance) or for any other reason, it should be placed after a more welcoming message and perhaps even downplayed through the use of properties such as font size or color.

Figure 6.15 shows an example of a web page that was designed in a much more welcoming manner. The text on this opening screen describes the survey in a nonthreatening way. As in this example, the opening screen should include the title of the survey, a brief description of its purpose, and instructions for how to proceed. Most opening screens also include a space for respondents to enter individual access codes, a topic covered in more depth in Chapter 7. This particular screen also includes additional information about participants' rights in the study and contact information that can be used if they have questions. The photo that is displayed was selected very carefully because of its appeal to those in the target population (more on this in Chapter 7). Such photos, however, should not be used without careful consideration of how they may affect both the decision to respond and the responses people give to individual questions.

Surveyors also frequently place sponsorship and other information on the welcome screen to encourage respondents to begin the survey. However, information of this sort should be arranged so that it does not interfere with the major function of the page (i.e., getting respondents into the survey), and it should be easily connected with other implementation features (see Chapter 7).

The message in the closing screen should also be written in a friendly, professional manner and should both tell the respondents that they have completed the survey and portray gratitude. In the example shown in Figure 6.15, respondents are informed that their questionnaire has been received, a message that tells them that they have entirely completed the survey task and can direct their browser to other web pages without losing information. In addition, consistent with social exchange, the final message respondents receive from the surveyor is a reward—gratitude for the effort they have put forth.

Guideline 6.25: Develop a Screen Format that Emphasizes the Respondent Rather than the Sponsor

When designing web questionnaires, it is important to approach design from the respondents' perspective and design pages that are appealing and interesting to respondents (similar to the welcome screen discussed previously). For example, repeating the title from the opening page and choosing a simple graphic that respondents identify with to repeat across each page can help encourage participation by focusing attention on respondents (see

Figure 6.15   Examples of interesting and informative welcome and closing pages for a web questionnaire.

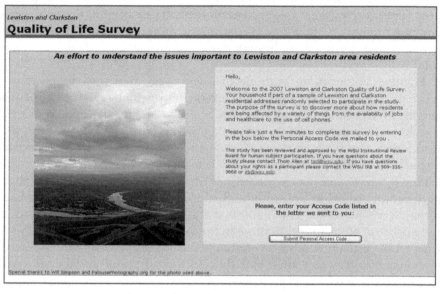

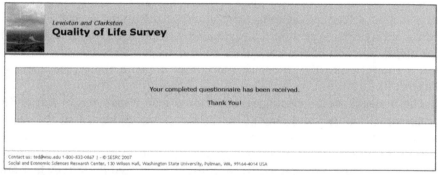

Source: "Combining Mail and Internet Methods to Conduct Household Surveys of the General Public: A New Methodology?" by D. A. Dillman, J. D. Smyth, L. M. Christian, and A. O'Neill, 2008, May, New Orleans, LA. Paper presented at the annual conference of the American Association for Public Opinion Research.

Figure 6.16). In contrast, a survey that includes a title such as "Annual Federal Assessment of Juvenile Delinquency" and images of multiple delinquent behaviors focuses more on the sponsor's needs and why the survey is being conducted than on the respondent. In addition, the use of selected images may even bias how respondents answer individual questions. For example, it has been found that people rate their own health better in web surveys

Figure 6.16   Example of a questionnaire screen that emphasizes the respondent.

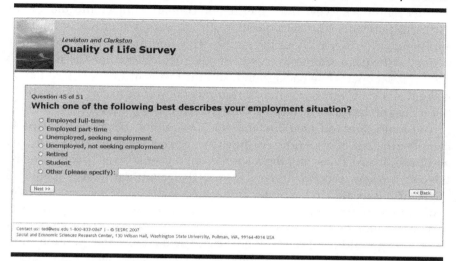

Source: "Combining Mail and Internet Methods to Conduct Household Surveys of the General Public: A New Methodology?" by D. A. Dillman, J. D. Smyth, L. M. Christian, and A. O'Neill, 2008, May, New Orleans, LA. Paper presented at the annual conference of the American Association for Public Opinion Research.

when presented with an image of a person who looks sick and worse when presented with an image of a person who looks healthy (Couper, Conrad, & Tourangeau, 2007). Similarly, in the previous example, people may rate their own behavior differently depending on what delinquent behaviors are pictured. Overall, it is important to focus on the respondent when designing web questionnaire screens, both in the choice of title and any imagery as well as in how information is presented on the page.

Guideline 6.26: Use a Consistent Page Layout across Screens and Visually Emphasize Question Information that Respondents Will Need to Complete the Survey While Deemphasizing Information that Is Not Essential to the Task

A consistent page layout across screens helps respondents easily process the basic organization of information on the screen and focus on the task of answering the questions. This can be especially important as the type of information requested and the question format changes across screens. In the examples in Figure 6.6 introduced earlier in this chapter, background colors, lines, and contours help respondents segment the page into three regions: the header or banner region, the main question area, and the footer.

The header and footer regions are often consistent across all screens. For the survey in Figure 6.6, the header region includes the name of the university and the title of the survey in white font against a dark gray background. This area may also include a small, very carefully selected graphic to help respondents identify with the survey. The footer region contains contact information for use by respondents who have questions for the surveyor or who would like additional information about the survey. This information is located at the bottom of the page, similar to contact or designer information for many web sites. It is set on a white background, and the text is in smaller black font to make it less visible (because not all respondents will need this information), but it can still be easily located by those who are looking for it.

The main question area contains the information respondents need to complete the task of responding to the survey question: the question stem, any additional instructions, and the response options or answer spaces. Because this area is where respondents need to focus their attention, it takes up most of the page, it is located in the center of the page, and a green background color is used to help draw attention to it. In addition, locating the components of each individual question in the same region (defined by the contours and the green background color) encourages respondents to see the question stem, any additional instructions or definitions, and the answer categories or spaces as a group that belong together.

Every question in the survey is designed following the guidelines for question design discussed in Chapter 4 (i.e., darker and larger print for the question stem, spacing to create subgrouping, visually standardized answer spaces, etc.). Looking across the question screens in Figure 6.6 also reveals, however, that great care was taken to ensure consistency in the visual appearance of the questions as a whole. For example, the question number (i.e., Question 1 of 27) is located in the same location on every screen (both vertically and horizontally), although it is in a smaller font than the question stem so respondents are encouraged to focus more on the question itself. Likewise, the distance that the response options and spaces are indented compared to the question stem is similar across the pages. Such consistency eases the response task as it allows the respondent to learn what to expect in the first screen or two and then apply that knowledge to the rest of the survey rather than having to reorient at every screen.

In many web surveys, designers provide custom navigation buttons for respondents to use when moving through the survey (i.e., different buttons from the "back" and "forward" buttons in their Internet browser). The benefit of these navigation buttons is that they allow greater control over how answers are saved as respondents proceed through the survey. As Figure 6.6 illustrates, the navigation buttons, if used, should be located in the central question area to make them more accessible to respondents as they move through the survey.

Experienced Internet users may notice that the navigation buttons pictured in Figure 6.6 are "backward" compared to how navigation buttons are generally displayed in Internet browsers. That is, the "back" button in

Internet browsers is usually located on the left and the "forward" button on the right. In the figure, the "back" button is located in the lower right corner of the question area and the "next question" button is located in the lower left corner. This swapping of sides from what is conventional in a web browser is very deliberate. The "next" button is placed directly under the question on the left side of the page both to make it more easily and quickly accessed by respondents and to encourage them to move forward through the survey. The "back" button is located on the same horizontal line but on the right side (i.e., outside of the foveal view) because fewer respondents will need to move backward in the survey (although it generally should be provided because some may need it for reasons described previously). We have seen no evidence that swapping the location of the navigation buttons in this way confuses respondents. Rather, they quickly learn where the buttons are and use them appropriately. What is most important, however, is that the location of the navigation buttons be consistent across screens as in this example.

Although screen layouts may differ somewhat from the one described here, the design of the web pages should help the respondent to organize the information on the page. Thus, it is important that surveyors use a consistent visual layout across web pages to aid respondents as the type of question or task changes and respondents move through individual pages or screens in the questionnaire.

Guideline 6.27: Do Not Require Responses to Questions Unless Absolutely Necessary for the Survey

The design and programming of web surveys allow surveyors to require responses to every question. Sometimes requiring responses to one or a few key questions can be essential to the goal of the survey and can save time and expense, such as when respondents would have to be called back by telephone to collect missing responses to key questions. However, for most surveys, requiring responses before respondents can move to the next screen, particularly for every question, can have detrimental effects on respondent motivation, on measurement, and on the likelihood that respondents will complete the entire survey. When respondents do not have an answer to a question but are required to provide one anyway, they have two options: get frustrated and terminate the survey, or lie and provide an answer that is not true for them. The first option will increase the likelihood of nonresponse error in the data, and the second will introduce measurement error.

Putting respondents into a situation where they feel they have to lie to get past a question may also have the undesirable side effect of making them more likely to provide inaccurate answers for questions later in the survey. An example of this was witnessed during a cognitive interview on a question that required people to indicate the degree they received from the community college they attended. One respondent explained that she only took one course, so could not answer the question. When the error message appeared telling her that she had to provide a response, she laughed and said, "Well it's a nice little college, and I always wanted a degree from there, so I guess now I have one. What year should I get it?" (Altheimer & Dillman, 2002).

In addition to increasing nonresponse and measurement error, requiring answers may be problematic for other reasons. For one, many institutional review boards require surveys to be designed so that respondents can skip questions they prefer not to answer (i.e., voluntary). Also, when web surveys are used as part of a mixed-mode survey with a mail survey, requiring answers may lead to different stimuli, and ultimately responses, across the two modes because answers cannot be required in mail surveys.

When we advise against requiring responses, we are often asked about situations in which respondents need to provide a response to an initial question so they can be routed to the appropriate follow-up question. Although requiring answers may be the only solution to this problem for some surveys, many surveys can be programmed so the respondent can be branched appropriately even when a response to the initial question is not provided. It may require more thought on the part of the surveyor to think about which questions the respondent should be asked next, but it will often improve the quality of responses received.

Regardless of the topic, most surveys have a few—and some have many—questions that cannot be honestly answered by respondents. As we have discussed, requiring responses often leads to nonresponse and measurement biases that can far outweigh the benefits of collecting responses for every question. If a response is going to be required to a question, it is important to ascertain whether this is necessary for the survey and what effects it will have on respondent behavior. In addition, it may be useful to include options such as "This question does not apply to me," "Prefer not to answer" or "Don't know" so that rather than choose a response that does not fit for them, respondents will be able to move on without having to provide an inaccurate answer or quit the survey out of frustration.

Guideline 6.28: Design Survey-Specific and Item-Specific Error Messages to Help Respondents Troubleshoot Any Issues They May Encounter

Sometimes technical issues may occur that require communicating with respondents what has happened and what they should do next. For example, respondents may not have entered their identification code correctly or they may not be able to view a page in the survey because it does not load, particularly if there are a lot of complex features and the respondents are on a slow connection. In another scenario, a respondent may be trying to return to the survey after answering a phone call or experiencing another interruption, but the survey may have timed out, making the person unable to continue.

In these cases, standard messages are often sent to respondents by the browser or server. However, often these generic messages may not be specific enough to help respondents troubleshoot the issue. For example, a generic message may say "This page cannot be found" and give some standard ways to try to fix the error. These messages are usually in a white background with black or red text and look very different from the survey pages. To the extent that these generic messages are unhelpful for the specific survey situation, they may frustrate respondents and cause some to stop trying to access the survey.

To help respondents troubleshoot these types of issues, we recommend designing and programming survey-specific messages that load in a new window and inform respondents of exactly what happened and how to get back on track. In our own web surveys we design survey-related error pages with the same look and feel of the regular survey pages. We do this so that instead of feeling as if they have left the survey, respondents mentally connect the error message to the rest of the survey. The first example in Figure 6.17

Figure 6.17   Examples of customized error messages.

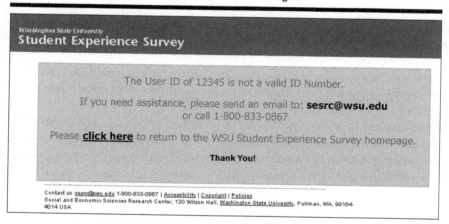

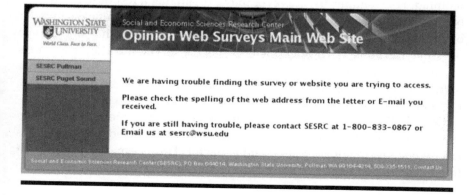

shows a survey-specific error message that a respondent might receive if she entered an incorrect access code. In this case, the respondent is told what has gone wrong (i.e., the user ID is invalid) and is given two options that are very specific and tailored to the survey—contact the sponsors for assistance, or return to the login page to try again. If the survey times out, one might explain in the message that the survey has timed out in order to conserve server resources but that the respondent can resume where he left off by reentering the access code on the login page. Likewise, if a page cannot load or there is another type of programming issue, a customized error page may say "We are sorry, but a programming error has occurred while answering the survey. By clicking here and reentering your ID number you will be returned to the correct page. If you have any questions, please contact us at ___." Regardless of the cause of the error message, it is important to always provide a link on the error page that will take respondents to where they need to go next. In social exchange terms, doing so will reduce the costs to respondents by making the process of getting back into the survey as easy as possible.

The second example in Figure 6.17 shows a screenshot of a custom-designed error page that respondents may encounter as they try to find the correct survey in the first place. Rather than a generic error message appearing, this page appears if respondents make a mistake in entering a survey's URL but get the domain correct. It provides immediate notification to the respondent that he or she is on the right track but may have made a slight error. It also provides contact information in case the respondent cannot resolve the problem.

In addition to these general survey-specific error messages, individual questions may require specific messages if the answer the respondent enters does not match the criteria programmed in a validation step. For example, if a response is needed for a particular question but a respondent leaves it blank, rather than using a generic message that says "Response required" or "You must provide a response to this question," a survey-specific message using the same page layout as the survey pages might explain why the response is required. For example, the surveyor may explain that a response is required because the main goal is for the federal government to determine the number of people in the household or that a response is required so that appropriate questions can be asked throughout the rest of the survey. If additional options are provided, such as "Prefer not to answer" or "This question does not apply to me," it may be helpful to remind respondents that they can provide these types of responses so they are able to move on to the next page.

Overall, these survey-specific and item-specific error messages can help improve respondent motivation when issues are encountered that would otherwise negatively impact respondent behavior. This is especially important to prevent respondents from terminating the survey, particularly if they are likely to be unfamiliar with web surveys or when responses are required for some of the questions in the survey.

Guideline 6.29: Evaluate Carefully the Use of Interactive Features, Balancing Improvements in Measurement with the Impact on Respondent Burden and the Implications for Mixed-Mode Surveys

Common interactive features on the Web include saving responses, branching respondents to appropriate questions based on their responses to previous questions (or previously collected data), and providing error message pages that communicate information about how to troubleshoot issues that may arise. Most of these types of features are considered essential for web surveys and should be included in all surveys.

However, additional interactive features are available as well. One example is that early responses or information already available from previous surveys or from sample records can be used to tailor later questions in the survey. This practice is especially common in establishment surveys and longitudinal surveys for which extensive information is available about the respondents ahead of time. Another example is that question wording can be customized, similar to computer-assisted telephone interviewing and computer-assisted personal interviewing (e.g., When you began your vacation in "July 2007" to "New Mexico," did you drive your "Toyota Avalon" or your "Toyota Rav4" or travel there in some other way?). In some surveys, an enormous amount of information can be brought forward to frame questions in a more direct manner for respondents. Although this ability can be incredibly useful, each of these inserts requires programming that should be extensively checked to make sure it is working properly.

In addition, web surveys can be designed so that if answers are not within a specified range, error messages are sent to respondents asking for corrections (i.e., validation steps). Although validation steps can improve the quality of the final data set for the surveyor and save data cleaning and editing time, they are usually designed from the viewpoint of the surveyor rather than the respondent. As such, they can be quite problematic for respondents. First, frequent error messages can be frustrating and burdensome, possibly leading to poor response behavior or even break-offs. Second, it often happens that scenarios that the surveyor did not think to include as possibilities apply to some respondents. In these cases, the data validation step often creates a situation much like that created by requiring respondents to answer before they can move on: It creates a roadblock that requires certain respondents to either give inaccurate data or quit the survey. Including data validation steps can also have negative effects for the surveyor. First and foremost, these steps are difficult to program, are very prone to mistakes that can have larger negative impacts on data quality, and are very expensive. In addition, the process of cleaning and editing data can be very informative with respect to how respondents interpreted the questions being asked of them. Interactive validation steps, in essence, "erase" this potentially useful information.

Other types of interactive features have been (and continue to be) developed for the Web, and the amount of research on these features varies greatly. Features such as drop-down menus, links to definitions or examples, automatic calculation tools, progress indicators, and visual analog scales have all been tested in web surveys and were discussed in Chapter 4. When deciding which interactive features to use, it is important to consider which are necessary and which are more of a novelty or do not directly help respondents as they complete the survey. This issue was summed up by a designer of many establishment surveys who commented that some respondents who completed the same survey each year expected such features to be included, especially for the purpose of avoiding callbacks, but that the same respondents often became frustrated when too many such features and feedback messages appeared in the survey. Oftentimes these interactive features cost more and take more time because they require more advanced programming and because the likelihood of programming errors increases. In addition, many of them require respondents to have JavaScript or other client-side scripting technologies enabled in order to work correctly, so no-script options (i.e., a different measurement stimulus) must also be programmed for those who have scripting disabled. Most important, these new features should be tested with respondents to see how they interact with them and whether the features help with or hinder survey completion.

Guideline 6.30: Use Audiovisual Capabilities of the Web Sparingly, and Evaluate the Differential Effect They May Have on Respondents

The Web allows for enhanced audiovisual capabilities that are not possible in combination with any other survey mode, other than perhaps face-to-face interviews. Many web surveyors are interested in using audio and video because it allows them to incorporate features such as voice and visual images that can make the Web more similar to interviewer-administered modes. For example, a survey may have a video of an interviewer who reads the survey questions or may include an audio recording of the question alongside the text version on the screen.

Although these features are generally included in an effort to assist respondents, they can be quite problematic for several reasons. First, many respondents may not have installed the necessary computer hardware capabilities, software, or additional plug-ins to run the video or audio components. In addition, these files often require high-speed Internet connections because they have shorter download times and better streaming capabilities. Even if it can be guaranteed that respondents have the needed Internet and computer capabilities, more simple things can go wrong, such as respondents having the volume on their computer turned down or off so that they cannot hear the audio components.

Moreover, research on these new features on the Web is rather limited. Thus, it is important to evaluate the effects of including audio or video components on respondent motivation and on the concepts being measured. As discussed previously, including pictures in surveys can have detrimental effects on measurement for particular questions, so the inclusion of audio or video may also have unknown effects on measurement or nonresponse. In addition, previous research on interview features may be important in evaluating audio–video components that include an interviewer reading the questions to respondents.

Guideline 6.31: Allow Respondents to Stop the Survey and Finish Completing It at Another Time

Most web survey respondents will complete the survey at one time rather than coming back and finishing it later, particularly if the survey is short and only one person is needed to answer the questions. However, sometimes respondents are interrupted (e.g., because of power outages or loss of Internet connectivity, to answer the phone, to respond to an urgent e-mail, to have a conversation with another person in the household, etc.) and need to finish the survey at another time. In addition, for more complex and longer surveys or for establishment surveys for which multiple people often need to be consulted to answer all of the questions, it is absolutely essential for respondents to be able to easily discontinue the survey and resume it later.

The ability to allow respondents to quit and return to the survey later comes standard with many software packages. When respondents return to the survey welcome page and enter their identification code, it is usually helpful to then route them to the page where they left off so they do not have to click through multiple screens to find where they stopped answering. However, it is also a good idea to allow respondents to go backward from the point they left off so they can remind themselves of the topic of the previous few questions if needed before proceeding with those that remain.

For establishment surveys and other complex surveys that are likely to be completed in multiple sessions, section headings or other types of tabs that describe the type of information requested may also help orient respondents when they resume the survey or when they are asked to complete a section they are particularly qualified for by someone else who has already completed another section. In such cases where different respondents need to complete different questions or sections of the survey, it is very helpful if respondents can click on a section heading to move directly to the relevant questions. For example, in an establishment survey headings may be organized by position (e.g., human resources, communications, research, etc.), or in an individual survey they may be organized based on the type of information requested (e.g., biographical information, employment history, political attitudes, etc.).

Overall, providing the ability to resume the survey at a later time shows that the surveyor is responsive to respondents' needs and is thinking about how they will complete the survey. As we mentioned, this feature is absolutely essential for surveys on particular topics, of longer lengths, and for particular types of populations. However, we recommend it for most surveys, even if only a few respondents may need to take advantage of this feature.

Guideline 6.32: Whenever Possible, Collect Paradata that Provide Feedback on How the Respondent Interacts with the Questionnaire

One of the most exciting developments in web surveys is the ability to collect server-side and especially client-side paradata that records the server's and client's interactions with the questionnaire. By collecting paradata, one can capture many types of interaction with the survey: how long it takes respondents to answer each question (and the entire survey), whether and how answers to each question are changed, and the sequence of clicks that respondents make on each page (Heerwegh, 2003; Heerwegh & Loosveldt, 2002b). This information can provide important feedback about how respondents answer specific questions and can be collected for all respondents, rather than only for a select few as is the case with laboratory studies or cognitive interviews. The following are ways in which paradata have recently been used to better understand questions and questionnaires.

- Christian et al. (in press) observed that respondents take longer to answer scalar questions when they are provided with a number box into which they must type the number corresponding with their response versus when they are provided with a labeled scale with circular radio buttons that correspond to each scale point.
- Smyth et al. (2006a) found that, on average, respondents to check-all questions answer quicker than respondents to forced-choice questions. In further analyses they were able to determine that those answering check-all questions the most quickly were also more likely to select options appearing in the top of the lists, indicating that they may have been satisficing (see Chapter 5, Guideline 5.18).
- Stern (in press) found that students were having considerable trouble discerning between two responses in a check-all question: "libraries" and "library instruction." When "library instruction" was presented before "libraries," many students selected that response but later changed it when they saw the "libraries" option. However, this was not a problem when "libraries" was presented first.

Overall, we have found that paradata can be a very valuable resource for evaluating responses to web surveys. One cautionary note, however, is that when paradata are collected, a large amount of information can be recorded, so it is particularly important to identify where paradata can be most useful in understanding response behavior in order to be able to focus analyses.

However, simple information such as response time is easy to compute, and many web surveyors now regularly include total response time when describing their web survey as well as question response times when reporting analyses from individual questions.

Guideline 6.33: Test the Survey Using a Variety of Platforms, Connection Speeds, Browsers, and User-Controlled Settings, and Test the Database to Ensure that Items Are Collected and Coded Correctly

Testing the web survey is one of the most important steps in the design process. Although paper surveys look the same for all respondents, web surveys cannot be controlled in the same way and are dependent on the respondents' individual setups. All of the hard work in designing and programming the survey does not matter if the survey does not work effectively on a variety of hardware and software configurations and across various connection speeds. Thus, it is important to test the survey using various technological configurations as determined earlier when assessing the capabilities of the survey population.

It should be standard web survey procedure to test the survey using all (or at least most) of the possible combinations of settings that potential respondents may use to complete the survey. Moreover, testing needs to be a systematic process whereby every page in the survey is viewed using these different combinations by multiple people and from different locations. One of the most important things to test is page download times to ensure that most pages download very quickly (a few seconds), even with slower connection speeds and processors. Another very important thing to test is what happens if scripting is disabled. It is important to both make sure that the web survey does not crash when accessed by a browser with scripting disabled and to make sure that a no-script option is available for each JavaScript (or other script) function in the survey. Although it is not ideal to have some respondents experiencing the JavaScript version and others experiencing the no-script version because the stimulus may differ between the two, JavaScript enables many important web survey functions and therefore is likely to be included to some degree in almost all web surveys. As such, tests need to be conducted with it both enabled and disabled. If the survey must utilize JavaScript, it should be able to detect if a respondent has scripting disabled. One option is to provide a polite explanation as to why scripting needs to be enabled for the survey and how to enable it.

Often web survey designers and programmers are on the cutting edge of new computer technology, have the most recent versions of web browsers, and are adept at customizing their own user settings. However, it is important to design and test the web survey from the respondent perspective; the respondent may not be as computer savvy or familiar with being online. In one of our recent student surveys, we decided to send a tester out to a number of different computer labs at our university because many respondents would be completing the survey on campus. In the process of testing, it was discovered that two labs on campus had not updated their browsers in 5 years. Although many students were aware of that and avoided using those labs, others did not know and may have completed the survey on those computers with the outdated browsers. We believe this situation is not unique and that even more variation exists in types and versions of browsers and in other hardware and connection speeds, as individual users have control over their own machines and how they run them. Under these conditions, seemingly small problems in the testing phase will often become much larger problems once the survey goes live.

In addition to testing the survey itself, it is also important to test the database. This step can be done in combination with testing the survey. As testers view the survey pages, they should enter responses and record what they entered so the responses can then be checked in the database. Every response option for every question should be tested at least once. Testing the database involves ensuring that a response is collected for every question, that the correct number is coded in the database for the response(s) selected, that open-ended text boxes are not truncating responses (unless desired by the researcher), and that any other response coding that may be unique to the survey is working correctly.

Guideline 6.34: Take Screenshots of Each Page of the Final Questionnaire for Testing and Documentation

Related to the testing process is the necessity of taking screenshots of each page of the final questionnaire so that people can see how the questionnaire pages appeared to respondents. These screenshots can serve as the documentation of the final version of the questionnaire, similar to copies of paper questionnaires. Once a survey has been removed from the Web it is often very difficult, if not impossible because of hardware and software upgrades, to repost it for viewing, especially if any amount of time has passed. The reality is that if no screenshots were taken to document the questionnaire, there may be no available record of the survey's appearance.

At a minimum, screenshots should be taken of the final questionnaire using the most common computer settings (i.e., on a PC using the most recent version of Internet Explorer with the default settings, and with common screen sizes and resolutions). However, a better standard is to take screenshots during the testing process as well as shots of the final questionnaire using a variety of platforms, browsers, and user-controlled settings. In addition to documenting the final version of the questionnaire, these screenshots can help surveyors compare how the survey looks across different configurations in the testing stage.

PRETESTING QUESTIONNAIRES

During a cognitive interview, a respondent who had recently earned her PhD and was entering answers into a newly developed web version of the National Science Foundation Survey of Earned Doctorates became visibly upset. She objected adamantly to the wording of the following question about her race:

C14. What is your racial background?
☐ American Indian or Alaska native (Please describe on next page)
☐ Native Hawaiian or other Pacific Islander
☐ Asian
☐ Black or African American
☐ White
☐ Decline to Answer

Turning to the interviewer, she said, "I am of mixed racial heritage, and it really makes me angry when you force me into one category. Why do you write questions like this?"

Several minutes of discussion followed as she elaborated on her concerns. Finally, the interviewer asked her to take another look at the question and see if there was any way she might be able to register an answer that was acceptable to her. It was then that her original concern turned to embarrassment as she realized the boxes in front of the answer categories, which were check boxes and not radio buttons, allowed her to choose as many answers as she liked for that question. The respondent was quite aware of this web page construction convention, but because she was so focused on the question wording, she missed completely what the answer categories allowed her to do (Altheimer & Dillman, 2002). The simple fix for this problem was to add the words "You may choose more than one response." This example illustrates the importance of evaluating questions and questionnaires prior to the start of data collection. No matter how hard one has worked in order to build a good questionnaire, the final essential test is what happens when respondents come face to face with the survey itself.

Traditionally, the term *pretesting* referred to delivering a questionnaire to individuals with special knowledge of the topic or members of the survey population and asking them to complete it and report any problems they experienced. In recent years, a variety of specific procedures have evolved for evaluating different kinds of questions and questionnaires. Many of these procedures are described in Presser et al. (2004), and each procedure contributes to the evaluative process in ways that each of the other procedures cannot. All are important for providing a comprehensive testing of questions and questionnaires, and as such we offer guidelines here that emphasize the strengths and weaknesses of each. Pretesting is also the point at which questionnaire design and survey implementation begin to intersect. Because of the crucial nature of this intersection, we discuss both here (even though implementation is the topic of the next chapter) to emphasize the essential linkage that must be achieved in the creation of an acceptable survey.

Guideline 6.35: Obtain Feedback on the Draft Questionnaire from a Number of People, Each of Whom Has Specialized Knowledge of Some Aspect of Questionnaire Quality

Some people are able to look at questions and provide feedback on whether they measure the concepts that the surveyor intends to measure. Others are able to look at a list of questions and identify the potential for unintended question order effects. Still others may look at a questionnaire and identify questions that should be asked but are not included. Some reviewers are able to evaluate question structures and identify response categories that are inappropriate. For example, a reviewer of a student-designed questionnaire that used five household income categories for a questionnaire, only one of which was more than $20,000 per year, pointed out to the designer that most respondents would be clustered in the highest category, thus limiting variation that would be helpful in the analysis. Some people have familiarity with how demographic data are collected in national surveys and are able to identify questions that are asked in a way that will preclude comparison with answers to the same general questions from other sources. An example of such a survey is the U.S. Census Bureau's American Community Survey, which is now relied on to supply detailed demographic data for the nation, its states, and most of its counties.

Other individuals may be able to identify technical problems with questions that people who are experts on other aspects of question construction may miss. We once had a reviewer comment simply that the preamble to a question was not true: The phrase "Police in this community are responsible for arresting and fining people who violate traffic laws ... " was inaccurate. Although police arrest people, it is the judicial system that actually levies fines. In another instance a reviewer with knowledge of the population to be surveyed informed us that it was very unlikely that all members of a survey population could answer a few specific questions among a series of items and recommended that "don't know" and "does not apply" categories be added.

It would be unusual for a single person to have the ability to identify all of the potential problems with questions and a questionnaire. Testing questionnaires for these items requires getting evaluations from people with technical knowledge about the survey topic, how demographic data are collected in comparison surveys, statistical analysis techniques, survey mode effects, and characteristics of the population to be surveyed.

Thus, this stage of pretesting requires consultation with a variety of different people whose areas of expertise are likely to be significantly different.

Many studies fail to achieve their objectives because surveyors limit this phase of pretesting only to colleagues down the hallway who are experts in some aspect of survey construction or, at the other extreme, to people who are members of the study population. Questionnaires fail for many reasons, and having a systematic approach to obtaining feedback from a variety of knowledgeable people on a complete draft of the questionnaire is essential for evaluating, in a preliminary way, potential survey design problems.

Guideline 6.36: Conduct Cognitive Interviews of the Complete Questionnaire in Order to Identify Wording, Question Order, Visual Design, and Navigation Problems

Cognitive interviews have now become the dominant mode of testing questions and questionnaires. Some organizations, such as the U.S. Census Bureau, which does many continuing surveys, have even mandated that before question wording changes can be made they must be tested. Cognitive interviews are considered an acceptable procedure for evaluating such changes.

Cognitive interviewing emerged in the early 1990s as a means of determining whether respondents comprehend questions as intended by the survey sponsor and whether questions can be answered accurately (Forsyth & Lessler, 1991). Potential survey respondents are asked individually to respond to a questionnaire in the presence of an interviewer who asks them to think out loud as they go through the draft questionnaire and tell the interviewer what is being thought about the questions and also how answers to questions are being formed. The interviewer probes in order to get an understanding of how each question is being interpreted and whether the surveyor's intent for each question is being realized.

When a think-aloud cognitive interview begins, an interviewer explains to the respondent that she will be asked to complete a questionnaire in a special way, which is outlined in Figure 6.18. The respondent is told that this includes telling the interviewer everything she is thinking as she develops and reports her answers. The respondent is then asked to complete a practice question in order to learn the technique. This part of the interview is critical, and we commonly ask two questions:

How many residences have you lived in since you were born?
_____ Number of residences

How many windows are in your home?
_____ Number of windows

The first question is often difficult for people to answer, especially if they have lived in a lot of different locations. Typically some people start counting from birth, whereas other people make an estimate. It has been our experience in more than 300 interviews in which this question has been used that

Figure 6.18 Example of protocol used for testing U.S. census questionnaires.

A. Introduction
Thank you for coming here today to help us out. The reason we asked for your help is that every ten years the U.S. Census Bureau conducts a complete count of everyone who is living in the United States. All residences are mailed the Census form with the request that people who live there complete and return it. Today I am going to ask you to look at Census forms that are being evaluated for possible use in the 2010 Census. Your reactions to these forms will provide us with information that will help make the form as easy to complete as possible. Okay?

B. Hand respondent confidentiality form
The first thing I need to do is to ask you to read and sign this consent form. But first let me explain what it is about. This interview is voluntary. It is being conducted by us for the U.S. Census Bureau, which is located in Washington D.C. Everything you write on the Census form is confidential. The only people who can see the information you provide are employees of the Census Bureau and those of us at Washington State University who will be conducting the interviews. We have been sworn by the Census Bureau to keep individual answers confidential, and we can be fined if we reveal peoples' specific answers in any way that makes the person identifiable. The statement we are asking you to sign indicates that you have volunteered for this interview. I will also sign it as well since I am the person conducting the interview and I want to assure you in writing of my promise to keep all of your information confidential.

C. Explain procedure
In a couple of minutes, I am going to hand you a Census form in an envelope. When I do, I would like you to talk out loud about your reactions to the form as you read questions and fill it out. I would like to know everything you think about it. Talking out loud about these sorts of things may seem a little unusual, so before I give you the Census mailing, I have a really short *practice* mailing. When I give it to you, please tell me everything you are thinking as you look at the envelope, and start deciding what to do with it and the form inside. I would like to know any thoughts you have about whether it strikes you in a favorable or unfavorable way, whether it is clear about what to do or not do, and so forth.

D. Hand respondent practice mail-out
Okay, please read the questions out loud and tell me everything you are thinking about while you fill it out.

(Provide positive reinforcement, e.g., *"Good, that's what we need to know."*)

(Encourage the respondent to provide other information, e.g., *"When you do the real Census form just be sure that you tell us about your reactions to everything, the envelope, the way the whole thing looks, whether it's clear what to do or not do, anything you don't understand, or anything that seems strange."*)

E. Hand first mail-out to respondent
Now here is the envelope that might arrive in the mailbox at the address for which you are completing the Census form in 2010. Please take your time and tell me any reactions you have to everything that you see in front of you. (Note: If person is responding for someone else, e.g., an elderly friend, mark here ☐ and make sure respondent understands our expectations.)

1. Any reactions to the mailing package:

2. Did they read the cover letter?
   ☐ Fully
   ☐ Partially
   ☐ Not at all

3. Did they react at all to the opportunity to fill out the form electronically (from the cover letter)? If so, how?

Based on procedure reported in more detail by Parsons, Mahon-Haft, and Dillman, 2005.

some people will think of cities in which they have lived, whereas others will think about individual residences. Regardless of which way people answer, we explain to respondents that when we have asked this question in such interviews some people have answered each way. We also explain that when we learn that people interpret the question differently it tells us that the question needs to be improved, and that is why we do interviews of this nature.

Figure 6.18 (*Continued*)

F. Ask respondent to fill out the form contained inside

Now, please fill out the census form and talk out loud about your impressions of it. We would like for you to read whatever you would read at home while filling it out; however, if there is anything you wouldn't read, don't read it here. We'd like for you to fill it out just like you would at home, except that you should talk out loud about it, and anything you read to yourself should be read out loud. Please go ahead.

Probes that might be used:

- *What are you thinking right now?*
- *Remember to read aloud for me—it's up to you what you read, but whatever you decide to read please do out loud so I know what you are looking at.*
- *Can you tell me more about that?*
- *Could you describe that for me?*
- *Don't forget to tell me what you are thinking as you do that.*

G. Record relevant comments, errors, hesitations, and other indicators of potential problems during completion (to be used to frame follow-up questions).

1. Did they read the note about filling out the form electronically?
   - ☐ Yes
   - ☐ No

2. What reactions did they volunteer, if any?

3. Did they read the roster instructions?
   - ☐ Fully
   - ☐ Partially
   - ☐ Skimmed
   - ☐ Not at all

4. Any reactions/hesitations/questions to the roster instructions?

H. Debriefing questions (first form)

1. Overall how easy or difficult was the form to complete?
   - ☐ Very easy
   - ☐ Somewhat easy
   - ☐ Somewhat difficult
   - ☐ Very difficult

2. Was there anything unclear or confusing about how to fill out this Census form?
   - ☐ Yes ➔(If yes) please explain:
   - ☐ No

3. If this form arrived at your residence in the mail, how soon do you think you would respond?
   - ☐ The same day
   - ☐ In 1 – 2 days
   - ☐ In a week or so
   - ☐ Two weeks or more
   - ☐ Not at all

People's answers to the question on windows usually allow us to begin to probe, for example asking whether they counted a sliding glass door, what they may have done with any multiple pane windows, and so on. By the time this practice questionnaire is complete, respondents have usually learned what the interview is designed to do and have become comfortable with thinking out loud. In addition, the entire interview experience has become far less threatening to them than it may have appeared at the beginning of the interview session. Practice questions shift the emphasis from providing answers that are right, and that may reflect on the respondent's competence, to helping the interviewer identify problems with the questions written by the surveyor.

In sum, the practice questions define expectations for the interview, provide respondents with the reasons for an out-loud answering process that probably seems unnatural to them, and help them understand why we are doing the interview. These crucial beginnings thus are designed to train the out-loud respondents as well as motivate them to be active participants in the process.

When the questionnaire to be evaluated is handed to respondents (or appears on the screen for web surveys), they are encouraged to continue to do what they have been doing with the practice questions. Detailed examples of protocols and questionnaire evaluations we have done that have utilized think-aloud techniques are available from this web site: www.sesrc.wsu.edu/dillman/.

Sometimes cognitive interviews are aimed primarily at evaluating whether people are interpreting the wording of questions in the same way and understanding the questions (Parsons, Mahon-Haft, & Dillman, 2007). In other cases, they may be aimed at determining whether people are able to navigate through a questionnaire appropriately (Dillman & Allen, 1995). When the latter is our primary concern, we have sometimes used a retrospective interviewing technique, asking people to complete a questionnaire silently, just as they might if they were home by themselves. We then simply observe the answering process and, in particular, whether mistakes get made. The reason for this process is that asking them to think aloud seems likely to encourage respondents to read questions slower and with greater attention to the wording and visual layout than they would at home. This technique enables us to get a better sense of how the graphical layout of a questionnaire is guiding respondents. With web surveys, this technique has allowed us to pick up mannerisms (e.g., forward and backward clicking as a means of trying to get a better comprehension of question context) to understand different ways that respondents navigate through questionnaires when not having to divide their attention between the interviewer, reading questions out loud (which is slower than doing it silently), and providing substantive answers (Sawyer & Dillman, 2002).

We cannot recall having completed a set of cognitive interviews without identifying at least a few potential problems with question wordings or questionnaire layouts, regardless of how much effort went into the initial design. However, it is also important to recognize that cognitive interviewing, as typically practiced, exhibits a number of shortcomings. Respondents tend to be volunteers obtained through advertisements or personal recruitment, because of being asked to come to a central location for the process to take place, and cannot be thought of as a random sample of a larger study population. Doing interviews is labor intensive, and as a general rule the number of such interviews conducted is often quite small (e.g., less than 20). Inasmuch as problems are often associated with particular characteristics of the respondent, conclusions are often based upon only one person having that particular characteristic. An example is cognitive interviews of Census forms that have focused (among other issues) on why newborns are often omitted from the Decennial Census form. An adequate cognitive test focused on this issue should in principle interview only individuals from households having a recently born child (Cork & Voss, 2006). In our experience it has been disconcerting to listen to strong recommendations for change from someone who has conducted relatively few interviews on a variety of issues, and then learn that the recommendation is sometimes based upon an occurrence in only one or perhaps two interviews or an interview with one respondent with a particular characteristic of interest. Under these circumstances it is difficult to know whether any problem that has been identified is a small isolated problem or something that will affect a significant number of respondents, and whether changing the question might then create problems for other respondents.

Another problem is that the labor-intensive nature of cognitive interviews often leads to their being conducted by entry-level personnel who are able to ask and record responses from individuals but who lack the skills or training needed for comprehending underlying causes of the problems and asking appropriate follow-up questions. A friend described it as the difference between a medical patient being examined by a physician and the physician's office assistant. Although the assistant may have medical training and as a result be able to ask appropriate questions, he probably lacks the in-depth knowledge needed for formulating the needed additional questions to rule out certain possibilities and better isolate the critical problems. We have observed some interviewers who are tremendously skilled at teasing out when interpretations of wording are problems and interacting with the respondent to identify words and phrases that are easier to understand. However, these same individuals are unable to pick up on the consequences of visual layout problems and how they might be corrected. The opposite situation also occurs. It is essential that individuals assigned to the cognitive interviewing task of evaluating web and paper surveys be knowledgeable in both of these areas.

Well-done cognitive interviews also require detailed reporting of procedures and evidence, just as is required for writing quantitative data reports. Doing that allows others to read the evidence and draw their own conclusions about its strength. Few things are as disconcerting as having the conductor of 20 cognitive interviews select a problem from one interview and simply declare that a question must be changed. Evidence is needed on what did or did not happen in the other 19 interviews to avoid making a correction to fix a problem experienced by one person, only to find that the revision creates problems for other respondents. This concern has led us to develop the practice of summarizing individual interviews in reports, making sure probes on the same topics are administered in as many interviews as possible and that the evidence is summarized in considerable detail (Dillman, Parsons, & Mahon-Haft, 2004; Parsons & Dillman, 2008).

The term *usability study* emerged in the past decade to describe tests of web surveys. These tend to be one-on-one interviews in which an individual attempts to complete a web survey. Initially, such usability studies tended to focus on the challenges individuals faced in using a computer to register responses. This practice has, over time, become somewhat blurred with cognitive interviews as evaluators have attempted to combine evaluation of the wording and sequence of questions with the manner in which they are presented and responded to while on a computer. In recent years the term *usability* has also been applied to evaluating paper questionnaires.

Occasionally, when we have proposed conducting cognitive interviews to evaluate a questionnaire, the survey designer has thought we were planning to do *focus groups*, in which a number of people are brought together in order to talk about questions in a questionnaire (Morgan, 1997). There is a considerable difference between cognitive interviews and focus groups. The latter tend to be a social experience in which people not only express their own opinions but listen to the opinions of others, which then may be taken into account as they express additional opinions. The group orientation of such interviews may lead to inappropriate conclusions when cultural considerations are related to the issue being studied.

Such an effect appeared to happen in a set of focus groups conducted in anticipation of a response rate experiment conducted in 1995. In preparation for the 2000 Decennial Census an extensive set of experiments was conducted with the aim of identifying factors that would improve response rates (Dillman, 2000a). The influences of 16 different factors were tested experimentally to determine the likelihood of their improving response rates. Only five factors were found to be significant, the most powerful of which was the inclusion of a box on the outgoing envelope that informed recipients "U.S. Census Form Enclosed; Your Response Is Required by Law" (improved response rates by about 10 percentage points). Smaller effects were also achieved by respondent-friendly design, prenotice letter, postcard reminder, and replacement questionnaire. However, four focus groups in two different cities that sought to determine whether such an announcement on the envelope should be used were unanimous in concluding that it would not affect response rates and that a more effective response-inducing strategy would be to place a different announcement on the envelope: "It Pays to Be Counted." A test of this message, carried out in the same national experiment, showed that it had absolutely no effect on response rate (Dillman, Singer, et al., 1996).

Guideline 6.37: When the Stakes Are High, Consider Doing Experimental Evaluations of Questionnaire Components

Once, when another critical decision was about to be made at the U.S. Census Bureau on the Decennial Census questionnaire, one of us was approached by a senior statistician who wanted to know the following: "Can't you just do a few cognitive interviews to find out whether it's okay to change to the newly proposed questionnaire format?" Doing that instead of an experiment would have been less costly and could have been completed much more quickly.

This incident illustrates a common dilemma faced in federal agencies as the practice of testing questions before changing them becomes a common expectation. Well-designed experiments can provide quantitative estimates of the effects of proposed changes in questionnaires and survey implementation procedures that are representative of the entire survey population, whereas cognitive interviews cannot. When a survey design decision needs to estimate the magnitude of a change in survey design, experimentation is needed.

In the 1990s the U.S. Census Bureau commissioned an outside firm to design two new mail-out envelopes and questionnaires, one of which was rolled out publicly as a new Census design to be used in the Decennial Census. Cognitive interviews suggested that neither of the designs were likely to work well, in part because the message that had previously been found experimentally to improve response rates by as much as 10 percentage points (i.e., "Your Response Is Required by Law") was graphically hidden in unusual print formats (Dillman, Jenkins, Martin, & DeMaio, 1996). An experimental test that was run at the same time as the cognitive interviews were conducted showed that indeed the two new designs lowered response rates by 9% and 5%, respectively, both of which were considered dramatic declines (Leslie, 1996). Inasmuch as a considerable commitment had been made by agency leadership to the new designs, it seemed quite unlikely that their use would have been rejected had only the cognitive interview report been available. However, the experimental results from a random sample of U.S. households provided an unquestioned quantitative basis for rejecting the designs, and this basis was strengthened even further by supportive reasoning as to why respondents were unfavorable toward the new designs that was revealed during cognitive testing with volunteers.

The parallel use of experimental and cognitive interview results is a particularly powerful basis for the evaluation of survey questions and questionnaires. Dillman and Redline (2004) reported three cases in which parallel experimental and cognitive interview studies were completed. Although the results of each of these companion efforts tended to point toward similar conclusions about the questions and procedures being tested, the experimental and cognitive interviews provided quite different kinds of information. The experiments allowed conclusions to be drawn about what would actually happen if a procedure were to be adopted but provided only minimal insight into why those differences occurred. In contrast, the cognitive interviews proved to be a rich source of hypotheses about the reasons those differences occurred. Neither method of testing can substitute for the other one.

Experiments on question wording and response rate concerns are not something that should be considered only when conducting national surveys for policy purposes. We have frequently interacted with survey designers in universities and private sector firms who have produced a questionnaire and proposed implementation procedure and have wanted to know whether people will give better answers to questions worded in a new way and what response rate they can expect with and without incentives. Because of the unique combination of content, length, and implementation procedures, it is usually impossible to provide anything other than a vague estimate of effects. An experiment involving a few hundred households can often provide insightful information that will prevent much larger amounts of money from being spent in pursuit of an unachievable objective. Thus, experimentation can play an essential and influential role in evaluating proposed questionnaires and implementation procedures.

Guideline 6.38: Conduct a Small Pilot Study with a Subsample of the Population in Order to Evaluate Interconnections among Questions, the Questionnaire, and the Implementation Procedures

A *pilot study* refers to a mini-study in which the proposed questionnaire and all implementation procedures are tested on the survey population in an attempt to identify problems with the questionnaire and related implementation procedures. The goal is to determine whether the proposed questionnaire and procedures are adequate for the larger study.

Although it is possible that experiments can be embedded in a pilot study, we distinguish between these methods of testing here because a pilot study provides critical information regardless of whether experiments are embedded in the design. It constitutes a final test of the exact procedures to be used in a study.

Pilot studies give a good sense of how the study procedures will work in practice. They are particularly useful for making quantitative estimates of response rates and thus may help in setting sample sizes for the full study. They may also identify item nonresponse problems and steps that may be taken to reduce them. If large enough, pilot studies can provide preliminary data sets that may be analyzed to determine the extent to which individual response categories are or are not used. They can also be used to get an indication of whether individual questions and scales appear to be working as intended (i.e., measuring concepts in the manner expected). Pilot studies are often deemed essential when a new survey questionnaire or new implementation procedures are to be used for a survey. They are also often necessary when implementation involves many different individuals and divisions within an organization. Pilot studies can provide important feedback on coordination among those individuals and groups and let them "practice" for the actual survey. An example is the "Dress Rehearsal" for the Decennial Census, which is usually conducted 2 years prior to the actual Census in small regions of the United States in order to give critical feedback on how well each component of the survey process and its connections to other components have been designed. Pilot studies are also especially valuable for obtaining cost estimates for the actual survey.

However, except for large costly surveys, most surveys now appear to be implemented without the conduct of pilot studies. We live in an age in which data are increasingly evaluated for timeliness and pressures have increased for doing surveys quickly, without taking time to conduct formal pilot studies. Not doing a pilot study can be disastrous for web surveys in particular.

As we discuss in the next chapter, a large number of things have to come together in the final preparations for fielding web surveys. The linking of e-mail administration, access code assignments, and programming for individual questions provides an enormous opportunity—if not likelihood—that something will be done wrong. We have experienced situations in which the programming was not finished, so answers to a particular category were recorded incorrectly in the database. We have also experienced situations in which users of a particular e-mail provider could not get the hyperlink to open the survey, and a poor choice of wording for access codes resulted in respondents entering student ID numbers instead of the access code provided to them. Unlike with mail surveys, respondents may not be able to just "skip over" a bad question. If respondents cannot get an access code to work, provide an answer to a particular question, or advance to the next question, then they are likely to quit, and it is unlikely they can be convinced to go back and do the survey after the problem is fixed. Yet the speed with which web surveys are often constructed and implemented means that there is a high likelihood that some errors will be made.

These concerns have led us to institute the practice of selecting a random sample of the survey population and inviting them to complete the survey a few hours or days ahead of others. Then, when no problems are encountered, the remaining respondents are contacted. In other cases, when a survey was particularly complex (e.g., involving frequent use of early answers in later questions, extensive branching constructions, questions with longer download times, and untested questions), we conducted a more traditional pilot study significantly ahead of the planned implementation so that response distributions and all other features of the survey could be more formally evaluated.

CONCLUSION

One of the significant impacts of the electronic age is that the line between constructing a questionnaire and implementing a survey is increasingly blurred, as is the line between writing a question and constructing a questionnaire. Although survey design has never been a linear process, the use of technology in both mail and Internet surveys now pushes surveyors even further down the path of constantly thinking about all aspects of the survey creation and implementation process. Our main focus in this chapter has been on what must happen when the decision is made to move from a listing of questions one wants to ask to the formatted questionnaire that respondents will experience, whether by mail or through the Web. In either case the last step of construction is pretesting, which has come a long way since its origins in the 1900s. It is no longer a catch-all, somewhat undefined technique for identifying potential survey problems. Much more precise methods are now available and need to be used, as discussed here. The next chapter takes this tested questionnaire toward completion of the survey design process. In it, we bring together sample and questionnaire decisions with the manner in which people are going to be approached with the request to complete the questionnaire.

LIST OF GUIDELINES

Ordering the Questions

Guideline 6.1:   *Group related questions that cover similar topics, and begin with questions likely to be salient to nearly all respondents*

Guideline 6.2:   *Choose the first question carefully*

Guideline 6.3:   *Place sensitive or potentially objectionable questions near the end of the questionnaire*

Guideline 6.4:   *Ask questions about events in the order the events occurred*

Guideline 6.5:   *Avoid unintended question order effects*

Creating a Common Visual Stimulus

Guideline 6.6:   *Establish consistency in the visual presentation of questions (across pages and screens), and use alignment and vertical spacing to help respondents organize the information on the page*

Guideline 6.7:   *Use color and contrast to help respondents recognize the components of the questions and the navigational path through the questionnaire*

Guideline 6.8:   *Visually group related information in regions through the use of contrast and enclosure*

Guideline 6.9:   *Consistently identify the beginning of each question and/or section*

Guideline 6.10:   *Use visual elements and properties consistently across questions and pages/screens to visually emphasize or deemphasize certain types of information*

Guideline 6.11:   *Avoid visual clutter*

Guideline 6.12:   *Minimize the use of matrixes and their complexity*

The Mail Questionnaire

Guideline 6.13:   *Determine whether keypunching or optical imaging and scanning will be used, and assess the limitations that may impose on designing and processing questionnaires*

Guideline 6.14:   *Construct paper questionnaires in booklet formats, and choose physical dimensions based upon printing and mailing considerations*

Guideline 6.15:   *Decide question layout and how questions will be arranged on each page*

Guideline 6.16:   *Use symbols, contrast, size, proximity, and pagination effectively when designing branching instructions to help respondents correctly execute them*

(continued)

Guideline 6.17: Create interesting and informative front and back cover pages that will have wide appeal to respondents

Guideline 6.18: Avoid placing questions side by side on a page so that respondents are asked to answer two questions at once

The Web Questionnaire

Guideline 6.19: Decide whether an electronic alternative to a web survey is more appropriate (e.g., fillable PDF or embedded e-mail survey)

Guideline 6.20: Choose how the survey will be programmed and hosted commensurate with the needs, skills, and sponsorship of each survey

Guideline 6.21: Evaluate the technological capabilities of the survey population

Guideline 6.22: Take steps to ensure that questions display similarly across different platforms, browsers, and user settings

Guideline 6.23: Decide how many questions will be presented on each web page and how questions will be arranged

Guideline 6.24: Create interesting and informative welcome and closing screens that will have wide appeal to respondents

Guideline 6.25: Develop a screen format that emphasizes the respondent rather than the sponsor

Guideline 6.26: Use a consistent page layout across screens and visually emphasize question information that respondents will need to complete the survey while deemphasizing information that is not essential to the task

Guideline 6.27: Do not require responses to questions unless absolutely necessary for the survey

Guideline 6.28: Design survey-specific and item-specific error messages to help respondents troubleshoot any issues they may encounter

Guideline 6.29: Evaluate carefully the use of interactive features, balancing improvements in measurement with the impact on respondent burden and the implications for mixed-mode surveys

(continued)

Guideline 6.30: Use audiovisual capabilities of the Web sparingly, and evaluate the differential effect they may have on respondents

Guideline 6.31: Allow respondents to stop the survey and finish completing it at another time

Guideline 6.32: Whenever possible, collect paradata that provide feedback on how the respondent interacts with the questionnaire

Guideline 6.33: Test the survey using a variety of platforms, connection speeds, browsers, and user-controlled settings, and test the database to ensure that items are collected and coded correctly

Guideline 6.34: Take screenshots of each page of the final questionnaire for testing and documentation

Pretesting Questionnaires

Guideline 6.35: Obtain feedback on the draft questionnaire from a number of people, each of whom has specialized knowledge of some aspect of questionnaire quality

Guideline 6.36: Conduct cognitive interviews of the complete questionnaire in order to identify wording, question order, visual design, and navigation problems

Guideline 6.37: When the stakes are high, consider doing experimental evaluations of questionnaire components

Guideline 6.38: Conduct a small pilot study with a subsample of the population in order to evaluate interconnections among questions, the questionnaire, and the implementation procedures

CHAPTER 7

Implementation Procedures

AS THE use of computers and the Internet has increased, people have become more inundated with requests for their time and attention, and people have become more guarded about providing their full contact information, the challenge of successfully implementing a survey has increased. One of the most perplexing difficulties facing surveyors now is how to conduct general population surveys. Those using the mail have long been challenged by the lack of an adequate sample frame, and with current challenges to random digit dial surveys, the telephone is becoming less and less of a desirable option for such surveys. The problems are similar for the Web: There is no available sample frame and response rates are often low. Moreover, as discussed previously, it is not considered ethical to contact individuals by e-mail unless a prior relationship exists.

This chapter is about finding new and innovative ways to overcome these challenges while still working from the social exchange perspective and within the tailored design framework. As such, the methods we advocate in this chapter for using address-based sample frames and applying both web and mail methods to general public surveys represent a significant departure from previous editions of this book, although many of the finer details will be familiar to readers of previous editions.

We provide the following example as a means for illustrating how address-based sampling frames along with mail and web modes can be used to conduct successful general population surveys. In 2007, the U.S. Postal Service Delivery Sequence File (DSF) described in Chapter 3 was used to obtain a random sample of households in a small metropolitan region of northern Idaho and eastern Washington. In an effort to examine different possibilities for conducting general population surveys, researchers designed several experimental treatments, and sampled households were randomly assigned to receive one of them. One treatment, mail preference, initially involved sending by postal mail a request to respond to a 12-page (8.5″ × 11″ booklet) questionnaire containing 51 questions that requested up to 81 answers. This group was later given the option to complete the survey by Web or mail when the replacement questionnaire was sent. Sample members in another treatment, web preference, were initially invited through a postal letter to respond to the same exact questions by Web but were informed that a mail questionnaire would be sent in about 2 weeks for those who did not have web access. The overall design for all treatment groups is summarized in Figure 7.1. Except for the technical details involved with responding by each mode, the contact materials used in each treatment were the same (examples can be seen throughout this chapter).

Overall, the mail preference treatment yielded a response rate of 71%, with only 1% responding by the Web. In comparison, the web preference treatment yielded a response rate of 55%, with 41% responding by the Web and 14% responding by mail. Two important conclusions can be drawn from these results. One is that mail methods for achieving reasonable response rates to household surveys continue to be effective, even when names are unavailable. The other is that it may also be possible to achieve response rates that approach those of mail through the use of address-based sampling and web surveys.

Figure 7.1 Experimental treatments for general population mail and web survey that used the Delivery Sequence File (DSF).

	Mail Preference	Web Preference
Nov. 2, 2007	Standard prenotice letter	Standard prenotice letter
Nov. 6, 2007	Invitation letter, $5 incentive, mail Questionnaire, and return envelope	Invitation letter including URL and access code, $5 incentive, and web survey instructions
Nov. 13, 2007	Postcard thank you/reminder	Postcard thank you/reminder with URL and access code
Nov. 29, 2007	Replacement questionnaire and return envelope with cover letter including URL and access code for web option	Reminder letter with URL, access code, and web survey instructions accompanied by a mail questionnaire and return envelope for the mail option
Outcome	**Responded by mail: 70%** **Responded by Web: 1%** **Total: 71%**	**Responded by mail: 14%** **Responded by Web: 41%** **Total: 55%**

Source: "Will a Mixed-Mode (Mail/Internet) Procedure Work for Random Household Surveys of the General Public?" by D. A. Dillman, J. D. Smyth, L. M. Christian, and A. O'Neill, 2008, May, New Orleans, LA. Paper presented at the annual conference of the American Association for Public Opinion Research.

In the design of this DSF study, we followed the advice of an old adage: "Don't put all your eggs in one basket." In other words, an enormous amount of effort was devoted to developing multiple and different aspects of the survey and implementation as a means to create appeal for many different types of respondents. The success of this study was not due to any one single characteristic or element of the survey or implementation; rather, it reflects a whole package of design and implementation decisions. Each decision was made with the goal of producing a personalized (although with no actual names) and highly salient questionnaire to be sent with implementation materials with a variety of appealing aspects, all of which are discussed throughout this chapter.

Results from this study were sufficiently promising that, in many cases, the guidelines we present in this chapter use examples from it. Nevertheless, the guidelines remain broad enough to be applied in a wide variety of survey situations. Moreover, although one of the specific challenges of this survey was the linkage between the availability of mail addresses and the desire to conduct the survey via the Internet, not all surveys will face this challenge. Therefore, in this chapter we discuss implementation procedures for mail and web surveys separately. However, behind the specifics of implementation for both of these modes is a common goal—to remove barriers to response and take steps to motivate as many potential respondents to complete the questionnaire as possible. Broadly speaking, one does that through minimizing the costs and maximizing the rewards of responding while also establishing trust.

MAIL SURVEY IMPLEMENTATION

Many surveyors we encounter have a tendency to shy away from mail surveys based on the belief that adequate response rates cannot be achieved using this mode. By comparison, we tend to give mail surveys more credit than that, and we continue to believe in their ability to produce good survey data if they are designed in a way that encourages response from as many different types of sample members as possible. When the questions and questionnaires are well designed in the ways discussed in previous chapters, and when solid implementation procedures are used, we see response rates of 50% to 70% time and time again. One key to this success is that implementation procedures cannot be planned at the last minute after spending extensive time on questionnaire design. The details of implementation are essential elements in the success of a mail survey and therefore must receive considerable thought and planning. We turn now to guidelines for mail survey implementation that are designed to help surveys appeal to as many sample members as possible.

Guideline 7.1: To the Extent Possible, Personalize All Contacts to Respondents (Even When Names Are Unavailable)

Social and behavioral scientists have long known that in emergency situations, the more bystanders there are, the less likely anyone is to step forward and help out. It is for this reason that many first aid courses emphasize the importance of personally singling out individuals to make requests for help: "You, go call 911!" Although less dramatic, the goal of personalizing survey contacts is quite similar: to draw the respondent out of the group. However, if the request is not personalized, it is very easy for respondents to ignore it, using the rationale that others in the group will surely respond. Moreover, personalization can be used to establish the authenticity of the survey sponsor and the survey itself and to gain the trust of respondents, both of which should improve the likelihood of response.

Correspondence can be personalized in many ways—the use of real letterhead printed on high-quality paper, real names instead of a preprinted salutation of "Dear Resident," blue ink signatures, or simply replacement mailings with the message "To the best of our knowledge you have not yet responded." Thus, in addition to using names when they are available, it is also important to look for other ways to personalize. In the DSF study discussed previously, the use of the address-based sampling frame meant that only addresses and not individual names were available, yet personalization played heavily in the design. The survey was strongly personalized to the community through the use of recognizable community-relevant graphics. These graphics appeared on the letters, the questionnaire, and the envelopes both to appeal to the respondents through their affiliation with the community and to help them make the mental connection between the questionnaire and all of the letters they had received. Personalization to the community was further enhanced through the use of questions that made meaningful reference to the community and to specific issues and events that occurred there. In addition, the request to complete the survey was framed as a request for help that only residents of this community could provide. What is more, even if names had been available, such attempts to highlight the personal importance of the survey for the respondent would have still been made.

However, because it is easy to use computer technology to insert information into form letters and e-mails, it is possible and very easy to over-personalize, as in the following example: "Dear Don Dillman, I am writing to inform you and your wife Joye that the XYZ Company has created a new dog food that we are sure your Boston Terrier, Crickett, will find to be very tasty. We would like to send a free sample to your home in Pullman, Washington." Such letters are impersonal precisely because of the extreme effort made to insert personal references. Therefore, it is important to strike a balance between producing generic contacts that could be sent to anyone and overpersonalizing contacts in a way that makes them seem intrusive. Personalization might best be thought of as what one would do in a letter sent to a business acquaintance who is not well known. It provides the look and feel of being from a real person rather than a carefully programmed computer, but it maintains professional distance.

A significant body of research has found such personalization to be an effective means for modestly increasing response to mail surveys. As just one example, Dillman et al. (2007) reported the results of nine experiments testing the effects in mail surveys of contacts that are personalized (insertion of name and address, use of sponsor's stationery, and blue ink signatures in each letter) versus unpersonalized (mass-copied letters with group salutations). The surveys included one nationwide survey, a statewide survey, three county or city surveys, and four surveys of special interest groups (e.g., Oregon ATV owners, New Hampshire mountain bikers, etc.). In the general population surveys, the personalization had a consistent and modest impact on response rates, increasing them from 3 to 12 percentage points. The effects of personalization in the surveys of special interest groups were less clear, however. In some cases appealing to the person's special interest (e.g., Dear ATV Owner), which may be considered a different kind of personalization, resulted in higher response than using the person's name, but this was not always the case and there was no predictable pattern in the data for when this effect may occur.

As more and more daily interactions occur with computers (i.e., automatic teller machines, self check-out at stores, global positioning system units that give driving directions, etc.) or products of computers (e.g., mass-produced letters and questionnaires), we believe that true authentic personalization will become more rare, thus making it even more important and effective when it is achieved. Inasmuch as authenticity and trust are integral parts of the tailored design method, so too is personalization.

Guideline 7.2: Send a Token of Appreciation with the Survey Request

One of the largest contributors to improved response rates, second only to multiple contacts (to be discussed later), is the appropriate use of prepaid token financial incentives. The token incentive serves two functions. It brings social exchange into play and encourages respondents to reciprocate by completing the survey. Equally important, though, it is a novel and unexpected gesture that brings additional attention to the request so that respondents read and contemplate it rather than just tossing it. Some examples of the effectiveness of various advance incentives on student and general public populations can be seen in Figure 7.2.

Perhaps more important than its influence on response rates is the effect that a token financial incentive has on nonresponse bias. Research is beginning to demonstrate that such incentives reduce *nonresponse bias* by pulling

Figure 7.2 Examples of the effects of advance token incentives in mail surveys.

Population/Year	Sample Size	Experimental Groups ($)	Response Rate (%)
Oregon State University students who left the College of Agricultural Sciences without graduating (1997, Mason)	133	0	28
	130	2 Check	44
	125	2 Bill	53
Recent graduates of the College of Agricultural Sciences at Oregon State University (1998, Mason)	129	0	59
	135	2 Bill	67
	141	5 Bill	81
Oregon State University distance education students (1997, Lesser)	249	0	20
	91	2 Check	25
	92	2 Bill	32
	87	5 Check	31
	97	5 Bill	32
Oregon State University June 1997 Graduates (1998, Lesser)	231	0	52
	234	2 Bill	65
New residents of Washington who obtained a state driver's license (1994, Dillman)	368	0	44
	357	2 Bill	63
New residents in Iowa who obtained an Iowa state driver's license (1997, Lorenz)	317	0	42
	313	2 Singles	70
	313	2 Bill	73
New residents of Idaho aged 50–70 (1996, Carlson)	526	0	53
	526	2 Bill	72
	524	300 Lottery	58
Centre County, Pennsylvania, residents (1998, Willits)	470	0	39
	288	2 Bill	62

Source: Quantifying the Influence of Incentives on Mail Survey Response Rates and Nonresponse Bias, by V. M. Lesser, D. A. Dillman, J. Carlson, F. Lorenz, R. Mason, and F. Willits, 2001, Atlanta, GA: American Statistical Association. Accessed June 20, 2008 at http://www.sesrc.wsu.edu/dillman/.

Figure 7.3 Effects of a $2 incentive on the age composition of a completed sample of new driver's license holders in Washington State.

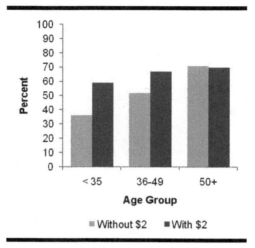

Source: The Influence of Different Techniques on Response Rates and Nonresponse Error in Mail Surveys, by K. J. Miller, 1996, Bellingham, WA: Western Washington University. Unpublished master's thesis.

in respondents who otherwise might not answer the questionnaire. Figure 7.3, for example, shows how a $2 incentive in a survey of new driver's license holders in Washington State pulled younger respondents into the sample, resulting in similar percentages of respondents completing the survey across age groups. Without the incentive, the completed sample would have considerably underrepresented younger respondents (Miller, 1996).

A more recent experiment demonstrated the power of incentives to reduce nonresponse bias in the estimates one is trying to make. Groves et al. (2006) found that respondents who reported high interest in birding were more likely than those who were uninterested in birding to respond to a mail questionnaire about birding, thus artificially inflating estimates of the prevalence of this activity among the population. When the surveyors included a prepaid token financial incentive with their survey request, however, more respondents who were relatively uninterested in birding completed the questionnaire, thus adjusting estimates of its prevalence down toward what one might expect the true value to be.

In an effort to save valuable resources, many surveyors opt to utilize promised or contingent incentives (i.e., payments sent after the questionnaire is completed and returned) instead of advance incentives. However, the question of advance versus promised incentives is one for which the evidence is quite clear. Token financial incentives included with the original survey request have been shown to be significantly more effective than much larger payments promised to respondents after they complete their questionnaires. As just one example, James and Bolstein (1992) achieved a 71% response rate with a four-contact response strategy including a $1 prepaid incentive but only a 57% response rate with the same contact strategy and a promised payment of $50 for those returning questionnaires. Likewise, in a meta-analysis of 38 experimental studies, Church (1993) found no statistically significant effect of promised incentives.

The problem with promised incentives is that many people view them as financial remuneration for answering a survey: "If you complete this questionnaire, I will pay you for it." In an economic exchange of this kind, if the price is too low or the person simply is not interested in doing the survey at any price, it is culturally acceptable not to respond. In contrast, token incentives provided in advance change the terms of exchange from economic to social, as discussed in Chapter 2. Sending a small amount of money with the questionnaire is a goodwill gesture that puts the sponsor and questionnaire in a positive light and sets the stage for the respondent to reciprocate by completing the questionnaire.

Because the incentive is meant to invoke a social exchange rather than a financial exchange, the value of the incentive can be kept quite small. From a practical standpoint, $1 is the smallest amount one can easily send, because coinage is difficult to process and handle. Some studies have found that larger amounts are more effective (Trussell & Lavrakas, 2004), but there are clearly diminished returns with far more of an increase coming from the first dollar than from 5 or 10 times that amount. Based on both evidence and experience, we recommend an incentive amount between $1 and $5 for surveys of most populations. One exception is with physicians—for which incentives of $25 to $100 have been found to be effective—but this is a very specialized population. In addition, we have seen few instances in which repeating incentives in later contacts is effective, and such practices are not consistent with the perspective that each contact with respondents should appeal to them differently. The exceptions are with establishment surveys, which are discussed in Chapter 12, and with surveys of physicians (Moore & An, 2001). Outside of these survey contexts, we recommend forgoing repeat incentives.

Many surveyors include nonmonetary, material incentives rather than cash incentives with their questionnaires. In some cases they use cash cards or gift cards to approximate a cash incentive. Other items that are used are packets of coffee, chocolate, ballpoint pens, regional park passes, phone cards, postage stamps, key rings, tea bags, and trading stamps, among other things. The reasons for opting to send such token gifts in lieu of a cash incentive vary widely. In some cases, material incentives are used because surveyors are bound by rules prohibiting them from sending cash. For example, cash cannot be sent through the mail in New Zealand or the Netherlands. In other cases, surveyors have opted to send material incentives because they can be bought in bulk, which saves money (i.e., buying a large number of $5 phone cards for $2.50 each; Teisl, Roe, & Vayda, 2005) or because the surveyor can be refunded for unused cash cards, whereas cash itself is gone for good once it is mailed (Bailey, Lavrakas, & Bennett, 2007).

The research, however, is consistent on the effects of such cash card and material incentives: They generally do increase response rates, but not as much as a small prepaid cash incentive. The aforementioned meta-analysis by Church (1993) found that material incentives improved response rates by 8 percentage points compared with 19 percentage points for token financial incentives. Likewise, Bailey et al. (2007) found that even a cash card worth twice the value resulted in significantly lower response rates than a $5 cash incentive. In addition, in a heterogeneous sample, it may be difficult to find a material incentive that will appeal similarly to everyone in the sample in the way that cash might. For example, one study in New Zealand found that chocolate increased response among young respondents, whereas postage stamps increased response among older respondents (Gendall & Healey, 2007). Thus, when it is allowable, providing a small token cash incentive has the largest effect on response rates, but when cash cannot be used, providing carefully selected material incentives can be beneficial.

Another incentive that has increased in popularity among surveyors is lotteries or prize drawings where respondents have a chance to win large-ticket items such as iPods or airline tickets. However, it appears that these offers have a relatively small, if any, effect on response. A comparison by Carlson (see Figure 7.2) of a $2 bill, a chance to win $300 in a lottery, and no incentive in a survey of new residents of Idaho resulted in a response rate of 53% for the control group compared to 58% for the lottery and 73% for the cash incentive. Another study that compared lotteries, cash, and contributions to charities showed that only prepaid cash incentives made a difference in response rates (Warriner, Goyder, Gjertsen, Hohner, & McSpurren, 1996). Even if prizes or lotteries can boost response a small amount, the effect when compared to sending a token cash incentive is quite small.

Guideline 7.3: Use Multiple Contacts, Each with a Different Look and Appeal

Multiple contacts are essential for maximizing response to mail surveys. Once when we suggested multiple contacts to a client, the immediate response was the following: "No problem. We'll just print a lot of extra questionnaire packets and stamp 'second notice' on the outside of the envelope." This meant that the dated letter and other contents would appear the same as those received earlier. As discussed in Chapter 2, under social exchange, stimuli that are different from previous ones are generally more powerful than the repetition of a previously used technique. People with whom the first letter was successful will not be subject to receiving a replacement questionnaire. Therefore, the later contacts need to be varied in an effort to increase their effectiveness with nonrespondents (who were not convinced to participate by tactics used in earlier requests). A system of five compatible contacts includes the following:

1. A brief *prenotice letter* that is sent to the respondent a few days prior to the questionnaire. It notes that a questionnaire for an important survey will arrive in a few days and that the person's response will be greatly appreciated.

2. A *questionnaire mailing* that includes a detailed cover letter explaining why a response is important, the questionnaire, a prepaid postage envelope, and a token incentive if one is to be provided.

3. A *thank you postcard* that is sent a few days to a week after the questionnaire. This mailing expresses appreciation for responding and indicates that if the completed questionnaire has not yet been mailed it is hoped that it will be returned soon.

4. A *replacement questionnaire* that is sent to nonrespondents 2 to 4 weeks after the previous questionnaire mailing. It indicates that the person's completed questionnaire has not yet been received and urges the recipient to respond.

5. A final contact made by a *different mode of delivery* 2 to 4 weeks after the previous mailing. The different mode of contact distinguishes each type of final contact from regular mail delivery. A "special" contact has been shown to improve overall response to mail surveys (Dillman et al., 1974; Heberlein & Baumgartner, 1978).

Although this five-contact system has worked effectively in many studies, there is some room for modification. For example, the DSF study that opened the chapter used only four contacts because the returns from the fourth contact were so small (suggesting returns from the fifth would also be small) as not to warrant the costs of an additional contact. Perhaps more important than whether three, four, or five contacts are used is that each communication differs from the previous one and conveys a sense of appropriate renewal of an effort to communicate. The prenotice indicates briefly that something will be coming and asks for no immediate response. The invitation to participate explains the nature of the request and asks for a response. The thank you contact has a different visual appearance and is expressed as gratitude. The reminder letter contains a powerful form of implicit personalization—"We've not yet heard from you. . . ." And the final contact expresses the importance of the response to the sponsor by showing the expenditure of considerably more effort and resources, as reflected by the cost of delivery by telephone, Federal Express, priority U.S. mail, or other special delivery.

The Prenotice Letter

Research has consistently shown that a prenotice will improve response rates to mail surveys by 3 to 6 percentage points (Dillman, 1991; Dillman, Clark, & Sinclair, 1995; Fox, Crask, & Kim, 1988; Kanuk & Berenson, 1975). The purpose of a prenotice letter is to provide a positive and timely notice that the recipient will be receiving a request to help with an important study or survey. It should be brief, personalized, positively worded, and aimed at engendering enthusiasm and building anticipation rather than providing the details or conditions for participation in the survey. If a small token of appreciation is to be provided with the questionnaire, it should be mentioned here without going into details. In addition, this letter should be sent by first-class mail and timed to arrive only days to a week ahead of the actual questionnaire. An example of such a prenotice letter is provided in Figure 7.4.

Crafting the prenotice letter in this way is central to its success. In one large sample pretest of a national government survey of Americans older than 65, a prenotice letter had no significant effect on response rates, leading some to argue that preletters are not useful. However, upon examination, the reasons the letter was unsuccessful become apparent. For one thing, the letter was sent nearly a month prior to receipt of the questionnaire, by which time it was likely to be a distant, if not forgotten, memory. Sending the letter only a few days ahead of the questionnaire avoids this problem. In addition, this letter was nearly two pages long, going into great detail about the reasons for the questionnaire, the fact that the request was voluntary, and other explanations that seemed likely to raise anxiety (and therefore "costs") but that the recipient could not resolve by being able to see the nonthreatening content of the questionnaire. Much of this information needed to be presented to the respondent, but the actual cover letter that accompanied the questionnaire would have been a much better place to present it. A more carefully crafted and timed prenotice letter would likely have produced higher response rates.

In surveys that are contracted to another organization for data collection, it may be useful to have the preletters come from the study sponsor on its stationery. An example is when a government agency contracts with a private firm to conduct the survey. Inasmuch as government sponsorship tends to improve response rates (Heberlein & Baumgartner, 1978), having the preletters processed on the appropriate government stationery is desirable. Such a preletter provides an opportunity to explain briefly that the survey is being conducted for that government agency by the XYZ Company, thereby invoking the exchange elements of authority and legitimacy.

Occasionally when a preletter has been recommended for starting the survey sequence, someone has objected to the format on the grounds that

Figure 7.4 Example of a postal mail prenotice letter used with an address-only sample.

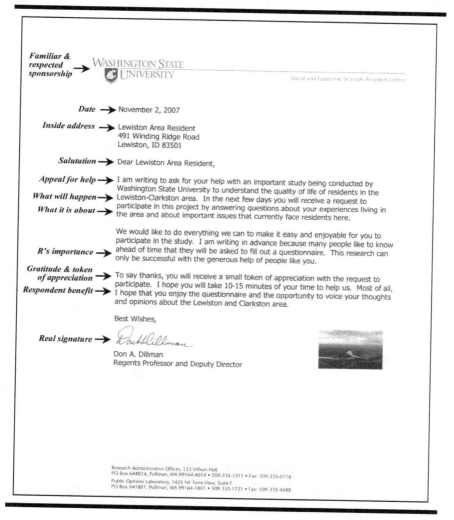

"I wouldn't open a letter, but I would look at a postcard." Although we are unaware of any mail survey tests, the effectiveness of letter versus postcard prenotices was examined with respect to a random-digit-dialing telephone survey. Hembroff, Rusz, Rafferty, McGee, and Ehrlich (2005) found that compared to not sending a prenotice, sending a prenotice letter increased the odds of completing the interview by 28%, whereas sending a postcard prenotice increased the odds of completing the interview by only 15%. In terms of response rates, this difference amounts to only about a 3 percentage point advantage for the letter over the postcard. However, in this study Hembroff et al. (2005) estimated that sending everyone the letter would have resulted in more than $5,000 savings (because of fewer follow-up calls to nonrespondents) compared to sending everyone the postcard and an $11,000 savings over sending no prenotice.

There are a number of reasons why sending a letter is more effective than sending a postcard. It takes perhaps 20 seconds to get an event into long-term memory. A postcard can be looked at, flipped over, and laid aside in only a few seconds. A letter takes longer to open and can contain more trust-inducing elements such as letterhead stationery, personalized address, and blue ink signature to help define the survey as important. The goal is to convey the idea that something important is about to be sent to the person to whom the letter is addressed. Consistent with the idea that variety by itself has value in making each mailing more salient, we save the postcard format for the third contact (the thank you/reminder), when it will be a fresh stimulus that appears quite different from previous contacts.

The Questionnaire Mailing

The next contact respondents should receive is the questionnaire mailing, but simply sending a questionnaire to potential respondents is unlikely to result in very high response rates. Instead, the questionnaire mailing should contain a number of important pieces that contribute to the goals of reducing barriers and increasing motivation to respond. These include a cover letter, postage-paid return envelope, token incentive if one is being used, and the questionnaire.

The goal of the cover letter is to provide certain critical pieces of information in a relatively short manner, preferably within one page. In a somewhat brief and engaging way, the cover letter needs to communicate to respondents what they are being asked to do, why they are being asked to do it, how they should go about doing it, and what benefit will come from doing it. Respondents also need to come away from reading the cover letter trusting the surveyor and with some confidence that their participation will not harm them. To this end, both the tone and the content of the cover letter need to be carefully considered and constructed.

Sometimes when people begin to draft letters, they immediately adopt an impersonal approach that treats the recipient more as an object than a person from whom they are about to request a favor. For example:

I am writing to people like yourself because it is necessary for my agency to complete a technical needs assessment as a matter of agency policy.

or

In order to help you do a better job of completing your future tax returns, we want to know what problems you have had in the past.

The first of these sentences conveys that the letter is being written to a lot of people and concerns something important only to the agency. The second example implies that the agency is going to help respondents do what they should have been doing all along. From an exchange standpoint, the first sentence immediately eliminates reward value, and the second one incurs cost by subordinating the respondent to the writer, as explained in Chapter 2.

To help avoid these tendencies, it is useful when writing cover letters to create a mental image of an acquaintance with an educational level a little lower than the average of the population to be surveyed and to compose a letter that communicates specifically to that person. The goal is to find a style and specific wording that reflects normal social interaction surrounding a diplomatic and socially appropriate request. To this end, the letter should convey an attitude of straightforward communication as would be done with any person with whom one hopes to maintain a mutually respectful relationship.

In order to strike the right balance between the professionalism that is needed to convey that the letter is important and the personalization that is needed to create a social exchange connection with the respondent, it is important to include in the letter several features commonly found in more formal communications (see Figure 7.5). One of these is the date. It is unlikely that someone would send a letter to a business acquaintance without putting the date at the top. The absence of the date serves as an immediate indicator that a letter is unimportant. Likewise, using an unconventional format for the date, such as "July, 2010," also communicates an air of unimportance and should be avoided.

Another sign of importance is the appearance of one's name and address just below the date (i.e., the inside address). The absence of this material indicates a lack of professionalism and, therefore, importance. Likewise, the choice of salutation can communicate a lot of information to respondents. A salutation that uses a general label such as "Dear Citizen" (or resident, friend, neighbor, or colleague) quickly tells respondents that they are receiving a form letter, not a personal correspondence. In other words, it highlights the disconnect or social distance between the surveyor and respondent rather than the personal connection that one will need in order to invoke social exchange.

The question of what is an appropriate salutation, however, is a difficult one, because the appropriateness of a salutation varies from one situation to another. For example, when the survey is intended to be answered by a specific, preknown person, that person's name should be used in the salutation. When there is no preexisting relationship between the sender and receiver but the gender is known, salutations such as "Dear Ms. Adamson" or "Dear Mr. Adamson" are appropriate. However, it is increasingly difficult to determine gender from a name (e.g., Pat, Chris, Kelly, Terry, etc.), and many names appear simply as initials. In such cases, the surveyor should omit the salutation rather than risk offending the recipient.

There are some instances, however, when it is inadvisable to use a name in the salutation. For example, when relying on a within-household selection process communicated in the letter (as was done in the example in Figure 7.5), using one household member's name may result in the unfortunate situation in which the named person answers the survey rather than follows the selection procedures. In this particular case, it was decided that the best

Figure 7.5   Example of a survey invitation cover letter.

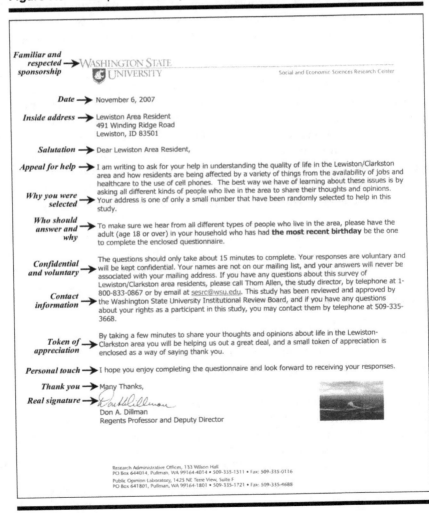

course of action was to use a general salutation but to personalize it in a way that was relevant to the survey topic. If a personalized salutation cannot be used because names are not available or because a within-household selection method is being employed, every attempt should be made to personalize in the other ways discussed previously.

Another important element to be included in the questionnaire mailing is a stamped return envelope. Within the social exchange framework, such an envelope serves three functions. First, it reduces costs to the respondent by making the return of the questionnaire as easy as possible. The respondent does not have to expend his own time and resources to find an envelope and stamp. Second, it encourages trust that the questionnaire is important, perhaps encouraging the respondent to think "Why else would this person have sent a stamped envelope that I can use for something else?" Third, sending a real stamp represents a goodwill gesture; the sender has sent something of value that the recipient can use for some other purpose if he likes. In addition, it is culturally difficult for many people to throw away something that has any monetary value. As a result, the enclosure of a stamped reply envelope seems likely to encourage the respondent to go ahead and complete the survey or at least to keep it in the household or office until the thank you postcard arrives.

One may be tempted to save money by using business reply envelopes rather than blank envelopes with real stamps. Such envelopes are processed by the U.S. Postal Service for a small annual charge for the permit necessary to use this service, and postage is paid only for envelopes that are returned. The use of business reply envelopes is becoming so common that receiving one will not seem unordinary. However, there is evidence that using a stamped envelope can improve response rates by a few percentage points over sending a business reply envelope (Armstrong & Luske, 1987; Dillman, Clark, et al., 1995). Responses also tend to come in more quickly with stamped envelopes, sometimes providing an advantage of 5 to 7 percentage points early in the fielding process so fewer incoming questionnaires cross in the mail with outgoing replacement questionnaires. In addition, business reply envelopes are processed differently by the post office than are first-class stamped envelopes. Because the post office has to keep an account of how many business reply envelopes are mailed back so that they can bill the organization correctly, it tends to hold them longer so that it can process them in groups. As a result, the returns to the surveyor are delayed and clustered much more than the small amount of delay and clustering that happens with first-class mail on the weekends and holidays.

Occasionally, in surveys that go to business employees, users of the tailored design method have objected to the use of stamped envelopes and even business reply envelopes on the basis that outgoing postage is essentially free to the respondent. Such an interpretation places the stamp in an economic rather than social exchange framework, much like the argument that incentives should be paid after the return of a questionnaire. It is the immediate effect on the recipient's mindset and behavior that is important when enclosing these items of small but real monetary value. Even when surveying organization executives, we normally use return envelopes with real stamps.

The Thank You Postcard

Most people who answer questionnaires, particularly for general public surveys, will do so almost immediately after they receive them. Repeated studies suggest that nearly half of the return envelopes are postmarked within 2 or 3 days of being received by respondents. After that time, the number of postmarked returns declines, sharply at first and then gradually. Those who fail to answer the questionnaire immediately are likely do so less because of conscious refusal than because of unrealized good intentions or the lack of any reaction at all. They likely lay the questionnaire aside with the vague intention of looking at it later, but as each day passes, it becomes a lower priority until it is completely forgotten, lost, or thrown away. As a result, the postcard follow-up is written not to overcome resistance but rather to jog memories and rearrange priorities. It is timed to arrive just after the original mailing has produced its major effect but before each person's questionnaire has had time to be buried under more recent mail or to be thrown away. One week is an appropriate interval of time for making an appeal that, if carefully worded, conveys a sense of importance without sounding impatient or unreasonable.

The choice of a postcard format over a letter is deliberate in that it should contrast with the prenotice letter, because new stimuli have greater effect than repeated stimuli. A letter format is used for the prenotice because it takes longer for the respondent to process cognitively and thus has a greater likelihood of being stored in long-term memory and recalled when the questionnaire arrives. In contrast, the function of a postcard is simply to jog one's memory so the fact that it can be quickly turned over and read is a benefit.

The precise wording of the card reflects still another concern. In the example in Figure 7.6, the first lines simply state that a questionnaire was sent to the respondent the previous week and why it was. This may appear to be a waste of precious space; however, for some respondents this is the first time they learn that a questionnaire was sent to them. The reasons for the original questionnaire not reaching a respondent extend well beyond it getting lost in the mail. The previous mail-out is sometimes addressed incorrectly or is not forwarded, whereas for some unexplained reason the postcard is. In still other cases, another member of the family opens the envelope containing the questionnaire and fails to give it to the desired respondent. Alternatively, it may have been skipped over when the respondent was looking through the mail and not opened at all. Whatever the reason, we often get telephone calls

Figure 7.6 Example of a postcard thank you/reminder.

Front

November 13, 2007

Last week a questionnaire was mailed to you because your household was randomly selected to help in a study about the quality of life in the Lewiston/Clarkston area.

If someone at your address has already completed and returned the questionnaire, please accept our sincere thanks. If not, please have the adult in your household who has had the **most recent birthday** do so right away. We are especially grateful for your help with this important study.

If you did not receive a questionnaire, or if it was misplaced, please call us at 1-800-833-0867 and we will get another one in the mail for you today.

Sincerely,

Don A. Dillman, Regents Professor and Deputy Director

Back

WASHINGTON STATE UNIVERSITY

110001

Social and Economic Sciences Research Center
PO Box 641801
Pullman, WA 99164-1801

Lewiston Area Resident
491 Winding Ridge Road
Lewiston, ID 83501

or letters after the postcard is mailed stating that the respondent would be willing to fill out a questionnaire if one were sent to them.

Most people who do not recall receiving a questionnaire will not bother to ask for one when they get the postcard. However, the knowledge that one was sent may stimulate them to query other members of their family (or organization) and may lead to its discovery. For others, the card may increase receptivity when a questionnaire finally does arrive in the mail, if it has been delayed. For those respondents who are fully aware of having received the questionnaire and still have it in their possession, the lead paragraph serves to remind them of it by coming quickly to the point.

The second paragraph of the card contains the crucial message that the postcard is designed to convey. People who have already returned their questionnaires are thanked, and those who have not are asked to do so right away. The urgency conveyed by asking for a response "right away" (or alternatively providing a time referent like "today") is consistent with the importance one wants to convey. In this particular study a household selection procedure was used, so an additional sentence was added to clearly communicate who should complete the questionnaire. The second paragraph is then finished with a sentence that subordinates the researcher to the respondents by indicating that their help is needed. In this way, respondents are made to feel important, which increases the benefit of participating in the survey.

The third and final paragraph is an invitation to call for a replacement questionnaire if one is needed. It is aimed at both those who did not receive the original questionnaire and those who lost or discarded it. A routine salutation and the researcher's name, signature, and title complete the thank you postcard message.

In addition to any identifying logos, the respondent's name and address are individually printed on the reverse side, exactly as was done for the envelope of the initial mail-out. The name is not repeated on the message side because this would require a further reduction of the print size used for the message and, if added mechanically, would exhibit an awkward contrast. In addition, when it is appropriate and not expected to influence answers to the survey questions, we sometimes include a relevant photograph or graphic on the reverse side of the postcard to help it stand out in the mail.

The decision to send this postcard to all questionnaire recipients whether they have responded or not is a practical one. About 1 week after the initial mailing is when the maximum number of returns usually arrive. Even in small surveys with a sample of a few hundred, there is usually no time to wait until a significant number of returns are in before addressing the postcard follow-up and still getting it mailed on schedule. Moreover, the monetary savings of doing so would be very small compared to the risk of sending the postcard too late. Another significant advantage of the blanket mailing is that the postcards can be (and should be) printed and addressed even before the first mail-out and stored so that this work does not interfere with the often confusing task of processing early returns.

The effect of the postcard reminder varies. A large factorial experiment of the preletter–postcard reminder sequence and a stamped return envelope on a national test of census questionnaires (where people were informed in a letter that their response was required by law) showed that the postcard reminder added 8 percentage points to the final response rate, compared with 6 percentage points for a preletter when tested alone (Dillman, Singer, Clark, & Treat, 1996). The combination of preletter and postcard added 13 percentage points, suggesting clearly that the effects are additive. The use of all three elements added 14 percentage points.

In a more recent examination of the effects of follow-up procedures, Roose, Lievens, and Waege (2007) reported a 12 percentage point increase in cooperation rates as a result of sending a postcard reminder to respondents who had responded to a brief questionnaire at a cultural performance and then been given a longer mail questionnaire to take home and complete. The cooperation rate for those who received no follow-up was 70% compared to 82% for those receiving only a postcard follow-up, 83% for those receiving both a postcard and a replacement questionnaire follow-up, and 89% for those receiving a postcard and two replacement questionnaire follow-ups.

Another experiment confirmed the importance of the format of the reminder contrasting with that of the prenotice. In this experiment, very similar postcards were used for the prenotice and reminder. Independently, the prenotice postcard improved response rates by 4 percentage points, and the reminder postcard improved them by 7 percentage points. In a treatment for which the prenotice and reminder postcards were both used, the response rate increased by 7 percentage points, the same as when the reminder was used alone (B. Ohm, personal communication, August 8, 1999). These results contrast sharply with the additive effect achieved in the census test mentioned previously, which relied on a prenotice letter and reminder postcard, and they provide additional evidence that contrasting stimuli are better for response than are repeated stimuli.

The Replacement Questionnaire

The next reminder letter should be sent about 3 weeks or so after the postcard reminder. Moreover, it is essential to send a replacement questionnaire with this follow-up letter because the time that has elapsed since the first questionnaire mailing makes it likely that the original questionnaire, if it has not been lost or thrown away, will be difficult to find. In one study, a researcher made the mistake of omitting a replacement questionnaire and as a result got a considerable quantity of cards and letters requesting a copy of the questionnaire (Dillman et al., 1974). Even after all of the effort of responding to these requests, the total response was only half that usually obtained for the second follow-up.

The packet of materials sent in this second follow-up will very much resemble that sent with the original questionnaire in that it should include a cover letter, questionnaire, and return envelope. What differs about this contact is that it should not contain a repeated incentive, as there is no evidence that repeated incentives are effective (except in certain establishment surveys, as is discussed in Chapter 12), and the tone of the cover letter should be very different (for an example, see Figure 7.7). This letter has a tone of insistence that the previous contacts lack. Its strongest aspect is the first paragraph,

Figure 7.7   Example of a postal mail follow-up letter.

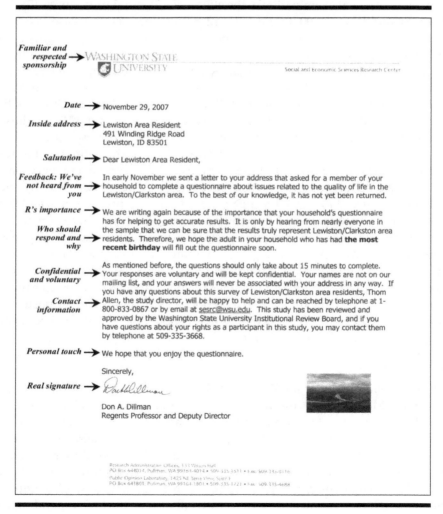

in which recipients are told that their completed questionnaire has not yet been received. This message is one of the strongest forms of personalization, communicating to respondents that they are indeed receiving individual attention. It reinforces messages contained in three previous contacts that the respondent is important to the success of the survey.

Most of this letter is devoted to a restatement of each respondent's importance to the study in terms quite different from those used in previous mailings. It conveys to the recipient, as a means of encouraging response, that others have responded. The social usefulness of the study is also reemphasized, implying that the usefulness of the study is dependent on the return of the questionnaire. The recipient is also reminded which member of the household is to complete the questionnaire, and participation is couched in "helping" terms to let the respondent know that he or she is important. The letter is completed with a reassurance of confidentiality, an implicit suggestion that the questionnaire should be enjoyable, the usual note of appreciation, and the now familiar blue ink signature. It is sent by first-class mail in the same type of envelope used for the initial mailing.

In developing the obviously stronger tone of this letter, it is important to neither over- nor under-sell. It needs to show a greater intensity than preceding letters, but not be so strong that potential respondents become disgruntled. The letter appears sterner and a little more demanding when considered in isolation than when read in the context of having already been asked to make a significant contribution to an important study. If the study lacked social importance or had a frivolous quality about it, the letter would probably seem inappropriate to the respondent and could produce a negative reaction.

Ordinarily this letter is not produced until questionnaires are returned from previous mailings in considerable quantity. The lapse of time provides an excellent opportunity to gather feedback on problems encountered by respondents. For every respondent who writes to ask a question, it is likely that many more have a similar question but do not take time to write. Thus, a postscript to the follow-up letter is sometimes added in hopes of answering questions that may have been suggested to the researcher by such feedback. When used in this way, the postscript also suggests that the study is important by indicating that the researcher is examining early returns and trying to deal with respondent concerns.

A replacement questionnaire creates certain processing challenges. It is possible that someone may fill out two questionnaires instead of only the one intended or may perhaps give the questionnaire to a spouse or friend to complete. Although this occasionally happens (as evidenced by returns with duplicate identification numbers and different handwriting), the frequency is so low as to be of little concern. Perhaps the greatest difficulty rests with those respondents who did fill out and return the earlier questionnaire, only to be informed that the researcher did not receive it. This underscores the great importance of an accurate identification system and the need to hold the follow-up mailing to the last minute so that respondents whose question-naires have just been received can be deleted from the mailing list.

The Final Contact

The important way in which this contact differs from those that precede it is in the packaging and delivery of the request. If one is considering simply sending a third copy of the questionnaire using the same type of envelope and another letter on the same stationery, it is hard to make this stimulus appear different from the second and fourth mailings. From an exchange per-spective, we expect that repeating any stimulus will decrease its effect each time it is used. After all, the stimulus failed to produce a response from the recipient the previous two times it was used. Thus, it seems unlikely that the recipient will get past the outward appearance to note any changes in the wording of the letter. This final contact differs from all previous con-tacts because of the packaging, the mode of delivery, and the speed by which it is delivered, all of which may be made noticeable before the letter is even opened. The effect being sought is to increase the perception of importance and of this being a legitimate request.

There are several different ways in which this perception of importance can be created. One method used with the original TDM was to send the final request by certified mail. Although this was a quite effective method in its time, increasing response rates between 10 and 20 percentage points (de Leeuw & Hox, 1988), we no longer use certified mail except in special cir-cumstances because it requires that someone be home to sign for the delivery. If nobody is home to sign for the letter, as is the case with many of today's dual-earner families, an attempted delivery notice is left and the individual may either sign that note and leave it for delivery the next day or go to the post office and pick up the letter. We consider it undesirable both from an exchange perspective and out of concern for the welfare of respondents to require people to go to the post office, which some recipients may be inclined to do. In addition, many alternatives to certified mail are now available that do not require signatures for delivery. They include courier delivery by one of several private companies such as Federal Express or United Parcel Service and priority mail delivery or special delivery by the U.S. Postal Service. The sole situation in which certified mail is recommended for use is when one is confident that someone is always present when postal deliveries are made, as might be the case in a business office.

An early study by Moore and Dillman (1980), which tested the use of special delivery and telephone follow-up calls as individual alternatives to certified mail, found that both alternatives worked about the same as certified mail (no significant difference), and both worked much better than another first-class mailing. We have observed many other tests of priority mail by courier in which an increment of additional response is attributable to use of courier or two-day priority U.S. Postal Service mail.

Sending this final contact by special mail requires using out-of-the-ordinary mailing procedures, which sometimes include different mailing forms and labels. Therefore, if one is contemplating using a particular service, it is imperative to talk with the provider. These delivery services are normally not set up to receive large numbers of such mailings at one time, and computerized procedures may be available for streamlining the process. In addition, costs may vary depending upon how many questionnaires are being dispatched. The variation in charges by distance, time of day that delivery is requested, whether a special promotional offer is being made, and whether the sponsor has a special contract or volume discount with the provider can affect both the possibilities and the costs. Current costs can range from about $2 per questionnaire up to as much as $25, or even more in the case of extremely long distances or when the fastest possible delivery time is selected.

Consequently, it is important to remember the total effect one is attempting to accomplish with this mailing. A different look is achieved by using a different outside container than in any previous mailings. An example is the light cardboard 9″ × 12″ carton used by some couriers. One also depends upon the special handling to convey that an attempt for rapid, assured delivery is being made. These attributes convey to the respondent that the survey is important. Finally, these external attributes are depended upon to get the recipient to read the letter, which differs significantly from the previous letters in that it is typically written in a softer tone, addresses any aspects of the survey that have been problematic for respondents, and includes an explanation of why the special contact procedure was used. In addition, enough time is allowed to elapse between the fourth and fifth contact so that little, if any, overlap occurs between this mail-out and late returns from the previous contact.

When telephone numbers are available, a telephone follow-up can be substituted for alternative mail delivery. In this case, a script is provided to interviewers so that they may inform respondents that a questionnaire was sent to them previously and explain that the call is being made to see if they have any questions about the study. Respondents are also encouraged to complete and return the survey. In some cases they may be given the opportunity to complete the survey on the telephone (see Chapter 8 for more on mixing modes) or told that another one can be sent to them if the previous one has been thrown away.

The switch in modes provides considerable contrast to the repetitive mail contacts and allows for immediate feedback from the respondent. Telephone follow-ups are preferred when the number of ineligible respondents is likely to be high. Typically, ineligible recipients of a questionnaire are more likely to ignore mailed requests to complete it, and learning that these people are ineligible by telephone allows the surveyor to drop them from the sample frame and allocate them properly in reports of response rates, cooperation rates, and so on. Telephone calls have also been found to be effective from the standpoint of reassuring people who do not understand the nature of the study and do not want to participate, as is sometimes the case with elderly respondents. The phone call also provides an opportunity to thank people for their consideration and assure them that they will not be contacted again.

When such a contact is used, it is important to make the call within a week after the fourth contact arrives by mail in order to increase the likelihood that the questionnaire has not been thrown away. It is also important that the interviewer be prepared to listen to concerns the respondent might have and be able to answer questions about the study and the questionnaire. This is not the type of call that can be turned over to someone instructed only to read a simple reminder notice to the questionnaire recipient.

The effectiveness of a carefully designed and deployed multiple-contact strategy can be seen in Figure 7.8, which charts the percentage of surveys

Figure 7.8 Percent returned per day in parallel general population mail and web surveys.

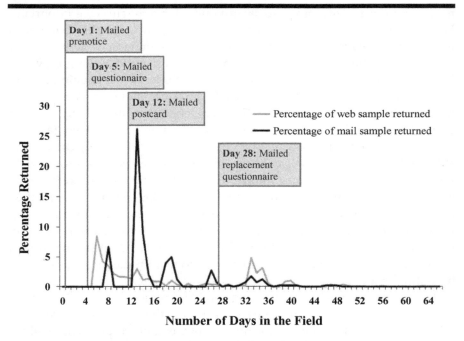

returned by day of the study for the general population DSF mail and web surveys discussed in the introduction to this chapter. The black line represents the mail returns from the contacts used as examples in this section. Although this study used a modified four-contact strategy, the figure quite clearly illustrates the spike in returns that occurred shortly after each contact was sent. It also reflects the clustering of mail sent in business reply envelopes (which is one of the reasons we prefer stamped first-class return envelopes) at the post office as well as how weekends and holidays affected returns (e.g., the spike occurring at Day 27 was due to incoming mail not being delivered over the Thanksgiving holiday and the weekend immediately following). The gray line in the figure represents returns from the parallel web survey, which is discussed in more depth later in the chapter.

A respondent-friendly questionnaire, personalization, a prepaid token financial incentive, and multiple contacts are the basic structural features around which an effective implementation system can be developed. But they are not the only elements of a good implementation system. Rather, they constitute the skeleton around which additional details are developed. It is these additional details to which we turn next.

Guideline 7.4: Carefully and Strategically Time All Contacts

As the previous discussion illustrated, each contact is intended to meet a specific goal. But each contact also has to work well within a set of other contacts. Sometimes it is the combined effects of multiple contacts that can be most powerful, and timing is central to those combined effects. For example, the prenotice should be given enough time to arrive and be processed before the questionnaire arrives, but it is important to get the questionnaire to the respondent before the prenotice is forgotten. Therefore, the first questionnaire mailing should be sent only a few days to a week after the prenotice and by first-class mail. In this way, when the respondent gets the questionnaire, he should immediately be able to make the connection between it and the prenotice letter he recently received: "Oh, this is the questionnaire they said they would be sending."

Likewise, the effectiveness of the postcard depends strongly on its arriving after the original request but before the questionnaire has been discarded or irretrievably lost. Therefore, it should be sent a few days to a week after the questionnaire. Scheduling the first replacement questionnaire follow-up a full 2 to 4 weeks after the postcard mailing is useful because it allows initial responses to dwindle to a small trickle, considerably lowering the chance that respondents who have just recently sent back their questionnaires will receive another one. Furthermore, the additional time, and subsequently smaller number of required follow-ups, reduces postage and clerical costs considerably. The strategy of waiting 2 to 4 weeks before sending the final contact serves the same purpose.

Guideline 7.5: Select All Mail-Out Dates with the Characteristics of the Population in Mind

Generally speaking, very few survey mail-out date "rules" apply to all populations. One exception might be that one should avoid certain holiday periods such as between Thanksgiving and Christmas, because people are often busier in these times. In addition, during this time as well as the day after any federal holiday, the U.S. Postal Service experiences higher than usual volume, which can create delivery problems. Other than these major holidays, the time of year or day of the week that a questionnaire is mailed does not seem to affect response rates.

Rather than attempting to find and follow general rules for mail-out timing, one should select a mail-out date based on the known characteristics of the population and the study's objectives. For example, in a survey of farm families, periods of planting and harvest, which are typically quite hectic, should be avoided. In northern climates this almost always means not doing such surveys in the spring or fall. Likewise, one should probably attempt to do surveys of grade school parents during the school year rather than in the summer because such a survey is more likely to be salient to the parents at that time. For targeting homogeneous groups such as these, changing salience and availability are prime considerations, and both are factors that cannot usually be identified for the general population.

Guideline 7.6: Place Information in the Mailing Exactly Where It Needs to Be Used

Initially, it is important to contemplate where the information to be included in the questionnaire mail-out best fits. For example, we have seen some questionnaires that provided information inside the questionnaire cover about who should respond and how. This information was then repeated almost word for word in the cover letter, a decision that contributed to the letter becoming three pages long! Sometimes separate sheets of instructions on how to answer certain questions are included. We have also seen mailing packages that included a second cover letter that was intended as support for the study but probably did no more than contribute to the bulk of the mail-out package. For these reasons, construction of the mail-out package begins by deciding what information should and should not be included and in which element it should be expressed. As noted in Chapter 4, there are compelling reasons for placing information exactly where it is to be used. If this is done, it tends to reduce the total number of words as well as the number of separate pieces that must be included in the mail-out, thereby reducing both stuffing and shipping costs.

It is also useful to determine which, if any, information needs to be repeated in multiple locations. One example is that the address to which the survey should be returned should be placed on the return envelope to ease the task of replying and also on the questionnaire itself in case the return envelope is misplaced. Likewise, it is sometimes useful to repeat within-household selection instructions both in the letter and on the questionnaire to help ensure that they get noticed and followed appropriately.

Guideline 7.7: Take Steps to Ensure that Mailings Will Not Be Mistaken for Junk Mail or Marketing Materials

When a legitimate survey arrives in the mailboxes of respondents, it arrives among a whole host of other pieces of mail such as merchandise catalogs, credit card offers, charity requests, campaign materials, messages from advocacy groups, personal correspondence, and bills, all vying for the recipients' attention. Because there are direct consequences attached to ignoring personal correspondence and bills, both of these are likely to get top priority from recipients, with the rest of the mail left to compete for attention and much of it thrown away unopened. Thus, it is important to differentiate the survey request and reminders from everyday junk mail. Doing so is absolutely critical when using address-only (i.e., no names) mailings, because the lack of a name in the address is an immediate indicator to recipients that a piece of mail is probably junk. In order to contribute to the impression that the survey is legitimate, authentic, and important, we recommend differentiating survey mail by professionalizing it in the following ways:

- Use standard and professional-appearing envelopes rather than those with flashy colors, those made of glossy paper, or those that are *artificially* made to look like express mail, air mail, or courier delivered.
- Provide a complete return address that clearly identifies the sender, in a way that is recognizable to respondents.
- If possible, use a recognized and respected logo with the return address.
- Except for the logo, limit print to standard print colors such as black or charcoal gray.
- Avoid buzzwords and phrases on envelopes such as "free gift," "easy," "hurry," "urgent," "immediate attention required," or "open at once."

Most of the tactics used by senders of junk mail are easily recognized as such by recipients. Thus, for the surveyor, it is useful to think of the envelope in a traditional sense, as a means to deliver an *enclosed* message to respondents. Except for those features meant to portray professionalism and perhaps sponsorship, the message one is delivering should be kept inside the envelope.

It is common to use a standard #10 business envelope (9.5" × 4.125") for many mail surveys, but sometimes the decision is made to use a larger envelope. Such was the case in the DSF survey discussed throughout this

Figure 7.9 Example of a large personalized envelope for mailing flat 8.5″ × 11″ booklet questionnaires.

chapter. A mock-up of the envelope used in that study can be seen in Figure 7.9. To help portray the importance of the contents and avoid the need to fold the questionnaire, we used a standard and plain 9″ × 13″ envelope. The Washington State University logo was added to the envelope on an address label in order to lend legitimacy to the package, and a recognizable return address was provided. For this particular study, we did add an extra graphic in addition to the logo, but for very strategic reasons. As discussed previously and as can be seen in the examples throughout this chapter, this same graphic (a photo of the communities being surveyed) was included on all of the letters as well as on the cover of the questionnaire itself. It was selected as a personalizing element because of the relevance it had for the particular population being surveyed, and it was included on the various elements of the survey package so that it could serve as an instant visual cue to help the respondents connect all of the pieces. Before even opening the envelope, respondents could recognize that the mailing was related to the letter they had recently received about an important study taking place in their community.

Guideline 7.8: Evaluate the Size and Weight of Mailing Materials on Mailing Costs

An unpleasant reality for mail surveyors in the United States is that postal expenses continue to increase. Whereas in the past postage was determined based on the weight (in ounces) of a mailing, in the round of postal price changes implemented in May 2007 package size and shape also became elements in determining postal costs for fairly standard types of mail (i.e., there have long been extra fees for irregular mail requiring special handling). For example, in the United States in early 2008 the rate for a standard letter or card (length, 5″–11.5″; height, 3.5″–6.125″; thickness, ≤.25″; weight, up to 3.5 oz) sent first class was 42 cents for one ounce and an additional 17 cents for each additional ounce. If mailed in a large envelope (length, ≥11.5″; height, ≥6.125″; thickness, ≤.75″) the first ounce cost 83 cents, with each additional ounce adding 17 cents. Given the reality of tight survey budgets, it is now important to consider both weight and size when calculating survey costs. Mailings that cannot fit into a standard #10 business envelope will be significantly more costly than those that can.

Guideline 7.9: Assemble the Mailings in a Way that Maximizes the Appealing Aspects of Each Element When the Package Is Opened

When it comes time to prepare each mail-out (except for the postcard), the first step is to assemble and insert the components—questionnaire, cover letter, return envelope, and (if appropriate) the token incentive. Often the planning of this step is ignored, leaving it up to the personnel who do it to find the most efficient way. However, this step is important and should be considered just as carefully as the content of the cover letter and the survey itself. Two things need to happen when the respondent opens the mail-out envelope: All enclosures need to come out of the envelope at once, and the appealing aspects of each element need to be immediately visible. Neither of these details should be left to chance.

In cognitive interviews designed to test mail-out packages, it has been observed repeatedly that one or more components often gets left in the envelope when the other contents are removed (Dillman et al., 1998). As a result of the desire to be as efficient as possible when assembling the mail-out, personnel typically fold the components individually and place them on top of one another before inserting them into the envelope. When the envelope is opened, the questionnaire typically gets removed because of its bulk, but the cover letter may be left in the envelope, which is often discarded before anyone realizes the mistake. When this happens, respondents have no explanation for why the questionnaire has been sent or what they are supposed to do with it. This can be particularly troublesome if the cover letter specifies who in the household is supposed to complete the questionnaire.

Fear of something getting lost has led to solutions that may compound the problem. One surveyor decided to insert a $2 bill into the reply envelope, reasoning that respondents would see it when inserting their completed questionnaires. This unfortunate decision did not take into account the importance of the respondent being able to see the token incentive immediately when opening the envelope in order to invoke social exchange. Moreover, those who decided not to complete the survey likely discarded the materials, including the incentive. Another surveyor decided to hide the incentive inside the pages of the booklet questionnaire, reasoning that the respondent would find it while answering the questions. Here again, the incentive was not immediately visible so that it could serve its social exchange function and, therefore, was probably unknowingly discarded by many.

Depending upon the size and shape of enclosures, somewhat different solutions are needed to avoid these problems. First, if one is using an 8.5" × 7" booklet questionnaire (i.e., legal-size paper folded in half the short way) with a standard 8.5" × 11" cover letter and a #10 business envelope, the following procedure is recommended. Fold the questionnaire vertically with the front cover on the outside of the fold. Insert the $2 bill on top of the folded questionnaire, and place the stamped reply envelope underneath. Then lay all three components on the middle third of the face-up cover letter. Fold the bottom third of the cover letter up and over these three components and complete the process by folding the top third of the cover letter down. The entire set of materials can then be picked up easily and inserted into the mail-out envelope (see the left panel of Figure 7.10). The advantage of this type of fold is that all materials must be removed together from the envelope. When the packet is unfolded, the respondent will simultaneously see every component. Another possibility is to use a Z fold, whereby the bottom third of the cover letter is folded upward over the middle third, and the top third is folded backward, so the paper forms a Z shape. The folded cover letter is then flipped over so that the top third of the letter is visible (and the portion of the letter on it is right side up), and the questionnaire and other materials are placed between the top and middle thirds so that they rest in the V formed by the fold. Placing the package into the envelope with the top portion of the letter right side up and facing forward ensures that when the letter is removed from the envelope, all of the other materials will come with it (see the right panel of Figure 7.10).

A thin 8.5" × 11" questionnaire stapled in the upper left corner and printed in the two-column format can be similarly folded. However, when initially folded for insertion, it should be done in accordion (or Z-fold) fashion so that the top of the front page displaying any masthead appears on the top of the fold, and underneath the token incentive, before being tucked inside the cover letter for insertion into the envelope.

Figure 7.10 Examples of ways to assemble mailings so that all pieces come out of the envelope at once and are immediately visible.

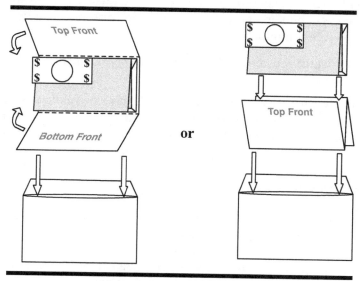

When the questionnaire has too many pages to allow for folding, flat mail-outs or U.S. Postal Service priority mail envelopes are often used. The chance of something getting left in this type of mail-out envelope is even greater. In these instances we are likely to use stickers to attach the token incentives to the cover letter or first page of the questionnaire. Attaching the mail-out components together with a metal binder clip is usually not done because of potential envelope tears from postal processing machines.

An important quality control issue surfaces during the folding and insertion process. The use of an identification number on the questionnaire for sample tracking purposes means that the right questionnaire has to be packaged with the right personally addressed cover letter and envelope (lest the wrong person be removed from the mailing list once the questionnaire is returned). In addition, the handling of cash (or checks written to individuals) requires that all of the right elements get into every mail-out in order for the implementation system to work. This is not a process that can be delegated to an organization's newest hires and forgotten. Like the rest of tailored design, it requires attention to detail.

When one is faced with the prospect of assembling thousands of mail-outs, rather than hundreds, or when one has access to machine assembly, it is tempting to forgo these methods in favor of separately folding and inserting each item as the machines encourage. We have observed many different mechanical processes and urge that anyone considering using them study prototype results carefully to control as much as possible whether and how respondents will be exposed to the results. The quality control for getting the right components in every mail-out package also needs to be carefully examined before committing to their use.

Guideline 7.10: Ensure that All Addresses in the Sample Comply with Current Postal Regulations

One relatively easy way to streamline a mail implementation system is to ensure that all addresses comply with current postal regulations prior to mailing. Doing so will considerably reduce the number of undeliverable pieces of mail returned by the post office. Some common rules to follow for mailing within the United States include the following (regulations may differ for other countries):

- Left-justify the delivery address.
- Capitalize everything in the delivery address.
- Use two-letter abbreviations for states.
- Do not use punctuation (periods or commas) in the delivery address.
- When possible, use zip +4 for more efficient delivery.

For example, "S.W. 705 Marcel St." should be changed to "705 SW MARCEL ST". In addition, the address should be printed large enough that it can be read when held at arm's length. Commercial software that will detect and correct such errors is available. With this software, it is much easier and more efficient to correct addresses ahead of time than to deal with individual pieces of returned mail once the survey is in the field, a topic to which we return later.

Guideline 7.11: Assign an Individual ID Number to Each Sample Member

Each questionnaire should have an individual identification number printed on it or printed on a label and affixed to it. An ID number is included so that follow-up mailings, an essential aspect of tailored design, can be sent only to nonrespondents (with the exception of returns that cross with the follow-up letter in the mail). Removing those who have already responded from the follow-up mailing list ensures that they are not inconvenienced, confused, or irritated by additional mailings that do not apply to them.

The ID number should be placed on the front or back cover of the questionnaire in plain view. Because some respondents are likely to tear off identification numbers, it is wise to place them in the corner of the questionnaire where their removal does not eliminate answers to questions (be sure to look at what is on the back side of the page too). Attempting to hide the numbers by placing them in small type on an inside page; embedding them into something that might be referred to as a *form, approval,* or *processing number* (e.g., "Approved Form 91854"); or printing them using invisible ink that will show up only under ultraviolet or other special light is unethical and inconsistent with the premise of making an honest effort to communicate openly with recipients. These are not trust-inducing strategies, and if respondents notice such attempts to hide ID numbers, their distrust will be heightened and their likelihood of participating reduced.

If one is highly concerned that respondents will object to the ID number, it might be best to disclose to them up front the reason for including such a number: "A questionnaire identification number is printed on the back cover of the questionnaire so that we can check your name off of the mailing list when your questionnaire is returned. The list of names is then destroyed so that individual names can never be connected to the results in any way." Informing respondents of the presence of an identification number in this way does not seem to have a serious negative effect on response rates, especially when compared to not being able to use the tailored follow-up that it facilitates.

If the data obtained by the questionnaire are considered so sensitive that the sponsor wishes not to be able to identify responses with an individual even momentarily (e.g., in questionnaires associated with litigation or those asking about sensitive behaviors), one might consider sending a stamped, self-addressed postcard that the respondent can return separately from the questionnaire to indicate that the questionnaire has been returned (see Figure 7.11

Figure 7.11 Example of separate return postcard used to facilitate anonymous return of questionnaires.

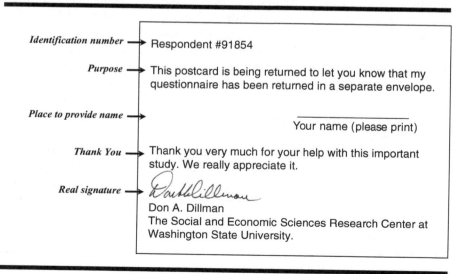

for an example). In this case, a message should be included in the cover letter along these lines:

> All answers to this questionnaire are completely anonymous. There is no identification number of any kind on the questionnaire. However, to let us know that your questionnaire has been returned, please sign the enclosed postcard and return it *separately* in the mail. This will allow us to check your name off of the mailing list so no further reminders will be sent to you.

In the few instances in which this procedure has been used, the number of postcards returned has corresponded closely, although not exactly, with the number of questionnaires returned, indicating that it is a quite effective alternative. However, such a strategy should be reserved only for the most sensitive questionnaires, because so much emphasis on protection with an ordinary questionnaire may discourage response by creating a false sense of concern among respondents that they are being "tricked" in some way. In addition, adding such a postcard is more expensive than using an identification number, and it adds considerable complexity to the mailing.

Guideline 7.12: Establish Procedures for Dealing with Undeliverable Mail

Usually one of the initial problems to present itself once contacts have been mailed is the return of undelivered mail. The first solution to this problem is to do everything possible to prevent it from happening, but despite the best of efforts some mail is still likely to be returned as undeliverable. Giving immediate attention to this mail often makes remailing possible and prevents wasting scheduled follow-ups.

The reasons provided by the U.S. Postal Service for nondelivery generally fit into three categories. The first relates to a change of residence by respondents. Occasionally people move without leaving a forwarding address. Others leave forwarding addresses, but the U.S. Postal Service only keeps them on record for 18 months. If the move was within the same city or county, it is sometimes possible to locate the person by consulting the local telephone directory or other listings. If only a telephone number is available, it may be necessary to call the household to get a mailing address. Through these efforts, it is often possible to remail a sizable portion of the questionnaires that were not forwarded.

The second reason for undelivered questionnaires is categorized here as "possible errors." This categorization seems appropriate because the main causes for "addressee unknown," "no such street," "no apartment number," "no residential delivery," and so on are clerical errors. When a questionnaire is returned for any of these reasons, processing procedures and sample sources need to be checked to see if an incorrect address was used. If this procedure does not identify the problem, then an attempt should be made to locate the respondent's telephone number and to call the household or business, thus reverting to the procedures used to locate those known to have moved. Some problems are unique to certain surveys. In one of our statewide surveys, nearly all of the letters for one rural community were returned. The reason for this problem was that the addresses reported in the sample list were different from those used by the U.S. Postal Service. A call to the local post office helped solve the problem.

The third category of problems reported in the notation system used by the U.S. Postal Service is that of letters that are refused or unclaimed. Generally, refusals are not a problem until later mailings when respondents recognize the envelope and presumably choose not to accept delivery. The questionnaires that are unclaimed from earlier mailings may have simply lain in the mailbox for a period of time without being picked up. This result suggests that the person may be temporarily gone, and remailing at a later time is often effective. However, some are clearly refusals, or the respondent chooses to leave the envelope in the mailbox. Out of respect for their rights, these respondents should not be contacted again. Finally, the U.S. Postal Service marks letters of persons who are deceased with that notation and returns them to the sender unless other arrangements for handling the deceased person's mail have been made.

The remailing of questionnaires requires establishing new mail-out dates for follow-up correspondence, creating additional work and complexity for the implementation of the study. However, the end result can be a significant increase of several percentage points in the final response rate.

Guideline 7.13: Establish Procedures for Dealing with Returned Incentives

In addition to creating a method for tracking and responding to returned mail, it is also important to establish a procedure for dealing with returned incentives. We quite commonly have respondents who send their incentive back to us because they do not want it, because they do not feel like they need incentive to respond, or for various other reasons. Likewise, incentives can come back in undeliverable mail. On one occasion a box of returned questionnaires that could not be remailed sat unopened in the mail center for weeks as other more pressing business was conducted. While on the way to discard these mailings, one of us decided to open one of the envelopes and found that it contained a $2 cash incentive, as did the rest of the envelopes in the box. As with this case, many surveyors are quite careful to account for every dollar when incentives are mailed out, but they often forget to plan ways to account for the money that is returned in undeliverable mail or by respondents. A system needs to be in place to deal with such returns and make sure all money is properly accounted for.

Guideline 7.14: Establish Procedures for Dealing with Respondent Inquiries

Another activity for which the researcher must be prepared is to answer respondent inquiries and comments. Each mailing is likely to bring reactions other than a completed questionnaire. Among the more frequent are the following:

- The person you want is out of town for a month and cannot do it until she returns.
- I would do the questionnaire except for the identification number on it.
- I would answer except for the personal questions, which I don't think are any of your business.
- I have only lived here for a few months, so I don't know enough about this community to answer your questions.
- I'm too old, but my daughter will fill it out if you really need it.
- I filled out a questionnaire like this one 6 months ago and don't want to do it again.
- Tell me how you got my name, and I'll do your questionnaire.

It would hardly be fair, or ethical, to send a questionnaire asking 50+ questions to someone and then ignore or refuse to answer their one or two resulting inquiries. Respondent questions, even strange ones, deserve a response. Thus, we make a point to answer each of them, but our response is determined by both philosophical concerns and response considerations. We explain why an identification number is used, why it is important to have old people as well as young people in the study, why the daughter would not be an acceptable substitute, and how the recipient's name was obtained. In general, one should respond to these types of queries as a well-trained interviewer would, attempting to convince people of their importance to the study. The most appropriate approach is to be straightforward and honest and to always thank the respondent for writing or calling.

In addition to these types of comments, letters are sometimes written by second parties on behalf of the questionnaire recipients. The most common of these indicate that the desired respondent is physically incapable of completing the survey, usually because of the infirmities of old age. Another fairly typical request comes from the spouse of the requested respondent, who reports that the person is temporarily out of town. These letters are responded to in much the same way that respondents' inquiries are answered, except that the acknowledgment letters are sent to the second parties who reported that the desired respondent cannot complete the questionnaire. The aim of these letters is to thank them and also to assure them that the person's name is being removed from the sample list, if that action is appropriate.

Still another kind of letter we have grown accustomed to seeing is from individuals who have simply heard about the study, perhaps because a friend showed them a questionnaire. These letters sometimes come from media people or from those who would find the results useful in their work. These inquiries are handled in as helpful a way as possible, consistent with the study's objectives. It is particularly important for large-scale surveys to be prepared with a policy for handling requests for interviews or news stories. An appropriate approach is to respond to such requests in much the same way one would answer respondents' questions, emphasizing the social usefulness of the study, the importance of every individual responding, and so on.

Guideline 7.15: Evaluate Early Returns for Problems that Can Be Addressed Mid-Stride

When returns begin to come in, one of the first priorities is to open the return envelopes and scrutinize the questionnaires. Besides providing for the quick location of items of concern that must be given attention in follow-up letters, this allows certain problems to be identified. For example, in one study it was learned that the ink used in printing the questionnaires caused some pages to stick together, resulting in sets of facing pages being skipped in many of the returned questionnaires (i.e., high item nonresponse). The immediate identification of this problem led to instituting a procedure whereby the missing two pages were photocopied, marked with the appropriate identification number, and returned to the respondent with a personalized note: "In our routine check for completeness we noticed two pages were missed. It appears they may have stuck together and thereby been inadvertently missed. . . ." Nearly two thirds of those contacted returned the missing pages, significantly improving the quality of the data. Usually, problems of this nature are not anticipated, making the close monitoring of early returns essential.

Each survey is different, with the survey topic, population, and sampling procedures all contributing to the existence of a unique set of circumstances. The important conclusion is that implementation activities do not simply take care of themselves once the survey questionnaires are in the mail. Much remains to be done.

WEB SURVEY IMPLEMENTATION

On the surface, many features of web survey implementation seem quite similar to those used for mail implementation, but because of the different technologies used (see Chapter 6), web implementation has to be handled somewhat differently than mail. One fundamental difference between mail and the Web is that with mail one delivers the questionnaire to the respondents, but with the Web one asks respondents to essentially go and get the questionnaire themselves, oftentimes through the use of technologies with which they are uncomfortable. As a result, making this task easy and comfortable for respondents becomes incredibly important. Another major difference is that with mail surveys it makes the most sense to send postal mail contacts (i.e., letters), because the questionnaire also has to be delivered by that method. But there are various ways contacts can be sent to ask people to complete a questionnaire on the Web, and the right choice depends on the specific survey situation. In some cases, respondents will need to be approached by e-mail only, a technique that works quite successfully for some surveys but is a major limitation for achieving good response rates to others. Yet in other instances, such as when only postal addresses are available as in the DSF study mentioned earlier in the chapter or when there is no prior relationship to justify sending e-mail contacts, respondents can only be approached by another mode (e.g., mail) and must be asked to go to the Web. In still other cases, the opportunity exists to approach respondents through both e-mail and mail. In these cases, we very deliberately take advantage of both for reasons described in this section. One needs to think very carefully about these multiple situations when starting to work on a web implementation system, because the mode of contact has serious consequences for other implementation features, such as the extent to which and how personalizing elements are used, whether and what type of incentives can be delivered, and how the delivery of contacts will be timed.

Guideline 7.16: To the Extent Possible, Personalize All Contacts to Respondents

Personalizing all contacts in web surveys is important for the same reason as in mail surveys—it establishes a connection between the surveyor and the respondent that is necessary to invoke social exchange, and it draws the respondent out of the group. However, the type of personalization one uses depends very much on the type of contact one is sending, and e-mail contacts can be particularly difficult to personalize, in part because e-mail is considered by many to be a less personal form of communication. In addition, many Internet users are keenly aware of the ease with which personalized e-mails can be mass produced. In fact, for experienced e-mail users, the appearance of one's name in certain locations within an e-mail—the subject line, for example—is an immediate indication that the message may be spam. Thus, the importance of striking a balance between adequately personalizing and overpersonalizing contacts may be even greater with e-mail contacts. However, a similar strategy to that used with postal mail contacts can also be used with e-mail contacts. That is, write the e-mail contacts as if writing an e-mail to a business acquaintance who is not well known. Doing so will help to strike the right tone and achieve the proper amount of personalization so that it is obvious that the message is from a real person (i.e., not computer generated) and that the request is legitimate and appropriate.

The effectiveness of e-mail invitation personalization was recently tested in a sample of first-year university students in Belgium. Students were randomly assigned to receive either a personalized (Dear [First name]

[Last name],) or an unpersonalized (Dear student,) e-mail invitation to participate in a web survey. The personalized invitations resulted in nearly an 8 percentage point increase in response rates over the unpersonalized invitations (Heerwegh, 2005). In another study, university students were asked to join an online survey panel for their university. Personalizing the invitation with "Dear [First name]" resulted in a 4.5 percentage point increase in the number of students joining the panel than did the less personal salutation "Dear Student" (Joinson & Reips, 2007). Further experimentation with the same panel also indicated that personalization has a stronger effect when survey invitations are sent from powerful individuals (e.g., professor and vice chancellor) than from less powerful individuals (Joinson & Reips, 2007).

Another strong indication that one is getting personal attention with e-mails is receiving individual, not bulk, messages. Stated another way, receiving a bulk e-mail (i.e., one sent to multiple recipients at once) is an immediate sign to individual recipients that they are unimportant. In this situation, it is easy for respondents to conclude that someone else will comply with the request and that their own response is not all that important, thus diffusing responsibility to others in the group. The same conclusion, however, is much more difficult to reach when the request is targeted to one individual in a more personal way.

Barron and Yechiam (2002) conducted an experiment to test this phenomenon. They e-mailed a simple question (i.e., "Is there a biology faculty in the institution?") to faculty, administrative staff members, and graduate students at a university, all of whom were likely to know the answer to such a question. Some of the requests were sent to groups of five individuals at a time, whereas others were sent to single individuals. Among those individuals who were sole recipients of the request for this information, about 65% replied, but among those who received the request as part of a group, only about 50% replied. Moreover, those who received individual requests and replied provided longer and more helpful responses to the question than did those who received the request along with others. This effect is much like the bystander effect that has long been studied in psychology, whereby the presence of bystanders decreases the likelihood of any one person stepping forward to help someone in need. Barron and Yechiam argued that virtual bystanders, represented by the presence of their e-mail addresses in the "To" field, invoke much the same effect.

In addition, the appearance of the e-mail addresses of multiple sample members in the "To" field raises serious ethical considerations, as confidentiality can no longer be ensured, and increases the likelihood that a message will be flagged as spam. As a result, in order to be ethical, to minimize the chance that contacts will be treated as spam, and to personalize contacts, avoid sending bulk e-mail contacts.

Guideline 7.17: Send a Token of Appreciation with the Survey Request

Inasmuch as one of the largest contributors to improved response rates in mail and telephone surveys is the appropriate use of prepaid token financial incentives, it stands to reason that the same would be true for web surveys. However, a pure Internet survey that uses e-mail contacts raises special problems for delivering prepaid financial incentives in that cash cannot be sent via e-mail. As a result, researchers have begun to explore different ways of delivering incentives, such as through electronic gift certificates, gift cards, or dispersal of incentives through such services as PayPal (Birnholtz, Horn, Finholt, & Bae, 2004). Incentives such as these have been shown to modestly increase response rates compared to sending no incentive. In a meta-analysis of 26 studies comparing incentive use to no incentive use in web surveys, Göritz (2006) found that providing material incentives increased the response rate by an average of 4.2 percentage points. This is likely a low estimate of the effect of material incentives, because most of the studies included in this meta-analysis utilized promised rather than advance incentives. Nevertheless, material incentives do not have as strong of an effect as a prepaid cash incentive. For example, Birnholtz et al. randomly assigned members of their web survey sample (all of whom were very experienced Internet users) to receive either (a) a $5 cash incentive with a survey invitation via postal mail, (b) a $5 Amazon.com gift certificate with a survey invitation via postal mail, or (c) a $5 Amazon.com gift certificate with a survey invitation via e-mail. The final response rates revealed that 57% of those receiving the cash incentive via postal mail completed the survey compared to 40% of those receiving the gift certificate via postal mail and only 32% of those receiving the gift certificate via e-mail.

The limited success of money and gift certificates sent electronically may very well stem from the added difficulty (i.e., costs) of redeeming them. For example, PayPal charges the recipients of money a fee to issue them a check (Birnholtz et al., 2004). In addition, it takes a fair amount of time, effort, and knowledge to set up an account with such services or to redeem gift certificates with particular online merchants. Moreover, there may be additional costs to respondents if the amount of the incentive only covers part of the cost of the item they are buying (Birnholtz et al., 2004). The costs (monetary and social exchange) of redeeming electronic incentives may be particularly high, and perhaps even prohibitive, for sample members who are relatively inexperienced with the Internet.

Another common response to the difficulty of providing incentives via e-mail is to utilize a lottery or prize drawing instead of a prepaid incentive. However, the research on the effectiveness of lotteries in Web-based surveys has generally shown that lotteries and prize drawings do not increase response rates significantly (Brennan, Rae, & Parackal, 1999; Cobanoglu & Cobanoglu, 2003; Porter & Whitcomb, 2003), with few exceptions (Bosnjak &

Tuten, 2003). Overall, then, the evidence strongly suggests that prize drawings and lotteries are not as effective as traditional cash incentives or material incentives, but there is some evidence to suggest that their effectiveness can be improved somewhat by informing respondents that they will receive the results of the prize drawing or lottery immediately upon completing the survey (Tuten, Galesic, & Bosnjak, 2004).

Like mail surveys, a prepaid cash incentive appears to be most effective at increasing response rates. Such an incentive, however, requires the surveyor to use a mode other than the Web to contact respondents and provide them with the incentive. Therefore, we advise using postal mail instead of or alongside e-mail contacts in order to provide sample members with a prepaid cash incentive whenever possible. Using postal mail to send invitations for Web-based surveys has other benefits as well that are discussed in Guideline 7.20.

Guideline 7.18: Use Multiple Contacts and Vary the Message across Them

As far as we are aware, sending multiple contacts to potential web survey respondents is the most effective way to increase response rates (Cook, Heath, & Thompson, 2000). As an illustration, in one study of college undergraduates, using four follow-up contacts resulted in a 37 percentage point increase in response rate over sending only a survey invitation and no follow-ups (Olsen, Call, & Wygant, 2005). However, very little research has been done on the optimal combination of contacts to use, and in some cases slight modification from the sequence used for postal mail surveys may be appropriate.

One such modification that we often make is the elimination of the prenotice. We often start our web survey implementation sequence straight away with a survey invitation that includes the uniform resource locator (URL) of the survey and instructions on how to access it along with the description of the study and why response is important. This initial invitation is then generally followed up with a number of reminder e-mails. Because sending additional e-mail contacts is relatively inexpensive, one can often leave the final decision on the number of follow-ups to send until well into the fielding process. If both the first and second follow-ups yield significant gains, a third follow-up may be useful as well. However, if previous follow-ups have only yielded a handful of responses, additional follow-ups may not be warranted as they may only irritate sample members (unless these follow-ups take a significantly different approach from previous contacts).

In the same way that it is important to vary the stimulus across postal contacts, it is also important to vary the stimulus across e-mail contacts. Sending the same e-mail over and over is unlikely to be effective at convincing sample members to reply. Moreover, if the first message gets flagged as spam, a repeat message is likely to meet the same fate. Varying the content of the e-mails both appeals in different ways to respondents and reduces the likelihood that all of the messages will be sorted out by spam filters.

In many ways the content of the e-mails can parallel the content that would be used in postal mail letters. For example, the original e-mail invitation should clearly state what is being asked of respondents, why they were selected, what the survey is about, and how they can contact someone to get their questions answered. It should also state that the data will be kept confidential. The biggest difference is that information should also be provided about how to find the survey on the Web and gain access to it. The first e-mail reminder message should parallel the postcard reminder in that it should explain that a survey invitation was sent, thank those who have responded, and ask those to respond who have yet to do so. The next follow-up should provide personalized feedback (e.g., "We've not heard from you") and emphasize the importance of the recipient's response. Additional contacts such as a prenotice or another follow-up can also parallel those that would be used for a postal mail survey.

Figure 7.12 shows an example of a three-contact strategy recently used in a survey of university students. Many of the features previously discussed for postal mail letters are paralleled in these three contacts. The first e-mail introduces the recipients to the survey and emphasizes why their response is important, along with providing the essential information needed for them to find and enter the survey. The second e-mail message serves as a thank you to those who have completed the survey and a reminder to those who have not and repeats the URL and access code. The third e-mail takes a different tone altogether, focusing, in a friendly way, on the short amount of time that is left to complete the survey and the importance of responding.

Although the content of e-mail contacts can and should parallel that of postal mail contacts, some of the features will differ. For example, the use of a date and inside address is less important in e-mail than in a postal letter because these features are not conventional in e-mail correspondence. In addition, this information is usually automatically included by e-mail software. Likewise a blue ballpoint pen signature is not possible in e-mails (although it can be replaced with a very high-quality scanned copy of one's signature).

Without some of these more formal features of the postal letters, the e-mail contacts may seem more relaxed. However, it is still important to maintain the professionalism of the contacts. To that end, one should avoid three e-mail practices commonly employed in other settings:

1. The first is ignoring common grammatical rules such as when to use capitalization or writing without punctuation another example is using. punctuation.in.unconventional.ways.such.as.instead.of.spaces.between .words
2. THE SECOND PRACTICE TO AVOID IS WRITING IN ALL CAPITAL LETTERS. NOT ONLY DOES THIS MAKE THE TEXT MORE

Figure 7.12   Example of three e-mail contact strategy.

Initial e-mail invitation

Professional sender info. →	From: Leah Melani Christian [survey@uga.edu] Sent: Tuesday, February 20, 2007 8:30 AM To: kschoon@uga.edu
Informative subject →	Subject: UGA Survey of Franklin College of Arts and Sciences Students
Date →	February 20, 2007

Appeal for help →
Why you were selected and what it's about →
We are writing to ask for your participation in a survey that we are conducting with the Latin American and Caribbean Studies Institute at the University of Georgia. We are asking undergraduate students like you, in the Franklin College of Arts and Sciences, to reflect on your interests and experiences as a student at UGA.

Usefulness of survey →
Your responses to this survey are very important and will help in advancing teaching and research in Latin American and Caribbean Studies at UGA. As part of the survey, we are also asking about your awareness of and interest in the new Latin American and Caribbean Studies major at UGA.

How to access the survey →
This is a short survey and should take you no more than ten minutes to complete. Please click on the link below to go to the survey website (or copy and paste the survey link into your Internet browser) and then enter the personal access code to begin the survey.

Clickable link → Survey Link: http://www.survey.uga.edu/lacsi/

Individualized ID → Personal Access Code: 458629

Confidential and voluntary →
Your participation in this survey is entirely voluntary and all of your responses will be kept confidential. The access code is used to remove you from the list once you have completed the survey. No personally identifiable information will be associated with your responses in any reports of this data. Should you have any further questions or

Contact information →
comments, please feel free to contact me at survey@uga.edu or 706-542-6234.

Thank you → We appreciate your time and consideration in completing the survey. Thank you for participating in this study! It is only through the help of students like you that we can

R's importance → provide information to help guide the direction of the Latin American and Caribbean Studies Institute at UGA.

Many thanks,

Leah Melani Christian
Survey Research Professional
Carl Vinson Institute of Government

Dr. Brent Berlin
Director
Latin American and Caribbean Studies Institute

DIFFICULT TO READ, BUT IT ALSO MAY GIVE THE IMPRESSION THAT ONE IS YELLING AT RESPONDENTS.

3. A third practice to avoid is using acronyms that have increased in popularity with the use of e-mail, text messaging, and instant messaging (e.g., BTW = by the way; FYI = for your information; LOL = laughing out loud; u r gr8 = you are great; etc.) but that instantly portray a lack of professionalism.

Figure 7.12 *(Continued)*

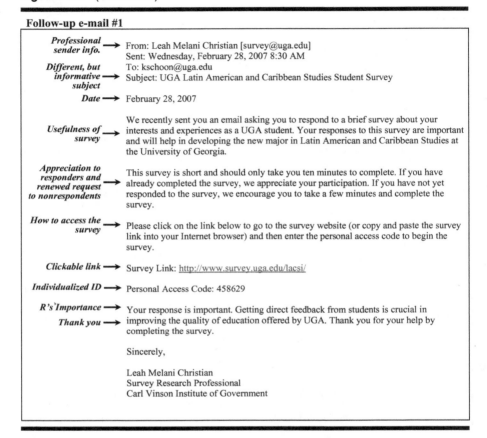

Follow-up e-mail #1

Professional sender info. →	From: Leah Melani Christian [survey@uga.edu] Sent: Wednesday, February 28, 2007 8:30 AM
Different, but informative subject →	To: kschoon@uga.edu Subject: UGA Latin American and Caribbean Studies Student Survey
Date →	February 28, 2007
Usefulness of survey →	We recently sent you an email asking you to respond to a brief survey about your interests and experiences as a UGA student. Your responses to this survey are important and will help in developing the new major in Latin American and Caribbean Studies at the University of Georgia.
Appreciation to responders and renewed request to nonrespondents →	This survey is short and should only take you ten minutes to complete. If you have already completed the survey, we appreciate your participation. If you have not yet responded to the survey, we encourage you to take a few minutes and complete the survey.
How to access the survey →	Please click on the link below to go to the survey website (or copy and paste the survey link into your Internet browser) and then enter the personal access code to begin the survey.
Clickable link →	Survey Link: http://www.survey.uga.edu/lacsi/
Individualized ID →	Personal Access Code: 458629
R's'Importance → *Thank you* →	Your response is important. Getting direct feedback from students is crucial in improving the quality of education offered by UGA. Thank you for your help by completing the survey.

Sincerely,

Leah Melani Christian
Survey Research Professional
Carl Vinson Institute of Government

Guideline 7.19: Carefully and Strategically Time All Contacts with the Population in Mind

As in the case of a mail survey (see Guideline 7.4), each contact for a web survey is designed to meet a specific goal but also has to work well within the entire set of contacts, and timing is important to the overall effect. If a prenotice is sent, it should be given adequate time to arrive and be processed, but not forgotten, before the survey invitation with the URL and access code arrives. Likewise, respondents need to be given adequate time to respond before reminders begin arriving, and waiting to send reminders gives the surveyor an opportunity to identify and address problems if they are occurring. However, one should not allow so much time to pass that the initial requests are forgotten.

Figure 7.12 *(Continued)*

Follow-up e-mail #2

Professional sender info. → From: Leah Melani Christian [survey@uga.edu]
Sent: Wednesday, March 6, 2007 8:30 AM
Different, but informative subject → To: kschoon@uga.edu
Subject: Please complete the UGA student survey

Date → March 6, 2007

Appeal for help → Spring is a busy time for students, and we understand how valuable your spare time is during the semester. We are hoping you may be able to give about ten minutes of your time before Spring Break to help us collect important information for the University of Georgia and the Latin American and Caribbean Studies Institute by completing a short survey.

Appreciation to responders and renewed request to nonrespondents → If you have already completed the survey, we really appreciate your participation. If you have not yet responded, we would like to urge you to complete the survey. We plan to end this study next week, so we wanted to email everyone who has not responded to make sure you had a chance to participate.

Time is running out →

How to access the survey → Please click on the link below to go to the survey website (or copy and paste the survey link into your Internet browser) and then enter the personal access code to begin the survey.

Clickable link → Survey Link: http://www.survey.uga.edu/lacsi/

Individual ID → Personal Access Code: 458629

Thank you → Thank you in advance for completing the survey. Your responses are important! Students
R's importance → are the best source of information to help shape the educational experience at UGA.

Sincerely,

Leah Melani Christian
Survey Research Professional
Carl Vinson Institute of Government

The optimal timing sequence for web surveys has not, we believe, been determined yet. Moreover, the timing will depend on the nature of the survey and the population being surveyed. As a result, we cannot offer hard and fast advice here. But we can mention some things to keep in mind when planning the timing of web survey contacts. First, the tempo of web surveys tends to be a little quicker than the tempo of mail surveys (see Figure 7.8). Because responses come in quicker from web surveys, the contacts can be sent out somewhat more quickly. In some ways, this is needed because an e-mail can more quickly be dismissed and forgotten than a piece of mail that physically lingers around the house until it is thrown away.

However, we have heard of several instances when two, three, and even four reminders were sent in only a couple of days or even in the same day. Unless there is a very strong survey- or population-related reason for doing this, we generally advise against such rapid-fire reminder sequences. The danger of sending multiple reminders too quickly is that they will seem pushy and irritate respondents. When thinking about contact timing, it might be useful to return to the comparison with how one would communicate with a business acquaintance whom one does not know very well. One would not likely send the same request to such an acquaintance multiple times in 1 day or even in 2 days for fear of alienating him. The same should be true for survey sample members.

Second, using e-mail contacts brings up a timing issue that is not relevant with postal contacts, that is, the time of day that the message is delivered. One has no control over what time mail is delivered to sample members, but e-mail messages will likely arrive in respondents' inboxes within minutes or even seconds of their being sent. There is some indication that e-mail invitations are most successful if they are delivered to recipients' inboxes early in the morning. In one study, e-mail contacts were intended to be sent before work hours on a Monday morning, but a technical difficulty resulted in only half of them being sent then and the rest being sent during lunchtime. It is interesting that those who received the invitation midday were significantly less likely to respond than those who received it before working hours (Trouteaud, 2004). The likely explanation for this finding is that an e-mail request received first thing in the morning can be handled before one gets into the major demands of the day, whereas one received midday is in direct competition with the ongoing demands of the day. Thus, one should consider when sample members are most likely to check their e-mail and be free from other demands and then attempt to have e-mail invitations delivered to their inboxes just prior to this time.

Guideline 7.20: Consider Contacting Respondents by Another Mode When Possible

E-mail contacts are popular because they can be sent very inexpensively and very quickly to the entire sample. However, as the previous guidelines indicate, they are somewhat of a risk because of the likelihood that they may not reach the intended recipients or they may never be opened and read by some recipients. An additional limitation of using e-mails for survey invitations is that they greatly limit the possibilities for sending token cash incentives. As a result, we recommend contacting respondents by another mode whenever this is possible (i.e., when the appropriate contact information is available). Contacting respondents by another mode is important when an incentive needs to be delivered to them and when it is particularly difficult to differentiate the survey from marketing and spam efforts because of its topic or sponsor. In some surveys where e-mail addresses were not available, we have forgone e-mail contacts altogether in favor of postal letters that directed respondents to the Web, whereas in others we have used a combination of e-mail and postal contacts. In both instances, the first request to complete the survey is sent by postal mail and contains the token financial incentive.

Figure 7.13 shows an example of a survey invitation sent by postal mail that directs the respondent to go to the Web to complete the questionnaire. This letter was sent with a $5 token incentive. It was preceded by the prenotice letter displayed in Figure 7.4, and it was followed by a postcard reminder

Figure 7.13   Web survey invitation sent by postal mail.

WASHINGTON STATE
UNIVERSITY

Social and Economic Sciences Research Center

November 6, 2007

Lewiston Area Resident
491 Winding Ridge Road
Lewiston, ID 83501

Dear Lewiston Area Resident,

I am writing to ask for your help in understanding the quality of life in the Lewiston/Clarkston area and how residents are being affected by a variety of things from the availability of jobs and healthcare to the use of cell phones. The best way we have of learning about these issues is by asking all different kinds of people who live in the area to share their thoughts and opinions. Your address is one of only a small number that have been randomly selected to help in this study.

To make sure we hear from all different types of people who live in the area, please have the adult (age 18 or over) in your household who has had **the most recent birthday** be the one to complete the questionnaire.

We are hoping that you will be able to complete the questionnaire on the Internet so that we can summarize results more quickly and accurately. Doing that is easy: just enter this web page address in your Internet browser, and then type in your access code to begin the survey.

http://www.opinion.wsu.edu/lewistonclarkston

Your access code: 440001

To help you complete the questionnaire on the web, we have enclosed step-by-step instructions that also show examples of the questions included in the survey. We realize that some households do not have Internet access. If you do not, we will send a paper questionnaire to all households we have not heard from in about 2 ½ weeks. If you would like one sooner, please contact Thom Allen by telephone at 1-800-833-0867.

The questions should only take about 15 minutes to complete. Your responses are voluntary and will be kept confidential. Your names are not on our mailing list, and your answers will never be associated with your mailing address. If you have any questions about this survey of Lewiston/Clarkston area residents, or if you have difficulties answering on the Internet, Thom Allen, the study director, will be happy to help and can be reached by telephone at the above 800 number or by email at sesrc@wsu.edu. This study has been reviewed and approved by the Washington State University Institutional Review Board, and if you have any questions about your rights as a participant in this study, you may contact them by telephone at 509-335-3668.

By taking a few minutes to share your thoughts and opinions about life in the Lewiston-Clarkston area you will be helping us out a great deal, and a small token of appreciation is enclosed as a way of saying thank you.

I hope you enjoy completing the questionnaire and look forward to receiving your responses.

Many Thanks,

Don A. Dillman
Regents Professor and Deputy Director

Research Administrative Offices, 133 Wilson Hall
PO Box 644014, Pullman, WA 99164-4014 • 509-335-1511 • Fax: 509-335-0116
Public Opinion Laboratory, 1425 NE Terre View, Suite F
PO Box 641801, Pullman, WA 99164-1801 • 509-335-1721 • Fax: 509-335-4688

and two follow-up reminders. As shown in Figure 7.1, this effort resulted in 41% of the sample completing the questionnaire on the Web. In this case, the decision to use only postal mail for all of the contacts was made because the survey was based on a general population sample for which e-mail addresses were not available. As a result, convincing respondents to go to the Internet to fill out the questionnaire and making it as easy as possible for them to do so was the main challenge.

The content of this letter has all of the features that the mail question-naire invitation letter displayed in Figure 7.5. In addition to these, it also provides the URL and personal access code needed to enter the survey, instructions for how to use these, and an explanation about the special instruc-tions for the survey that accompanied the letter (more on this in Guideline 7.24). Recipients are also told what to do if they are unable to do the survey because they do not have access to the Internet. This extra information is included in each of the follow-up contacts as well.

Figure 7.14 shows the first two in a series of postal and e-mail contacts used to survey Washington State University undergraduate students about their experiences at the university. The decision to use both postal and e-mail contacts was made in this survey because the postal contacts provided a way to send a $2 incentive to each student at the outset of the survey and a way to contact all respondents, whereas e-mail provided a second source of stimulus for approximately two thirds of the sample who had an e-mail address registered with the university. The e-mail was also particularly appropriate for (and likely to be noticed by) the university students, and it was a vehicle for providing a clickable URL that would take students straight to the web survey. As a result, e-mail recipients could fill out the survey immediately upon receiving the notice, whereas those who received only a postal letter had to remember to take the letter along with them when they went to a computer to get online, thus adding an additional logistical step to completing the questionnaire. This combination of postal and e-mail contacts has resulted in response rates ranging from 50% to 59% across a series of 5 student experience web surveys conducted from Spring 2003 to Spring 2007.

Guideline 7.21: Keep E-Mail Contacts Short and to the Point

The key to getting respondents to read all of the important information in the e-mail invitation and follow-ups is to keep these contacts short and engaging. Whereas one page is the standard length for a printed letter, e-mail communi-cations tend to be shorter on average. As a result, the survey contacts should provide the information that is required for respondents to understand what is being asked of them, why they are being asked, and what they should do, but the contacts should do this in as short of a format as possible (without

Figure 7.14 Initial postal and e-mail contacts for a student experience survey.

Initial postal contact (the first contact made)

WASHINGTON STATE UNIVERSITY

Social and Economic Sciences Research Center

November 4, 2004

Bailey Stevens
145 Sunrise Drive
Pullman, WA 45667

Dear Bailey,

Students are the best source for evaluating Washington State University as a place to go to school. I am writing to ask for your help in better understanding how you feel about your educational experience at WSU.

You are one of a sample of Washington State University undergraduates being surveyed about your student experience at the WSU Pullman campus – the survey questionnaire is short, only 25 questions, and should take less than ten minutes to complete.

I would really appreciate your taking a few minutes on a computer to go to the following website and enter your code to gain access to the survey:

http://www.sesrc.wsu.edu/studentexperience
Your Access Code 743839

This survey is confidential. Your participation is voluntary, and if you come to any question you prefer not to answer please skip it and go on to the next. This project has been reviewed and approved by the WSU Institutional Review Board and if you have questions about your rights as a participant you can contact them at 335-9661. Should you have any other questions or comments please contact Thom Allen, the study director, or me, at the Social and Economic Sciences Research Center, 335-1511 or sesrc@wsu.edu.

I am enclosing a small token of appreciation with this letter as a way of saying thank you for participating in this important assessment of the student experience at WSU.

Many Thanks.

Don A. Dillman
Regents' Professor and Deputy Director

Research Administrative Offices, 133 Wilson Hall
PO Box 644014, Pullman, WA 99164-4014 • 509-335-1511 • Fax: 509-335-0116
Public Opinion Laboratory, 1425 NE Terre View, Suite F
PO Box 641801, Pullman, WA 99164-1801 • 509-335-1721 • Fax: 509-335-4688

Figure 7.14   *(Continued)*

Initial e-mail contact

From: Don A. Dillman [sesrc@wsu.edu]
Sent: Friday, November 12, 2004 8:30 AM
To: bstevens@wsu.edu
Subject: WSU Student Experience Survey

Dear Bailey,

Recently, we sent you a letter asking you to respond to a very brief Internet questionnaire about your experience as a student at WSU. The questionnaire is short - 25 questions and should take less than ten minutes to complete.

If you have already completed the survey, we would like to thank you for your time, as your responses are very important to our research! If you have not yet answered the questionnaire, we'd like to urge you to take a few minutes to do so. By sending this email with your access code and a link to the web site, we thought it might be easier to respond.

http://www.sesrc.wsu.edu/studentexperience
Your access code : 743839

Please make sure to enter the access code provided above when prompted and not your WSU student ID number.

Thank you for your help. This questionnaire is important. It is one of the few ways available for getting truly representative opinions of the student experience at WSU.

Sincerely,

Dr. Don A. Dillman
Regents' Professor and Deputy Director
Social and Economic Sciences Research Center
Washington State University
(509) 335-1511

---

taking a blunt tone) in order to increase the likelihood that they will be read in their entirety.

Guideline 7.22: Take Steps to Ensure that E-Mails Are Not Flagged as Spam

Almost all of us who regularly use e-mail have had an important message get routed by our e-mail software to a "junk" or "bulk" mail folder because it was mistaken for *spam* (i.e., unsolicited bulk messages for which there is no preexisting relationship between the sender and recipient). Oftentimes we do not even know we missed the important message until the sender contacts us in another way and brings it to our attention. Although all of us appreciate them for what they do, spam filters pose special problems for web surveyors. The problem of e-mail contacts being labeled as "junk mail" is particularly severe, because the decision is often not in sample members' hands, as is the case with postal mail. Rather, spam filters can prevent large segments of the sample from receiving contacts altogether.

A quick search will turn up long lists of advice for how to minimize the likelihood of survey e-mails being flagged as spam. Some common examples include the following:

- Talk to your Internet service provider or survey vendor—make sure the Internet protocol (IP) address you will be sending from is not already flagged by major e-mail providers your sample members use. This may involve opening e-mail accounts with those providers and sending yourself simple test messages. If the IP address is flagged, resulting in your not receiving the test messages or their being routed to junk mail folders, insist on a different IP address for your survey mailings.
- Use text messages rather than HTML messages because many people, and spam filters, closely associate the formatting and graphics available in HTML messages with spam.
- Send individual e-mails rather than using bulk mailing options, and do not use the "CC" or "BCC" fields.
- Avoid words such as *offer, free, cash, win, promo, prize,* and so on.

The list could go on and on. In fact, many spam filters use hundreds and even thousands of criteria to create scores to classify messages as legitimate or as spam. To complicate matters further, the advice provided here may quickly become obsolete, because spam filters are constantly being updated to catch increasingly creative spammers. Therefore, perhaps the most useful advice we can give is to research spam filters close to the time one will be doing the survey and to test the messages using a spam analyzer, a number of which are now available on the Web. These programs will examine the message for common content that is known to trigger spam filters. They then provide feedback on how likely the message is to be flagged as spam and what components of the message are particularly problematic so that one can make appropriate changes.

Guideline 7.23: Carefully Select the Sender Name and Address and the Subject Line Text for E-Mail Communications

Once an e-mail gets past spam filters and delivered into an inbox, the recipient generally has only two sources of information to use in determining whether to open the message: the text that appears in the "From" field and the subject line. As a result, these two pieces of information need to convince the respondent that this is an important message from a reputable sender. Thus, it is important to send the e-mail requests from a professional-appearing e-mail sender and address. For example, jolene.smyth@xyzuniversity.edu seems much more reputable than joeeebean@lentil_lovers.com. Likewise, it is advisable to have a full, formal name appear in the "From" field rather than a nickname (i.e., Jolene Smyth vs. joeeebean).

In addition to communicating the professionalism of the e-mail, the material in the "From" line should also help respondents make connections between the various e-mails they will receive about a survey. For this reason, all contacts should be sent from the same e-mail address so that they are recognizable to respondents and so that respondents can quickly sort their messages by sender to find related e-mails.

The subject line should also be professional and informative. It should immediately tell the respondent that the e-mail is about a survey, who the sponsor is, and what the topic is (e.g., "Washington State University student experience survey"). Consistent with the social exchange perspective, some research has found that stating the subject as a request for help rather than an offer to let respondents share their opinions results in increased response. For example, Trouteaud (2004) found that the subject line "Please help [name of company] with your advice and opinions" resulted in a 5% increase in response rates compared to the subject line "Share your advice and opinions now with [name of company]."

Guideline 7.24: Provide Clear Instructions for How to Access the Survey

Regardless of the method of contacting and inviting respondents to take a web survey, one needs to provide clear instructions for how to access it. Most people generally know the basics of applying pencil to paper to answer a mail survey, but there is much more variation within the population with respect to how to operate a computer or find and use a web page. Therefore, at the very least, respondents should be provided with the instruction to type in the web address, click the link, or copy and paste the address into their web browser and then to enter their access code.

However, one can go considerably further to help respondents access and complete web surveys, especially respondents who are expected to be less experienced and skillful with computers and the Internet. When surveying such populations, or even populations in which one can expect great variation in ability to use the Internet and in comfort level and confidence doing so, it may be helpful to also include a more explicit instruction for how to access the survey and complete questions. Figure 7.15 shows an example of such instructional materials that was sent to web sample members in the DSF study discussed throughout this chapter. This instruction is designed to boil down the answer process into five easy steps. It tells and shows respondents where to enter the survey URL on their web browser, where to enter their access code, where to get additional instructions for navigating the survey, what the questions will look like, and how they will know when they have completed the survey.

However, this instruction sheet also includes a number of other important elements. First, it is designed with its own simple logic and navigational

Figure 7.15   Additional instructions for a web survey of a general population sample.

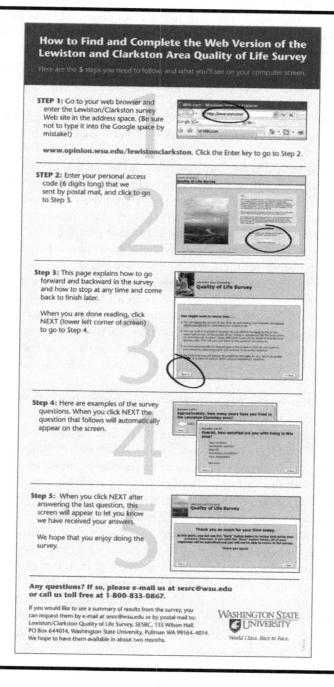

path so that it is easy to read and process. This starts with a clear title that tells what this insert is and continues with clear numbering of the steps and clear delineation between each step using visual elements and properties in much the same way as they are used in question and questionnaire design (see Chapters 4 and 5). The instructions are brief and are written at a very accessible, although not demeaning, level. This is important, because if unsure respondents cannot process the instructions, they may conclude that the whole survey is too difficult for them. The instructions need to be designed in a way that encourages and empowers respondents, leaving them with the impression that "I can do this." In this way, some of the costs or barriers to completing the questionnaire are removed. Second, the additional instruction sheet also includes the familiar logo of the survey sponsor, lending it credibility and authenticity. Third, it is tailored to the situation in that it incorporates actual screenshots of the survey that the respondents are being asked to complete, and it is printed in color in order to accurately represent the questionnaire. The purpose of doing this is twofold: It ensures that when respondents get to the survey they will not be surprised by seeing something vastly different on their screen than what is on the instructions, and it communicates the importance of this specific survey and topic. A generic set of instructions designed to be used with all Internet surveys cannot do these two things. Fourth, the instruction sheet clearly provides additional resources for respondents to use if they have questions or need further assistance. Finally, it was printed on 5.75″ × 12.75″ cardstock, a feature intended both to provide novelty so it would be noticed and to provide stability in the envelope.

Designed in this way, the instruction sheet serves two functions. The first is its intended function of making it as simple as possible for respondents who are not comfortable with the Internet to find, access, and complete the survey. The second function that we suspect it serves is to communicate to all respondents the importance of the survey and the professionalism behind it. This is done both through the use of the survey sponsor's logo and through the professional design of the instruction sheet as well as its tailoring to the exact survey the respondents are being asked to complete.

Although we are unable to say how much influence the instruction had, when we used it we received a 41% response rate via the Web in the general population survey described in the introduction to this chapter. That we were able to get more than a third of the sample to complete the survey by Web bodes well for the future of web surveys and suggests that with careful implementation, the Web may become a viable survey mode for general population surveys. But until Internet access and computer skills are much more universal, instructions like these may be helpful in getting some recipients of the survey request to respond.

Guideline 7.25: Make Obvious Connections between the Opening Screen and Other Implementation Features

One of the most important functions of the opening screen of a web survey is that it informs the respondents that they are in the proper location and describes what steps they should take next. As a result, it is useful to think about this page as another type of contact in the implementation process. In the same way that the prenotice, cover letter, and all other contacts should draw on social exchange concepts to encourage response, so too should the opening screen, and it should be readily apparent that the opening screen respondents have arrived at is the correct screen for the study they were invited to participate in.

The opening screen pictured in Figure 6.15 in Chapter 6 provides an example of how to design such a screen to connect to the other implementation elements that sample members receive. Perhaps the most obvious connection to the contact letters is the appearance of the graphic. A smaller version of this same picture appeared in each postal letter respondents received about this survey, as well as on the additional instructions for how to access the survey. As such, it serves as an immediate visual affirmation that the respondent has reached the right web page. Another way the welcoming page connects to the letters is by the direct mention of them where respondents are instructed to enter their access code: "Please enter your Access Code listed *in the letter we sent you*." Finally, the substantive content of the welcome page very closely parallels the messages sent in the invitation letter and follow-ups. With these connections to all of the previous information respondents have received about this survey, they will very quickly realize that they have accessed the correct web page. Moreover, the design of the page, as discussed in Chapter 6, along with the text instructions will guide respondents through the next steps to enter the survey.

Guideline 7.26: Assign Each Sample Member a Unique ID Number

The unique identification number for web respondents serves all of the same purposes as for mail respondents. It allows the surveyor to keep track of who has responded and to remove respondents' contact information from follow-up lists so that they do not continue to receive reminders. However, in web surveys the unique identification number serves an additional function in that it can be used as a unique access code that can, and should, be required in order to enter the web survey. Requiring respondents to enter a code in order to access the survey helps protect the integrity of the sample and survey data by ensuring that unsampled people who stumble upon the survey are not able to access it. It also provides a way to ensure that each respondent answers the survey only once, as the access code can be inactivated after the respondent submits the completed survey.

Some respondents, however, legitimately need to stop the survey and return to it at a later time to finish. As a result, inactivating access codes after they have been entered once is not a desirable practice. For this reason, we typically program our surveys so that if respondents stop before completing the survey and then come back to it later, they are returned to the question where they previously quit. They can leave and reenter the survey in this way as many times as they desire. However, once respondents submit the completed survey, their access code is inactivated (see Guideline 6.31 in Chapter 6). We have found this to be a quite useful strategy because the bulk of respondents who start the survey will finish it in the same sitting if there are no offensive questions or technical difficulties that lead to artificially high break-off rates. Although this seems to work well for most of our surveys, other strategies may be more appropriate in other situations.

That one should assign an access code raises the issue of how one should require that access code to be used. Currently two main strategies are used: manual and automatic login. In manual login, respondents are sent a URL and access code. Once they get to the introductory web page using the URL, they are asked to key their access code into a designated space to gain access to the survey. In automatic login, the unique access code is contained within the URL so that entering the URL in their web browser (or clicking on it if it is sent by e-mail) will automatically gain respondents entrance into the survey.

Several studies have compared the use of these two strategies. Crawford et al. (2001) found that providing an automatic login significantly increased response rates by nearly 5 percentage points over a manual login condition in which respondents had to enter both a password and access code. Heerwegh and Loosveldt (2003) reported a similar but nonsignificant finding (a 3 percentage point advantage for automatic login). However, they also found that a semiautomatic login procedure in which the password was included in a URL but the respondent still had to key in an access code resulted in an 8 percentage point increase in response rate over the manual login procedure. Both of these studies as well as an additional study by Heerwegh and Loosveldt (2002c) also reported some evidence that respondents who log in manually (or semiautomatically) provide more complete data. In particular, Heerwegh and Loosveldt (2002c) reported that respondents who log in manually are more likely to complete more of the survey and are more likely to provide substantive answers to sensitive questions, an effect they attributed to respondents believing their data are more secure when they have to key in an access code.

Based on these findings, it seems advisable to require respondents to key in an access code rather than to provide automatic login. But it is also important to use access codes large enough that one is unlikely to wrongfully enter the survey, whether by accident (i.e., a typo in entering one's own code) or by guessing a code. If, for example, one wants to use a four-digit numerical (i.e., digits 0–9) access code, the total number of possible codes that can be generated is 10,000. If one is surveying 1,000 respondents, 1 in every 10 possible access codes will be assigned to a respondent. With a five-digit access code, however, there are 100,000 possibilities, meaning that only 1 in every 100 possible codes will be assigned to a respondent. The likelihood of somebody wrongfully accessing the survey by guessing an access code or making a typo in entering his own code is considerably less with a five-digit access code. However, the use of longer access codes should be balanced with considerations of the difficulty of transferring the access code from the contact letter or e-mail to the web site. One of us recently received a customer satisfaction web survey invitation through the mail with the following access code: 250801141029692. Correctly entering such long access codes into a space on a web page can be quite difficult because of the large number of digits that have to be entered.

In addition to considering the length of the access code, one should also be sure to avoid using adjacent numbers for different respondents. For example, using the access codes 10001, 10002, 10003, and so on would make it quite simple for a respondent to answer the survey multiple times by simply altering his own access code by one digit. Thus, it is important to build in an interval greater than 1 between access codes. However, one should also avoid regular intervals, as in the following sequence: 10101, 10201, 10301, and so on. Instead, a random interval of between 50 and 300 digits should be used; this can be easily accomplished using the random functions included in common software.

It is also important to make sure that the access codes one provides are not easily mistaken with other codes respondents deal with on a daily basis. For example, we once sent e-mail invitations for a student experience survey to a sample of undergraduate students. The invitation included a clickable link to the survey and respondents' ID number for accessing the survey. Shortly after sending the first batch of e-mails, we began getting messages back from students claiming that their ID did not work. It was only when one student included her ID number in her message that we realized that the students were entering their school ID numbers rather than the randomly generated ID numbers we had sent them in the e-mail. When surveying this type of group, we now make it a point to refer to the survey ID numbers as "access codes" to help differentiate them from what students more commonly think of as their ID. We also now specify "Please enter your access code listed in the letter we sent you" on the login page rather than the less specific "Please enter your ID." The types of specialized groups who can be surveyed via the Web oftentimes have preexisting ID numbers, membership numbers, or access codes that they use regularly. It is good practice to look into this ahead of time and take steps to differentiate survey access codes from these more common, group-specific identifiers.

Guideline 7.27: Know and Respect the Capabilities and Limits of the Web Server(s)

Although conducting a survey using computer and Internet technology gives one a wealth of new possibilities, it also means that one is constrained by the limits of those technologies. One of those limits that can be very damaging to a survey project if exceeded is the capacity of the web server(s). Web servers can only handle so much outgoing or incoming traffic before they begin to bog down or even crash. As a result, it is important to know ahead of time what effect sending or receiving mass amounts of survey-related information might have on one's server(s) and to plan accordingly.

Based on the advice of our information technology professionals, we very rarely send e-mail survey invitations or reminders to the entire sample at one time (the exception is for small samples) because, although our e-mail program will allow us to do so, our server cannot handle that many outgoing e-mails at once. The risk is that some of the messages will be lost or will be bounced back to the sender, leading to the incredibly complex task of trying to sort through who got the e-mail and who did not. Instead, we send our e-mail communications in batches of a few hundred at a time over the course of a day or, better yet, in the late evening when the servers are less busy and the messages can arrive before recipients check their e-mail the next morning. This is slightly more labor intensive, but it is not nearly the amount of work that sorting out bounced e-mails would be.

In addition to considering the effects of outgoing communications, it is also important to consider the effects of incoming survey activity on the server(s). The nature of the Internet is such that many sample members can receive their invitations at virtually the same time, and all of them can immediately try to access and complete the survey. However, if too many people try to access the same survey on the same server all at once (or if responses are coming into the same server for different surveys all at once), the likely results could range from significant slowdowns that might lead some to quit the survey to a server crash that would cut every respondent off. Neither of these outcomes, nor any point in between, is desirable. When we have large survey projects that pose such challenges, we send invitations in batches over longer time periods so that the responses come in smaller waves rather than in one large spike. Another strategy we often employ is to have our server disconnect from respondents' computers if the computers are idle for a specified amount of time. We do this so that server resources can be devoted to respondents who are actively completing the questionnaire. When the idle respondents return to their computers and try to continue, they are provided with a friendly message that explains what happened and tells them how to return to their previous place in the survey.

The main point, though, is that it is important to know the limits of the hosting server(s) and plan accordingly. The best advice we can give here is to consult one's information technology professional or Internet service provider well in advance to work out an implementation and survey management strategy that works well within the limits of the server(s) one will be using.

Guideline 7.28: Establish a Procedure for Dealing with Bounced E-Mails

Whenever we field a web survey using e-mail contacts, we expect that many of the e-mails, even sometimes hundreds, will bounce back to us as undeliverable. Some come back because the e-mail address is unknown, others because the recipients' mailboxes are full, and still others for a variety of other reasons. A similar thing happens with undeliverable postal mail, but with e-mails it occurs with much higher frequency and much more rapidly. The benefit is that some problems can be addressed quickly and the e-mails re-sent, even the same day as the original message. The downside, though, is that tracking the delivery status of e-mails and following up with potentially hundreds of bounced e-mails can be a very daunting process. For this reason, the fielding period is not the time to be trying to figure out how to deal with bounced e-mails. The procedures that will be followed should be planned before the first set of contacts is sent out.

We have found that in many cases, the problems that cause the e-mail to be returned to us are only temporary, and the message can be re-sent at a later date. But depending on how much later the message is sent, this may mean that future contacts have to be delayed as well. In other cases, it may be necessary to examine the e-mail addresses for errors or to attempt to contact respondents by an alternative mode.

Guideline 7.29: Establish Procedures for Dealing with Returned Incentives

Just as with mail surveys, it is important with web surveys to ensure that all returned incentives are properly accounted for. This may mean monitoring undeliverable and returned mail if a prepaid cash incentive was used, but it may also mean remembering, months after the survey has been completed, to work with the cash card company or other provider of electronic incentives to retrieve the value of the incentives that were not used before they expired, assuming such an arrangement was made in the beginning. Forgetting these follow-through steps may entirely nullify any cost savings of using these types of incentives in the first place and is simply not good business.

Guideline 7.30: Establish Procedures for Dealing with Respondent Inquiries

The need to respond to inquires is just as important in web surveys as it is in mail surveys, and many of the same tactics should be used in doing so (see Guideline 7.14). However, web surveys bring into play a whole host of difficulties not generally faced with mail surveys because people are dealing with more complex technology. Oftentimes the only way for the surveyor to know about such difficulties is by paying close attention to what respondents are saying in their inquiries. For example, the mix-up of university student ID numbers and survey access codes discussed previously was recognized as the cause of many login errors only because a student e-mailed an inquiry in which she listed her student ID as her access code. The project director recognized the difference in the number of digits and followed up, only then identifying the problem that so many respondents were having. Had this e-mail been skipped over or even just ignored for a day or two, many more respondents may have had the same problem and may have written off the survey. In another instance, we received the following e-mail:

> Dear Professor Dillman,
>
> When I enter my access code into the window that says, "Welcome to the WSU Student Experience Survey" I enter my number and it opens up the same window??? I'm not real sure if this is a system error or an operator error?
>
> Thanks,
>
> Kayla

After some investigation, it was discovered that this error was occurring for respondents with common free, Web-based e-mail accounts because this e-mail program was putting a frame around the survey web page that was interfering with the survey programming. Once this was recognized, the respondents who e-mailed were advised to copy and paste the link into their browser instead of clicking on it in order to avoid the frame. Similar advice was then included in the next e-mail contact to the entire group of nonrespondents. A short time later a programming solution was discovered to automatically break out of such frames. Given the large portion of students who had their university e-mail forwarded to this and other e-mail providers that also use frames, this was an issue that could have caused major problems had it gone undetected or unacknowledged.

Guideline 7.31: Implement a System for Monitoring Progress and Evaluating Early Completes

One of the most remarkable differences between web and mail surveys is the increased speed with which things begin to happen when a web survey goes live. In a mail survey there are usually a few days of lag while the letters make their way through the mail to their destination and the completed surveys make their way back to the surveyor. If the surveys are being sent a great distance, this lag can be a week or longer. The same is not true for web surveys; completed surveys can start rolling in only minutes after a contact is sent by e-mail. If contacts are sent by postal mail, surveys can be completed as soon as the mail is delivered, saving the time return post would take with a mail survey. For the DSF survey discussed in the introduction of the chapter, Figure 7.8 illustrates this difference in timing and tempo by showing the percentage of web surveys completed by day of study for the web treatment (gray line) and the percentage of mail returns by day for the mail treatment (black line).

The fact that web survey responses come in so much quicker than mail survey responses and that they are already in electronic form means that quicker and improved progress monitoring on the part of the surveyor is possible. However, it also means that the surveyor has to be ready and have systems for progress monitoring in place immediately when survey notices go out. Many established research organizations have web pages on which the survey sponsor and project managers can monitor results as they come in, and many survey software packages include similar tools. In one organization, these progress monitoring web pages are jokingly referred to as the "sanity pages" because they allow the surveyors to watch closely to ensure that their costly projects are going well.

Such a page might include a summary of response dispositions (i.e., partial completes, completes, refusals, return to sender, and nonresponse rates) that updates as additional information comes in. Another good feature for progress monitoring is a list of case IDs that have accessed the survey, the date each accessed it, and the outcome (i.e., the last question completed). Having this information available and updated regularly makes it possible to quickly find problem areas if they exist. For example, if a large proportion of those who access the survey drop out at a specific question, one can reexamine that question and the survey programming underlying it to determine what the problem may be. In web surveys, unlike mail surveys, changes to the questionnaire can be made very quickly even after the survey is fielded to correct any problems due to question wording, design, or programming, provided these problems are identified and fixed very early in the fielding process.

Unfortunately, not every surveyor has the resources to also have a progress monitoring web site that automatically updates as surveys come in. But even if such a luxury is not available, it is still important to set up some sort of system for this type of progress monitoring. At the very least, a manual accounting of case dispositions and break-off points for those returning partially completed surveys should be taken once daily starting when the survey goes live. Regardless of how and how often the progress monitoring is going to occur, one should have the progress monitoring system or protocol in place before the survey goes live. If one has to take the time to establish a system while the survey is in the field, by the time he gets around to actually looking closely at the returns, the damage may already be done.

In addition to monitoring completion rates and break-off points, one should also closely monitor the data. In one of our surveys that included open-ended questions we inadvertently set a character limit on the answer box so that only the first 255 characters that were entered got recorded into the database, a mistake that was caught by examining early returns. It is also important to monitor server logs to see what types of errors are being registered, as these logs will let the researcher know if respondents are experiencing things like browser incompatibilities, data transfer errors, or other obscure errors that may have been missed in the testing phase. In one instance we mistakenly had a maximum byte limit set for each record (i.e., respondent) so that an error occurred if people tried to submit too much information. Checking too many items on a check-all question or entering too much text into text boxes triggered these errors. One cannot catch these types of problems by looking at completion rates or even the data, but server logs of errors can reveal that such problems are occurring. It is imperative to examine the data set and the server logs throughout the fielding process. Again, such monitoring should start immediately when returns start coming in so that corrective action can be taken quickly to minimize the damage caused by easy-to-make mistakes like these examples.

CONCLUSION

Readers of the previous edition of this book are likely to have noticed three major differences between the way we approached survey implementation here and in the previous edition. First, we no longer assume for mail surveys that one has or must use a respondent name in contact letters. In fact, most of the implementation examples used in this chapter came from a random sample of households drawn from an address list that did not include names. The promise of these address-based lists for obtaining random samples of households with good coverage means that more and more mail surveys are probably going to be conducted without respondent names. However, as we have outlined in this chapter, there are many other ways to personalize these surveys to appeal to all types of respondents and keep response rates high.

Second, we have developed methods of using postal contacts to support surveys on the Internet, and in initial tests these methods have been quite successful. One of these methods involves using only postal contacts to invite sample members to access and complete a web survey, whereas the other involves using postal contacts along with e-mail contacts. The primary benefits of using the mail to get people to go to the Web are that it enables surveyors to send incentives directly to sample members, it ensures that those without e-mail or who check their e-mail very rarely have an opportunity to hear about the survey, and it provides a way to bypass e-mail spam filters that may prevent some sample members from receiving survey contacts. Third, we have described other implementation procedures for web surveys that were not yet well developed when the previous edition of this book was written.

This chapter completes the systematic description of how to design and implement self-administered surveys using the tailored design method to reduce the four major sources of error. Together with the chapters that preceded it, it sets the context for the more in-depth discussion of tailoring one's survey methods to a variety of situations and concepts that comes in the rest of this book. The types of survey situations that are discussed include mixed-mode surveys (Chapter 8), longitudinal and Internet panel surveys (Chapter 9), satisfaction surveys (Chapter 10), survey sponsorship (Chapter 11), and surveying establishments rather than individuals (Chapter 12).

LIST OF GUIDELINES

Mail Survey Implementation

Guideline 7.1: *To the extent possible, personalize all contacts to respondents (even when names are unavailable)*

Guideline 7.2: *Send a token of appreciation with the survey request*

Guideline 7.3: *Use multiple contacts, each with a different look and appeal*

Guideline 7.4: *Carefully and strategically time all contacts*

Guideline 7.5: *Select all mail-out dates with the characteristics of the population in mind*

Guideline 7.6: *Place information in the mailing exactly where it needs to be used*

Guideline 7.7: *Take steps to ensure that mailings will not be mistaken for junk mail or marketing materials*

Guideline 7.8: *Evaluate the size and weight of mailing materials on mailing costs*

Guideline 7.9: *Assemble the mailings in a way that maximizes the appealing aspects of each element when the package is opened*

(continued)

Guideline 7.10: *Ensure that all addresses in the sample comply with current postal regulations*

Guideline 7.11: *Assign an individual ID number to each sample member*

Guideline 7.12: *Establish procedures for dealing with undeliverable mail*

Guideline 7.13: *Establish procedures for dealing with returned incentives*

Guideline 7.14: *Establish procedures for dealing with respondent inquiries*

Guideline 7.15: *Evaluate early returns for problems that can be addressed mid-stride*

Web Survey Implementation

Guideline 7.16: *To the extent possible, personalize all contacts to respondents*

Guideline 7.17: *Send a token of appreciation with the survey request*

Guideline 7.18: *Use multiple contacts and vary the message across them*

Guideline 7.19: *Carefully and strategically time all contacts with the population in mind*

Guideline 7.20: *Consider contacting respondents by another mode when possible*

Guideline 7.21: *Keep e-mail contacts short and to the point*

Guideline 7.22: *Take steps to ensure that e-mails are not flagged as spam*

Guideline 7.23: *Carefully select the sender name and address and the subject line text for e-mail communications*

Guideline 7.24: *Provide clear instructions for how to access the survey*

Guideline 7.25: *Make obvious connections between the opening screen and other implementation features*

Guideline 7.26: *Assign each sample member a unique ID number*

Guideline 7.27: *Know and respect the capabilities and limits of the web server(s)*

Guideline 7.28: *Establish a procedure for dealing with bounced e-mails*

(continued)

Guideline 7.29: Establish procedures for dealing with returned incentives

Guideline 7.30: Establish procedures for dealing with respondent inquiries

Guideline 7.31: Implement a system for monitoring progress and evaluating early completes

CHAPTER 8

When More than One Survey Mode Is Needed

IN THE past 10 years, mixed-mode survey designs have gone from being a novelty to a necessity for many survey situations. They have even been described by some as the "norm" for survey design (Biemer & Lyberg, 2003). The increase in mixed-mode surveys is directly related to the technological and cultural changes and their impact on survey practices that we discussed in Chapter 1.

Throughout this book, we have responded to this change in the importance of mixed-mode survey designs by developing procedures for sampling, writing questions, constructing questionnaires, and implementing surveys that anticipate the likelihood of mixed-mode designs. In this chapter, we address the fundamental reasons for using multiple survey modes and the likely consequences of doing so.

THE BIG CHANGE

Advocacy for the use of mixed-mode data collection has been evident for decades (Payne, 1964), and in some surveys the use of different survey modes is an established procedure. For example, the U.S. Decennial Census has combined the use of mail surveys followed by personal enumeration since 1970 (almost 50 years). However, the relative rarity of mixed-mode designs in the twentieth century is illustrated by an analysis of all active federal surveys. As of August 1981, 80% of federal surveys used a single data collection mode, 10% used two modes, and only 3% used three modes; information was not available on the remaining 7% (U.S. Office of Management and Budget, 1984).

The barriers to conducting mixed-mode surveys were substantial. In the early 1990s, one of us was asked by the director of a large ongoing survey of health provider organizations how response might be improved. This survey had started with multiple mail contacts and then switched to telephone for additional contacts when mail responses slowed. After noting the fact that mailings were addressed only to establishments and not to individual people, it was proposed to the director that all of the businesses be called first to find out the name of the person who could provide the information being requested. The telephone call would serve as a prenotice and ensure that the questionnaire and all subsequent mailings were addressed specifically to the correct individual to help keep them from going astray as sometimes happens in large organizations.

After a slight hesitation, the survey director, who worked in a large organization with separate divisions for mail and telephone surveys, responded, "Look, I'm willing to send a survey from mail operations to telephone operations once, but sending it to the telephone group first, then to mail, and then back to telephone again, is something I cannot do; the time and effort is unthinkable." His response describes the enormous difficulty that existed only a decade and a half ago with shifting survey operations from one mode to another. Left unexplained by him was the lack of management and computer systems that would allow simultaneous implementation of telephone and mail data collection procedures and the shifting of the survey from telephone to mail and back again.

Thus, it should not be surprising that the research available for guiding mixed-mode designs prior to the 1990s was limited or that one of the early treatments of the topic in relation to telephone surveys was the final chapter in a 32-chapter book (Groves & Lyberg, 1988), the only one to focus on mixed-mode surveys. Its title, "Administrative Issues in Mixed-Mode Surveys," also reflected the complications of implementing surveys by multiple modes, the major mixed-mode problem of that time (Dillman & Tarnai, 1988).

An enormous shift has occurred with new developments in computers and software as well as e-mail, file sharing, and servers that make it easier to conduct mixed-mode surveys. These developments have allowed surveyors to integrate systems to contact respondents, design and program questionnaires, manage and track data collection, and analyze data from different modes with speed and accuracy; this integration is necessary for conducting mixed-mode surveys. However, surveyors need to have a general understanding of all modes to be able to effectively design mixed-mode studies. In addition, planning and implementing mixed-mode surveys requires effective communication and coordination among people with different expertise and often among multiple operational divisions within a survey organization.

Other factors beyond technological developments are fueling this trend toward mixed-mode surveys. Surveyors are increasingly looking to compensate for the biases in survey estimates that may arise because of the coverage, sampling, and nonresponse errors in single-mode surveys. In addition, surveyors balancing increasingly tighter budgets and the demand for quick survey results are attracted to collecting data with new and inexpensive modes, such as Web and interactive voice response (IVR). The rapidly expanding literature on the possibilities as well as the pitfalls of introducing a second or third mode into survey designs demonstrates the growing interest in mixed-mode surveys (de Leeuw, 2005; Dillman, in press; Dillman & Christian, 2005).

WHY CONSIDER A MIXED-MODE SURVEY DESIGN

Surveyors often turn to mixed-mode survey designs when it is difficult to achieve the desired results using a single mode alone. As mentioned in the earlier chapters, individual modes may have limitations that prevent surveyors from using a single mode to achieve the high-quality data results they need.

LOWER COSTS

One of the most compelling reasons for considering the use of multiple survey modes is to lower costs. Many mixed-mode survey designs begin with less expensive modes and then move to more costly modes for those who do not respond initially. An example of using multiple modes to reduce survey costs is the U.S. Decennial Census, for which questionnaires are mailed to all U.S. households (nearly 120 million in 2000) to get initial responses (nearly 70%) and then more costly personal enumeration is used to collect the remaining responses. Another example is the Agricultural Resource Management Survey conducted by the U.S. Department of Agriculture National Agricultural Statistics Service, which uses an initial self-administered paper questionnaire sent to 30,000 farm operations (and obtains responses from about 40%) before sending interviewers to collect data from the remainder of the businesses (Beckler & Ott, 2006). Other surveys of populations for which a list of e-mail addresses is available may first collect responses via the Web and then switch to mail or telephone for those who did not respond via the Internet. Likewise, some survey organizations attempt to lower costs for certain telephone interviews by calling people on the telephone and then asking them to complete an automated telephone survey. Those who agree are transferred to an IVR interview (Steiger & Conroy, 2008).

IMPROVE TIMELINESS

Mixed-mode surveys may also allow surveyors to collect responses more quickly. For example, a longitudinal survey of doctoral degree recipients conducted by the National Science Foundation asked which mode (Web, paper, or telephone) respondents preferred in a 2003 data collection and then offered the preferred method in 2006. This shortened significantly the length of time needed to complete the follow-up (Hoffer, Grigorian, & Fecso, 2007).

As another example, the Current Employment Statistics (CES) survey, conducted each month by the Bureau of Labor Statistics, uses six different modes (mail, computer assisted telephone interviewing, fax, touchtone data entry, electronic data exchange, and Web) to collect employment data from businesses. Businesses are matched with the mode that is most convenient for them to respond by in an effort to improve the speed of response because a 14-day turnaround is critical for reporting national employment data (Rosen, 2007). Similarly, one of the largest regularly conducted surveys in the United States, the Current Population Survey (CPS), which collects data monthly from nearly 60,000 households, initially contacts those households in person. However, when telephone numbers are obtained from households that have them, those households are then contacted by telephone for reinterviews in subsequent months to help reduce data collection costs. Initially contacting respondents in person improves coverage over using the telephone alone by including households without telephones, which is essential for this survey that estimates monthly unemployment rates in the United States, and using the telephone follow-up cuts the costs of reinterviews (see www.census.gov/apsd/techdoc/cps/cps-main.html).

REDUCE COVERAGE ERROR

In addition to reducing survey costs and improving timeliness, mixed-mode surveys are also used to improve coverage when a single mode cannot adequately cover the population of interest or when contact information is not available for the desired mode of data collection. For example, the general population survey discussed in Chapter 7 successfully used postal mail to contact respondents and ask them to respond to a web survey. To resolve coverage issues, paper questionnaires were mailed to respondents who were unable to respond via the Web. An alternative mode, such as in-person or telephone interviews, is also often used to recruit respondents for web panels so that all households, including those who do not have Internet access, can be covered as well as randomly sampled (this is discussed in more detail in Chapter 9).

Another example is from the Washington State University Student Experience Survey conducted via the Web annually since 2003. Because e-mail addresses are available for only about two thirds of the students, all respondents are first contacted via postal mail with the survey request and to deliver a small token incentive (discussed later). Subsequent contacts are also made via e-mail for those students who have provided e-mail addresses to the university. In 2003, the response rate was 46% for students who could be contacted only by postal mail; however, it improved to 61% for students who could be contacted by both postal mail and e-mail.

DELIVER INCENTIVES

One of the most effective ways of improving response rates in surveys, as discussed in Chapter 7, is to provide token cash incentives of a few dollars at the time of the survey request. Postal mail can be an effective way to provide small cash incentives for modes where incentives cannot otherwise be easily delivered (e.g., for telephone or web data collection). Although some incentives can be delivered electronically through the Web, many people are still suspicious of electronic financial exchanges, and taking advantage of these methods is often more difficult for respondents than simply opening a letter with cash inside.

For example, the mailed letters for the aforementioned student experience survey included $2 as a token of appreciation to help improve responses via the Web. In addition, when this survey was conducted as a web and telephone mixed-mode survey in 2005 and 2006, postal mail was also used to send token cash incentives to the telephone portion of the sample in advance of the initial telephone calls.

IMPROVE RESPONSE RATES AND REDUCE NONRESPONSE ERROR

One of the most important ways that mixed-mode surveys have been shown to enhance data quality is by improving response rates. One of the core reasons for using an alternative mode to deliver incentives is to improve response rates and reduce nonresponse error, but this is only one of the ways in which multiple modes can be used to improve response. Concern with low response rates for all modes, but particularly for telephone surveys, combined with the recognition that people have different preferences for being surveyed, has led to the offering of alternative survey modes for the purpose of improving overall response rates and reducing nonresponse bias. This justification for the use of mixed-mode surveys has become increasingly important in recent years and is one of the most important driving forces in the decision to switch from a single-mode to a multiple-mode survey design.

One aspect of the decision to use multiple modes is the recognition that some people prefer certain modes and may not respond via other modes. Preference is perhaps more complicated than it seems on the surface. Offering people a choice of survey mode has sometimes been shown to cause people to switch modes, but it may not result in an overall improvement in response (Dillman, Clark, & West, 1994). In fact, in an additional experimental treatment in the study summarized in the introduction of Chapter 7, we gave respondents a choice from the beginning between the mail and web versions of the survey. The result was a 9 percentage point decrease in response rates compared to the mail preference treatment (Dillman et al., 2008). The same effect (i.e., response rate decreases in the range of 1 to 9 percentage points) has been found in at least three similar experiments comparing a paper version to a web/paper choice version, one with the Arbitron Radio Diaries (Gentry, 2008), another with the American Community Survey (Griffen, Fischer, & Morgan, 2001), and the third with the National Science Foundation's Survey of Doctorate Recipients (Grigorian & Hoffer, 2008). As a result of these findings, we advise against letting respondents choose from among several survey modes.

However, assigning respondents to one mode ahead of time based on their preference, if it is known, can be useful. Offering people the mode they prefer increases the speed by which they respond (as discussed earlier). In addition, offering people one mode but then, when a response is not forthcoming, offering a second mode in effect increases the total number of contacts, a factor known to have a strong effect on improving response rates and reducing nonresponse error. Thus, the effect of accounting for mode preference on response rates may be realized in different ways.

Offering a second or even third mode to nonrespondents can improve response rates and reduce error by getting responses from people who may be difficult to reach via the initial mode of data collection. However, achieving high response rates does not always mean that nonresponse error is reduced (Dillman et al., in press; Groves, 2006). Thus, it is important that the use of multiple modes actually help to improve the representativeness of the responses received such that nonrespondents are not different in significant ways from those who do respond. For example, if people included in a particular survey population are unskilled computer users or are uncomfortable with responding to web surveys, offering a second mode such as mail or telephone may serve as an important way of reducing nonresponse error. A type of survey in which this may be important is when one wishes to use web surveys for populations that include a number of people who are older or who have less education, as discussed in Chapter 9.

REDUCE MEASUREMENT ERROR

Using mixed-mode surveys to reduce measurement error may be one of the oldest and most generally recognized reasons for conducting mixed-mode surveys. When in-person interviews were the primary means of collecting data, respondents often had to provide answers out loud in the presence of other household family members, in addition to the interviewer, which often led to more socially desirable responses for sensitive questions (e.g., sexual behaviors or the use of drugs and alcohol). The need to ask sensitive questions in ways that were not embarrassing led to the practice of handing people a brief paper questionnaire for them to record their responses without saying their answers out loud. A modern version of this practice is to simply offer respondents the same computer used by the interviewer to record answers so they have the opportunity to read and answer questions themselves (i.e., mixing computer-assisted personal interviewing with computer-assisted self-administration). In a more advanced version, the respondent can be provided with earphones to listen to questions and can answer them by marking answers on a screen where no one, including the respondent, can see the questions. This practice is particularly common in health interview surveys.

COMBINED EFFECTS

In general, it would be a mistake to attribute the trend toward using multiple modes to only one of these causes. More often, a combination of concerns leads to the decision to use a mixed-mode survey design. The substantial increase in the use of mixed-mode surveys throughout the world has been fueled by surveyors balancing the often competing demands of budget and time while striving to improve data quality by reducing coverage, sampling, nonresponse, and measurement errors. In addition, the computerized manipulation of question, address, and other files needed to conduct mixed-mode surveys now provides surveyors with the means for easily controlling the quality of the implementation processes and improving the speed at which these studies can be conducted, two factors that for so many decades thwarted most attempts to effectively use mixed-mode survey designs.

Creating the best survey design involves choosing the optimal mode or combination of modes to minimize overall total survey error. Thus, in deciding whether to employ a mixed-mode survey design, surveyors should consider the best mode or modes for the target population and research question under study within the budget and time frame for the particular study.

FOUR TYPES OF MIXED-MODE SURVEYS

Although the specific reasons for using multiple-mode approaches to conduct surveys vary greatly, there are four major ways that modes are often mixed, each of which has quite different effects on the overall results. The nature of each type of mixed-mode survey and the impacts on data quality are summarized in Figure 8.1.

Figure 8.1   Types of mixed-mode surveys and their implications.

Type	Motivation	Limitations
I Use one mode to contact respondents and to encourage response by a different mode	• Improve response rates • Reduce coverage and nonresponse error	• Increased implementation costs
II Use a second mode to collect responses from the same respondents for specific questions within a questionnaire	• Reduce measurement error • Reduce social desirability bias for sensitive questions	• Increased design costs • Increased nonresponse if respondent must respond by other mode at a later time
III Use alternative modes for different respondents in the same survey period	• Improve response rates • Reduce coverage and nonresponse error • Reduce survey costs	• Increased design costs • Measurement error from mode differences that may be confounded with differences among subgroups
IV Use a different mode to survey the same respondents in a later data collection period	• Different modes become available to survey respondents • Reduce survey costs	• Increased design costs • Measurement error from mode differences that impact the ability to measure change over time

Type I. Use One Mode to Contact Respondents and to Encourage Response by a Different Mode

One type of mixed-mode survey is where one mode is used to contact respondents and to encourage response by a different mode; that is, the mode of contact is used to support data collection by another mode, but not to actually collect survey responses. An alternative mode(s) can be used for any of the steps in the contact process: screening and recruitment, prenotice, survey invitation, and follow-up reminders.

In Chapter 7, we discussed the possibility of using the U.S. Postal Service Delivery Sequence File to send letters to household samples in order to invite them to respond to Internet surveys (i.e., mail implementation and web data collection). We also discussed other contexts in which postal mail is used to reach listed samples of individuals for whom Internet addresses are unavailable, to deliver incentives, and to improve response rates to Internet surveys. Other examples come from Nielsen Media Research and Arbitron, who used both postal mail and telephone to contact and recruit respondents to complete paper diaries about television viewing and radio listening and also to make reminder contacts.

Yet another example is the mailing of paper questionnaires to potential respondents with the explicit request that they *not* respond by mail but instead go to a web page to send answers (i.e., mail copy of paper questionnaire to use as a reference in completing a web survey). This strategy is commonly used in establishment surveys when the respondent will likely have to organize or collect information from multiple sources to be able to complete the web survey (see Chapter 12).

Mixing modes in this way is increasingly common. The motivation for using an alternative mode to contact respondents and to support data collection by another mode is to reduce the coverage error associated with some modes (e.g., the Internet) and to improve response rates in an effort to reduce nonresponse error. Unlike some other mixed-mode techniques that we discuss, this strategy for using multiple modes does not introduce potential measurement error. The only drawback to this use of a second or third mode may be increased implementation costs; however, in general this cost is minor compared to the likely benefit.

TYPE II. USE A SECOND MODE TO COLLECT RESPONSES FROM THE SAME RESPONDENTS FOR SPECIFIC QUESTIONS WITHIN A QUESTIONNAIRE

A second mode may be used to collect responses to a subset of questions from the same respondents. For example, respondents who are interviewed face to face or via telephone may be asked to complete a self-administered component and return or submit it after the interview is completed. This strategy can be used when the interview survey is quite long, when respondents need to record some form of daily activity, or for sensitive questions. For example, this strategy is often used when respondents need to record certain behaviors (e.g., food consumption, recreational activities, or media usage) at the time they occur for a period of time.

A more common use of a self-administered mode for a subset of questions for all respondents occurs when sensitive questions must be asked. Interview respondents may be switched from an interview to a self-administered paper or computer survey to enhance privacy so that their answers are not affected by the presence of the interviewer (or anyone who may be within earshot). This strategy is used in the U.S. National Survey on Drug Use and Health. A second mode might also be used when requesting extensive financial information from individuals or businesses to allow people the time to gather the specific information requested (before or after the interview) so that the data will be more accurate.

The motivation for using this type of mixed-mode survey is to improve data quality by reducing measurement error that can occur due to social desirability or respondent fatigue from a long interview. Surveyors are usually not concerned about measurement error that results from using multiple modes of data collection for this purpose because (a) the expected outcome is to improve measurement by obtaining more honest and accurate answers, and (b) all respondents answer the subset of questions using the same mode (i.e., responses are not compared across modes). The only limitations to this type of mixed-mode survey are the increased design costs of using a second mode for data collection and the potential that respondents may not complete or return the self-administered component if the questions are not answered as part of the initial interview. This type of mixed-mode survey is not our main focus in this chapter.

TYPE III. USE ALTERNATIVE MODES FOR DIFFERENT RESPONDENTS IN THE SAME SURVEY PERIOD

The practice of asking some respondents to reply to a survey by one mode and other respondents to respond via a different mode is increasingly common. This type of mixed-mode survey can offer multiple modes of data collection at one time in the field period (e.g., respondents can be offered a paper or web version of the survey from the beginning). Another strategy is to offer multiple modes in a specific sequence. For example, the American Community Survey, through which the U.S. Census Bureau provides reliable statistical information about all geographic areas of the United States, uses an initial mail contact followed by web, telephone, and face-to-face contacts with nonrespondents (see www.census.gov/acs/www/SBasics/DataColl.htm). This type of mixed-mode survey is also used for surveys of people in different regions or countries to respond to cultural differences and variations in survey capabilities. For example, the Pew Global Attitudes Project interviews people in some countries via telephone and others in person.

The motivation for using this type of mixed-mode data collection strategy is to reduce coverage and nonresponse error and sometimes to lower the costs of data collection, although there are additional costs associated with designing and implementing the survey via multiple modes. Alternative modes may be offered because of the lack of contact information for a particular mode; however, it is also increasingly likely that surveyors will give respondents an alternative mode of responding because they think it is preferred by respondents and will help improve response rates. Offering different respondents alternative survey modes raises the critical question of whether people answer questions in the same way in different modes. Compelling evidence exists that this type of mixed-mode survey may introduce measurement error because of how characteristics of different modes can influence how people respond, especially when a switch is made from an aural to visual mode or vice versa. In addition, the measurement error may be confounded with differences among respondents because those with different characteristics may respond by different modes. Thus, this type of mixed-mode survey raises the difficult question of whether the gains in coverage and response rates will offset any measurement differences that may occur.

TYPE IV. USE A DIFFERENT MODE TO SURVEY THE SAME RESPONDENTS IN A LATER DATA COLLECTION PERIOD

Longitudinal surveys, discussed in more detail in the next chapter, typically involve going back to respondents so that change over time can be measured. Oftentimes the data collection mode will be changed between survey periods to reduce survey costs or because new modes are available. A common example is when initial surveys were conducted via in-person interview or in a group self-administered setting, but then respondents are surveyed months or years later via another mode because people have dispersed geographically. In these cases, surveyors often switch to telephone or individual paper self-administration for follow-up surveys because the costs associated with sending interviewers to geographically dispersed areas or asking respondents to regroup in a common location prohibit them from using the original mode of data collection. In addition, the availability of the Web and IVR, which were not available when some current longitudinal surveys were begun, now provide an even more favorable cost advantage.

However, when different modes are used at different times to collect information, the change in the mode of data collection can introduce differences in measurement and threaten the ability to accurately measure change in attitudes, opinions, or behaviors. When the objective is to measure change between survey data collections, it is critical that questions be presented in the same way so that measurement error is minimized. The overall goal of the survey can be threatened when mode changes introduce systematic measurement differences at different data collection periods (see Chapter 9 for more on this topic). One strategy for assessing the impact of a mode change is to continue to collect data from a random subset of respondents using the original mode so that additional analyses can help one understand the impact of the change in mode on the rest of the respondents.

WHY DIFFERENT SURVEY MODES SOMETIMES PRODUCE DIFFERENT ANSWERS TO SURVEY QUESTIONS

A significant limitation to using multiple modes of data collection is that survey modes introduce measurement error because people may provide different answers to the same questions depending on the mode being used to ask the question. Three fundamental factors affect why people provide different responses: interviewer presence, aural versus visual communication of information, and differences in question construction.

In interviewer-administered surveys, the interviewer controls the delivery of the questions, and the social interaction with the interviewer may influence how a respondent answers. In addition, whether respondents perceive the survey questions aurally or visually can influence how they comprehend what is being asked and the answers they provide. Similarly, different visual layouts for asking questions may produce different responses (as discussed in Chapters 4, 5, and 6), which introduces the challenge of identifying the visual formats that can produce equivalent answers to interview surveys. Lastly, one of the largest sources of mode effects results from differences in how questions are constructed for each survey mode, because ways of constructing various types of questions have evolved over time into conventions associated with particular modes.

A rich literature has developed on the many ways in which these three factors may influence answers to survey questions. The results from this literature have become increasingly complicated to interpret, as these three factors often work together to influence how people respond to survey questions. Thus, questions are often constructed differently for each mode of data collection to respond to the presence versus absence of an interviewer, the differences in aural versus visual communication, and the conventions associated with each mode. In addition, as the number of available survey modes has increased, the variety in how questions are constructed and what type of formats respondents can use to report their answers has also increased.

Presence versus Absence of an Interviewer

The presence of an interviewer influences the level of control respondents have over the delivery of the survey questions and significantly increases the level of social interaction that occurs. The lack of control over the delivery of the questions may reduce the influence of question order on responses (i.e., question order effects), thus improving measurement, but the increased social interaction will likely increase the extent to which social norms are invoked when responding, thus potentially increasing bias due to social desirability, acquiescence, and other social norms.

Locus of Control

In interviewer-administered surveys, the interviewer controls the delivery of the stimulus, including the pace and flow of the conversation and the order in which questions are read and answered. In contrast, the respondents control the delivery in self-administered surveys, so they can answer at their own pace and complete the survey in the order they choose rather than be constrained by the interviewer. This can have a significant impact on how much time respondents spend answering each question and how question order may impact responses.

Normative Question Order Effects

Another potential contributor to differences between self-administered and interviewer-administered questionnaires is that people may adjust their answers to later questions to take into account their answer to an early question or questions. This behavior may be less likely to occur in self-administered surveys because respondents can preview questions to come or go back and change answers after responding to a later question, and social norms are not invoked as strongly as when an interviewer is present. Inconsistencies in one's presentation of self are more tolerable when there is no interviewer to witness them and potentially pass judgment.

For example, Bishop, Hippler, Schwarz, and Strack (1988) asked the following in separate surveys of U.S. and German students: "Do you think that the American government should be allowed to set limits on how much Japanese industry can sell in the United States (Germany)?" This was immediately followed by this question: "Do you think that the Japanese government should be allowed to set limits on how much American (German) industry can sell in Japan?" Not only did asking these questions by telephone in this order result in greater agreement than when asked in reverse order, but the effect was eliminated in the self-administered version. The explanation offered by the authors is that asking the question in this order on the telephone evokes a sense of fairness such that respondents feel their answer to the second question must be similar to their answer to the first. In contrast, respondents to self-administered questionnaires can look ahead and take into account the second question when answering the earlier one, or even change their answer afterward. This explanation invokes both cognitive and normative considerations as explanations (see Chapter 6 for a full discussion of question order effects).

A replication of this test on a different topic in the United States by Sangster (1993) found that although the norm of evenhandedness was evoked, the effects for mail and telephone were about the same. One possible explanation for these different results is that the evaluation by Bishop et al. (1988) examined the self-administered differences in a classroom setting where students might have approached answering the questions more as taking a test, in which it is normal to examine question sequences before answering and to change answers. In contrast, the mail questionnaires used in the Sangster study were sent to people's homes. In this setting, respondents seemed more likely to go straight through them without looking back and to worry less about consistency.

Other research, some of which was discussed extensively in Chapter 6, has revealed the existence of question order effects for which mail and telephone comparisons result in no differences. The lack of mode differences for these question order effects is likely due to the fact that they stem from cognitive, not normative, processes. Therefore, the presence or absence of an interviewer makes little difference in how they occur.

Social Desirability

Many years ago the administrator of a large regional hospital in Florida asked for advice on two customer satisfaction surveys of similar samples of former patients. One set of data had been obtained by a mail survey and the other by telephone interviews. Results from the mail questionnaires showed much lower satisfaction ratings. The request to examine the results came with his casually offered comment that the hospital had tentatively decided to discontinue the mail survey because of the belief that only unhappy patients seemed to be responding, but the sponsor wondered why that was the case. When asked for more information about the procedures, he indicated that in order to keep costs low, the telephone sample had been interviewed by nursing staff on the evening shift, many of whom had cared for the former patients they were asked to call, whereas the mail portion of the sample was able to respond anonymously (no identification number was printed on the return questionnaire). In light of this information, these results were not surprising. It seemed likely that patients would offer more positive, socially desirable answers by telephone when interviewed by the nursing staff; respondents' answers reflected what they thought the person who had provided the service hoped to hear. The advice given to the administrator was to at least change who did the interviews (i.e., contract to an outside firm), but even with this change the elimination of social desirability could not be guaranteed.

Because of the interaction with another person, interview surveys are more likely to produce socially desirable answers for sensitive questions, particularly for questions about potentially embarrassing behavior such as drug use or cheating on one's spouse. Similarly, socially desirable responses are also likely to be offered for drinking behavior, which is usually considered unacceptable. For example, one study asked the question "How often do you drive a car after drinking alcoholic beverages? Frequently, Occasionally, Seldom, Never, or Don't Know." Whereas 52% of the mail survey respondents responded "never," a significantly higher percentage (63%) of the telephone respondents said "never" (Dillman & Tarnai, 1991). Another finding supported by various studies is that respondents are more likely to say they have shoplifted something from a store when asked in self-administered surveys than in interviewer-administered surveys (Aquilino, 1994; de Leeuw, 1992; de Leeuw & van der Zouwen, 1988; DeMaio, 1984; Dillman, Sangster, Tarnai, & Rockwood, 1996).

Social desirability even operates at a threshold far below what one thinks of as sensitive behavior, because even very ordinary questions that seem on the surface to have little social desirability consistently exhibit this effect. For example, consider the following: "How would you describe your current health? Excellent, Good, Fair, or Poor." Compared to interviewer-administered surveys, self-administered surveys consistently produce lower proportions of respondents who choose "excellent" (Biemer, 1997; Hochstim,

1967). When one person meets another on the street and offers the conventional American greeting "How are you?" the person typically responds "Fine" regardless of how she is truly feeling. A more negative answer often requires additional explanation. Overall, when deciding whether to use interviewer- and self-administered modes in a mixed-mode survey design, one should routinely expect social desirability differences with sensitive questions. But these effects also need to be considered for less sensitive questions. Moreover, different populations often consider different topics sensitive. Therefore, it is advisable to try to detect sensitive questions during any pretesting.

Acquiescence

Acquiescence is a culturally based tendency to agree with others. In most cultures, it is easier to agree than to disagree, especially when interacting with another person (Javeline, 1999). For example, a classic interview experiment by Schuman and Presser (1981) showed that 60% of one national sample of respondents agreed with the following statement: "Individuals are more to blame than social conditions for crime and lawlessness in this country." However, 57% of a control group agreed with the exact reverse of this statement: "Social conditions are more to blame than individuals." Five months later respondents were resurveyed and given the opposite statement of the one they had in the initial survey. A quarter of respondents agreed to both of these opposing statements across these two data collection periods, indicating a tendency toward agreement. Moreover, changing the question structure to a forced choice between the two items produced an intermediate response.

An experiment by Dillman and Tarnai (1991) found that in seven comparisons assessing opinions of whether proposals for increasing seatbelt use would work, telephone respondents were significantly more likely than a comparable sample of mail respondents to agree. Differences ranged from 5 to 23 percentage points. A similar pattern was observed by Jordan, Marcus, and Reeder (1980). However, a meta-analysis by de Leeuw (1992) failed to detect any differences, revealing that the literature is not entirely consistent on this issue. Nonetheless, surveyors should watch carefully for differences between modes on agree/disagree types of questions, or try to avoid these formats as discussed in Chapter 4.

AURAL VERSUS VISUAL COMMUNICATION EFFECTS

Whether respondents receive survey questions aurally or visually can have a significant influence on how they perceive and comprehend the questions, the information they retrieve, the judgment they form, and the responses they report. When one person talks to another, the respondent must listen and recall the words that form each question and the associated answer choices. In addition, voice inflection, tone, and other paralinguistic features of the interviewer's voice convey additional meaning and may influence how respondents interpret what the interviewer says. When communication is visual, the words and other visual elements that respondents perceive are important. The visual presentation of words and other visual elements impacts responses to written questions just as voice characteristics influence answers to aurally administered questions (see Chapters 4 through 6).

Primacy/Recency Effects

One type of mode measurement difference that stems from the type of communication is the tendency to more frequently choose from among the first categories offered (called a *primacy effect*) or the last categories offered (called a *recency effect*) depending on how the categories are communicated. The explanation for these effects is based primarily on cognitive considerations. According to the cognitive elaboration model of response order effects, each response option is a short persuasive communication that brings to mind either confirming or disconfirming cognitive elaborations. The more time respondents have to think about each item, which is a direct function of the survey mode and the position of the item in the list, the more confirming or disconfirming information will come to mind (Schwarz, Hippler, & Noelle-Neumann, 1992; Sudman, Bradburn, & Schwarz, 1996). In self-administered (i.e., visual) survey modes, respondents can deeply process items appearing early in the list, but as they move through the list their minds become more cluttered and their ability to process becomes increasingly limited (Krosnick & Alwin, 1987). Thus, if early response options are plausible and bring to mind confirmatory thoughts, they are more likely to be endorsed, resulting in primacy effects (see Figure 8.2). However, if early items are implausible and bring to mind disconfirming thoughts, later items are more likely to be selected, resulting in recency effects. The expectations are a bit different for interviewer-administered surveys without show cards (i.e., aural interviews). In these modes there is typically not enough time for respondents to process all of the response categories as they are being read by the interviewer. Consequently, when the time comes to respond, the last categories that are heard are more likely to be remembered and are processed more deeply than the earlier ones (Krosnick & Alwin, 1987). Thus, if the last categories are plausible, a recency effect is expected, but if they are implausible, a primacy effect is expected. Under typical survey conditions, in which researchers try to avoid providing implausible response options, one would expect primacy effects in self-administered surveys and recency effects in interviewer-administered surveys.

Figure 8.2   Cognitive elaboration model of response order effects.

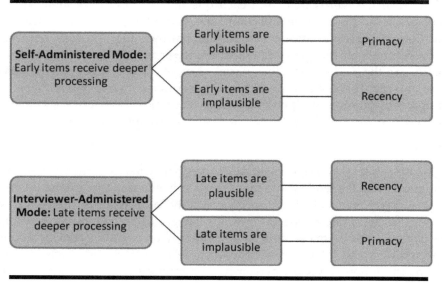

Evidence for the existence of pure primacy/recency effects is decidedly mixed. Although recency effects have been observed in telephone surveys by several researchers (Moore, 1997; Schuman & Presser, 1981), these same authors have also noted exceptions. Relatively few mixed-mode comparisons have been done (for one exception, see Schwarz et al., 1992). However, an analysis of 82 experiments (in 12 separate surveys conducted in seven states) found that primacy and recency effects occurred in both mail and telephone surveys (Dillman, Brown, et al., 1995).

We conclude that despite the extensive discussion of these effects in the literature, much remains to be learned about the conditions under which primacy and recency occur in surveys, some aspects of which may be entangled with other effects of visual versus aural communication of survey questions. The occurrence of primacy effects in self-administered surveys and recency effects in telephone surveys is far from predictable, and further experimentation needs to be done until this issue is settled.

SCALAR QUESTIONS: IS THE TYPE OF COMMUNICATION OR LEVEL OF SOCIAL INTERACTION PRODUCING DIFFERENT RESPONSES?

For more than 2 decades, studies have shown substantial differences in responses to scalar questions when asked by telephone versus visual modes. This research has shown that respondents provide more positive responses when surveyed by telephone than when presented with a visual scale (in mail, web, or in face-to-face surveys when show cards are used). A handful of explanations have been offered up for why these effects may occur, but as the research summarized here shows, none of the explanations seems able to adequately account for these differences.

One commonly offered explanation for such differences is social desirability, but the effects have been found consistently on questions that would not seem particularly sensitive or otherwise subject to social desirability. Another common explanation is higher incidence of acquiescence on the telephone, but the research has shown that the effects are consistently found on many types of scales that would not seem prone to acquiescence in addition to on agree/disagree scales that may exhibit acquiescence. Moreover, the telephone has been shown to produce more extreme responses than face-to-face surveys using show cards. That an interviewer was present in both modes and the extremeness on the telephone still occurred suggests that the effect has more to do with visual versus aural communication differences between the modes than with any normative effects that might occur due to the presence or absence of an interviewer (i.e., social desirability or acquiescence). Yet another explanation that has been offered up is that primacy and recency effects may underlie the extremeness on the telephone. However, as the research presented here shows, the effects continue to exist regardless of whether the most positive categories are offered first or last, so primacy and recency do not seem like plausible explanations either.

Three studies comparing responses to scalar questions across interviewer-administered surveys found that respondents were more likely to select the extreme positive category when surveyed by telephone than when surveyed by face-to-face interview with show cards used to visually display the scale. In two of these studies, the most positive category was presented first in both modes (Groves & Kahn, 1979; Jordan et al., 1980). In the third, de Leeuw (1992) found that even when the most positive category was presented last, telephone respondents were more likely to select it than both face-to-face respondents who received a show card and mail respondents. Because interviewers were present in all of these comparisons of telephone and face-to-face responses, social desirability and acquiescence would not seem likely to have caused these differences. Similarly, primacy/recency cannot explain these findings, because the extremeness occurred regardless of whether the positive or negative end of the scale was presented first. Thus, the visual presentation of the response categories on a show card seems to be what resulted in more extreme responses.

In another study, Dillman and Mason (1984) compared responses to a series of questions about how problematic several community issues were ("not a problem," "a small problem," "a serious problem," or "you don't know on this issue") from face-to-face, telephone, and mail surveys of general public samples. They found that face-to-face (with no show card) and telephone

Figure 8.3   Average percentage using the most extreme positive category ("not a problem") for interview and paper self-administered respondents in three studies.

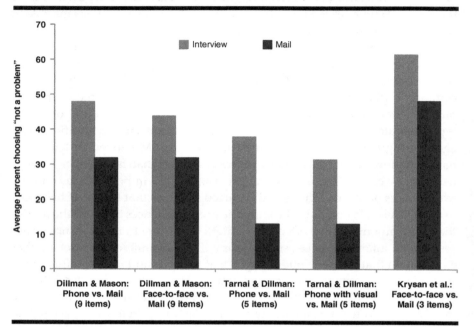

Source: "The Influence of Survey Method on Question Response," by D. A. Dillman and R. G. Mason, May 1984, Delevan, WI. Paper presented at the annual conference of the American Association for Public Opinion Research; "Questionnaire Context as a Source of Response Differences in Mail versus Telephone Surveys" (pp. 115–129), by J. Tarnai and D. A. Dillman, in *Context Effects in Social and Psychological Research,* N. Schwarz and S. Sudman (Eds.), 1992, New York: Springer-Verlag; and "Response Rates and Response Content in Mail Versus Face-to-Face Surveys," by M. Krysan, H. Schuman, L. J. Scott, and P. Beatty, 1994, *Public Opinion Quarterly, 58,* pp. 381–399.

respondents were more likely than mail respondents to choose the extreme positive option ("not a problem") when this option was presented first. This effect occurred for all nine of the items, with individual differences ranging from 4 to 19 percentage points (see Figure 8.3). This study also noted a similar tendency to choose the most positive end of scales for 15 other items about community and neighborhood qualities.

In an effort to decipher potential reasons for the differences observed in this study, a near replication of five items from the survey was conducted by Tarnai and Dillman (1992) using a college student sample (the topic was changed from satisfaction with community features to campus features). The differences found in this study were even larger, with differences for use of the "not a problem" category ranging from 13 to 38 percentage points, and with the telephone respondents averaging 25 points higher than mail respondents (see Figure 8.3). This study also tested the independent effects of visually presenting the response scale to respondents by experimentally comparing responses from the telephone and mail respondents to those of another group who received a copy of the questionnaire in the mail for them to use while responding via telephone. The group interviewed by telephone with the questionnaire in front of them averaged an 18 percentage point higher use of the "not a problem" category than the self-administered group, which was 7 percentage points less than the telephone-only group (see Figure 8.3). Based on this finding, it was concluded that the differences in aural versus visual communication were partly, but not entirely, responsible for the extremeness on the telephone.

Krysan et al. (1994) reported similar results for three questions asking whether (1) city services, (2) property not being kept up, and (3) crime were "always, often, sometimes, or never a problem" for respondents. Responses to the most positive category ("never") were 7 to 17 percentage points higher for interviewed respondents than for a comparable sample of respondents to self-administered questionnaires (see Figure 8.3). Again, the fact that the category order for this study was the reverse of that used in the aforementioned studies (Dillman & Mason, 1984; Tarnai & Dillman, 1992) suggests that something other than primacy and recency explanations is necessary for explaining these differences.

All three of these studies may have exhibited a low threshold of social desirability for respondents interviewed by telephone; that is, people are invested in their neighborhood, campus, or community and are predisposed to responding in a more positive light when interacting with an interviewer. However, the three studies showed similar results between telephone and in-person respondents when the presence of an interviewer was controlled, because interviewers administered the questions in both modes and the extremeness still occurred.

Another study was undertaken to compare mail and telephone responses as well as those of two newer modes: Web (a second visual method) and IVR (a second aural method). This study used a general population sample for which both telephone numbers and postal addresses were available (Dillman et al., in press). The survey was only 10 questions long, with 5 of the questions using a polar-point scalar question format (e.g., "Overall how satisfied are you with your long distance company? Please use a 1 to 5 scale where 1 means not at all satisfied and 5 means extremely satisfied."). The results indicated that telephone and IVR respondents provided more positive responses than mail and web respondents for all 5 polar-point questions (see Figure 8.4). It should also be noted that the direction of the scalar categories was reversed for half of the telephone sample, and no evidence of a recency effect was found.

Consistent with previous findings, in two mixed-mode telephone and web surveys of college undergraduates conducted in 2004 and 2006, telephone

Figure 8.4   Percentage of respondents endorsing the positive endpoint on scalar questions across four survey modes, by question.

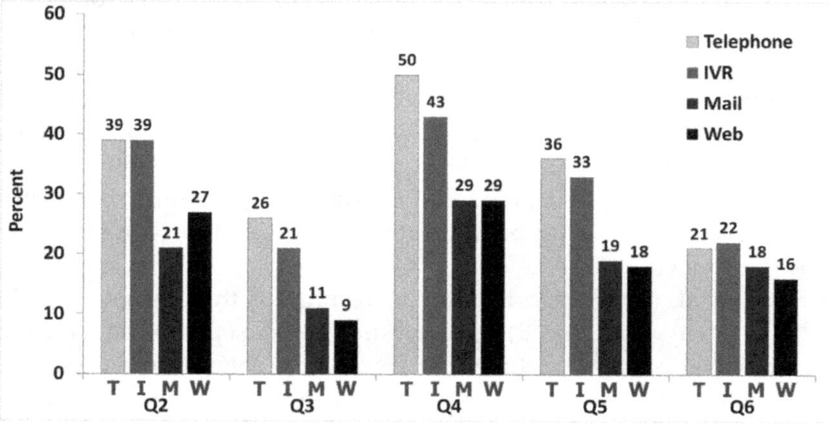

Source: "Response Rate and Measurement Differences in Mixed Mode Surveys Using Mail, Telephone, Interactive Voice Response, and the Internet," by D. A. Dillman et al., in press, *Social Science Research.*

respondents provided significantly more positive ratings than web respondents for 36 of the 46 scalar questions across various types of response scales and a variety of different question topics and scale labels (Christian, 2007). Telephone respondents provided more positive ratings than web respondents (a) regardless of whether all of the categories or only the endpoints were verbally labeled, (b) regardless of whether all of the categories were presented in one step or in two steps (the first step asked respondents to report the direction, positive or negative; the second step asked respondents to evaluate the strength of their position), and (c) across a variety of scale lengths.

The results of all of these studies indicate that the same scalar questions may produce more positive responses when no visual display of the scale is present, and these differences can oftentimes be quite large in magnitude. The likelihood that these differences will occur cannot be ignored, and we believe that attributing the differences to social desirability, acquiescence, or primacy/recency effects oversimplifies a much more complex situation. The consistency of the evidence across all types of attitude and opinion items is such that we suggest caution when combining responses to scalar questions from telephone surveys with those collected by other modes and when comparing estimates from surveys using these different modes. Because scalar questions are used quite frequently in surveys, this issue is one that cannot be ignored for most mixed-mode surveys that combine telephone with other modes of data collection. This is an area in which more research may be needed so that statistical adjustments can be developed to correct for these measurement differences.

HOW THE CHOICE OF MODE INFLUENCES
THE CONSTRUCTION OF QUESTIONS

Although the importance of the other two sources of mode differences should not be underestimated, changes in question wording and format may be the biggest source of differences across survey modes. Each of the survey modes is subject to conventions that have evolved over time and that sometimes create substantial pressures against constructing questions similarly for mixed-mode surveys. In this way, designers for each mode can actually enhance unwanted measurement error in mixed-mode surveys.

Several years ago a colleague called to indicate that conversion of a telephone survey to a web survey, in which nearly 10,000 people were being interviewed each month, resulted in a change in responses to the question "What is your marital status?" This is not a question that one would expect to produce variations in answers when asked in different survey modes. Further investigation revealed that this question was asked in an open-ended format on the telephone, and interviewers simply checked one of five options—single, married, separated, divorced, or widowed—depending on what the respondent said. On the Web, respondents were explicitly presented the categories and chose one of them themselves. In the closed-ended web format, 4.5% fewer respondents each month reported being single or married, whereas 3.5% more reported being separated and 1% more reported being divorced or widowed. The likely explanation for this difference is that when one is asked this question in an open-ended fashion, "single" or "married" are the usual responses one would provide, and someone would be less likely to volunteer the more specific responses of "separated," "divorced," or "widowed" unless it is apparent the questioner wants those categories to be considered, as was the case in the web survey.

When it was proposed that the problem could be solved by offering the options explicitly on the telephone the same way they were being presented on the Web, a concern was raised in the telephone survey unit because this is how the question was asked in nearly all telephone surveys conducted at this organization. Standard practice or tradition is a powerful force that results in questions being changed from one wording or format to another when asked in a different mode to conform to existing practices, even when this results in different question constructions for different modes from which data will be compared.

Traditionally, show cards that present response categories, or even full question wordings, have been used for face-to-face interviews so that respondents can hear and read the response categories. This has been true particularly for more complex questions or ones with longer lists of categories. In telephone surveys the practice quickly evolved of splitting complex questions into multiple parts, shortening longer scales by offering fewer categories, or removing scale labels (e.g., switching from fully labeled scales to scales with only the polar points labeled) in order to make responding easier. When it is proposed for face-to-face surveys that scales be shortened and show cards abandoned in order to provide equivalent stimuli with telephone surveys, opposition is often substantial, yet, as discussed earlier (Tarnai & Dillman, 1992), allowing people to read questions while responding verbally may influence answers in a significant way.

Even the Web has quickly evolved so that certain practices have become set in designers' minds as "best practices" that differ from those used in other modes. One example that was discussed in more depth in Chapter 6 has been to use different symbols to denote single- versus multiple-answer questions (e.g., radio buttons vs. html boxes) rather than to word questions in a way that indicate whether one or multiple answers can be provided.

Likewise, as discussed in Chapter 5, designers of self-administered questionnaires have converted questions that were asked in a forced-choice manner in interviewer-administered surveys (e.g., "Please indicate whether each of the following is or is not a reason that you chose to attend this university") to a check-all format (e.g., "For which of the following reasons did you choose to attend this university?"). The trend toward using this format has been further encouraged in web survey design because of the programming distinction between html boxes and radio buttons. However, research now makes it clear that respondents are likely to more deeply process all items, which encourages the endorsement of more items, when a forced-choice format is used for such questions (Smyth et al., 2006a) and that answers for the telephone and the Web are more likely to correspond when the forced-choice format is used for both modes (Smyth et al., 2008).

A MIXED-MODE DESIGN PROBLEM: THE 2010 U.S. DECENNIAL CENSUS

The U.S. Decennial Census consists of six questions (name, sex, age, date of birth, Spanish/Hispanic/Latino ethnicity, and race) asked about each member of the household, plus two general questions about the household. As preparations were being made for the 2010 Census and questionnaires were being developed for mail, Web, small handheld computer (although it has since been decided that handheld computers will not be used), and telephone administration, it became apparent that substantial differences existed among the ways these questions were being asked in each of the modes. Some of these differences were the following:

- The computer-assisted telephone questionnaire asked "Are you Spanish, Hispanic, or Latino?" The paper questionnaire asked the same question, but immediately provided categories, including "No, Not Spanish/Hispanic/Latino," "Yes, Mexican, Mexican Am./Chicano," and so on.

- The paper questionnaire used answer category boxes for all questions that required the selection of one or more answers; however, the Internet designers used radio buttons for single-answer questions (e.g., male/female) and html boxes for check-all questions for which multiple answers could be recorded (e.g., race and ethnicity).
- The Internet designers placed date of birth ahead of age so people's age could be automatically calculated and filled in based on the date of birth, whereas paper designers reversed the order because of evidence of less item nonresponse when age is asked before date of birth.
- The Internet designers allowed write-ins of unlimited length for each person's name and race categories, but paper designers could only use as many spaces as would fit in the columns on the page.
- The paper form used a person-based approach, whereby all six questions were asked for one person before moving to the next person in the household. In contrast, the Internet form used a topic-based approach (e.g., asking everyone's gender before proceeding to the next topic, age, which was asked about each person before moving to each of the following topics).
- On paper and the Internet, the question about how each member of the household was related to others showed 10 "related" categories and 5 other categories prefaced by the heading "IF NOT RELATED to Person 1." For the handheld computer mode, people were first asked if a person was related to Person 1, and only the "related" categories were shown.

When the various question formats were examined side by side, it was immediately apparent that the questions had been changed in well-intentioned efforts to make the items work better for each specific mode without attention to comparisons across modes. In response to these differences and because of the importance of this national survey that is, by law, used to allocate funds to states and communities, a 20-member task force worked for nearly a year to develop 30 guidelines (see Figure 8.5) so that the questions would be designed consistently across survey modes (Martin et al., 2007). The underlying principle for these guidelines was described as

> Universal Presentation: all respondents should be presented with the same question and response categories, regardless of mode. . . . Universal presentation says that the meaning and intent of the question and response options must be consistent. The goal is that instruments collect equivalent information regardless of mode . . . the same respondent would give the same substantive answer to a question regardless of the mode of administration. (p. 2)

As shown in Figure 8.5, these guidelines are focused on many aspects of writing questions that go far beyond choice of words and phrasing. They include the use of preambles and instructions, use of the same punctuation,

Figure 8.5   Proposed design guidelines for use in the 2010 U.S. Decennial Census for achieving commonality across mail, web, telephone, and handheld computer modes.

1. Every effort should be made to maintain the same wording of questions across survey modes. When variant wording for a particular mode is proposed, the decision to change wording should be based upon evidence (from Census Bureau tests or other sources) that a difference in wording is more likely than the same wording to produce consistent meaning and equivalent answers.

2. Preambles and instructions on the answering process may require different wording to be appropriate to the individual mode. They should not vary within modes.

3. Fills (e.g., for name) in the question are permissible in automated instruments, and should have the same format. If name (or other) fills are used, the format (e.g., first name + middle initial + last name) should be consistent across all automated modes and questions.

4. The elements of a question may be reordered if necessary to ensure that respondents are exposed to all essential information in interviewer-administered modes. Any reordering should be constant within mode.

5. Substantive instructions and explanations should be consistent across modes.

6. The underlying response task posed by a question should be consistent across modes, even if the implementation differs.

7. Question punctuation should be consistent and appropriate for the response task.

8. Question wording may be simplified for questions to be repeated for multiple household members.

9. The same examples, in the same order, should be presented in a question in all modes. Exceptions may be made if evidence exists that adding or deleting examples in one mode improves data quality (e.g., reduces item nonresponse) and does not bias response distributions. Unless such evidence exists, examples should not be introduced into (or eliminated from) a single mode.

10. Placement and presentation of examples may vary by mode, consistent with the principle of universal presentation.

11. Examples should be shown on the screen in internet applications, rather than being available only behind hyperlinks.

12. Identical response categories should be used across all modes.

13. For closed questions (i.e., those with fixed categories), instruments in all modes should be designed and administered to expose respondents to the response categories, in the same order, and to present response categories with the question.

14. When "Don't Know" is presented to respondents as an explicit response option in one mode, it should be offered in all.

15. When compiling a household roster, prefilling the last name given by the previous person listed is an acceptable practice in automated instruments used by experienced interviewers.

Figure 8.5 *(Continued)*

16. Formats for answer spaces should be applied consistently within mode.

17. Maintain the check box/radio button distinction in the internet form. Use verbal instructions, which do not have to be the same across modes, to reinforce the use of check boxes for multiple responses.

18. The amount and arrangement of space for write-in boxes should be consistent across all modes and appropriate for the required response. (Use of shared write-in spaces is an exception by necessity.) Other aspects of visual layout and design differences should be carefully reviewed and tested if possible for their impacts on responses.

19. The use of selective emphasis should be consistent across modes. The convention (boldface, underlining, capitalization, italics, etc.) used to communicate it may vary across modes although consistency is preferable.

20. Include a marker to uniquely identify each question in an instrument.

21. Question order should be constant for all modes unless there is empirical evidence to show data quality is improved in one mode, and comparability of data between modes is not reduced, by using a different order.

22. Whether an instrument is person- or topic-based should be decided based on evidence about data quality and ease of administration in each mode, and the comparability of data across modes.

23. Extra questions (asked in some modes but not others) should if possible be asked after rather than before the core short-form questions, to avoid introducing order effects. When this is not possible, they should be carefully reviewed to ensure that they do not introduce new concepts, terms, or meanings that might influence answers to subsequent, core questions.

24. When used, the content and design of a flashcard should be developed to best achieve the objectives of a question.

25. When flashcards are used, their use should be scripted for the interviewer.

26. If more than five response options are presented to the respondent, the question should if possible, be adapted for interviewer administration (by use of a flashcard, a branching question, or other adaptation).

27. Soft edits should be applied across all automated instruments when they increase data completeness and consistency.

28. Easily interpreted and relevant help should be provided across all modes in some form.

29. Help for all modes should come from the same source, such as an improved Questionnaire Reference Book.

30. Help should be user-initiated, reasonably accessible in each mode, and require low levels of effort to obtain.

Source: Guidelines for Designing Questionnaires for Administration in Different Modes (pp. 5–26), by E. Martin et al., 2007, Suitland, MD: U.S. Census Bureau.

presentation of "don't know" responses, and many other issues that were handled in quite different ways when each mode's format was developed independently.

UNIFIED VERSUS MODE-SPECIFIC DESIGN

Because there are different ways of combining modes and a variety of reasons for using a mixed-mode approach, there are also different approaches for constructing questionnaires for mixed-mode surveys. There are three main approaches to designing mixed-mode questionnaires: unified mode, mode-specific, and mode-enhancement construction (see Figure 8.6). When each of these types of construction is used depends on the goals of the particular mixed-mode study. Unified mode construction is recommended when all modes are equally important to the study, whereas mode-specific and mode-enhancement construction may be better suited when there is a dominant mode of data collection with another mode or modes used to supplement it.

Unified (or unimode) construction has a similar goal to the "universal presentation" principle developed for the 2010 U.S. Decennial Census. *Unified mode construction* involves writing and presenting questions the same or nearly the same across different survey modes to ensure that respondents in both modes receive the same mental stimulus. The goal is to find a common ground such that the meaning of the question stays the same regardless of what mode is used so that items are measured equivalently across modes. In

Figure 8.6   Types of mixed-mode construction and their suggested use.

Type	Definition	Use
Unified mode	Writing and presenting questions the same or nearly the same across different survey modes to ensure respondents perceive a common mental stimulus	To eliminate needless differences in how questions are constructed for alternate modes
Mode-specific	Modifying how questions are worded or presented for different modes based on the particular capabilities of each mode	When technology and communication factors of different modes require different formats to achieve the same stimulus
Mode-enhancement	Using features that are not available in all modes to improve the quality of responses to that mode	When the highest quality answers are desired and equivalency across modes is of lesser importance

practice, this type of construction involves providing similar question wording and offering the same response categories in all modes. Unified mode construction is best used to eliminate needless and inadvertent differences in how questions are constructed for alternative modes (see Figure 8.6).

As mentioned earlier, many of the differences in how questions are constructed for each mode persist simply because of tradition. One example of eliminating needless differences in question construction is to explicitly offer responses such as "both," "never heard of," or "don't know" in telephone, mail, and web modes (rather than accept them only when volunteered on the telephone and present them with the other response options in the mail and on the Web). In addition, one may decide to withhold show cards in face-to-face interviews in order to remove that visual component when respondents to telephone surveys are not able to have an equivalent visual component. Another example is to use forced-choice questions ("yes" or "no" for each of the presented items) in all modes (rather than check-all in self-administered modes) because they have been shown to produce more equivalent answers across telephone and web modes (Smyth et al., 2008). A different kind of example is to avoid requiring an answer to questions in web surveys, because neither telephone nor mail surveys have the parallel capability of requiring respondents to answer every question. These are only a few of the many differences in construction that exist primarily because questionnaires for individual modes are often constructed by specialists working within the experiences of a particular mode rather than thinking about constructing questions to work across multiple modes.

An example of developing a unified mode construction between the Web and telephone was achieved in a series of surveys conducted by the Research Triangle Institute (Wine, Cominole, Heuer, & Riccobono, 2006). This effort involved conducting each survey initially by the Web with a computer-assisted telephone interview follow-up to everyone who did not respond on the Web. To achieve mode equivalency, researchers followed a unimode approach of using the same screens for telephone interviews as those used for web respondents. This required building the screens in ways quite different from those typically used for telephone interviewing that include interviewer prompts and similar information that is not to be read to respondents. Follow-up analysis by the authors indicated that this unified design produced virtually no differences between modes.

Mode-specific construction is a different perspective on writing questions and administering them. It starts with the premise that different survey modes are inherently different in their capabilities, as well as in their fundamental means of communication, so questions may need to be modified for different modes. Thus, different question structures, wording, or presentations may be needed in order to provide respondents with a common stimulus that produces equivalent answers across survey modes (see Figure 8.6). The basis of this approach is that the unique capabilities of each particular mode are strategically employed to improve the chance of obtaining equivalent data across modes.

Mode-specific construction should be used when communication and technology differences require different formats to achieve the same stimuli for respondents. For example, interviewers act as an intelligent system to clarify information for telephone and face-to-face respondents, interpret their responses, or probe for additional clarification, but they are not available to fulfill these functions for self-administered surveys. Thus, additional design features may be needed in mail and web surveys to improve the quality of responses and make them more comparable to those obtained in interviewer-administered surveys.

An example of this stems from the role of answer spaces in communicating respondent expectations in mail and web surveys. In Chapter 4 we discussed research pertaining to how to get respondents to report answers to the simple question of what month and year they began classes at a university. This research showed that answers were greatly affected by the size of the answer spaces and how they were labeled (Christian, 2007; Christian et al., 2008). Thus, in self-administered surveys, the way answer spaces and categories are displayed visually can fulfill some of the functions interviewers perform in telephone and face-to-face surveys. Research has also shown that respondents are likely to make errors interpreting scales when it is necessary to transfer information in question stems to answer spaces. Thus, mode-specific construction may be quite valuable for increasing the likelihood that equivalent data will be obtained across survey modes.

Mode-specific construction is sometimes used to pursue a quite different objective, particularly when there is one primary mode of data collection where responses should be optimized and then one or more secondary modes. To differentiate this use of mode-specific construction, we refer to it here as *mode-enhancement construction*. In this type of construction the objective is to produce the highest quality answers for one mode, even though another mode in the mixed-mode survey may not be capable of producing similar responses. In other words, the goal here is to enhance the quality of responses to one mode when the equivalency across modes is of lesser importance (see Figure 8.6).

Sometimes a survey may collect the most responses by one mode, using another as a secondary mode to collect responses from a smaller number of respondents. One reason for mode-enhancement construction might be the consideration that the few questionnaires obtained in the final stages of data collection are of much less importance than any advantages that might be gained by using mode-enhancement construction to collect the bulk of the data. In longitudinal surveys, even though a mode is changed in later years for some respondents, sponsors may choose to stick with a type of survey construction that works better for the previous mode than the new one.

Mode-enhancement approaches to mixed-mode surveys are common. There is a history in survey methodology of thinking of individual modes in terms of advantages and disadvantages, and this perspective is likely to persist. Just as face-to-face surveyors are reluctant to give up show cards when also using telephone surveys, telephone surveyors are often reluctant to agree to longer scales that are fully labeled and may be desired by users of other survey modes. In-person, telephone, and web surveyors who can change category orders (even randomizing them), or who can use responses to previous questions to formulate later questions, may be reluctant to give up these capabilities when mail surveys are also used. In particular, the advent of the Web has encouraged surveyors to generate totals automatically, provide error messages, require answers to every question to eliminate item nonresponse, use drop-down menus to avoid coding incomplete information, and use other new response formats. In addition, the use of handheld devices for responding to surveys has created pressures for breaking questions into smaller parts (so they can be displayed entirely on a small screen). For all of these reasons, we expect the interest in mode-enhancement construction to remain strong.

CONCLUSION

Recently, an ambitious student approached one of us to discuss her preliminary plans for a mixed-mode survey of the general public on a controversial retail development planned for the community. She intended to administer an initial survey and then repeat the survey 1 or 2 years later to see if concerns expressed before the development had actually been realized after the development. The student planned to use the U.S. Postal Service Delivery Sequence File to get a good address list. She also proposed giving respondents a choice of answering by Web or mail as a means of improving response rate. Because she knew that some of the Delivery Sequence File addresses could be matched with telephone records, she planned to recontact nonrespondents for whom a number could be found with a request to complete the survey over the telephone in order to try to improve response rates. The telephone follow-up would also obtain responses from those who would not answer by the other survey modes. In addition, she was concerned about the effects of question order on people's answers to certain items and thus wanted to randomly rotate response category order for certain questions on the Web and telephone.

Our response to her was that although mail and the Web could probably be used without producing significant measurement differences, it was not likely that simply offering both would significantly improve response rates.

We also suggested that surveying some people by the Web or mail and others by telephone was likely to introduce significant measurement differences for the opinion questions, which were a significant part of her survey. Instead we proposed that if she wanted to use the telephone, she should use it as a follow-up reminder in which interviewers offered to answer respondents' questions and encouraged respondents to complete the mail or web questionnaire. We also encouraged her not to randomly rotate categories on the Web or telephone, if used, because it was unlikely she could do that effectively on the mail questionnaire. Thus, we concluded that not only would a mixed-mode survey of the nature she proposed be costly and difficult to complete, but results could be difficult to interpret. Sometimes the best decision is not to attempt a mixed-mode survey.

In contrast, we have also talked with people who propose survey designs that are impossible to conduct by a single mode. Sometimes it is the lack of a complete address list for a single mode. In other instances it is the reality of needing to boost response by switching to another mode. In still other instances it is a lapse of time that makes it impossible to approach people who were surveyed at an earlier time with the previously used mode. Although mixed-mode surveys are increasingly important, they are not to be used without careful consideration of the costs, error, and management consequences, both positive and negative.

The four types of mixed-mode surveys discussed in this chapter describe quite different uses of second and third modes for a particular study, some with large consequences for measurement and others without such impacts. We continue in Chapter 9 with two situations in which changing or not changing modes between periods of data collection may affect greatly the quality of data being collected.

CHAPTER 9

Longitudinal and Internet Panel Surveys

BECAUSE THE goal of longitudinal surveys is often to measure change over time, these surveys are particularly sensitive to the mode changes discussed in Chapter 8. Switching modes between data collection periods makes it difficult to determine whether changes in the trends result from differences in how people respond to the new survey mode or from actual changes in people's opinions, attitudes, or behaviors. In addition, longitudinal surveys face additional challenges because of (a) the increased potential for nonresponse error, as oftentimes sample members quit between surveys (i.e., attrition); and (b) measurement error due to respondent conditioning (i.e., respondents answering differently because of prior survey experiences). Although all surveys have the potential for nonresponse and measurement error, the danger of these errors occurring in longitudinal surveys is magnified because of the task of surveying the same respondents multiple times. These errors are also significant problems for Internet panels, in which the same respondents are usually asked to respond to different questionnaires on a variety of topics. Because both types of surveys must deal with the effects of a previous administration on the next period of data collection, we consider them together in this chapter.

Despite these commonalities, these types of surveys also exhibit sharp contrasts. For example, in longitudinal surveys there is often great pressure to change modes between data collection periods. In contrast, some Internet panels attempt to avoid the mixed-mode problem completely by asking people to respond only via the Internet, thereby limiting responses to those who have Internet access. However, by doing so, they create serious potential for coverage error. Other Internet panels may use another mode to recruit respondents into the panel or may even provide respondents without Internet access an alternative mode for responding (e.g., paper surveys).

In addition, whereas for many longitudinal surveys years may elapse between data collections, Internet panel surveys may allow only days or weeks between surveys, and one survey may be unrelated to the next topically. As a result, the danger of measurement error resulting from respondent conditioning is often magnified in Internet panels, although it remains a problem for both types of surveys. Both longitudinal surveys and Internet panels require surveyors to make different decisions from those they typically need to make for independent cross-sectional surveys, and because of the unique challenge of keeping respondents motivated over time and over multiple surveys, the need for a tailored design strategy that takes into account costs, rewards, and trust is intensified for both.

LONGITUDINAL SURVEYS

Every year an enormous number of longitudinal surveys are conducted throughout the world. Some are long-standing and may track and interview people periodically for 20 or 30 years or even longer. An example is a survey that follows individuals from high school to retirement from the workforce. Other longitudinal surveys are fairly simple. A short-course instructor may ask respondents to complete a questionnaire at the end of the course to evaluate what they learned and then may decide 6 months later to ask the same respondents the same or similar questions to see whether the course had a lasting impact. Thus, it is not surprising that the objectives of, as well as resources devoted to, longitudinal surveys vary enormously.

Longitudinal surveys deal with many difficult issues, ranging from how to track respondents over many decades to how to keep them responding to each of the follow-up surveys. A number of sources written over many years provide a wealth of detail on how to design and implement longitudinal surveys effectively (Call, Otto, & Spencer, 1982; Lynn, 2008; Willits, Crider, & Bealer, 1969).

One of the special challenges faced by longitudinal surveys is that there are often enormous pressures to change the survey mode in subsequent waves of data collection. High school students surveyed by paper in a classroom prior to graduation cannot easily and cost-effectively be reassembled and surveyed in the same classroom 1 or 2 decades later. Likewise, surveys started many years ago could not have anticipated the development of modern survey methods and alternatives, such as the Internet. However, the reality of budgeting expenses and getting funding years after the initial data collection to conduct additional waves often necessitates the use of these less expensive modes. Other surveys may change modes or use multiple modes in an effort to maximize response from all members, because attrition in longitudinal surveys not only affects the current wave of data collection but also the potential for losing the trend line associated with previously collected data. In still other instances, survey directors have been known to switch modes simply because using a more modern mode seems like a "better" choice. For all of these reasons, many longitudinal surveys change modes of data collection; some would not be able to complete future waves without doing so.

At the same time, it is apparent that longitudinal surveys are particularly sensitive to mode differences and other context effects because of their goal to measure change over time. When one is attempting to determine answers to questions such as "How satisfied are you with your work?" or "How would you rate your health?" many considerations may influence whether people are responding to the same stimulus they were exposed to during the previous round of data collection (a requirement for reliable measurement). Chief among those concerns is whether the context surrounding the question has changed. Oftentimes the context changes because the order of questions has been changed, the order of response options has been changed, or new questions have been added. When these questionnaire changes occur, they may also change the cognitive and normative processes underlying how people respond to the questions, leading to measurement error.

As discussed in Chapter 8, respondents' answers may be influenced by the presence of an interviewer (e.g., changes in respondent control, social desirability, acquiescence, and question order effects), by a change from a mode that relies primarily on aural communication to a mode that uses predominantly visual communication (e.g., primacy/recency effects, visual design influences), and by whether the structure of the question is inadvertently changed (e.g., using a check-all format rather than a forced-choice format or explicitly offering some response options in one mode but not in another). It also now seems probable that changing from aural to visual modes will change answers to ordinal scale questions, as was discussed in Chapters 5 and 8. In addition, the technology associated with each mode may produce unintended measurement differences. These concerns about how the choice of survey mode influences responses lead us to exercise considerable caution when considering a change in survey modes for longitudinal surveys.

GUIDELINES FOR LONGITUDINAL SURVEYS

Guideline 9.1: Plan ahead by Selecting a Longitudinal Survey Mode that Can Be Used in Future Years, and Adopt a Conservative Stance on whether to Change Modes for Follow-Up Data Collections

When longitudinal surveys are started, sponsors often do not think about the long-term consequences of their choice of mode. In hindsight, some initial survey data collections that were completed on paper in classroom settings might have been conducted by interview in order to establish baselines for expected follow-ups to be conducted by interviewers. Today, one might choose the Web for the initial data collection simply because it seems likely to be available and usable in a less costly way in future years.

Sometimes mode changes are made by surveyors for nonessential reasons. A change may be made to be able to contract with a particular organization or to give a more modern appearance to the survey. Sometimes people are given an option as to which mode they can use as a favor to the respondent and in hopes that overall response rates may be improved slightly. However, as discussed in Chapter 8, there is little compelling evidence that giving people a choice will improve response. Changes also get made for the sake of convenience to the sponsor. Because the risks of mode changes to data quality are so great, one should be careful about changing modes for these simple reasons. The influence on data quality may far outweigh any advantages gained. An example of a survey that began with paper questionnaires in 1975 and continues to use them to avoid potential mode effects is the University of Michigan Institute for Social Research's Monitoring the Future project, which collects information on the behaviors, attitudes, and values of U.S. adolescents and young adults (Bachman et al., 2008).

In addition, effective alternatives to switching the mode of data collection may exist. For example, a Type I mixed-mode survey (see Figure 8.1 in Chapter 8) uses one mode to encourage response by a different mode. In this context, one may use any of the modes to encourage people to respond by any of the other modes without anticipating increases in measurement error as long as only one mode is used for data collection. For example, one might contact people by telephone or the Internet to get them to complete a mail survey in order to increase response rates while also maintaining continuity with data collected by mail in the past. One of the current strengths of surveys is that different modes can be used to support data collection by other modes, whether by taking advantage of an address not available to other modes or delivering an incentive or other appeal not easily sent by another means.

Guideline 9.2: Be Especially Cautious about Switching from a Visual Self-Administered Mode of Data Collection to an Aural Interviewer-Administered Mode or Vice Versa

It is becoming increasingly evident that the presence or absence of an interviewer in the survey process has significant effects on respondents' answers. Likewise, adding or removing a visual stimulus can significantly impact answers. As a result, if a change in mode is necessary, it is best to select a different mode that relies on the same type of administration and communication as the initial mode. For example, if costs are driving a mode switch and the first survey was conducted face to face, a telephone survey may be the best alternative for the next data collection mode because both modes (a) have an interviewer present and (b) rely primarily on aural communication. Moreover, although differences between personal and telephone interviews have been observed, they have for the most part been relatively minor. However, ample evidence now exists that respondents may give different answers to interview and noninterview surveys for many reasons, ranging from social desirability and control over the order of processing to differences in how questions are constructed. Thus, the survey is at great risk when switching between visual self-administered and aural interviewer-administered modes of surveying.

Guideline 9.3: When Changes in Visual Modes Are Made, Maintain Similar Visual Layouts in Order to Minimize Measurement Error due to Inadvertent Design Changes

Research now shows that visual layout effects are quite similar in postal and web surveys (Dillman, 2007). This evidence exists for a number of different kinds of questions ranging from scales to open-ended answer boxes. Thus, it seems prudent to maintain similarity in the visual layout across survey modes to avoid potential differences in measurement. As we discussed in Chapter 7, it is now possible to achieve greater similarity between the design of web screens and the design of paper surveys. However, following this guideline may sometimes mean holding back on the use of drop-down menus and other measurement formats that are available in web surveys but not on paper. These are issues that should continue to be addressed in future research.

Guideline 9.4: Avoid Offering Respondents a Choice of Survey Mode

In recent years, as telephone response rates have declined and it has become possible to conduct surveys simultaneously with multiple modes of data collection, a tendency has developed to allow respondents to choose the mode by which they would prefer to respond. Evidence is lacking that offering a choice of mode will necessarily improve response, and doing so may even decrease it. One of the consequences of giving respondents a choice of survey mode is that measurement differences based on the survey mode may be confounded with differences in people who choose to respond via one mode versus another. The undesirable consequence of this change will likely be to make it even more difficult to discern whether changes in data are due to the mode change or are due to actual changes in the attitudes and behaviors of respondents.

In sum, the consequences of mode change for longitudinal surveys may be substantial, and therefore changes need to be carried out cautiously, if at all, and only after considering the likely effects on the important goal of measuring changes over time.

INTERNET PANELS

The development of Internet panels, in which people are asked to respond regularly to a number of survey requests rather than only once (as tends to be done with most surveys), has been a response to many of the changes in survey research discussed in Chapter 1. The decline in telephone survey response rates in the 1990s and the emergence of the trend toward cellular phones replacing landlines led many surveyors, particularly those interested in surveying young people, to examine other alternatives. At the same time, the rapid increase in Internet access rates and the hope that most people would someday soon have the skill levels needed to complete web surveys made such surveys a likely solution to the challenges being faced by telephone surveyors. Layer on top of that the recognition that once a web survey was set up, the marginal costs of contacting and getting responses from additional respondents would be smaller than for any other survey mode, and the situation was ripe for the rapid development of web surveying.

However, there are a number of difficulties with conducting general population surveys via the Web. First, surveyors have historically had access to the general public through both the telephone and postal mail because both of these utilities were publicly regulated, making it possible for anyone to attempt to reach anyone else when contact information was available. In contrast, many Internet providers are privately owned and are not treated by government as a public utility, meaning that Internet providers have the right to prevent access to customers. Moreover, some organizations that enforce the professional norms and standards of surveying have taken the position that a "prior relationship" is necessary to legitimate sending survey requests to people via e-mail (see www.casro.org/codeofstandards.cfm). In addition to these preventive factors, as was discussed in Chapter 3 there is no available sampling frame for Internet users and no standard way of assigning e-mail addresses that would facilitate sampling through an algorithm as is done with random-digit dialing.

Within this context of great opportunities clashing with great difficulties, one practical solution was to compile and maintain very large lists of Internet users who were willing and able to answer web surveys. Once their name was added to the list, it made sense to ask them to complete multiple surveys over time. Hence, the first Internet panels were born. Initially Internet panels consisted of individuals who "volunteered" to receive and respond to surveys. When the individuals volunteered (usually in response to a general advertisement, as is discussed later) and provided their e-mail address, they were establishing a relationship that then allowed the surveyor to ethically send them e-mail requests to complete surveys. More recently, a number of attempts have been made to develop web panels by using other survey modes, such as telephone or mail, to employ a probability-based selection strategy to identify and recruit possible panel members who would subsequently receive and respond to surveys via the Web. We discuss these two very different types of Internet panels in turn.

VOLUNTEER INTERNET PANELS

In many ways, today's volunteer Internet panels are a Web-specific extension of an earlier tradition of convenience, purposive, and quota samples that have often been used in marketing and other nongovernmental research (Bethlehem & Stoop, 2007). Because web surveyors have to have a prior relationship with a respondent in order to send a survey request, the most common method of recruiting panel members quickly has become through banner ads, pop-up ads, or e-mail advertisements. Excerpts from several such advertisements or recruitment notices that we have recently received are displayed in Figure 9.1. As these notices clearly indicate, in return for

Figure 9.1   Examples of web panel recruitment notices.

If you're a USA resident, and you'd like to earn money by taking surveys, then welcome to the greatest job on earth! [Website name] will give you links to companies that are paying for surveys. You may register for as many as you like. . . . These companies will send you emails with paid surveys, which you will complete and return. It's the perfect job for women who want to stay at home with their children, or anyone who needs extra money.

Dear Student,
We will pay your university fees? Believe it or not, your opinion is worth a paycheck. Companies are willing to pay people like you good money for their opinions. . . . $5 to $75 per hour just to fill out simple online surveys from the comfort of your own home.

Your opinion could be worth $500.

[Panel name] only needs about 10 minutes of your time to register. Best of all, it's FREE!

Join our nationwide online community of experts and get rewarded for sharing your opinions! What are you waiting for!

Visit the [web address] member site to learn about additional member benefits, points, sweepstakes, and much more. Complete the registration and [company name] will grant you 3,000 points and an automatic entry into a $500 sweepstakes drawing!

As a member of the [panel name], you will be invited to participate in regular surveys and opinion polls about the products you buy, the services you use, the places you shop, and more. With each survey you complete, you are granted more points and sweepstakes entries!

responding, volunteers are typically offered chances to win awards, sweepstakes prizes, reward points that can be redeemed for merchandise, and direct payments.

When Internet users respond to an ad (i.e., are recruited into the panel), they are asked to provide basic information about themselves. This information is generally taken at face value and is rarely verified by those managing the panel. Once the panel has enough members, members can be sampled to complete various surveys, perhaps several or many times per month. Generally, samples are drawn from the volunteers in ways that ensure that the reported background characteristics of the selected panel members match those of the target populations for each survey. The sampled subset of panel members is then asked to complete the relevant survey. Response rates are typically less than 25% (Lee, 2006).

A brief look at volunteer Internet panels illustrates the divergence of these panels from the traditional four-cornerstone model of surveying introduced in earlier chapters of this book.

- *Coverage error problems:* Because only 70% of households have Internet coverage, and within households an unknown additional number of people lack the skills needed for responding to web surveys, a significant portion of the general public cannot respond to Internet surveys (undercoverage). Moreover, those who have Internet access differ in important ways from those who do not (see Chapter 3). Thus, it is highly likely that those who join Internet panels will differ from those who do not in ways that result in coverage error, and attempts to generalize results from these surveys beyond those who respond will be undermined.

- *Self-selection and sampling error problems:* Only people who happen across a recruitment advertisement or receive one from a third party via e-mail will have the opportunity to volunteer, and only a portion of those people will actually volunteer. Such self-selection further undermines the extent to which the composition of the panel mirrors the composition of the general public and likely leads to biased results. Bethlehem and Stoop (2007), for example, compared election predictions for the 2003 and 2006 Dutch parliamentary elections from polls of volunteers, polls of samples of volunteer Internet panel members, and polls of respondents selected through probability methods (i.e., nonvolunteers). The polls relying on probability sampling predicted the actual election outcomes more accurately than any of the volunteer-based polls, including those for which members of volunteer panels were selected to mirror the sociodemographic and voting characteristics of the general Dutch public.

Because of the dependence on volunteers, there is no basis for calculating sampling error for volunteer web panels or determining the precision of statistical estimates obtained in surveys of web panel members (unless one defines the panel itself as the population of interest). Thus, the fundamental notion that the larger the completed sample size, the more precise the survey estimates (discussed in Chapter 3) has no meaning. In fact, in the Bethlehem and Stoop (2007) comparisons, the volunteer polls and the survey of members of a volunteer panel had much larger numbers of respondents than the probability-based poll but did a worse job of predicting outcomes. Without a probability sample, one cannot make statements such as "I am 95% confident that my sample of 400 respondents produces estimates that are within 5 percentage points of all members of the general public." In short, sample size loses its meaning as an indicator of the precision of survey estimates in volunteer Internet panel surveys.

• *Measurement error problems:* Asking respondents to complete multiple surveys each month places surveyors in the somewhat uncharted territory of not knowing the precise effects of repeated surveying. Evidence now exists that conditioning effects (i.e., changes in responses due to having completed multiple surveys) occur in at least some panel surveys; the less time that elapses between surveys, the more pronounced they are (Cartwright & Nancarrow, 2006). In addition, concern exists about respondents who do not give honest or careful answers (Smith & Hofma-Brown, 2006), particularly when monetary compensation is involved, an issue that also relates to nonresponse error concerns at both the item and questionnaire levels (see "Who Responds to Volunteer Web Panel Surveys?" in Box 9.1).

• *Nonresponse error problems:* Although the nonprobability nature of the sample already undermines the generalizability of the results, it is useful to consider additional problems that can arise because of nonresponse. Typical response rates of less than 25% mean that there is significant risk of nonresponse error beyond the issue of coverage error, even within the sample for a single survey.

Thus, volunteer Internet panels operate outside the framework of the four cornerstones of survey error. Surveying only Internet users means large segments of the population are left out of such panels. Inviting all willing respondents to complete the survey eliminates the ability to estimate sampling error and the ability to generalize results with statistical confidence to any larger population. In addition, repeated surveying with a significant and continuing financial motivation may lead to measurement error and response selectivity, both of which can undermine data quality in ways that are not yet well understood. Thus, although volunteer Internet panels are touted as being advantageous because of their ability to get very large sample sizes and to do so quickly, their weaknesses are substantial.

Box 9.1: Who Responds to Volunteer Web Panel Surveys?

A recent study in the Netherlands, where Internet penetration is reported to be above 80%, provides valuable insight into web panel participation (Willems, van Ossenbruggen, & Vonk, 2006). In that study, 19 of the more than 25 commercial online access panels in the Netherlands agreed to conduct the same survey with the same initial sample size of 1,000 panel members. The results indicated that significant portions of the adult population were missing from the panels. For example, ethnic minorities, including Turks and Moroccans, who compose 9% of the overall population and 30% in major cities, tended to be missing from most of the panels. In contrast, voters were overrepresented, composing 90% of panel respondents but only 79% of the national population. Within the voters surveyed, voters for Christian Democrats were underrepresented (16% vs. 29% in the general population), and Socialist Party voters were overrepresented (14% vs. 6% in the general population). People who attended church also tended to be underrepresented. In short, the panelists as a whole fell far short of being a defensible sample of the Dutch adult population.

The study also revealed significant overlap across panels, with one third of panel members belonging to four or more of the panels. Based on these analyses, the researchers estimated that among the 1,650,000 panelists registered to the 19 panels, there were only about 900,000 unique individuals. Moreover, about 40% of the panelists reported that they had completed four or more surveys during the preceding 4 weeks. Overall, about 22% of the panel members were found to be completing approximately 80% of all surveys.

When asked why they participated in online research, 81% indicated that they love completing questionnaires or love to express themselves. One third of the respondents reported participating because of the financial compensation. Certainly it is the rewards that are stressed in the recruitment samples shown in Figure 9.1.

Findings such as these fuel concerns about the quality of answers received from web panel respondents. Some very important questions that have been raised are the following: Does participation in numerous surveys and panels change the way respondents answer? Are those with high participation rates different in a meaningful way from those with low or no participation? Do some respondents give halfhearted or even fraudulent answers to quickly get through the survey and collect their reward? If so, how do surveyors identify them? Does the information in one survey change the way respondents answer another?

Research is just beginning to address these concerns, and researchers are beginning to identify typologies of respondents. For example, one analysis classified respondents as hyperactive (participants who join numerous panels), fraudulent (participants who misrepresent themselves and may join the same panel under multiple names or addresses), inattentive (respondents who answer quickly and incompletely), and conditioned (respondents whose answers are affected by their participation in many different surveys in a short time period; Smith & Hofma-Brown, 2006).

In the Dutch study, respondents were divided into three groups: professional (or hyperactive), loyal (doing what was requested in an apparently thoughtful manner), or inattentive. Answers varied widely among the three groups on such issues as the importance of financial rewards, interest in politics, and brand familiarity. Thus, part of panel management now involves finding ways to identify and even eliminate the responses of those whose behavior may undermine data quality.

Nonetheless, the use of volunteer Internet panels has grown rapidly, especially in countries with particularly high Internet penetration such as the Netherlands and Australia, and particularly for marketing research, for which there is a long tradition of nonprobability surveys. And in most cases, the response to the lack of representativeness is to weight the survey results in an attempt to match those that might be attained from the general public. For example, if fewer retired people are in a panel than are in the population, the responses of those retired people who are in the panel and respond to a specific survey are given more influence or weight in the final tabulations.

One particular type of weighting that is becoming increasingly popular among those conducting volunteer web panel surveys is propensity weighting. In the broadest sense, *propensity weighting* amounts to adjusting the sample distribution of the volunteer web panel survey to closely match that of a similar survey that used probability-based sampling methods. The overall goal of propensity weighting is to minimize any selection bias due to the nonprobability nature of the sample. More specifically, propensity weighting consists of the following three steps:

1. Collecting reference survey data through a smaller data collection procedure that runs parallel to the volunteer web survey, uses probability sampling, uses a traditional survey mode (presumably with less coverage error), and has higher response rates.
2. Combining the two sources of data and using logistic regression to determine the probability of participating in the volunteer web panel as

opposed to the reference survey (i.e., the propensity score) as a function of covariates (i.e., demographic and substantive variables) that were measured in both the volunteer panel survey and the reference survey.

3. Using the propensity scores (and weighting formulas that are outside the scope of this book) to adjust the distribution of the volunteer web sample so that it matches the distribution of the reference survey sample.

For more information on how propensity weighting is used in web surveys, we recommend consulting Lee (2006). The application of propensity scoring to web surveying is relatively new, meaning that the extent to which it reduces selection bias is still an empirical question.

However, the practice of weighting Internet panel data faces a number of problems that are still unresolved. First, to the extent that the 30% of the population who do not have Internet access differ in their attitudes, beliefs, and behaviors from those who do have Internet access, they will not be represented regardless of weighting (Bethlehem & Stoop, 2007). In other words, weighting implicitly assumes that, for example, retired people (or any type of group) with Internet access will answer questions the same way as retired people without Internet access, but this may or may not be a tenable assumption depending on the topic of the survey. If retired people without Internet access would have answered in different ways from those with Internet access, then the practice of giving more weight to the responses of those with Internet access would increase, not decrease, bias.

Second, the success of any weighting effort depends largely on the researcher being able to include the right covariates in the models. In other words, one can only weight data on observed or measured characteristics of respondents. As a result, even after extensive weighting there may still be bias as a result of unobserved characteristics. As a simple example, if one is trying to measure opinions on animal rights issues, there is no way to account for bias due to disproportionate representation of pet owners in the panel if pet ownership was not measured but, as would likely be the case, is related to opinions on animal rights issues. In addition, weighting on income can be especially problematic because of the high rates of item nonresponse for this type of question.

In many instances, convincing arguments can be made that all of the important covariates have been included in a weighting procedure based on previous research that has identified them as important. For example, some of the earliest and most prevalent uses of panels were, and still are, for conducting political and election polls, because much surveying has been done on these topics and there is a substantial literature on the correlates between respondent characteristics and voting behavior. However, major difficulties for postsurvey weighting will arise in situations in which new topics are being explored for which there is little knowledge of the appropriate covariates. In these cases, surveys designed within the four-cornerstone tradition become increasingly important.

In summary, volunteer Internet panel surveys are developed around a very different model from the four-cornerstone error model followed in this book. The assumptions one is required to make and the models one uses to adjust volunteer panel data are relatively new and require further research. It remains to be seen whether the use of volunteer web panels will persist and for what purposes, and what techniques will be used to compensate for errors that threaten the quality of the data from these surveys. Bethlehem and Stoop's (2007) general conclusion, and one that we largely agree with, is that volunteer Internet panels may serve as "a useful tool for exploratory studies, experiments, tests and other purposes *as long as undisputed results—both point estimates and the size of relationships—are not the aim of the study*" (p. 128; emphasis added).

PROBABILITY-BASED PANELS

Another approach to building an Internet panel of the general public involves using probability methods for identifying a random sample of households or individuals for inclusion regardless of whether they have Internet access. Often these types of Internet panels use an alternative mode, such as in-person or telephone surveys, to recruit people into the panel and to cover those who do not have Internet access so that probability-based sampling methods can be used. Those who do not have Internet access may be given equipment and access as well as training for responding, or they may be given another option for inclusion such as a different mode (e.g., mail or telephone). Three different examples of such panels are described here.

In the Netherlands, a web panel has been developed with the goal of regularly surveying a panel of 5,000 Dutch households (the LISS panel). The households were selected from a sample frame of households and initially contacted through face-to-face interviews by Statistics Netherlands, the national statistical agency. People who do not have Internet access are provided a computer and Internet access, as well as extensive support and training, in an attempt to motivate them to respond to the panel surveys. They are provided with an incentive when asked to join the panel and are asked to respond to up to four surveys per month, each of which is about 30 minutes long.

Development of this panel, now in its early stages, is of particular interest because of the high Internet penetration rate (above 80%) that exists in the Netherlands as a result of a deliberate government policy to encourage providing high-speed access to as many households as possible. It is also of interest because of its use of face-to-face recruitment to attempt to overcome coverage error by giving all Dutch households a known, nonzero chance of being included in the panel. The LISS panel builds upon a tradition started in 1986 when home computers were placed in the homes of panel members, the first such attempt of which we are aware to create an electronic panel. Sampled individuals were asked to download questionnaires and upload answers by means of telephone and modem (Saris, 1998).

A different method of recruiting respondents is used in a U.S. probability-based panel begun in the 1990s by Knowledge Networks that is now reported to have about 40,000 panel members. This panel recruits households through random-digit-dial telephone calls asking whether people are willing to participate in the Internet panel. If the people do not have Internet access, they are provided with it and with the hardware needed for responding to Internet surveys. They are asked to complete three to four surveys per month averaging 15 minutes in length. An incentive system has been developed that allows points to be redeemed for cash and other prizes. In addition, the incentives are not contingent on whether respondents qualify to complete the survey.

A third approach to probability-based general public sample surveys is used by the Gallup Organization. Recruiting for The Gallup Panel starts by contacting households through random-digit-dial telephone calls. Respondents who agree to participate are then sent an initial mail questionnaire in which all household members are invited to sign up for panel participation. This panel is unique from the other two we discussed here in that it uses a mixed-mode data collection strategy whereby panel members are assigned to either Internet or mail questionnaires depending upon their frequency of Internet use and their preference. No monetary incentives for responding are provided to respondents; the survey instead relies on the long history of Gallup and its established reputation as conductor of the Gallup Poll to encourage response. In addition, results of the panel surveys are made available to respondents through several media in an effort to communicate to panelists that their participation is a way for their voices to be heard. An effort is made to avoid potential mode differences by maintaining very similar visual layouts for the web and mail surveys.

Analysis of selected 2006 Gallup panel data revealed that those who responded by mail (nearly half of the panel members) were quite different from those who responded by the Internet (Rookey, Hanway, & Dillman, 2008). Not unexpectedly, mail respondents were older, had lower incomes, and were less likely to be married. The analysis also found that for many questions, quite different response distributions were obtained from mail respondents than from web respondents, and the differences did not disappear when normal weighting procedures were followed. Moreover, collecting data from both the web and mail portions of the panel through an independent mode—the telephone—produced more accurate predictions of election outcomes than did collecting the data from only the web portion of the panel (Rookey et al., 2008). These findings suggest that having certain types of respondents respond by mail adds value to this data collection effort by reducing coverage and nonresponse errors.

Probability-based panels like the ones described here attempt to overcome the two main problems of volunteer Internet-only surveys by starting with random samples of the general public and by ensuring that those who typically do not have Internet access are still able to respond. However, there is also much that remains to be learned about their effectiveness in overcoming these problems. For example, to the extent that samples obtained through random-digit dialing that only includes landline telephones (and not cell phones) are becoming less and less representative of the U.S. population, these samples are less effective for recruiting an Internet panel that is representative. As an alternative to telephone survey recruitment, in Chapter 7 we discussed the emerging potential of using mail and address-based sampling lists such as the U.S. Postal Service Delivery Sequence File to contact random samples of households, but much also remains to be learned about this list's potential as a sampling frame and a tool for establishing panels. Moreover, two of the probability samples discussed here use only the Internet to collect data, but it is not yet known whether trying to bring non-Internet users to the Internet is a successful strategy for getting them to respond. These are just some of the challenges that those building probability-based Internet panels will have to address as they continue to find innovative ways to survey the general public amid the current context of great opportunities clashing with great difficulties.

ISSUES OF PANEL MANAGEMENT: ATTRITION AND CONDITIONING

Although probability-based panels have taken measures to minimize coverage and sampling error, they still face several challenges that, not coincidentally, are also common to longitudinal surveys and volunteer web panels. The first is the problem of *panel attrition,* or people dropping out of the panel. The second is *panel conditioning,* a term that refers to the tendency for respondents to answer survey questions differently because of their participation in previous surveys. Although research exists on both of these topics, neither problem is well understood, a situation that is due in part to the difficulty of disentangling the effects of real change, change due to attrition, and change due to conditioning over time (and sometimes change in the survey mode).

Panel attrition becomes particularly problematic when the people who leave the panel are systematically different from people who continue to participate with respect to the variable of interest, which contributes significantly to nonresponse error and makes the panel as a whole less representative of the target population. In fact, even the best designed longitudinal surveys can expect to lose about 10% of respondents at each wave of data collection (Hansen, 2008). A common method for trying to minimize the impact of panel attrition is to replace those who drop out with similar individuals sampled from the target population. However, such a practice is problematic in three ways. First, it results in a loss of continuity in the sample, which can reduce the precision of estimates over time (Sharot, 1991). Second, it reduces the sample size that is available for analyses at the respondent level (Sharot, 1991), a consequence that can be particularly problematic for longitudinal surveys, where the goal is often to be able to explore the factors affecting individual outcomes over time. Third, it is possible to match those who dropped out to new sample members only on observed characteristics, which are often very limited with new sample members.

As a result of these difficulties, a better strategy is to devote resources to minimizing panel attrition from the beginning rather than trying to correct for it once it has occurred. Many of the strategies for encouraging trust, increasing rewards, and reducing costs discussed in Chapter 2 can be employed to encourage participation and minimize attrition. A small body of research has begun to explore ways to do just that. Topics that have been studied thus far include initial recruitment strategies, contact strategies, incentive and reward use, length of surveys, and frequency of surveys. However, this research is still in its infancy, and many of the findings are specific to a certain panel and cannot be generalized across panels. Much more research needs to be conducted before researchers can get to the root sources of attrition.

Panel conditioning is different from panel attrition in that some types of conditioning can be advantageous. For example, if respondents learn how to navigate the questionnaire or use specialized measurement instruments (e.g., drop-down boxes, grids, etc.) more efficiently in later surveys, they may be able to provide better answers (Das, Toepoel, & van Soest, 2007). However, it is also possible that respondents may learn to give less optimal answers to reduce the amount of effort they have to invest, thereby altering their responses in a way that creates measurement error. Another possibility is that early surveys will cause respondents to think about questions in subsequent surveys in ways they would not have if they had not completed the previous surveys. In perhaps the most extreme example of panel conditioning, respondents may actually change their behavior because of their participation in the survey. For example, Veroff, Hatchett, and Douvan (1992) found some support for the notion that couples who participated in surveys about their marriages more often and answered more questions developed better adjusted marriages than did couples who participated less often and in less detail. Respondents may also be more likely to satisfice when they participate in multiple surveys over a short time period. In each of these types of scenarios, the end result is that early surveys affect respondents in ways that make them less representative of the general public on the measures of interest.

Sometimes the goals of minimizing attrition and reducing conditioning effects can be in conflict. Whereas the challenge of panel attrition is to keep respondents active members in the panel, a common response to panel conditioning, especially in web panels, is to retire respondents out of the sample after a set amount of time or if they begin to show evidence of poor response behavior. The sample is then refreshed with newly selected sample members, a practice that raises the same problems of reduced sample continuity and reduced sample size for respondent-level analyses as the replacement strategies used to address attrition. For many web panels, however, these costs are bearable because respondent-level analysis over long periods of time is not the primary concern or purpose.

THE PANEL RESPONDENT: CHEAP LABOR OR SOMEONE IMPORTANT?

Perhaps one of the most disturbing issues associated with the development of Internet panels and one that is likely to have long-term ramifications for the survey field as a whole is how the big-numbers mentality of such panels has affected the way in which some respondents are treated. To be fair, the approach taken toward respondents varies greatly from panel to panel, with some making great efforts to be respectful of respondents and their needs. For example, some explain to respondents how data will be used and even produce newsletters, web sites, and e-mails to communicate the purpose of surveys and share their results with respondents. In this way, respondents get to see what they have participated in producing. By action as well as words, it is communicated to respondents that not only do those operating the panels want honest answers, but those answers are important and appreciated.

However, a notable number of panels appear to be quite disrespectful of respondents. Once respondents join the panel they receive the briefest of messages about surveys (e.g., "This time we are sending you a survey on financial services you use"). Oftentimes, no broader effort is made to explain in what way answers might be useful. Sometimes the surveys are programmed such that each question must be answered before the respondent can move to the next question (discussed in Chapter 6), a practice that invites dishonest answers, especially when, as is often the case, such programming is coupled with policies of offering chances to win prizes or receive other awards contingent on completing the survey. In some cases, respondents are lured with promises of entrance into prize drawings, but the odds of winning are not disclosed. In these cases, respondents seem to be treated as casual labor—like the surveyors are doing them a favor by allowing them to fill out surveys. Viewing respondents in this way is inconsistent with the social exchange perspective that underlies the methods discussed in this book, and it has the potential to negatively impact the way thousands of people view surveys and the trust they have in surveyors and survey data (after all, the same people who are survey respondents in one context are consumers of survey data in other contexts).

Given that many web panels put such a strong emphasis on small financial rewards as one—and sometimes the only—motivating factor for joining the panel and completing the surveys, it is not surprising that one of the major issues being faced by sponsors of volunteer panels is that answers are sometimes not thoughtfully and carefully given. Reward policies that emphasize quantity rather than quality create a situation in which it is in the best interests of respondents to complete surveys quickly and perhaps even to lie about their eligibility for some surveys so that they can be eligible for the rewards connected to them. As a result, terms such as *fraudulent, dishonest, imposter, bogus, inattentive,* and so on have been used to describe respondents, and some organizations post on their web sites the means they use to identify such respondents. For example, some surveyors have described how they introduce trap questions, reverse the wording of an item (e.g., insert a "not" into a set of positive statements), insert questions that are completely out of context (e.g., check the "strongly agree" box to tell us where you are), and make up bogus products in order to "catch" such respondents. Another tactic sometimes used is putting in low-incidence items to catch people who are trying especially hard to qualify for studies and thus get rewarded. The problem with taking measures such as these is threefold. First, it puts the onus on respondents when, in fact, it is the survey situation itself with its focus on rewards as the sole motivation for participation that sets the stage for such poor survey behavior in the first place. Second, respondents are able to see through these kinds of efforts as easily as surveyors can insert them into their surveys, making these tactics rather ineffective in the long term. Third, such practices encourage a tit-for-tat mentality, pitting surveyors against respondents.

In short, these tactics do not create a favorable social exchange relationship, and using them is simply not good survey practice. The norm of reciprocity suggests that people who convey sincerity will receive sincerity in return. It would also suggest that people who game respondents will be gamed in return. It is not surprising that these topics receive a great deal of discussion in professional meetings (Smith & Hofma-Brown, 2006). One of the important challenges facing all survey methodologists is to be respectful and honest with respondents in order that respondents treat our surveys in the same way. We return to this topic in Chapter 11.

GUIDELINES FOR INTERNET PANEL SURVEYS

The guidelines presented here are brief and consistent with the probability-based methods advocated throughout this book and the four cornerstones introduced in Chapter 2. We doubt that readers of this book will be attempting to create their own panel. However, these guidelines may be helpful in contemplating whether and how to use or not use panel data, analyses of which are beginning to appear in the research literature.

Guideline 9.5: When Internet or Other Panels Are Designed to Represent a Specific Population, Find a Means for Recruiting Respondents in a Way that Gives All Members of the Population a Known, Nonzero Probability of Being Included

Allowing panel participation on a volunteer basis rather than selecting panel members through a probability process means that the concepts of sampling error and completed number of questionnaires lose all meaning as indicators of survey quality. There is no mathematical or theoretical basis for generalizing results beyond the volunteer panel itself. This means that panels need to rely on probability-based selection methods in recruiting panel members unless they are to be used solely for exploratory research.

Guideline 9.6: For Panels Relying Only on the Internet, Provide an Alternative Mode of Response for Respondents Who Lack Access or Skills for Using the Internet

The need to use probability samples to recruit representative panels means that one needs to find a way either to bring the Internet to respondents who would not otherwise have it or to provide alternative means for them to respond. The rapid rise in Internet use is tapering off, as typically happens for most innovations. Although we still expect the proportion of households with Internet access to increase over the next few years, it also seems that non-Internet households will continue to exist. Moreover, as the Internet becomes more accessible, it is likely that those who continue to lack access will be more and more different from those who do have access (i.e., they are likely to be the most extreme cases in the digital divide). We also expect that whereas some people in a household with Internet access will have the skills necessary to use it, there will be more variation in people's familiarity with responding to surveys via the Internet. All respondents without access need to be provided with Internet access if they have the skills to use it or with an alternative mode in which to respond.

In addition, we have repeatedly observed the reluctance of some Internet users to complete surveys on the Internet, and, when given a choice, there tends to be a preference among some for mail questionnaires (Dillman et al., 2008). We do not know the reasons for this preference. It could be that paper questionnaires can be completed when people are tired of being on the Internet, or the survey can be done when using a computer or being online is inconvenient. Whatever the reason, for some surveys, an alternative mode of responding (such as mail) may remain important even for those who have Internet access.

There are cases, however, when an alternative mode may not be as important. For example, we have heard of attempts to build feedback panels for certain groups in which nearly everyone has Internet access and uses it regularly (e.g., members of professional associations or purchasers of computer equipment). In these cases, a different survey mode is unnecessary, and we would encourage the limiting of mode changes for many of the same reasons that we think longitudinal surveys should avoid using multiple modes.

Guideline 9.7: Anticipate and Evaluate Effects from the Use of Incentives

As discussed previously, many panels rely strongly on incentives that are received after the survey is completed, in essence paying respondents for each questionnaire they complete. In Europe in 2006, we frequently heard that the general norm among surveyors was 1 Euro for every 10 minutes spent responding. Offering to pay people cash or reward points or to send gifts in this way turns the completion of surveys into a sort of employment, as suggested by the recruitment notices shown in Figure 9.1. This may change the nature of the surveyor/respondent relationship in undesirable ways, which may in turn have real effects on the quality of the resulting data.

It is important that careful evaluations be made of how incentives of this nature affect respondents, whether respondents in such systems are as likely to give honest answers, and what happens to people when they in essence become professional respondents. This is not something with which surveyors have had extensive experience as yet, but the stakes are quite high, especially because Internet panels touch so many potential respondents.

Guideline 9.8: Anticipate and Evaluate the Effects of Attrition and Conditioning

One of the shared characteristics of probability and nonprobability surveys is concern with attrition and conditioning effects. Although such effects have long been a concern in longitudinal surveys, they are a much greater concern in modern panel surveys because of the greater frequency with which people are surveyed. Evidence is accumulating that both of these effects happen, and they need to be considered. Hopefully, future research will provide much more guidance here.

CONCLUSION

At the most basic level, longitudinal and Internet panel surveys have a similar underlying goal—collect data from the same people multiple times. As such, they share many of the same challenges and difficulties, such as how to minimize attrition and the effects of conditioning. At a deeper level, however, these two types of surveys begin to diverge. Whereas the use of a second or third mode can greatly undermine the goals of longitudinal surveys, it seems to be a necessary element of recruiting respondents and collecting quality data using an Internet panel. Likewise, respondents to longitudinal surveys are usually asked to answer at intervals of months or even years, whereas Internet panel respondents are often asked to complete three or more surveys per month. The frequency with which Internet panel members are surveyed means that the challenges usually associated with keeping respondents motivated and engaged are magnified. It also means that a balance has to be struck between sample continuity and sample turnover. How to find the appropriate balance is not yet known.

When the previous edition of this book was published in 2000, Internet panels were just beginning to emerge. Now they have become a full-fledged industry. Yet the research upon which they rest is thin. In the coming years, we expect to see continued discussion, energetic debate, and fundamental research aimed at better understanding and directing the future use of such panels in an attempt to navigate the opportunities and pressures currently facing the survey industry. The major issues discussed in this chapter will likely be at the fore of such debates and discussions. One issue that has not been explicitly discussed, but that may also deserve attention, is the impact of so many thousands of people being exposed to surveys through Internet panels. As such, an important question surveyors may need to ask themselves is what effect does the Internet panel experience, whether it consists of participating in a panel or simply receiving a recruitment advertisement, have on people's perceptions of surveys and the survey industry as a whole? These are not easy questions to answer.

LIST OF GUIDELINES

Longitudinal Surveys

Guideline 9.1: *Plan ahead by selecting a longitudinal survey mode that can be used in future years, and adopt a conservative stance on whether to change modes for follow-up data collections*

Guideline 9.2: *Be especially cautious about switching from a visual self-administered mode of data collection to an aural interviewer-administered mode or vice versa*

Guideline 9.3: *When changes in visual modes are made, maintain similar visual layouts in order to minimize measurement error due to inadvertent design changes*

Guideline 9.4: *Avoid offering respondents a choice of survey mode*

(continued)

Web Panel Surveys

Guideline 9.5: When Internet or other panels are designed to represent a specific population, find a means for recruiting respondents in a way that gives all members of the population a known, nonzero probability of being included

Guideline 9.6: For panels relying only on the Internet, provide an alternative mode of response for respondents who lack access or skills for using the Internet

Guideline 9.7: Anticipate and evaluate effects from the use of incentives

Guideline 9.8: Anticipate and evaluate the effects of attrition and conditioning

CHAPTER 10

Customer Feedback Surveys and Alternative Delivery Technologies

EACH YEAR millions of people are asked to complete surveys about a product or service they have purchased, the store where they purchased it, or the web site they visited for information. The range of items or experiences evaluated seems infinite, from meals in restaurants to massages to oil changes for cars. Some customer surveys evaluate seminars or classes taken, programs watched on television, or stations listened to on the radio. Others ask mostly about particular product features, whereas still others focus on satisfaction with the use of a product or service and the overall customer experience. A wide variety of methodologies are used to conduct such surveys, some of which give accurate and useful information and others of which do neither.

In this chapter, we discuss tailoring the procedures discussed in earlier chapters of this book to the special challenges of customer surveys, which are often targeted toward different kinds of populations and use a variety of technologies. Some of the unique challenges encountered in designing customer surveys arise because lists of customers that can be used for sampling often do not exist. In this case, paper surveys may be administered in person to individuals or groups as they visit the organization, or requests for survey participation through a telephone call or by accessing the Web may appear at the bottom of cash register receipts. In addition, customer surveys have been quick to adopt newer technologies such as the Web, interactive voice response (IVR), and handheld computers and may use a combination of modes to encourage people to respond. Although our focus in this chapter is on customer use and satisfaction surveys, the alternative methods for delivering surveys that we discuss can be used for many other situations as well.

A CUSTOMER SURVEY EXPERIENCE

One of us checked into a hotel recently where a small tented card on the guest room desk contained the following message:

> After your departure, you may receive a survey from us. It is our goal to earn a perfect 10. If you feel that you cannot score us in this manner, please contact our Guest Service Hotline so that we may address the situation immediately.

A dated letter with the guest's name inserted was also on the desk. Between the hotel letterhead and the date was this information.

"10"

Our goal is to exceed all of your expectations. If for any reason your stay is not a "perfect 10" please notify our Guest Service Hotline and we will immediately address the situation.

At breakfast the next morning, a slip of paper was received from the server near the end of the meal along with a verbal explanation that bonus points in the hotel's rewards program could be earned by calling the telephone number listed within a few days and completing an automated telephone survey or by using a computer and going to a web address that was listed on the slip of paper to do the survey. In either case, the server advised it would be necessary to enter the access code printed on the slip of paper, the server's number that was handwritten in, and the guest's Hotel Frequent Rewards Guest number. The server explained that the last number was important because entering it would make it possible to receive the bonus points for completing the survey. On the second day of the stay at this hotel, another slip of paper with the same instructions was delivered by that day's waitperson in a friendly manner and with similar instructions.

The questionnaire was the same on the telephone and Web and consisted mostly of satisfaction questions using fully labeled 5-point scales. While completing the web survey, an attempt was made to leave the following question blank:

Rate your server's knowledge of the menu and ability to answer questions.

- ☐ Excellent
- ☐ Very Good
- ☐ Good
- ☐ Fair
- ☐ Poor

The reason for not wanting to answer this item was not because of the way the question was worded (although its unbalanced scale—with more positive than negative categories—runs counter to our recommendation in Guideline 5.23 in Chapter 5 to use only balanced scales), but because an honest answer could not be provided given the categories offered. The guest had opted for the breakfast buffet and had not asked any questions of the waitperson. An attempt to leave the answer choices blank produced an immediate error message indicating that the question must be answered in order to proceed (which we do not recommend for most surveys, as discussed in Chapter 6, Guideline 6.27). The programming for this survey required that each question be answered before going to the next item, making it necessary for the guest to "create" an appropriate answer when a question did not apply. In order to complete the survey, the guest somewhat randomly chose a category for such questions because no options for "does not apply" or "prefer not to answer" were provided with any of the questions. When attempting to complete the second day's survey through the IVR system, the guest was repeatedly and persistently instructed by a recorded voice "Please answer now," and again no items could be left unanswered.

The general satisfaction web survey, with its 10-point scales, that was mentioned on the tented card and letter on the desk was never received by the guest. However, two other surveys from different hotels in the same chain had been completed recently, so it may not have been sent for that reason. The other questionnaires had been sent within 5 days of each visit to the e-mail address associated with the account from which the hotel reservations had been made. The e-mail invitations began by saying thank you for staying at the hotel on the specific date. They also contained hyperlinks to the survey that could be clicked on or copied and pasted into the recipient's browser. Those surveys each took about 15 to 20 minutes to complete and asked for responses to about 80 different items, including thirty 11-point scales. The questions, each of which required an answer in order to proceed, covered nearly all hotel services and features, most of which the visitor did not experience. The surveys also asked a number of questions about any problems experienced, previous stays at other hotels, and participation in other frequent guest programs. At the end, the survey asked if the respondent was willing to respond to other questions about stays at this company's hotels.

When the 2000 edition of this book was written, it was most common for hotels to use paper surveys. Some companies used similarly long and detailed questionnaires mailed after the hotel visit. They commonly covered every conceivable guest experience, including many that were unlikely to be experienced by most guests, corresponding to the complete service menus of the hotels. In these paper surveys, respondents could easily skip questions that did not apply to their stay. Other hotels used brief paper surveys, each on a different topic (service from the staff, meals, hotel appearance and cleanliness of the rooms, check-in procedures, or other hotel services), that could be picked up from the desk at the time of departure, provided with the respondent's meal, or included in the hotel room. These shorter surveys could be submitted immediately or mailed back later.

These recent hotel and restaurant experiences compared to those experienced less than a decade ago illustrate (a) the increased intensity of survey efforts now being undertaken by many organizations to measure customer satisfaction and (b) the use of new methods such as IVR and the Web, as well as mixed-mode strategies, to achieve responses to those surveys. When such automated systems are used to collect and summarize results, it is possible to attempt to survey nearly every customer at little additional cost. Moreover, because hotels assign numbers to individual wait staff and have information about guests' stays, they can use the results to provide evaluations of individual staff who service those customers. In addition, these examples illustrate the use of different types of incentives or rewards (such as bonus points) that are being offered for participation.

Use of these methods, particularly the one described in the opening of this chapter, suggests that the satisfaction survey may have changed from being an attempt to get honest assessments of the hotel guest experience to being more of a marketing campaign aimed at improving scores through delivering messages that attempt to produce higher, more positive ratings. This experience brought back the memory of having purchased a new automobile several years ago. The salesman, after explaining how features of the car worked, made considerable effort to explain that a survey would be arriving soon. He also noted that he had been the top salesman in his district for several years and that any numbers lower than the highest score of "5" just did not "cut it" with his company. In addition, he requested that if a "5" could not be given for something (e.g., an explanation of how to program the garage door opener), the customer should call or drop by and he would go through it so that it would be possible for the customer to offer the highest rating.

Efforts like those of the hotel, the wait person, and the salesman suggest to the customer that the survey is not really an effort to understand whether customers are truly satisfied with these services. Instead, the survey may be viewed as an employee monitoring system that is likely to have potential consequences for those who receive poor ratings. In addition, when employees have control over who is asked to participate and when they understand the impact of the evaluations on their jobs, it can directly affect the responses likely to be received. The intensity of being confronted with multiple surveys for one customer experience, each of which can be identified with the customer and employee(s) who served that customer with no promise of confidentiality, and the realization that if one responds it may be necessary to provide inaccurate answers in order to get reward points, does not bode well for these kinds of surveys. It should not be surprising that response rates to such attempts often turn out to be quite low, so that only a few completed questionnaires are available to evaluate individual employees or services.

DESIGNING CUSTOMER FEEDBACK SURVEYS

Customer experience surveys represent, to some degree, the ultimate survey situation in need of tailored design. The following issues that are common to many such surveys illustrate the variety of problems that can arise and for which a tailored solution is needed:

- Survey modes often need to be selected that allow the questionnaire to be delivered at the time when customers are experiencing the product or service to be evaluated.
- Some sponsors have considerable information on clients and attempt to link that information to the survey questions by using it either to ask different questions of different respondents (e.g., "How does this hotel visit compare to your experience when you stayed at the Manado Beach Hotel?") or to analyze how respondent characteristics (e.g., frequency of staying at that company's hotels) influence satisfaction ratings.
- Many customer surveys are carefully designed to gather feedback that will be used to inform business decisions. Others are ad hoc evaluations that must be quickly constructed and implemented to respond to requests that are part of a review process or to construct advertising materials.
- Oftentimes no list exists for sampling the population of interest (e.g., visitors to a museum or event).
- Surveyors are faced with the challenge of encouraging responses from a diverse mix of customers, some of whom are very pleased and others who are quite disappointed with the product or service under evaluation.
- Customer satisfaction surveys rely heavily on ordinal rating scales, which are very susceptible to measurement error induced by design decisions.
- Results must often be communicated effectively and convincingly to people who are tasked with making fundamental business decisions based on them.

Each of these situations requires making careful and thoughtful design decisions to maximize the quality of data obtained within the constraints of the particular study by minimizing sampling, coverage, nonresponse, and measurement errors. Constructing any survey requires making difficult decisions to minimize errors, but what makes customer satisfaction surveys uniquely challenging is that people who have a vested interest in their producing the highest possible ratings are often highly involved in their design and implementation. The guidelines that follow are intended both to highlight how this context can undermine satisfaction surveys if left unchecked and to suggest ways of obtaining true measures of satisfaction that can be accurately used to evaluate the nature of a customer's experience.

SAMPLING METHODS

Guideline 10.1: Consider Randomly Sampling Portions of the Population instead of Trying to Survey the Entire Population, Especially When the Latter Leads to People Being Surveyed Repeatedly and Unnecessarily

Electronic administration along with the potential to build extensive organization-specific feedback systems has led some to survey all customers (i.e., take a census) rather than only a sample of customers, and to survey them frequently. We were once approached by a national nonprofit organization of about 10,000 members whose executive director was excited about the potential for using web surveys to get monthly feedback from members on what the organization should or should not be doing on behalf of the membership. They were planning to send monthly 30-minute surveys to all members, with each survey introducing a different topic or topics. The organization leaders thought they could build the capacity to conduct such surveys and felt that even if only 1,000 members (10%) responded each month, that would be enough to give an accurate reading of member preferences.

Our initial reaction to these plans was one of considerable skepticism. One concern was the high likelihood that there would be considerable selectivity among those who responded based in part on survey topic. Another concern was that the number of responses would not be meaningful because probability sampling was not employed, as explained in Chapter 3. We were also very concerned that such frequent surveying would not engender goodwill for responding to survey requests among the organization's members. Thus, we recommended against doing a census of the organization (i.e., surveying the complete population) and instead encouraged the leadership to think about surveying only a tenth of the membership each month and including follow-up reminders that would emphasize the importance of each survey.

Our recommendation was intended to minimize nonresponse error by reducing the likelihood that only members with particular interest in the topic would respond, by encouraging different types of organization members to respond, and by avoiding overburdening members with too many survey requests. To further address the issue of burnout and to improve overall response quality, we also encouraged the organization's leadership to reduce the frequency with which the surveys would be conducted and to reduce the number of questions in each survey. With more time between surveys, better questions could be crafted, better implementation procedures could be designed with effective follow-ups for nonrespondents, and a better job could be done analyzing the results of each survey. Taking this amount of care would be difficult if monthly surveys were to be conducted, particularly if the necessary resources were not available or if staff had little experience in survey research.

Overall, randomly sampling portions of the population rather than surveying the entire population is essential to obtaining high-quality responses from customers. Oversurveying customers can create an environment in which they do not want to respond to these types of surveys at all or in which whether and how they respond is impacted in ways that introduce nonresponse and measurement error.

Guideline 10.2: Develop Procedures for Ensuring that Onsite Sampling Is Carefully Executed and Will Not Be Affected by Personal Preference

Many surveyors face the challenge of needing to select customers for a satisfaction survey when a list is unavailable from which to draw a random sample. In addition, timeliness is often of key importance because many surveys of this nature require sampling people at the time they are experiencing the service being provided (e.g., while visiting a restaurant, museum, or park). In these situations, *intercept surveys* are often used, in which every nth customer or visitor is surveyed, usually at different periods throughout the day, week, and year.

One of the most common threats to the quality of customer survey results is when employees have control over selecting who to sample (i.e., which customers should get surveys and which ones should not). It is not surprising that employees, especially those whose performance evaluations depend on customer feedback, may make a greater effort to distribute the requests for feedback to those who seem most likely to give higher ratings and may avoid distributing requests to those who they think will provide poor ratings. Employees may read clues, either consciously or unconsciously, about the ratings customers are likely to provide. For example, if a server notices that a customer is enjoying his or her experience, has complimented the server or the food in any way, or overall seems pleasant about the experience, the server may be more likely to ask that person to complete the survey. In contrast, customers who are more negative or who do not seem to be in a good mood may be less likely to be invited to complete the survey. In some situations, employees may fear that asking someone to complete a survey will impact them directly (e.g., reduce the tip the customer is likely to give), or they may not feel that they have established enough rapport to ask such a favor. It also seems likely that surveys are more likely to be administered when it is more convenient for the employee (e.g., when the business is less busy or when people seem interested in providing feedback). Thus, the potential for bias may emerge from questionnaires being disproportionately distributed to happy versus unhappy customers, single parties versus multiperson parties, people who do not seem to be in a hurry versus those who are, and so on. There are many ways that results can be misleading, and the challenge faced here is to avoid misleading results because of the way customers are selected to complete the survey.

One way employers have tried to overcome the potential for such sampling selectivity is to print requests on cash register receipts. Some establishments print the request on every receipt, but others attempt to survey only a sample of their customers by printing requests on only selected receipts (e.g., print a request on every 10th receipt or using some other selection technique). In most instances the receipt includes a number to call to take a survey using an IVR system, or it includes a web site customers can access to complete the survey. The benefit of this sampling method is that it takes the sampling decision out of the hands of the employees whose performance is likely to be evaluated; however, it is also important to recognize that cash register receipts sometimes cover multiple people. Thus, the sample can shift from individuals to groups in ways that are unknown and are often not controlled for in the survey. For example, providing survey requests with receipts might result in not gathering the opinions of the people who are not paying, or it might result in the person who is paying trying to represent the views of everyone in the group rather than just her own. Moreover, as we discuss later, the procedures for inviting response once a customer is selected by the receipt method oftentimes have the potential to increase nonresponse bias.

NONRESPONSE ISSUES

Nonresponse is a delicate issue for many sponsors of satisfaction surveys because of the sampling issues discussed previously. In order for the sample to be representative, the views of all types of customers need to be included. People conducting customer satisfaction surveys do not want to have low response rates, but the use of follow-up reminders, which remains the most powerful way of improving response rates (as discussed in Chapter 7), can be challenging, especially when contact information is unavailable for respondents (e.g., in many intercept surveys and for invitations included on receipts). In addition, there is some reluctance to using follow-up reminders for some customer satisfaction surveys because of the worry that customers will feel hassled and get angry. Concern about sending any reminders is probably greater for surveys of this nature than for most other situations, but sending reminders is an integral part of minimizing nonresponse error.

Guideline 10.3: Actively Seek Means of Using Follow-Up Reminders in Order to Reduce Nonresponse Error

Nonresponse to customer surveys is, in many cases, the greatest threat to the quality of results. In the nonprofit organization example discussed earlier, we encouraged lowering both the number of people being selected to complete a survey and the frequency of surveying so that reminders could be sent with less fear of a backlash. Many people would be annoyed by requests to participate in a survey each month and would probably be even more frustrated if they received several reminders for each monthly survey, resulting in a total of 30 to 50 contacts each year. In this case, just as the sound of a television or traffic becomes easier to ignore the more that one is around it, the survey requests would become easier to ignore. However, by reducing the frequency of requests and the length of the surveys, one could avoid annoying sample members in this way. In this more amenable context, follow-up contacts would likely have their intended effect of politely and respectfully reinforcing the importance of respondents to the success of the important survey they have been asked to complete.

When reminders are sent, they need to be worded carefully and in ways that explain why they are being sent. For example, a reminder might explain the following: "We are sending this reminder because we want to be sure that we hear from all types of respondents including women and men, people of all ages, and both those who use our product only a little and those who use it a lot so that we better understand ways we might improve it for everyone." The use of reminders indicates the seriousness with which a survey is being taken by the sponsor but must also connect with the kind of questionnaire being used. A carefully constructed questionnaire with questions that are meaningful to respondents is also important in encouraging people to respond.

The challenge of sending multiple contacts has led to the use of in-person delivery techniques for many customer satisfaction surveys so that the initial experience can create interest in the survey and may even increase the social obligation to respond. Some surveys focus a lot of effort on using the personal delivery situation that is needed for sampling to also strongly encourage response and even use it as a basis for getting contact information that makes follow-ups possible. We return to the topic of in-person delivery later.

Guideline 10.4: Provide All Selected Respondents with Similar Amounts and Types of Encouragement to Respond

The danger of increased nonresponse bias due to different types of respondents receiving different amounts or types of encouragement to respond is magnified in many customer satisfaction surveys because of the nature of the procedures commonly used to implement the surveys. One such procedure that was talked about in a slightly different way in Guideline 10.2 is having the people who are providing the service that is being evaluated be the ones responsible for inviting customers to take the survey, a practice that is very common in restaurants. Although randomly selecting respondents through the cash register receipt method can eliminate employee preference in the selection method, problems can arise when the extent to which a customer is encouraged to complete the survey differs based on the amount of rapport that has developed throughout previous interactions. For example, if a waiter has had a particularly poor experience with a customer and that customer is selected for the survey, the invitation will most likely be delivered in as quick and short a manner as possible. Even if the waiter is totally innocent and has no intention of trying to influence his "scores," the displeasing social situation itself will likely encourage the waiter to make the contact with this customer as short and quick as possible. If the same waiter makes a particularly good connection with another customer who is also selected as a respondent, it is likely that the task of inviting that customer to take part in the survey will be much more comfortable and perhaps even enjoyable. In this situation, the waiter is more likely to take his time and explain the survey and procedures in more depth. The end result is that one customer will have received minimal encouragement to respond or information about how to respond, and another will have received a lot more encouragement and information. It is very likely that these two customers would rate their experiences quite differently, but the person who had a poor experience will probably be less likely to respond (i.e., nonresponse error).

Another common customer satisfaction survey procedure that can become problematic from the standpoint of nonresponse error is tying the incentive to respond to the product or service being evaluated. Many businesses do this because they can offer their own product or service as a survey incentive much more easily and cheaply than they can offer other types of incentives such as the token cash incentives discussed in Chapter 7. For example, it is very common for businesses or organizations who put their survey requests on receipts to provide respondents with a code at the end of the survey that, if written on the receipt and brought along on a future visit to the same establishment, entitles them to a discount on their purchase. This type of discount might be very motivating to individuals who are already regular customers and are generally satisfied, thus increasing response rates among them. However, the same offer of a discount has little to no value among customers who are dissatisfied with the product or service and have little or no intention of purchasing it in the future. Thus, the incentive will likely have a different effect on the likelihood of these two different types of customers responding that will increase nonresponse bias. To a large degree the problem here is that the survey incentive is closely related to what is being evaluated. In some small part this problem is also due to the surveyors providing the reward only after the survey has been completed. As discussed in Chapter 2, incentives of this nature shift the survey request from a social exchange to an economic exchange wherein the incentive comes to be seen as compensation.

In this framework, different respondents will have very different views about what constitutes enough compensation to merit their response. Thus, the best practice may be to offer an incentive that is not related to the product being evaluated, but when that is not possible it is advisable to use the incentive in the spirit of social rather than economic exchange. This means providing it to every sample member at the time of the survey invitation.

MEASUREMENT ISSUES

Accurate measurement of customer satisfaction is particularly difficult in an environment where the goal of many people involved in their design and implementation is to achieve high satisfaction ratings. For this reason, in this section we provide a series of guidelines intended to help minimize types of measurement error that can be unique to customer satisfaction surveys. In Chapter 5 we presented a number of guidelines (5.20–5.27) for designing ordinal scales that also apply to the construction of scales for customer satisfaction surveys. However, attempts to measure customer satisfaction are particularly challenging from a measurement standpoint because of the implications of using different kinds of scales and the manner in which results are interpreted, so we include in this chapter specific guidelines for designing scales for customer satisfaction ratings. One of the challenges associated with designing such scales is to get an accurate measure of how people feel about their customer experience that can be easily communicated to users of the results, so we also address that issue.

Guideline 10.5: Avoid Encouraging Higher Ratings during the Delivery of the Survey Request

It is human to want to succeed. However, it is unfortunate when getting a high satisfaction rating itself becomes the object of a person's or organization's efforts, rather than providing quality service that will warrant a high rating. When people are, in essence, being asked or pressured to provide the highest possible rating, as suggested by the hotel signage in the introduction to this chapter, the entire process loses credibility.

In light of the explicit linkage often made between customer satisfaction scores and employees who are providing the services, it is not surprising that individuals, such as the car salesman discussed previously, take actions to improve the service they offer to sampled customers (but not customers who are not sampled) and to encourage those customers to give them high scores. Such behavior can easily create a situation in which respondents feel uneasy or guilty about providing honest responses. We have observed similar, not-so-subtle encouragement of high ratings when seminar speakers mention that whether they get invited back to do a short course depends upon whether evaluations get completed and the nature of those evaluations. We have also observed internal reward programs in organizations that regularly report the number of people who achieved the top score of "5." Likewise, we commonly encounter signage in businesses that reports the number of consecutive months that the business has received all "5 star" ratings from customers and expresses the importance of continuing to do so.

It is the function of the survey to measure customers' satisfaction, not create it. Moreover, it is not in the best interest of businesses to bias measurement in this way, because ultimately it gets in the way of their discovering what their customers really think and how they can improve their product or service to improve their business. Thus, any activity that is intended to improve customer satisfaction needs to be carried out prior to and entirely separately from the customer satisfaction survey. The survey itself needs to be designed and administered in ways that allow the business to fairly and accurately assess customers' opinions. To that end, extra steps should be taken to avoid creating a situation in which the people delivering the questionnaire or the environment in which it is delivered encourage respondents to report high satisfaction when that may not be the case.

Guideline 10.6: Obtain Responses from Customers When They Are Best Able to Provide Them

Customer surveys provide a number of challenges with regard to timing. Many customer experiences need to be reported immediately after they happen in order for them to be remembered. It is unlikely that many people will easily remember specific experiences, such as eating at a restaurant or purchasing a product in a store, after several other similar experiences have occurred. In addition, people who do these activities more frequently may be even less likely than those who do them less frequently to be able to remember specific occurrences, particularly in detail. One of the most extreme challenges of this nature is obtaining information about radio listening or television viewing behavior (i.e., which stations, programs, or channels were listened to or watched) because these activities are so frequent and mundane for many respondents. Because it is so difficult to get accurate reports about these types of behaviors in retrospect, diaries are commonly used that ask people to record their listening or viewing behavior as it happens for a full week. In sharp contrast, training programs designed to have a lasting impact are often evaluated a few weeks or even months after they occur because of the desire to measure long-term impacts instead of immediate impressions. The issue of timing has considerable impacts on the choice of the technologies used to survey respondents.

Guideline 10.7: Choose Measurement Devices that Will Have Credibility with Those Who Will Use the Results as Well as with Respondents

Many years ago a debate emerged among researchers who had been measuring community satisfaction with a simple question of whether people were very, somewhat, a little, or not at all satisfied with the community in which they lived. Because most people at the time were "very satisfied" with where they lived, the researchers developed what became known as the "delighted–terrible" scale, with the following categories: Delighted, Pleased, Mostly Satisfied, Mixed (about equally satisfied and dissatisfied), Mostly Dissatisfied, Unhappy, Terrible (Andrews & Withey, 1976). This modification was successful in achieving more variation in people's answers. At the time that this scale was developed, interest in social indicators of people's well-being was quite high among political leaders, and as a result a discussion emerged about whether political leaders would take a report seriously if it claimed "x% were delighted and y% thought their community was terrible." The realization that some might not take such a finding seriously has led us to avoid this particular scale ever since. As this example illustrates, it is important to keep in mind the users of the customer satisfaction survey results when designing questions and to consider whether those users will take the results seriously or might interpret the measures as whimsical and question their accuracy.

We have also observed decision makers in some organizations being uncomfortable with satisfaction questions that used polar-point-labeled scales (e.g., a scale of 1 to 5, where 1 means *not at all satisfied* and 5 means *very satisfied;* see Chapter 5). In one instance, the reason for the decision makers' discomfort was that they had difficulty assigning meaning to categories that only had numerical labels or deciding how to interpret the average rating (e.g., what does a 3.6 mean on a scale of 1 to 5?). After a long explanation of such a scale and how it was converted to numbers, one of the board members listening to the report grew impatient and interrupted the presenter to ask "Does this mean people are satisfied with the performance of county government or not?" The numerical reporting of findings had less meaning to her than would a statement such as "60% of county residents are satisfied with county services, whereas 20% are very dissatisfied." Whereas some audiences may be completely comfortable with numerical ratings, even insisting on their use because of the mathematical precision that facilitates statistical analyses, the use of these ratings may not meet the needs of other survey sponsors or the intended audience for the results.

It is also important that respondents find scales comfortable to use and that the results are easily interpreted. Few survey designers would make the mistake illustrated by the example in the top panel in Figure 10.1. In this case, local companies built a simple satisfaction form but did not label

Figure 10.1　Examples of poorly constructed scales used in customer feedback surveys.

<u>*Scales with unspecified meaning*</u>

Using this 1 to 5 scale, rate how well our product has met your needs ....5　4　3　2　1

How would you rate the speed of delivery for the product you purchased?.............A　B　C　D　F

<u>*A scale that is unnecessarily indirect and difficult to comprehend*</u>

To what extent do you agree or disagree that you are satisfied with the service received during your last visit to a branch of our bank?

☐ Strongly agree
☐ Somewhat agree
☐ Neither agree nor disagree
☐ Somewhat disagree
☐ Strongly disagree

<u>*Scales that combine different concepts that may confuse respondents*</u>

How did our people treat you?......................☐ Like royalty
　　　　　　　　　　　　　　　　　☐ Attentive
　　　　　　　　　　　　　　　　　☐ Okay, I guess
　　　　　　　　　　　　　　　　　☐ Could have been better
　　　　　　　　　　　　　　　　　☐ What service?

Handling of my baggage? ....☐ Excellent
　　　　　　　　　　　　　　　　　☐ Good
　　　　　　　　　　　　　　　　　☐ Satisfactory
　　　　　　　　　　　　　　　　　☐ Unsatisfactory
　　　　　　　　　　　　　　　　　☐ Poor

<u>*A scale that may please some respondents but make it difficult to interpret results*</u>

Which of these faces best describes the way you were treated during your most recent visit to a branch of our bank?

　A　　　B　　　C　　　D　　　E　　　F　　　G

<u>*Unbalanced scales*</u>

How well did our staff treat you? ..... 　☐　　　　☐　　　　☐　　　　☐
　　　　　　　　　　　　　　 Outstanding　Excellent　　Good　　　Poor

How was the quality of the food?....... 　☐　　　　☐　　　　☐　　　　☐　　　　☐
　　　　　　　　　　　　　　 Excellent　Very Good　Good　　Fair　　Poor

---

the numeric or alphanumeric points so respondents would know which end of the scale was positive and which was negative. Although many may assume that 5 is higher than 1 and that A is more positive than F (using an academic grading system), the design of this scale is such that respondents themselves must determine the meaning of the points and may interpret them differently.

We have also seen surveys that use an unnecessarily indirect approach in which respondents are asked to indicate the extent to which they agree or disagree that they are satisfied, as shown in the second example (see the second panel of Figure 10.1). Asking such a question makes it more difficult because respondents have to think along two dimensions—agreement and satisfaction; they have to translate their judgment about how satisfied they are to the agree/disagree categories provided (see Guideline 5.21 in Chapter 5 for more discussion of the importance of using construct-specific rather than indirect scales). Another common design error is to combine two different concepts in the scale categories offered, as shown in the third panel in Figure 10.1. Designs such as these force respondents to try to compare categories that are not immediately and directly comparable.

Guideline 10.8: Avoid Choosing Measurement Devices Primarily because of Their Potential for Improving Response Rates

Sometimes, designers have attempted to make questionnaires more interesting—and thus more likely to be filled out—by trying to make them fun to complete. An example is a questionnaire from a bank that contained the question in the third panel of Figure 10.1 asking how one had been treated. For this question, the first category was labeled "Like royalty" and the last category asked rhetorically, "What service?" A restaurant used a similar tactic when they anchored the positive end of a scale measuring satisfaction with servers, "I want to marry my server." The facial expressions in the fourth panel of Figure 10.1 also fall into the category of a scale designed to be more interesting or entertaining at the expense of measurement. It is not uncommon for restaurants and businesses with mascots to display their mascots with different faces in this way in satisfaction scales to make their surveys more entertaining and fun for respondents. However, many survey sponsors may be uneasy when trying to interpret and report the results from scales using these types of descriptors. Balancing respondent preferences and needs with those of survey users is extremely important but can also raise a number of challenges.

The problem with using answer responses of this nature is that cuteness gets in the way of interpretation and of comparisons with other scales for which the same cuteness was not used. It is difficult to define specific meaning for answers such as these and to communicate results to dispassionate observers. Most important, very little research has been conducted to suggest that these types of scales actually improve response rates or to examine how they affect measurement. Although it is not often done, we recommend pretesting questions in customer satisfaction surveys using the procedures discussed in Chapter 6.

Guideline 10.9: Be Sure that Scales Are Balanced and the Measurement Procedure Fully Revealed When Reporting Satisfaction Survey Results

For the reasons discussed previously, some satisfaction survey designers tend to prefer fully labeled scales so they can report the percentage in each response category along with a word meaning for each of the categories. It is common to see scales of this nature: "excellent," "very good," "good," "fair," "poor," as shown in the bottom panel of Figure 10.1. As discussed in Guideline 5.23 in Chapter 5, respondents tend to draw information not only from the words that describe categories but also from the number and positioning of categories. In the scale in this example, "good" becomes the middle or average category, and there are three clearly positive categories, one fairly neutral category, and only one negative category. We conducted an experiment comparing results from this scale with those from one that used the categories "excellent," "good," "fair," "poor," "very poor." A total of 80% of students rated their experience as a student as "good or better," when "good" was the middle category in the unbalanced scale and three of the categories were good or better. However, when only two categories were good or better (in the balanced scale), 66% rated their experience in that way (Dillman, 2002). The unbalanced scale artificially made the ratings more positive. Thus, one of the critical goals that needs to be achieved with satisfaction scales is to make sure they are balanced, especially when one wishes to make summary statements with evaluative meeting (e.g., the percentage who report a good or higher degree of satisfaction).

We were once asked to comment on a proposed satisfaction survey being designed to evaluate a retirement community in the Pacific Northwest that had independent as well as assisted living and nursing home residential arrangements. The survey population consisted of people who tended to move into the community with the intent of staying for the rest of their life. The survey contained this question: "How satisfied are you with living in X community?" and the choices included "wonderful," "excellent," "good," "fair," and "poor." When we pointed out that the scale was unbalanced because of "good" being the middle category and because of the use of the word "wonderful" and proposed instead a more balanced 4-point scale consisting of "excellent," "good," "fair," and "poor," a board member responded that the organization did not want to do that because the purpose of this organized retirement community as communicated regularly to residents and prospective residents was to "provide a *wonderful* life to all of the residents." It was further explained that if the community was not doing that, then they needed to work to improve the situation. As a result, the final draft of the questionnaire used the 6-point scale of "wonderful," "excellent," "good," "fair," "poor," "very poor." We mention this example because the fit of a scale with the culture of the group being evaluated seemed an appropriate goal to be respected, and the extension to a 6-point scale made the scale more balanced while retaining the word *wonderful* that seemed to carry special meaning to members of the community. Our effort on this survey was aimed at finding a measurement device that was comfortable for both sponsors and respondents and that minimized measurement error.

It is also useful to recall from Chapter 5 that fully labeled scales tend to produce more responses in the extreme positive category than do polar-point-labeled scales, in which more people choose the middle category when one is offered. When faced with differences between fully labeled and polar-point-labeled scales, survey sponsors often ask which is more accurate. Answering this question is not easy because of the use of vague quantifiers. Although all types of scales are aimed at placing respondents higher or lower on a measurement device, respondents do not typically possess knowledge of satisfaction in the way they do age or a level of education. That the measurement of satisfaction (and related opinions) is so susceptible to scale design effects makes it especially important for surveyors to reveal exactly how they have measured this concept when reporting results to others.

Guideline 10.10: Carefully Evaluate the Impact of Using Both Aural and Visual Modes to Measure Satisfaction

Customer satisfaction surveys of either the same or different samples of customers are often conducted on a continuing basis to assess changes over time in the customer experience. The trend toward offering multiple modes, as noted in the example with which we began this chapter where customers could respond by Web or IVR, may create special problems. As discussed in Chapter 8, considerable research using ordinal scale questions has shown that responses are likely to differ across survey modes such that responses are more positive by telephone than modes where a visual display of the scale is provided, regardless of scale type or length. Thus, changes in mode from one survey to another should be made with care so as not to impact the trends over time. Because we know of no solution to this tendency for telephone surveys to produce more positive answers to ordinal scale questions, if a change of modes is necessary, responses should be collected by both modes for several surveys in order to assess the impact of the mode change on responses. In addition, the decision to use multiple modes may influence the ability to compare responses to the different modes, particularly when telephone or IVR is one of the modes and a visual mode is the other. In this case, the tendency to get more positive results on the telephone is often confounded by the fact that different types of respondents tend to prefer to respond to different modes. When modes are changed or when multiple modes are used, there is no way to control for the influence of the mode of administration on the measurement of responses.

A CONCLUDING THOUGHT ON CUSTOMER FEEDBACK SURVEYS

We strongly encourage those who conduct customer satisfaction surveys to disclose their methods when reporting results or at minimum to make them available upon request. Because of the variety of sampling and implementation procedures and the diversity of measurement devices used, it is imperative for those who interpret and use results from these surveys to understand how the different sources of error may be impacting responses. With full transparency, when customers are trying to evaluate whether to stay at one hotel or another or to purchase a product from one store over another they can understand the meaning behind the customer service ratings being reported. Likewise, business leaders will be in a position to make decisions about how to better serve customers if they understand how the data were collected.

ENHANCING THE ACCURACY OF CUSTOMER SURVEYS THROUGH SELECTION OF DELIVERY METHODS

Many customer surveys are delivered like most other surveys, by contacts through e-mail or postal mail as described in previous chapters. In other cases, specialized delivery procedures have been developed and are used in ways that improve survey quality. One of the challenges with regard to delivery method is matching the method to the type of feedback request being made of customers. We consider some of these procedures in the examples that follow. In addition, these examples illustrate different ways of conducting satisfaction surveys with a focus on reducing sampling, nonresponse, and measurement error as discussed in the previous guidelines.

IN-PERSON APPEALS WITH DIVERSE FOLLOW-UP PROCEDURES

When one has to identify people as they participate in an event in order to obtain a random sample, one also needs to be concerned about achieving high response rates with minimal nonresponse error as well as accurate measurement. On the one hand, this challenge can be quite daunting. On the other hand, the human interaction can be used to encourage response. In addition, it may also be possible to take steps that allow for follow-up even though the contact between the customer and surveyor is quite brief.

Recently surveyors studying people who attended dance, music, and theater performances in Belgium randomly sampled audience members and asked them to fill out a questionnaire during the performance and return it at the end before they left (Roose et al., 2007). When the questionnaire was returned, respondents were given a second questionnaire to take home that was more extensive, and a random sample of audience members was asked to provide their postal address. Sending follow-up letters, including two replacement copies of the questionnaire, to nonrespondents improved cooperation from 70% to 89%. More important, the analysis showed that attendees with less interest in the survey topic were significantly more likely to respond if they received the follow-up letters and replacement questionnaires, thus reducing nonresponse error. This analysis shows the importance of using multiple contacts in improving responses and relying on more than simply handing people a questionnaire in hopes that they will return it.

The delivery method in the Belgian study utilized a foot-in-the-door technique, in which people are more likely to comply with a large request (the second questionnaire) if they first agree to a smaller request. This technique and others have been successfully used for many years by the U.S. National Park Service (NPS) to obtain feedback in order to improve visitors' experiences in the nation's parks.

From 1988 through 2007, the U.S. NPS implemented 184 surveys ranging from 12 to 16 pages in length and obtaining an average response rate of 75% (Littlejohn, 2008). The procedure used for conducting these surveys has been described in detail elsewhere (Dillman & Carley-Baxter, 2001; Dillman, Dolsen, et al., 1995). People (or vehicles) are selected and asked to talk briefly to a uniformed staff member of the NPS after they have paid the entrance fee (if applicable) to the park. It is explained to the person (or people) that a visitor survey is being conducted and that their cooperation with the survey would be appreciated. They are informed that the NPS staff member will ask them three initial questions that day—(1) who, if anyone, the visitor is traveling with; (2) how many people are in the group; and (3) the person's age. These questions are asked to gain insight into potential nonresponse error to the longer questionnaire.

If they agree to help, the respondents are told about how long the full survey will take and that they will need to mail it back after their visit, and they are asked to write their name and address on a mailing label that will be sent to them on a postcard to thank them for visiting the National Park and to remind them to return the questionnaire if it has not already been returned. Respondents who prefer not to use their real name or who want to provide only their address can do so. The questionnaire itself is printed as a small booklet (8.5" × 5") using black type on colored paper. For the first several years, 12-page booklets were used, but they have now expanded to 16 pages. The number of questions asked has increased by about one third as a result of the increased number of pages and more crowded spacing, although the exact number of questions varies somewhat for each park.

The request to complete these surveys combines several elements that may influence response. One of them is making the request salient to individuals by having them walk (or drive) a very short distance to where the NPS representative is waiting to talk to them and explain the purpose of the study. That the NPS staff wears uniforms may be seen as an effort to invoke an appeal from a legitimate authority who works for the government. Similar to the Belgian study, this effort uses a foot-in-the-door approach by asking three simple questions at the beginning and following that with the larger request to complete the survey.

The postcard reminder that is typically used includes a picture on one side, much like one might buy at the visitor's center, and a printed message on half of the back side from the park superintendent thanking the visitor as well as reminding him to return the questionnaire if he has not yet done so. The postcard arrives about 2 weeks after the visit to the park. Sending it sooner seems inappropriate for this tailored use because many people are on vacation when visiting a national park and might still be traveling. It is important that the postcard not be sitting in a large stack of mail when they return.

The method used prior to the adoption of this delivery procedure, which involved simply handing people the questionnaire with no follow-up, produced an average response rate of 38% between 1985 and 1987 (and there was no way of assessing the impact of nonresponse). The new procedure, which, as mentioned previously, has an average response rate of 75%, has exhibited a minimal decline in response rates over the 20-year period of its use despite using slightly longer questionnaires containing more questions. Procedures now used for these surveys and the questionnaires are located at http://psu.uidaho.edu.

The kinds of procedures used for these surveys of cultural performances in Belgium and National Park visits can be modified for a wide variety of situations. If one were to survey visitors to an art museum, it would seem appropriate to have someone dressed as a docent provide information about the visitor survey. Visitors could be randomly selected after entering the museum or paying their admission fee. In addition, the postcard reminder could show a picture of one of the memorable art objects in the museum. It might also be possible to provide an incentive to people when the request is made (e.g., a poster from a current exhibit).

We have gone into some detail on in-person delivery of the survey request to suggest that what at first seems a negative (i.e., not having a list of people to survey) may be turned into a positive whereby one capitalizes on the opportunity to talk with people in order to encourage a response. Having a face-to-face interaction opens up the possibility of using that brief interaction to make follow-up contacts possible that may help reduce nonresponse error, which is one of the biggest concerns among those who conduct customer surveys. In addition, similar to the procedure used in the National Park study, the initial interaction can be used to ask people to respond to a few key questions either because the questions are the most important to the study or because they can later help assess the impact of nonresponse on data quality.

The applicability of in-person delivery methods goes well beyond customer surveys. These methods can also be used in many other situations where lists do not exist and one has to select people and talk with them in an effort to obtain a survey response. As we have tried to explain here, the key to success is making this initial encounter much more than just asking someone to respond.

INTERACTIVE VOICE RESPONSE METHODS

The 2000 edition of this book introduced touchtone data entry, a predecessor of IVR, as a technology that was growing in importance during the 1990s and described a number of principles to be followed in constructing surveys using this technology (Dillman, 2000a, pp. 402–411). This technology, which requires a touchtone phone, has been used successfully by the U.S. Bureau of Labor Statistics to collect current employment statistics (Rosen, Clayton, & Wolf, 1993). It has also been used successfully in the medical field (e.g., to obtain preoperative self-assessments from surgery patients; Mingay et al., 1999). Yet another use was as a substitute for telephone interviews, whereby individuals were called by telephone and then asked to switch to an automated system for responding. Attempts have also been made to use IVR, which, in its current form, can record verbatim answers for processing as well as information entered by punching numbers.

The IVR data collection mode uses a prerecorded script in which people are read questions and informed how to respond. For example: "On a 5-point scale, how satisfied were you with your recent meal at Friendly Times Restaurant? To answer, press or say '5' for very satisfied, '4' for somewhat satisfied, '3' for neither satisfied nor dissatisfied, '2' for somewhat dissatisfied, or '1' for very dissatisfied."

Although IVR can be very useful and cost effective, it brings into play several specific challenges. First, research has shown that if polar-point-labeled scales are used and the interim numbers (2, 3, and 4) are not mentioned, respondents are more likely to select the endpoints (Srinivasan & Hanway, 1999). Thus, it is important to explicitly mention all categories. Second, prerecorded messages have to be provided and programmed to appear if there is no answer or if the respondent presses an invalid answer. Respondents can even be asked to press numbers corresponding to reasons why they did not respond. Third, the response process can be tedious for respondents, especially if the question formats change frequently. Fourth, inasmuch as more and more use is being made of cell phones and fewer phones have keypads that are separate from the earpiece, IVR responses may be more difficult now for some people than in the past. Even in the best of circumstances, one must listen carefully as well as follow the use of the keypad visually to make sure the desired response is recorded. And finally, a further challenge for the use of IVR is the fact that surveyors sometimes require some answers to be given verbally, rather than through the use of the phone keypad. Because of the trend toward greater use of cell phones and calling that occurs in busy places, it becomes increasingly difficult for verbal answers to be "heard" by the IVR system above the background noise.

As web survey technology improves, the use of IVR for surveys in general may be declining. However, it remains important for certain survey situations and continues to see wide use for some satisfaction surveys. Requests containing a toll-free number to call to complete a survey can be handed to respondents in retail stores, restaurants, hotels, and other locations and even printed on cash register receipts as previously discussed. Moreover, most people have access to touchtone telephones, whereas many do not have web connections. In addition, the respondent can complete an IVR survey from anywhere rather than having to wait until a computer is available. Even if web access is available, people need to remember the request and complete the survey at some later time, and accurately typing in often long or complex web addresses remains one of the significant barriers to getting people to respond via the Internet.

The use of IVR, and its requirement that the stimulus be delivered aurally without the presence of an interviewer to anticipate and respond to problems, creates pressures toward simplifying questions and shortening scales, even more so than in standard telephone interviews. This mode is also primarily aural but has some visual elements, such as when respondents enter numbers from their keypad. One surveyor, for example, found that the use of a 1-to-10 scale resulted in a substantial increase in the use of "9" in 21 of 22 items (with an average difference of 11 percentage points) compared to a paper survey (Mu, 1999). This result is not surprising inasmuch as typing in "10" requires pressing two keys compared to only one for the other answers. In addition, when one is contemplating the use of a 5-point scale, the numbers 1, 2, and 3 are on the first row of the keypad, whereas the numbers 4 and 5 are on the second row, thus creating an artificial visual break in the scale.

Because completion of IVR surveys can be somewhat awkward for respondents, some surveyors have attempted to make the process easier by providing written instructions that explain to respondents how to make the call and what to do if they get into difficulty. In addition, these handouts may even show the format of the primary scale to be used for responding to questions, along with the corresponding numbers that the respondent will be asked to press. Some short interviews have even included the entire script of the questions in an effort to convince people that it is easy to do.

Using IVR in mixed-mode situations can present challenges. Evaluations have found that IVR interviewing systems produce less social desirability in people's answers than telephone interviews with a live interviewer. However, they have also found that personalizing the wording of IVR recordings (e.g., "Now I will ask you...") resulted in respondents making significantly fewer embarrassing admissions (Toureangeau et al., 2002). For less sensitive question wordings, IVR has produced slightly lower satisfaction ratings than traditional telephone surveys (i.e., computer-assisted telephone interviewing). Other research has shown that the results are intermediate between those produced by Web and mail on the one hand and computer-assisted telephone interviewing on the other (Dillman et al., in press).

DIARIES THAT CAPTURE CUSTOMER BEHAVIOR WHEN IT HAPPENS

Many customer surveys are focused on reporting behavior other than satisfaction. Among such surveys, few are more demanding than diaries that require respondents to report behaviors they engage in as they happen over the course of a few days, a week, a month, or sometimes longer. Examples include food consumption, household purchases, and travel diaries. These types of surveys are conducted by a variety of sponsors, from university faculty and federal agencies to private companies.

Our attention here is focused on two of the most common uses of diaries. The radio listening diaries conducted by Arbitron and the television viewing diaries conducted by Nielsen Media Research share many similarities. These diaries are important to broadcasters in setting advertising rates for their programming and in getting general feedback on individual station performance in attracting listeners or viewers. Because data are collected frequently and in large quantities in order to provide information for the hundreds of television and radio markets, considerable research has been conducted to understand what works and what does not work for obtaining accurate responses from carefully designed household samples. The unique challenges of conducting diary surveys illustrate the value of a greater degree of tailoring than occurs for most surveys.

For many situations discussed in this book, only a few contacts are made, and they may be made over a period of months. In contrast, diary surveys may concentrate six, seven, or even more contacts with respondents within a 3- to 4-week period, with most of the contacts being made within a 10-day period surrounding the respondent's diary week (Frederick & O'Hare, 2005; Trussell & Lavrakas, 2004). For many years, household units have been sampled and identified using random-digit dialing. Although contact procedures vary, when telephone numbers can be matched to addresses, respondents are sent a prenotice letter indicating a telephone call will be coming. The telephone call then asks households to participate, and that call is immediately followed up with a letter. Households that do not answer or are not interested in responding may be sent an appropriately tailored request to reconsider. The diaries are then mailed just before the designated week begins. Postcards and/or telephone calls are made during the week when listening or viewing is to occur, and a final follow-up letter or postcard contact may be made when the diary week comes to an end. So many contacts in such a short time would seem unreasonable for most surveys, but because of the nature of diary surveys where respondents have to record their behavior throughout the week, this likely does not seem unreasonable to most respondents.

These general public diaries also face coverage difficulties because of fewer households having landline telephones. Thus, it is significant that research is occurring on the use of addressed-based sampling using the U.S. Postal Service Delivery Sequence File. Addresses obtained from the Delivery Sequence File are then matched with other lists to obtain as many telephone numbers as possible in order to apply the implementation procedures outlined previously. This sample source allows surveyors to access cell-phone-only households and is planned as a replacement for random-digit dialing (Shuttles, Link, & Smarr, 2008).

Financial and other incentives are normally used in diary surveys. Sometimes cash incentives are sent only once, and in other cases both cash and material incentives are given to respondents at different times during the process. In addition, households in locations for which lower response rates are typically obtained may be sent larger incentives. Such incentives may also be targeted to characteristics of respondents, from age to race or ethnicity, in order to improve responses from these subgroups. Thus, some households may receive different contacts and incentives than others with the result that improved representation across subpopulations is obtained and poststratification weights can be reduced (O'Hare, 2008). In general, larger incentives lead to higher response rates (Trussell & Lavrakas, 2004). Even the packaging of surveys may be manipulated to improve response rates. For example, a box that looks similar to one that might contain a half pound of chocolates has been found to improve response over that achieved using envelopes for radio diaries (Patchen, Woodard, Caralley, & Hess, 1994).

Designing diaries and implementation procedures so that respondents can provide accurate information is enormously challenging. Through the years, the number of potential television channels has increased from only a few in the antenna age to hundreds with cable and satellite, and people can have many different combinations of channels. Homes are also much more likely to have multiple television sets than in the past. In addition, television programs are now commonly recorded for delayed viewing, and people watch movies and videos. Also, people are often unaware of the name of the program or even the channel they are watching. Radio diaries face their own challenges inasmuch as they must be portable because radios may be listened to more often in cars and away from one's home than at home. Similarly, more people are listening to satellite radio, streaming radio over the Internet, and recordings of their favorite radio shows. Implementation procedures and the diaries themselves must be designed to take these contingencies into account.

The reliance on mail and paper surveys in such a short window for data collection would seem to strongly encourage the development of electronic reporting. An Internet alternative for diary reporting has been developed, and appears to be preferred by some respondents. However, initial tests in situations where respondents are given a choice of responding by mail or the Web have resulted in declines in overall response between 3 and 4 percentage points (Gentry, 2008).

It is clear that diary surveys by these major organizations are in a period of transition. It is also evident that this research is being guided by efforts to tailor design in ways that will reduce survey error from multiple sources in order to preserve the high quality for which these organizations have gained a reputation.

Group Administration

Group administration of questionnaires remains an important means of conducting satisfaction as well as other types of surveys, but the ways in which it is accomplished are now quite varied.

In universities, students are often asked to complete instructor evaluation forms. One of our universities uses a procedure whereby paper evaluation forms are handed out in class, and a volunteer agrees to accept the returned forms and take them to the department's main office, where they are given to a staff person. When people participate in seminars, short courses, or brief professional meetings, they are often asked to complete formal evaluation forms near the end of the experience and turn them in immediately to the sponsor.

Paper remains a favored method of administering such forms, because very few people are likely to go online after the class or short course is over and complete the survey. In addition, it is often important to obtain such evaluations before memory of the content has faded, especially when, as often happens, the evaluations ask about specific aspects of the experience. Because getting responses immediately is so important for some evaluations, we have observed situations in which forms are forgotten until people start to leave, and members of the group are admonished "Don't forget to turn in the evaluation form" as they are leaving the room or the conference.

We have also noted a trend toward shifting the evaluation process for group experiences to the Web. Such shifts happen in different ways and for different reasons. In the simplest case, instruction happens on computers or in computer laboratories, and people simply receive evaluation forms as part of regular assignments and are expected to complete them in order to provide feedback on instruction and content. In other situations, people may be e-mailed and asked to respond to a web survey within hours or days of the course, particularly in populations with high rates of computer use.

Computerized evaluations increase the likelihood that more open-ended information can be collected from respondents, inasmuch as research has shown that open-ended questions produce more complete and detailed information on the Web than on paper, as discussed in Chapter 5. The advantages of an automated feedback system that can provide information more quickly and completely than the processing of paper forms suggest to us that paper feedback systems may be used less in the future.

CONCLUSION

After having lunch in a local restaurant while the three of us were working on this book, we received the bill along with an evaluation questionnaire and a computerized handheld device that resembled a calculator. By having us respond to the questions on the device, the restaurant had our immediate reactions to the quality of our meals and general dining experience. An advantage of this evaluation is that we could respond accurately about our impressions of the service, temperature of the food when it came, and other specifics that a restaurant finds important to know about while we were still in the environment of the restaurant and our memories were still very fresh. It was also a "group" response in that the three of us together provided responses.

The novelty of the experience was such that we responded to the questionnaire promptly and thoughtfully. Would we respond the same if it were an evening meal with a partner or spouse? What about if each time we went to a restaurant we faced the prospect of receiving not only a bill, but a request to complete a questionnaire while the waitperson was processing our bill? That is difficult to say.

Perhaps this experience summarizes the situation with regard to satisfaction questionnaires and delivery mechanisms. There is an enormous variety of ways in which questionnaires can now be delivered and people encouraged to complete them. The overall trend toward increased measurement of people's satisfaction is higher than at any time in history, in part the result of society's movement into the electronic world. Yet the fundamental question remains the same: Do threats from coverage, sampling (when sampling is done), nonresponse, and measurement error allow for appropriate conclusions to be made?

We have devoted an entire chapter to customer surveys for two important reasons. The first is that the number of such surveys conducted each year is enormous and is likely to become greater. The second is that sponsors and those who affect the delivery and retrieval of such surveys often have a vested interest in the outcome in ways that create a unique survey situation. When the providers of customer services begin to encourage a certain type of answer over others, when scales are developed in ways that encourage more positive answers than would other scales, and when reporting is done in selective ways to emphasize the most positive features of the evaluation, the dangers to valid measurement are substantial. Although it is difficult to imagine an interviewer for the U.S. Decennial Census intentionally encouraging respondents to report that they own instead of rent their home or that they are of one race rather than another, the same appears not to be the case for some satisfaction surveys. The intimate ties between the questionnaires, the sponsors, and those who implement them make such surveys especially sensitive to design issues that promote certain outcomes. The science that underlies valid sampling procedures and measurement should not be sacrificed in favor of fun and innovative data collection methods that in the end produce invalid or unusable measures of use and satisfaction.

LIST OF GUIDELINES

Guideline 10.1: Consider randomly sampling portions of the population instead of trying to survey the entire population, especially when the latter leads to people being surveyed repeatedly and unnecessarily

Guideline 10.2: Develop procedures for ensuring that onsite sampling is carefully executed and will not be affected by personal preference

Guideline 10.3: Actively seek means of using follow-up reminders in order to reduce nonresponse error

Guideline 10.4: Provide all selected respondents with similar amounts and types of encouragement to respond

Guideline 10.5: Avoid encouraging higher ratings during the delivery of the survey request

Guideline 10.6: Obtain responses from customers when they are best able to provide them

Guideline 10.7: Choose measurement devices that will have credibility with those who will use the results as well as with respondents

(continued)

Guideline 10.8: Avoid choosing measurement devices primarily because of their potential for improving response rates

Guideline 10.9: Be sure that scales are balanced and the measurement procedure fully revealed when reporting satisfaction survey results

Guideline 10.10: Carefully evaluate the impact of using both aural and visual modes to measure satisfaction

CHAPTER 11

Effects of Sponsorship and the Data Collection Organization

IN CHAPTER 7, we reported the results of an experiment on the effectiveness of prenotice letters and postcards on the U.S. Census. The story behind that particular set of experiments illustrates very well some of the types of challenges that often arise around survey sponsorship. In the early 1990s, the U.S. Census Bureau was looking for ways to improve mail-back response rates for the 2000 U.S. Decennial Census because they had declined significantly in the 1990 Census. One of us proposed that a postcard reminder be sent a few days after delivery of the Census Form. Research had shown that a reminder of this nature was quite effective at improving response rates to mail surveys, and it was an integral part of the original total design method (Dillman, 1978).

However, Census officials immediately rejected the proposal on the grounds that Title 13, the federal law that governs procedures used in this survey of all U.S. households, would not allow it. Although no individual names are used on Decennial Census correspondence, it was explained that the text of the postcard could be read easily by the postal delivery person or someone else, thus letting an unauthorized person know that people living at the address shown on the other side of the postcard were included in the Census. It was reasoned that if that happened, it would be a violation of the confidentiality that Census employees are legally obliged to protect under Title 13.

Inasmuch as every other household in the United States would be sent the same questionnaire and postcard, this interpretation of the law seemed extreme. Discussion of the proposal with Census Bureau legal counsel confirmed that this office would not allow the postcard to be used if it included wording stating that this household had been sent the Decennial Census

Form. However, it was deemed acceptable by legal counsel for us to state that a brief "census form" had been mailed to that address, leaving unnamed the specific survey. Based on this interpretation of the law, the experiment on the effectiveness of prenotice letters and postcards described in Chapter 7 was designed, and it was found that the use of a postcard would improve response rates considerably. Because of these findings and the great concern about improving mail-back response rates, a prenotice letter and postcard reminder were subsequently included in the implementation procedures for the 2000 Census.

This example illustrates how rules and laws, and the ways they are interpreted, may conflict with best practices for survey data collection. It also shows how an acceptable alternative can sometimes be found. Survey *sponsors* (i.e., the individuals and organizations who pay for or otherwise support surveys) and the organizations that carry out the actual data collection are often invaluable for lending authority to a survey and encouraging responses, thereby improving final data quality. But they can, just as often, pose barriers to the use of effective data collection strategies. Our focus in this chapter is on the many and varied effects of sponsorship and how to overcome challenges that may arise because of sponsorship.

U.S. OFFICE OF MANAGEMENT AND BUDGET

In the United States, approval of the U.S. Office of Management and Budget (OMB) is required for surveys sponsored by the federal government. This law applies to all data collection efforts that are either government financed or collected by a government agency or office. The requirement for OMB approval is established in the Paperwork Reduction Act of 1995, which requires government agencies to get approval from OMB prior to obtaining or soliciting *identical* information from 10 or more respondents. The most recent guidelines for OMB approval were announced in the *Federal Register* in September 2006 (U.S. Office of Management and Budget, 2006b).

Broadly speaking, the procedure for requesting OMB approval requires potential surveyors to publish a 60-day notice in the *Federal Register* that summarizes their data collection plan so that the public can comment. Surveyors then submit an Information Collection Request for approval by OMB. This form typically requires a justification for every question proposed as well as a detailed description of the proposed implementation procedures. At this time, they are required to publish a second, 30-day notice in the *Federal Register* that informs the public that OMB approval is being sought and that public comments on the project can be submitted to OMB. Once an Information Collection Request is submitted, OMB has 60 days to make its decision. The entire process, from preparation to *Federal Register* notices to an OMB decision, can take well over 120 days or 4 months (U.S. Office of Management and

Budget, 2006a). The development of these OMB approval requirements and the rigorous and sometimes lengthy approval process occurred because of concerns about survey quality, duplication of survey efforts by different arms of government, and the survey burden imposed on individual respondents.

Government and OMB concern about data quality for sample surveys is broad based (Harris-Kojetin, 2007). There are 20 published standards that focus on multiple aspects of survey design, from development of concepts, design, and data collection to data analysis and dissemination of results (U.S. Office of Management and Budget, 2006b). The four cornerstones discussed in Chapter 2 are a major focus of the approved 20 standards. However, perhaps the most discussed standard among surveyors is the following:

> Survey Response Rates, Standard 1.3. Agencies must design the survey to achieve the highest practical rates of response, commensurate with the importance of survey use, respondent burden, and data collection costs, to ensure that survey results are representative of the target population so that they can be used with confidence to inform decisions. Nonresponse bias analyses must be conducted when unit or item response rates or other factors suggest the potential for bias to occur. (U.S. Office of Management and Budget, 2006b, p. 8)

The guidelines further stipulate that the bias analysis must be planned for when the expected unit response rate is less than 80% and when any item response rate is less than 70%. Overall response rates less than 60% are generally considered unacceptable.

Surveys approved by OMB are expected to carry a statement that explains the nature of OMB approval, the response burden expressed as the expected time required to complete the form or questionnaire, and who to contact with questions. Respondents may also be informed that they are not required to respond to a questionnaire unless the request is within the approval period specified on the questionnaire. Figure 11.1 illustrates how one agency informs respondents about OMB approval on a questionnaire.

The practical effect of OMB requirements on government surveys is to encourage strenuous efforts to obtain high response rates. To meet OMB standards, surveyors often must use a wide array of response-inducing techniques such as many follow-up reminders, explicit refusal conversions, and additional survey modes when one mode alone cannot obtain a satisfactory response rate. As a result, survey designers sometimes consider OMB guidelines onerous and overly difficult to accomplish. Achieving satisfactory quality can also be quite costly (Detlefsen, 2007). However, it is important to recognize that survey data are central to making and implementing government policy. Government survey results are used to allocate enormous amounts of money to agencies, states, and other organizations. In addition, laws are frequently proposed and passed based upon findings from

Figure 11.1   Example of a U.S. Office of Management and Budget approval notice for a Census Bureau questionnaire.

Printed on the first page of the questionnaire:

OMB No. 0607-0919-DR Approval Expires 8/30/2010

Printed on the back page of the questionnaire:

The Census Bureau estimates that, for the average respondent, this form will take about 5 minutes to complete, including the time for reviewing the instructions and answers. Send comments regarding the burden estimate or any other aspect of this burden to: Paperwork Reduction Project 0607-0919-DR, U.S. Census Bureau, 4700 Silver Hill Road, AMSD-3K138, Washington DC 20233. You may email comments to Paperwork@census.gov; use "Paperwork Project 0607-0919-DR as the subject.

Respondents are not required to respond to any information collection unless it displays a valid approval number from the Office of Management and Budget.

government-sponsored surveys. Because of the importance of survey results in this context, the matter of survey quality is not something that can or should be taken lightly.

INSTITUTIONAL REVIEW BOARDS

In some organizations, anyone proposing to conduct a survey is required to have the questionnaire and implementation protocol reviewed and approved by an institutional review board (IRB). This group is charged with ensuring that the proper steps are being taken to protect the rights and well-being of human research subjects. Institutional review boards were established and codified into law (Title 15, Part 46, of the Code of Federal Regulations) by the National Research Act of 1974 to guard against research abuses that had been occurring largely, although not solely, in the biomedical field. Originally, IRB approval was required only for research that received funding from federal health agencies, but in the years since, coverage has been expanded to all research involving "human subjects," including surveys.

Institutional review boards now exist in universities, state agencies, and many private research firms throughout the United States. In contrast to OMB, which serves as a centralized and unified authority for survey approval, IRBs vary enormously. Their expectations and procedures reflect the background and experiences of the members who serve on those boards as well as the policy interests of the sponsoring institutions. At some universities, any data collection by students, staff, or faculty, in addition to secondary analyses of previously collected data, must be approved by an IRB.

The wide breadth of activities covered by IRBs and the diversity of members that serve on them sometimes lead to challenges for survey researchers seeking project approval. The professionals who serve on IRBs often have specialties in areas other than survey methodology. The IRB staff who review proposals may have little or no background in survey design and measurement and may lack knowledge of the sources or consequences of survey error. One IRB staff person, for example, indicated his displeasure that any follow-up contacts would be made after an initial survey mailing. His reasoning was that in psychological experiments valid data were obtained simply by asking for volunteers. The concepts of sampling, coverage, and nonresponse errors, as discussed in Chapter 3, were not viewed by him as important.

Many IRBs have also attempted to apply standard practices to all surveys. We were told of one IRB that wanted to obtain written consent forms for all surveys regardless of content, survey mode, or location of respondents. However, this practice was impractical for telephone surveys and unnecessary in mail and web surveys when it had already been explained to respondents that the survey was voluntary and that they could skip any question they did not wish to answer. In some studies, the consent forms would contain names of respondents and sometimes other identifying information that otherwise would not be collected as part of the survey itself, thereby introducing concerns about confidentiality.

In another instance, a standard statement was developed by IRB staff to inform people how to contact the IRB office if they had questions. Problems arose when it was required that this statement, along with an accompanying phone number that was not toll free, be given to possible survey respondents in a foreign country. The standard form of the statement was inappropriate in this context because many of the respondents were unlikely to speak English, and they were a population in which literacy rates were quite low. Moreover, only a few questions were to be asked of each respondent. In another instance, the same IRB office informed a study investigator conducting a mail survey that every communication with respondents had to contain a standard and somewhat lengthy IRB statement. However, placing it on the postcard thank you/reminder, a form of contact discussed in Chapter 7, would have utilized most of the available space for a written message. We have also experienced situations in which IRBs insisted respondents be given a standard statement that answering each question is voluntary while at the same time approving a web questionnaire with programming that would require an answer for every question. To work out these contradictions, the designers added a "prefer not to answer" or "no opinion" category to respond to the IRB request that otherwise would not have been used substantively by the surveyors.

Another common tendency that most likely stems from their origins in medical research is for IRBs to require survey researchers to implement the detailed and stringent consent protocols often needed to protect the rights of participants in medical research. However, these procedures tend to evoke unwarranted anxiety in potential survey respondents and, from a social exchange perspective, discourage survey participation by increasing perceived costs. We also know of situations in which investigators have been told that they must obtain signatures on a lengthy consent form when people are asked to complete mail questionnaires. Though an unusual requirement, it was once posed by a committee that was quite familiar with medical experiments done on volunteers who were paid for their participation, and the committee members did not think such a consent form would prevent randomly sampled members of the general public from responding to a survey.

Once IRB approval is received, it is common practice for surveyors to be required to inform respondents of that approval and of whom to contact at the IRB if a respondent has questions. This information must often be included along with OMB approval for federally sponsored surveys. If contact information is also provided for the person conducting the study, this means that three separate phone numbers and e-mail addresses may need to be included for three different organizations or individuals.

The difficulties faced with IRBs can become even more challenging when multiple funding sources and collaborators are involved with a project and all of them have to gain approval from their respective IRBs. We learned recently of the plight of an investigator who was funded by a state health agency to conduct a survey jointly with two universities. Each university required that standard IRB statements and procedures be used, but the standards differed across the universities, resulting in disagreement about which procedures were to be used for the proposed study. That the two IRBs also had different time lines for doing their reviews did not help matters. The result was a long and arduous process. We have also heard of situations in which approval is needed from two IRBs, but each, working independently of the other, informs the researcher that it will not grant approval until the other has done so. When multiple IRBs are involved, the challenges of gaining approval can be magnified significantly.

We are not suggesting that IRB impacts on survey design are all negative. Rather, we believe strongly that IRBs serve a legitimate and important purpose. They have been effective at ensuring that respondent confidentiality is protected and at requiring that potential respondents are told that completing a questionnaire is voluntary. They also prevent last-minute, poorly conceived study designs from being implemented. Yet, as these examples illustrate, IRBs may also often develop and enforce procedures that undermine the collection of quality survey data and that can even lead to increased anxiety among study participants and sometimes even increased respondent burden. Many of the problems between surveyors and IRBs surface because of the desire on the part of IRBs to have standard procedures and methodologies for all surveys, rather than allowing surveyors to be sensitive to differences in survey populations, survey modes, and particular data collection situations. Unfortunately, the standard procedures that are developed and implemented may directly conflict with or prevent the use of methods that would ensure a better experience for respondents and, as a result, improve respondent cooperation.

Figure 11.2 The institutional review board and response rate dilemma.

	Low ethics	High ethics
High response rate	**1** Unacceptable procedures with good data quality	**2** Acceptable procedures with good data quality
Low response rate	**3** Unacceptable procedures with poor data quality!	**4** Acceptable procedures with poor data quality

The dilemma is illustrated in Figure 11.2. Institutional review boards were formulated and their regulations written with the good intentions of eliminating the unethical research that fits into Boxes 1 and 3. However, some requirements that are often imposed on survey research result in research that falls into Box 4. The research is ethical from an IRB standpoint, but the procedures utilized to ensure that it is ethical undermine survey data quality, resulting in both the surveyor's and the respondents' time and resources being wasted. Nevertheless, the organization-specific nature of IRBs provides an opportunity to work out locally an appropriate balance between protecting respondent rights and allowing researchers the flexibility to respond to the specific characteristics of each particular study with methods for achieving high response quality; in other words, to conduct high-quality and ethical research that would be classified as belonging in Box 2.

Some of the most complicated situations occur when federal funding, with OMB requirements, is superimposed upon local IRB requirements. In many respects there is a built-in tension between IRB efforts to protect human subjects and OMB requirements for achieving high response rates. For example, OMB requirements encourage more contacts to increase response rates, whereas IRBs may urge investigators to use fewer contacts in order to protect respondents from the intrusion. A contractor who was asked to consider bidding on a proposed study once began the discussion with two simple questions: "Will this survey require OMB approval?" and "How many IRB approvals will be needed?" The contractor then explained that the answers to these two questions would probably determine whether the study could be done within the desired time frame and budget.

ACCOMMODATION OF DISABILITIES

Many populations that one may want to sample and survey include individuals with disabilities. In order to collect data from these individuals, surveyors often have to take additional steps to make the surveys accessible. Such steps are *required* if the survey is conducted by a federal department or agency. Section 508 of the Rehabilitation Act of 1973 as amended (*United States Code*, Title 29, Section 794d) requires that individuals with disabilities who are members of the public seeking information or services from a federal agency have access to information that is comparable to that provided to members of the public who are not individuals with disabilities, unless an undue burden would be imposed on the agency. Surveys are only one of the many activities to which the Rehabilitation Act applies. Details about this law and for accomplishing compliance are available from http://section508.gov.

The American Community Survey, which the U.S. Census Bureau mails to hundreds of thousands of households each year, provides one example of an effort being made to accommodate a disability. For individuals who are deaf, the following statement is printed on the front page of the survey: "Telephone Device for the Deaf (TDD): Call 1-800-xxx-xxxx. The telephone call is free."

The web age has brought with it an enormous amount of effort aimed at making web pages accessible to everyone (e.g., www.w3.org/WAI/ and www.webAIM.org). The guidelines that have developed out of these efforts have diffused rapidly throughout nearly all organizations that post web pages of any kind and are now being brought to the attention of web surveyors (Harrison & Coburn, 2007). Some common guidelines include providing text equivalents for every nontext element, such as images or graphical representations; ensuring that all information conveyed with color is also available without color to compensate for color blindness; making sure that any audio features have alternative tags that allow those with hearing difficulties to read what the audio is attempting to convey to respondents; and developing logical ways to navigate pages without using a mouse for those who are unable to do so.

ORGANIZATIONAL RULES AND PRACTICES

In addition to OMB and IRB rules and accessibility laws that surveyors with certain sources of funding are expected to follow, many sponsorship influences stem from rules and standard practices of the survey organization. Some of these practices are specific to the conduct of surveys, whereas others are general organizational rules that often limit indirectly how surveys can be designed and implemented. The effect of such standardized rules is to constrain the ability of surveyors to tailor designs toward maximizing response rates and quality.

Although some survey design constraints stem from specific laws, as did the examples introduced previously, other constraints stem from normal operating procedures within organizations. Still others stem from the predilections of individuals who have authority over what can and cannot be done when asking people to complete a survey. In addition, the nature of the organization (e.g., government, university, private business, or nonprofit) can provide both opportunities for and constraints on how surveys are conducted.

FEDERAL GOVERNMENT SPONSORSHIP

A meta-analysis of surveys done many years ago showed that response rates to government-sponsored surveys were higher than for surveys with any other type of sponsor, whereas those sponsored by private companies were the lowest (Heberlein & Baumgartner, 1978). We know of no evidence to indicate that this situation has changed. Response rates to government surveys remain quite high, as suggested indirectly by the current OMB standards. This is not surprising, as a government survey often has greater legitimacy than a survey done by someone in the private sector, a nonprofit group, or a university. This situation results in a more supportive context for the effective application of the social exchange principles discussed in Chapter 2. Inasmuch as government surveys are often used to implement federal laws, allocate funds, and set policy, it is often relatively easy to formulate a compelling argument that a proposed survey is socially useful. For example, the request to complete a 2000 U.S. Decennial Census form, to which all households are required to respond, explained that the number of representatives each state has in Congress depends on the number of people living in the state as counted by the Census, and that the amount of government money received by communities also depends upon answers to the Census.

With that said, there are cases in which sponsorship, and even government sponsorship, has the potential to increase nonresponse bias. For example, we once enlisted the help of a state government agency to get a sampling frame for a mail survey. In interviews conducted prior to the survey, some respondents expressed dissatisfaction with this particular agency's current policies and communicated that because of their dissatisfaction they were unwilling to participate in research conducted by or for that agency. Although the research in question was not being conducted by or for the agency, this experience serves as a good example of how the effects of sponsorship may be unknown, and even surprising, to the researcher. As a result, the best advice may be to examine the effects of sponsorship prior to fielding the survey through pretests, focus groups, or other means.

Although they can be enormously helpful from a sponsorship perspective, government survey organizations sometimes face enormous challenges in developing surveys that are acceptable to sponsors and stakeholders and also sensible to respondents. For some surveys, Congress and its individual members may become involved, even to the extent of proposing and insisting on specific wording for questions. Stakeholder groups, from formal advisory committees to interest groups, may similarly influence question wording or how other aspects of surveys are designed. Formal reviews by organizations such as the National Academy of Sciences may also have major effects on surveys and the questions they contain (Cork & Voss, 2006).

In addition, many federal government surveys are done on a continuing basis, and a tension is often created between the desire to keep questions the same to protect trend lines and the desire to change items so that they communicate more effectively with respondents. For example, one of the response options to a question in the Decennial Census for many decades has been whether people pay "Cash Rent" for the dwelling they occupy. Few people now pay for rent with cash. Yet because it is a part of a more complex question asking about ownership versus renting arrangements, and because it was used in many previous censuses, it remained in use through the 2000 Census.

Reconciling these different viewpoints and expectations for specific government surveys is often enormously time consuming. However, the need to arbitrate such conflicting points of view is also a significant source of survey improvement inasmuch as the requests for change often lead to the conducting of important experimental research that can inform the decision-making process. Research produced out of such debates is an important source of innovation in government surveys.

Some of the rules that guide surveys stem from the existence of multiple stakeholders in the outcome, and the influence of political leaders, even on seemingly small things, should not be underestimated. At one point during the development of the 2000 Decennial Census Short Form, the numbering of questions on page 1 began with 1 for number of people living in the household, 2 for whether one's residence was rented or owned, and then started over again with 1 for the householder's name, and each of five other questions asked about each individual in the household. Many survey methodologists were concerned that this numbering system would cause people to skip the first two questions and instead start with the second number 1, which was visually more prominent because of the large answer space provided for writing the respondent's name. Several attempts were made to get approval for changing the numbering to 1 through 8, but they all failed. Finally a high-level Census official explained that Congress had been promised that there would be only six questions about each person who lived in each residence, and renumbering the questions would make it appear that there were eight questions about the first person. Although the numbering was eventually changed, this example illustrates the degree to which concerns of stakeholders become represented in the design of questionnaires and, in effect, can become rules for construction. In many different government agencies, we have listened to detailed descriptions of how questions must be asked in specific ways because of the position of the person who proposed it, an advisory committee that insisted on it, another agency that was paying for it, or a specific analyst who wanted it asked in a particular way.

Conducting surveys in large government survey agencies often leads to challenging situations. Once when tracing out objections to a proposal (which had originated in a federal agency) for sending out checks as prepayments for a national survey that had received OMB approval, the surveyor mistakenly assumed that someone in the agency objected to paying respondents, which at the time was an unusual procedure for a government survey. When the source of the objection was located, it was found to be the chief of the accounting division. He was concerned about the likelihood of there being many un-cashed checks that would have to be carried on the agency's books for several years. When the proposal was changed to sending cash and acceptable procedures for monitoring its use had been developed, the request was immediately approved. In other organizations, the opposite has occurred; that is, checks have been required and cash could not be used.

A similar problem occurred when designing cover letters for one survey. Time and time again drafts of the letters would be returned from the agency with dates removed. After considerable investigation it was found that one person was responsible for the management of all correspondence signed by the agency director. Inasmuch as dates for mailings were sometimes not known, dates on all letters were simply removed, and once the letters were approved the dates could not be added back on.

When Internet surveying began in earnest, we learned that one federal agency required for security reasons that passwords and access codes for completing a business survey be sent in a postal mailing and not by e-mail. It also required that they be sent separately from a mailing that transmitted a paper copy of the questionnaire, and that they could only be sent after a specific respondent had been identified (i.e., not to the business). One result of this practice was a lower response rate than desired, which probably stemmed in part from the difficulty of locating and bringing together disparate pieces of information relevant to accessing and completing the survey. Security and confidentiality remain driving issues that have limited the use of Internet survey methods by some U.S. government agencies, as discussed further in Chapter 12.

The electronic age has ushered in a variety of other sponsorship issues as well. For example, some organizations have established policies that all communications sent outside the organization must have an approved logo. For web surveys that means placing a sponsor logo on each and every page of the web survey. The need to include logos in this way can lead to frustrating results. For example, one of the largest conductors of federal surveys developed an in-house web survey procedure that agency rules required branding with multiple established agency and division logos. When customers such as other federal agencies came to that organization for doing a survey, it was common for the client to ask for its own agency logos to be added to each page as well. The effect was to produce web pages with a header as well as a footer, each of which contained several agency logos and other sponsorship information. The presence of different brightly colored logos of different sizes located somewhat randomly in the available header and footer space gave the entire page a cluttered appearance, making it more difficult to see and follow the desired navigational path for answering each question. In addition, the amount of usable space for presenting survey questions on each screen was also decreased considerably so that on some screens respondents could not see the entire question without vertically scrolling.

UNIVERSITY SPONSORSHIP

Large numbers of surveys are also conducted in universities and colleges. Many of these educational institutions have survey research centers that conduct surveys for university faculty and administrative units and may also conduct them for clients from outside the institution. At the same time, faculty and graduate students frequently design and implement their own surveys, often on shoestring budgets and using whatever resources they can scrape together.

In general, these institutions exert considerably less control over response rate and quality expectations than is the case for government surveys because they lack an oversight organization such as OMB (although OMB becomes a factor for university research funded by federal sources). As a result, it should not be surprising that tremendous variations exist in survey quality in these settings. Inasmuch as IRBs constitute the main influence on surveys in the academic setting, procedures used in these surveys are less likely to emphasize obtaining high response rates and minimizing the four sources of error than is the case with government-sponsored research.

Surveys in universities also constitute a rich source of innovation in survey methodology as the nature of the research process, which is a key aspect of many universities, encourages the development, testing, and publication of new knowledge. However, constraints on university surveys can also be substantial.

An example of such constraints occurred when a university faculty member attempted to conduct a survey using contract funds from an international organization. The faculty member was to collect the U.S. portion of an international survey, and the organization spearheading the survey was unwilling to allow the U.S. portion to be analyzed separately from the rest of the international data. However, in an attempt to protect the research independence of its faculty, the university had a policy preventing any data from being collected by a unit of that university unless the faculty member had an explicit right to analyze and publish all information that was collected. It took several weeks to hammer out an agreement acceptable to both parties. In the end, the agreement was reached based on a declaration by the faculty member that he wanted to do the survey because of the opportunity for methodological experimentation it provided him and that he had no interest in analyzing or publishing the substantive data. However, during the negotiation process much time was lost because both organizations objected to changing their standard wording, making it necessary to add additional wording that provided adequate clarifications.

Sometimes presumed university rules or practices are used to justify inadequate survey methods. Several years ago a research proposal for conducting a statewide survey of the general public that included respondent incentives was submitted to a national competitive grants program by a university faculty member. In the research plan, the faculty member proposed to pay each respondent a modest amount for completing the questionnaire. A scientific review proposed that the researcher send a token cash incentive to each person in the sample because of the lack of research showing postsurvey payments to be effective. The researcher responded that it was against her university's policy to allow token cash incentives in advance because some people (nonrespondents) would, in effect, be paid for doing something that they did not do (completing a questionnaire). This situation immediately raised the question of whether this was a rule that was being imposed by the department, the college, the university itself, or an office somewhere within the university (e.g., financial accounting or the IRB). It also raised the question of whether it applied specifically to surveys or was more of a general rule for all financial matters at the university. One could speculate whether the organizational source of the rule understood why one might choose to use token incentives in advance that were likely to improve response rates and reduce nonresponse error rather than postsurvey payments that would probably not. Although laborious, it is sometimes necessary to trace out the sources of rules to figure out why they exist and sometimes whether they even exist at all.

Another benefit of conducting surveys within universities is the speed with which research projects can be planned, implemented, and reported. When one of us went from a university to the federal government on a 2-year assignment, a significant portion of the government orientation was to explain that the federal government was not like a university in this respect.

Whereas researchers at a university are pretty much free to make their own design decisions on a survey and can often put an experiment into the field in a few months or even weeks, for government surveys there is at least a 1- to 2-year, and sometimes longer, planning horizon within which researchers need to work. Compared to the federal government, universities provide opportunities to move quickly if one has funding available and can secure IRB approval in a timely manner, but their advantage in this regard is much less than in the private sector.

Private Sector Sponsorship

Private sector survey organizations are a critical part of the nation's infrastructure. They also do a tremendous amount of survey research and development and can provide an effective feedback capability for businesses that typically emphasize quick turnaround when needed. Many such organizations also successfully compete for government-funded surveys. In many cases, because they are in the private sector, they are able to respond more quickly to new opportunities than can either government or university surveyors.

In general, private sector organizations also tend to innovate more quickly than others, testing new technologies as they attempt to maintain a competitive edge over other survey organizations. For example, private sector surveyors are ahead of government agencies and universities in their efforts to use interactive voice response and web survey methods, just as telephone survey methods were first developed in private sector organizations in the 1970s (Blankenship, 1977). One of us recalls the tortuous multiyear process of getting a new, but fairly straightforward, construction feature accepted in a federal government agency. However, within a month of mentioning the same proposed construction feature to a private sector organization, it was put into practice in all of that organization's surveys.

Some private sector organizations that use surveys to improve their business also exhibit a tendency to be more fluid between strict sample survey methods and more general needs assessments. An example is the hotel customer satisfaction surveys discussed in Chapter 10, for which blanket survey mailings without follow-ups are often used in hopes of identifying specific organizational problems that need to be solved. Oftentimes in these surveys, relatively little concern is focused on whether results will be representative of all people who stayed at the hotel. Instead, the need to maintain a good relationship with clients tends to discourage the use of intensive follow-up procedures aimed at pushing response rates higher, as OMB requirements encourage in government surveys and the peer-review publication process often does for university-based surveys.

One of the standards we have observed in some private sector organizations is to produce data that are good enough to guide a decision, rather than data that are as accurate as possible, within reasonable cost limits. This standard seems to underlie the tendency of some private sector organizations to embrace voluntary web panel surveys, as discussed in Chapter 9. Because of the variation in private survey organizations and the types of surveys they conduct, some private sector survey data are of very high quality, whereas other data are not, as is also the case with university-sponsored surveys.

ORGANIZATIONAL SIZE AND COMPLEXITY

The size of the organization may have a significant effect on survey design, regardless of the specific company or agency that is conducting the survey. For example, the larger the organization and the more surveys it conducts, the more likely established rules exist that will influence what can and cannot be done to encourage survey response. This is especially likely to be true when survey tasks are organized across the multiple organizational divisions that size tends to produce. In the early 1990s, one federal agency had an established practice of printing key codes used in data entry in large bold type inside the answer spaces on paper questionnaires. A request to remove them on a single questionnaire being developed for another federal agency produced immediate objections. A visit to the keypunching center that was located in another city quickly revealed the basis of the objections. Keypunchers at that centralized facility were paid a bonus for speed and accuracy. The larger and easier the key codes were for them to see, the faster they could find and use them. Efforts to change the "system" pitted employee satisfaction and work quality on the one side against ease of respondent reporting on the other. Because the keypunching division did not have a direct interest in easing the task of the respondent, it lobbied quite effectively to make key codes as prominent as possible. The lack of advocacy for respondent-friendly questionnaires meant that this institutionalized practice was exceedingly difficult to change. When this problem was pointed out to a division chief, her response was, "Well, we have divisions for forms design, field operations, and question topics. If the respondent perspective is ever going to be represented in survey design negotiations, I guess that means we need a Division of the Respondent."

An analysis of survey design decisions in the U.S. Census Bureau done in the mid-1990s revealed that needed innovations in survey design were often thwarted in multiple ways (Dillman, 1996). Because of the extremely large and complex surveys that were routinely undertaken, two professional cultures and the staffs who identified with each came into frequent conflict. An essential operations culture whose staff members had little research methodology training but were vitally concerned about the efficiency of survey implementation viewed research aimed at improvements in survey procedures as primarily an opportunity to improve survey operation activities but had little interest in conducting controlled experiments. However, the research division, who identified with experimental testing and had as a goal the publication of results in scientific journals, was focused on controlled tests of ideas rather than addressing survey implementation problems. These different orientations often led to extensive debates over what research was to be conducted. Resolution of differences was through a strong hierarchical system of control, part of which was outside the control of the agency, which made resolving their differences quite difficult. The inevitable compromises often resulted in studies that produced uninterpretable results that satisfied no one. In addition, arriving at decisions on specific experiments or tests was also affected by quite different views among researchers as well as among operations staff about which sources of survey error (e.g., coverage vs. measurement vs. nonresponse) should be given the highest priority (Dillman, 2000b).

A recent example of the effects of organization size illustrates the occasional need for rules to emerge in order to standardize work across divisions. As was discussed in Chapter 8, in preparation for the 2010 Census, an effort was being made by the Census Bureau to develop questionnaires for four different survey modes—mail, Web, handheld computers (although this mode was later dropped for the 2010 Census), and telephone. It became apparent in 2005 that a different group was responsible for questionnaire development in each mode and that each group was constructing its questionnaire in what appeared to be the best way for that individual mode, resulting in significant differences in question construction across the modes (examples of the differences are provided in Chapter 8). A similar problem was observed in a private sector organization that had physically separated its telephone, Web, interactive voice response, and mail units, which allowed each to design according to what was best for its individual mode, and, as a consequence, wording and structure differed greatly for the various modes.

Technology

As discussed in Chapters 6 and 7, technology can greatly influence the capabilities available for designing mail and web questionnaires and implementing survey designs. The technology that an agency or organization has can also limit how surveys are designed. In general, it is to the benefit of organizations to purchase one type of software for conducting web surveys and to use common procedures for constructing and processing paper surveys. This sometimes leads to less flexibility in how surveys can be designed and implemented or to the institutionalization of practices that constrain how surveys can be designed even though different software may be readily available.

One organization we observed developed optical scanning and imaging procedures for mail surveys in which guide marks were placed on questionnaires in ways that interfered significantly with respondent comprehension. Another organization used a quite different procedure that was much more consistent with good visual design principles. The important point here is that to gain economies in survey design, all surveys within each organization had to go through the same template. Thus, every survey was affected by the technology system that had been adopted for general use. As this example illustrates, organizational adoption policies can be either a substantial facilitator or an equally substantial hindrance to good survey design that individual project directors cannot influence.

Rules with considerable benefit overall may also introduce problems. It is increasingly common for established surveys that are conducted repeatedly over a number of years to require testing of any proposed changes. The desirable impact of such a rule is to encourage survey designers to conduct experiments on the effects of changes before they propose that the changes actually get made. More commonly, these rules encourage surveyors to systematically conduct cognitive interviews or focus groups to gain insight into how respondents are likely to be affected by the proposed changes. However, rules such as this also produce a convenient excuse—"It hasn't been tested"—for avoiding simple but important changes if an individual or group within a large organization is opposed to the change, especially when time is short.

A final organizational issue that has arisen in recent years is the development and increasingly common practice of branding the products of a company, agency, or university on web pages. For example, rules have evolved that require the use of specific font styles, sizes of fonts, and colors and the identification of organizational themes on all company products. These rules are often applied to individual web pages, including survey questionnaire pages. However, people need to process and use web pages intended to collect information (i.e., web surveys) differently than they process and use web pages intended to disseminate information (e.g., the organization's home page). As a result, the styles chosen to represent the organization on its home page or on other products may be quite inappropriate for use in a web survey sponsored by that organization.

An intriguing problem of organizational rules being layered on top of one another surfaced at the U.S. Census Bureau in preparation for the 2008 Census Dress Rehearsal. When printing the envelope, a logo prepared for use in the 2010 Census was accompanied by the words "2008 Census Dress Rehearsal" beside it. Those words were the same size as the message that response was required by U.S. law, which was also printed on the envelope. An attempt to decrease the size of the Dress Rehearsal message ran into the rule created by those concerned with marketing that census that when words were used with the logo, they had to be the same size as the complete logo (which had a small font for "United States" written above "Census 2010" in a much larger font). Consequently, the Dress Rehearsal language became dominant over the required-by-law language, which itself had been shown in previous research to increase response by as much as 10 percentage points (Dillman, Singer, et al., 1996). Sometimes rules make sense to those creating them but when applied to a different situation make no sense at all. Getting the Dress Rehearsal words downsized was a significant challenge. This is only one example of how small seemingly insignificant rules can become major problems in the design of surveys.

GUIDELINES

Against the background of these sponsorship influences, certain guidelines seem useful in attempting to respond positively to the challenges that can arise.

Guideline 11.1: When U.S. Office of Management and Budget or Institutional Review Board Approval Is Necessary, Allow Sufficient Time for the Approval Process

Few things can be as frustrating as having a survey completely designed with staff ready to implement it, and then watching them sit idle while one waits on OMB and IRB approvals. The prominence of these organizations in the decision-making process has led to changes in the design procedures often used for surveys. The design has to be created sooner than it often was in the past and has to be shepherded through an approval process that once was associated more with grant writing than survey implementation. One is well-advised to start this process early and monitor it closely in case revisions are needed in order to get final approval.

Guideline 11.2: Recognize that Sponsorship and How it Is Communicated to Questionnaire Recipients Is Likely to Influence Survey Response

Frequently, we are asked what kind of response rate is likely to result from a particular survey. This is a difficult question to answer until we know who is financing the survey, who is actually conducting it, and how sponsorship is likely to be conveyed to respondents. Often federal government surveys are contracted to private organizations for implementation. In some cases, we have noted that the contractor tends to emphasize its role in conducting the survey while deemphasizing the fact that it is a government survey. In general, we expect surveys conducted by the government to obtain higher responses rates than those conducted by universities, which in turn will obtain higher response rates than those conducted by private sector organizations. Thus, unless there is good reason to believe that it will have negative effects, it is important not to hide government sponsorship from respondents or to deemphasize it under the mistaken view that private sector sponsorship will be better received by the survey respondents. To take advantage of the benefits of sponsorship, many surveys develop procedures whereby appeals for response are sent directly from sponsoring agencies as well as the data collection organization.

Guideline 11.3: When Choosing a Data Collection Organization, Determine What Constraints the Selected Organization Will Place on Design and Implementation

Survey units that design and administer surveys for others, regardless of whether located in government, university, or private sector organizations, tend to develop particular ways of conducting surveys. One of the most obvious examples is web software. Increasingly, survey organizations have adopted a single software solution. It is an advantage for organizations to be able to use the same software and design procedures for as many of their surveys as possible. We have observed in most large organizations a tendency to regress survey design on all topics toward a common way of doing the survey in which the agency or company has a significant investment. As occurred in the early years of telephone interviewing, there now exists a very wide variety of web survey software, some developed within organizations and some purchased or leased from providers of such software. As such, decisions on which survey organization to use may affect the overall visual design of the survey, the editing capacity that can be built into it, whether information offered in response to early questions can be used to frame later questions, how confidentiality is protected, how e-mail addresses are handled, whether postal mailings can be used to support data collection via the Web, the usual way that questions are worded, and many other features of design.

Similar constraints are also apparent in organizations that do mail surveys. Printing equipment, optical scanning and imaging equipment, envelope sizes, questionnaire sizes, color versus black and white printing, cover designs, and capability for intelligent printing vary enormously among organizations. Thus, sponsors need to be aware of the limitations, as well as the unique possibilities, available in certain organizations that will influence many of the questionnaire design and implementation procedures discussed in Chapters 6 and 7.

It is critical to know what survey organizations can and cannot provide when deciding which organization to use. As an analogy, when one decides to fly between two distant cities, there is often a choice of airlines. Number of flights, locations of the connecting cities, and the total time required for the trip can be examined to determine which flight best meets one's needs. The same is now true for choosing an organization to implement one's survey.

CONCLUSION

In this chapter, we have described some of the many sponsorship and organizational attributes that sometimes influence survey design. Some of these features have positive effects on survey quality, whereas others have undesirable effects. We have included a discussion of these issues because over a period of many years we have observed the inordinate amounts of time needed to deal with how to comply with, obtain exemptions from, or even change the policies of the organization to facilitate the development and use of good survey practices that will effectively reduce survey error.

It is also clear that different survey requests and modes may need different adaptations of organizational rules. Well-intentioned laws, rules, and organizational procedures may be helpful for certain surveys but have unanticipated negative effects on others. An example happened as a result of the passage of the Confidential Information Protection and Statistical Efficiency Act of 2002 (CIPSEA), which improved confidentiality protection for respondents to many business surveys. When procedures were applied to several mandatory surveys conducted by mail by the Energy Information Administration, response rates were unaffected and, in some cases, may even have increased. However, when the Energy Information Administration's Motor Gasoline Price Survey was conducted by telephone, OMB required new CIPSEA information about confidentiality to be included in the telephone script, resulting in a different effect. The week that the new confidentiality protection notice had to be read to respondents, the response rate immediately fell 10 percentage points from 98% to 88% (Bournazian, 2007). This particular survey is very brief, as it collects only the current price for each grade of gasoline being sold at sampled gas stations. It seems likely that what had seemed a simple survey to most respondents, often as easy as reading prices off of signs outside the gas station window, became puzzling and maybe even threatening when confidentiality was so strongly emphasized.

We doubt that the differential effects of policy requirements across surveys that are observed in this case are unusual. We are in an era when those who develop and enforce rules and procedures try to identify standard statements and procedures that can be used across multiple survey modes and situations. In other cases, organizational effects are simply due to standard policies being applied to surveys when they were developed with no expectation that they would be applied to the design of surveys.

The one-size-fits-all paradigm for survey design no longer exists, because it was not viable given the variety and complexity of different surveys being conducted. It was replaced with a paradigm of tailoring survey procedures to the many different survey populations and situations that arise in an effort to achieve optimal data quality (i.e., the tailored design method). It is important to recognize that a focus on attempting to enforce standard organizational statements, rules, and procedures for all survey situations runs contrary to the tailored design method. Whether the policy comes from OMB, IRB, the government, a university, the private sector, or any one group or individual, if it is blindly applied across survey situations, the likely effect will be a reduction in data quality.

LIST OF GUIDELINES

Guideline 11.1: When U.S. Office of Management and Budget or institutional review board approval is necessary, allow sufficient time for the approval process

Guideline 11.2: Recognize that sponsorship and how it is communicated to questionnaire recipients is likely to influence survey response

Guideline 11.3: When choosing a data collection organization, determine what constraints the selected organization will place on design and implementation

CHAPTER 12

Surveying Businesses and Other Establishments

One of the most challenging data collection situations occurs when individuals are no longer the respondent, but instead an organization is asked to respond to a survey request. Although an individual (or perhaps multiple people) is asked to complete a questionnaire on behalf of the business, agency, educational institution, or some other organized entity, that person is not doing so of her own accord or providing information primarily about herself. These conditions call for many changes in the ways in which one should design questionnaires and effectively appeal for them to be completed. In addition, the tailoring required for business surveys is affected by nearly all of the issues discussed in previous chapters, including mixing modes, conducting repeated surveys of the same units, and taking into account respondent preferences. However, it also involves new issues because of the need to pass questionnaires from one person to another within the responding organization, and it involves implementation situations that are more complex than any so far discussed in this book.

Establishment surveys are among the most critical surveys done in societies throughout the world. They are used to assess the amount of new housing constructed, employment practices, money borrowing, research and development expenditures, the societal production of scientists and engineers, energy use, manufacturing output, and imports and exports, to mention only a few. In the United States, they are relied upon to provide a variety of information critical to providing statistical guidance to the Federal Reserve Board and other entities responsible for maintaining the smooth operation of national and international economies. They also provide information relied on for developing new laws and government regulations.

Thousands of surveys such as these are conducted in the United States and other countries each year, especially by government agencies. Although most establishment surveys are conducted by government entities, these surveys are also conducted by universities, nonprofit organizations, and businesses themselves (Kriauciunas, Parmigiani, & Rivera-Santos, 2007; Tomaskovic-Devey, Leiter, & Thompson, 1994). Thus, procedures for surveying establishments must take into account sponsorship as well as the entities to be surveyed.

Establishment surveys are in a state of transition; the methods used for conducting them are changing. In the past, establishment questionnaires were more likely than surveys of any other population to be conducted by mail. Often, the questionnaires were designed more as forms—with questions forced into the least space possible and divider lines putting questions into spaces of various sizes and shapes—than as attractive questionnaires. Visual principles for design were not generally used to guide respondents, as illustrated by the relatively recent questionnaire on industrial research and development shown in Figure 12.1. This questionnaire is printed in a horizontal rather than vertical format, and the page is filled by information items and questions that are not placed in an easy-to-follow navigational path. In addition, paper questionnaires like this one were usually accompanied by separately printed and lengthy instruction booklets that provided definitions and answers for nearly every question that designers believed any respondent might ask. We return to this questionnaire later in this chapter.

Of all of the populations discussed in this book, establishments, particularly larger ones, may be far closer than most others to having universal web access. Employees who complete questionnaires are likely to have good computer skills and are usually comfortable using the Web. This makes the establishment survey a likely candidate for being transitioned completely to the Web. However, that goal remains far from being realized, even though the advantages to establishments of providing the detailed data that are requested of them electronically are considerable, especially when organizations must report for multiple entities within a firm (e.g., franchise restaurants).

Although the transition to the Web or other types of electronic data collection is nearly complete for some establishment surveys, other surveys continue to be conducted predominantly by mail. Still others use multiple survey modes as they attempt to target different segments of the establishment survey population. For example:

- The Current Employment Statistics (CES) survey conducted monthly by the U.S. Bureau of Labor Statistics offers reporting firms a variety of options in a deliberate attempt to match businesses with their preferred response mode. This monthly survey of a sample of 300,000

Figure 12.1 Example of an old-style mail establishment questionnaire that lacks a clear navigational path.

PLEASE RETURN BY:

OMB No. 3145-0027: Approval Expires 1/31/2005

FORM **RD-1** (3-5-XXXX)

Economics and Statistics Administration, U.S. CENSUS BUREAU
U.S. DEPARTMENT OF COMMERCE
COLLECTING AND COMPILING AGENT FOR
THE NATIONAL SCIENCE FOUNDATION

SURVEY OF INDUSTRIAL RESEARCH AND DEVELOPMENT DURING 2002

In correspondence pertaining to this report refer to this **IDENTIFICATION NUMBER (ID) (11 digits)** ▶

NOTICE – YOUR RESPONSE IS REQUIRED BY LAW. Title 13, United States Code, requires businesses and other organizations that receive this questionnaire to answer the questions and return the report to the U.S. Census Bureau. By the same law, **YOUR REPORT IS CONFIDENTIAL.** It may be seen only by persons sworn to uphold the confidentiality of Census Bureau information and may be used only for statistical purposes. Further, copies retained in respondents' files are immune from legal process.

RETURN TO

U.S. Census Bureau
1201 East 10th Street
Jeffersonville, IN 47132-0001

Name of person who supplied 2001 data

MANDATORY REPORTING REQUIREMENTS

Data supplied in all items for 2002 on this form will satisfy the mandatory reporting requirements. (Title 13, U.S. Code.)

PLEASE READ ENCLOSED INSTRUCTIONS BEFORE COMPLETING THIS FORM.

THIS REPORT SHOULD COVER YOUR ENTIRE CONSOLIDATED DOMESTIC ENTERPRISE, INCLUDING ALL U.S. SUBSIDIARIES AND DIVISIONS.

The term "company" on this form refers to the consolidated domestic enterprise.

- Please complete this form by the date printed at the top of this page and return it in the envelope provided. Make a copy for your records.
- Please read the enclosed instructions before completing this form.

- Report figures in thousands of dollars. Reasonable estimates are acceptable.
- Explain significant changes in year-to-year data in the remarks section.

(Please correct any error in name and address, including ZIP Code.)

COVERAGE REVIEW

Was this company owned or controlled by another company on December 31, 2002?

001 ☐ Yes – See instructions for Coverage Review.

☐ No – Continue with item 1

Section I – GENERAL COMPANY DATA

Item 1 – RECEIPTS AND EMPLOYMENT FOR THE COMPANY

A. Sales, operating receipts and revenues from all domestic operations of the company, net of returns and allowances. *(Report in thousands of dollars.)*

EXCLUDE domestic intra-company transfers and sales by foreign subsidiaries.

INCLUDE receipts for sales of products and services provided to other companies, individuals, U.S. Government agencies, and foreign countries.

B. Domestic company employment in all activities during the period which includes the 12th of March 2002 (Item 1 of I.R.S. Form 941, if one Form 941 was filled for the entire company.)

	2002			2001		
	Bil.	Mil.	Thou.	Bil.	Mil.	Thou.
102						

Number
112

Item 2 – NUMBER OF RESEARCH AND DEVELOPMENT SCIENTISTS AND ENGINEERS

Apportion on a full-time equivalent basis. *See page 4 of the instruction booklet for more detail.*

	January 2003	January 2002
	Number	Number
A. Federal research and development	204	
B. Company and other research and development	205	
C. TOTAL – *Sum of lines 2A and 2B* ▶	206	

PLEASE CONTINUE ON REVERSE.

business establishments obtains responses by six different modes: mail, 8%; computer-assisted telephone interviewing (CATI), 23%; fax, 18%; touchtone data entry, 20%; electronic data exchange, 30%; and Web, 1% (Rosen, 2007).

- The Economic Census conducted by the U.S. Census Bureau every 5 years remains in large part a mail census. A variety of factors ranging from the construction of the sample frame, the lack of e-mail addresses, and security concerns over reporting via the Internet have resulted in mail remaining the dominant mode of response, although an electronic option is provided that is used mostly by large firms.
- The Graduate Student Survey, conducted annually by the National Science Foundation, is a complex survey that identifies a coordinator at each university to collect information from departmental representatives on the number and race/ethnicity of graduate students supported by each department during a specific term. Prior to 2008, much of the communication and data collection occurred by mail. Beginning in 2008, both the coordinator and respondents for individual departments were transitioned to e-mail and the Web for responding. Paper forms are now sent only by special request.
- The Survey of Earned Doctorates, also conducted by the National Science Foundation, involves contacting all doctorate-granting universities in the United States and asking for all students completing doctorates to complete and return a questionnaire that is used nationally to count the number of doctoral degrees granted each year. An Internet option for completing this survey has been provided for several years; however, only about 5% of new doctorates complete the questionnaire on the Web. The explanation for this low percentage is that the questionnaire is distributed to students through an office at their university as they complete the requirements for their degree. Most of these offices provide a paper copy of the questionnaire to students along with other paperwork that needs to be completed in order to receive their degree (S. Hill, personal communication, February 13, 2007). That individual people (new doctorates) complete this questionnaire makes this seem like an individual-person survey, but its distribution and collection occurs through universities, making it a type of establishment survey.

Other establishment surveys also seem in certain respects to be individual-person surveys. For example, some respondents to surveys of physician offices, farm operations, accounting firms, and other establishments are individual proprietors, thus blurring the line between the survey being of an establishment versus an individual person. This often occurs without the survey sponsor being aware of the exact nature of the businesses to be surveyed and the variety within the population. Despite the occasional fine line between establishment surveys being business and individual-person surveys, the design and implementation procedures that become important for surveying organizations are often quite different from those used when individuals are reporting only for themselves.

SIXTEEN QUESTIONS TO BE ASKED WHEN DEVELOPING AN ESTABLISHMENT SURVEY

The challenge of surveying businesses and other establishments is determined in part by the intersection between the nature of the organization to be surveyed and the type of information being sought. It involves asking a series of questions summarized in Figure 12.2 that are often quite different from those asked when beginning to plan an individual-person survey. The heterogeneity among types of organizations is enormous and has a considerable impact on survey procedures. The questions posed here are aimed at helping the surveyor obtain relevant information to guide the establishment survey design process.

1. HOW LARGE IS THE SAMPLE OR POPULATION TO BE SURVEYED?

Surveying only a few hundred entities is very different from surveying thousands or even millions. Large business surveys are not unusual. Hundreds of thousands of businesses are surveyed in the Census of Manufacturers conducted by the U.S. Census Bureau, and about 2 million farms are now in the Census of Agriculture conducted by the U.S. Department of Agriculture's National Agricultural Statistics Service (USDA-NASS). Many surveys seek cooperation from all establishments (and thus constitute censuses), whereas others are limited to samples. The number of establishments to be surveyed can make an enormous difference in which kinds of response-inducing procedures (e.g., individual contact and personalization) can and cannot be used.

2. HOW MUCH VARIATION EXISTS IN THE SIZE AND STRUCTURE OF THE SURVEY UNITS?

If one desires to survey manufacturers, retail stores, nursing homes, travel agencies, consulting firms, law firms, or businesses of any other type, there is considerable likelihood that some firms in the population are quite large and others are quite small. Variation in the size of establishments has increased as the availability of information-age technologies has made it possible for individuals operating out of their homes to do work that formerly required a central location and public visibility. In fact, one person may operate several organizations, a phenomenon encouraged by many tax laws. The trend has also been fueled in the United States by the movement away from

Figure 12.2 Sixteen important questions to ask when designing an establishment survey.

1. How large is the sample or population to be surveyed?	Enormous variation exists.
2. How much variation exists in the size and structure of the survey units?	Some samples are quite heterogeneous.
3. Does the establishment still exist?	Names and ownership change frequently.
4. What is the name of the establishment?	Names used for business purposes may differ from the publicly recognized name.
5. What is the organizational entity?	Establishments may organize themselves differently than how they are presented to customers or the public.
6. Where is the establishment located?	It may not be where the buildings are.
7. Does the establishment have a survey policy?	Responding may require an approval process.
8. Who should be the respondent?	Increasingly, only specialists can answer important survey questions.
9. Is it necessary to go through a gatekeeper?	Some people who need to answer must be approached through other people.
10. Who is the sponsor?	Sponsorship has an especially heavy effect on whether a business will respond.
11. Is a response required by law?	If so, confidentiality requirements may be extraordinary.
12. Does a reporting deadline exist?	Producing organization information often takes time.
13. How difficult are the questions, and will records need to be consulted?	The response process and time needed for a response may increase.
14. Are detailed instructions needed?	Producing simple numbers may require considerable detail.
15. Is the survey repeated at regular intervals with the same respondents?	If so, the implementation procedures are likely to be affected.
16. Will the customer orientation of the organizations help obtain a response?	The customer orientation of businesses may make attempted contacts less likely to be ignored.

manufacturing to a service- and information-based economy, which makes it possible for small consulting firms and other entities to achieve enormous reach with their activities.

In small organizations, all incoming correspondence may be seen by the owner or manager. In large organizations, executives may not open their own postal mail, or even their own e-mail. In addition, mail that can be handled by someone else, such as an invitation to respond to a survey, may not be shown to them. The effect is to increase the difficulty of writing questionnaires, instructions, and correspondence that take into account these variations in a way that does not overwhelm respondents with details relevant only to other businesses in the sample. Different communications and even questionnaires may need to be developed to respond to the variation within the population. As we discuss later, extensive cognitive testing and pre-survey telephone contacts may be especially helpful in understanding the heterogeneity in samples and how to design to deal with it.

3. DOES THE ESTABLISHMENT STILL EXIST?

Establishments are created and terminated regularly. Sometimes they are re-organized or changed by buying or selling components, or simply by changing their names to create a different public image. In surveys of businesses, finding an adequate list is often difficult. Even tax revenue lists get outdated very quickly, as some businesses terminate or are sold while other businesses are being created. Therefore, it is imperative that tax or other lists used for sampling be as up to date as possible. In addition, it may be necessary to determine whether a business has been recreated under a different name or entity.

4. WHAT IS THE NAME OF THE ESTABLISHMENT?

Frequently, the name of a business for accounting and tax purposes is not the same as the name provided to the public. This is especially true for businesses that have public visibility and multiple locations. In one survey of businesses, a chain of restaurants located in many cities with a well-known public name was listed on all records we could find with an innocuous name like "KAG Incorporated." Consequently, surveyors need to be aware that the establishment they identify by one name may be referred to as something else by the respondent.

5. WHAT IS THE ORGANIZATIONAL ENTITY?

The sponsor of a survey may define each restaurant or nursing home with a name and location in a particular community as a separate business. However, the establishment's owner may view it as one of several locations within a single organization. Both parties have a legitimate perspective. In a survey of businesses within one city or county, the survey sponsor may be correct in identifying each specific location as a business. The owner, however, may see each as a component of a unified, indivisible larger business that spans cities or counties and for which separate accounting information may not even be kept. Depending on the type of information requested, respondents may not even be able to separate information for one location from another. It is important that establishment surveys specify what constitutes a separate organization for purposes of the survey and find ways to reconcile differences between how they define separate units and how the business owners define separate units in ways that allow for the development of appropriate sample designs and questionnaire development.

6. Where Is the Establishment Located?

The location where a business provides its service or product to buyers may not be where business affairs are handled. A list of businesses may contain one address but not the other, making sampling and coverage issues particularly difficult to handle. An example of this difficulty occurred in a multistage sample of businesses that drew counties as a second-stage sampling unit. This process led to the inclusion of some business outlets that, although physically located in the sampled county, had mailing addresses in an adjacent county that was within the urban area but technically outside the sample area and therefore ineligible for a proposed survey. Often, unforeseen issues of this nature can easily be resolved by survey designers, but the likelihood of this happening cannot be ignored. This issue has become far more complex as international corporations have expanded and both headquarters and subunits have been located in different countries, as well as in different states and even counties within states because of tax and other jurisdictional rules.

7. Does the Establishment Have a Survey Policy?

Many organizations have policies that address whether they will cooperate with survey requests and an approval process for questionnaires that do get completed and information that can be released. In some organizations, one person is responsible for all questionnaires, or at least needs to approve them, whereas in other businesses making survey decisions is a time-consuming process involving many people. A policy of not responding to questionnaires provides a convenient means of immediately dispatching requests for completion of questionnaires with the simple statement "It's against company policy." In many cases, such policies apply to certain questionnaire modes (interview but not paper, or vice versa). It also appears that a policy of nonresponse to questionnaires sometimes exists as a convenient means of getting rid of most requests, but the policy may be far from absolute. Persistent but careful attempts to obtain an exception to policy for an "important purpose" may therefore be required. More important, perhaps, is that if one knows what kind of communication a survey request sets off, one can plan for it at an early stage of design.

8. Who Should Be the Respondent?

Work in many organizations is increasingly specialized, with people in one part of an organization knowing very little about what is done in another part. Human resources officials may have little understanding of computer security issues, and information technology employees may know very little about the work that happens in the human resources department. Likewise, people with accounting responsibilities may have little knowledge of strategic planning or production issues. In some organizations, one person is in charge of hiring policies, another is in charge of setting wages, another is in charge of continuing education, another person makes equipment decisions, and still another has chief responsibility for long-range planning. Thus, questionnaires that require information about specific areas of an organization may be directed from the person who initially receives the questionnaire to a particular office or person who can accurately provide the needed information, and in some cases the questionnaire may need to be passed through several offices or people in order to obtain all of the information requested.

In fact, one of the important recent trends in some establishment surveys is to ask for different sections of questionnaires to be completed by different respondents, thus making one organizational staff member a sort of "coordinator" for survey implementation. This is happening because of the increasingly specialized knowledge of individual employees, but it adds a layer of complexity to data collection that has important design consequences. In these cases, the variety of questions being asked may require considerable behind-the-scenes communication before someone enters answers, a process that may include getting approval to report certain information. In contrast, in small organizations one person may handle all of the decisions and compile all of the responses himself or herself. The more topics and people involved in responding to a survey, especially one that involves requests for specific numbers rather than broad estimates, the more difficult and time consuming it is likely to be to get a completed survey from the organization.

9. Is It Necessary to Go through a Gatekeeper?

In many organizations, the person who opens mail or answers the telephone often screens requests for survey participation, even without knowing what the request is about. Although e-mail is a direct way for approaching many people, higher level organizational representatives sometimes use e-mail addresses that are not provided outside the company or that are screened by someone else. A questionnaire sent by postal mail may be thrown away without the person to whom it is addressed even knowing it was received. Having methods of getting past gatekeepers, who are often as effective by stalling as by saying no, is critical for achieving a response to self-administered surveys. We suspect that much of the success of token financial incentives in obtaining responses to surveys from, for example, physicians is that their inclusion enables the questionnaire to get beyond gatekeepers who are authorized to say no but are not authorized to accept or dispose of money without the approval of the addressee. We return to this topic later in this chapter.

10. Who Is the Sponsor?

One of the largest sponsors of business surveys is the federal government. As indicated previously, many of these surveys are of great national importance, especially with respect to making economic and policy decisions. Moreover, just as individuals are required by law to respond to the U.S. Decennial Census, businesses are required by the same law (Title 13) to respond to certain surveys, as we discuss in the next section. The requirement to respond is balanced by guarantees of confidentiality. Other federal surveys are voluntary and cannot utilize government authority in the same way. In yet other cases, businesses occasionally conduct surveys of other businesses, raising the possibility of one business being asked to provide proprietary information to a competitor. University-sponsored surveys, by contrast, may not present the threat of a competitor asking about a company's business. As discussed in Chapter 11, survey sponsorship influences both how a questionnaire is viewed by the recipient and that person's likelihood of responding.

11. Is a Response Required by Law?

Whereas most individual surveys are voluntary, a number of establishment surveys conducted by the federal government require by law that the organizations respond. One result of this requirement is that the question faced by organizations may not be whether they should respond, but when it is convenient for them to do so. This places a different kind of context around the way in which questionnaires are received and handled. Organizations (or their representatives) that prefer not to respond may focus more on delaying or negotiating why some data cannot be provided than on making a straightforward refusal to respond. In addition, the requirement that organizations respond may also necessitate the use of extraordinarily stringent confidentiality requirements that influence how electronic reporting methods can be used.

12. DOES A REPORTING DEADLINE EXIST?

Data collected from some establishments often need to be reported by certain dates. For example, some survey data are the key to calculating important economic performance indicators and must be available by a certain date each month. This challenge has contributed to the development of fax, embedded e-mail, and other electronic forms as means of getting business surveys completed. For other surveys, there is no firm completion date. These differences have a substantial influence on the kinds of methods that may be used, especially with respect to the mode used and the ability to send follow-ups.

13. HOW DIFFICULT ARE THE QUESTIONS, AND WILL RECORDS NEED TO BE CONSULTED?

In general, questions asked in business surveys tend to be more difficult than those asked in individual-person surveys and may require that respondents consult records to find the answers. We have been asked to help with surveys that ask the exact size of boat engines and the year boats were purchased, the number of employees who received a particular kind of training in the past 18 months, income information that appears only on tax records, exact numbers of livestock bought and sold in a specific time period, and quantities of power produced from independent power producers as opposed to co-generators and other sources. In each of these cases, respondents likely have to check records in order to provide an accurate answer.

Asking people to check records makes it more difficult to obtain responses, because an important reason for nonresponse stems from whether records are available. Likewise, the burdensome and oftentimes tedious nature of consulting records may greatly increase the social exchange costs of completing the survey. In some surveys, it may be possible to ask more general questions with categorical answers, such as the following: "About how many head of cattle did you sell last year? (a) less than 35, (b) 35 to 74, (c) 75 to 149, or (d) 150 or more." An answer to this question might easily be provided without having to find the sales records. However, the sponsors of many surveys, and particularly economic surveys conducted for policy purposes, may feel that only precise numbers are acceptable (e.g., they may ask for the exact number of cattle sold rather than accept a range). As a result, obtaining responses to these surveys is more difficult.

14. ARE DETAILED INSTRUCTIONS NEEDED?

The complexity of questions often means that extensive sets of instructions are deemed necessary and separate instruction booklets must be provided.

In several instances, we have observed instruction books that are longer than the questionnaires themselves. These instructions are provided primarily for surveys for which the respondent is being asked to consult records, and they become yet another design challenge to overcome in order to obtain a satisfactory response.

15. Is the Survey Repeated at Regular Intervals with the Same Respondents?

Many federal government surveys are conducted with the same establishments yearly or even monthly. This situation sometimes leads to the development of understandings and policies that aim to ease the reporting task by not making changes in data collection procedures, developing reporting relationships with particular individuals within companies, and implementing other procedures that are unique to particular surveys. Although this may help some respondents, it also leads to the retention of out-of-date procedures that can make responding more difficult for new establishments that are added to the sample.

Another challenge arises when surveys are repeated frequently with the same businesses. In these cases, a special emphasis is placed on getting questions to be understood and answered in the same way in every data collection period. One way this consistency can be facilitated is by providing establishments with their answers from the previous survey along with the current questionnaire to use as an answering guide (see Figures 12.3 and 12.4, discussed later in this chapter, for examples). This process is facilitated by the use of new technologies that allow each firm's questionnaire to be uniquely printed so as to include data collected from the firm for the previous year. Tailoring the questionnaire in this way requires a different printing and distribution procedure than might otherwise be used. Similarly, web surveys allow previous responses to be prefilled or even used as a verification step for the responses provided in the current survey.

16. Will the Customer Orientation of the Organizations Help Obtain a Response?

Most of these questions point out some of the difficulties of surveying businesses. By contrast, a positive customer orientation is a decidedly positive attribute for surveyors. Surveys of individuals often produce adamant, emotionally charged refusals. In addition, individuals may go to great lengths to make it hard for surveyors to locate telephone numbers or to get through an answering machine. Although businesses can react the same way, they are generally more concerned about providing convenient access to customers and clients. Phone numbers for businesses are likely to be listed rather than unlisted, and increasingly employees are trained to be responsive to callers. The desire to be responsive to callers is of considerable help in resolving many of the potential difficulties outlined previously. For example, what is the company's name? Is the location in Sioux Falls a separate business entity? Who is the person to whom a request for information about the business should be addressed?

There are several benefits of talking with a representative of an organization. They range from determining eligibility for a survey to identifying to whom a questionnaire should be addressed, and even encouraging response at a later time. Moreover, the relative ease of locating telephone numbers has led to the use of the telephone to encourage or augment mail and electronic methods for most organizational surveys.

CHOOSING THE MOST APPROPRIATE MODE

The list of alternative modes now being regularly used for conducting establishment surveys goes well beyond mail and the Web. Establishment surveyors can choose from a variety of survey modes to tailor to specific situations and even individual organizations within the population. This tailoring is much greater than that typically applied to individual-person surveys. Moreover, the various needs of many establishment surveys now encourage a multimode approach.

A summary of modes used in eight major Bureau of Labor Statistics surveys in 2007 reveals the following percentages of respondents reporting in each of the following ways (Rosen, 2007):

Mode	Percentage
Mail	44
Web	13
Fax	12
Electronic data exchange	10
CATI	8
Touchtone data entry	6
Telephone prompting	5
Personal visit	1
More than one mode	1

As these numbers indicate, mail was more than 3 times as likely to be used than was Web, fax, CATI, and other types of telephone interviews. Underlying these data is the use of mixed-mode approaches, whereby organizations respond by different modes. Each of the eight surveys used a minimum of three different modes, with two surveys using six different modes. Mail was used for all eight surveys, electronic data exchange for seven of them, fax for six, and the Web for four, with the remainder of the modes used for three or fewer surveys. The top three reasons for using the multiple-mode approach were (1) respondent preference, (2) reduction of cost, and (3) improved response rates (Rosen, 2007). Thus, a combination of considerations influenced the choice of modes.

In contrast, the Energy Information Administration, which conducts a number of mandatory surveys on the production and consumption of energy, uses mail for contacts but does not receive any responses by mail. One reason is that the 9/11 catastrophe, followed closely by the anthrax scare in mail communication, led the government to institute screening of mail addressed to government agencies. This screening has produced long delays in delivery that cannot be tolerated given the survey time lines. To avoid these delays, the Energy Information Administration provides a fax option for returning questionnaires and is moving toward more Web-based data collection strategies for many of its surveys. Even with this move, paper forms remain very important, as many respondents prefer to complete the information on paper and use the Web for entering the data and transmitting it to the Energy Information Administration.

The U.S. Census Bureau, perhaps the world's largest conductor of establishment surveys, has encouraged the evolution of three different models for conducting such surveys (Morrison et al., in press). Certain surveys are conducted mostly over the Internet using an in-house system known as Census Taker. It encourages the use of a common set of agency procedures for conducting Internet surveys. Other surveys deemed inappropriate for the Internet use a Questionnaire User Interface and the Generalized Instrument Design System (QUI-GIDS). This system was initially developed for the 2002 Economic Census. It allows one to pull questions and related material from a metadata repository containing approximately 550 previously used industry-specific questionnaires to build both paper and electronic questionnaires. Building questionnaires using QUI-GIDS provides paper instruments that are ready for key-from-image data capture, whereby the entire questionnaire is optically scanned and operators review answers to correct or add those not captured accurately by the system. A third design approach is to develop surveys for unique survey situations as negotiated with clients. These surveys, though heavily mail oriented, may also use fax or telephone as well as e-mail support for data collection.

Although it is clear that a movement exists in transitioning previously mail-only surveys to other modes, success varies by agency. It also varies depending upon survey topic, whether the survey is mandatory or voluntary, whether the survey is long or short, and a variety of other characteristics. A summary of the dominant mode options and a discussion of each of their strengths and limitations follow.

MAIL

The persistence of mail as the primary establishment survey mode is in part because some sample frames do not include e-mail contact information. In addition, some business populations lack adequate penetration of high-speed Internet access (e.g., small businesses, including many farms or other family-based businesses), especially in rural locations. Moreover, the investment required to ensure response security over the Internet, agency rules on how password and security codes can be sent, and other slow-to-change policies mean that the challenge of moving away from the use of mail is sometimes substantial.

For many surveys, electronic means acceptable to the survey sponsor are not available. In other instances, respondents are unable or unwilling to use desired electronic substitutes. In these cases, mail is a viable alternative. It also provides an effective survey means for individual researchers (e.g., university students and professors) to obtain business survey responses. For example, in one survey effort, university-based surveyors utilized a mail implementation strategy to obtain responses from a variety of industrial firms in multiple countries (Kriauciunas et al., 2007).

The USDA-NASS now offers web response for some of its surveys. By July 2007, 57 USDA-NASS surveys were online, but only 2% of the total number of responses from those surveys were received through the Internet; however, 8.2% of the questionnaires from agribusinesses were returned over the Web, compared to 1.3% of those from farm/ranch operators (Gregory & Earp, 2007). As these numbers indicate, a significant push to convert respondents to the Web has not yet been made, in part because of poorer quality Internet service in rural places where many responding organizations are located.

At the same time, the USDA-NASS has made significant investments in improving the visual layout of questionnaires so that they are easier for respondents to complete (Dillman et al., 2005). For example, the Agricultural Resource Management Survey, which is used to survey a national sample of thousands of farmers and is estimated to take 2.5 hours to complete, was shifted in part from personal enumeration to a mail survey with enumerator follow-up. Use of the revised questionnaire with a $20 automatic teller machine card cash incentive in 2004 resulted in 44% of the surveys being returned by mail before personal enumerators were employed to collect the remaining responses. Collecting 44% of the surveys by mail produced a substantial cost savings. The final response rate was 72% (Ott & Beckler, 2007).

THE WEB

Certain surveys completely dependent upon the mail mode in past years have now been transformed almost entirely to being hosted on the Internet. An example is the National Science Foundation Survey of Science and Engineering Research Facilities, which assesses space and other resource uses by scientific fields at nearly 500 colleges and universities and 200 independent hospitals and other nonprofit biomedical organizations (Smith, Gray, & Christovich, 2007). When it was started in 1986, this survey used only a paper questionnaire. In 1996, a Windows-based application on a diskette was introduced and was successful in obtaining responses from 27% of the organizations. Beginning in 1998, respondents were given the option of responding by the Web, and 53% responded in that way. By 2005, 96% of the academic institutions and 83% of the biomedical organizations responded on the Web, although all respondents were given a choice of responding by mail or Web. Currently, the response process begins with a postal letter that is then followed with a paper questionnaire and instructions for how to access the web survey. Response is further encouraged with e-mail and telephone follow-ups. In addition to the creation of a web version, a fairly complete transformation of the previously used mail questionnaire moved away from a traditional mail format to a visual design and layout that was consistent in wording and page formatting to that used on the Web. It was further supported by nearly 100 online data checks to help identify problems. In addition, respondents could print the completed questionnaire in order to review it and maintain a paper file copy if desired, something that is often needed by many organizations. Evidence of the success of this process is that slightly more of the mail respondents than web respondents (88% vs. 73%) required edit resolution follow-up.

This example illustrates an underlying process of moving respondents from paper to the Web that is time consuming but that is occurring in many other countries throughout the world as well. Statistics Sweden, which conducts many of that nation's government-sponsored establishment surveys, now offers enterprises in Sweden the opportunity to respond by the Web. However, the initial contacts are through a paper form with web access information provided on the form. Response by the Web typically ranges from 5% to 20%. In Norway, virtually all business surveys are offered by the Web, and the proportion of businesses that respond electronically is steadily increasing. In 2005, about 33% of businesses reported electronically, a figure that increased to 36% in 2006 and approximately 48% in 2007, an increase of 15 percentage points in only 2 years. Most of this reporting is over the Web, although as much as 10% may be by other electronic means (G. Haraldsen, personal communication, March 18, 2008).

Reporting by the Web is advantageous in business surveys for many reasons. For one thing, the emphasis on collecting numbers and data that are compiled from organizations' records means that the response task may be simplified by allowing respondents to simply transfer data from company records to the establishment questionnaire. Use of the Web or other methods of electronic reporting can ease this task, and web surveys make possible the addition of automatic editing (e.g., providing totals for columns and verification steps that identify answers that are inconsistent with other answers). In addition, instructions can be made more accessible when they are needed on the Web. Also, page length requirements that were a major constraint for mail are relaxed because of there being only minor cost implications of using more space, which can also improve the visual design and layout of questions.

However, several considerations seem to undermine the successful movement away from paper and toward the Web. One of them is the ability to provide sufficient security and to guarantee confidentiality for the electronic transmission of data. Survey sponsors are reluctant to use the Web for surveys until they can be absolutely sure that the transmission of data is secure. To ensure this, they sometimes insist on respondents using passwords and other access information that is complex and must be changed frequently, and some even require that this information be sent to respondents separately from the request to complete a survey. In addition, it is sometimes required that such information not be transmitted electronically but instead be sent by postal mail or transmitted in some other way. Such stringent security requirements have been an inhibitor to transitioning surveys to the Web (Rosen, 2007).

Another barrier to conducting web surveys stems from the need for respondents to understand what data need to be assembled, and from whom they must be obtained, prior to filling in the form. Web surveys that cannot be perused in their entirety in order to contemplate what information needs to be assembled prior to reporting greatly discourage businesses from responding over the Web. Likewise, those that cannot be accessed multiple times can be particularly challenging to complete when information must be entered from several divisions or people within an establishment. For these reasons, paper forms are often used, even when data are transmitted via the Web or other electronic means.

WEB-LITE

One agency fielding a very brief survey that requested a small number of data items on a monthly basis found that it was taking respondents longer to log on than to enter their data because of somewhat complicated security procedures (Fredrickson-Mele, 2007). The underlying concern was that response rates were being negatively affected. The approach this agency used and labeled *Web-lite* streamlined the authentication process by requiring only that surveyed respondents report a number and a word verification using CAPTCHA (Completely Automated Public Turing Test to Tell Computers and Humans Apart). Developed by researchers at Carnegie Mellon University, CAPTCHA is a visual display of characters that a human can read and then enter into a survey but a computer cannot, thus providing an additional layer of security (Rosen, Harrell, & Yu, 2007). In addition, the agency decided that no respondent identifying information or historical data would be sent with the request to complete the questionnaire, thus easing previous security concerns. The procedure the agency developed also allowed fewer edits to be performed and required that data be entered in one session on the computer. The resulting advantages included respondents spending less time reporting, respondents not having to remember an account number and password, and the survey being easier to use. This procedure was found to produce higher response rates but was recognized as not being appropriate for complex surveys when a respondent is likely to have to interrupt the process of responding to look up data or obtain them from someone else.

EMBEDDED E-MAIL

Although asking respondents to answer questions embedded in e-mails preceded use of the Web as a usable survey technique, it was often a frustrating response mechanism for both survey sponsors and respondents (Dillman, 2000a, pp. 361–372; Schaefer & Dillman, 1997). In essence, it involved inserting a text reply into a message; however, the added text changed some of the usual structures and visual presentation of the questions. For example, adding an X or numbers to an answer space would shift the original text to the right, sometimes causing it to wrap onto the next line and thereby affecting all lines below it. Simply put, responding to a text e-mail message was awkward. In addition, summarizing answers involved printing out the full text of a returned e-mail and performing separate data entry. Yet for very short surveys, this somewhat primitive technique was quite useful.

Software now exists that allows survey designers to embed formatted questions into e-mails. For example, the International Price Program has tested the use of e-mail using commercial software to develop, send, and retrieve data (Fast, 2006). Switching to e-mail is convenient for respondents. However, current applications have been limited because some respondents' e-mail applications do not support HTML formatting, and the software allows only limited editing to be done. Sending and responding to e-mails also appears to have greater security risks than other forms of responding. Nonetheless, its use in a pilot test obtained response rates comparable to or higher than those obtained by touchtone data entry and resulted in considerable positive feedback.

The U.S. Bureau of Labor Statistics also uses e-mail and off-the-shelf software for the CES survey data collection. Concerns with its use include not being able to perform data edits due to security issues. Also, some Internet service providers with aggressive spam blockers may prevent the questionnaire from going through to respondents. The search for ways to improve e-mail data collection continues, and in February 2007 e-mail was incorporated as one of the CES survey data collection modes (Rosen et al., 2007).

Electronic Data Collection

In contrast to web and Web-lite applications, electronic data collection uses printable forms in a portable document file (PDF) format. The Bureau of Economic Analysis uses this method to collect data for 16 mandatory establishment surveys on direct investments, multinational company operations, and trade in services (Ku-Graf, 2007). Java applets in the respondent's browser are used to collect data on printable forms that can be answered online or offline. Developmental efforts were begun in the late 1990s and implemented in early 2000. To address security issues, data collected by the Bureau of Economic Analysis are encrypted in transit using unique passwords for each respondent.

The percentage of questionnaires completed electronically increased from about 10% in 2001 to 22% in 2006, but mail remains the major source for responses. The advantages of this form of electronic data collection are improved timeliness, reduced costs and time frame for accessing reported data, and increased data integrity through the elimination of keypunch errors. But this mode also has high maintenance costs and requires attention to password maintenance (Ku-Graf, 2007). This system of responding is now being expanded to all Bureau of Economic Analysis surveys.

The Energy Information Administration also uses electronic data collection but in a different way. They provide spreadsheets to respondents that can be completed and returned through a secure electronic system. The Australian Bureau of Statistics has also developed the use of spreadsheets in response to the Australian Electronic Transnation Act of 1999, which requires that all businesses that want to report electronically be accommodated. Although they are not used as the principal mode of collection, 40 different Australian Bureau of Statistics surveys make some use of spreadsheet forms for reporting establishment data (Farrell, Hewett, Rowley, Van Ede, & Burnside, 2007).

Another electronic option that seems likely to see greater use in the future is a combination of these two forms, whereby respondents enter data into fillable PDF forms that are set up so that responses can be read directly into a spreadsheet, thus eliminating printing or data entry. As familiarity with and use of this technology develop, this option seems likely to be used by more survey organizations as an alternative to the Web. It also has the potential for dealing with encryption in a more efficient way than do certain other modes of responding.

Fax

Often when people are asked to transfer bank account, Social Security, and other sensitive information, they use a facsimile machine just to be on the "safe side." Using faxes that go through telephone landlines is perceived as a safer mode of sending information than doing it over the Internet. In addition, for some faxing is simply easier because it does not require passwords and encoding. In essence, faxing is sending paper forms back in a quicker way than postal mail allows.

Automated fax machines are now quite different than the slow, one-page-at-a-time communication devices once used for sending interoffice messages. These high-volume machines are used in several notable surveys, such as the monthly CES survey in which data collection is carried out in an approximately 2-week window. The Energy Information Administration also uses faxing to avoid slowdowns caused by mail screening, as discussed previously. Respondents who do not want to respond electronically to their surveys are provided with the alternative of returning their forms by fax. Thus, fax remains an important way for many establishments to collect completed paper surveys.

TOUCHTONE DATA ENTRY

Touchtone data entry involves calling a toll-free number, listening to a written script in conjunction with directions given over the telephone, and then punching in answers to questions using numbers on the telephone keypad or in some instances speaking them out loud. This method has been used for a number of years for establishment surveys. It was introduced for this purpose in 1986 by the Bureau of Labor Statistics in the CES survey and was followed by the addition of voice recognition in 1988. The CES survey is a fairly simple survey requiring the reporting of a few employment numbers each month, so respondents who use touchtone data entry become quite familiar with both the survey and the way to enter their answers. Yet it is a laborious method of reporting, requiring concentration and the careful punching of numbers. It also requires reminders of when the numbers need to be reported. Touchtone data entry response for this survey increased from 8% in 1993 to 59% in 2000. However, by May 2003, it decreased to 33% and in 2007 was down to about 20% (Rosen, 2007). Over time, greater use of the fax, electronic data interchange, and CATI have tended to reduce the use of touchtone data entry (Rosen, 2007).

WHICH MODE IS BEST?

When we began writing this chapter, we were impressed with how much change had occurred since the publication of the previous edition of this book in 2000. We were even more intrigued with how much additional change seems likely to continue. However, the trajectory of that change seems consistent with the overall theme of this book, that is, greater use of mixed-mode designs and tailoring designs to the quite different populations and situations that surveyors face.

It seems likely that more and more establishment surveys will be conducted at least in part electronically. Yet there are many barriers to achieving 100% electronic surveying, ranging from the development of capabilities for conducting surveys in different ways to the amount of security needed and how easily it can be achieved. It is against this background that we suggest some guidelines for contemplating how to achieve quality results from establishment surveys.

GUIDELINES

Guideline 12.1: Seek Answers to the 16 Questions Posed in This Chapter in Order to Methodically Plan and Develop the Establishment Survey

Discussions with first-time designers of establishment surveys have suggested to us that one of the main reasons for failing at doing establishment surveys is that sponsors do not recognize how different such surveys are than the typical individual-person surveys described in survey methods texts. Moreover, the enormous differences among establishment surveys add an additional layer of complexity. Answering the 16 questions posed earlier in this chapter helps one consider the many aspects that must be given attention at various stages of the design process.

One of the changes we have observed since completing the second edition of this book is how much more likely designers of major establishment surveys are to interact with likely respondents during the initial design stages in order to get a sense of procedures that will work or not work in surveying certain types of establishments. One aspect of this is conducting cognitive interviews to test proposed questionnaires, a process that was not routinely done in the 1990s but has now become required in some agencies. In addition, informal contacts with potential respondents have been used to pose many of the 16 questions presented earlier in this chapter, so that from the beginning of the design process procedures are proposed that have a greater likelihood of succeeding.

Guideline 12.2: Plan from the Beginning for a Mixed-Mode Data Collection Process

It is evident from the experiences of many surveyors that the use of multiple modes encourages response to establishment surveys. However, that encouragement happens in different ways and for different reasons in various types of establishment surveys. Some surveys have benefited from assigning different modes of response to different establishments. Respondents have preferences, and acceding to those preferences seems to encourage responses in establishment surveys (Hoffer et al., 2007). Other establishment surveys have benefited from using a mail response form to help respondents see what data are needed and begin to draft answers when the Web or some other electronic means is the desired response mechanism (Snijkers, Onat, & Vis-Visschers, 2007). It is apparent from a perusal of the practices used by a variety of government agencies and by others that surveyors have gravitated toward using multiple means of improving the speed, quality, and quantity of responses to establishment surveys.

Guideline 12.3: Identify the Most Appropriate Respondent for a Business Survey and Develop Multiple Ways of Contacting That Person

When the unit being surveyed is a business, it is often hard to know who the respondent should or will be. Thus, when contacts sent to the organization are addressed only to the organization but not to named individuals and are followed by similarly addressed reminders, it is possible that the initial contact and various follow-ups will be delivered to different people, thereby losing their effectiveness. Knowing at the beginning who the likely respondent will be (a) helps surveyors focus their communications on motivating an individual to respond, an important factor in improving responses to establishment surveys; and (b) provides assurance that their communications are being received.

Also, many of the most effective surveys use postal, e-mail, and telephone modes to interact with the same respondent. Collecting contact information at the beginning of the survey process allows one to build a communication strategy with careful articulation of contacts by different means. Postal addresses can be used to send a paper copy of the questionnaire and general instructions for helping recipients organize the preparation of data for responding electronically. E-mail can be used for brief reminders, and having established an e-mail contact allows respondents to more easily ask questions of the survey sponsor. In addition to identifying the proper respondent, telephone contacts can be used at the data processing stage to clarify answers to questions and seek answers that may not have been provided by the respondent in the initial questionnaire.

Having multiple means of contact provides additional opportunities for tailoring the data collection approach to the particular survey. For example, for surveys conducted annually, such as the National Science Foundation's Graduate Student Survey (which identifies numbers, support, and minority status of students enrolled in science and engineering departments), an initial e-mail to the coordinator from the prior year is used to determine whether that person or some other person will be responsible for the current year's data collection and to confirm contact information.

Guideline 12.4: Develop a Printable Questionnaire to Support Completion of Electronic Questionnaires

The need for respondents to collect and organize exact data that may require consulting records from multiple sources within an establishment makes it important that a printed copy of each establishment survey be available to respondents, even when mail responses are not being solicited. A study by Snijkers and Lammers (2007) used paradata to examine the sequential process by which establishment survey respondents completed a web survey. Respondents used the option to print a questionnaire at different times during the response process. Some printed a copy prior to entering any responses. Others printed sections of the questionnaire midway through the response process. Printing was also done after an attempt had been made to answer all of the questions, perhaps as a means to review the responses entered or simply to obtain a copy for their records. Extensive cognitive interviews about another establishment questionnaire for which printed copies had not been provided led to requests for such a copy. It was desired because "they want to know where they are and what data they have already entered. . . . When other departments have to be consulted, separate sections of the questionnaire can be passed on in hard copy" (Snijkers et al., 2007, p. 9). A similar conclusion was reached by Dowling (2005) and Smith et al. (2007).

In some periodic national surveys, sponsors are reluctant to produce and make available printed copies of questionnaires. One reason is that the previously used paper questionnaires were formatted quite differently, and use of those questionnaires in a prior mailing or as printable PDF files may be more likely to confuse respondents than to help them. Defenders of this practice (i.e., sending web surveys without paper copies or a simple way of printing out the entire web survey) sometimes point out that web questionnaires can be printed one page at a time. However, printing in this manner often makes it difficult to reconstruct the questionnaire, especially when question numbers are not used, as is the practice of some web surveyors.

Printed copies can be delivered in multiple ways; one is through postal delivery. Another is to provide a feature in the web design that allows copies of the entire questionnaire and sections, as well as any overall instructions, to be printed during the response process, such as in the study reported by Snijkers and Lammers (2007) that was described previously. It is also possible to deliver PDFs as e-mail attachments that introduce the survey and try to help respondents organize the response process.

Guideline 12.5: Use Principles of Visual Design to Guide Respondents through the Pages of Questionnaires

In Chapters 4, 5, and 6, we presented concepts and principles for designing questions and constructing questionnaires in ways that enhance comprehension and understanding. These concepts also need to be applied to the development of establishment surveys, which by their nature tend to be more complex. At the beginning of this chapter, we showed a questionnaire developed in an older construction style that lacked a navigational path (see Figure 12.1). The next page of that questionnaire, which is shown in Figure 12.3, asks

Figure 12.3 Difficult-to-navigate page from old-style mail industrial research and development questionnaire.

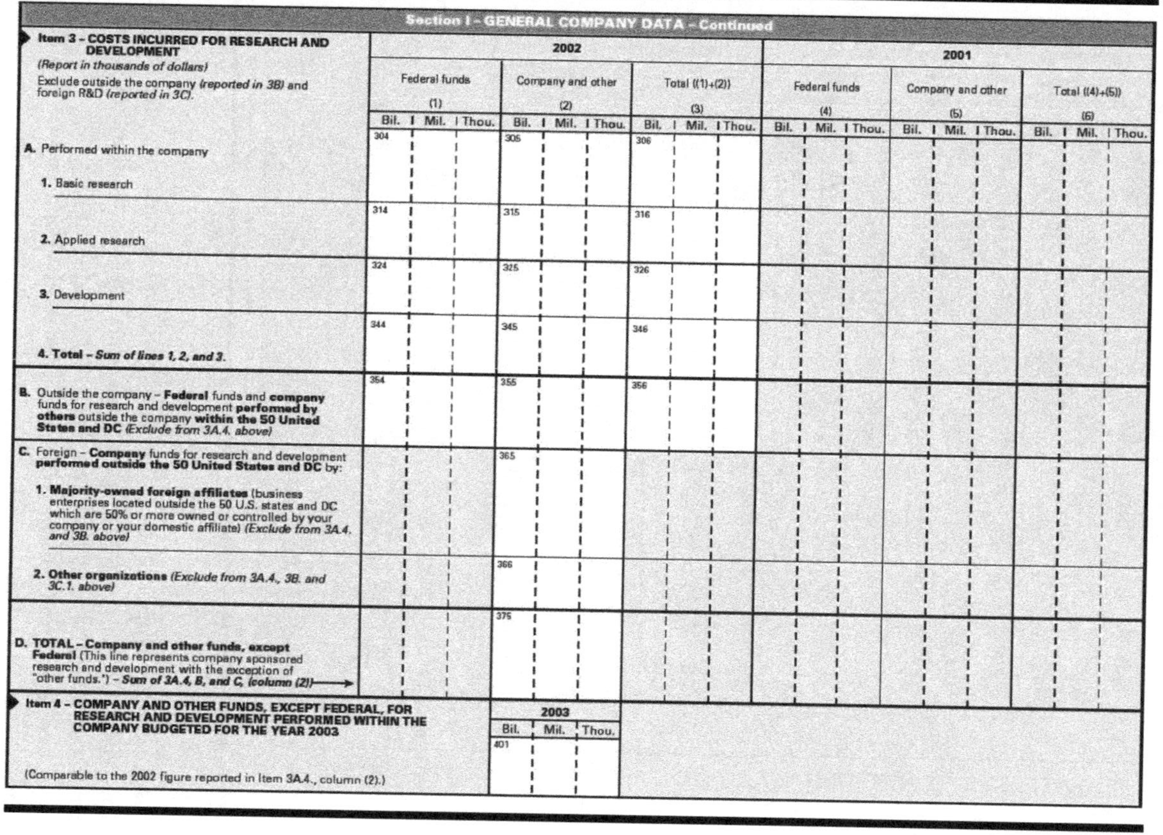

Figure 12.4 Test revision of page from Figure 12.3 done to simplify and clarify communication and navigation.

SECTION 1. GENERAL COMPANY DATA - Continued

DRAFT 2

▷ **Item 3** – How much of the costs incurred by your company for research and development in 2002 was: *(Report in thousands of dollars)*

	Federal funds spent within your company (1)			Company and other funds (2)			Total ((1) + (2)) (3)		
	Bil.	Mil.	Thou.	Bil.	Mil.	Thou.	Bil.	Mil.	Thou.
A Performed within the company									
1. Basic research 2002									
Amount reported in 2001	4	500	000	1	100	000	5	600	000
2. Applied research 2002									
Amount reported in 2001	4	230	000	1	000	000	5	230	000
3. Development 2002									
Amount reported in 2001	24	300	000	4	500	000	28	800	000
4. Total (Sum of lines 1,2, and 3) 2002									
Amount reported in 2001	33	159	000	5	600	000	39	759	000

B Performed by others within the United States and DC, but outside the company *(Exclude from A above)* 2002

Amount reported in 2001 | 2 | 457 | 000 | 1 | 080 | 000 | 3 | 517 | 000

C Performed outside the 50 United States and DC by:

	Bil.	Mil.	Thou.
1. Majority-owned foreign affiliates (business enterprises located outside the 50 U.S. States and DC which are 50% or more owned or controlled by your company or your domestic affiliate)*(Exclude from A and B above)* 2002			
Amount reported in 2001	2	500	000
2. Other organizations *(Exclude from A, B and C1 above)* 2002			
Amount reported in 2001	1	123	900

D TOTAL – Company and other funds, except Federal (This line represents company sponsored research and development with the exception of "other funds") – Sum of A.4, B and 3C.1 (column (2)) 2002

Amount reported in 2001 | 4 | 500 | 000

▷ **Item 4** – How much of the costs incurred for research and development performed within the company was budgeted for the year 2003 *(Report in thousands of dollars)* 2003

Company and other funds budgeted for 2003 | Bil. | Mil. | Thou.

respondents to report costs incurred for research and development for 2002 in the white areas. To assist respondents, the costs reported in 2001 are printed in brown (seen here as gray) areas.

A proposed revision of this form that uses visual layout principles discussed earlier in this book is presented in Figure 12.4. In this revision, the page has been rotated into a more normal portrait position, and the dividing lines between questions have been removed in favor of a more open format. The Gestalt principle of proximity (i.e., information placed together will be seen as belonging to the same group) has been invoked to place the previous year's information underneath the white space with which it is associated, thus bringing it within the foveal view of the answer spaces for the current year's data. Items 2 and 3 have also been reworded as questions rather than truncated phrases (as recommended in Guideline 4.7 in Chapter 4). The goal of redesigning the questionnaire in this way was to make it easier to comprehend and navigate. This is only one example of how visual design principles might be used and applied to improve questionnaires. Other examples are included in Morrison et al. (in press), Snijkers et al. (2007), Conrad (2007), and Dillman et al. (2005).

Guideline 12.6: Apply Similar Principles of Visual Layout to Both Paper and Electronic Questionnaires, Including Numbering All Questions

The "culture" of developing web questionnaires has encouraged many surveyors to think of them as needing to be different than paper questionnaires. One example is discouraging designers from numbering questions on the Web. This somewhat conventional web design decision is problematic in establishment surveys because the lack of numbering makes it difficult for respondents to make connections between an electronic and paper version of the same questionnaire. Other examples of differences include using circles (radio buttons) for single-answer questions and check boxes for multiple-answer questions (e.g., race and ethnicity categories) and reserving underlining to signify hyperlinks on the Web. But the use of these elements is quite different in paper questionnaires. In addition, web questionnaires can have definitions that float above words and periodic messages that summarize previously given answers so respondents can know whether answers to a series of questions were given correctly. For example, after a series of questions about one's farming operation, the respondent is informed as follows: "You have indicated that in 2006 you owned 2,400 acres, rented an additional 1,200 acres, and 3,100 of these 3,600 acres were planted to crops in that year." Messages like this help respondents overcome inadvertent errors. It is also possible to provide error messages when an answer is outside the range of expected answers and to provide automatic calculation tools to keep running totals (percentage of time allocated to different tasks), which are especially important in many establishment surveys. In our view, these are appropriate differences between the Web and mail. However, they should not prevent presenting respondents with a paper or printable version of the questions that has basic similarities in how questions are worded, ordered, and numbered. In addition, a similar visual layout (spacing, use of bold types, size and shape of answer spaces, and other graphical features) should be used for both.

The process of achieving such similarity may be more difficult than it seems at first glance. In 2002, the USDA-NASS began the process of converting an interview instrument to a mail format but with plans to ultimately develop a web version. The mail format was developed using common word

Figure 12.5 Construction rules for redesigning the Agricultural Resource Management Survey questionnaire to encourage consistency in communication and improve usability.

1. Provide a figure/ground composition that highlights answer spaces.

2. Delineate separate regions to identify thematic sections.

3. Make agency-only information less visible to respondents.

4. Use reverse print to support preattentive processing and definition of navigational path.

5. Use wording that enables sections and questions to stand alone.

6. Establish consistency in use of all symbols and graphical arrangements across questions.

7. Build in mechanisms for correcting errors.

8. Establish visual connections between pages.

9. Make hidden questions more visible.

10. Simplify each matrix by building consistency, regularity, and completeness across the many parts.

11. Place codes that the respondent is required to use near where they are to be used.

12. Provide strong visual guides for changes in respondent use of answer spaces.

Source: "Achieving Usability in Establishment Surveys through the Application of Visual Design Principles," by D. A. Dillman, A. Gertseva, and T. Mahon-Haft, 2005, *Journal of Official Statistics, 21,* pp. 183–214.

processing software rather than specialized questionnaire design software, because doing so would facilitate later development of the web questionnaire. After several revisions, certain rules of construction were developed in order to build consistency into the design. These rules are summarized in Figure 12.5 and have been described elsewhere in much greater detail (Dillman et al., 2005). The goal of this redesign was to build successful affective and cognitive usability, as described by Norman (1988, 2004), by applying visual design principles. Considerable emphasis was placed on consistency in how symbols and graphical arrangements were used across questions. An example of a paper questionnaire that followed these rules of construction is shown in Figure 12.6.

When the web page formats were constructed after the redesign was complete, scrolling was used within sections rather than asking each question on a different page. This was done to allow respondents to move up and down on the screen to check their answers and look for completeness. It also allowed for the provision of more descriptions at the beginning of each section of how questions were to be answered. These design elements were anticipated in the paper version of the questionnaire, which was built with sections that would be appropriate for the web screens. Although the web formats that were eventually developed deviated somewhat from the paper questionnaire, the transition was made much easier as a result of the design of the paper questionnaire. Moreover, the similarities between the paper and web questionnaires facilitated use of the paper format by respondents for organizing their information for later entry into the web version of the questionnaire.

Guideline 12.7: Incorporate Instructions Directly into Questions by Shortening Them and Providing Additional Detail When Necessary on Separate Web Pages

It was once commonplace to write separate instruction booklets for completing paper establishment surveys and many individual-person or household surveys. Such booklets were often as long as or longer than the questionnaire itself, as the writers attempted to anticipate every possible situation the respondent might face. Placing so much detail in these booklets allowed questionnaire designers to write questions that were shorter and to reduce the number of pages in the paper format. Inadvertently, this led to writing questions in cryptic phrases rather than as complete sentences (see Guideline 4.7 in Chapter 4). However, many of these instruction booklets (discussed in more detail in Dillman, 2000a) were rarely used by respondents when answering the questionnaires.

The shift toward designing web questionnaires made it possible to present instructions in different ways. First, the pressure for limiting the number of pages was reduced. Second, the need to make individual pages more self-standing was recognized. Thus, essential instructions could be, and needed to be, inserted with the question itself. In addition, it became possible to allow the definition of a word to appear by floating the cursor above the word. It also became possible to place the answer to an anticipated question one click away behind a hyperlink.

However, research on the use of instructions is not particularly encouraging with respect to how often respondents use them. A series of studies discussed by Tourangeau et al. (2007) showed that the more effort respondents have to make in accessing instructions, the less likely they are to access

Figure 12.6 Old and revised Agricultural Resource Management Survey questionnaire using rules from Figure 12.5.

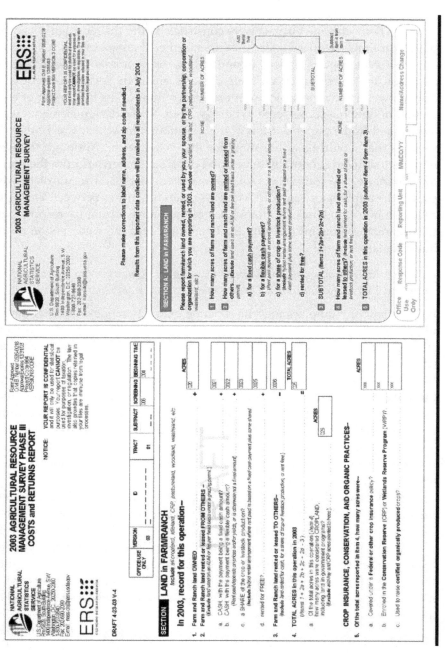

Source: "Achieving Usability in Establishment Surveys through the Application of Visual Design Principles," by D. A. Dillman, A.

and use them. For example, placing material in the periphery of screens makes it less likely to be used, and the likelihood of use also decreases with increases in the number of mouse clicks needed to access material (i.e., no click is best, followed by a single click and then multiple clicks).

In many respects, the little-used instruction books were a product of an earlier time when communication between surveyors and respondents was more difficult and survey designers attempted to anticipate every possible question and make an answer available in writing. Now, e-mail contacts make it possible to get quick answers to questions that only a few people might like to know. Even when studies are conducted completely by postal mail and the telephone, it is still possible to place answers to questions on a web page in an easily searchable format, making the detailed printed instruction booklets a thing of the past. An example of incorporating instructions directly into questions is shown in Figure 12.7. This example is from the Annual Enterprise Survey conducted by Statistics New Zealand. Incorporation of instructions has long been used in this survey and is facilitated by the use of a lighter shading around the instructions, which are located appropriately between the query and the answer space where they will be most needed.

Guideline 12.8: Incorporate Editing Functions into Interactive Electronic Questionnaires, but Do So Judiciously

One of the advantages of web questionnaires is the ability to build in edits (i.e., verification steps) that help respondents correct errors and avoid leaving questions blank and that provide totals for respondents to see whether they have answered questions correctly (e.g., percentage of office time spent on a number of different activities). These verification steps can be quite effective in eliminating logical errors in surveys, pointing out conflicting answers to respondents, and saving survey staff a considerable amount of time and effort needed for calling respondents to correct errors. Although they can be helpful, they can also cause problems if their use is pushed to an extreme by not allowing a correct (though extreme) answer to be reported. They can also have the unintended consequence of preventing a respondent from moving forward until a particular question is answered, even though the respondent cannot correctly answer it.

Two schools of thought have emerged on the use of edits in business surveys. One school is to maximize their use in order to save the time and effort of the survey staff. The other is to minimize the use of edits to avoid making respondents angry. An argument for moderation in their use has been offered by Erikson (2007). Although noting that increasing the burden at the responding stage eliminates the need to recontact respondents, he also noted that the use of edits to overcome the weaknesses of a question is a bad survey practice. Our discussion of this issue with a number of survey designers has

Figure 12.7 Example of respondent-friendly business survey page from the New Zealand Annual Enterprise Survey that effectively incorporates instructions with questions.

Page 5

Expenditure

12 **Payments to subcontractors and labour only contractors** 1211 $ 000

13 **Purchase of goods and materials** 1101 $ 000

Include items such as:
- Purchase of materials and equipment
- Goods purchased for resale

14 **For any of the items in questions 12 to 13, please advise any significant differences between this financial year and the previous financial year (eg increase in expenditure due to a lower exchange rate)**

15 **Workplace injury insurance expenses**

Include items such as:
- Workplace injury insurance premiums
- Employer levies paid to ACC (Accident Compensation Corporation)

On behalf of working proprietors and partners	+	Paid employees	=	Total payments to insurers/ACC
2601 $ 000		2611 $ 000		1401 $ 000

16 **Employer contributions to superannuation, pension, and welfare schemes**

Include items such as:
- Withholding tax on contributions to superannuation funds
- Payments for healthcare and medical insurance

On behalf of working proprietors and partners	+	Paid employees	=	Total employer contributions
2602 $ 000		2612 $ 000		1402 $ 000

17 **Salaries and wages paid**

Include items such as:
- Employee ACC contributions
- Severance and redundancy payments
- Sick and holiday pay
- Directors' fees
- Bonus and other performance payments (eg commissions)
- Other employment related expenses

Exclude:
- Capitalised salaries and wages
- Fringe Benefit Tax

Paid to working proprietors and partners	+	Paid employees	=	Total salaries and wages paid
2603 $ 000		2613 $ 000		1403 $ 000

Please estimate the amount included in the above total salaries and wages paid that was:

a) Severance and redundancy payments 2649 $ 000

b) Bonus payments 2650 $ 000

Source: Annual Enterprise Survey, 2002–2003, by Statistics New Zealand, accessed June 2, 2008, from http://www2.stats.govt.nz/domino/external/quest/sddquest.nsf/byName?openview.

also produced concern that building in too many edits may force a respondent to provide dishonest answers when it would often be more useful to ask why the respondent cannot answer a particular question. Another downside of building in edits is that the more such edits are used, the more likely it is that errors will be made in programming the survey. This issue remains controversial in the design of business surveys. For now surveyors should balance their needs for obtaining high-quality data from respondents and decreasing clarification follow-ups against reducing respondent burden and providing ways for respondents to move on when answers do not conform with designer assumptions and expectations.

Guideline 12.9: Tailor the Communication Strategy toward Function and Timing as Well as Response Rate Concerns

In the mail-only era, discussions of communication strategies often started by deciding how many contacts were to be made and when. For certain large economic surveys, this led to the practice of contacts being sent multiple mailings weeks or months apart (e.g., an initial mailing that included the questionnaire and when it was due [often 2–3 months away]; a reminder near the due date; a later follow-up that return of the questionnaire was overdue; second and third reminders, often using the same verbiage, that the questionnaire was overdue; and then a shift to telephone for selected respondents such as the largest employers who accounted for a disproportionate part of the activity in a particular industry). Each contact took effort and entailed cost. In addition, a great deal of time was often spent deciding what information would go into each letter and what information would not, making it necessary to satisfy the interests of many different people and divisions within an organization.

The ease of sending communications in the computerized world makes it possible to think differently about the frequency and content of communications and also the most appropriate mode of contact. A focus can be placed on the task each communication needs to accomplish, when it is best for it to occur, and how it will support the overall response process (as discussed in Chapter 7). Moreover, because of the mandatory response requirement, some government surveys' response rates may be less of a concern than the length of time required for getting a survey finished.

An attempt to remedy the problem of shortening a nearly 8-month data collection period for a survey was reported by Britt and Featherston (2007). The National Science Foundation Survey of Research and Development Expenditures is an annual voluntary survey conducted of some 700 colleges and universities since 1973. It has established a pattern of being able to obtain a response rate of more than 90% each year. The data, which are of national policy interest, are also of considerable interest to the institutions that provide them as they allow participants to see how they rank compared to all other universities. During the past decade the number of contacts made with institutions increased significantly, but the length of time required to reach closeout appeared stuck at around 30 weeks. Many of those contacts were similar if not identical e-mails reminding participants that they had not yet responded and emphasizing the need to ask for and receive an "extension" for submitting their responses. As many as 15 contacts were thus sent to a single person. In addition, some e-mails had gravitated toward being system oriented (e.g., having to go to a web site and check in after the first contact rather that only replying to an e-mail) just to let the sponsors know that the previous year's respondent was correct for the coming year.

The contact strategy developed by Britt and Featherston was significantly different (e.g., asking for a simple reply to an e-mail about whether the person was the correct respondent for the new year's data collection). The strategy also used fewer contacts, with a change in emphasis from set deadlines toward the need to release the final results more quickly so they could be more useful. To encourage the last holdouts to reply, the surveyors explained to the respondents that the National Science Foundation did not want to release the data without presidents of the institutions being aware that their institution would not be included in the new data set. The result of this change in procedure led to a slight increase in response rates for 2006 (97% compared to 93%–94% for the previous 3 years). But, even more important, closeout was achieved in only 17 weeks instead of the 26 to 34 weeks it took in the previous 3 years.

The importance of this redeveloped strategy is that it represented a rethinking of the approach used for communicating with respondents. Specific communications were aimed more at developing a thoughtful, mutually supportive set of communications (as described in Chapter 7) within the context of a survey valued by the leaders of the responding institutions. The procedure of bombarding nonrespondents with nearly the same message over and over, made easy by the use of e-mails and telephone for this relatively small survey, was replaced with a strategy that was tailored to the response situation.

In the mail survey era of the 1990s, discussions about communications were often budget discussions in which sponsors would discuss the number of contacts that could be afforded, the content of each contact, and the timing. The decisions were heavily influenced by a one-size-fits-all approach of using quite similar strategies across all surveys or across all respondents in the population. We believe it is increasingly essential, as well as possible, to tailor communication strategies to the survey situation.

Guideline 12.10: Make Access Codes and Passwords for Respondents Easy to Locate and Use

The difficulty of sending, receiving, and using passwords and other access information in order to fill out establishment surveys remains one of the major barriers to the greater use of the Web and other electronic means. A conversation several years ago with sponsors of an industry survey illustrates the problem being faced in one agency. It was determined by agency administrators that because of security concerns and confidentiality promises, none of the survey access information could be sent by e-mail. This meant that the receiver would not be able to simply click on a link and enter the password. It was also determined that the information had to be sent separately from the postal mailing that included the questionnaire and instructions for how to respond to the survey. In addition, because of the size of the survey and different locations from which the information would be sent, the contacts were spaced as much as 2 weeks apart. Thus, it was left to the recipient of the request to connect three separate contacts—two postal and one e-mail—in order to respond to the survey. Moreover, as a consequence of these delivery rules, if the access information was lost, it could not be obtained by e-mail or telephone. Instead it had to be sent by postal mail a second time. The situation was not helped by the fact that the password and access information were quite long and contained a random combination of letters and numbers that made them virtually impossible to remember and difficult to enter correctly. Moreover, they could not be changed. Finally, because the survey was repeated annually, it was expected that each year there would be a new set of passwords used to gain entrance.

It is difficult to argue against reasonable security requirements in today's world, especially for surveys that involve confidential information that the organization being surveyed does not want others to know. However, having to connect disparate pieces of information sent in separate communications adds significantly to the burden of responding and greatly complicates the already challenging task of getting all survey communications past gatekeepers and into the hands of the proper respondent. The need to find a middle ground between designing laborious, hard-to-navigate security procedures that are both difficult and annoying to respondents on the one hand, and providing an adequate level of security on the other hand, remains one of the most significant barriers to the use of the Web and other electronic reporting procedures for some agencies.

Guideline 12.11: When Supporting Information Comes from Multiple Senders,
Consider Limiting the Sources of the Contacts and Use a Common Return Address

Among the defining attributes of the computerized world are a sharp division of labor, the efficiency of communication that stems from individual e-mail addresses, and the ability of many people to interact with one another at any given time. Unfortunately, these otherwise desirable features of organizational efficiency can create problems for survey implementation.

Frequently, surveys sponsored by a federal agency are contracted out to an organization that implements them. In an effort to define a survey as legitimate, it may be decided that the agency director as well as the project administrator should communicate directly with respondents as needed. Within the data contracting organization, it may also be decided that different people may have separate needs to communicate with respondents for various reasons, from answering questions about why a postal mailing was not received or how to obtain password information to discussing how to upload data files appropriately. Also, some of the mailings may contain a variety of e-mail addresses and phone numbers for different purposes, from contact information for an institutional review board to contact information for different people in both the sponsoring agency and contracting organization. When the respondent receives postal letters and e-mails from a variety of people and addresses, confusion often results, especially when the recipient tries to retrieve an essential piece of information but cannot remember the name of the person or the e-mail address from which it originated. Thus, what starts out as an effort to increase efficiency and effectiveness by the agency and contractor creates a high-cost situation for respondents. This can also undermine the importance of using multiple contacts if respondents do not connect the various contacts with one another.

To simplify the process for the respondent, it is desirable to limit the number of different people using their own e-mail addresses or postal return addresses who have direct contact with respondents. It is also important to make sure that information on e-mail addresses (and the name of the sender that will show up in one's reader file if different from the e-mail address) is in postal mailings and to either use a common e-mail address for all communications or make secondary reference in e-mails to other addresses. Few things can be as frustrating for respondents as deciding in response to one communication to complete a survey but not being able to locate essential information provided earlier from another source.

Guideline 12.12: Use Incentives When Appropriate, but Cautiously

Small financial incentives can be useful in certain kinds of establishment surveys but not others. Some organizations have rules against employees receiving any money or gifts, and if this is the case sending something in appreciation for completing a survey would be inappropriate as well as actually discourage a survey response. At the other extreme, the use of incentives is traditional, for example in physician surveys.

The closer a business comes to being an individually owned and operated organization, the more likely it is that incentives will be considered appropriate and will be effective. As discussed in Chapter 7, token financial incentives are very powerful as a means of encouraging survey response when provided in advance. They can be similarly powerful in certain establishment surveys, for example to get past gatekeepers.

As discussed in Chapter 7, Moore and Ollinger (2007) showed that cash incentives can be effective in a variety of settings. For example, in a survey of physicians in health maintenance organizations, response rates were nearly doubled from 43% to 80% by using priority (rather than regular first-class) mail and including $10 with both the initial and replacement mailing. One feature of this experiment that is unusual with regard to incentives is that the use of an incentive in a replacement mailing was effective, adding 10 percentage points when it was used. In a separate experiment, they showed that the double use of incentives was similarly effective in surveys of meat manufacturers, grain warehouses and shippers, and environmental management groups in various industries (Ollinger & Moore, 2007). The breadth of their findings across groups is considerable, thus suggesting that incentives have an important role to play in obtaining responses to certain establishment surveys and that their effect may differ in establishment surveys from that in individual-person surveys (i.e., incentives included with the second contact have not been found to be effective in individual-person surveys).

Many sponsors of government establishment surveys are reluctant to use cash incentives for these surveys because of the image that the sending of cash by mail may convey with regard to the use of government funds. For example, instead of sending cash, a study conducted by the USDA provided a $20 cash card that could be redeemed by the recipient in any automatic teller machine. Use of this procedure resulted in response rates of 41% when sent in regular mail and 44% when sent by priority mail compared to only 30% for no incentive by regular mail. Follow-up by enumerators raised the response rates to 70% and 72%, respectively, compared to 63% for the control. Because enumerator costs were reduced significantly, the overall costs per respondent were about $20 less when the incentive was used than were costs for the control group (Ott & Beckler, 2007). Respondents were far more likely than nonrespondents to convert the card for cash. Overall, the incentive method used here, and demonstration of its effectiveness for obtaining response to a long difficult survey, suggests a procedure easier to defend in a federal government survey than simply sending cash to all sample units. Finally, these studies as well as others suggest that cash or cash equivalent incentives can be quite effective for improving response rates in certain kinds of establishment surveys.

CONCLUSION

In 2000, when the second edition of this book appeared, we were cautiously optimistic that the transition to Internet data collection for establishment surveys would be fairly quick. It also seemed to us that the Internet would help eliminate out-of-date mail construction methods and encourage the development of compatibility between mail and the Web. Whereas for some establishment surveys that has happened, for others it has clearly not. Instead, we have witnessed the development of a variety of electronic procedures, resulting in a greater degree of tailoring than had previously been imagined.

The great heterogeneity in how establishment surveys are conducted discussed in this chapter is partly the result of sponsorship effects, which we described in Chapter 11. However, it also stems from enormous differences in the nature of such surveys that range from collecting answers to a few questions every month to making one-time efforts to collect information for surveys that have not been previously undertaken.

The challenge now facing designers of establishment web surveys seems to us to have little to do with the limitations of web technology or a general inability or unwillingness of potential respondents to use it. Instead, the barriers seem to be associated more with the difficulty of ensuring adequate security for surveys to which responses are sometimes mandatory, integrating communications and those security requirements with requests to be surveyed, mixing modes in response to preferences of respondents, and, in general, handling the interface between potential respondents and the survey. Few surveying challenges are as difficult as achieving the Web's potential for collecting information from establishments. We continue our discussion of some of the challenges of continuing the transition to greater use of the Web in the final chapter of this book.

LIST OF GUIDELINES

Guideline 12.1: *Seek answers to the 16 questions posed in this chapter in order to methodically plan and develop the establishment survey*

Guideline 12.2: *Plan from the beginning for a mixed-mode data collection process*

Guideline 12.3: *Identify the most appropriate respondent for a business survey and develop multiple ways of contacting that person*

Guideline 12.4: *Develop a printable questionnaire to support completion of electronic questionnaires*

Guideline 12.5: *Use principles of visual design to guide respondents through the pages of questionnaires*

Guideline 12.6: *Apply similar principles of visual layout to both paper and electronic questionnaires, including numbering all questions*

(continued)

Guideline 12.7: Incorporate instructions directly into questions by shortening them and providing additional detail when necessary on separate web pages

Guideline 12.8: Incorporate editing functions into interactive electronic questionnaires, but do so judiciously

Guideline 12.9: Tailor the communication strategy toward function and timing as well as response rate concerns

Guideline 12.10: Make access codes and passwords for respondents easy to locate and use

Guideline 12.11: When supporting information comes from multiple senders, consider limiting the sources of the contacts and use a common return address

Guideline 12.12: Use incentives when appropriate, but cautiously

CHAPTER 13

Coping with Uncertainty

THE TECHNOLOGICAL and cultural changes introduced in Chapter 1 and discussed throughout this book have dramatically increased the number and variety of surveys being conducted. The diversity and complexity of the surveys conducted in this rapidly changing survey environment have magnified the importance of tailoring survey designs to respond to the needs of the particular survey situation. As surveyors strive to meet their goals within tighter budgets and often shorter survey periods, tailoring to the survey topic, sponsorship, and population continue to be critical; however, the diversity within populations requires even more tailoring throughout the design. In addition, the challenge of balancing the four sources of survey error (coverage, sampling, nonresponse, and measurement) has intensified as new modes have been introduced, respondents have become more difficult to reach, and the use of mixed-mode surveys has increased.

In this turbulent survey environment, the Internet or other new technologies have not completely replaced more established modes such as in-person, mail, and telephone surveys, nor does this seem likely to happen in the near future. Instead, the survey community is faced with a situation, which we expect to continue, in which surveyors need to understand the strengths and weaknesses of each survey mode and how these modes can be used together in different ways to conduct high-quality sample surveys. Thus, in this final chapter we discuss the future of Internet, mail, and mixed-mode surveys as well as the larger survey environment.

WHY ARE ALL SURVEYS NOT CONDUCTED VIA THE INTERNET?

In today's world, there are fewer and fewer important transactions that cannot be done over the Internet, and increasingly the Internet has become a primary source of information for many. Using the Internet offers significant reductions in time, energy, and cost from other ways of accomplishing many tasks. Even a casual look at lifestyles in the United States makes it clear that the Internet is now a central aspect of most people's lives. For example:

- Answers to specific questions such as how to get from one place to another, how to contact a local business, and what the treatments are for specific health conditions can often be obtained more quickly and in more detail than through any other source.
- Searches for virtually any information that in the past required a trip or trips to a good library or bookstore and hours or even days to complete can now be done electronically in minutes, and a variety of sources can be consulted, including multiple libraries across the country and world.
- Communication among friends and relatives, whether they are within the same city or countries apart, can be maintained at very low cost through the immediate sharing of pictures and experiences by e-mail and instant messaging as well as through faxes and telephone calls placed over the Internet.
- Songs, entire albums, television shows, and movies can be listened to or watched online or can be purchased and downloaded for later use on a variety of devices.
- Purchasers of airline tickets and hotel rooms experience greater choice and often lower prices when using the Internet rather than a telephone operator or travel agency.
- Weather and travel advisories can be obtained more quickly, more reliably, and in greater detail than through any other means.
- Items that cannot be purchased locally can be purchased over the Internet, often at low prices, in a few minutes and with a few clicks of a mouse.
- Newspaper, magazine, and other deliveries can be started and stopped over the Internet.
- Up-to-date bank, investment, and credit card balances are available over the Internet, and people who wish to do so can make payments electronically. In addition, federal and many state tax returns can be filed electronically, and a refund may often be received within days or weeks, rather than months.

- Eligible people can sign up for Social Security and other government programs online with much less effort than by making an appointment to visit a government office.

For many people, doing without Internet services such as those listed here would be a hardship, and for a lot of them, inconceivable. Increasingly, people without reliable Internet access and the skills to use it find themselves penalized when seeking needed information and services. In this context, it would seem that surveying would fall in line to occur mostly over the Internet. Yet that has not yet happened for a number of reasons.

THE UNCONNECTED AND THE POORLY CONNECTED

As discussed in Chapter 3, the major challenge facing those who wish to conduct Internet surveys in the United States is that a substantial portion of the general public are not connected at all (so they cannot respond to web surveys) or are connected via slow lines (and thus are hampered in responding). In addition, the demographic characteristics of individuals who lack Internet access are quite different from those who have access. Older people (particularly those 65 and older), non-Whites, people with lower income, less educated people, and people living in rural areas have lower Internet access rates than their counterparts and are less likely to have high-speed connections. Therefore, they are more likely to be left out of Internet surveys, and people within these groups who have Internet access may differ considerably from those who do not.

Good high-speed connections are becoming critical for encouraging people to connect to web surveys and respond. However, although many argue that complete Internet coverage will happen in the near future, society has not yet reached that reality and is unlikely to do so in the short term. The speed of adoption of broadband connections has slowed considerably (Horrigan & Smith, 2007), as has been the case with most innovations after a critical mass has been reached. This situation also reflects the substantial education and wealth disparities that now characterize the United States and that may be growing wider. The cost of purchasing computers, software, and broadband connections has contributed to the slowing of Internet adoption. In addition, even if some people want to purchase a high-speed Internet connection, their location may make it difficult for them to access it, particularly at affordable prices.

Thus, surveyors cannot ignore people who are not connected to the Internet. The coverage issue means that many households are not included in Internet surveys, and the groups who are even less likely to be connected are often of great interest to government and policy makers as well as other surveyors wishing to accurately represent the general population in the

United States. Attempts to use an "Internet-only" approach to surveying have resulted in the development of volunteer panels whose members are surveyed repeatedly, with inevitable conditioning and attrition effects (as discussed in Chapter 9). These panels, the theoretical basis for which falls outside of the scientific probability model emphasized in this book, remain unacceptable for U.S. government–sponsored surveys and many others. Moreover, applying weighting techniques to account for those who are unconnected does not ensure accurate survey results.

In contrast, probability-based Internet panels will likely continue in the future; however, they may suffer from some of the challenges we discuss next. These and other mixed-mode strategies discussed in this book are a product of the effort to capture the cost efficiencies of Internet surveying and the speed at which responses can be received, while also maintaining a scientific approach to the design and implementation of sample surveys.

COMFORT AND SAFETY

Computers and methods of connecting to the Internet remain troublesome for many people, although less so than when the second edition of this book was written. Many lack the needed skills for using computers effectively, downloading browsers and other software, connecting to the Internet, avoiding viruses, and troubleshooting other problems. When automobiles were relatively new during the early part of the twentieth century, they broke down constantly and needed frequent repair. The same was true of color television sets during the middle of the century, although both have become far more reliable in recent decades. But even now, as familiarity increases and breakdowns and system crashes become less common, the variation in people's computer knowledge and technical abilities is expanding. In addition, once people have a computer system that seems reliable and effective, they also seem less likely to constantly update and change it, perhaps following the adage "If it's not broke, don't fix it." This, too, limits the ability of people to respond to state-of-the-art web surveys.

Even when Internet coverage exists for nearly all members of a survey population, such as in some European countries, it is still difficult to get responses to Internet surveys. Whereas highly salient surveys that are well done and sent to specialized populations can obtain excellent response rates, many others obtain much lower response rates. It remains unclear whether low response stems from the fact that the task of responding to a survey on the Web is an unfamiliar experience that many try to avoid. If unfamiliarity and related discomfort is the case, the problem of low response to Internet surveys may go away with time. However, it is unclear whether people's apprehension over whether it is "safe" to respond to a survey from an unknown party will remain a barrier to response (as people become more familiar with the Internet there are also more scams being run on it).

There is a growing literature about how the web experience can be reshaped through improved survey design to increase responsiveness. Many design features—such as required responses to every question, excessive error messages, and features that take a long time to download—have been shown to increase break-offs and decrease overall response (see Chapter 6). Moreover, whereas the expense of adding additional questions in many modes encourages designers to keep their surveys short, the low marginal costs of additional questions in web surveys mean that many long questionnaires are fielded that respondents likely find tedious or even boring and that also decrease response. In addition, many web surveyors have adopted a financial exchange perspective, using postpayments for completing surveys, rather than the social exchange perspective of providing small token cash incentives in advance (see Chapter 7).

We have seen a proliferation of requests to complete web surveys and greater variation in the quality of surveys being conducted. Web surveys can now easily be conducted by individuals with programming skills or by those who lack these skills but who can use available software packages or an online service. These services have improved greatly over the past several years, and surveys of good quality can be conducted in this manner; however, many web surveys of poor quality are still being conducted. Much remains to be learned on these topics.

COMMUNICATION SYSTEMS AND TECHNOLOGY

The major Internet concern in 2000, when the previous edition of this book appeared, was whether people could connect to it, receive surveys, and respond to them. Although this remains an important concern for some groups, a major shift has occurred as the widespread use of web surveys has led to the development of more complex surveys that require equally complex, efficient, and safe e-mail-based implementation procedures. For example, some web surveys require information for a single survey to be collected from multiple respondents but lack an efficient e-mail communication system that helps respondents pass information back and forth in order to compile responses. In addition, we have seen rigid confidentiality and privacy requirements that are codified in laws and company policies make the needed efficient exchange of information impossible to achieve. In some cases, respondents have been asked to answer via the Web yet have not been allowed to communicate with the sponsor by e-mail. In other cases, such as the example discussed in Chapter 12 (Guideline 12.10), security concerns have dictated that passwords be sent only by postal contacts, separate from the survey invitation that included the web address. Both of these situations are akin to providing drivers with fast new cars without also building inter-state highways for them to drive on. In other words, the infrastructure does not yet exist to efficiently support some of the more complex web surveys that have been developed. In addition to issues of Internet penetration and online safety, the new challenge of needing an efficient communication infrastructure to support web surveys also has a restraining effect on the use of Internet surveys.

In early 2008 an interagency committee met to discuss the conversion of an establishment survey that had been conducted annually for many years by paper to the Web. Part of the conversion plan was to improve data quality by taking advantage of people's specialized knowledge, which meant having the respondent from previous years plus up to three others who could more accurately answer questions about information technology, human resources, and accounting practices complete the questionnaire. In general, using the Internet seemed the most efficient way to communicate with the primary respondent and individuals identified by her as the best people to provide the additional technical responses. The meeting began with much optimism because it was known that virtually all of the businesses to be surveyed had broadband Internet connections, and results from cognitive interviewing suggested that recipients would prefer responding over the Internet rather than by paper.

The group's optimism soon shifted to pessimism for several reasons. First, they realized that the considerable changes being proposed would likely result in respondents having many questions for the sponsor, but because of the confidentiality requirements for this survey, recipients would not be provided with an e-mail address they could use to obtain help unless a very complicated procedure for a secure transmission route was used. Second, it became clear that separate passwords might be necessary for respondents within a single establishment in order to protect the confidentiality of each respondent's answer in accordance with an applicable federal law. Not only would this requirement add a layer of complexity to the procedures, but the need to protect everyone's confidentiality in this way might also prohibit the use of a primary contact who could coordinate responses within each establishment. Third, the need to protect everyone's confidentiality greatly complicated the process of obtaining the names and contact information of the separate respondents within the organization in a timely manner. In addition, the group learned that it was not possible for passwords to be sent to anyone through e-mail, so even if the proper names were obtained, the process of getting them access to the survey would be slowed considerably. This survey ran the risk of breaking down not because of technical problems of developing, posting, and getting people to respond to an Internet survey, but because it could not be supported by an efficient electronic communication system.

Despite considerable gains in surveyors' knowledge of how to collect survey data via the Internet, this mode has not replaced other modes but instead exists alongside them. That the Internet has not become the primary survey mode of the times stems from remaining coverage limits, people's lack of comfort with and trust in Internet technology, and lack of communication systems that can support complex web surveys. In addition, the turbulence of the current survey world demands flexibility in all aspects of surveying, including what mode is selected.

THE CONTINUED RELEVANCE OF MAIL AND PAPER SURVEYS

As many of the examples we have discussed in this book illustrate, paper surveys and postal mail continue to be widely used for single-mode surveys but also increasingly in combination with other modes. In a time when declining response rates are a major concern, response rates for mail surveys can be significantly higher than those obtained by telephone and web surveys. In addition, evidence is abundant that for many surveys mail response rates have not declined over the past few decades to nearly the same extent that they have for telephone surveys (Hox & de Leeuw, 1994). There is also evidence that many people still prefer to respond to paper surveys via postal mail rather than to Internet surveys (Couper, 2005; Dillman et al., 2008). Mail and paper surveys continue to be relevant for a number of reasons, including the availability of address-based sampling lists such as the Delivery Sequence File (DSF) providing good coverage, the ability to deliver incentives and multiple follow-ups, their cost-effectiveness (especially as initial modes to precede face-to-face follow-up), and the ease with which they can be used when no sample frame exists (e.g., in customer satisfaction surveys).

Paper versus Web Surveys

One significant factor motivating the use of mail surveys is that people can design and conduct their own paper surveys but cannot do this easily for either telephone or in-person interviews. Many individuals can even take advantage of newly available technologies to improve the design of mail questionnaires and the implementation materials sent to respondents. This access remains an important aspect of the continued use of mail surveys. However, having widespread access to design and implementation tools is also becoming increasingly possible for web surveys, with new software packages that people can easily use and services available to host the survey for them.

Although mail surveys can provide adequate coverage for many populations (e.g., general population surveys) and can still produce high response rates, significant barriers remain. One of the main barriers that they face is the higher costs associated with implementing them, particularly when compared to Internet surveys, as questionnaires and contact letters must be printed, mailed, and processed for each member of the sample, and the multiple contacts necessary for high response rates also require additional resources. In addition, the lengthy field period required to conduct high-quality mail surveys prevents their use for many survey situations. Lastly, people who cannot read or who cannot read the language used in the questionnaire and those with lower levels of education are less likely to respond to mail surveys.

PAPER SURVEYS ARE EASY AND ARE PREFERRED BY SOME

Recently, while we were talking to the director of a probability-based household Internet panel in another country, the conversation turned to the extreme difficulty those researchers were having getting people who did not have Internet access to accept and use the Web as a means of responding, even when it was provided for free. She was questioning both the high cost of providing web access and of keeping such respondents in the panel. When she was asked whether a paper option had been considered for those households, and we indicated that there was very little, if any, evidence that measurement would be adversely affected in some way, her reply was immediate: "But mail is so old fashioned, I don't think that we would want to do that."

This example illustrates the coverage problem with many Internet surveys, but it also illuminates how people view mail as a "traditional" method. However, it is exactly this tradition and comfort with postal mail and the familiarity with providing information on paper forms that remain one of the strengths of this mode. There is no technological barrier with mail surveys in that most people receive and are comfortable opening postal mail (in contrast to e-mails with attachments, which many still fear opening).

In addition, there still seems to be a general preference among people for responding by mail rather than the Internet. In Chapter 7, we discussed an experiment in which significantly more people responded by mail (a) when offered that option initially and then a web option later, and (b) when offered a choice between mail and the Web from the beginning. These findings echo others in which researchers have found that when given a choice, people tend to prefer mail. Another example is the Gallup panel discussed in Chapter 9, where people who were not likely to respond via the Internet could be included in the panel by returning paper surveys by postal mail. Perhaps part of the preference for paper questionnaires is because completing them can fit more easily into downtime (e.g., when traveling, relaxing) or times when people cannot be connected online, even for those who spend a lot of time online. More research is needed to understand the basis of this apparent preference and whether it will diminish over time.

ENHANCED COVERAGE AND HIGH RESPONSE RATES

As surveyors face a situation where the incomplete coverage of web surveys remains a barrier to their use for many situations and random-digit-dialing frames are threatened by cell-only households, the U.S. Postal Service DSF provides new opportunities as a sampling frame for mail surveys. Previously, mail surveys relied on samples of listed telephone numbers for which addresses could be matched; however, the DSF includes all addresses to which the U.S. Postal Service delivers mail (see Chapter 3 for a full discussion of the DSF as a sampling frame). The excitement around this new frame is evident in the pilot study using this frame conducted in the Behavioral Risk Factor Surveillance System, sponsored by the Centers for Disease Control and Prevention (Link et al., 2008). In addition, address-based sampling is now planned as a replacement for random-digit dialing for the Nielsen TV diaries (Shuttles et al., 2008).

Early studies using this frame have shown that it can produce high response rates. The study we discussed in Chapter 7 achieved a response rate of 71% for the mail-only treatment even when individual names, which have previously been shown to increase response rates, were not used. This was considerably higher than the 55% response rate achieved in the comparison group that was asked in a postal mail letter to respond via the Web (with nonrespondents provided a paper questionnaire in follow-up contacts). In addition, Link et al. (2008) showed that response rates were significantly higher for the DSF group than for a random-digit-dialing comparison group, but mail did not do as well in reaching lower socioeconomic status groups. However, it was successful in reaching households that had cellular phones only. Their experiment also showed that the addition of names to household addresses where possible did not improve response over the address-only treatment (Link et al., 2008). These and other studies now suggest that the DSF can help overcome the coverage limits that have long plagued mail surveys and that this mode, once considered the least capable of achieving high response rates, may now be capable of achieving higher response rates than either web or telephone surveys.

PAPER AND MAIL IN MIXED-MODE DESIGNS

Another strength of mail and paper surveys is that they can be used effectively in mixed-mode design strategies (as discussed in Chapter 8). The DSF sampling frame enhances the potential for using mail in combination with other modes. Mail can be an effective way to contact people for data collection by another mode and can be used to provide token cash incentives in advance, which have been shown to increase response rates and reduce nonresponse error (see Chapter 7).

As the study discussed in Chapter 7 demonstrated, mail can be used for web surveys when no sampling frame is available to contact people and request that they respond to a survey via the Internet. Contacting respondents by mail also allows one to easily include detailed instructions (designed to help people respond via the Internet) and incentives with the contact letter. In addition, mail surveys can be an effective way to supplement web surveys, as a mail alternative can be provided for those who do not have Internet access or who are unlikely to use it even when it is provided to them (see Chapter 9 for a discussion of this as it relates to Internet panels).

Mail surveys have also been used effectively in combination with interview surveys for some time. Most often, mail is used with another mode(s) in sequence, such that people are first mailed paper questionnaires and then nonrespondents are followed up by telephone or in-person interview. The U.S. Decennial Census uses this strategy, starting with mailed questionnaires and following up via in-person interviews. In addition, handing out paper questionnaires in person remains an attractive possibility, and even a necessity, for some surveys, as discussed in Chapter 10, when no sampling frame exists for the population to be surveyed. Lastly, combining mail with telephone may be an effective way to ensure that respondents with lower education levels and household incomes will respond.

MIXED-MODE SURVEYS: A SOLUTION TO TODAY'S TURBULENCE?

Mixed-mode surveys are increasingly being conducted to respond to coverage and response rate issues facing single-mode surveys. Landline telephone coverage is declining rapidly, and declining response rates, particularly among certain groups such as young people, are a major concern for telephone surveyors. In addition, the cost and logistics of surveying people on their cell phones introduces many new challenges.

As new communication devices become available, people have changed how they relate to the telephone. In particular, the increase in the number of cell phones has resulted in the phone becoming an individually owned and controlled device rather than a household one. For a variety of reasons discussed in Chapter 1, the telephone has changed from being a required form of communication to one that is optional, where people choose when to answer it based on what they are doing, the time of day, and who is calling. These changes in telephone use also relate to people's use of computers, the Web, and other communication devices.

Although the Web offers enticing possibilities for lower cost surveying, the coverage issues facing Internet surveys remain substantial. In addition, there is no systematic way to sample e-mail addresses, and a prior relationship is needed to send e-mails to people. E-mail has quickly evolved as a source of large numbers of unwanted contacts that may even put one's computer at risk. Similarly, response rates to Internet surveys remain low, except among certain populations. Unfortunately, as happens during times of rapid change, the declining culture of favorable response surrounding the use of the telephone to complete surveys has not been replaced by a culture that is favorable to response by the Web. The fears and frustration associated with both affect what is and is not possible for conducting high-quality surveys using these methods.

Finding new ways to combat these challenges has resulted in a variety of types of mixed-mode surveys (as discussed in Chapter 8). The costs and coordination involved in conducting mixed-mode surveys have declined significantly because survey questionnaires and data can be easily moved from one mode to another and implementation can more easily be coordinated across multiple people and units. In addition, research increasingly shows that some survey modes can be used effectively to increase the likelihood that people will respond by other modes, and that it is sometimes desirable to give people alternative ways of responding to a given survey. This is particularly important because sample frames for many surveys are more likely than in the past to have incomplete listings for any single contact method as people exert greater control over how others can contact them. Overall, the challenges created by these many trends and realities have given considerable momentum to the practice of designing and implementing mixed-mode surveys. However, conducting mixed-mode surveys also raises the fundamental question of whether reductions in coverage and nonresponse error may be offset by increases in measurement error when data collected from different modes are combined or compared.

Throughout this book, we have argued that not every survey can or should be a mixed-mode design. We have discussed situations in which paper, web, and even telephone, interactive voice response, and in-person surveys can be effective stand-alone survey modes. However, we have also described increasingly prevalent situations in which one mode is insufficient for obtaining high-quality survey data, particularly when coverage and nonresponse biases for individual modes cannot be ignored. Sometimes the best decision is to use multiple modes for a survey, whereas other times the best decision is to use a single mode. In some cases it is better to avoid one mode in favor of another. Making these decisions about when to use a mixed-mode design strategy is often difficult. The tailored design approach is essential in helping with these decisions as the particular goals of the survey need to be balanced with the time and budget as well as the overall data quality required.

We have three key recommendations for the use of mixed-mode surveys. First, use one mode to encourage response by another mode in order to reduce coverage and nonresponse error. However, when possible, collect responses by only one mode to avoid introducing measurement error due to mode differences. As we have discussed throughout this book, this mixed-mode strategy can be effective for a variety of survey situations.

Second, be cautious about using more than one mode of data collection. In particular, be conservative about switching modes for different respondents as respondent differences may be confounded with measurement differences, and research has suggested that offering respondents a choice of modes can even lower response rates (see Chapter 8). Similarly, think ahead when planning longitudinal surveys, as changing modes between waves can impact the ability to effectively measure trends over time. However, for Internet panel surveys, a second mode can be used to create probability-based panels, and mail can be an effective way to survey respondents who are less likely or unable to respond via the Internet.

Third, for surveys that involve multiple modes of data collection, whenever possible first choose modes that rely on similar forms of communication (e.g., mail and the Web both rely on visual communication, whereas telephone uses aural communication, and both types of communication can be used for in-person interviews). In addition, primarily use unified mode construction, where the same question structure and wording is used in all modes to ensure that people are interpreting the question similarly across modes. However, because of the inherent differences in the capabilities of individual modes, it may be necessary to occasionally use mode-specific construction to achieve equivalency, particularly when moving across aural versus visual communication and interviewer- versus self-administered surveys.

THE IMPACT OF VISUAL DESIGN RESEARCH

Throughout the twentieth century, the focus in question and questionnaire design was on wording questions and instructions, as if only writing questions was important and not other aspects of question and questionnaire design. Cognitive interviewing was focused almost entirely on words—what do you understand this sentence to mean, what do you think that word means, and so on—and the pretesting of questionnaires also emphasized these same concerns and how interviewers influenced responses when present.

The past 20 years have seen a significant shift, as more surveyors are focusing not only on question wording but also on the visual design of questions and questionnaires. Considerable research has now shown that the visual design and layout of survey questionnaires makes a difference in how respondents organize the information and navigate the questionnaire as well as how they interpret and respond to individual questions (see detailed discussions in Chapters 4, 5, and 6). In particular, the evidence is compelling that visual design influences how people interpret the meaning of items in the questionnaire. This research has important implications for the design not only of single-mode surveys but also of mixed-mode surveys, as we have discussed in Chapter 8 and elsewhere.

For example, answer spaces convey important information in mail and web surveys, and some respondents may even focus more attention on them than on the wording of the question. The size of answer spaces and the labels provided with them influence the type and amount of information people provide. A few years ago when evaluating a proposed Decennial Census questionnaire, we noticed that some respondents tended to look at a response space before looking at the long question that preceded it. When asked the reason for this, some respondents indicated that the question looked complicated, and they explained that they commonly look first to the answer spaces to see what information is being asked for. If they cannot figure it out from the spaces, they then look to the question stem. That some respondents process in this way means that the design of questions and how response categories and spaces are labeled in mail and web surveys may be as important as the question wording in obtaining the desired answer. This situation is very different from telephone and even in-person interviews, for which a question is carefully worded so that it contains all of the detail and explanation respondents need because no visual cues can be used to help improve understanding and meaning. These issues have important implications for the design of mail and web surveys and for the design of mixed-mode data collections in which equivalency is desired across modes.

Research has consistently shown that if similar visual layouts are used for mail and web surveys, comparable results can be obtained. Thus, combining mail and the Web can be an effective way to conduct mixed-mode surveys where mail can be used to help overcome the coverage limitations of web surveys as well as the other limitations that prevent their widespread use. Similarly, the low cost of the Web means it can be used to supplement mail for respondents, especially younger ones, who are hard to reach by other modes, who are comfortable responding on the Web, and who may even prefer that mode.

THE FUTURE AND EVEN MORE INTENSE TAILORING

It was apparent in the 1990s that tailoring methods to the survey situation—and in particular populations, sponsorship, and content—was occurring with increased frequency. However, since that time, tailoring has occurred to a far greater degree than expected as surveyors have taken advantage of new as well as varied electronic alternatives and their increased abilities to match methods with multiple aspects of proposed surveys to achieve greater efficiency. Tailoring is now aimed at controlling costs; increasing the speed of response; adapting to difficult coverage, survey length, and measurement concerns; treating different people in different ways; and a host of other factors. Yet in the coming decades we expect tailoring to become even more intense.

One of the business surveys discussed in this book uses six different modes of data collection—fax, interactive voice response, Web, telephone, mail, and electronic data exchange—in an effort to give respondents what they want so they will provide a quick response that will allow reporting of results within about 2 weeks. The computerization of the survey world allows for connecting data together from multiple sources within severe time constraints. The use of multiple devices and means for responding seems likely to increase.

Another increasingly common trend in surveys is tailoring procedures to different people and organizations within one's sample frame. Many sample sources now come with additional information that can be used to decide whether to use another contact, a different kind of incentive, or even a different sequence of modes to achieve the desired response. Considering respondents' mode preference, which hardly seemed feasible in the past, is now frequently being done to decide which modes to use in both individual-person and establishment surveys. Whereas in the past surveyors often thought of questionnaires and implementation procedures separately, in today's world the communication processes that support implementation have, for some surveys, become mini-data collection processes to support the next steps of survey implementation.

Tailoring is also taking on increased importance for deciding how to ask specific questions in order to get valid measurement. Recently, one of us reviewed a questionnaire for a national survey of several hundred universities in which the respondent was being asked a series of general questions about university facilities. Because of the addition of some highly technical questions about information technology infrastructure in the last part of the questionnaire, a question was posed asking whether the respondent's university had certain technological elements. Three choices were given: yes, no, and uncertain. On the one hand, the "uncertain" category was important to offer because it was unlikely that everyone would know the answer. On the other hand, respondents who chose "uncertain" at that juncture of the questionnaire would then proceed not to answer many of the remaining follow-up questions. The proposed solution for this problem was to redesign this aspect of the questionnaire, making a greater effort just prior to the question to emphasize its importance and request that the respondent consult with someone who had the technical knowledge to answer it. Thus, an "uncertain" category that seemed an obvious choice for a technical question became an item that needed to be evaluated in terms of its effect on allowing certain respondents to continue answering when the survey objectives called for "convincing" the respondent to get help from a different respondent.

When the second edition of this book was published in 2000, the increased emphasis that the division of labor in organizations would place on finding ways to actively encourage, and even require, that respondents get help from others in providing answers to questions in establishment surveys was not anticipated. Thus, whereas "uncertain" seems such a reasonable choice for questions that are difficult to answer, the situation of providing an "out" to unknowledgeable respondents came as something of a surprise. When one shifts the survey design emphasis from tailoring a questionnaire to an individual to encouraging a multiple-person response process, it is a level of surveying that is enormously challenging.

Likewise, as the value of longitudinal surveys becomes apparent for achieving a better understanding of people's lives, new survey designs are being proposed that were simply unthinkable in the past. Recently, we learned of a proposed survey design that involved sampling women before they became pregnant and following their children into adulthood. This study would involve multiple modes of data collection as well as physical examinations and the collection of biological information. The huge initial sample sizes and selection, the necessity of obtaining equivalent measurement across modes of contact, the building of an effective communication strategy for obtaining and maintaining involvement in the study and reducing nonresponse error, and the approval of institutional review boards seem in some ways overwhelming. Yet this is the kind of survey that seems to fit well with providing the knowledge and insight that less ambitious surveys cannot provide and that society now needs.

Another growing challenge for surveyors is that multiple-language surveys, once rare, are increasingly becoming the norm for very important national surveys, a trend that coincides with larger cultural changes. That the possibility of choosing a language in which to interact is becoming a part of normal culture in the United States is evident in many settings. As just one example, automatic teller machines now commonly begin transactions by asking which language the user prefers. As a result of these changes, receiving a document in multiple languages and choosing one in which to respond, once a very uncomfortable occurrence for some in the United States, is now coming to be considered normal and oftentimes does not receive a second thought from recipients.

Surveyors have responded to the need for surveys in multiple languages in a variety of ways. Telephone interviews are often offered in English and Spanish, and there is increasing demand for bilingual interviewers so respondents do not have to be transferred to another interviewer or called back to be able to respond in another language. Similar to automatic teller machines, web surveys can begin by asking respondents which language they prefer and then routing them to the correct version of the questionnaire based on their choice. Paper surveyors can print separate questionnaires in multiple languages, or they can provide questions in multiple languages within the same questionnaire. For example, a letter was sent to most households in the United States indicating that the 2000 Decennial Census questionnaire could be requested in five different languages. A common method for constructing dual-language questionnaires is to use a double-column format whereby questions are provided in one language, such as English, in the left column and another, such as Spanish, in the right column. Another strategy is used in Canada, whereby complete questionnaires are printed in French in one half of the booklet but in English in the other half. To switch languages one has only to turn the questionnaire over and allow the top to become the bottom. A similar goal has been accomplished in opinion questionnaires by printing queries in different languages on alternate lines. For each of these structures, colored background fields or different colored fonts can be used to help guide people through the different languages.

One of the most important challenges for multiple-language surveys is how questionnaires are translated. The focus should not be on direct translation of words but instead on accurately translating concepts across different languages (Harkness, 2003; Harkness, Van de Vijver, & Johnson, 2003). This is because oftentimes literal translation of specific words will change the meaning that is conveyed by a question, and such changes will not be detected by back-translation strategies that also focus on literal translation (i.e., having a second translator translate the question back into the original language to check for changes in meaning). To avoid this problem, translation should focus on ensuring that each language maintains the meaning of the question and concepts within it, even if doing so means deviating from a literal translation.

Yet another survey design challenge that can benefit greatly from a tailored design approach is the international survey. There can be little doubt that data collection efforts will increasingly be focused on conducting the same survey simultaneously in multiple countries (de Leeuw et al., 2008). In fact, this may be one of the fastest growing trends in the survey industry, a primary example of which comes from the European Union, with its 27 member countries. Sample surveys, including many on opinion issues, are done regularly in the European Union, requiring designers to deal with both cultural and language differences. The European Social Survey is one of many examples (www.europeansocialsurvey.org/).

A particularly important and ambitious survey effort, the Gallup World Poll, has as a goal to ask the same survey questions in as many as 130 different countries. One important strategy the organizers of this survey have developed is the use of dichotomous yes/no questions in order to limit the use of certain scalar questions, which, with their common use of vague quantifiers, are incredibly difficult to translate across languages and cultures. This survey also has to deal with the necessity of using different modes in various countries because of country-specific variation in the availability of different technologies. Each of these challenges and how it is dealt with has important consequences for data quality and for the ability to compare data collected across countries.

The trend toward international surveys is also evident within corporations and other organizations as their structures cross borders. Recently, we helped with a survey by a professional organization that had many international members. Previously the international members had not been included in surveys simply because of the cost and length of time it required to contact them by mail. Likewise, telephone had not been considered because of the costs associated with that mode of data collection. However, provided it is available to the population of interest (as was the case with this survey), the Internet now makes it possible to obtain responses as quickly from someone from another country as from someone in the office next door.

Trends toward making cross-country comparisons possible, as well as widespread interest in such data, lead us to wonder if worldwide surveys and polls may someday become as commonplace as national ones are now. However, the complexity of designing and conducting such surveys, and the necessity of using different modes in different countries, suggests the need to respond to challenges on a scale not previously faced by the survey community. The issues raised by these types of data collection efforts provide some of the most important and challenging new frontiers that surveyors are beginning to address (de Leeuw et al., 2008; Harkness et al., 2003).

In part because of the technological innovations of the past 2 decades, the survey community seems to be transitioning from an era of relatively simple and straightforward surveys (although they may not have seemed simple and straightforward at the time!) to an era of incredibly complex and intensive surveys. The options for surveying are now greater than ever, as is the need for creatively using survey knowledge and tools to successfully create and execute ever more ambitious survey designs. Within this era, tailored design takes on increasing importance.

CONCLUSION

Our discussion in Chapter 1 of the turbulence now being experienced by survey methodology may lead one to think that, as in the flight of an airplane, the turbulence is temporary and only a prelude to smoother flight. We doubt that to be the case for survey design.

When one thinks of the nearly 8 decades of surveying and its transition from mostly in-person methods to greater use of the mail and telephone to the invention of not just the Internet but other electronic modes of data collection as well, it is apparent that change has not only occurred but accelerated. It also seems likely that the knowledge base that now exists for ways in which surveys might be designed is greater than it was at any time in history. This does not seem like a time when a slowdown in innovation will produce stabilization or a return to commonness in how surveys are conducted.

In our conversations with people who experienced early decades of surveying, we have been struck by the general inability of surveyors to predict what comes next. The telephone was not foreseen by in-person surveyors in the 1950s and 1960s as the dominating data collection mode it became some 20 years later. And telephone surveyors of the 1970s and 1980s found it hard, if not impossible, to imagine cell phones and the Internet and how they now dominate our daily lives, if not yet our surveys.

It would be presumptuous, and probably inaccurate, for us to predict the survey methods that will be effective in the coming decades other than to say they are likely to be different than those now in use. We also expect that part of the power of the survey method will rest with how well surveyors learn to reduce errors from coverage, sampling, measurement, and nonresponse. Yet there seems little doubt that the turbulence will continue as possibilities change in the coming era of complex and intense surveying.

References

Altheimer, I., & Dillman, D. A. (2002). *Results from cognitive interviews of NSF earned doctorate web survey* (Tech. Rep. No. 02-30). Pullman: Washington State University, Social and Economic Sciences Research Center.

American Association for Public Opinion Research. (2007). *What is a "push" poll?* Available from www.aapor.org/whatisapushpoll.

American Association for Public Opinion Research. (2008). *Standard definitions: Final dispositions of case codes and outcome rates for surveys.* Available from www.aapor.org/uploads/Standard_Definitions_04_08_Final.pdf.

Andrews, F. M., & Withey, S. B. (1976). *Social indicators of well-being.* New York: Plenum Press.

Aquilino, W. S. (1994). Interview mode effects in surveys of drug and alcohol use: A field experiment. *Public Opinion Quarterly, 58,* 210–240.

Armstrong, J. S., & Luske, E. J. (1987). Return postage in mail surveys: A meta-analysis. *Public Opinion Quarterly, 51,* 233–248.

Bachman, J. G., O'Malley, P. M., Schulenberg, J. E., Johnston, L. D., Freedeman-Doan, P., & Messersmith, E. E. (2008). *The education-drug use connection.* New York: Erlbaum.

Bailey, J. T., Lavrakas, P. J., & Bennett, M. A. (2007, May). *Cash, credit, or check: A test of monetary alternatives to cash incentives.* Paper presented at the annual conference of the American Association for Public Opinion Research, Anaheim, CA.

Barron, G., & Yechiam, E. (2002). Private e-mail requests and the diffusion of responsibility. *Computers in Human Behavior, 18,* 507–520.

Battaglia, M. P., Link, M. W., Frankel, M. R., Osborn, L., & Mokdad, A. H. (2005, August). *An evaluation of respondent selection methods for household mail surveys.* Paper presented at the Joint Statistical meetings, Minneapolis, MN.

Beckler, D., & Ott, K. (2006). Indirect monetary incentives with a complex agricultural establishment survey. *Proceedings of the Survey Research Methods Section, American Statistical Association.* Retrieved from www.amstat.org/Sections/Srms/Proceedings/y2006/Files/JSM2006–000059.pdf.

Belli, R. F. (1998). The structure of autobiographical memory and the event history calendar: Potential improvements in the quality of retrospective reports in surveys. *Memory, 6*(4), 383–406.

Bethlehem, J., & Stoop, I. (2007, September). *Online panels—A paradigm theft?* Paper presented at the meeting of the Association for Survey Computing, Southampton, England. Retrieved from www2.asc.org.uk/ASC/Sep2007/Conference/files/papers/asc13Jelke %20Bethlehem.pdf.

Biemer, P. P. (1997). [Health insurance finance agency evaluation]. Unpublished data. Research Triangle, NC: Research Triangle Institute.

Biemer, P. P., & Lyberg, L. E. (2003). *Introduction to survey quality* (Wiley Series in Survey Methodology). Hoboken, NJ: Wiley.

Birnholtz, J. P., Horn, D. B., Finholt, T. A., & Bae, S. J. (2004). Cash, electronic, and paper gift certificates as respondent incentives for a web-based survey of technologically sophisticated respondents. *Social Science Computer Review, 22,* 355–362.

Bishop, G., Hippler, H. J., Schwarz, N., & Strack, F. (1988). A comparison of response effects in self-administered and telephone surveys. In R. M. Groves, P. P. Biemer, L. E. Lysberg, J. T. Massey, W. L. Nicholls II, & J. Wakesberg (Eds.), *Telephone survey methodology* (pp. 321–340). New York: Wiley.

Blankenship, A. B. (1977). *Professional telephone surveys.* New York: McGraw-Hill.

Blau, P. M. (1964). *Exchange and power in social life.* New York: Wiley.

Blumberg, S. J., & Luke, J. V. (2006). *Wireless substitution: Preliminary data from the January–June 2006* (National Health Interview Survey, U.S. Department of Health and Human Services Centers for Disease Control and Prevention, National Center for Health Statistics). Retrieved March 14, 2007, from www.cdc.gov/nchs/products/pubs/pubd/hestats/wireless2006/wireless2006.htm.

Blumberg, S. J., & Luke, J. V. (2008). *Wireless substitution: Early release of estimates from the National Health Interview Survey, July–December 2007.* National Center for Health Statistics. Available from http://www.cdc.gov/nchs.nhis.htm.

Blumberg, S. J., Luke, J. V., & Cynamon, M. L. (2006). Telephone coverage and health survey estimates: Evaluating the need for concern about wireless substitution. *American Journal of Public Health, 96*(5), 926–931.

Bosnjak, M., & Tuten, T. L. (2003). Prepaid and promised incentives in web surveys: An experiment. *Social Science Computer Review, 21,* 208–217.

Bournazian, J. (2007, June). *A surgical approach to applying CIPSEA.* Paper presented at the ICES III International Conference on Establishment Surveys, Montreal, Quebec, Canada.

Brennan, M., Rae, N., & Parackal, M. (1999). Survey-based experimental research via the web: Some observations. *Marketing Bulletin, 10,* 57–65.

Britt, R., & Featherston, F. (2007, June). *Increasing survey cooperation: Motivating chronic late responders to an annual survey.* Paper presented at the ICES III International Conference on Establishment Surveys, Montreal, Quebec, Canada.

Call, V. R. A., Otto, L. B., & Spenner, K. I. (1982). *Tracking respondents: A multi-method approach.* Lexington, MA: Lexington Books.

Cape, P. (2006, November). *How not to kill the goose that lays the golden egg: A new approach to incentives in online access panels. Proceedings from the ESOMAR World Research Conference, Panel Research 2006: Vol. 317* (pp. 208–214). Amsterdam: ESOMAR.

Cartwright, T., & Nancarrow, C. (2006, November). The effect of conditioning when re-interviewing: A Pan-European study. *Proceedings from the ESOMAR World Research Conference, Panel Research 2006: Vol. 317* (pp. 22–28). Amsterdam: ESOMAR.

Chestnut, J. (2008). *Effects of using a grid versus a sequential form on the ACS basic demographic data* (Memorandum Series Chapter No. ASC-MP-09). Washington, DC: U.S. Census Bureau, DSSD American Community Survey Methods Panel.

Christian, L. M. (2003). *The influence of visual layout on scalar questions in web surveys.* Unpublished master's thesis. Retrieved April 1, 2006, from Washington State University, Social and Economic Sciences Research Center Web site: www.sesrc.wsu.edu/dillman/papers.htm.

Christian, L. M. (2007). *How mixed-mode surveys are transforming social research: The influence of survey mode on measurement in web and telephone surveys.* Unpublished doctoral dissertation, Washington State University, Pullman, WA.

Christian, L. M., & Dillman, D. A. (2004). The influence of graphical and symbolic language manipulations on responses to self-administered questions. *Public Opinion Quarterly, 68*(1), 58–81.

Christian, L. M., Dillman, D. A, & Smyth, J. D. (2007a, May). *After a decade of development: A visual design framework for how respondents process survey information.* Paper presented at the annual conference of the American Association for Public Opinion Research, Anaheim, CA.

Christian, L. M., Dillman, D. A., & Smyth, J. D. (2007b). Helping respondents get it right the first time: The influence of words, symbols, and graphics in web surveys. *Public Opinion Quarterly, 71*(1), 113–125.

Christian, L. M., Dillman, D. A., & Smyth, J. D. (2008). The effects of mode and format on answers to scalar questions in telephone and web surveys. In J. M. Lepkowski, C. Tucker, J. M. Brick, E. de Leeuw, L. Japec, P. J. Lavrakas, et al. (Eds.), *Advances in telephone survey methodology* (pp. 250–275). Hoboken, NJ: Wiley.

Christian, L. M., Parsons, N. L, & Dillman, D. A. (in press). Measurement in web surveys: Understanding the consequences of visual design and layout. *Sociological Methods and Research.*

Church, A. H. (1993). Estimating the effect of incentives on mail survey response rates: A meta-analysis. *Public Opinion Quarterly, 57,* 62–79.

Cialdini, R. B. (1984). *Influence: The new psychology of modern persuasion.* New York: Quill.

Cialdini, R. B., Levy, A., Herman, P., & Evenbeck, S. (1973). Attitudinal politics: The strategy of moderation. *Journal of Personality and Social Psychology, 25*(1), 100–108.

Cobanoglu, C., & Cobanoglu, N. (2003). The effect of incentives in web surveys: Application and ethical considerations. *International Journal of Market Research, 45*(4), 475–488.

Cochran, W. G. (1977). *Sampling techniques* (3rd ed.). New York: Wiley.

Comley, P. (2006, November). The games we play: A psychoanalysis of the relationship between panel owners and panel participants. *Proceedings from the ESOMAR World Research Conference, Panel Research 2006: Vol. 317* (pp. 123–132). Amsterdam: ESOMAR.

Connelly, N. A., Brown, T. L., & Decker, J. D. (2003). Factors affecting response rates to natural resource focused mail surveys: Empirical evidence of declining rates over time. *Society and Natural Resources, 26,* 541–549.

Conrad, A. (2007, September). *Questionnaire design in web surveys.* Paper presented at the Workshop on Internet Survey Methodology. Lillehammer, Norway.

Cook, C., Heath, F., & Thompson, R. L. (2000). A meta-analysis of response rates in web- or internet-based surveys. *Educational and Psychology Measurement, 60*(6), 821–836.

Cork, D. L., & Voss, P. R. (2006). *Once, only once, and in the right place: Residence rules in the decennial census.* Washington, DC: National Academy Press.

Council of American Survey Research Organizations. (2007). *CASRO Code of Standards and Ethics for Survey Research*. Retrieved March 17, 2008, from http://casro.org/pdfs/CodeVertical-FINAL.pdf.

Couper, M. P. (2005). Technology trends in survey data collection. *Social Science Computer Review, 23*(4), 486–501.

Couper, M. P., Conrad, F. G., & Tourangeau, R. (2007). Visual context effects in web surveys. *Public Opinion Quarterly, 71*(4), 623–634.

Couper, M. P., Tourangeau, R., Conrad, F. G., & Crawford, S. D. (2004). What they see is what we get: Response options for web surveys. *Social Science Computer Review, 22*(1), 111–127.

Couper, M. P., Tourangeau, R., Conrad, F. G., & Singer, E. (2006). Evaluating the effectiveness of visual analog scales: A web experiment. *Social Science Computer Review, 24*(2), 227–245.

Couper, M. P., Traugott, M. W., & Lamias, M. J. (2001). Web survey design and administration. *Public Opinion Quarterly, 65*(2), 230–253.

Crawford, S. D., Couper, M. P., & Lamias, M. J. (2001). Web surveys: Perceptions of burden. *Social Science Computer Review, 19*, 146–162.

Crowe, J. (2008). *Discrepancies between the pursuit and implementation of economic development in the nonmetropolitan west: How much do natural, physical, and social factors matter?* Unpublished doctoral dissertation, Washington State University, Pullman, WA.

Das, M., Toepoel, V., & van Soest, A. (2007). *Can I use a panel? Panel conditioning and attrition bias in panel surveys* (CentER Discussion Series No. 2007-56). Tilburg, The Netherlands: CentER. Retrieved March 19, 2008, from http://papers.ssrn.com/sol3/papers.cfm?abstract_id=1012252.

de Leeuw, E. D. (1992). *Data quality in mail, telephone, and face-to-face surveys*. Amsterdam: TT Publications.

de Leeuw, E. D. (2005). To mix or not to mix data collection modes in surveys. *Journal of Official Statistics, 21*(2), 233–255.

de Leeuw, E. D., & Hox, J. J. (1988). The effects of response-stimulating factors on response rates and data quality in mail surveys: A test of Dillman's Total Design Method. *Journal of Official Statistics, 4*, 241–249.

de Leeuw, E. D., Hox, J. J., & Dillman, D. A. (Eds.). (2008). *International handbook of survey methodology*. New York: Psychology Press.

de Leeuw, E. D., & van der Zouwen, J. (1988). Data quality in telephone and face-to-face surveys: A comparative analysis. In R. M. Groves, P. P. Biemer, L. E. Lyberg, J. T. Massey, W. L. Nicholls II, & J. Wakesberg (Eds.), *Telephone survey methodology* (pp. 283–299). New York: Wiley.

DeMaio, T. J. (1984). Social desirability and survey measurement: A review. In C. F. Turner & E. Martin (Eds.), *Surveying subjective phenomena* (Vol. 2, pp. 257–282). New York: Russell Sage Foundation.

Detlefsen, R. (2007, December). *Issues related to achieving target response rates for economic surveys at the U.S. Census Bureau*. Paper presented to the Federal Economic Statistics Advisory Committee, Washington, DC.

Dillehay, R. C., & Jernigan, L. R. (1970). The biased questionnaire as an instrument of opinion change. *Journal of Personality and Social Psychology, 15*(2), 144–150.

Dillman, D. A. (1978). *Mail and telephone surveys: The total design method.* New York: Wiley-Interscience.

Dillman, D. A. (1991). The design and administration of mail surveys. *Annual Review of Sociology, 17,* 225–249.

Dillman, D. A. (1995). *Image optimization test: Summary of 15 taped interviews in Moscow, Idaho, Pullman, Washington, and Spokane, Washington* (Tech. Rep. No. 95-40). Pullman, WA: Washington State University, Social and Economic Sciences Research Center.

Dillman, D. A. (1996). Why innovation is difficult in government surveys. *Journal of Official Statistics, 12*(2), 113–124.

Dillman, D. A. (2000a). *Mail and internet surveys: The tailored design method* (2nd ed.). New York: Wiley.

Dillman, D. A. (2000b). The role of behavioral survey methodologists in national statistical agencies. *International Statistical Review, 68*(2), 199–220.

Dillman, D. A. (2002). [2002 Washington State University student experience survey]. Unpublished data. Social and Economic Sciences Research Center, Pullman, WA.

Dillman, D. A. (2005a). Telephone surveys. In K. Kemph-Leonard (Ed.), *Volume 3: Encyclopedia of social measurement* (pp. 757–762). London: Elsevier Press.

Dillman, D. A. (2005b). Mail surveys. In K. Kemph-Leonard (Ed.), *Volume 3: Encyclopedia of social measurement* (pp. 617–621). London: Elsevier Press.

Dillman, D. A. (2007). *Mail and internet surveys: The tailored design method* (2nd ed.). Hoboken, NJ: Wiley.

Dillman, D. A. (2008). The logic and psychology of constructing questionnaires. In E. D. de Leeuw, J. J. Hox, & D. A. Dillman (Eds.), *International handbook of survey methodology* (pp. 161–175). New York: Psychology Press.

Dillman, D. A. (in press). The total design method. In P. Lavrakas (Ed.), *Encyclopedia of survey research methods.* Thousand Oaks, CA: Sage.

Dillman, D. A., & Allen, T. B. (1995). *Census Booklet Questionnaire Evaluation Test: Phase I—Summary of 20 taped interviews* (Tech. Rep. No. 95-41). Pullman, WA: Washington State University, Social and Economic Sciences Research Center.

Dillman, D. A., Brown, T. L., Carlson, J., Carpenter, E. H., Lorenz, F. O., Mason, R., et al. (1995). Effects of category order on answers to mail and telephone surveys. *Rural Sociology, 60,* 674–687.

Dillman, D. A., & Carley-Baxter, L. R. (2001). *Structural determinants of mail survey response rates over a 12-year period, 1988–1999.* Paper presented at the American Statistical Association Survey Methods Section, Alexandria, VA. Retrieved April 1, 2006, from www.sesrc.wsu.edu/dillman/papers.htm.

Dillman, D. A., Christenson, J. A., Carpenter, E. H., & Brooks, R. (1974). Increasing mail questionnaire response: A four-state comparison. *American Sociological Review, 39,* 744–756.

Dillman, D. A., & Christian, L. M. (2005). Survey mode as a source of instability across surveys. *Field Methods, 17*(1), 30–52.

Dillman, D. A., Clark, J. R., & Sinclair, M. A. (1995). How prenotice letters, stamped return envelopes, and reminder postcards affect mailback response rates for census questionnaires. *Survey Methodology, 21,* 1–7.

Dillman, D. A., Clark, J. R., & West, K. K. (1994). Influence of an invitation to answer by telephone on response to census questionnaires. *Public Opinion Quarterly, 58,* 557–568.

Dillman, D. A., Dolsen, D. E., & Machlis, G. E. (1995). Increasing response to personally-delivered mail-back questionnaires by combining foot-in-the-door and social exchange methods. *Journal of Official Statistics, 11,* 129–139.

Dillman, D. A., Gertseva, A., & Mahon-Haft, T. (2005). Achieving usability in establishment surveys through the application of visual design principles. *Journal of Official Statistics, 21,* 183–214.

Dillman, D. A., Jackson, A., Pavlov, R., & Schaefer, D. (1998). *Results from cognitive tests of 6-person accordion versus bi-fold census forms* (Tech. Rep. No. 98-15). Pullman, WA: Washington State University, Social and Economic Sciences Research Center.

Dillman, D. A., Jenkins, C., Martin, B., & DeMaio, T. (1996). *Cognitive and motivational properties of three proposed decennial census forms* (Tech. Rep. No. 96-29). Pullman, WA: Washington State University, Social and Economic Sciences Research Center.

Dillman, D. A., Lesser, V., Mason, R., Carlson, J., Willits, F., Robertson, R., et al. (2007). Personalization of mail surveys for general public and populations with a group identity: results from nine studies. *Rural Sociology, 72*(4), 632–646.

Dillman, D. A., & Mason, R. G. (1984, May). *The influence of survey method on question response.* Paper presented at the annual conference of the American Association for Public Opinion Research, Delevan, WI.

Dillman, D. A., & Parsons, N. L. (2006). Self-administered paper surveys. In W. Donsbach & M. Traugott (Eds.), *Handbook of public opinion research.* Thousand Oaks, CA: Sage.

Dillman, D. A., Parsons, N. L., & Mahon-Haft, T. (2004). *Connections between optical features and respondent friendly design: Cognitive interview comparisons of the census 2000 form and new possibilities* (Tech. Rep. No. 04-030). Pullman, WA: Washington State University, Social and Economic Sciences Research Center.

Dillman, D. A., Phelps, G., Tortora, R., Swift, K., Kohrell, J., Berck, J., et al. (in press). Response rate and measurement differences in mixed mode surveys using mail, telephone, interactive voice response, and the Internet. *Social Science Research.*

Dillman, D. A., & Redline, C. D. (2004). Testing paper self-administered questionnaires: Cognitive interview and field test comparisons. In S. Presser, J. M. Rothgeb, M. P. Couper, J. T. Lesser, J. Martin, & E. Singer (Eds.), *Methods for testing and evaluating survey questionnaires* (pp. 299–317). New York: Wiley-Interscience.

Dillman, D. A., Sangster, R. L., Tarnai, J., & Rockwood, T. (1996). Understanding differences in people's answers to telephone and mail surveys. In M. T. Braverman & J. K. Slater (Eds.), *New directions for evaluation series: Vol. 70. Advances in survey research* (pp. 45–62). San Francisco: Jossey-Bass.

Dillman, D. A., Sinclair, M. D., & Clark, J. R. (1993). Effects of questionnaire length, respondent-friendly design, and a difficult question on response rates for occupant-addressed census mail surveys. *Public Opinion Quarterly, 57,* 289–304.

Dillman, D. A., Singer, E., Clark, J. R., & Treat, J. B. (1996). Effects of benefit appeals, mandatory appeals and variations in confidentiality on completion rates of census questionnaires. *Public Opinion Quarterly, 60,* 376–389.

Dillman, D. A., Smyth, J. D., Christian, L. M., & O'Neill, A. (2008, May). *Will a mixed-mode (mail/Internet) procedure work for random household surveys of the general public?* Paper presented at the annual conference of the American Association for Public Opinion Research, New Orleans, LA.

Dillman, D. A., & Tarnai, J. (1988). Administrative issues in mixed mode surveys. In R. M. Groves, P. P. Biemer, L. E. Lyberg, J. T. Massey, W. L. Nicholls II, & J. Wakesberg (Eds.), *Telephone survey methodology* (pp. 509–528). New York: Wiley.

Dillman, D. A., & Tarnai, J. (1991). Mode effects of cognitively-designed recall questions: A comparison of answers to telephone and mail surveys. In P. P. Beimer, R. M. Groves, L. E. Lyberg, N. A. Mathiowetz, & S. Sudman (Eds.), *Measurement errors in surveys* (pp. 73–93). New York: Wiley.

Dowling, Z. (2005, September). *Web data collection for mandatory business surveys: The respondents' perspective.* Paper presented at European Science Foundation/Standing Committee for the Social Sciences Exploratory Workshop, Dubrovnick, Croatia.

Erikson, J. (2007, September). *Error messages and editing in web questionnaires: The present situation in Sweden.* Paper presented at the International Survey Methodology Workshop, Lillehammer, Norway.

Farrell, E., Hewett, K., Rowley, T., Van Ede, L., & Burnside, R. (2007, June). *Interface design and testing for electronic self administered survey forms using Excel.* Paper presented at the International Conference on Conference Surveys, Montreal, Quebec, Canada.

Fast, D. (2006, December). *Email data collection.* Paper presented to the Federal Statistics Advisory Committee, Washington, DC.

Forsyth, B. H., & Lessler, J. T. (1991). Cognitive laboratory methods: A taxonomy. In P. P. Beimer, R. M. Groves, L. E. Lysber, N. A. Mathiowetz, & S. Sudman (Eds.), *Measurement errors in surveys* (pp. 393–418). New York: Wiley.

Fox, C. R. (2000). *A vote for Buchanan is a vote for Gore? An analysis of the 2000 presidential election results in Palm Beach, Florida.* Unpublished manuscript, UCLA Anderson School.

Fox, R. J., Crask, M. R., & Kim, J. (1988). Mail survey response rate: A meta-analysis of selected techniques for inducing response. *Public Opinion Quarterly, 59,* 467–491.

Frederick, C., & O'Hare, B. C. (2005, May). *Individualized treatments within a household: Can targeted incentives raise young male response?* Paper presented at the annual conference of the American Association for Public Opinion Research, Miami Beach, FL.

Frederickson-Mele, K. (2007, December). *Using a web-lite approach to collecting data via the web.* Paper presented to the Federal Statistics Advisory Committee, Washington, DC.

Gaziano, C. (2005). Comparative analysis of within-household respondent selection techniques. *Public Opinion Quarterly, 69*(1), 124–157.

Gendall, P., & Healey, B. (2007, May). *Alternatives to prepaid monetary incentives in mail surveys.* Paper presented at the annual conference of the American Association for Public Opinion Research, Anaheim, CA.

Gentry, R. (2008, March). *Offering respondents a choice of survey mode.* Paper presented at the CMOR Respondent Cooperation Workshop, Las Vegas, NV.

Göritz, A. S. (2006). Incentives in web studies: Methodological issues and a review. *International Journal of Internet Science, 1*(1), 58–70.

Gregory, G., & Earp, M. (2007, June). *Evolution of web surveys at USDA's National Agricultural Statistics Service*. Paper presented at the International Conference on Conference Surveys, Montreal, Quebec, Canada.

Griffin, D. H., Fischer, D. P., & Morgan, M. T. (2001, May). *Testing an Internet response option for the American Community Survey*. Paper presented at the American Association for Public Opinion Research. Montreal, Quebec, Canada.

Grigorian, K., & Hoffer, T. B. (2008, March). *2006 Survey of Doctorate Recipients mode assignment analysis report*. Prepared for the National Science Foundation by the National Opinion Research Center

Groves, R. M. (1989). *Survey errors and survey costs*. New York: Wiley.

Groves, R. M. (2006). Nonresponse rates and nonresponse bias in household surveys. *Public Opinion Quarterly, 70*(5), 646–675.

Groves, R. M., Cialdini, R., & Couper, M. P. (1992). Understanding the decision to participate in a survey. *Public Opinion Quarterly, 56*, 475–495.

Groves, R. M., Couper, M. P., Presser, S., Singer, E., Tourangeau, R., Acosta, G. P., et al. (2006). Experiments in producing nonresponse bias. *Public Opinion Quarterly, 70*(5), 720–736.

Groves, R. M., & Kahn, R. L. (1979). *Surveys by telephone: A national comparison with personal interviews*. New York: Academic Press.

Groves, R. M., & Lyberg, L. E. (1988). An overview of nonresponse issues in telephone surveys. In R. M. Groves, P. P. Beimer, L. E. Lyberg, J. T. Massey, W. L. Nichols II, & J. Wakesberg (Eds.), *Telephone survey methodology* (pp. 191–211). New York: Wiley.

Groves, R. M., & Magilavy, L. J. (1981). Increasing response rates to telephone surveys: A door in the face or foot-in-the-door? *Public Opinion Quarterly, 45*(3), 346–358.

Groves, R. M., Presser, S., & Dipko, S. (2004). The role of topic interest in survey participation decisions. *Public Opinion Quarterly, 68*(1), 2–31.

Groves, R. M., Singer, E., & Corning, A. (2000). Leverage-saliency theory of survey participation: Description and an illustration. *Public Opinion Quarterly, 64*(3), 299–308.

Hansen, J. (2008). Panel surveys. In W. Donsbach & M. W. Traugott (Eds.), *The Sage handbook of public opinion research* (pp. 330–339). Thousand Oaks, CA: Sage.

Harkness, J. (2003). Questionnaire translation. In J. A. Harkness, F. J. R. Van de Vijver, & P. P. Mohler (Eds.), *Cross-cultural survey methods* (pp. 35–56). Hoboken, NJ: Wiley.

Harkness, J., Van de Vijver, F. J. R., & Johnson, T. P. (2003). Questionnaire design in comparative research. In J. A. Harkness, F. J. R. Van de Vijver, & P. P. Mohler (Eds.), *Crosscultural survey methods* (pp. 19–34). Hoboken, NJ: Wiley.

Harris-Kojetin, B. A. (2007, December). *OMB standards and guidelines for statistical surveys: Nonresponse bias analyses*. Paper presented to the Federal Economic Statistics Advisory Committee, Washington, DC.

Harrison, H. L., & Coburn, J. (2007, May). *Universal accessibility in web survey design: Practical guidelines for implementation*. Paper presented at the annual conference of American Association for Public Opinion Research, Anaheim, CA.

Heberlein, T. A., & Baumgartner, R. (1978). Factors affecting response rates to mailed questionnaires: A quantitative analysis of the published literature. *American Sociological Review, 43*, 447–462.

Heerwegh, D. (2003). Explaining response latencies and changing answers using client-side paradata from a web survey. *Social Science Computer Review, 21*, 360–373.

Heerwegh, D. (2005). Effects of personal salutations in e-mail invitations to participate in a web survey. *Public Opinion Quarterly, 69*(4), 588–598.

Heerwegh, D., & Loosveldt, G. (2002a). An evaluation of the effects of response formats on data quality in web surveys. *Social Science Computer Review, 20*, 469–482.

Heerwegh, D., & Loosveldt, G. (2002b, October). *Describing response behavior in web-surveys using client side paradata.* Paper presented at the International Workshop on Web Surveys, Mannheim, Germany.

Heerwegh, D., & Loosveldt, G. (2002c). Web surveys: The effect of controlling survey access using PIN numbers. *Social Science Computer Review, 20*, 10–21.

Heerwegh, D., & Loosveldt, G. (2003). An evaluation of the semiautomatic login procedure to control web survey access. *Social Science Computer Review, 21*, 223–234.

Hembroff, L. A., Rusz, D., Rafferty, A., McGee, H., & Ehrlich, N. (2005). The cost-effectiveness of alternative advance mailings in a telephone survey. *Public Opinion Quarterly, 69*(2), 232–245.

Hochstim, J. R. (1967). A critical comparison of three strategies of collecting data from households. *Journal of the American Statistical Association, 62*, 976–989.

Hoffer, T. B., Grigorian, K., & Fecso, R. (2007, July). *Assessing the effectiveness of using panel respondent preferences.* Paper presented at the Joint Statistical Meetings, Salt Lake City, UT.

Hoffman, D. D. (2004). *Visual intelligence.* New York: Norton.

Holland, J., & Christian, L. M. (2007, October). *The influence of interactive probing on response to open-ended questions in a web survey.* Paper presented at the Southern Association for Public Opinion Research annual conference, Raleigh, NC.

Homans, G. (1961). *Social behavior: Its elementary forms.* New York: Harcourt, Brace & World.

Horrigan, J. B., & Smith, A. (2007, June). *Home broadband adoption 2007.* Retrieved from www.pewinternet.org/pdfs/PIP_Broadband%202007.pdf.

Hox, J. J., & de Leeuw, E. D. (1994). A comparison of nonresponse in mail, telephone, and face-to-face surveys. *Quality and Quantity, 28*, 329–344.

Hyman, H. H., & Sheatsley, P. B. (1950). The current status of American public opinion. In J. C. Payne (Ed.), *The teaching of contemporary affairs: Twenty-first yearbook of the National Council for the Social Studies* (pp. 11–34). New York: National Education Association.

Iannacchione, V. G., Staab, J. M., & Redden, D. T. (2003). Evaluating the use of residential mailing addresses in a metropolitan household survey. *Public Opinion Quarterly, 67*, 202–210.

Israel, G. D. (2005, August). *Visual cues and response format effects in mail surveys.* Paper presented at the annual meeting of the Rural Sociological Society, Tampa, FL.

Israel, G. D., & Taylor, C. L. (1990). Can response order bias evaluations? *Evaluation and Program Planning, 13*, 1–7.

James, J. M., & Bolstein, R. (1990). The effect of monetary incentives and follow-up mailings on the response rate and response quality in mail surveys. *Public Opinion Quarterly, 54*, 346–361.

James, J. M., & Bolstein, R. (1992). Large monetary incentives and their effect on mail survey response rates. *Public Opinion Quarterly, 56*, 442–453.

Javeline, D. (1999). Response effects in polite cultures: A test of acquiescence in Kazakhstan. *Public Opinion Quarterly, 63*(1), 1–28.

Jenkins, C., & Dillman, D. A. (1997). Towards a theory of self-administered question-naire design. In L. E. Lyberg, P. Biemer, M. Collins, E. D. de Leeuw, C. Dippo, N. Schwarz, et al. (Eds.), *Survey measurement and process quality* (pp. 165–196). New York: Wiley-Interscience.

Johnson, T., & McLaughlin, S. (1990). *GMAT registrant survey design report.* Los Angeles: Los Angeles Graduate Admission Council.

Joinson, A. N., & Reips, U. (2007). Personalized salutation, power of sender, and response rates to web-based surveys. *Computers in Human Behavior, 23,* 1372–1383.

Jordan, L. A., Marcus, A. C., & Reeder, L. G. (1980). Response styles in telephone and household interviewing: A field experiment. *Public Opinion Quarterly, 44,* 210–222.

Kanuk, L., & Berenson, C. (1975). Mail surveys and response rates: A literature review. *Journal of Marketing Research, 12,* 400–453.

Kerlinger, F. N. (1965). *Foundations of behavioral research.* New York: Holt, Rinehart and Winston.

Kish, L. (1949). A procedure for objective respondent selection within the household. *Journal of American Statistical Association, 44,* 380–387.

Kish, L. (1965). *Survey sampling.* New York: Wiley.

Kriauciunas, A., Parmigiani, A., & Rivera-Santos, M. (2007). *Surveys in nontraditional contexts: The importance of establishing trust and mitigating risk.* Unpublished paper.

Krosnick, J. A. (1991). Response strategies for coping with the cognitive demands of attitude measures in surveys. *Applied Cognitive Psychology, 5,* 213–236.

Krosnick, J. A., & Alwin, D. F. (1987). An evaluation of a cognitive theory of response-order effects in survey measurement. *Public Opinion Quarterly, 51,* 201–219.

Krosnick, J. A., & Fabrigar, L. R. (1997). Designing rating scales for effective mea-surement in surveys. In L. Lyberg, P. Biemer, M. Collins, L. Decker, E. de Leeuw, C. Dippo, et al. (Eds.), *Survey measurement and process quality.* New York: Wiley-Interscience.

Krysan, M., Schuman, H., Scott, L. J., & Beatty, P. (1994). Response rates and response content in mail versus face-to-face surveys. *Public Opinion Quarterly, 58,* 381–399.

Ku-Graf, L. (2007, June). *Electronic data collection at the U.S. Bureau of Economic Analysis.* Paper presented at the ICES III International Conference on Establishment Surveys, Montreal, Quebec, Canada.

Lavrakas, P. J. (Ed.). (2007). Cell phone numbers and telephone surveying in the U.S. [Special issue]. *Public Opinion Quarterly, 71*(5).

Lavrakas, P. J., Stasny, E. A., & Harpuder, B. (2000). A further investigation of the last-birthday respondent selection method and within-unit coverage error. *Proceedings of the Survey Research Methods Section, American Statistical Association* (pp. 890–895). Retrieved from www.amstat.org/sections/srms/Proceedings/.

Lee, S. (2006). Propensity score adjustment as a weighting scheme for volunteer panel web surveys. *Journal of Official Statistics, 22*(2), 329–349.

Lepkowski, J. M., Tucker, C., Brick, J. M., de Leeuw, E., Japec, L., Lavrakas, P. J., et al. (2008). *Advances in telephone survey methodology.* Hoboken, NJ: Wiley.

Leslie, T. F. (1996). *1996 National Content Survey results* (Internal DSSD Memorandum No. 3). Washington, DC: U.S. Census Bureau.

Leslie, T. F. (1997). Comparing two approaches to questionnaire design: Official government versus public information design. *Proceedings of the American Statistical Association* (pp. 336–341). Anaheim, CA: American Statistical Association.

Lesser, V. M., Dillman, D. A., Carlson, J., Lorenz, F., Mason, R., & Willits, F. (2001). Quantifying the Influence of Incentives on Mail Survey Response Rates and Nonresponsive Bias. American Statistical Association. Retrieved June 20, 2008 at http://www.sesrc.wsu.edu/dillman/.

Lidwell, W., Holden, K., & Butler, J. (2003). *Universal principles of design.* Gloucester, MA: Rockport.

Link, M. W., Battaglia, M. P., Frankel, M., Osborn, L., & Mokdad, A. (2008). Comparison of address-based sampling (ABS) versus random-digit dialing (RDD) for general population surveys. *Public Opinion Quarterly, 72*(1), 6–27.

Link, M. W., Battaglia, M. P., Giambo, P., Frankel, M. R., Mokdad, A. H., & Rao, R. S. (2005, May). *Assessment of address frame replacements for RDD sampling frames.* Paper presented at the annual conference of the American Association for Public Opinion Research, Miami Beach, FL.

Littlejohn, M. (2008). [Visitor survey project]. Unpublished raw data. University of Idaho, Moscow, ID.

Lohr, S. L. (1999). *Sampling: Design and analysis.* Pacific Grove, CA: Duxbury Press.

Lynn, P. (2008). *Methodology of longitudinal surveys.* Chichester, West Sussex, England: Wiley.

Manfreda, K. L., Batagelj, Z., & Vehovar, V. (2002). Design of web survey questionnaires: Three basic experiments. *Journal of Computer Mediated Communication, 7*(3). Retrieved from http://jcmc.indiana.edu/vol7/issue3/vehovar.html.

Martin, E., Childs, J. H., DeMaio, T., Hill, J., Reiser, C., Gerber, E., et al. (2007). *Guidelines for designing questionnaires for administration in different modes.* Suitland, MD: U.S. Census Bureau.

Mason, R., Carlson, J. E., & Tourangeau, R. (1994). Contrast effects and subtraction in part-whole questions. *Public Opinion Quarterly, 58*(4), 569–578.

Maxim, P. S. (1999). *Quantitative research methods in the social sciences.* New York: Oxford University Press.

Miller, K. J. (1996). *The influence of different techniques on response rates and nonresponse error in mail surveys.* Unpublished master's thesis, Western Washington University, Bellingham, WA.

Mingay, D. J., Belkin, M., Kim, R., Farrell, S., Headley, L., Khokha, P., et al. (1999, May). *In-home evaluations of an automated touch-tone telephone system to administer a health questionnaire.* Paper presented at the annual conference of the American Association for Public Opinion Research, St. Petersburg, FL.

Moore, D. E., & Dillman, D. A. (1980). *Response rate of certified mail and alternatives.* Unpublished paper, Pennsylvania State University.

Moore, D. L., & An, L. (2001, August). The effect of repetitive token incentives and priority mail on response to physician surveys. *Proceedings of the annual meeting of the American Statistical Association.* Retrieved from www.amstat.org/sections/srms/proceedings/y2001/Proceed/00186.pdf.

Moore, D. L., & Ollinger, M. (2007, June). *Effectiveness of monetary incentives and other stimuli across establishment survey populations.* Paper presented at the ICES III International Conference on Establishment Surveys, Montreal, Quebec, Canada.

Moore, D. W. (1997). Perils of polling '96: Myth and fallacy. *Polling Report, 12,* 1FF.

Moore, D. W. (2002). Measuring new types of question order effects: Additive and subtractive. *Public Opinion Quarterly, 66,* 80–91.

Morgan, D. L. (1997). *Focus groups as qualitative research* (2nd ed.). Thousand Oaks, CA: Sage.

Morrison, R., Dillman, D. A., & Christian, L. M. (in press). Guidelines for designing establishment surveys. *Journal of Official Statistics.*

Mowen, J. C., & Cialdini, R. B. (1980). On implementing the door in the face compliance technique in a business context. *Journal of Marketing Research, 17,* 253–258.

Mu, X. (1999). *IVR and distribution of responses: An evaluation of the effects of IVR on collecting and interpreting survey data.* Unpublished paper. Princeton, NJ: Gallup Organization.

Neubarth, W. (2008). Online measurement of (drag & drop) moveable objects. In S. S. Gosling & J. A. Johnson (Eds.), *Advanced methods for behavioral research on the internet.* Washington, DC: American Psychological Association.

Norman, D. A. (1988). *The psychology of everyday things.* New York: Basic Books.

Norman, D. A. (2004). *Why we love (or hate) everyday things.* Cambridge, MA: Basic Books.

O'Hare, B. (2008, March). Surveys in the private sector. Paper presented at the Council of Professional Associations on Federal Statistics seminar on Survey Respondent Incentives: Research and Practice, Washington D.C.

Ollinger, M., & Moore, D. L. (2007). Food safety approaches to examining HACCP costs and performance and technologies. *Agribusiness, 23*(2), 193–210.

Olsen, D., Call, V., & Wygant, S. (2005, May). *Comparative analyses of parallel paper, phone, and web surveys with and without incentives: What differences do incentive and mode make?* Paper presented at the annual conference of the American Association for Public Opinion Research, Miami Beach, FL.

O'Muircheartaigh, C., English, E. M., & Eckman, S. (2007, May). *Predicting the relative quality of alternative sampling frames.* Paper presented at the annual conference of the American Association for Public Opinion Research, Anaheim, CA.

Ott, K., & Beckler, D. (2007, June). *Incentives in surveys with farmers.* Paper presented at the ICES III International Conference on Establishment Surveys, Montreal, Quebec, Canada.

Otto, L., Call, V. R. A., & Spenner, K. (1976). *Design for a study of entry into careers.* Lexington, MA: Lexington Books.

Palmer, S. E. (1999). *Vision science: Photons to phenomenology.* London: Bradford Books.

Parsons, N., & Dillman, D. A. (2008). *Alternative questions for reporting the time periods during which the NSRCG respondents took community college classes: A cognitive evaluation* (Tech. Rep. No. 08-003). Pullman, WA: Washington State University, Social and Economic Sciences Research Center.

Parsons, N., Mahon-Haft, T., & Dillman, D. A. (2005) *Cognitive evaluations of three census form design features: The Internet option message, roster instructions, and identifying person 1* (Tech. Rep. No. 05-022). Pullman, WA: Washington State University, Social and Economic Sciences Research Center.

Parsons, N., Mahon-Haft, T., & Dillman, D. A. (2007). *Cognitive evaluations of potential questions for SESTAT surveys to determine the influence of community college on educational and work choices: Round 2* (Tech. Rep. No. 07-58). Pullman, WA: Washington State University, Social and Economic Sciences Research Center.

Parten, M. (1950). *Surveys, polls, and samples: Practical procedures.* New York: Harper and Brothers.

Patchen, R. H., Woodard, D. S., Caralley, M. D., & Hess, D. L. (1994, May). *Outside the box thinking about survey mailing packages: A report on the return rate effects of using boxes instead of envelopes for packaging outgoing mail questionnaires.* Paper presented at the annual meeting of the American Association for Public Opinion Research, Danvers, MA.

Payne, S. L. (1964). Combination of survey methods. *Journal of Marketing Research, 1,* 61–62.

Petrie, R., Moore, D. L., & Dillman, D. A. (1998). Establishment surveys: The effect of multi-mode sequence on response rates. *Proceedings of Survey Methods Section* (pp. 981–987). Alexandria, VA: American Statistical Association.

Pew Internet & American Life Project. (2007). *Demographics of internet users.* Retrieved February 12, 2007, from www.pewinternet.org/trends/User_Demo_6.15.07.htm.

Porter, S., & Whitcomb, M. E. (2003). The impact of lottery incentives on student survey response rates. *Research in Higher Education, 44*(4), 389–407.

Postman, D. (2005, March 4). Builders group uses trickery to check out voters' signatures. *Seattle Times.* Retrieved from http://seattletimes.nwsource.com/html/localnews/2002196557_mccabe04m.html.

Potaka, L. (2008). Comparability and usability: Key issues in the design of Internet forms for New Zealand's 2006 census of populations and dwellings. *Survey Research Methods, 2,* 1–10.

Presser, S., Rothgeb, J. M., Couper, M. P., Lessler, J. T., Martin, E., Martin, J., et al. (2004). *Methods for testing and evaluating survey questionnaires.* New York: Wiley-Interscience.

Redline, C. D., & Dillman, D. A. (2002). The influence of alternative visual design on respondents' performance with branching instructions in self-administered questionnaires. In R. Groves, D. Dillman, J. Eltinge, & R. Little (Eds.), *Survey nonresponse* (pp. 179–196). Hoboken, NJ: Wiley.

Redline, C. D., Dillman, D. A., Carley-Baxter, L., & Creecy, R. H. (2005). Factors that influence reading and comprehension of branching instructions in self-administered questionnaires. *Allgemeines Statistiches Archiv (Journal of the German Statistical Society), 89*(1), 21–38.

Redline, C. D., Dillman, D. A., Dajani, A. N., & Scaggs, M. A. (2003). Improving navigational performance in U.S. Census 2000 by altering the visual administered languages of branching instructions. *Journal of Official Statistics, 19,* 403–419.

Rockwood, T. H., Sangster, R. L., & Dillman, D. A. (1997). The effect of response categories in questionnaire answers: Context and mode effects. *Sociological Methods and Research, 26*(1), 118–140.

Rokeach, M. (1973). *The nature of human values.* New York: Free Press.

Rookey, B. D., Hanway, S., & Dillman, D. A. (2008, May). *Does the inclusion of mail and web alternatives in a probability-based household panel improve the accuracy of results?* Paper presented at the annual conference of the American Association for Public Opinion Research, New Orleans, LA.

Roose, H., Lievens, J., & Waege, H. (2007). The joint effect of topic interest and follow-up procedures on the response in a mail questionnaire: An empirical test of the leverage-saliency theory in audience research. *Sociological Methods and Research, 35*(3), 410–428.

Rosen, R. J. (2007, June). *Multi-mode data collection: Why, when, how.* Paper presented at the ICES III International Conference on Establishment Surveys, Montreal, Quebec, Canada.

Rosen, R. J., Clayton, R. L., & Wolf, L. L. (1993). Long-term retention of sample members under automated self-response data collection. *Proceedings of section of survey research methods* (pp. 748–752). Washington, DC: American Sociological Association.

Rosen, R. J., Harrell, L., & Yu, H. (2007, June). *Respondent acceptance of web and e-mail data reporting for an establishment survey.* Paper presented at the ICES III International Conference on Establishment Surveys, Montreal, Quebec, Canada.

Sangster, R. L. (1993). *Question order effects: Are they really less prevalent in mail surveys?* Unpublished doctoral dissertation, Washington State University, Pullman, WA.

Saris, W. E. (1998). Ten years of interviewing without interviewers: The telepanel. In M. P. Couper, R. P. Baker, J. Bethlehem, C. Clark, J. Martin, L. Nicholls II, et al. (Eds.), *Computer assisted survey information collection* (pp. 409–431). New York: Wiley.

Saris, W. E., & Krosnick, J. A. (2000, May). *The damaging effect of acquiescence response bias on answers to agree/disagree questions.* Paper presented at the annual conference of the American Association for Public Opinion Research, Portland, OR.

Sawyer, S., & Dillman, D. A. (2002). *How graphical, numerical, and verbal languages affect the completion of the Gallup Q-12 on self-administered questionnaires: Results from 22 cognitive interviews and field experiment* (Tech. Rep. No. 02–26). Pullman, WA: Washington State University, Social and Economic Sciences Research Center.

Schaefer, D., & Dillman, D. A. (1997). Development of a standard e-mail methodology: Results of an experiment. *Public Opinion Quarterly, 62,* 378–397.

Schaeffer, N. C., & Pressor, S. (2003). The science of asking questions. *Annual Review of Sociology, 29,* 65–88.

Schuman, H., & Presser, S. (1981). *Questions and answers in attitude surveys: Experiments on question form, wording, and context.* New York: Academic Press.

Schwarz, N. (1996). *Cognition and communication: Judgmental biases, research methods, and the logic of conversation.* Mahwah, NJ: Erlbaum.

Schwarz, N., & Clore, G. L. (1983). Mood, misattribution, and judgments of well-being: Informative and directive functions of affective states. *Journal of Personality and Social Psychology, 45*(3), 513–523.

Schwarz, N., Grayson, C. E., & Knäuper, B. (1998). Formal features of rating scales and the interpretation of question meaning. *International Journal of Public Opinion Research, 10*(2), 177–183.

Schwarz, N., Hippler, H. J., & Noelle-Neumann, E. (1992). A cognitive model of response-order effects in survey measurement. In N. Schwarz & S. Sudman (Eds.), *Context effects in social and psychological research* (pp. 187–199). New York: Springer-Verlag.

Schwarz, N., Knauper, B., Hippler, H. J., Noelle-Neumann, E., & Clark, L. (1991). Rating scales: Numeric values may change the meaning of scale labels. *Public Opinion Quarterly, 55*(4), 570–582.

Sharot, T. (1991). Attrition and rotation in panel surveys. *Statistician, 40*(3), 325–331.

Shuttles, C., Link, M., & Smarr, J. (2008, March). *Addressed based sampling.* Paper presented at the CMOR Respondent Cooperation Workshop, Las Vegas, NV.

Slocum, W. L., Empey, T., & Swanson, H. S. (1956). Increasing response to questionnaires and structure interviews. *American Sociological Review, 21,* 221–225.

Smith, R., & Hofma-Brown, H. (2006). Comparing metrics and assessing claims. *Proceedings from the ESOMAR World Research Conference, Panel Research 2006: Vol. 317* (pp. 9–21). Amsterdam: ESOMAR.

Smith, T., Gray, C., & Christovich, L. J. (2007, June). *Survey of science and engineering research facilities fiscal year 2005.* Paper presented at ICESIII the International Conference on Establishment Surveys, Montreal, Quebec, Canada.

Smith, T. W. (1993). *Little things matter: A sampler of how differences in questionnaire format can affect survey response* (GSS Methodological Rep. No. 78). Chicago: University of Chicago, National Opinion Research Center.

Smyth, J. D. (2007). *Doing gender when home and work are blurred: Women and sex-atypical tasks in family farming.* Unpublished doctoral dissertation, Washington State University, Pullman, WA.

Smyth, J. D., Christian, L. M., & Dillman, D. A. (2008). Does "Yes or No" on the telephone mean the same as "Check-All-That-Apply" on the web? *Public Opinion Quarterly, 72,* 103–113.

Smyth, J. D., Dillman, D. A., & Christian, L. M. (2007a). Context effects in web surveys: New issues and evidence. In A. Joinson, K. McKenna, T. Postmes, & U. Reips (Eds.), *The Oxford handbook of Internet psychology* (pp. 427–443). New York: Oxford University Press.

Smyth, J. D., Dillman, D. A., & Christian, L. M. (2007b, May). *Improving response quality in list-style open-ended questions in web and telephone surveys.* Paper presented at the annual conference of American Association for Public Opinion Research, Anaheim, CA.

Smyth, J. D., Dillman, D. A., Christian, L. M., & McBride, M. (2006, May). *Open ended questions in telephone and web surveys.* Paper presented at the World Association of Public Opinion Research Conference, Montreal, Quebec, Canada.

Smyth, J. D., Dillman, D. A., Christian, L. M., & McBride, M. (in press). Open-ended questions in web surveys: Can increasing the size of answer boxes and providing extra verbal instructions improve response quality? *Public Opinion Quarterly.*

Smyth, J. D., Dillman, D. A., Christian, L. M., & Stern, M. J. (2005). *Comparing check-all and forced-choice question formats in web surveys: The role of satisfying, depth of processing, and acquiescence in explaining differences* (Tech. Rep. No. 05-029). Pullman, WA: Washington State University, Social and Economic Sciences Research Center. Retrieved from http://survey.sesrc.wsu.edu/dillman/papers.htm.

Smyth, J. D., Dillman, D. A., Christian, L. M., & Stern, M. J. (2006a). Comparing check-all and forced-choice question formats in web surveys. *Public Opinion Quarterly, 70,* 66–77.

Smyth, J. D., Dillman, D. A., Christian, L. M., & Stern, M. J. (2006b). Effects of using visual design principles to group response options in web surveys. *International Journal of Internet Science, 1*(1), 6–16.

Snijkers, G., & Lammers, L. (2007, September). *Audit trails and completion behavior in the Annual Structural Business Survey*. Paper presented at the International Survey Methodology Workshop, Lillehammer, Norway.

Snijkers, G., Onat, E., & Vis-Visschers, R. (2007, June). *The Annual Business Survey: Developing and testing an electronic form*. Paper presented at the International Conference on Establishment Surveys, Montreal, Quebec, Canada.

Srinivasan, R., & Hanway, S. (1999, May). *A new kind of survey mode difference: Experimental results from a test of inbound voice recognition and mail surveys*. Paper presented at the annual conference of the American Association for Public Opinion Research, St. Pete Beach, FL.

Statistics New Zealand. (2006). 2006 census final questionnaire design. Retrieved March 14, 2008, from www.stats.govt.nz/NR/rdonlyres/4A31B200–D2D7–D44B8–C937–E037F30070A6/0/2006CensusFinalQuestionnaireDesign.pdf.

Steiger, D. M., & Conroy, B. (2008). IVR: Interactive voice response. In E. D. de Leeuw, J. J. Hox, & D. A. Dillman (Eds.), *International handbook of survey methodology* (pp. 285–298). New York: Psychology Press.

Stern, M. J. (2006). *How use of the internet impacts community participation and the maintenance of core social ties: An empirical study*. Unpublished doctoral dissertation, Washington State University, Pullman, WA.

Stern, M. J. (in press). The use of client side paradata in analyzing the effects of visual layout on changing responses in web surveys. *Field Methods*.

Steve, K., Dally, G., Lavrakas, P. J., Yancey, T., & Kulp, D. (2007, May). *R&D studies to replace the RDD-frame with an ABS-frame*. Paper presented at the annual conference of the American Association for Public Opinion Research, Anaheim, CA.

Sudman, S., Bradburn, N., & Schwarz, N. (1996). *Thinking about answers*. San Francisco: Jossey-Bass.

Tarnai, J., & Dillman, D. A. (1992). Questionnaire context as a source of response differences in mail versus telephone surveys. In N. Schwarz & S. Sudman (Eds.), *Context effects in social and psychological research* (pp. 115–129). New York: Springer-Verlag.

Teisl, M. F., Roe, B., & Vayda, M. (2005). Incentive effects on response rates, data quality, and survey administration costs. *International Journal of Public Opinion Research, 18*(3), 364–373.

Thibaut, J. W., & Kelley, H. H. (1959). *The social psychology of groups*. New York: Wiley.

Thomas, R. K., & Couper, M. P. (2007, March). *A comparison of visual analog and graphic ratings scales*. Paper presented at the General Online Research Conference, Leipzig, Germany.

Todorov, A. (2000). The accessibility and applicability of knowledge: Predicting context effects in national surveys. *Public Opinion Quarterly, 64*(4), 429–451.

Toepoel, V., Das, M., & van Soest, A. (2006). Design of web questionnaires: The effect of layout in rating scales (CentER Discussion Series No. 2006-30). Tilburg, The Netherlands: CentER. Retrieved March 19, 2008, from http://arno.uvt.nl/show.cgi?fid=53906.

Tomaskovic-Devey, D., Leiter, J., & Thompson, S. (1994). Organizational survey nonresponse. *Administrative Science Quarterly, 39*, 439–467.

Tortora, R. D., Dillman, D. A., & Bolstein, R. (1992). *Considerations related to how incentives influence survey response.* Paper prepared for Symposium on Providing Incentives to Survey Respondents, John F. Kennedy School of Government, Harvard University, Cambridge, MA.

Tourangeau, R. (1992). Context effects on response to attitude surveys: Attitudes as memory structure. In N. Schwarz & S. Sudman (Eds.), *Context effects in social and psychological research* (pp. 35–48). New York: Springer-Verlag.

Tourangeau, R., Couper, M., & Conrad, F. (2004). Spacing position, and order: Interpretive heuristics for visual features of survey questions. *Public Opinion Quarterly, 68*, 368–393.

Tourangeau, R., Couper, M., & Conrad, F. (2007). Color, labels, and interpretive heuristics for response scales. *Public Opinion Quarterly, 71*(1), 91–112.

Tourangeau, R. Steiger, D. M., & Wilson, D. (2002). Self-administered questionnaires by telephone: Evaluating interactive voice response. *Public Opinion Quarterly, 66*, 265–278.

Trouteaud, A. R. (2004). How you ask counts: A test of internet-related components of response rates to a web-based survey. *Social Science Computer Review, 22*, 385–392.

Trussell, N., & Lavrakas, P. J. (2004). The influence of incremental increases in token cash incentives on mail survey response: Is there an optimal amount? *Public Opinion Quarterly, 68*(3), 349–367.

Tulp, D. R., Jr., How, C. E., Kusch, G. L., & Cole, S. J. (1991). Nonresponse under mandatory versus voluntary reporting in the 1980 Survey of Pollution Abatement Costs and Expenditures (PACE). *Proceedings of the survey research methods section* (pp. 272–277). Alexandria, VA: American Statistical Association.

Tuten, T. L., Galesic, M., & Bosnjak, M. (2004). Effects of immediate versus delayed notification of prize draw results on response behavior in web surveys. *Social Science Computer Review, 22*, 377–384.

U.S. Office of Management and Budget. (1984). The role of telephone data collection in federal statistics. *Statistical Policy Working Paper No. 1.* Washington, DC: U.S. Government Printing Office.

U.S. Office of Management and Budget. (2006a). *Questions and answers when designing surveys for information collections.* Retrieved January 7, 2008, from www.whitehouse.gov/omb/inforeg/pmc_survey_guidance_2006.pdf.

U.S. Office of Management and Budget. (2006b). *Standards and guidelines for statistical surveys.* Retrieved January 7, 2008, from www.whitehouse.gov/omb/inforeg/statpolicy/standards_stat_surveys.pdf.

Veroff, J., Hatchett, S., & Douvan, E. (1992). Consequences of participating in a longitudinal study of marriage. *Public Opinion Quarterly, 56*(3), 315–327.

Wand, J. N., Shotts, K. W., Sekhon, J. S., Mebane, W. R., Jr., Herron, M. C., & Brady, H. E. (2001). The butterfly did it: The aberrant vote for Buchanan in Palm Beach County, Florida. *American Political Science Review, 95*(4), 793–810.

Ware, C. (2004). *Information visualization: Perception for design.* San Francisco: Morgan Kaufmann.

Warriner, K., Goyder, J., Gjertsen, H., Hohner, P., & McSpurren, K. (1996). Charities, no; Lotteries, no; Cash, yes: Main effects and interactions in a Canadian incentives experiment. *Public Opinion Quarterly, 60,* 542–562.

Willems, P., van Ossenbruggen, R., & Vonk, T. (2006). The effects of panel recruitment and management on research results: A study across 19 online panels. *Proceedings from the ESOMAR World Research Conference, Panel Research 2006: Vol. 317* (pp. 79–99). Amsterdam: ESOMAR.

Willits, F. K., Crider, D. M., & Bealer, R. C. (1969). *A design and assessment of techniques for locating respondents in longitudinal sociological studies.* Report to National Institute of Mental Health, Contract #PH-43-68-76. University Park: Pennsylvania State University.

Willits, F. K., & Janota, J. (1996, August). *A matter of order: Effects of response order on answers to surveys.* Paper presented at the meeting of the Rural Sociology Society, Des Moines, IA.

Willits, F. K., & Saltiel, J. (1995). Question order effects on subjective measures of quality of life. *Rural Sociology, 60,* 654–665.

Wine, J., Cominole, M., Heuer, R., & Riccobono, J. (2006, January). *Challenges of designing and implementing multimode instruments.* Paper presented at the Telephone Survey Methodology II Conference, Miami, FL.

Index